Theoretical Aspects of Object-Oriented Programming

Foundations of Computing
Michael Garey and Albert Meyer, editors

Theoretical Aspects of Object-Oriented Programming
Types, Semantics, and Language Design

edited by
Carl A. Gunter and John C. Mitchell

The MIT Press
Cambridge, Massachusetts
London, England

The book was set in Times Roman by Asco Trade Typesetting Ltd., Hong Kong, and was printed and bound in the United States of America.

Library of Congress Cataloging-in-Publication Data

Theoretical aspects of object-oriented programming: types, semantics, and language design / edited by
  Carl A. Gunter and John C. Mitchell.
     p.   cm. — (Foundations of computing)
  Includes bibliographical references.
  ISBN 0-262-07155-X
  1. Object-oriented programming (Computer science) 2. Programming languages
(Electronic computers) I. Gunter, Carl A. II. Mitchell, John C. III. Series.
  QA76.64.T49   1993
  005.1—dc20   93-28984
                                                                          CIP

Contents

Series Foreword

Theoretical computer science has now undergone several decades of development. The "classical" topics of automata theory, formal languages, and computational complexity have become firmly established, and their importance to other theoretical work and to practice is widely recognized. Stimulated by technological advances, theoreticians have been rapidly expanding the areas under study, and the time delay between theoretical progress and its practical impact has been decreasing dramatically. Much publicity has been given recently to breakthroughs in cryptography and linear programming, and steady progress is being made on programming language semantics, computational geometry, and efficient data structures. Newer, more speculative, areas of study include relational databases, VLSI theory, and parallel and distributed computation. As this list of topics continues expanding, it is becoming more and more difficult to stay abreast of the progress that is being made and increasingly important that the most significant work be distilled and communicated in a manner that will facilitate further research and application of this work. By publishing comprehensive books and specialized monographs on the theoretical aspects of computer science, the series on Foundations of Computing provides a forum in which important research topics can be presented in their entirety and placed in perspective for researchers, students, and practitioners alike.

Michael R. Garey
Albert R. Meyer

Theoretical Aspects of Object-Oriented Programming

Introduction

This volume comprises fifteen chapters, by selected authors, on theoretical aspects of object-oriented programming languages. The focus is on type systems and semantic models, and how advances in these areas can contribute to new language designs. The collection is divided into five parts: Objects and Subtypes, Type Inference, Coherence, Record Calculi, and Inheritance. The chapters are organized approximately in order of increasing complexity of the language constructs they consider. Put briefly, the collection begins with variations on Pascal- and Algol-like languages, develops the theory of illustrative record object models, and concludes with research directions for developing a more comprehensive theory of object-oriented programming languages.

Part I discusses the similarities and differences between "objects" and algebraic-style abstract data types, and addresses general problems associated with subtyping (or subclasses) in the presence of operations that may be applied to objects of more than one type.

Parts II–IV, which form the core of the collection, are concerned with what may be called the *record model* of object-oriented languages. More specifically, these chapters discuss static and dynamic semantics of languages with simple object models that include a type or class hierarchy but do not all provide what is often called "dynamic binding" or "dynamic method lookup." Part II develops the record model incrementally, beginning with a simple extension of the record operations from the language ML. The denotational semantics of these languages are considered in part III, with more elaborate record object models and more precise connections with object-oriented methodology developed in part IV.

Extensions and modifications to record object models are considered in part V. These chapters bring us closer to the full complexity of practical object-oriented languages; however, the complete theoretical underpinnings of the language features discussed in part V remain a topic for future research.

Objects and Subtypes

The first two chapters of the volume, which form part I, are also the first two works chronologically. Both chapters were written by John Reynolds, and they discuss themes that are echoed throughout the rest of the volume. Chapter 1 reprints an often-overlooked paper on data abstraction, discussing the difference between the algebraic view, in which data types consist of a type or sort and associated functions, and what Reynolds called *procedural data structures*, which are essentially *objects* (though limited to having a single method). The chapter uses a case study to illustrate the tradeoffs between these two approaches to data abstraction. This is the idea underlying the philosophies of data abstraction that differentiate the designs of languages such as Ada and ML from those of languages that emphasize an *object-oriented* approach.

To understand the work in chapter 2, it is helpful to appreciate its historical context. The original paper was presented at a conference on semantics-directed compiler generation and was intended to provide a challenge to researchers in this area. The primary topic is that of *subtypes*. The motivating example is a familiar one: the type of integers is to be viewed as a subtype of that of reals. Given this, one asks what relationship, if any, should hold between the operation of addition on integers and reals. Given a mapping from subclass (integer) to superclass (real), should it be the case that the commands

```
x := integer-to-real(m) + integer-to-real(n)
```

and

```
x := integer-to-real(m+n)
```

have the same meaning? This question illustrates two of the most fundamental themes in studying the semantics of subtypes. The first of these is the notion of a *coercion* map. Such maps can be *explicit*, as in the preceding programs, or *implicit*, as in programs where the compiler can infer the coercion without the need for programmer annotations. The second is the notion of *coherence*. The equivalence of the preceding programs is a typical coherence question. A closely related property says that if there are coercions c_1, c_2, c_3 having types $r \to s$ and $s \to t$ and $r \to t$ respectively, then the composition of the coercions c_1 and c_2 is a coercion from r to t this is equal to c_3. Chapter 2 provides a categorical treatment of the issue of the semantics of subtypes for an ALGOL-like language. Reynolds's concluding remarks in this chapter also include the description of a system of subtyping on records, variants, and function spaces that anticipates many of the ideas in subtyping that would become a focus of study in works such as those in part III, which expand the discussion to languages that include *parametric polymorphism*.

Types and Type Inference

One of the central objectives of studies in this volume is ensuring desirable characteristics of the run-time behavior of programs. A valuable class of such characteristics can be ensured through the imposition of a *phase distinction* between compile-time and run-time if this separation exploits a *static type discipline* to filter programs that may have undesirable run-time properties. In programs that do not impose such a discipline, programming is less restrained, but fewer assumptions can be made about run-time errors. An example of a language with no type discipline (an *untyped language*) is considered in chapter 13, but most of the chapters of this volume focus on typed languages.

There are several gradations in typing systems one may impose. One approach is to impose a system of programmer type annotations that is then checked by a decidable or semi-decidable type verification algorithm. On the other hand, one may define a type discipline with the property that a *most general* type can be decidably *inferred* for a program even when the program has few or no explicit (programmer) type annotations. The practical utility of such type disciplines has been demonstrated by the language ML [MT91, MTH90, Pau91], which uses the Hindley-Milner type inference algorithm [Hin69, Mil78] to generate type schemes for programs with very few type annotations. The development of similar systems for languages with object-oriented features such as flexible record types has been one focus of research, and it is the topic of part II of this volume.

The study of type inference for systems with more flexible record types began with a seminal paper of Mitchell Wand [Wan87]. Part II consists of three works that forged further directions toward a system of type inference for languages with flexible records. The first of these, chapter 3, offers a proposal by Didier Rémy of a type inference system for a language extending ML. Rémy's type system allows functions to be applied to all records that have at least some minimum set of components required by the function body. This problem is essentially the same as the problem of type-checking programs that manipulate objects, allowing any object to be replaced by another with at least as many methods. Chapter 4 employs a similar system and demonstrates how some of the fundamental concepts of object-oriented languages can be encoded in a system with type inference. In particular, Wand focuses on the concepts of *instance variable* and *inheritance*. The notion of an instance variable is modeled functionally in that chapter, as in most of the rest of this volume, using record fields. The result is a clear analysis in a type system that is easy to understand and has very good properties. This work should be compared with other treatments of inheritance that appear as the central topic of part V. Chapter 5 describes an approach of Atsushi Ohori and Peter Buneman to achieving flexible record types in a system with type inference. Their system is based on the notion of *conditional types* that annotate type variables with restrictions, an idea reminiscent of *bounded quantification*, which is studied in subsequence chapters. Unlike the systems using bounded quantification, however, Ohori's and Buneman system has inferred principle types. This chapter also discusses the programming of database primitives in the proposed system.

Semantics and Coherence

Whereas the chapters forming part II all consider ways to make a record system more flexible through quantification over type variables, the common theme of part III is to combine such quantification with the idea of subtyping along the lines discussed at the end of chapter 2. A central theme of part III is the idea of *coherence*. Although coherence was already discussed in chapter 2, the form in which it is studied in part II involves a number of new ideas. Prior to Reynolds's work most of the work on the semantics of subtypes focused on interpreting subtypes as subsets. Chapter 2 breaks with this idea and proposes that there are important instances in which subtypes should not be considered subsets from a semantic perspective. Chapter 6, by Kim Bruce and Giuseppe Longo, proposes a new idea for understanding the semantics of subtyping in a way that has the intuitive flavor of interpreting subtypes as subsets but also addresses the problem that the coercion from a subtype into a supertype may not be an injection (1-1 mapping). Surprisingly enough, though, the structure of the model is such that coercions are computed by (indices of) the identity function and contravariance of $\rightarrow$ is faithfully preserved. Bruce and Longo's idea is to use *partial equivalence relations (PERs)* over Kleene's applicative algebra of partial recursive functions to serve as the interpretations of types. The coercion of a subtype into a supertype could then be given as the "inclusion" between PERs in a sense compatible with the idea that the coercion need not be an injection. Proving that the corresponding meaning function is well-defined—the coherence problem for the PER interpretation—is one of the primary results of chapter 6. A different approach to coherence for essentially the same language is pursued in chapter 7, by Val Breazu-Tannen, Thierry Coquand, Carl A. Gunter, and Andre Scedrov. Rather than interpreting the system of interest directly, they translate the calculus syntactically into an extension of the Girard-Reynolds polymorphic λ-calculus that has an explicit notion of coercion but no subtyping relation. The translation is defined by induction on the height of a derivation of a type for a term; to give a well-defined semantics, they then show that the translation is coherent in the sense that no matter which derivation of a given term is used for the translation, the result is always the same up to provable equality in the target calculus. This shows that any model of the target calculus can be seen as a model of the calculus with subtyping; since the models of the former are fairly well understood, this provides a simple system for generating models. The proofs of coherence in chapters 6 and 7 are among the most technically intricate ones in this volume. In chapter 8, the final chapter of part III, Pierre-Louis Curien and Giorgio Ghelli address the question of how to prove such results using term rewriting techniques. Their exposition is based on a calculus called $F_{\leq}$ (pronounced "F sub") that simplifies the syntax of the language being studied without changing the central issues involved in proving coherence for languages such as those considered in the two previous chapters. Rather than defining rewriting directly for proofs in $F_\leq$, Curien and Ghelli define an auxiliary type system in which terms carry complete information about their typing derivations. A normalizing rewriting system is defined for terms in this langue; properties of this rewriting system can then be related to the proofs of $F_\leq$ in a way that implies the desired coherence result.

Varieties of Record Calculi

Several different illustrative languages are used in presenting semantic models in part III. A common core of all of these languages is a typed lambda calculus with polymorphism and subtyping. Although originally formulated by Cardelli and Wegner as part of a language called *Bounded Fun* [CW85], this language is now known by the name $F_\leq$. The polymorphic lambda calculus with subtyping is an extension of Girard's original polymorphic lambda calculus [Gir71, Gir72], which he called *System F*. The difference between $F_\leq$ and F is that $F_\leq$ has a subtype relation on types, which is often written using the symbol $\leq$ (or, alternatively, $<:$ or $\subseteq$).

While $F_\leq$ provides a framework for studying object-oriented languages, many important features are apparently missing from $F_\leq$. The most notable is that $F_\leq$ does not have any constructs resembling objects. Therefore, to represent the basic concepts of object-oriented languages in a simple way, it seems natural to add some form of objects to $F_\leq$. Beginning with Cardelli's seminal paper on records and subtyping [Car88] (which originally appeared in conference form in 1984), it has been traditional to regard objects as derived from record structures in some way. Therefore, a substantial portion of the research on foundations of object-oriented languages is concerned with record operations that could be added to $F_\leq$. In this volume, this line of work is represented by first three chapters of part IV.

The first chapter of part IV, written by Luca Cardelli and John Mitchell, begins by summarizing a number of calculi of record operations that had been developed prior to the original publication of this chapter and then presents a calculus of record operations that subsumes most of the prior proposals. The main operations on records in this chapter are (i) add a field, or component, to a record, (ii) remove a field of a record, and (iii) select the value of a specified component of a record. Along with these operations, the main focus of the paper is a form of polymorphism over record types that allows a single function to manipulate all types of records sharing certain specified fields. The importance and relevance of this form of polymorphism may be illustrated by example. In a program where there are several kinds of two-dimensional (geometric) points, it would be useful to be able to move all, or almost all, kinds of points using the same function. Thus we would like a single `move` function to be applicable to ordinary points with only x, y-coordinates, colored points having an additional `color` field, and other extensions of the basic class of points. This was originally addressed in the language *Bounded Fun* of [CW85]; however, as discussed in section 6 of chapter 6, *Bounded Fun* has significant limitations. These are lifted in chapter 9.

One limitation of the record operations in chapter 9 is that it is impossible to type concatenation of records in a direct manner. (This is discussed in section 4.4 of chapter 9.) One programming situation that calls for record concatenation is relational databases, where it seems natural to represent a relation as a finite sets of records. The join of two relatons is obtained by concatenating all pairs of records (one from each relation) that agree at appropriate fields. A straightforward approach to record concatenation is presented in chapter 10, by Didier Rémy. This chapter gives a general method for defining record concatenation in any language that allows records to be extended with new fields and that has sufficient functional programming capabilities. This method also shows how multiple inheritance can be reduced to single inheritance, in principle.

A surprising feature of $F_\le$, explained in detail in chapter 11 by Luca Cardelli, is that a range of record operations may in fact be encoded directly in $F_\le$. In this encoding, records are represented as a certain form of polymorphic function. Although the encoding is probably too inefficient to be useful in practice, it shows that, from a semantic or theoretical point of view, a substantial range of record operations may be represented in the "basic" language $F_\le$ with no record operations at all.

Whereas part II is concerned with the existence of algorithms for type checking, or with inferring types for expressions containing record operations, these algorithmic concerns are absent from the first three chapters of part IV. The final chapter of part IV, written by Benjamin Pierce, shows that there is no typing algorithm for $F_\le$. This holds regardless of whether the types of variables and formal function parameters are written explicitly in programs. The reason is that the subtype relation itself is undecidable. This shows that there would be significant implementation problems in building a practical programming language around full $F_\le$, but the concluding section of the chapter gives some suggestions for avoiding this algorithmic problem in practice.

Inheritance

Records provide the most basic feature of objects, aggregation of functions and data. In addition to records, the record calculi of parts II–IV also provide forms of subtyping and parametric polymorphism that allow programs to operate uniformly over all records (or objects) that share common properties. Roughly speaking, the languages considered in parts II–IV are more concerned with operations on objects than with the ways that objects are created or defined. In part V, which contains the final three chapters of the collection, the focus changes to inheritance mechanisms, which are used to define objects or classes of objects incrementally by specifying how a new object should differ from those already defined.

The first chapter of part V, written by Samuel Kamin and Uday Reddy, presents a series of model languages that illustrate the difference between Pascal-style records and the form of object and class declarations that appear in languages such as SMALLTALK [GR83], Eiffel [Mey92], and C^{++} [ES90]. The first language, called *ObjectTalk*, provides only a simple form of object with instance variables and methods. The semantic interpretation of an *ObjectTalk* object is a "message environment" binding message names to their methods. This is essentially the same as a record associating a value with each component (or field) name; however, as pointed out in the chapter, an object denotes a recursively defined message environment (or record), since the methods of an object may refer to each other recursively. In effect, the language *ObjectTalk* shows how recursive definitions allow us to model objects as records.

The subsequent languages of chapter 13 are *ClassTalk*, *InheritTalk*, and *SmallTalk*, the final language being an abstraction of SMALLTALK-80. The first, *ClassTalk*, has a form of class, which is a function that creates objects sharing a common set of methods. Since most common object-oriented languages are class-based, this brings us closer to the form of language generally encountered in practice. *ClassTalk*, however, is easily translated into *ObjectTalk*. (This may again be interpreted as a positive result about the record model.) *InheritTalk* adds a form of inheritance to *ClassTalk*, allowing one class to be defined from another. The final example language, *SmallTalk*, differs from *InheritTalk* in that when class *A* inherits from class *B*, and message to an object of type *A* results in invocation of a method of class *B*, any reference to *self* in this method leads to the method of class *A* rather than class *B*. This rather technical-sounding difference is important in object-oriented programming and is explained in more detail in the chapter. Whereas most chapters use typed *functional* languages, with no notion of global store, to illustrate the main ideas, chapter 13 uses untyped imperative languages. These are given denotational semantics using the traditional Scott-Strachey approach, which reduces imperative programs to functional programs with store operations.

The remaining chapters are chapter 14, by William Cook, Walter Hill, and Peter Canning, and chapter 15, by John Mitchell. Both are concerned with inheritance, chapter 14 in a class-based language and chapter 15 in a delegation-based language. The main difference between class- and delegation-based languages is that in class-based languages, every object is created by a class and the class determines the implementation of each method. In contrast, delegation-based languages allow one object to be created by "cloning" another, with the implementation of each inherited method determined by the object that is cloned. Although these two approaches to inheritance may sound very different, the basic nature of inheritance, as a mechanism for reusing methods, is very similar in both cases. (Some comparison between class- and delegation-based languages may be found in [Ste87].)

Chapters 14 and 15 are both concerned with typing and its relation to inheritance. A significant issue in both papers is that (stated in class-based terms) if one class is defined from another by inheritance, it may be desirable to change the types of some of the inherited methods. This is significant since it may make objects created by the inheriting class unusable as substitutes for objects for the base (or super) class. For example, suppose we have a class Point of points with x, y-coordinates, and some associated methods, including an equality method eq. If we define a class Colored_Point of points with x, y-coordinates and color, inheriting eq and other methods, then it would be natural to redefine eq for colored points. Specifically, if we compare two objects of class Point, they should be equal if they have the same x, y-coordinates. In contrast, two objects of class Colored_Point would only be equal if they have the same x, y-coordinates *and* color. In this situation, the eq method of a Colored_Point may only be used for comparison with another Colored_Point.

We may understand the title, "Inheritance Is Not Subtyping," of Chapter 14 using the example of points and colored points. The definition of subtyping that is used is that A is a subtype of B precisely if any object of type A may be used in any context where an object of type B is required, without producing a type error. Suppose Point and Colored_Point are as just described, with p an object of class Point and q an object of type Colored_Point. Then clearly p eq p is sensible, since the equality method of p allows p to be compared with any other Point, including itself. If Colored_Point were a subtype of Point, then we would expect to be able to replace either occurrence of p by q without causing a type error. The expression p eq p does not cause any problem, since the eq method of p only requires the x, y-coordinates of q. But if we replace the first occurrence of p by q, resulting in q eq p, then we have an error. Specifically, the eq method of q requires the x, y-coordinates and color of p, but p does not have a color. This produces the error *message not understood* in SMALLTALK-like systems. From the point of view of chapters 14 and 15, this is a type error. Thus inheritance does not produce a subtype.

A difference between chapters 14 and 15 is the way that objects are represented. The first chapter uses recursively defined records, in a calculus allowing record concatenation (or "combination," as it is called in the chapter), while the second uses, essentially, self-applicaton in place of recursive definition. Some comparison between these two approaches appears in section 7 of chapter 14 and in the conference paper [Bru92], which was written after this collection was assembled. In both cases it is possible to use record operations to account for inheritance. A point that is not made in either comparison is that the recursively defined records diverge under call-by-value evaluation order, while the alternative representation is satisfactory under both call-by-value and call-by-name.

Acknowledgments

We would like to thank Bob Prior, our editor at MIT Press, for suggesting the idea of collecting a selection of the work on this subject into a single volume. We are also indebted to the authors of the articles in the collection for their cooperation and their enthusiasm for the project.

Most of the articles in the volume are reprinted from previous publications where they have received varying levels of review. New submissions appearing in the volume were not subjected to a formal review process prior to their inclusion.

Bibliography

[Bru92] K. Bruce. The equivalence of two semantic definitions of inheritance in object-oriented languages. In *Proc. Mathematical Foundations of Programming Language Semantics*, pages 102–124, Berlin, 1992. Springer LNCS 598.

[Car88] L. Cardelli. A semantics of multiple inheritance. *Information and Computation*, 76:138–164, 1988. Special issue devoted to *Symp. on Semantics of Data Types*, Sophia-Antipolis (France), 1984.

[CW85] L. Cardelli and P. Wegner. On understanding types, data abstraction, and polymorphism. *Computing Surveys*, 17(4):471–522, 1985.

[ES90] M. Ellis and B. Stroustrop. *The Annotated C^{++} Reference Manual*. Addison-Wesley, 1990.

[Gir71] J.-Y. Girard. Une extension de l'interpretation de Gödel à l'analyse, et son application à l'élimination des coupures dans l'analyse et la théorie des types. In J. E. Fenstad, editor, *2nd Scandinavian Logic Symposium*, pages 63–92. North-Holland, Amsterdam, 1971.

[Gir72] J.-Y. Girard. Interpretation fonctionelle et elimination des coupures de l'arithmetique d'ordre superieur. Thèse D'Etat, Université Paris VII, 1972.

[GR83] A. Goldberg and D. Robson. *Smalltalk-80: The Language and its Implementation*. Addison-Wesley, 1983.

[Hin69] J. R. Hindley. The principal type-scheme of an object in combinatory logic. *Trans. AMS*, 146:29–60, 1969.

[Mey92] B. Meyer. *Eiffel: The Language*. Prentice-Hall, 1992.

[Mil78]   R. Milner. A theory of type polymorphism in programming. *JCSS*, 17:348–375, 1978.

[MT91]   Robin Milner and Mads Tofte. *Commentary on Standard ML*. MIT Press, 1991.

[MTH90]   Robin Milner, Mads Tofte, and Robert Harper. *The Definition of Standard ML*. MIT Press, 1990.

[Pau91]   L. C. Paulson. *ML for the Working Programmer*. Cambridge Univ. Press, 1991.

[Ste87]   L. A. Stein. Delegation is inheritance. In *Proc. ACM Conference on Object-Oriented Programming Systems, Languages, and Applications*, pages 138–146, 1987.

[Wan87]   M. Wand. Complete type inference for simple objects. In *Proc. IEEE Symp. on Logic in Computer Science*, pages 37–44, 1987. Corrigendum in *Proc. IEEE Symp. on Logic in Computer Science*, page 132, 1988.

I OBJECTS AND SUBTYPES

1 User-Defined Types and Procedural Data Structures as Complementary Approaches to Data Abstraction

John C. Reynolds

Abstract

User-defined types (or modes) and procedural (or functional) data structures are complementary methods for data abstraction, each providing a capability lacked by the other. With user-defined types, all information about the representation of a particular kind of data is centralized in a type definition and hidden from the rest of the program. With procedural data structures, each part of the program which creates data can specify its own representation, independently of any representations used elsewhere for the same kind of data. However, this decentralization of the description of data is achieved at the cost of prohibiting primitive operations from accessing the representations of more than one data item. The contrast between these approaches is illustrated by a simple example.

Introduction

User-defined types and procedural data structures have both been proposed as methods for data abstraction, i.e., for limiting and segregating the portion of a program that depends upon the representation used for some kind of data. In this paper we suggest, by means of a simple example, that these methods are complementary, each providing a capability lacked by the other.

The idea of user-defined types has been developed by Morris [1, 2], Liskov and Zilles [3], Fischer and Fischer [4], and Wulf [5], and has its roots in earlier work by Hoare and Dahl [6]. In this approach, each particular conceptual kind of data is called a *type*, and for each type used in a program, the program is divided into two parts: a type definition and an "outer" or "abstract" program. The type definition specifies the representation to be used for the data type and a set of primitive operations (and perhaps constants), each defined in terms of the representaton. The choice of representation is hidden from the outer program by requiring all manipulations of the data type in the outer program to be expressed in terms of the primitive operations. The heart of the matter is that any consistent change in the data representation can be effected by altering the type definition without changing the outer program.

Various notions of procedural (or functional) data structures have been developed by Reynolds [7], Landin [8], and Balzer [9]. In this approach, the abstract form of

First appeared in Stephen A. Schuman, editor, *New Directions in Algorithmic Languages*, 1975, IFIP Working Group 2.1 on Algol, INRIA, pages 157–168. Reprinted in David Gries, editor, *Programming Methodology, A Collection of Papers by Members of IFIP WG 2.3*, 1978, Springer-Verlag, pages 309–317. © Springer-Verlag, attn: Permissions Dept., 175 Fifth Ave, 19 Flr, New York, NY 10010.

data is characterized by the primitive operations which can be performed upon it, and an item of data is simply a procedure or collection of procedures for performing these operations. The essence of the idea is seen most clearly in its implementation: an item of procedural data is a kind of record called a *closure* that contains both an internal representation of the data and a pointer (or flag field) to code for procedures for manipulating this representation. A program with access to a closure record is only permitted to examine or access the internal representation by executing the code indicated by the pointer, so that this code serves to close off or protect the internal representation.

In comparison with user-defined types, procedural data structures provide a decentralized form of data abstraction. Each part of the program which creates procedural data will specify its own form of representation, independently of the representations used elsewhere for the same kind of data, and will provide versions of the primitive operations (the components of the procedural data item) suitable for this representation. There need be no part of the program, corresponding to a type definition, in which all forms of representation for the same kind of data are known. But a price must be paid for this decentralization: a primitive operation can have access to the representation of only a single data item, the item of which the operation is a component.

Apparently this price is inevitable. If an operation is to have access to the representation of more than one item of data, each of which may have several possible representations, then its definition cannot be "decentralized" into one part for each representation, since one must provide for every possible *combination* of representations. Presumably this requires the definition to occur at a point in the program where all possible representations of the operands are known.

Linguistic Preliminaries

Before illustrating these ideas, we must digress to explain (informally) the language we will use. It is an applicative language, similar to pure LISP [10] or the applicative subsets of GEDANKEN [7], PAL [11], or ISWIM [12], but with a complete type structure somewhat like Algol 68 [13]. Types will be indicated by writing $\in \tau$, where τ is a type expression, after binding occurrences of identifiers (except where the type is obvious from context). Type expressions are constructed with the operators $\rightarrow$ denoting functional procedures, $\times$ denoting a Cartesian product, and $+$ denoting a named disjoint union.

The named disjoint union is sufficiently novel to require a more detailed explanation. If $\tau_1, \ldots, \tau_n$ are type expressions denoting the sets $S_1, \ldots, S_n$ and $i_1, \ldots, i_n$ are distinct identifiers, then

$$i_1 : \tau_1 + \cdots + i_n : \tau_n$$

is a type expression denoting the set of pairs

$$\{\langle i_k, x \rangle \mid 1 \leq k \leq n \text{ and } x \in S_k\}.$$

If e is an expression of type τ_k with value x, then

inject $i_k e$

is an expression of type $i_1 : \tau_1 + \cdots + i_n : \tau_n$ with value $\langle i_k, x \rangle$.

Let e be an expression of type $i_1 : \tau_1 + \cdots + i_n : \tau_n$ with value $\langle i, x \rangle$, let $i_{k_1}, \ldots, i_{k_m}$ be distinct members of the set of identifiers $\{i_1, \ldots, i_n\}$, for $1 \leq j \leq m$ let l_j be an expression of type $\tau_{k_j} \to \tau'$ with value f_j, and let e' be an expression of type τ' with value x'. Then

unioncase e **of** $(i_{k_1} : l_1, \ldots, i_{k_m} : l_m, \textbf{other} : e')$

is an expression of type τ' with the value

$$\textbf{if} \begin{bmatrix} i = i_{k_1} \\ \vdots \\ i = i_{k_m} \\ \text{otherwise} \end{bmatrix} \textbf{then} \begin{bmatrix} f_1(x) \\ \vdots \\ f_m(x) \\ x' \end{bmatrix}$$

When $m = n$, the **other** clause will be omitted.

We use the type expression **nilset** to denote a standard one-element set, whose unique member is denoted by ( ).

Integer Sets as a User-Defined Type

Our example is an implementation of the abstract concept of sets of integers. Using the approach of user-defined types, we wish to define a type *set* and primitive constants and functions

none $\in$ *set*

all $\in$ *set*

limit $\in$ **integer** $\times$ **integer** $\times$ *set* $\to$ *set*

union $\in$ set $\times$ set $\to$ set

exists ∈ **integer** × **integer** × *set* → **Boolean**

satisfying the specifications

none = { }

all = The set of all (machine-representable) integers

$limit(m, n, s) = s \cap \{k | m \le k \le n\}$

$union(s1, s2) = s1 \cup s2$

when $m \le n$, $exists(m, n, s) = (\exists k)\, m \le k \le n$ and $k \in s$

To make our solution seem more realistic, we require that the execution of *limit* and *union* should require time and space bounded by constants which are independent of their arguments. Of course this will exact a price in the speed of *exists*.

An appropriate and simple solution is to represent a set by a list structure that records the way in which the set is constructed via primitive operations. Thus the representation of a set is a disjoint union, over the four set-valued primitive functions (including constants), of sets of possible arguments for these functions. More precisely, this representation is defined by the recursive type declaration:

set = *nonef* : **nilset** + *allf* : **nilset** + *limitf* : **integer** × **integer** × *set* + *unionf* : *set* × *set*

and the effect of *none*, *all*, *limit*, or *union* is to imbed its arguments into the appropriate kind of list element:

none = **inject** *nonef* ( )

all = **inject** *allf* ( )

$limit(m, n, s)$ = **inject** $limitf\ (m, n, s)$

$union(s1, s2)$ = **inject** $unionf\ (s1, s2)$

(Roughly speaking, we are representing sets by a free algebra with constants *none* and *all*, and operators *limit* and *union*.) The entire computational burden of interpreting this representation falls upon the function *exists*:

$exists(m, n, s)$ = **unioncase** *s* **of**
        $(nonef : \lambda(\ )\,.$ **false**,
        $allf : \lambda(\ )\,.$ **true**,
        $limitf : \lambda(m1, n1, s1)\,.\, max(m, m1) \le min(n, n1)$
                and $exists(max(m, m1), min(n, n1), s)$,
        $unionf : \lambda(s1, s2)\,.\, exists(m, n, s1)$ **or** $exists(m, n, s2))$

(We assume that the operations **and** and **or** do not evaluate their second operand when the first operand is sufficient to determine their result.)

Although the above is a definition of the type *set* which meets our specifications, it can be easily improved, even within the time and space constraints imposed upon *limit* and *union*. For example, both *limit* and *union* can be optimized by taking advantage of some obvious properties of sets—the result of *limit* can be simplified when its last argument is *none* or another application of *limit*, and the result of *union* can be simplified when either argument is *none* or *all*:

$limit(m, n, s) =$ **unioncase** s **of**
    $(nonef : \lambda(\ ) . none,$
    $limitf : \lambda(m1, n1, s1) .$ **if** $max(m, m1) \leq min(n, n1)$
          then inject $limitf\ (max(m, m1), min(n, n1), s1)$ **else** $none,$
    other : **inject** $limitf\ (m, n, s))$
$union(s1, s2) =$ **unioncase** $s1$ **of**
    $(nonef : \lambda(\ ) . s2, allf : \lambda(\ ) . all,$
    other : **unioncase** $s2$ **of**
        $(nonef : \lambda(\ ) . s1, allf : \lambda(\ ) . all,$
        other : **inject** $unionf\ (s1, s2)))$

In conclusion, we show how our specification of integer sets might be "packaged" in a language permitting user-defined types:

newtype $set = nonef :$ **nilset** $+ allf :$ **nilset** $+ limitf :$ **integer** $\times$ **integer** $\times set$
    $+ unionf : set \times set$
with $none \in set =$ **inject** $nonef\ (\ ),$
    $all \in set =$ **inject** $allf\ (\ ),$
    $limit \in$ **integer** $\times$ **integer** $\times set \to set =$
        $\lambda(m, n, s) .$ **unioncase** s **of**
        $(nonef : \lambda(\ ) . none,$
        $limitf : \lambda(m1, n1, s1) .$ **if** $max(m, m1) \leq min(n, n1)$
                then inject $limitf\ (max(m, m1), min(n, n1), s1)$ **else** $none,$
        other : **inject** $limitf\ (m, n, s)),$
    $union \in set \times set \to set =$
        $\lambda(s1, s2) .$ **unioncase** $s1$ **of**
        $(nonef : \lambda(\ ) . s2, allf : \lambda(\ ) . all,$
        other : **unioncase** $s2$ **of**
            $(nonef : \lambda(\ ) . s1, allf : \lambda(\ ) . all,$
            other : **inject** $unionf\ (s1, s2))),$

$exists \in$ **integer** $\times$ **integer** $\times$ $set \to$ **Boolean** $=$
$\lambda(m, n, s)$. **unioncase** s **of**
$(nonef: \lambda(\ )$. **false**,
$allf: \lambda(\ )$. **true**,
$limitf: \lambda(m1, n1, s1)$. $max(m, m1) \leq min(n, n1)$
            and $exists(max(m, m1), min(n, n1), s)$,
$unionf: \lambda(s1, s2)$. $exists(m, n, s1)$ **or** $exists(m, n, s2))$

in $\langle$ outer program $\rangle$

The language used here is an outgrowth of the ideas discussed in reference [14]. A complete exposition of this language is beyond the scope of this paper, but the following salient points should be noted:

1. The type declaration between **newtype** and **with** binds all occurrences of the type identifier set throughout the above expression (including occurrences in $\langle$ outer program $\rangle$). The ordinary declarations between **with** and **in** bind all occurrences of the ordinary identifiers $none$, all, $limit$, $union$, and $exists$ throughout the expression.

2. With regard to occurrences of set between **with** and **in**, the type declaration behaves like a mode definition in Algol 68, i.e., set is equivalent to the type expression on the right side of the type declaration, and the type-correctness of the text in **with...in** depends upon this type expression.

3. In $\langle$ outer program $\rangle$ occurrences of set behave like a primitive type, e.g., **integer** or **Boolean**. In other words, $\langle$ outer program $\rangle$ must be a correctly typed expression regardless of what type expression might be equivalent to set. This insures that all manipulations of the user-defined type in $\langle$ outer program $\rangle$ must be expressed in terms of the primitives declared in **with...in**.

4. Although it is not illustrated by our example, it should be possible to declare simultaneously several related user-defined types between **newtype** and **with**. This ability is needed to permit the definition of multiargument primitive functions that act upon more than one user-defined type. An example might be the use of the types $point$ and $line$ in a program for performing geometrical calculations.

Integer Sets as Procedural Data Structures

We now develop integer sets as procedural data structures. The starting point is the realization that all we ever want to do to a set s, aside from using it to construct other sets, is to evaluate the Boolean expression $exists(m, n, s)$. This suggests that we can simply equate the set s with the Boolean function $\lambda(m, n) \cdot exists(m, n, s)$ that characterizes the only information we want to extract from the set.

Thus we define

$$set = \textbf{integer} \times \textbf{integer} \rightarrow \textbf{Boolean}$$

and specify that if $s \in set$ represents the "mathematical" set s_0, then for $m \leq n$,

$$s(m, n) = (\exists k)\, m \leq k \leq n \text{ and } k \in s_0.$$

The need for defining the primitive function $exists$ has vanished since this function has been *internalized*—its value for a particular set is simply the (only component of the) set itself. The remaining primitive constants and functions are easily defined by:

$$none = \lambda(m, n) \cdot \textbf{false}$$
$$all = \lambda(m, n) \cdot \textbf{true}$$
$$limit(m, n, s) = \lambda(n1, n1),$$
$$max(m, m1) \leq min(n, n1) \textbf{ and } s(max(m, m1), min(n, n1))$$
$$union(s1, s2) = \lambda(m, n) \cdot s1(m, n) \textbf{ or } s2(m, n)$$

In this approach, there is no "outer program" from which the definition $set = $ **integer** $\times$ **integer** $\rightarrow$ **Boolean** is hidden. Any part of the program can create a set by giving an appropriate function whose internal representation (the collecton of values of global variables which form the fields of the closure record) can be arbitrary. For example, in augmenting an existing program, one might write

$$\lambda(m, n) \cdot even(m) \textbf{ or } (m < n)$$

to denote the set of even integers, or

letrec $s = \lambda(m, n) \cdot (m \leq n) \textbf{ and } (p(m) \textbf{ or } s(m + 1, n))$ **in** s

to denote the set of integers satisfying the predicate p. The procedural approach insures that these definitions will mesh correctly with the rest of the program, even though they introduce novel representations.

This kind of extensional capability, which is the main advantage of the procedural approach, is offset by two limitations. In the first place, although (ignoring computability considerations) every set can be represented by a function in **integer** $\times$ **integer** $\rightarrow$ **Boolean**, the converse is false. To represent a set, a function s must satisfy

$$s(m, n) = \bigvee_{k=m}^{n} s(k, k)$$

for all m and n such that $m \leq n$. This kind of condition, which cannot be checked syntactically, must be satisfied by all parts of the program which create sets.

A more important limitation is that only the function *exists*, which has been internalized as (the only component of) a procedural data item, is truly primitive in the sense of having access to the internal representation of a set. Essentially, we have been forced to express the functions *limit* and *union* in terms of the internalized *exists*. We are fortunate that our example permits us to do this at all. Even so, we are prevented from optimizing *limit* and *union* as we did in the user-defined-type development. There is no practically effective way that $limit(m, n, s)$ can "see" whether s has the form *none* or $limit(m1, n1, s1)$, or that $union(s1, s2)$ can "see" whether $s1$ or $s2$ has the form *none* or *all*.

In fact, this difficulty can be surmounted for *limit* but not for *union*. The solution is to internalize *limit* as well as *exists*, so that both functions have access to internal representations. Thus we represent sets by pairs of functions:

$$set = (\textbf{integer} \times \textbf{integer} \rightarrow \textbf{Boolean}) \times (\textbf{integer} \times \textbf{integer} \rightarrow set)$$

and specify that if s represents the mathematical set s_0 then for $m \leq n$,

$$s.1(m, n) = (\exists k) \, m \leq k \leq n \text{ and } k \in s_0,$$

and for all m and n, $s.2(m, n)$ represents the mathematical set

$$s_0 \cap \{k | m \leq k \leq n\}$$

(Here $s.1$ and $s.2$ denote the components of the pair s.)

In this approach, we may define *none* by:

$$none = (\lambda(m, n). \textbf{false}, \lambda(m, n). none)$$

Note the peculiar kind of recursion that is characteristic of this style of programming: the second component of *none* is a function which does not call itself but rather returns itself as a component of its result.

To define *all* and *union* we first define an "external" $limit \in \textbf{integer} \times \textbf{integer} \times set \rightarrow set$ which will be called upon by the internal limiting functions (i.e., the second components) of *all* and *union*:

$$limit(m, n, s) =$$
$$(\lambda(m1, n1). max(m, m1) \leq min(n, n1) \textbf{ and } s.1(max(m, m1), min(n, n1)),$$
$$\lambda(m1, n1). \textbf{if } max(m, m1) \leq min(n, n1) \textbf{ then }$$
$$limit(max(m, m1), min(n, n1), s) \textbf{ else } none)$$

Then

$$all = (\lambda(m, n) . \textbf{true}, \lambda(m, n) . limit(m, n, all))$$
$$union(s1, s2) = (\lambda(m, n) . s1 . 1(m, n) \textbf{ or } s2 . 1(m, n),$$
$$\lambda(m, n) . limit(m, n, union(s1, s2))).$$

With these definitions, the internal limiting functions perform simplifications analogous to those performed by *limit* in the user-defined-type approach. Indeed, if one examines the behavior of the closures that would represent sets in an implementation of this definition, one finds that they mimic the list structures of the type approach almost exactly (except for the simplifications performed by *union*).

But even to someone who is experienced with procedural data structures, the internalization of *limit* is more a tour de force than a specimen of clear programming. Moreover, internalization cannot be applied to give a function such as *union* access to the internal representation of more than one argument, i.e., we could convert *union*(s1, s2) to a component of s1 or of s2 but not both.

Conclusions

In comparison with user-defined types, procedural data structures offer a more decentralized method of data abstraction that precludes any interaction between different representations of the same kind of data. This offers the advantage of easier extensibility at the price of prohibiting primitive operations from accessing the representations of more than one data item.

Of course, the two approaches can be combined. For example, we can augment our user-defined-type definition to include an additional primitive *functset* ∈ (**integer** × **integer** → **Boolean**) → *set* which accepts a functional set (in the sense of the first part of the previous section) and produces an equivalent value of type *set*. It is sufficient to add one more kind of record to the disjoint union defining *set* and one more alternative to the branches defining *exists*:

newtype *set* = ⋯ + *functsetf* : (**integer** × **integer** → **Boolean**)
with ...
    functset ∈ (**integer** × **integer** → **Boolean**) → *set* = λf . **inject** *functsetf* f,
    exists ∈ **integer** × **integer** × *set* → **Boolean** =
        $\lambda(m, n, s)$. **unioncase** *s* **of**
        (... *functsetf* : $\lambda f . f(m, n)$)
in ⟨outer program⟩

However, this kind of combination is hardly a unification. To some extent, the data-representation structuring approach of Hoare and Dahl [6] unifies the concepts of user-defined types and procedural data structures, but only at the expense of combining their limitations. It appears that this is inevitable; that the two concepts are inherently distinct and complementary.

The reader should be cautioned that this is a working paper describing ongoing research. In particular, the linguistic constructs we have used are tentative and will require considerable study and evolution before they can be integrated into a complete programming language. The extension of these constructs to languages with imperative features is a particularly murky area.

Note

Work supported by National Science Foundation Grant GJ-41540.

References

1. [Morris 73] Morris, James H., Jr. "Types Are Not Sets" *Conference Record of ACM Symposium on Principles of Programming Languages* (1973), 120–124.

2. [Morris 74] Morris, James H., Jr. "Towards More Flexible Type Systems" *Programming Symposium: Proceedings of Colloque sur la Programmation* Berlin: Springer-Verlag (1974), 377–384.

3. [Liskov 74] Liskov, Barbara H. and Zilles, Stephen "Programming with Abstract Data Types" *Proceedings of a Symposium on Very High Level Languages* (1974) 50–59.

4. [Fischer 73] Fischer, Alice E. and Fischer, Michael J. "Mode Modules as Representations of Domains—Preliminary Report" *Conference Record of ACM Symposium on Principles of Programming Languages*, 139–143.

5. [Wulf 74] Wulf, William A. "ALPHARD: Toward a Language to Support Structured Programs" Technical Report, Computer Science Department, Carnegie-Mellon University, April 30, 1974. See also in Shaw, Mary (editor) *ALPHARD: Form and Content*, New York: Springer-Verlag, 1981.

6. [Dahl 72] Dahl, O.-J., Dijkstra, Edsger W., and Hoare, C. A. R. *Structured Programming* London: Academic Press, 1972.

7. [Reynolds 70] Reynolds, John C. "GEDANKEN—A Simple Typeless Language Based on the Principle of Completeness and the Reference Concept" *Communications of the ACM* 13, 5 (May, 1970), 308–319.

8. [Landin 65] Landin, Peter J. "A Correspondence Between ALGOL 60 and Church's Lambda-Notation" *Communications of the ACM* 8, 2–3 (February–March, 1965), 89–101 and 158–165.

9. [Balzer 67] Balzer, Robert M. "Dataless Programming" *Proceedings AFIPS 1967 Fall Joint Computer Conference* Washington, D.C.: Thompson Books (1967), 535–544.

10. [McCarthy 60] McCarthy, John "Recursive Functions of Symbolic Expressions and Their Computation by Machine, Part I" *Communications of the ACM* 3, 4 (April, 1960), 184–195.

11. [Evans 68] Evans, Arthur, Jr. "PAL—A Language Designed for Teaching Programming Linguistics" *Proceedings 23rd National ACM Conference*, Princeton, N.J.: Brandin Systems Press (1968), 395–403.

12. [Landin 66]   Landin, Peter J. "The Next 700 Programming Languages" *Communications of the ACM* 9, 3 (March, 1966), 157–166.

13. [van Winjngaarden 75]   van Winjngaarden, A., Mailloux, B. J., Peck, J. E. L., Koster, C. H. A., Sintzoff, M., Lindsey, C. H., Meertens, L. G. L. T., and Fisker, R. G. "Revised Report on the Algorithmic Language ALGOL 68" *Acta Informatica* 5, 1–3, (1975), 1–236.

14. [Reynolds 74]   Reynolds, John C. "Towards a Theory of Type Structure" *Programming Symposium: Proceedings of Colloque sur la Programmation* Berlin: Springer-Verlag (1974), 408–425.

2 Using Category Theory to Design Implicit Conversions and Generic Operators

John C. Reynolds

Abstract

A generalization of many-sorted algebras, called category-sorted algebras, is defined and applied to the language-design problem of avoiding anomalies in the interaction of implicit conversions and generic operators. The definition of a simple imperative language (without any binding mechanisms) is used as an example.

Introduction

A significant problem in the design of programming languages is the treatment of implicit conversions, sometimes called coercions, between types. A failure to provide implicit conversions can degrade the conciseness and readability of a language. On the other hand, unless great care is taken in the design of such conversions, and their interaction with operators that can be applied to operands of several types, the resulting language will exhibit anomalies that will be a rich source of programming errors. (In the author's opinion, PL/I and Algol 68 exemplify this danger.)

As a simple illustration, consider assigning the sum of two integer variables to a real variable. In the absence of an implicit conversion from **integer** to **real**, one would have to write either

$$x := \text{integer-to-real}(m) + \text{integer-to-real}(n)$$

or

$$x := \text{integer-to-real}(m + n).$$

Clearly, one would prefer to write $x := m + n$. If the language permits this, however, one can ask whether the implicit conversion precedes or follows the addition, i.e., which of the above statements is equivalent to $x := m + n$.

It is generally believed that a precise language definition must answer this question unambiguously. However, if one were to ask the question of a mathematician (at least one who didn't know too much about programming), he would probably reply that it doesn't matter, since both of the above statements have the same meaning, and that

First appeared in Neil D. Jones, editor, *Semantics-Directed Compiler Generation*, Springer-Verlag Lecture Notes in Computer Science 94, 1980, pages 211–258. © Springer-Verlag, attn: Permissions Dept., 175 Fifth Ave, 19 Flr, New York, NY 10010.

indeed the whole point of permitting the same operator + to be applied to arguments of different type which are connected by an implicit conversion is that the resulting ambiguity should not affect the meaning.

In a sense, of course, the mathematician is wrong: some computers provide a floating-point representation with such limited precision that the ambiguity in question does affect meaning. But in a deeper sense the mathematician is right. One intuitively expects that the above statements should have nearly the same meaning, and in analogous cases where numerical approximation or overflow is not involved, one expects exactly the same meaning.

To see this, replace **real** by **character string** in the above example, and suppose that integers are implicitly converted into character strings giving their decimal representation, and that + denotes both addition of integers and concatenation of strings. Then the two possible meanings of $x := m + n$ are radically different. This case is clearly a mistake in language design that would be likely to cause programming errors.

In this paper we will describe a method for avoiding such errors. The underlying mathematical tool will be a generalization of many-sorted algebras called category-sorted algebras, which are closely related to the order-sorted algebras invented by Goguen [1].

Beyond the specific goal of treating implicit conversions, our presentation is intended to illustrate the potential of category theory in the area of language definition and to suggest that the "standard" denotational semantics developed by Scott and Strachey may not be the final solution to the language-definition problem. There is nothing incorrect about the Scott-Strachey methodology, and it has provided fundamental insights into many aspects of programming languages such as recursion. But it has not been so helpful in other areas of language design such as type structure. We suspect that clearer insights into these areas will require quite different applications of mathematics.

Conventional Many-Sorted Algebras

Our use of algebras is based on the ideas of Goguen, Thatcher, Wagner, and Wright [2], which have roots as far back as Burstall and Landin [3]. In [2] a language is viewed as an initial algebra and its semantic function as the unique homomorphism from this initial algebra into some target algebra, so that defining the target algebra is tantamount to defining semantics. Here we will adopt the slightly more elaborate view that (roughly speaking) a language is the free algebra generated by some set of identifiers, that an environment is a mapping of these identifiers into the carrier of the target algebra, and that the semantic function is the function mapping each environment into its unique extension as a homomorphism from the free algebra to the target algebra.

We propose to treat implicit conversions in this framework by generalizing the concept of an algebra appropriately. To motivate this proposal we will proceed through a sequence of increasingly general definitions of "algebra".

The standard concept of a many-sorted algebra used in algebraic semantics is due to Birkhoff and Lipson [4], who called it an "heterogeneous" algebra. According to Birkhoff and Lipson, but with changes of notation and terminology to reveal the similarity to later definitions:

(1) A *signature* consists of:

   (1a) A set Ω of *sorts*. (Informally, the sorts correspond to types in a programming language.)

   (1b) A family, indexed by nonnegative integers, of disjoint sets Δ_n of *operators* of rank n.

   (1c) For each $n \geq 0$ and $\delta \in \Delta_n$, a *specification* $\Gamma_\delta \in \Omega^n \times \Omega$. (Informally, if $\Gamma_\delta = \langle\langle \omega_1, \ldots, \omega_n \rangle, \omega \rangle$ then the operator δ accepts operands of sorts $\omega_1, \ldots, \omega_n$ and yields a result of sort ω.)

(2) An $\Omega\Delta\Gamma$-*algebra* consists of:

   (2a) A *carrier* B, which is an Ω-indexed family of sets. (Informally $B(\omega)$ is the set of meanings appropriate for phrases of type ω.)

   (2b) For each $n \geq 0$ and $\delta \in \Delta_n$, an *interpretation* $\gamma_\delta \in B(\omega_1) \times \cdots \times B(\omega_n) \to B(\omega)$, where $\langle\langle \omega_1, \ldots, \omega_n \rangle, \omega \rangle = \Gamma_\delta$.

(3) If B, γ and B', γ' are $\Omega\Delta\Gamma$-algebras, then a *homomorphism* from B, γ to B', γ' is an Ω-indexed family of functions $\theta(\omega) \in B(\omega) \to B'(\omega)$ such that, for all $n \geq 0$ and $\delta \in \Delta_n$, the diagram

$$
\begin{array}{ccc}
B(\omega_1) \times \cdots \times B(\omega_n) & \xrightarrow{\ \gamma_\delta\ } & B(\omega) \\
\Big\downarrow {\scriptstyle \theta(\omega_1) \times \cdots \times \theta(\omega_n)} & & \Big\downarrow {\scriptstyle \theta(\omega)} \\
B'(\omega_1) \times \cdots \times B'(\omega_n) & \xrightarrow{\ \gamma'_\delta\ } & B'(\omega)
\end{array}
$$

commutes. Here $\langle\langle \omega_1, \ldots, \omega_n \rangle, \omega \rangle = \Gamma_\delta$ and $f_1 \times \cdots \times f_n$ denotes the function such that $(f_1 \times \cdots \times f_n)(x_1, \ldots, x_n) = \langle f_1(x_1), \ldots, f_n(x_n) \rangle$.

Unfortunately, it is difficult to pose the implicit-conversion problem within this concept of algebra since there is no mechanism for grouping operators that are represented by the same symbol. For example, integer addition and real addition would be distinct members of Δ_2 (with specifications $\langle\langle\textbf{integer},\textbf{integer}\rangle,\textbf{integer}\rangle$ and $\langle\langle\textbf{real},\textbf{real}\rangle,\textbf{real}\rangle$), and there is no mechanism for relating their interpretations more closely than, say, integer addition and multiplication.

Many-Sorted Algebras with Generic Operators

To solve this problem, we will employ an alternative concept of many-sorted algebras due to Higgins [5]. In this approach, the operators are (in programming jargon) generic. The specification of an operator of rank n is a partial function from Ω^n to Ω that is defined for the combinations of sorts of operands to which the operator is applicable, and that maps each such combination into the sort of the result yielded by the operand. (Notice that this captures the idea of bottom-up type determination.) Then the interpretation of the operator is a family of n-ary functions indexed by the domain of its specification.

In our own development we will insist that the specification be a total function from Ω^n to Ω. At first sight, this simplification might appear to be untenable since it implies that every operator can be applied to operands of arbitrary sorts. Formally, however, the situation can be saved by introducing a "nonsense" sort **ns**, which is the sort of "type-incorrect" phrases. (If a phrase is type-incorrect whenever any of its subphrases are type-incorrect, then every specification will yield **ns** whenever any of the sorts to which it is applied is **ns**. However, one can conceive of contexts, such as the application of a constant function, where this assumption might be relaxed.)

With this simplification, and a few changes of notation and terminology, Higgins' concept of a many-sorted algebra is:

(1) A *signature* consists of:

    (1a) (as before) A set Ω of *sorts*.

    (1b) (as before) A family, indexed by nonnegative integers, of disjoint sets Δ_n of *operators* of rank n.

    (1c) For each $n \geq 0$ and $\delta \in \Delta_n$, a *specification* $\Gamma_\delta \in \Omega^n \to \Omega$. (Informally, $\Gamma_\delta(\omega_1,\ldots,\omega_n)$ is the sort of result yielded by the generic operator δ when applied to operands of sorts $\omega_1,\ldots,\omega_n$.)

(2) An $\Omega\Delta\Gamma$-*algebra* consists of:

    (2a) (as before) A *carrier* B, which is an Ω-indexed family of sets.

    (2b) For each $n \geq 0$ and $\delta \in \Delta_n$, an *interpretation* γ_δ, which is an Ω^n-indexed family of functions $\gamma_\delta(\omega_1, \ldots, \omega_n) \in B(\omega_1) \times \cdots \times B(\omega_n) \to B(\Gamma_\delta(\omega_1, \ldots, \omega_n))$. (Informally, $\gamma_\delta(\omega_1, \ldots, \omega_n)$ is the interpretation of the version of the generic operator δ which is applicable to sorts $\omega_1, \ldots, \omega_n$.)

(3) If B, γ and B', γ' are $\Omega\Delta\Gamma$-algebras, then an *homomorphism* from B, γ to B', γ' is an Ω-indexed family of functions $\theta(\omega) \in B(\omega) \to B'(\omega)$ such that, for all $n \geq 0$, $\delta \in \Delta_n$, and $\omega_1, \ldots, \omega_n \in \Omega$, the diagram

$$
\begin{array}{ccc}
B(\omega_1) \times \cdots \times B(\omega_n) & \xrightarrow{\gamma_\delta(\omega_1, \ldots, \omega_n)} & B(\Gamma_\delta(\omega_1, \ldots, \omega_n)) \\
\Big\downarrow{\scriptstyle \theta(\omega_1) \times \cdots \times \theta(\omega_n)} & & \Big\downarrow{\scriptstyle \theta(\Gamma_\delta(\omega_1, \ldots, \omega_n))} \\
B'(\omega_1) \times \cdots \times B'(\omega_n) & \xrightarrow{\gamma'_\delta(\omega_1, \ldots, \omega_n)} & B'(\Gamma_\delta(\omega_1, \ldots, \omega_n))
\end{array}
\tag{I}
$$

commutes.

Algebras with Ordered Sorts

We can now introduce the notion of implicit conversion. When there is an implicit conversion from sort ω to sort ω', we write $\omega \leq \omega'$ and say that ω is a *subsort* (or *subtype*) of ω'. Syntactically, this means that a phrase of sort ω can occur in any context that permits a phrase of sort ω'.

It is reasonable to expect that $\omega \leq \omega$ and that $\omega \leq \omega'$ and $\omega' \leq \omega''$ implies $\omega \leq \omega''$. Thus the relation $\leq$ is a preordering (sometimes called a quasiordering) of the set Ω. Actually, in all of the examples in this paper $\leq$ will be a partial ordering, i.e., $\omega \leq \omega'$ and $\omega' \leq \omega$ will only hold when $\omega = \omega'$. However, our general theory will not impose this additional requirement upon $\leq$.

Now suppose δ is an operator of rank n, and $\omega_1, \ldots, \omega_n$ and $\omega'_1, \ldots, \omega'_n$ are sorts such that $\omega_i \leq \omega'_i$ for each i from one to n. Then a context that permits a phrase of sort $\Gamma_\delta(\omega'_1, \ldots \omega'_n)$ will permit an application of δ to operands of sorts $\omega'_1, \ldots, \omega'_n$. But the context of the ith operand will also permit an operand of sort ω_i, so that the overall context must also permit an application of δ to operands of sort $\omega_1, \ldots, \omega_n$, which has sort $\Gamma_\delta(\omega_1, \ldots, \omega_n)$. Thus we expect that $\Gamma_\delta(\omega_1, \ldots, \omega_n) \leq \Gamma_\delta(\omega'_1, \ldots, \omega'_n)$ or, more abstractly, that the specification Γ_δ will be a monotone function.

If $\omega \leq \omega'$ then an algebra must specify a conversion function from the set $B(\omega)$ of meanings appropriate to ω to the set $B(\omega')$ of meanings appropriate to ω'. At first sight, one might expect that this can only occur when $B(\omega)$ is a subset of $B(\omega')$, and that the conversion function must be the corresponding identity injection. For example, **integer** can be taken as a subsort of **real** because the integers are a subset of the reals.

However there are other situations in which this is too limited a view of implicit conversion. For example, we would like to say that **integer variable** is a subsort of **integer expression**, so that integer variables can occur in any context which permits an integer expression. But it is difficult to regard the meanings of integer variables as a subset of the meanings of integer expressions. In fact, we will regard the meaning of an integer variable as a pair of functions: an acceptor function, which maps integers into state transformations, and an evaluator function, which maps state into integers. Then the meaning of an expression will just be an evaluator function, and the implicit conversion function from variables to expressions will be a function on pairs that forgets their first components.

In general, we will permit implicit conversion functions that forget information and are therefore not injective. To paraphrase Jim Morris [6], subtypes are not subsets. This is the main difference between our approach and that of Goguen [1]. (There are some more technical differences, particularly in the definition of the signatures, whose implications are not completely clear to this author.)

However, there are still some restrictions that should be imposed upon implicit conversion functions. The conversion function from any type to itself should be an identity function. Moreover, if $\omega \leq \omega'$ and $\omega' \leq \omega''$ then the conversion function from $B(\omega)$ to $B(\omega'')$ should be the composition of the functions from $B(\omega)$ to $B(\omega')$ and from $B(\omega')$ to $B(\omega'')$. This will insure that a conversion from one sort to another will not depend upon the choice of a particular path in the preordering of sorts.

These restrictions can be stated more succinctly by invoking category theory. A preordered set such as Ω can be viewed as a category with the members of Ω as objects, in which there is a single morphism from ω to ω' if $\omega \leq \omega'$ and no such morphism otherwise. Suppose we write $\omega \leq \omega'$ to stand for the unique morphism from ω to ω' (as well as for the condition that this morphism exists), and require the carrier B to map each $\omega \leq \omega'$ into the conversion function from $B(\omega)$ to $B(\omega')$. Then we have

(i) $B(\omega \leq \omega') \in B(\omega) \to B(\omega')$.

(ii) $B(\omega \leq \omega) = I_{B(\omega)}$.

(iii) If $\omega \leq \omega'$ and $\omega' \leq \omega''$ then $B(\omega \leq \omega'') = B(\omega \leq \omega'); B(\omega' \leq \omega'')$.

(Thoughout this paper we will use semicolons to indicate composition in diagrammatic order, i.e., $(f; g)(x) = g(f(x))$.) These requirements are equivalent to saying that B must be a functor from Ω to the category SET, in which the objects are sets and the morphisms from S to S' are the functions from S to S'.

This leads to the following definition:

(1) A *signature* consists of:

   (1a) A preordered set Ω of *sorts*.

   (1b) (as before) A family, indexed by nonnegative integers, of disjoint sets Δ_n of *operators* of rank n.

   (1c) For each $n \geq 0$ and $\delta \in \Delta_n$, a *specification* Γ_δ, which is a monotone function from Ω^n to Ω.

(2) An $\Omega\Delta\Gamma$-*algebra* consists of:

   (2a) A *carrier* B, which is a functor from Ω to SET.

   (2b) For each $n \geq 0$ and $\delta \in \Delta_n$, an *interpretation* γ_δ, which is an Ω^n-indexed family of functions $\gamma_\delta(\omega_1, \ldots, \omega_n) \in B(\omega_1) \times \cdots \times B(\omega_n) \to B(\Gamma_\delta(\omega_1, \ldots, \omega_n))$ such that, whenever $\omega_1 \leq \omega'_1, \ldots, \omega_n \leq \omega'_n$, the diagram

$$
\begin{array}{ccc}
B(\omega_1) \times \cdots \times B(\omega_n) & \xrightarrow{\ \gamma_\delta(\omega_1, \ldots, \omega_n)\ } & B(\Gamma_\delta(\omega_1, \ldots, \omega_n)) \\
\Big\downarrow{\scriptstyle B(\omega_1 \leq \omega'_1) \times \cdots \times B(\omega_n \leq \omega'_n)} & & \Big\downarrow{\scriptstyle B(\Gamma_\delta(\omega_1, \ldots, \omega_n) \leq \Gamma_\delta(\omega'_1, \ldots, \omega'_n))} \\
B(\omega'_1) \times \cdots \times B(\omega'_n) & \xrightarrow{\ \gamma_\delta(\omega'_1, \ldots, \omega'_n)\ } & B(\Gamma_\delta(\omega'_1, \ldots, \omega'_n))
\end{array}
\qquad \text{(II)}
$$

   commutes.

The above diagram asserts the relationship between generic operators and implicit conversions that originally motivated our development. To recapture our original example, suppose **integer**, **real** $\in \Omega$, **integer** $\leq$ **real**, $+ \in \Delta_2$, $\Gamma_+(\textbf{integer}, \textbf{integer}) = $ **integer**, and $\Gamma_+(\textbf{real}, \textbf{real}) = $ **real**. Then a particular instance of the above diagram is

$$
\begin{array}{ccc}
B(\textbf{integer}) \times B(\textbf{integer}) & \xrightarrow{\ \gamma_+(\textbf{integer}, \textbf{integer})\ } & B(\textbf{integer}) \\
\Big\downarrow{\scriptstyle B(\textbf{integer} \leq \textbf{real}) \times B(\textbf{integer} \leq \textbf{real})} & & \Big\downarrow{\scriptstyle B(\textbf{integer} \leq \textbf{real})} \\
B(\textbf{real}) \times B(\textbf{real}) & \xrightarrow{\ \gamma_+(\textbf{real}, \textbf{real})\ } & B(\textbf{real})
\end{array}
$$

In other words, the result of adding two integers and converting their sum to a real number must be the same as the result of converting the integers and adding the converted operands.

In essence, the key to insuring that implicit conversions and generic operators mesh nicely is to require a commutative relationship between these entities. An analogous relationship must also be required between implicit conversions and homomorphisms:

(3) If B, γ and B', γ' are $\Omega\Delta\Gamma$-algebras, then an *homomorphism* from B, γ to B', γ' is an Ω-indexed family of functions $\theta(\omega) \in B(\omega) \to B'(\omega)$ such that, whenever $\omega \leq \omega'$, the diagram

$$
\begin{array}{ccc}
B(\omega) & \xrightarrow{\ \theta(\omega)\ } & B'(\omega) \\
\downarrow{\scriptstyle B(\omega \leq \omega')} & & \downarrow{\scriptstyle B'(\omega \leq \omega')} \\
B(\omega') & \xrightarrow{\ \theta(\omega')\ } & B'(\omega')
\end{array}
\qquad\qquad \text{(III)}
$$

commutes, and (as before) for all $n \geq 0$, $\delta \in \Delta_n$, and $\omega_1, \ldots, \omega_n \in \Omega$, the diagram (I) commutes.

Category-Sorted Algebras

By viewing the preordered set of sorts as a category, we have been able to use the category-theoretic concept of a functor to express appropriate restrictions on implicit conversion functions. In a similar vein, we can use the concept of a natural transformation to express the relationship between implicit conversion functions and interpretations given by diagram (II) and the relationship between implicit conversion functions and homomorphisms given by diagram (III).

In fact, diagram (III) is simply an assertion that the homomorphism θ is a natural transformation from the functor B to the functor B'. Diagram (II), however, is more complex. To express this diagram as a natural transformation, we must first define some notation for the exponentiation of categories and functors, and for the Cartesian product functor on SET:

(1) For any category K, we write:

    (a) $|K|$ for the set (or collection) of objects of K.

    (b) $X \xrightarrow[K]{} X'$ for the set of morphisms from X to X' in K.

    (c) I_X^K for the identity morphism of X in K.

    (d) $;_K$ for composition in K.

(2) For any category K, we write K^n to denote the category such that:

    (a) $|K^n| = |K|^n$, i.e. the n-fold Cartesian product of $|K|$.

(b) $\langle X_1,\ldots,X_n\rangle \underset{K^n}{\to} \langle X'_1,\ldots,X'_n\rangle = (X_1 \underset{K}{\to} X'_1) \times \cdots \times (X_n \underset{K}{\to} X'_n)$.

(c) $I^{K^n}_{\langle X_1,\ldots,X_n\rangle} = \langle I^K_{X_1},\ldots,I^K_{X_n}\rangle$.

(d) $\langle \rho_1,\ldots,\rho_n\rangle \,;_{K^n} \langle \rho'_1,\ldots,\rho'_n\rangle = \langle \rho_1 \,;_K \rho'_1,\ldots,\rho_n \,;_K \rho'_n\rangle$.

(Notice that when K is a preorder (e.g. Ω) this definition is consistent with the usual notion (e.g. Ω^n) of exponentiation of a preorder.)

(3) For any functor F from K to K', we write F^n to denote the functor from K^n to K'^n such that:

(a) $F^n(X_1,\ldots,X_n) = \langle F(X_1),\ldots,F(X_n)\rangle$.

(b) $F^n(\rho_1,\ldots,\rho_n) = \langle F(\rho_1),\ldots,F(\rho_n)\rangle$.

(4) We write $\times^{(n)}$ to denote the functor from SET^n to SET such that:

(a) $\times^{(n)}(S_1,\ldots,S_n) = S_1 \times \cdots \times S_n$.

(b) $\times^{(n)}(f_1,\ldots,f_n) = f_1 \times \cdots \times f_n$.

Next, we note that when Ω^n and Ω are viewed as categories, the monotone function Γ_δ can be viewed as a functor from Ω^n to Ω by defining its action on morphisms to be $\Gamma_\delta(\omega_1 \le \omega'_1,\ldots,\omega_n \le \omega'_n) = \Gamma_\delta(\omega_1,\ldots,\omega_n) \le \Gamma_\delta(\omega'_1,\ldots,\omega'_n)$. Then

$$\Omega^n \overset{B^n}{\to} \text{SET}^n \overset{\times^{(n)}}{\to} \text{SET}$$

and

$$\Omega^n \overset{\Gamma_\delta}{\to} \Omega \overset{B}{\to} \text{SET}$$

are compositions of functors that can be used to rewrite diagram (II) as:

$$
\begin{array}{ccc}
(B^n ; \times^{(n)})(\omega_1,\ldots,\omega_n) & \xrightarrow{\ \gamma_\delta(\omega_1,\ldots,\omega_n)\ } & (\Gamma_\delta ; B)(\omega_1,\ldots,\omega_n) \\
{\scriptstyle (B^n;\, \times^{(n)})(\omega_1 \le \omega'_1,\ldots,\omega_n \le \omega'_n)}\big\downarrow & & \big\downarrow{\scriptstyle (\Gamma_\delta;\, B)(\omega_1 \le \omega'_1,\ldots,\omega_n \le \omega'_n)} \\
(B^n ; \times^{(n)})(\omega'_1,\ldots,\omega'_n) & \xrightarrow[\ \gamma_\delta(\omega'_1,\ldots,\omega'_n)\ ]{} & (\Gamma_\delta ; B)(\omega'_1,\ldots,\omega'_n).
\end{array}
$$

In this form, the diagram is clearly an assertion that γ_δ is a natural transformation from the functor $B^n ; \times^{(n)}$ to the functor $\Gamma_\delta ; B$.

At this stage we have come to regard Ω entirely as a category. Indeed, we can justify the term "category-sorted algebra" by extending our definition to the case where Ω is an arbitrary category:

(1) A *signature* consists of:

(1a) A category Ω of *sorts*.

(1b) A family, indexed by nonnegative integers, of disjoint sets Δ_n of *operators* of rank n.

(1c) For each $n \geq 0$ and $\delta \in \Delta_n$, a *specification* Γ_δ, which is a functor from Ω^n to Ω.

(2) An $\Omega\Delta\Gamma$-*algebra* consists of:

   (2a) A *carrier* B, which is a functor from Ω to SET.

   (2b) For each $n \geq 0$ and $\delta \in \Delta_n$, an *interpretation* γ_δ, which is a natural transformation from $B^n ; \times^{(n)}$ to $\Gamma_\delta ; B$.

(3) If B, γ and B', γ' are $\Omega\Delta\Gamma$-algebras, then an *homomorphism* from B, γ to B', γ' is a natural transformation from B to B' such that, for all $n \geq 0$, $\delta \in \Delta_n$, and $\omega_1, \ldots,$ $\omega_n \in \Omega$, the diagram (I) commutes.

This is a clear illustration of what we mean by applying category theory to language definition. Our intention is not to use any deep theorems of category theory, but merely to employ the basic concepts of this field as organizing principles. This might appear as a desire to be concise at the expense of being esoteric. But in designing a programming language, the central problem is to organize a variety of concepts in a way that exhibits uniformity and generality. Substantial leverage can be gained in attacking this problem if these concepts can be defined concisely within a framework that has already proven its ability to impose uniformity and generality upon a wide variety of mathematics.

It is easy to verify that $\Omega\Delta\Gamma$-algebras and their homomorphisms form a category, which we will call $\text{ALG}_{\Omega\Delta\Gamma}$. It is also evident that these category-sorted algebras reduce to the Higgins algebras (with total specifications) discussed earlier when Ω is a discrete category (i.e., a partially ordered set in which $\omega \leq \omega'$ only holds when $\omega = \omega'$).

Algebraic Semantics

We can now explicate our claim that defining semantics is tantamount to defining a target algebra. Suppose the target algebra is a category-sorted $\Omega\Delta\Gamma$-algebra B, γ. Then $B(\omega)$ is the set of meanings of type ω. Thus we can define the set M of all meanings to be the disjoint union of $B(\omega)$ over $\omega \in |\Omega|$, i.e.,

$$M = \{\omega, x \mid \omega \in |\Omega| \text{ and } x \in B(\omega)\}.$$

We can also define the function $\tau_M \in M \to |\Omega|$ such that

$$\tau_M(\omega, x) = \omega,$$

which gives the type of each meaning in M.

Now let I be a set of identifiers and $\tau_I \in I \to |\Omega|$ be an assignment of types to each identifier in I. Then an environment e for I, τ_I is a function from I to M that maps each identifier into a meaning of the appropriate type, i.e., that makes the diagram

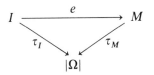

of functions commute.

To describe this situation in category-theoretic terms, we define the category $\text{SET} \downarrow |\Omega|$ of sets with type assignments. This is the category such that

(a) The objects of $\text{SET} \downarrow |\Omega|$ are pairs S, τ, where S is a set and $\tau \in S \to |\Omega|$,

(b) $S, \tau \underset{\text{SET}\downarrow|\Omega|}{\to} S'$, τ' is the set of functions f from S to S' such that the diagram

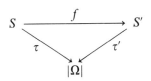

commutes,

(c) Composition and identities in $\text{SET} \downarrow |\Omega|$ are the same as in SET.

Then an environment for I, τ_I is a morphism in I, $\tau_{I\,\text{SET}\downarrow|\Omega|} \to M$, τ_M. We call this set $\text{Env}(I, \tau_I)$.

Next we define U to be the functor from $\text{ALG}_{\Omega\Delta\Gamma}$ to $\text{SET} \downarrow |\Omega|$ whose action on an $\Omega\Delta\Gamma$-algbra B, γ is given by

$$U(B, \gamma) = S, \tau \quad \text{where} \quad S = \{\omega, x \,|\, \omega \in |\Omega| \text{ and } x \in B(\omega)\},$$

$\tau \in S \to |\Omega|$ is the function such that $\tau(\omega, x) = \omega$,

and whose action on an homomorphism θ from B, γ to B', γ' is given by

$$U(\theta) \in U(B, \gamma) \underset{\text{SET}\downarrow|\Omega|}{\to} U(B', \gamma') \text{ is the function such that} \quad U(\theta)(\omega, x) = \omega, \theta(\omega)(x).$$

Then M, τ_M is the result of applying U to the target algebra B, γ, so that $\text{Env}(I, \tau_I) = I$, $\tau_{I\,\text{SET}\downarrow|\Omega|} \to U(B, \gamma)$. More generally, U is the "forgetful" functor that forgets both interpretations and implicit conversions, and maps a category-sorted algebra into the disjoint union of its carrier, along with an appropriate assignment of types to this disjoint union.

In the appendix, we will show that for any object I, τ_I of SET $\downarrow |\Omega|$ there is an algebra $F(I, \tau_I)$, called the *free $\Omega\Delta\Gamma$-algebra generated by I, τ_I*, and a morphism $\eta(I, \tau_I) \in I, \tau_I$ ${}_{\text{SET}\downarrow|\Omega|}^{\longrightarrow} U(F(I, \tau_I))$, called the *embedding of I, τ_I into its free algebra*, such that:

For any $B, \gamma \in |\text{ALG}_{\Omega\Delta\Gamma}|$ and $e \in I, \tau_I {}_{\text{SET}\downarrow|\Omega|}^{\longrightarrow} U(B, \gamma)$, there is exactly one homomorphism $\hat{e} \in F(I, \tau_I) {}_{\text{ALG}_{\Omega\Delta\Gamma}}^{\longrightarrow} B, \gamma$ such that the diagram

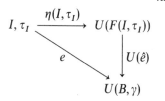

in SET $\downarrow |\Omega|$ commutes.

Suppose $F(I, \tau_I) = B_0, \gamma_0$. Then each $B_0(\omega)$ is the set of phrases of type ω that can be constructed from identifiers in I whose types are given by τ_I. Each $\hat{e}(\omega)$ maps the phrases of type ω into their meanings in $B(\omega)$. Moreover, suppose $R, \tau_R = U(B_0, \gamma_0) = U(F(I, \tau_I))$. Then R is the set of phrases of all types, τ_R maps these phrases into their types, and $U(\hat{e})$ maps these phrases into their meanings in a way that preserves types.

The embedding $\eta(I, \tau_I)$ maps each identifier into the phrase which consists of that identifier. Thus the above diagram shows that the meaning $U(\hat{e})(\eta(I, \tau_I)(i))$ of the phrase consisting of i is the meaning $e(i)$ given to i by the environment e.

For a given I, τ_I, one can define the $|\Omega|$-indexed family of semantic functions

$$\mu(\omega) \in B_0(\omega) \to (\text{Env}(I, \tau_I) \to B(\omega))$$

such that

$$\mu(\omega)(r)(e) = \hat{e}(\omega)(r).$$

Then each $\mu(\omega)$ maps phrases of type ω into functions from environments to meanings of type ω. Alternatively, one can define the single semantic function

$$\mu \in R \to (\text{Env}(I, \tau_I) \to M)$$

such that

$$\mu(r)(e) = U(\hat{e})(r).$$

This function maps phrases of all types into functions from environments to meanings.

It is evident that the linguistic applicaton of category-sorted algebras depends crucially upon the existence of free algebras or, more abstractly, upon the existence of a left adjoint to the forgetful functor U. In general, if U is any functor from a category

K' to a category K, F is a functor from K to K', and η is a natural transformation from I_K to F; U such that:

For all $X \in |K|$, $X' \in |K'|$, and $\rho \in X \xrightarrow{K} U(X')$, there is exactly one morphism $\hat{\rho} \in F(X) \xrightarrow{K'} X'$ such that

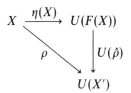

commutes in K,

then F is said to be a *left adjoint of U*, with *associated natural transformation η*. The triple F, U, η is called an *adjunction* from K to K'.

In the appendix, we show the existence of free category-sorted algebras by constructing a left adjoint and associated natural transformation for the forgetful functor U from $\mathrm{ALG}_{\Omega\Delta\Gamma}$ to $\mathrm{SET} \downarrow |\Omega|$.

Data Algebras

To illustrate the application of category-sorted algebras, we will consider several variations of Algol 60. However, since we do not yet know how to treat binding mechanisms elegantly in an algebraic framework, we will limit ourselves to the subset of Algol that excludes the binding of identifiers, i.e., to the simple imperative language that underlies Algol. Although this is a substantial limitation, we will still be able to show the potential of our methodology for disciplining the design of implicit conversions and generic operators.

As discussed in [7] and [8], we believe that a fundamental characteristic of Algol-like languages is the presence of two kinds of type: data types, which describe variables (or expressions) and their ranges of values, and phrase types (called program types in [7]), which describe identifiers (or phrases that can be bound to identifiers) and their sets of meanings.

Algebraically, Ω should be a set of data types in order to define the values of expressions. In this case, the carrier of the free algebra is a data-type-indexed family of sets of expressions, and the carrier of the target algebra, which we will call a *data algebra*, is a data-type-indexed family of sets of values.

In Algol 60 itself there are three data types: **integer**, **real**, and **boolean**, to which we must add the nonsense type **ns**. To avoid implicit conversions, we would take Ω to be

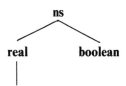

integer   real   boolean.

Notice that **ns** is the greatest element in this partial ordering, reflecting the notion that any sensible expression can occur in a context which permits nonsense.

On the other hand, to introduce an implicit conversion from **integer** to **real**, we would take **integer** to be a subtype of **real**:

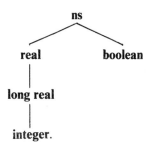

A more interesting situation arises when **long real** is introduced. One might expect **real** to be a subtype of **long real**, but an implicit conversion from **real** to **long real** would be dangerous from the viewpoint of numerical analysis, since a real value does not provide enough information to completely determine a long real value. In fact, it is the opposite implicit conversion that is numerically safe, so that **long real** should be a subtype of **real**:

```
            ns
         /      \
     real       boolean
      |
   long real
      |
    integer.
```

In a language definition that was sufficiently concrete to make sense of the distinction between **real** and **long real**, one might take $B(\textbf{real})$ and $B(\textbf{long real})$ to be sets of real numbers with single and double precision representations, respectively, and $B(\textbf{long real} \leq \textbf{real})$ to be the truncation or roundoff function from $B(\textbf{long real})$ to $B(\textbf{real})$. Notice that this function is not an injection, reflecting the fact that a conversion from **long real** to **real** loses information.

However, although this is suggestive, our methodology is not really adequate for dealing with the problems of roundoff or overflow. For this reason, we will omit the type **long real** and define our language at the level of abstraction where roundoff and overflow are ignored.

In the rest of this paper we will take Ω to be:

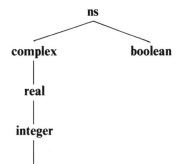

digit string.

It should be emphasized that this choice of Ω—particularly the use of **digit string**—is purely for illustrative purposes, and is not put forth as desirable for a real programming language.

In the carrier of our target algebra we will have:

$B(\textbf{digit string})$ = the set of strings of digits,

$B(\textbf{integer})$ = the set of integers,

$B(\textbf{real})$ = the set of real numbers,

$B(\textbf{complex})$ = the set of complex numbers,

$B(\textbf{boolean})$ = $\{\textbf{true}, \textbf{false}\}$,

with the conversion functions

$B(\textbf{digit string} \leq \textbf{integer})$ = the function which maps each digit string into the integer of which it is a decimal representation.

$B(\textbf{integer} \leq \textbf{real})$ = the identity injection from integers to real numbers.

$B(\textbf{real} \leq \textbf{complex})$ = the identity injection from real numbers to complex numbers.

Notice that, because of the possible presence of leading zeros, the function $B(\textbf{digit string} \leq \textbf{integer})$ is not an injection.

We must also specify $B(\textbf{ns})$ and the conversion functions into this set. For these conversion functions to exist, $B(\textbf{ns})$ must be nonempty, i.e., we must give some kind of meaning to nonsense expressions. The closest we can come to saying that they do not make sense is to give them all the same meaning by taking $B(\mathbf{ns})$ to be a singleton set. This insures (since a singleton set is a terminal element in the category SET), that there will be exactly one possible conversion function from any data type to $\mathbf{ns}$:

$$B(\mathbf{ns}) = \{\langle\ \rangle\},$$

$B(\omega \leq \mathbf{ns}) = $ the unique function from $B(\omega)$ to $\{\langle\ \rangle\}$.

As an example of an operator, let $+$ be a member of Δ_2, with the specification

$\Gamma_+(\omega_1, \omega_2) = $ **if** $\omega_1 \leq$ **integer and** $\omega_2 \leq$ **integer then integer**
       else if $\omega_1 \leq$ **real and** $\omega_2 \leq$ **real then real**
       else if $\omega_1 \leq$ **complex and** $\omega_2 \leq$ **complex then complex**
       else ns

and the interpretation

$\gamma_+(\omega_1, \omega_2) = $ **if** $\omega_1 \leq$ **integer and** $\omega_2 \leq$ **integer then**
      $\lambda(x, y)$. **let** $x' = B(\omega_1 \leq$ **integer**$)(x)$ **and** $y' = B(\omega_2 \leq$ **integer**$)(y)$
          in integer-addition(x', y')
    else if $\omega_1 \leq$ **real and** $\omega_2 \leq$ **real then**
      $\lambda(x, y)$. **let** $x' = B(\omega_1 \leq$ **real**$)(x)$ **and** $y' = B(\omega_2 \leq$ **real**$)(y)$
          in real-addition(x', y')
    else if $\omega_1 \leq$ **complex and** $\omega_2 \leq$ **complex then**
      $\lambda(x, y)$. **let** $x' = B(\omega_1 \leq$ **complex**$)(x)$ **and** $y' = B(\omega_2 \leq$ **complex**$)(y)$
          in complex-addition(x', y')
    else $\lambda(x, y). \langle\ \rangle$.

Although the above definition makes $+$ a purely numerical operator, it can be extended to encompass nonnumerical "addition":

$\Gamma_+(\omega_1, \omega_2) = $ **if** $\omega_1 \leq$ **boolean and** $\omega_2 \leq$ **boolean then boolean**
       else if $\omega_1 \leq$ **digit string and** $\omega_2 \leq$ **digit string then digit string**
       else ... (as before)
$\gamma_+(\omega_1, \omega_2) = $ **if** $\omega_1 \leq$ **boolean and** $\omega_2 \leq$ **boolean then**
      $\lambda(x, y)$. **let** $x' = B(\omega_1 \leq$ **boolean**$)(x)$ **and** $y' = B(\omega_2 \leq$ **boolean**$)(y)$
          in boolean-addition(x', y')
    else if $\omega_1 \leq$ **digit string and** $\omega_2 \leq$ **digit string then**
      $\lambda(x, y)$. **let** $x' = B(\omega_1 \leq$ **digit string**$)(x)$
           and $y' = B(\omega_2 \leq$ **digit string**$)(y)$
          in digit-string-addition(x', y')
    else ... (as before).

Since there are no implicit conversions between **boolean** and any other type than **ns**, we are free to choose "boolean addition" to be any function from pairs of truth values to truth value. On the other hand, "digit-string addition" is tightly constrained by the implicit conversion from **digit string** to **integer**, which gives rise to the requirement that

$$B(\text{digit string}) \times B(\text{digit string}) \xrightarrow{\quad\text{digit-string addition}\quad} B(\text{digit string})$$

$$\Big\downarrow \begin{matrix} B(\text{digit string} \leq \text{integer}) \\ \times\, B(\text{digit string} \leq \text{integer}) \end{matrix} \qquad\qquad\qquad \Big\downarrow B(\text{digit string} \leq \text{integer})$$

$$B(\text{integer}) \times B(\text{integer}) \xrightarrow{\quad\text{integer addition}\quad} B(\text{integer})$$

commute. In other words, the sum of two digit strings must be a decimal representation of the sum of the integers that are represented by those two strings. The only freedom we have in defining digit-string addition is in the treatment of leading zeros in the result.

The definition of $+$ suggests that a typical operator will have a significant specification and interpretation for certain "key" sorts of operands, and that its specification and interpretation for other sorts of operands can be obtained by implicitly converting the operands to key sorts. To formalize this idea, let

1. Λ_δ be a category of *keys*.

2. Φ_δ be a functor from Λ_δ to Ω^n.

3. $\overline{\Gamma}_\delta$ be a functor from Λ_δ to Ω.

4. $\overline{\gamma}_\delta$ be a natural transformation from $\Phi_\delta; B^n; \times^{(n)}$ to $\overline{\Gamma}_\delta; B$.

Intuitively, for each key $\lambda \in |\Lambda_\delta|$, $\Phi_\delta(\lambda)$ is the n-tuple of sorts to which the "λ-version" of δ is applicable, $\overline{\Gamma}_\delta(\lambda)$ is the sort of the result of the λ-version of δ, and $\overline{\gamma}_\delta(\lambda) \in \times^{(n)}$ $(B^n(\Phi_\delta(\lambda))) \to B(\overline{\Gamma}_\delta(\lambda))$ is the interpretation of the λ-version of δ.

These entities can be extended to all sorts of operands if the functor Φ_δ possesses a left adjoint Ψ_δ, which will be a functor from Ω^n to Λ, and an associated natural transformation η_δ, which will be a natural transformation from I_{Ω^n} to $\Psi_\delta; \Phi_\delta$. Then we can define the specification

$$\Gamma_\delta = \Psi_\delta; \overline{\Gamma}_\delta \in \Omega^n \to \Omega,$$

and the interpretation

$$\gamma_\delta(\omega_1, \ldots, \omega_n) = \times^{(n)}(B^n(\eta_\delta(\omega_1, \ldots, \omega_n))); \overline{\gamma}_\delta(\Psi_\delta(\omega_1, \ldots, \omega_n)),$$

which can easily be shown to be a natural transformation from $B^n; \times^{(n)}$ to $\Gamma_\delta; B$. Intuitively, $\Psi_\delta(\omega_1, \ldots, \omega_n)$ can be thought of as the key determining the version of δ

to be used for operands of sorts $\omega_1, \ldots, \omega_n$, and $\eta_\delta(\omega_1, \ldots, \omega_n)$ as the implicit conversion to be applied to these operands.

In the special case where Λ_δ and Ω are partially ordered sets, it can be shown [9, p. 93] that Ψ_δ will be a left adjoint of Φ_δ if and only if $\overline{\omega} \le \Phi_\delta(\Psi_\delta(\overline{\omega}))$ for all $\overline{\omega} \in \Omega^n$ and $\Psi_\delta(\Phi_\delta(\lambda)) \le \lambda$ for all $\lambda \in \Lambda_\delta$. In this case $\eta_\delta(\overline{\omega})$ will be the unique morphism $\overline{\omega} \le \Phi_\delta(\Psi_\delta(\overline{\omega}))$, and γ_δ will be

$$\gamma_\delta(\overline{\omega}) = \times^{(n)}(B^n(\overline{\omega} \le \Phi_\delta(\Psi_\delta(\overline{\omega})))) ; \overline{\gamma}_\delta(\Psi_\delta(\overline{\omega})).$$

Moreover, as shown by the following proposition, Ψ_δ will be uniquely determined by Φ_δ:

PROPOSITION   Suppose Φ is a monotone function from Λ to Ω^n, where Λ and Ω^n are partially ordered sets, such that

1. For all $\overline{\omega} \in \Omega^n$, the set $\{\lambda | \lambda \in \Lambda$ and $\overline{\omega} \le \Phi(\lambda)\}$ has a greatest lower bound in Λ.

2. For all $\overline{\omega} \in \Omega^n$, $\Phi(\bigsqcap_\Lambda \{\lambda | \lambda \in \Lambda$ and $\overline{\omega} \le \Phi(\lambda)\})$ is the greatest lower bound in Ω^n of $\{\Phi(\lambda) | \lambda \in \Lambda$ and $\overline{\omega} \le \Phi(\lambda)\}$.

Then $\Psi(\overline{\omega}) = \bigsqcap_\Lambda \{\lambda | \lambda \in \Lambda$ and $\overline{\omega} \le \Phi(\lambda)\}$ is the unique monotone function from Ω^n to Λ such that Ψ is a left adjoint of Φ.

Proof Ψ is obviously monotone. For any $\lambda \in \Lambda$, $\Psi(\Phi(\lambda))$ is the greatest lower bound of $\{\lambda' | \lambda' \in \Lambda$ and $\Phi(\lambda) \le \Phi(\lambda')\}$ and, since λ belongs to this set, $\Psi(\Phi(\lambda)) \le \lambda$. For any $\omega \in \Omega^n$, $\Phi(\Psi(\overline{\omega})) = \Phi(\bigsqcap_\Lambda \{\lambda | \lambda \in \Lambda$ and $\overline{\omega} \le \Phi(\lambda)\})$ is the greatest lower bound of $\{\Phi(\lambda) | \lambda \in \Lambda$ and $\overline{\omega} \le \Phi(\lambda)\}$ and, since $\overline{\omega}$ is a lower bound of this set, $\overline{\omega} \le \Phi(\Psi(\overline{\omega}))$.

Suppose Ψ is a left adjoint of Φ. If $\overline{\omega} \le \Phi(\lambda)$ then $\Psi(\overline{\omega}) \le \Psi(\Phi(\lambda)) \le \lambda$. Thus $\Psi(\overline{\omega})$ is a lower bound of $\{\lambda | \lambda \in \Lambda$ and $\overline{\omega} \le \Phi(\lambda)\}$. Moreover, this set contains $\Psi(\overline{\omega})$ since $\overline{\omega} \le \Phi(\Psi(\overline{\omega}))$. Thus any lower bound of this set must be less than $\Psi(\overline{\omega})$, so that $\Psi(\overline{\omega})$ is the greatest lower bound.   ■

The conditions in this proposition will hold if Λ contains greatest lower bounds of all of its subsets, i.e., if Λ is a complete lattice, and Φ preserves all greatest lower bounds However, we will sometimes use Λ's which are not complete lattices.

As an example, the purely numeric definition of $+$ given earlier can be recast more concisely by using the set of keys

$$\Lambda_+ = \{\textbf{integer}, \textbf{real}, \textbf{complex}, \textbf{ns}\}$$

with the same partial ordering as Ω. Then the specification Γ_+ is determined by the functions Φ_+ and $\overline{\Gamma}_+$ such that

λ	$\Phi_+(\lambda)$	$\overline{\Gamma}_+(\lambda)$
integer	**integer, integer**	**integer**
real	**real, real**	**real**
complex	**complex, complex**	**complex**
ns	**ns, ns**	**ns**

and the interpretation γ_+ is determined by

$\overline{\gamma}_+(\mathbf{integer})$ = integer addition

$\overline{\gamma}_+(\mathbf{real})$ = real addition

$\overline{\gamma}_+(\mathbf{complex})$ = complex addition

$\overline{\gamma}_+(\mathbf{ns}) = \lambda(x, y).\langle\ \rangle.$

To extend this definition to nonnumeric types, one adds **boolean** and **digit string** to Λ_+, with

λ	$\Phi_+(\lambda)$	$\overline{\Gamma}_+(\lambda)$
boolean	**boolean, boolean**	**boolean**
digit string	**digit string, digit string**	**digit string**

and

$\overline{\gamma}_+(\mathbf{boolean})$ = boolean addition

$\overline{\gamma}_+(\mathbf{digit\ string})$ = digit-string addition.

(Notice that in this case Λ_+ is not a complete lattice, but the necessary conditions for the existence of a left adjoint to Φ_+ are still met.)

In the remainder of this section we will illustrate our approach by defining a few other binary operators. In each case Λ_+ is the listed subset of Ω, with the same partial ordering as Ω.

For the division operators / and $\div$ we can define

λ	$\Phi_/(\lambda)$	$\overline{\Gamma}_/(\lambda)$
real	**real, real**	**real**
complex	**complex, complex**	**complex**
ns	**ns, ns**	**ns**

$\bar{\gamma}_/(\textbf{real}) = $ real division

$\bar{\gamma}_/(\textbf{complex}) = $ complex division

$\bar{\gamma}_/(\textbf{ns}) = \lambda(x, y). \langle\ \rangle$

and

λ	$\Phi_\div(\lambda)$	$\overline{\Gamma}_\div(\lambda)$
integer	**integer, integer**	**integer**
ns	**ns, ns**	**ns**

$\bar{\gamma}_\div(\textbf{integer}) = \lambda(x, y).$ the unique integer q such that
$\qquad x = q \times y + r$ where
$\qquad$ **if** $x \geq 0$ **then** $0 \leq r < |y|$ **else** $-|y| < r \leq 0,$

$\bar{\gamma}_\div(\textbf{ns}) = \lambda(x, y). \langle\ \rangle.$

These operations cannot be combined into a single operator since, for example, $3/2 = 1.5$ but $3 \div 2 = 1$. On the other hand, since the definition of $\gamma_\div(\textbf{integer})$ extends sensibly to the case where x and y are real, one could generalize $\div$ by taking $\Phi_\div(\textbf{integer}) = \textbf{real, real}$.

Since nonnegative integers have not been introduced as a data type and, for example, 3^{-2} is not an integer, there are no operand sorts for which exponentiation always yields an integer result. If exponents are limited to integers, one can define

$\lambda_\uparrow$	$\Phi_\uparrow(\lambda)$	$\overline{\Gamma}_\uparrow(\lambda)$
real	**real, integer**	**real**
complex	**complex, integer**	**complex**
ns	**ns, ns**	**ns**

$\bar{\gamma}_\uparrow(\textbf{real}) = \lambda(x, n). x^n$

$\bar{\gamma}_\uparrow(\textbf{complex}) = \lambda(x, n). x^n$

$\bar{\gamma}_\uparrow(\textbf{ns}) = \lambda(x, y). \langle\ \rangle.$

This can be extended to noninteger exponents by taking $\Phi_\uparrow(\textbf{complex}) = \textbf{complex},$ **complex**, but the multi-valued nature of complex exponentiation (as well as the time required to compute the necessary logarithms and exponentials) would probably make this unwise.

Finally, we define an equality operation:

λ	$\Phi_=(\lambda)$	$\overline{\Gamma}_=(\lambda)$
boolean	**boolean, boolean**	**boolean**
integer	**integer, integer**	**boolean**
real	**real, real**	**boolean**
complex	**complex, complex**	**boolean**
ns	**ns, ns**	**ns**

$\overline{\gamma}_=(\lambda) =$ **if** $\lambda \neq$ **ns then** the equality relation for $B(\lambda)$
     else $\lambda(x, y) . \langle \ \rangle$.

One might be tempted to add **digit string** to $\Lambda_=$, with $\Phi_=($**digit string**$) =$ **digit string, digit string**, $\overline{\Gamma}_=($**digit string**$) =$ **boolean**, and $\overline{\gamma}_=($**digit string**$) =$ the equality relation for $B($**digit string**$)$. However, the diagram

$$
\begin{array}{ccc}
B(\textbf{digit string}) \times B(\textbf{digit string}) & \xrightarrow{\ =\ \textbf{digit string}\ } & B(\textbf{boolean}) \\
\Big\downarrow {\scriptstyle B(\textbf{digit string} \leq \textbf{integer})} & & \Big\downarrow {\scriptstyle I_{B(\textbf{boolean})}} \\
{\scriptstyle \times\ B(\textbf{digit string} \leq \textbf{integer})} & & \\
B(\textbf{integer}) \times B(\textbf{integer}) & \xrightarrow{\ =\ \textbf{integer}\ } & B(\textbf{boolean})
\end{array}
$$

does not commute, since $B($**digit string** $\leq$ **integer**$)$ is not an injection. (For example, 6 and 06 are unequal digit strings that convert to equal integers.) Indeed, one can never use the same operator for the equality relation on different data types when the data types are connected by an implicit conversion function that is not an injection. (At the more concrete level where roundoff error is taken into account, this suggests, quite correctly, that there are special perils surrounding an equality operation for real numbers.)

Algebras for Simple Imperative Languages

Now we move from data algebras, which describe languages of expressions, to algebras that describe simple imperative programming languages, i.e., languages with variables, expressions, and commands, but without binding operations. The sorts of our algebras will change from data types to phrase types, which can be thought of as phrase class names of the abstract syntax for the language being defined. For example, in place of the set of data types {**integer**, **real**, **boolean**}, Ω might be the following partially ordered set of phrase types:

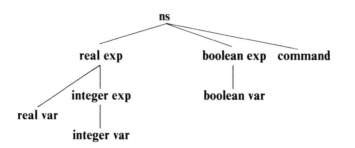

It is evident that for each data type τ there will be two phrase types τ **exp**(ression) and τ **var**(iable), and that τ **exp** will be a subtype of τ' **exp** whenever the data type τ is a subtype of τ'. Moreover, τ **var** will be a subtype of τ **exp** since a variable can be used in any context that permits an expression of the same data type. On the other hand, the subtype relation will never hold between variables of distinct data types. For example, an integer variable cannot be used as a real variable since it cannot accept a noninteger value, and a real variable cannot be used as an integer variable since it might produce a noninteger value.

This kind of phrase-type structure, which describes many programming languages, is unpleasantly asymmetric. For each data type, there are variables, which can accept or produce values, and expressions, which can only produce values. Thus one might expect another kind of phrase, called an *acceptor*, which can only accept value. If acceptors for each data type are added to Ω, we have:

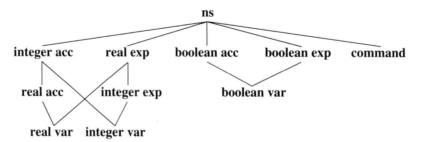

Notice that the subtype relation among acceptors is the dual of that for data types or expressions. For example, a real acceptor can be used as an integer acceptor since an integer value can be converted into a real value.

The above partial ordering has the peculiarity that there is a pair of phrase types, **real var** and **integer var**, that have no least upper bound. In general this might not be a problem, but we will find that there is one language construct, the general conditional phrase, that requires the existence of binary least upper bounds. To see the problem, suppose n is an integer variable and x is a real variable, and consider the conditional variable

if p **then** n **else** x.

In a context that calls for an expression, this phrase must be considered a real expression, since when p is false it can produce a noninteger value. But in a context that calls for an acceptor, the phrase must be considered an integer acceptor, since when p is true it cannot accept a noninteger value. The phrase type that describes this situation must be a subtype of both **integer acc** and **real exp** that in turn has **real var** and **integer var** as its subtypes. In other words, it must be the least upper bound of **real var** and **integer var**.

The way out of this difficulty is to characterize variables by both the data type that they accept and the data type that they produce. For example, a **real var** is actually a "real-accepting, real-producing" variable, an **integer var** is actually an "integer-accepting, integer-producing" variable, and the above conditional variable is an "integer-accepting, real-producing" variable. If we write $\tau_1 \tau_2$ **var** to abbreviate "τ_1-accepting, τ_2-producing" variable, then we have the ordering

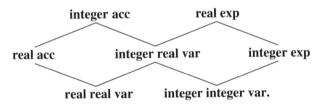

Implicit in this discussion is the idea that phrase types are constructed from data types. More generally, since the meaning of expressions can be described by a data algebra, and expressions are a major constituent of an imperative programming language, it should be possible to define the algebra describing the programming language in terms of the data algebra describing its expressions. To emphasize this possibility we will construct a programming-language algebra for an arbitrary data algebra, with signature $\Omega^D, \Delta^D, \Gamma^D$, carrier B^D, and interpretation γ^D. The main restrictions we will place upon this data algebra are that **ns** must be the greatest sort in Ω^D, and that $\Gamma^D(\omega_1, \ldots, \omega_n) = $ **ns** must hold when any ω_i is **ns**.

The set of phrase types is

$$\Omega = \{\tau \textbf{ exp} | \tau \in \Omega^D - \{\textbf{ns}\}\} \cup \{\tau \textbf{ acc} | \tau \in \Omega^D - \{\textbf{ns}\}\} \cup \{\tau_1 \tau_2 \textbf{ var} | \tau_1, \tau_2 \in \Omega^D - \{\textbf{ns}\}\}$$

$$\cup \{\textbf{comm}, \textbf{ns}\},$$

with the least partial ordering such that

if $\tau \leq^D \tau'$ then τ **exp** $\leq \tau'$ **exp**

if $\tau' \leq^D \tau$ then τ **acc** $\leq \tau'$ **acc**

if $\tau_1' \leq^D \tau_1$ and $\tau_2 \leq^D \tau_2'$ then $\tau_1 \tau_2$ **var** $\leq \tau_1' \tau_2'$ **var**

$\tau_1 \tau_2$ **var** $\leq \tau_1$ **acc**

$\tau_1 \tau_2$ **var** $\leq \tau_2$ **exp**

$\omega \leq$ **ns**.

Our target algebra describes direct semantics. (Continuation semantics can be treated in much the same way, but it leads to more complex definitions without providing any additional insights into the concerns of this paper.) The carrier of this target algebra will map each sort into a domain (a partially ordered set containing a least element $\bot$ and least upper bounds of its directed subsets), with implicit conversion functions that are strict and continuous (i.e., that preserve $\bot$ and least upper bounds of directed sets). Specifically, the following carrier is appropriate for direct semantics:

$B(\tau \ \textbf{exp}) = S \rightarrow [B^D(\tau)]_\bot$

$B(\textbf{comm}) = S \rightarrow [S]_\bot$

$B(\tau \ \textbf{acc}) = B^D(\tau) \rightarrow B(\textbf{comm})$

$B(\tau_1 \tau_2 \ \textbf{var}) = B(\tau_1 \ \textbf{acc}) \times B(\tau_2 \ \textbf{exp})$

$B(\textbf{ns}) = \{\bot\}$

$B(\tau \ \textbf{exp} \leq \tau' \ \textbf{exp}) = \lambda v . v ; [B^D(\tau \leq \tau')]_\bot$

$B(\tau \ \textbf{acc} \leq \tau' \ \textbf{acc}) = \lambda a . B^D(\tau' \leq \tau) ; a$

$B(\tau_1 \tau_2 \ \textbf{var} \leq \tau_1 \ \textbf{acc}) = \lambda(a, v) . a$

$B(\tau_1 \tau_2 \ \textbf{var} \leq \tau_2 \ \textbf{exp}) = \lambda(a, v) . v$

$B(\tau_1 \tau_2 \ \textbf{var} \leq \tau_1' \tau_2' \ \textbf{var}) = B(\tau_1 \ \textbf{acc} \leq \tau_1' \ \textbf{acc}) \times B(\tau_2 \ \textbf{exp} \leq \tau_2' \ \textbf{exp})$

$B(\omega \leq \textbf{ns}) = \lambda x . \bot_{B(\textbf{ns})}$.

Here S is an unspecified set of store states. For any set X, $[X]_\bot$ denotes the flat domain obtained by adding $\bot$ to X. For any function $f \in X \rightarrow X'$, $[f]_\bot$ denotes the strict extension of f to $[X]_\bot \rightarrow [X']_\bot$.

Basically, the meaning of a command is a state transition function (with result $\perp$ for nontermination), the meaning of an acceptor is a function from data values to state transition functions, and the meaning of a variable is a pair giving both the meaning of an acceptor and of an expression. Notice that this way of defining variables avoids the mention of any entities such as Strachey's L-values. (As a consequence, our definition permits strangely behaved variables akin to the implicit references in GEDANKEN [10]).

Next we consider operators. Each operator of the data algebra becomes an expression-producing operator of the imperative-language algebra. If $\delta \in \Delta_n^D$, then $\delta \in \Delta_n$, with the specification given by:

$$\Lambda_\delta = (\Omega^D)^n$$

$$\Phi_\delta = \phi^n, \text{ where } \phi \in \Omega^D \to \Omega \text{ is the function such that } \phi(\tau) = \text{if } \tau = \text{ns then ns else } \tau \text{ exp},$$

$$\overline{\Gamma}_\delta = \Gamma_\delta^D ; \phi.$$

To define the interpretation of δ we must give a natural transformation $\overline{\gamma}_\delta$ from $\Phi_\delta ; B^n ; \times^{(n)} = \phi^n ; B^n ; \times^{(n)}$ to $\overline{\Gamma}_\delta ; B = \Gamma_\delta^D ; \phi ; B$. Thus $\overline{\gamma}_\delta(\tau_1, \dots, \tau_n)$ must be a function from $B(\phi(\tau_1)) \times \cdots \times B(\phi(\tau_n))$ to $B(\phi(\Gamma_\delta^D(\tau_1, \dots, \tau_n)))$. If $\Gamma_\delta^D(\tau_1, \dots, \tau_n)$ is **ns**, then $\overline{\gamma}_\delta(\tau_1, \dots, \tau_n)$ will be the unique function from $B(\phi(\tau_1)) \times \cdots \times B(\phi(\tau_n))$ to $B(\textbf{ns})$. Otherwise, none of the τ_i will be **ns**, and $\overline{\gamma}_\delta(\tau_1, \dots, \tau_n)$ will be the function from $B(\tau_1 \textbf{ exp}) \times \cdots \times B(\tau_n \textbf{ exp}) = (S \to [B^D(\tau_1)]_\perp) \times \cdots \times (S \to [B^D(\tau_n)]_\perp)$ to $B(\Gamma_\delta^D(\tau_1, \dots, \tau_n) \textbf{exp}) = S \to [B^D(\Gamma_\delta^D(\tau_1, \dots, \tau_n))]_\perp$ such that

$$\overline{\gamma}_\delta(\tau_1, \dots, \tau_n)(v_1, \dots, v_n) = \lambda\sigma \in S . [\gamma_\delta^D(\tau_1, \dots, \tau_n)]_{\perp\perp}(v_1(\sigma), \dots, v_n(\sigma)),$$

where $[\gamma_\delta^D(\tau_1, \dots, \tau_n)]_{\perp\perp}$ denotes the extension of $\gamma_\delta^D(\tau_1, \dots, \tau_n)$ such that $[\gamma_\delta^D(\tau_1, \dots, \tau_n)]_{\perp\perp}(x_1, \dots, x_n) = \perp$ if any $x_i = \perp$.

Assignment is an operator $:= \,\in \Delta_2$. This is the one case which we cannot define by using an adjunction from a set of keys. The specification is

$$\Gamma_{:=}(\omega_1, \omega_2) = \text{if } (\exists \tau \in \Omega^D - \{\textbf{ns}\}) \, \omega_1 \leq \tau \textbf{ acc and } \omega_2 \leq \tau \textbf{ exp then comm else ns}$$

If a data type τ meeting the above condition exists, then the interpretation is

$$\gamma_{:=}(\omega_1, \omega_2) = \lambda(a, v) . \textbf{ let } a' = B(\omega_1 \leq \tau \textbf{ acc})(a) \textbf{ and } v' = B(\omega_2 \leq \tau \textbf{ exp})(v)$$

$$\textbf{in } D_{\textbf{comm}}(v' ; [a']_\oplus);$$

otherwise

$$\gamma_{:=}(\omega_1, \omega_2) = \lambda(a, v) . \perp_{B(\textbf{ns})}.$$

Here $[a']_\perp$ is the $\perp$-preserving extension of a' from $B^D(\tau) \to B(\textbf{comm})$ to $[B^D(\tau)]_\perp \to B(\textbf{comm})$, and $D_{\textbf{comm}} \in (S \to B(\textbf{comm})) \to B(\textbf{comm})$ is the diagonalizing function such that

$$D_{\textbf{comm}}(h)(\sigma) = h(\sigma)(\sigma).$$

A subtlety in this definition is that the data type τ may not be unique. For example, if ω_1 is **real acc** and ω_2 is **integer exp** then τ can be either **integer** or **real**. However, the definition still gives a unique meaning to $\gamma_{:=}$. Basically, this is because the structure of Ω insures that, if

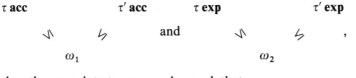

then there are data types τ_1 and τ_2 such that

$$\begin{array}{ccccccc}
\tau\ \textbf{acc} & & \tau'\ \textbf{acc} & \tau\ \textbf{exp} & & \tau'\ \textbf{exp} \\
\diagdown & \diagup & & & \diagdown & \diagup \\
& \tau_1\ \textbf{acc} & & \text{and} & \tau_2\ \textbf{exp} & \\
& \shortmid & & & \shortmid & \\
& \omega_1 & & & \omega_2 &
\end{array}$$

Then the definition of B for the implicit conversion of acceptors and expressions implies that the diagram

$$\begin{array}{ccc}
B(\omega_1) \times B(\omega_2) & & \\
\Big\downarrow {\scriptstyle B(\omega_1 \leq \tau_1\ \textbf{acc}) \times B(\omega_2 \leq \tau_2\ \textbf{exp})} & & \\
B(\tau_1\ \textbf{acc}) \times B(\tau_2\ \textbf{exp}) & \xrightarrow{\ B(\tau_1\ \textbf{acc} \leq \tau\ \textbf{acc}) \times B(\tau_2\ \textbf{exp} \leq \tau\ \textbf{exp})\ } & B(\tau\ \textbf{acc}) \times B(\tau\ \textbf{exp}) \\
\Big\downarrow {\scriptstyle B(\tau_1\ \textbf{acc} \leq \tau'\ \textbf{acc}) \times B(\tau_2\ \textbf{exp} \leq \tau'\ \textbf{exp})} & & \Big\downarrow {\scriptstyle \lambda(a,v).\,D_{\textrm comm}(v;[a]_{\textcircled{1}})} \\
B(\tau'\ \textbf{acc}) \times B(\tau'\ \textbf{exp}) & \xrightarrow{\ \lambda(a',v').\,D_{\textrm comm}(v';[a']_{\textcircled{1}})\ } & B(\textbf{comm})
\end{array}$$

of functions commutes. A slight extension of this argument shows that $\gamma_{:=}$ is a natural transformation.

Next we consider conditional phrases. It is trivial to define a particular type of conditional phrase such as a conditional command, but the definition of a generic conditional, applicable to arbitrary phrase types, is more challenging. Obviously, **boolean** must be a data type, with $B^D(\textbf{boolean}) = \{\textbf{true, false}\}$. Less obviously, Ω must possess all binary least upper bounds. (Note that this imposes a restriction upon Ω^D.)

Under these conditions, we can define **if** $\in \Delta_3$, with the specification

$$\Lambda_{\textbf{if}} = \Omega$$

$$\Phi_{\textbf{if}} \in \Omega \to \Omega^3 \quad \text{is the function such that}$$

$$\Phi_{\textbf{if}}(\omega) = \textbf{if } \omega = \textbf{ns then } \langle \textbf{ns, ns, ns} \rangle \textbf{ else } \langle \textbf{boolean exp}, \omega, \omega \rangle$$

$$\overline{\Gamma}_{\textbf{if}} = I_\Omega.$$

Then the left adjoint of $\Phi_{\textbf{if}}$ is the function $\Psi_{\textbf{if}} \in \Omega^3 \to \Omega$ such that

$$\Psi_{\textbf{if}}(\omega_1, \omega_2, \omega_3) = \textbf{if } \omega_1 \leq \textbf{boolean exp then } \omega_2 \sqcup \omega_3 \textbf{ else ns}.$$

(From the proposition in the previous section, it can be shown that if there are ω_2, ω_3 in Ω that do not possess a least upper bound then Φ has no left adjoint.)

To determine the interpretation of **if**, we must give a natural transformation $\overline{\gamma}_{\textbf{if}}$ from $\Phi; B^3; \times^{(3)}$ to $\overline{\Gamma}; B = B$. When $\omega = \textbf{ns}$, $\overline{\gamma}_{\textbf{if}}(\omega)$ is the unique function from $B(\textbf{ns}) \times B(\textbf{ns}) \times B(\textbf{ns})$ to $B(\textbf{ns})$. Otherwise it is the function from $B(\textbf{boolean exp}) \times B(\omega) \times B(\omega)$ to $B(\omega)$ such that

$$\overline{\gamma}_{\textbf{if}}(\omega)(v, f, g) = D_\omega(v; [\lambda b \in \{\textbf{true, false}\} . \textbf{if } b \textbf{ then } f \textbf{ else } g]_{\bigoplus}),$$

where D is the Ω-indexed family of diagonalizing functions, $D_\omega \in (S \to B(\omega)) \to B(\omega)$ such that

$$D_{\tau \, \textbf{exp}} = \lambda h \in S \to (S \to [B^D(\tau)]_\perp) . \lambda \sigma \in S . h(\sigma)(\sigma)$$

$$D_{\textbf{comm}} = \lambda h \in S \to (S \to [S]_\perp) . \lambda \sigma \in S . h(\sigma)(\sigma)$$

$$D_{\tau \, \textbf{acc}} = \lambda h \in S \to (B^D(\tau) \to (S \to [S]_\perp)) . \lambda x \in B^D(\tau) . \lambda \sigma \in S . h(\sigma)(x)(\sigma)$$

$$D_{\tau_1 \tau_2 \, \textbf{var}} = \lambda h \in S \to B(\tau_1 \, \textbf{acc}) \times B(\tau_2 \, \textbf{exp}) .$$

$$\langle D_{\tau_1 \, \textbf{acc}}(h; (\lambda(a, v) . a)), D_{\tau_2 \, \textbf{exp}}(h; (\lambda(a, v) . v)) \rangle$$

$$D_{\textbf{ns}} = \lambda h \in S \to B(\textbf{ns}) . \perp_{B(\textbf{ns})}.$$

(Notice that $D_{\textbf{comm}}$ also occurred in the definition of assignment.) This family has the property that, for all $\omega, \omega' \in \Omega$ such that $\omega \leq \omega'$ and all $h \in S \to B(\omega)$,

$$B(\omega \leq \omega')(D_\omega(h)) = D_{\omega'}(h; B(\omega \leq \omega')).$$

It is this property that insures that $\overline{\gamma}_{\textbf{if}}$ is a natural transformation.

Finally, for completeness, we define operators for statement sequencing and a **while** statement. Since these operators are not generic, their definition is straightforward:

$; \in \Delta_2$, **while** $\in \Delta_2$

$\Lambda_; = \Lambda_{\textbf{while}} = \{\textbf{comm, ns}\}$ with the same partial ordering as Ω.

$\Phi_;(\textbf{comm}) = \langle \textbf{comm, comm} \rangle$, $\Phi_{\textbf{while}}(\textbf{comm}) = \langle \textbf{boolean exp, comm} \rangle$

$\Phi_;(\textbf{ns}) = \Phi_{\textbf{while}}(\textbf{ns}) = \langle \textbf{ns, ns} \rangle$

$\overline{\Gamma}_;(\textbf{comm}) = \overline{\Gamma}_{\textbf{while}}(\textbf{comm}) = \textbf{comm}$

$\overline{\Gamma}_;(\textbf{ns}) = \overline{\Gamma}_{\textbf{while}}(\textbf{ns}) = \textbf{ns}$

$\overline{\gamma}_;(\textbf{ns}) = \overline{\gamma}_{\textbf{while}}(\textbf{ns})$ is the unique function from $B(\textbf{ns}) \times B(\textbf{ns})$ to $B(\textbf{ns})$.

$\overline{\gamma}_;(\textbf{comm}) = \lambda(c_1 \in S \rightarrow [S]_\perp, c_2 \in S \rightarrow [S]_\perp) . c_1 ; [c_2]_{\textcircled{\scriptsize 1}}$

$\overline{\gamma}_{\textbf{while}}(\textbf{comm}) = \lambda(v \in S \rightarrow [\{\textbf{true, false}\}]_\perp, c_1 \in S \rightarrow [S]_\perp).$

$$Y(\lambda c_2 \in S \rightarrow [S]_\perp . D_{\textbf{comm}}(v ; [\lambda b . \textbf{if } b \textbf{ then } (c_1 ; [c_2]_{\textcircled{\scriptsize 1}}) \textbf{ else } J]_{\textcircled{\scriptsize 1}}).$$

Here J is the identity injection from S to $[S]_\perp$ and Y is the least-fixed-point operator for the domain $S \rightarrow [S]_\perp$.

Future Directions

The approach described in this paper is still far from being able to encompass a full-blown programming language. In particular, the following areas need investigation:

1. Binding mechanisms, i.e. declarations and procedures.
2. Products of types, i.e. records or class elements.
3. Sums of types, i.e. disjoint unions.
4. Type definitions, including recursive type definitions.
5. Syntactic control of interference [7].

In the first three of these areas, our ideas have progressed far enough to suggest the form of the partially ordered set of phrase types. One wants a set Ω satisfying

$$\Omega = \Omega_{\text{primitive}} + \Omega_{\text{procedure}} + \Omega_{\text{product}} + \Omega_{\text{sum}}.$$

Here + denotes some kind of sum of partially ordered sets. (At present, it is not clear how this sum should treat the greatest type **ns** or a possible least type.) The partially ordered set $\Omega_{\text{primitive}}$ is similar to the Ω described in the previous section, and

$$\Omega_{\text{procedure}} = \{\omega_1 \to \omega_2 | \omega_1, \omega_2 \in \Omega\}$$

$$\Omega_{\text{product}} = \{\mathbf{product}(\omega_1, \ldots, \omega_n) | n \geq 0 \text{ and } \omega_1, \ldots, \omega_n \in \Omega\}$$

$$\Omega_{\text{sum}} = \{\mathbf{sum}(\omega_1, \ldots, \omega_n) | n \geq 0 \text{ and } \omega_1, \ldots, \omega_n \in \Omega\}$$

The main novelty is the partial ordering of $\Omega_{\text{procedure}}$. One wants procedure types to satisfy

$$(\omega_1 \to \omega_2) \leq (\omega'_1 \to \omega'_2) \text{ if and only if } \omega'_1 \leq \omega_1 \text{ and } \omega_2 \leq \omega'_2,$$

so that the type operator $\to$ is antimonotone in its first argument. For example, suppose **integer exp** $\leq$ **real exp**. Then a procedure of type **real exp** $\to$ **boolean exp**, which can accept any real expression as argument, can also accept any integer expression as argument, and should therefore be permissible in any context which permits a procedure of type **integer exp** $\to$ **boolean exp**. Thus (**real exp** $\to$ **boolean exp**) $\leq$ (**integer exp** $\to$ **boolean exp**).

It follows that $\Omega_{\text{procedure}}$ will be isomorphic to $\Omega^{\text{op}} \times \Omega$, where Ω^{op} denotes the dual of Ω. This raises the question of how one solves the recursive equation describing Ω. The simplest answer is to impose an appropriate ordering on the least set satisfying this equation. The resulting Ω, however, will not contain certain limits which will be needed to deal with recursive type definitions. One would like to use Scott's methods to treat recursive definitions, but these methods do not encompass the operation of dualizing a partial ordering.

This difficulty does not arise for products or sums, where conventional pointwise ordering seems natural. However, a richer ordering becomes attractive when named, rather than numbered, products and sums are considered. Suppose we redefine

$$\Omega_{\text{product}} = \{\mathbf{product}(\overline{\omega}) | \overline{\omega} \in N \to \Omega \text{ for some finite set } N \text{ of names}\},$$

and similarly for Ω_{sum}. Then the following ordering can be used:

$\mathbf{product}(\overline{\omega}) \leq \mathbf{product}(\overline{\omega}')$ whenever $\text{domain}(\overline{\omega}) \supseteq \text{domain}(\overline{\omega}')$ and

$(\forall n \in \text{domain}(\overline{\omega}')) \, \overline{\omega}(n) \leqslant \overline{\omega}'(n),$

$\mathbf{sum}(\overline{\omega}) \leq \mathbf{sum}(\overline{\omega}')$ whenever $\text{domain}(\overline{\omega}) \subseteq \text{domain}(\overline{\omega}')$ and

$(\forall n \in \text{domain}(\overline{\omega})) \, \overline{\omega}(n) \leq \overline{\omega}'(n).$

The first ordering permits implicit record conversions which forget fields. The second ordering permits implicit conversions of disjoint unions which broaden the number of alternatives in a union.

In particular, the second ordering solves a long-standing problem in the type-checking of disjoint union expressions. Suppose p is a phrase of type ω, and **make-n** denotes the injection into a disjoint union corresponding to the alternative named n. Using bottom-up type analysis, how does one determine the type of **make-$n(p)$**? The answer is that the type is **sum**$(n:\omega)$, which is a subtype of any sum of the form **sum**$(\ldots, n:\omega, \ldots)$.

Appendix

In this appendix we will demonstrate the existence of free category-sorted algebras by constructing an appropriate adjunction. Our basic approach will be to connect category-sorted algebras with ordinary one-sorted algebras in order to use the known existence of free ordinary algebras. We begin by stating several general properties of adjunctions which will be used in our development.

PROPOSITION   Suppose U is a functor from K' to K, F is a function from $|K|$ to $|K'|$, and η is a $|K|$-indexed family of morphisms $\eta(X) \in X \underset{K}{\to} U(F(X))$ such that:

For all $X \in |K|$, $X' \in |K'|$, and $\rho \in X \underset{K}{\to} U(X')$ there is exactly one morphism $\hat{\rho} \in F(X) \underset{K'}{\to} X'$ such that

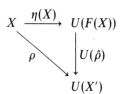

commutes in K.

Then there is exactly one way of extending F to be a functor from K to K' such that F is the left adjoint of U with η as the associated natural transformation. Namely, for each $\theta \in X \underset{K}{\to} X'$, $F(\theta)$ must be the unique morphism such that

$$X \xrightarrow{\eta(X)} U(F(X))$$
$$\downarrow \theta \qquad\qquad \downarrow U(F(\theta))$$
$$X' \xrightarrow{\eta(X')} U(F(X'))$$

commutes in K.

We omit the proof (11, p. 116), the main point of which is to show that the extension of F preserves composition and identities. The utility of this proposition is that, in specifying adjunctions it is only necessary to specify the object part of the left adjoint.

Next, we consider the composition of adjunctions:

PROPOSITION   Suppose U is a functor from K' to K with left adjoint F and associated natural transformation η, and U' is a functor from K'' to K' with left adjoint F' and associated natural transformation η'. Let

$$U'' = U'; U$$

$$F'' = F; F'$$

$$\eta''(X) = \eta(X); {}_K U(\eta'(F(X))).$$

Then U'' is a functor from K'' to K with left adjoint F'' and associated natural transformation η''.

Again we omit the proof (9, p. 101).

Finally, we introduce the construction of categories over distinguished objects, and show that an adjunction between such categories can be built out of an adjunction between the categories from which they have been constructed.

Let K be a category and $T \in |K|$. Then $K \downarrow T$, called the **category of objects over** T, is the category such that

(a) $|K \downarrow T| = \{X, \tau \mid X \in |K| \text{ and } \tau \in X \underset{K}{\to} T\}$,

(b) $X, \tau \underset{K \downarrow T}{\to} X', \tau'$ is the set of morphisms $\rho \in X \underset{K}{\to} X'$ such that

commutes in K.

(c) Composition and identities are the same as in K.

Then:

PROPOSITION   Suppose U is a functor from K' to K with left adjoint F and associated natural transformation η. Suppose $T' \in |K'|$ and $T = U(T')$. Let $\overline{U}$ be the functor from $K' \downarrow T'$ to $K \downarrow T$ such that $\overline{U}(X', \tau') = U(X'), U(\tau')$ and $\overline{U}(\rho) = U(\rho)$. Then $\overline{U}$ has a left adjoint $\overline{F}$ and an associated natural transformation η such that

$$\overline{F}(X, .) = F(X), \hat{\tau}$$

$$\overline{\eta}(X, \tau) = \eta(X),$$

where $\hat{\tau} \in F(X) \underset{K'}{\to} T'$ is the unique morphism such that

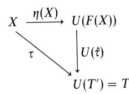

commutes in K.

Proof   We leave it to the reader to verify that $\overline{U}$ is a functor from $K' \downarrow T'$ to $K \downarrow T$, that $\overline{F}$ is (the object part of) a functor from $K \downarrow T$ to $K' \downarrow T'$, and that $\overline{\eta}(X, \tau) \in X, \tau \underset{K \downarrow T}{\to} \overline{U}(\overline{F}(X, \tau))$. To show the adjunction property, suppose $X, \tau \in |K \downarrow T|$, $X', \tau' \in |K' \downarrow T'|$, and $\rho \in X, \tau \underset{K \downarrow T}{\to} \overline{U}(X', \tau')$. Then we must show that there is exactly one $\hat{\rho} \in \overline{F}(X, \tau) \underset{K' \downarrow T'}{\to} X', \tau'$ such that

$$X, \tau \xrightarrow{\ \overline{\eta}(X, \tau) = \eta(X)\ } \overline{U}(\overline{F}(X, \tau)) = U(F(X)), U(\hat{\tau})$$

with ρ and $\overline{U}(\hat{\rho}) = U(\hat{\rho})$ to $\overline{U}(X', \tau') = U(X'), U(\tau')$

commutes in $K \downarrow T$.

Since composition is the same in $K \downarrow T$ as in K, $\hat{\rho}$ can only be the unique morphism in $F(X) \underset{K'}{\to} X'$ such that

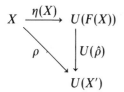

commutes in K.

However, we must show that $\hat{\rho}$ actually belongs to the more restricted set of morphisms $\overline{F}(X,\tau) \underset{K' \downarrow T'}{\rightarrow} X'$, τ'. To establish this, we note that $\rho \in X$, $\tau \underset{K \downarrow T}{\rightarrow} \overline{U}(X',\tau') = X$, $\tau \underset{K \downarrow T}{\rightarrow} U(X')$, $U(\tau')$ implies that

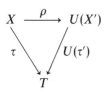

commutes in K, which in conjunction with the previous diagram implies that

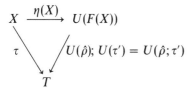

commutes in K. Then the uniqueness of $\hat{\tau}$ gives $\hat{\rho}$; $\tau' = \hat{\tau}$, so that $\hat{\rho} \in F(X)$, $\tau' \underset{K' \downarrow T'}{\rightarrow} X'$, $\tau' = \overline{F}(X,\tau) \underset{K' \downarrow T'}{\rightarrow} X'$, τ'.

Now we can apply these general results to the specific case of interest. Let $\Omega\Delta\Gamma$ be a fixed but arbitrary category-sorted signature, let CALG (called $ALG_{\Omega\Delta\Gamma}$ in the main text) be the category of $\Omega\Delta\Gamma$-algebras and their homomorphisms, and let ALG be the category of Δ-algebras and their homomorphisms:

(1) A Δ-algebra consists of:

    (1a) A *carrier* R, which is a set.

    (1b) For each $n \geq 0$ and $\delta \in \Delta_n$, an *interpretation* $\sigma_\delta \in R^n \to R$.

(2) If R, σ and R', σ' are Δ-algebras, then a *homomorphism* from R, σ to R', σ' is a function $h \in R \to R'$ such that, for all $n \geq 0$ and $\delta \in \Delta_n$, the diagram

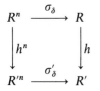

of functions commutes.

The known existence of ordinary free algebras can be stated in the language of adjunctions by:

Let U_A be the functor from ALG to SET that maps algebras into their carriers and homomorphism into themselves. Then U_A possesses a left adjoint F_A with an associated natural transformation η_A.

Here $F_A(S)$ is the free Δ-algebra generated by S, $\eta_A(S)$ is the embedding of S into the carrier of $F_A(S)$.

Of particular importance is the Δ-algebra, which we will call T, in which the carrier members are sorts and the interpretation of each operator is its category-sorted specification. More precisely, T is the Δ-algebra $|\Omega|, \Gamma_{ob}$, where each $\Gamma_{ob,\delta}$ is the object part of the functor Γ_δ.

We now introduce the categories ALG $\downarrow T$ and SET $\downarrow |\Omega|$. An object of ALG $\downarrow T$ can be thought of as a Δ-algebra equipped with an assignment of sorts to the members of its carrier. Similarly, an object of SET $\downarrow |\Omega|$ can be thought of as a set equipped with an assignment of sorts to its members. Since $|\Omega| = U_A(T)$, our last general proposition gives:

Let U_T be the functor from ALG $\downarrow T$ to SET $\downarrow |\Omega|$ such that $U_T(\langle R, \sigma \rangle, \tau) = U_A(R, \sigma)$, $U_A(\tau) = R$, τ, and $U_T(h) = U_A(h) = h$. Then U_T has a left adjoint F_T and an associated natural transformation η_T such that

$F_T(S, \tau) = F_A(S), \hat{\tau}$

$\eta_T(S, \tau) = \eta_A(S),$

where $\hat{\tau} \in F_A(S) \underset{\text{ALG}}{\rightarrow} T$ is the unique morphism such that

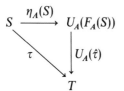

commutes in SET.

Informally, a type assignment to a set can be extended to the free Δ-algebra generated by that set by using the specification Γ to interpret the operators in Δ.

Our final (and most complicated) task is to construct an adjunction from $\text{ALG} \downarrow T$ to CALG. Let U_C be a functor from CALG to $\text{ALG} \downarrow T$ whose action on objects is given by:

$$U_C(B', \gamma') = \langle R', \sigma' \rangle, \tau' \quad \text{where} \quad R' = \{\omega, x' \mid \omega \in |\Omega| \text{ and } x' \in B'(\omega)\},$$

$$\sigma'_\delta \in R'^n \to R' \quad \text{is the function such that} \quad \sigma'_\delta(\langle \omega_1, x'_1 \rangle, \dots, \langle \omega_n, x'_n \rangle)$$

$$= \Gamma_\delta(\omega_1, \dots, \omega_n), \gamma'_\delta(\omega_1, \dots, \omega_n)(x'_1, \dots, x'_n),$$

$$\tau' \in R' \to |\Omega| \text{ is the function such that} \quad \tau'(\omega, x') = \omega. \tag{1}$$

(The variables in this definition have been primed to facilitate its application to later developments.) The reader may verify that τ' is an homomorphism from R', σ' to T, so that $\langle R', \sigma' \rangle, \tau'$ is an object of $\text{ALG} \downarrow T$. Intuitively, the action of U_C on objects is to forget the morphism part of B' (i.e., the implicit conversion functions) and to collapse the object part of B' into a disjoint union R' of its components, with a type assignment τ' that remembers which component of B' was the source of each member of R'.

To specify the action of U_C on morphisms, suppose $\theta \in B, \gamma \underset{\text{CALG}}{\to} B', \gamma'$, and let $\langle R, \sigma \rangle, \tau = U_C(B, \gamma)$ and $\langle R', \sigma' \rangle, \tau' = U_C(B', \gamma')$. Then

$$U_C(\theta) \in R \to R' \quad \text{is the function such that} \quad U_C(\theta)(\omega, x) = \omega, \theta(\omega)(x).$$

The reader may verify that $U_C(\theta)$ is an homomorphism from R, σ to R', σ' (which depends upon the fact that θ is an homomorphism from B, γ to B', γ'), that

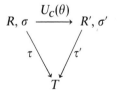

commutes in ALG, so that $U_C(\theta) \in \langle R, \sigma \rangle, \tau \underset{\text{ALG}\downarrow T}{\to} \langle R', \sigma' \rangle, \tau'$, and that U_C preserves composition and identities.

Next, let F_C be the functor from $\text{ALG} \downarrow T$ to CALG such that $F_C(\langle R, \sigma \rangle, \tau) = B, \gamma$ where

$$B(\omega) = \{r, \iota \mid r \in R \text{ and } \iota \in \tau(r) \underset{\Omega}{\to} \omega\},$$

$$B(\rho \in \omega \underset{\Omega}{\to} \omega') \in B(\omega) \to B(\omega') \text{ is the function such that}$$

$$B(\rho)(r, \iota) = r, (\iota; {}_\Omega \rho),$$

$$\gamma_\delta(\omega_1,\ldots,\omega_n) \in B(\omega_1) \times \cdots \times B(\omega_n) \to B(\Gamma_\delta(\omega_1,\ldots,\omega_n))$$

is the function such that

$$\gamma_\delta(\omega_1,\ldots,\omega_n)(\langle r_1, \iota_1\rangle,\ldots,\langle r_n, \iota_n\rangle) = \sigma_\delta(r_1,\ldots,r_n), \Gamma_\delta(\iota_1,\ldots,\iota_n). \tag{2}$$

To see that $\gamma_\delta(\omega_1,\ldots,\omega_n)$ is a function of the correct type, suppose that, for $1 \leq i \leq n$, $\langle r_i, \iota_i\rangle \in B(\omega_i)$. Then each $\iota_i \in \tau(r_i) \underset{\Omega}{\to} \omega$. Thus $\Gamma_\delta(\iota_1,\ldots,\iota_n) \in \Gamma_\delta(\tau(r_1),\ldots,\tau(r_n)) \underset{\Omega}{\to} \Gamma_\delta(\omega_1,\ldots,\omega_n)$. But since τ is an homomorphism from R, σ to $T = |\Omega|, \Gamma_{\mathrm{ob}}$, this set is also $\tau(\sigma_\delta(r_1,\ldots,r_n)) \underset{\Omega}{\to} \Gamma_\delta(\omega_1,\ldots,\omega_n))$. Thus $\langle \sigma_\delta(r_1,\ldots,r_n), \Gamma_\delta(\iota_1,\ldots,\iota_n)\rangle \in B(\Gamma_\delta(\omega_1,\ldots,\omega_n))$. The reader may also verify that B is a functor from Ω to SET and γ_δ is a natural transformation from $B^n;\ \times^{(n)}$ to $\Gamma; B$.

Intuitively, one can think of τ as assigning a "minimal" type to each member of R, and of a member of $B(\omega)$ as a member of R paired with an implicit conversion from its minimal type to ω.

For any object $\langle R, \sigma\rangle, \tau$ of ALG $\downarrow T$,

$$U_C(F_C(\langle R, \sigma\rangle, \tau)) = \langle \bar{R}, \bar{\sigma}\rangle, \bar{\tau} \quad \text{where}$$

$$\bar{R} = \{\omega, \langle r, \iota\rangle \mid \omega \in |\Omega| \text{ and } r \in R \text{ and } \iota \in \tau(r) \underset{\Omega}{\to} \omega\},$$

$\bar{\sigma}_\delta \in \bar{R}^n \to \bar{R}$ is the function such that

$$\bar{\sigma}_\delta(\langle \omega_1, \langle r_1, \iota_1\rangle\rangle,\ldots,\langle \omega_n, \langle r_n, \iota_n\rangle\rangle) = \Gamma_\delta(\omega_1,\ldots,\omega_n), \langle \sigma_\delta(r_1,\ldots,r_n), \Gamma_\delta(\iota_1,\ldots,\iota_n)\rangle,$$

$\bar{\tau} \in \bar{R} \to |\Omega|$ is the function such that $\bar{\tau}(\omega, \langle r, \iota\rangle) = \omega$.

Let

$\eta_C(\langle R, \sigma\rangle, \tau) \in R \to \bar{R}$ be the function such that

$$\eta_C(\langle R, \sigma\rangle, \tau)(r) = \tau(r), \langle r, I_{\tau(r)}^\Omega\rangle.$$

The reader may verify that $\eta_C(\langle R, \sigma\rangle, \tau)$ is an homomorphism from R, σ to $\bar{R}, \bar{\sigma}$ (which depends upon the fact that τ is an homomorphism from R, σ to $T = |\Omega|, \Gamma_{\mathrm{ob}}$), and that

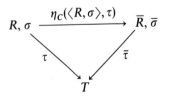

commutes in ALG. Thus $\eta_C(\langle R, \sigma\rangle, \tau) \in \langle R, \sigma\rangle, \tau \underset{\mathrm{ALG}\downarrow T}{\to} \langle \bar{R}, \bar{\sigma}\rangle, \bar{\tau} = \langle R, \sigma\rangle, \tau \underset{\mathrm{ALG}\downarrow T}{\to} U_C(F_C(\langle R, \sigma\rangle, \tau)).$

Now we will show that F_C is a left adjoint of U_C, with associated natural transformation η_C. Let $\langle R, \sigma \rangle$, τ be an object of ALG $\downarrow T$, let B', γ' be an object of CALG, and let h be a morphism in ALG $\downarrow T$ from $\langle R, \sigma \rangle$, τ to $U_C(B', \gamma')$, where $U_C(B', \gamma') = \langle R', \sigma' \rangle$, τ' is described by (1).

Since h is a function from R to R', the definition of R' implies that $h(r)$ will be a pair ω, x', where $x' \in B'(\omega)$. Moreover, since h is a morphism in ALG $\downarrow T$,

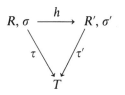

must commute in ALG, so that $\tau(r) = \tau'(h(r)) = \tau'(\omega, x') = \omega$. Thus $[h(r)]_1 = \tau(r)$ and $[h(r)]_2 \in B'(\tau(r))$.

Now suppose $\hat{h}$ is any morphism in $F_C(\langle R, \sigma \rangle, \tau) \xrightarrow[\text{CALG}]{} B'$, γ', where $F_C(\langle R, \sigma \rangle, \tau) = B, \gamma$ is described by (2), and consider the diagram

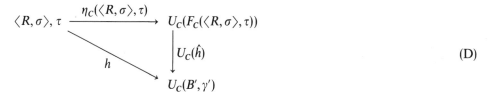

(D)

in ALG $\downarrow T$.

From the definitions of η_C and of the action of U_C on morphisms, we have

$$U_C(\hat{h})(\eta_C(\langle R, \sigma \rangle, \tau)(r)) = U_C(\hat{h})(\tau(r), \langle r, I^{\Omega}_{\tau(r)} \rangle) = \tau(r), \hat{h}(\tau(r))(r, I^{\Omega}_{\tau(r)}).$$

Thus the diagram (D) will commute if and only if, for all $r \in R$,

$$\hat{h}(\tau(r))(r, I^{\Omega}_{\tau(r)}) = [h(r)]_2.$$

Moreover, since $\hat{h}$ is a category-sorted homomorphism from B, γ to B', γ', it is a natural transformation from B to B'. Thus for all $r \in R$, $\omega \in |\Omega|$, and $\iota \in \tau(r) \xrightarrow{\Omega} \omega$,

$$
\begin{array}{ccc}
B(\tau(r)) & \xrightarrow{\hat{h}(\tau(r))} & B'(\tau(r)) \\
\downarrow{\scriptstyle B(\iota)} & & \downarrow{\scriptstyle B'(\iota)} \\
B(\omega) & \xrightarrow{\hat{h}(\omega)} & B'(\omega)
\end{array}
$$

commutes in SET. In conjunction with the action of B on morphisms, this gives

$$\hat{h}(\omega)(\langle r, \iota \rangle) = \hat{h}(\omega)(B(\iota)(r, I^{\Omega}_{\tau(r)})) = B'(\iota)(\hat{h}(\tau(r))(r, I^{\Omega}_{\tau(r)})).$$

Thus diagram (D) will commute if and only if

$$\hat{h}(\omega)(\langle r, \iota \rangle) = B'(\iota)([h(r)]_2)$$

holds for all $r \in R$, $\omega \in |\Omega|$, and $\iota \in \tau(r) \underset{\Omega}{\to} \omega$.

Since this equation completely determines $\hat{h}$, the adjunction property will hold if the resulting $\hat{h}$ is actually a category-sorted homomorphism from B, γ to B', γ'. We leave it to the reader to verify that $\hat{h}(\omega) \in B(\omega) \to B'(\omega)$, and that, because of the action of B on morphisms, $\hat{h}$ is a natural transformation from B to B'. The one nontrivial property to be shown is that $\hat{h}$ satisfies the homomorphic relationship with the interpretations γ and γ', i.e., that for all $n \geq 0$, $\delta \in \Delta_n$, and $\omega_1, \ldots, \omega_n \in |\Omega|$,

$$
\begin{array}{ccc}
B(\omega_1) \times \cdots \times B(\omega_n) & \xrightarrow{\;\gamma_\delta(\omega_1, \ldots, \omega_n)\;} & B(\Gamma_\delta(\omega_1, \ldots, \omega_n)) \\[2pt]
\Big\downarrow {\scriptstyle \hat{h}(\omega_1) \times \cdots \times \hat{h}(\omega_n)} & & \Big\downarrow {\scriptstyle \hat{h}(\Gamma_\delta(\omega_1, \ldots, \omega_n))} \\[2pt]
B'(\omega_1) \times \cdots \times B'(\omega_n) & \xrightarrow{\;\gamma'_\delta(\omega_1, \ldots, \omega_n)\;} & B'(\Gamma_\delta(\omega_1, \ldots, \omega_n))
\end{array}
$$

commutes in SET.

To see this, suppose $\langle r_1, \iota_1 \rangle, \ldots, \langle r_n, \iota_n \rangle \in B(\omega_1) \times \cdots \times B(\omega_n)$. Then

$$\hat{h}(\Gamma_\delta(\omega_1, \ldots, \omega_n))(\gamma_\delta(\omega_1, \ldots, \omega_n)(\langle r_1, \iota_1 \rangle, \ldots, \langle r_n, \iota_n \rangle))$$

$$= \hat{h}(\Gamma_\delta(\omega_1, \ldots, \omega_n))(\sigma_\delta(r_1, \ldots, r_n), \Gamma_\delta(\iota_1, \ldots, \iota_n))$$

$$= B'(\Gamma_\delta(\iota_1, \ldots, \iota_n))([h(\sigma_\delta(r_1, \ldots, r_n))]_2) = B'(\Gamma_\delta(\iota_1, \ldots, \iota_n))([\sigma'_\delta(h(r_1), \ldots, h(r_n))]_2)$$

since h is an homomorphism from R, σ to R', σ'

$$= B'(\Gamma_\delta(\iota_1, \ldots, \iota_n))(\gamma'_\delta(\tau(r_1), \ldots, \tau(r_n))([h(r_1)]_2, \ldots, [h(r_n)]_2))$$

by the definition of σ'_δ given in (1)

$$= \gamma'_\delta(\omega_1, \ldots, \omega_n)(B'(\iota_1)([h(r_1)]_2), \ldots, B'(\iota_n)([h(r_n)]_2))$$

since γ'_δ is a natural transformation from B'^n; $\times^{(n)}$ to Γ_δ; B'

$$= \gamma'_\delta(\omega_1, \ldots, \omega_n)(\hat{h}(\omega_1)(r_1, \iota_1), \ldots, \hat{h}(\omega_n)(r_n, \iota_n)).$$

In summary, we have constructed the adjunctions

$$\text{SET} \downarrow |\Omega| \underset{U_T}{\overset{F_T}{\rightleftarrows}} \text{ALG} \downarrow T \underset{U_C}{\overset{F_C}{\rightleftarrows}} \text{CALG}$$

with associated natural transformations η_T and η_C. The adjunction used in the main text is the composition of these adjunctions:

$$U = U_C; U_T$$

$$F = F_T; F_C$$

$$\eta(S, \tau_S) = \eta_T(S, \tau_S);_{\text{SET}\downarrow|\Omega|} U_T(\eta_C(F_T(S, \tau_S))).$$

The free $\Omega\Delta\Gamma$-algebra $F(S, \tau_S)$ generated by S, τ_S is given explicitly by (2), where R, σ is the free Δ-algebra generated by S and $\tau \in R \to |\Omega|$ is the unique homomorphism such that $\eta_A(S); \tau = \tau_S$.

In the special case where Ω is a preordered set, there is at most one $\iota \in \tau(r) \underset{\Omega}{\to} \omega$, so that (2) is isomorphic to the much simpler definition:

$$B(\omega) = \{r | r \in R \text{ and } \tau(r) \le \omega\}$$

$B(\omega \le \omega')$ is the identity inclusion from $B(\omega)$ to $B(\omega')$,

$$\gamma_\delta(\omega_1, \ldots, \omega_n)(r_1, \ldots, r_n) = \sigma_\delta(r_1, \ldots, r_n).$$

In this case, $B(\omega)$ is simply the subset of the terms of the ordinary free Δ-algebra whose minimal sort is a subsort of ω, the implicit conversion functions are all identity inclusions, and the operators are interpreted the same way as in the ordinary free algebra.

Note

Work supported by National Science Foundation Grant MCS 75-22002.

References

1. [Goguen 78]   Goguen, Joseph A. "Order Sorted Algebras: Exceptions and Error Sorts, Coercions and Overloaded Operators" Semantics and Theory of Computation Report 14, Computer Science Dept., UCLA, December, 1978.

2. [Goguen 77]   Goguen, Joseph A., Thatcher, James W., Wagner, Eric G., and Wright, Jesse B. "Initial Algebra Semantics and Continuous Algebras" Communications of the ACM 24, 1 (January, 1977), 68–95.

3. [Burstall 69]   Burstall, Rodney M. and Landin, Peter J. "Programs and their Proofs: An Algebraic Approach" Meltzer, Bernard and Michie, Donald *Machine Intelligence* 4 Edinburgh: Edinburgh University Press (1969), 17–43.

4. [Birkhoff 70]   Birkhoff, Garrett and Lipson, John D. "Heterogeneous Algebras" *Journal of Combinatorial Theory* 8, 1 (January, 1970), 115–133.

5. [Higgins 63]   Higgins, Philip J. "Algebras with a Scheme of Operators" *Mathematische Nachrichten* 27 (1963), 115–132.

6. [Morris 73]   Morris, James H. Jr. "Types Are Not Sets" *Conference Record ACM Symposium on Principles of Programming Languages* (1973), 120–124.

7. [Reynolds 78]   Reynolds, John C. "Syntactic Control of Interference" *Conference Record of the Fifth Annual ACM Symposium on Principles of Programming Languages* (1978), 39–46.

8. [Reynolds 81]   Reynolds, John C. *The Craft of Programming* London: Prentice-Hall International (1981).

9. [Mac Lane 71]   Mac Lane, Saunders *Categories for the Working Mathematician* New York: Springer-Verlag (1971).

10. [Reynolds 70]   Reynolds, John C. "GEDANKEN—A Simple Typeless Language Based on the Principle of Completeness and the Reference Concept" *Communications of the ACM* 13, 5 (May, 1970), 308–319.

11. [Arbib 75]   Arbib, Michael A. and Manes, Ernest G. *Arrows, Structures, and Functors—The Categorical Imperative* New York: Academic Press (1975).

II TYPE INFERENCE

3 Type Inference for Records in a Natural Extension of ML

Didier Rémy

Abstract

We describe an extension of ML with records where inheritance is given by ML generic polymorphism. All common operations on records but concatenation are supported, in particular the free extension of records. Other operations such as renaming of fields are added. The solution relies on an extension of ML, where the language of types is sorted and considered modulo equations, and on a record extension of types. The solution is simple and modular and the type inference algorithm is efficient in practice.

Introduction

The aim of typechecking is to guarantee that well-typed programs will not produce runtime errors. A type error is usually due to a programmer's mistake, and thus typechecking also helps him in debugging his programs. Some programmers do not like writing the types of their programs by hand. In the ML language for instance, type inference requires as little type information as the declaration of data structures; then all types of programs will be automatically computed.

Our goal is to provide type inference for labeled products, a data structure commonly called records, allowing some inheritance between them: records with more labels should be allowed where records with fewer labels are required.

After defining the operations on records and recalling related work, we first review the solution for a finite (and small) set of labels, which was presented in [Rém89], then we extend it to a denumerable set of labels. In the last part we discuss the power and weakness of the solution, we describe some variations, and suggest improvements.

Without records, data structures are built using product types, as in ML, for instance.

```
("Peter", "John", "Professor", 27, 5467567, 56478356,
 ("toyota", "old", 8929901))
```

With records one would write, instead:

```
{name = "Peter"; lastname = "John"; job = "Professor";
 age = 27; id = 5467567; license = 56478356;
 vehicle = {name = "Toyota"; id = 8929901; age = "old"}}
```

The latter program is definitely more readable than the former. It is also more precise, since components are named. Records can also be used to name several arguments or several results of a function. More generally, in communication between processes records permit the naming of the different ports on which processes can exchange information. One nice example of this is the LCS language [Ber88], which is a combination of ML and Milner's CCS [Mil80].

Besides typechecking records, the challenge is to avoid record type declarations and fix size records. Extensible records introduced by Wand [Wan89, CM89] can be built from older records by adding new fields. This feature is the basis of inheritance in the view of objects as records [Wan89, CM89].

The main operations on records are introduced by examples, using a syntax similar to CAML syntax [CH89, Wei89]. Like variable names, labels do not have particular meanings, though choosing good names (good is subjective) helps in writing and reading programs. Names can, of course, be reused in different records, even to build fields of different types. This is illustrated in the following three examples:

```
let car = {name = "Toyota"; age = "old"; id = 7866};;
let truck = {name = "Blazer"; id = 6587867567};;
let person = {name = "Tim"; age = 31; id = 5656787};;
```

Remark that no declaration is required before the use of labels. The record person is defined on exactly the same fields as the record car, though those fields do not have the same intuitive meaning. The field age holds values of different types in car and in person.

All these records have been created in one step. Records can also be build from older ones. For instance, a value driver can be defined as being a copy of the record person but with one more field, vehicle, filled with the previously defined car object.

```
let driver = {person with vehicle = car};;
```

Note that there is no sharing between the records person and driver. You can simply think as if the former were copied into a new empty record before adding a field car to build the latter. This construction is called the *extension* of a record with a new field. In this example the newly defined field was not present in the record person, but that should not be a restriction. For instance, if our driver needs a more robust vehicle, we write:

```
let truck_driver = {driver with vehicle = truck};;
```

As previously, the operation is not a physical replacement of the vehicle field by a new value. We do not wish the old and the new value of the vehicle field to have the same type. To distinguish between the two kinds of extensions of a record with a new field, we will say that the extension is *strict* when the new field must not be previously defined, and *free* otherwise.

A more general operation than extension is concatenation, which constructs a new record from two previously defined ones, taking the union of their defined fields. If the car has a rusty body but a good engine, one could think of building the hybrid vehicle:

```
let repaired_truck = {car and truck};;
```

This raises the question: what value should be assigned to fields which are defined in both car and truck? When there is a conflict (the same field is defined in both records), priority could be given to the last record. As with free extension, the last record would eventually overwrite fields of the first one. But one might also expect a typechecker to prevent this situation from happening. Although concatenation is less common in the literature, probably because it causes more trouble, it seems interesting in some cases. Concatenation is used in the standard ML language [HMT91] when a structure is opened and extended with another one. In the LCS language, the visible ports of two processes run in parallel are exactly the ports visible in any of them. And as shown by Mitchell Wand [Wan89] multiple inheritance can be coded with concatenation.

The constructions described above are not exhaustive but are the most common ones. We should also mention the permutation, renaming and erasure of fields. We described how to build records, but of course we also want to read them. There is actually a unique construction for this purpose.

```
let id x = x.id;;
```

```
let age x = x.age;;
```

Accessing some field a of a record x can be abstracted over x, but not over a: Labels are not values and there is no function which could take a label as argument and would access the field of some fixed record corresponding to that label. Thus, we need one extraction function per label, as for id and age above. Then, they can be applied to different records of different types but all possessing the field to access. For instance,

```
age person, age driver;;
```

They can also be passed to other functions, as in:

```
let car_info field = field car;;

car_info age;;
```

The testing function `eq` below should of course accept arguments of different types provided they have an `id` field of the same type.

```
let eq x y = equal x.id y.id;;

eq car truck;;
```

These examples were very simple. We will typecheck them below, but we will also meet more tricky ones.

Related Work

Luca Cardelli has always claimed that functional languages should have record operations. In 1986, when he designed Amber, his choice was to provide the language with records rather than polymorphism. Later, he introduced bounded quantification in the language FUN, which he extended to higher order bounded quantification in the language QUEST. Bounded quantification is an extension of ordinary quantification where quantified variables range in the subset of types that are all subtypes of the bound. The subtyping relation is a lattice on types. In this language, subtyping is essential for having some inheritance between records. A slight but significant improvement of bounded quantification has been made in [CCH$^+$89] to better consider recursive objects; a more general but less tractable system weas studied by Pavel Curtis [Cur87]. Today, the trend seems to be the simplification rather than the enrichment of existing systems [LC90, HP90, Car91]. For instance, an interesting goal was to remove the subtype relation in bounded quantification [HP90]. Records have also been formulated with explicit labeled conjunctive types in the language Forsythe [Rey88].

In contrast, records in implicitly typed languages have been less studied, and the proposed extensions of ML are still very restrictive. The language Amber [Car84, Car86] is monomorphic and inheritance is obtained by type inclusion. A major step toward combining records and type inference has been Wand's proposal [Wan87] where inheritance is obtained from ML generic polymorphism. Though type inference is incomplete for this system, it remains a reference, for it was the first concrete proposal for extending ML with records having inheritance. The year after, complete type inference algorithms were found for a strong restriction of this system [JM88, OB88]. The restriction only allows the strict extension of a record. Then, the author proposed a complete type inference algorithm for Wand's system [Rém89], but it was formalized only in the case of a finite set of labels (a previous solution given by Wand in 1988 did not admit principal types but complete sets of principal types, and was exponential in size in practice). Mitchell Wand revisited this approach and extended it with an "and" operation[1] but did not provide correctness proofs. The case of an infinite set of labels has been addressed in [Rém90], which we review in this article.

1   A Simple Solution When the Set of Labels Is Finite

Though the solution below will be made obsolete by the extension to a denumerable set of labels, we choose to present it first, since it is very simple and the extension will be based on the same ideas. It will also be a decent solution in cases where only few labels are needed. And it will emphasize a method for getting more polymorphism in ML (in fact, we will not put more polymorphism in ML but we will make more use of it, sometimes in unexpected ways).

We will sketch the path from Wand's proposal to this solution, for it may be of some interest to describe the method which we think could be applied in other situations. As intuitions are rather subjective, and ours may not be yours, the section 1.1 can be skipped whenever it does not help.

1.1   The Method

Records are partial functions from a set $\mathscr{L}$ of labels to the set of values. We simplify the problem by considering only three labels a, b and c. Records can be represented in three field boxes, once labels have been ordered:

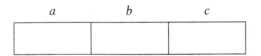

Defining a record is the same as filling some of the fields with values. For example, we will put the values 1 and *true* in the a and c fields respectively and leave the b field undefined.

1		*true*

Typechecking means forgetting some information about values. For instance, it does not distinguish two numbers but only remember them as being numbers. The structure of types usually reflects the structure of values, but with fewer details. It is thus natural to type record values with partial functions from labels ($\mathscr{L}$) to types ($\mathscr{T}$), that is, elements of $\mathscr{L} \to \mathscr{T}$. We first make record types total functions on labels using an explicitly undefined constant *abs* ("absent"): $\mathscr{L} \to \mathscr{T} \cup \{abs\}$. In fact, we replace the union by the sum $pre(\mathscr{T}) + abs$. Finally, we decompose record types as follows:

$$\mathscr{L} \longrightarrow [1, Card(\mathscr{L})] \longrightarrow pre(\mathscr{T}) + abs$$

The first function is an ordering from $\mathscr{L}$ to the segment $[1, Card(\mathscr{L})]$ and can be set once and for all. Thus record types can be represented only by the second component, which is a tuple of length $Card(\mathscr{L})$ of types in $pre(\mathscr{T}) + abs$. The previous example is typed by

1		*true*

$\Pi(\, pre(num) \quad , \qquad abs \qquad , \quad pre(bool)\,)$

A function $\_.\,a$ reading the a field accepts as argument any record having the a field defined with a value M, and returns M. The a field of the type of the argument must be $pre(\tau)$ if τ is the type of M. We do not care whether other fields are defined or not, so their types may be anything. We choose to represent them by variables θ and ε. The result has type α.

$$\_.\,a : \Pi(pre(\alpha), \theta, \varepsilon) \to \alpha$$

1.2   A Formulation

We are given a collection of symbols $\mathscr{C}$ with their arities $(\mathscr{C}^n)_{n \in N}$ that contains at least an arrow symbol $\to$ of arity 2, a unary symbol *pre* and a nullary symbol *abs*. We are also given two sorts *type* and *field*. The signature of a symbol is a sequence of sorts, written ι for a nullary symbol and $\iota_1 \ldots \otimes \iota_n \Rightarrow \iota$ for a symbol of arity n. The signature $\mathscr{S}$ is defined by the following assertions (we write $\mathscr{S} \vdash f :: \iota$ for $(f, \iota) \in \mathscr{S}$):

$\mathscr{S} \vdash pre :: type \Rightarrow field$

$\mathscr{S} \vdash abs :: field$

$\mathscr{S} \vdash \Pi :: field^{card(\mathscr{L})} \Rightarrow type$

$\mathscr{S} \vdash f :: type^n \Rightarrow type \qquad f \in \mathscr{C}^n \backslash \{pre, abs, \Pi\}$

The language of types is the free sorted algebra $\mathscr{T}(\mathscr{S}, \mathscr{V})$. The extension of ML with sorted types is straightforward. We will not formalize it further, since this will be subsumed in the next section. The inference rules are the same as in ML though the language of types is sorted. The typing relation defined by these rules is still decidable and admits principal typings (see next section for a precise formulation). In this language, we assume the following primitive environment:

Basic constants for ΠML_{fin}

$\{\ \}: \Pi(abs, \ldots abs)$

$\_. a: \Pi(\theta_1 \ldots, pre(\alpha), \ldots \theta_l) \to \alpha$

$\{\_\ with\ a = \_\}: \Pi(\theta_1, \ldots \theta_l) \to \alpha \to \Pi(\theta_1 \ldots, pre(\alpha), \ldots \theta_l)$

The constant $\{\ \}$ is the empty record. The $\_. a$ constant reads the a field from its argument, we write $r . a$ the application $(\_. a)\ r$. Similarly $\{r\ with\ a = M\}$ extends the records r on label a with value M.

2 Extension to Large Records

Though the previous solution is simple, and perfect when there are only two or three labels involved, it is clearly no longer acceptable when the set of labels is getting larger. This is because the size of record types is proportional to the size of this set—even for the type of the null record, which has no field defined. When a local use of records is needed, labels may be fewer than ten and the solution works perfectly. But in large systems where some records are used globally, the number of labels will quickly be over one hundred.

In any program, the number of labels will always be finite, but with modular programming, the whole set of labels is not known at the beginning (though in this case, some of the labels may be local to a module and solved independently). In practice, it is thus interesting to reason on an "open", i.e. countable, set of labels. From a theoretical point of view, it is the only way to avoid reasoning outside of the formalism and show that any computation done in a system with a small set of labels would still be valid in a system with a larger set of labels, and that the typing in the latter case could be deduced from the typing in the former case. A better solution consists in working in a system where all potential labels are taken into account from the beginning.

In the first part, we will illustrate the discussion above and describe the intuitions. Then we formalize the solution in three steps. First we extend types with record types in a more general framework of sorted algebras; record types will be sorted types modulo equations. The next step describes an extension of ML with sorts and equations on types. Last, we apply the reults to a special case, re-using the same encoding as for the finite case.

2.1   An Intuitive Approach

We first assume that there are only two labels a and b. Let r be the record $\{a = 1;$ $b = true\}$ and f the function that reads the a field. Assuming f has type $\tau \to \tau'$ and r has type σ, f can be applied to r if the two types τ and σ are unifiable. In our example, we have

$$\tau = \Pi(a:pre(\alpha);b:\theta_b),$$

$$\sigma = \Pi(a:pre(num);b:pre(bool)),$$

and τ' is equal to α. The unification of τ and σ is done field by field and their most general unifier is:

$$\begin{cases} \alpha \mapsto num \\ \theta_b \mapsto pre(bool) \end{cases}$$

If we had one more label c, the types τ and σ would be

$$\tau = \Pi(a:pre(\alpha);b:\theta_b;c:\theta_c),$$

$$\sigma = \Pi(a:pre(num);b:pre(bool);c:abs).$$

and their most general unifier

$$\begin{cases} \alpha \mapsto num \\ \theta_b \mapsto pre(bool) \\ \theta_c \mapsto abs \end{cases}$$

We can play again with one more label d. The types would be

$$\tau = \Pi(a:pre(\alpha);b:\theta_b;c:\theta_c;d:\theta_d),$$

$$\sigma = \Pi(a:pre(num);b:pre(bool);c:abs;d:abs).$$

whose most general unifier is:

$$\begin{cases} \alpha \mapsto num \\ \theta_b \mapsto pre(bool) \\ \theta_c \mapsto abs \\ \theta_d \mapsto abs \end{cases}$$

Since labels c and d appear neither in the expressions r nor in f, it is clear that fields c and d behave the same, and that all their type components in the types of f and r are equal up to renaming of variables (they are isomorphic types). So we can guess the component of the most general unifier on any new field l simply by taking a copy of its component on the c field or on the d field. Instead of writing types of all fields, we only need to write a template type for all fields whose types are isomorphic, in addition to the types of significant fields, that is those which are not isomorphic to the template.

$\tau = \Pi(a : pre(\alpha); b : \theta_b; \infty : \theta_\infty)$,

$\sigma = \Pi(a : pre(num); b : pre(bool); \infty : abs)$.

The expression $\Pi((l : \tau_l)_{l \in I}; \infty : \sigma_\infty)$ should be read as

$$\prod_{l \in \mathscr{L}} \left(l : \begin{cases} \tau_l & \text{if } l \in I \\ \sigma_l & \text{otherwise, where } \sigma_l \text{ is a copy of } \sigma_\infty \end{cases} \right)$$

The most general unifier can be computed without developing this expression, thus allowing the set of labels to be infinite. We summarize the successive steps studied above in this figure:

Labels	a	b	c	d	∞
τ	$pre(\alpha)$	θ_b	θ_c	θ_d	θ_∞
σ	$pre(num)$	$pre(bool)$	abs	abs	abs
$\tau \wedge \sigma$	$pre(num)$	$pre(bool)$	abs	abs	abs

This approach is so intuitive that it seems very simple. There is a difficulty though, due to the sharing between templates. Sometimes a field has to be extracted from its template, because it must be unified with a significant field.

The macroscopic operation that we need is the transformation of a template τ into a copy τ' (the type of the extracted field) and another copy τ'' (the new template). We regenerate the template during an extraction mainly because of sharing. But it is also intuitive that once a field has been extracted, the retained template should remember that, and thus it cannot be the same. In order to keep sharing, we must extract a field step by step, starting from the leaves.

For a template variable α, the extraction consists in replacing that variable by two fresh variables β and γ, more precisely by the term $l:\beta;\gamma$. This is exactly the substitution

$$\alpha \mapsto l:\beta;\gamma$$

For a term $f(\alpha)$, assuming that we have already extracted field l from α, i.e. we have $f(l:\beta;\gamma)$, we now want to replace it by $l:f(\alpha);f(\gamma)$. The solution is simply to ask it to be true, that is, to assume the axiom

$$f(l:\beta;\gamma) = l:f(\alpha);f(\gamma)$$

for every given symbol f but Π.

2.2 Extending a Free Algebra with a Record Algebra

The intuitions of previous sections are formalized by the algebra of record terms. The algebra of record terms is introduced for an arbitrary free algebra; record types are an instance. The record algebra was introduced in [Rém90] and revisited in [Rém92b]. We summarize it below but we recommend [Rém92b] for a more thorough presentation.

We are given a set of variables $\mathcal{V}$ and a set of symbols $\mathcal{C}$ with their arities $(\mathcal{C}_n)_{n \in N}$.

Raw Terms   We call *unsorted record terms* the terms of the free unsorted algebra $\mathcal{T}'(\mathcal{D}', \mathcal{V})$ where $\mathcal{D}'$ is the set of symbols composed of $\mathcal{C}$ plus a unary symbol Π and a collection of projection symbols $\{(l:\_;\_)|l \in \mathcal{L}\}$ of arity two. Projection symbols associate to the right, that is $(a:\tau;b:\sigma;\tau')$ stands for $(a:\tau;(b:\sigma;\tau'))$.

EXAMPLE 1   The expressions

$$\Pi(a:pre(num);c:pre(bool);abs) \quad \text{and} \quad \Pi(a:pre(b:num;num);abs)$$

are raw terms. In section 2.4 we will consider the former as a possible type for the record $\{a = 1; c = true\}$ but we will not give a meaning to the latter. There are too many raw terms. The raw term $\{a:\alpha;\chi\} \to \chi$ must also be rejected since the template composed of the raw variable χ should define the a field on the right but should not on the left. We define record terms using sorts to constrain their formation. Only a few of the raw terms will have associated record terms.

Record Terms   Let $\mathcal{L}$ be a denumerable set of labels. Let $\mathcal{K}$ be composed of a sort *Type*, and a finite collection of sorts $(Row(L))$ where L range over finite subsets of labels. Let $\mathcal{S}$ be the signature composed of the following symbols given with their sorts:

$\mathscr{S} \vdash \Pi :: Row(\emptyset) \Rightarrow Type$

$\mathscr{S} \vdash f^K :: K^n \Rightarrow K \qquad f \in \mathscr{C}^n, K \in \mathscr{K}$

$\mathscr{S} \vdash (l^L : \_ ; \_) :: Type \otimes Row(L \cup \{l\}) \Rightarrow Row(L) \qquad l \in \mathscr{L}, L \in \mathscr{P}_{fin}(\mathscr{L} \setminus \{l\})$

The superscripts are parts of symbols, so that the signature $\mathscr{S}$ is not overloaded, that is, every symbol has a unique signature. We write $\mathscr{D}$ the set of symbols in $\mathscr{S}$.

DEFINITION 1   *Record terms* are the terms of the free sorted algebra $\mathscr{T}(\mathscr{S}, \mathscr{V})$.

EXAMPLE 2   The left term below is a record term. On the right, we drew a raw term with the same structure.

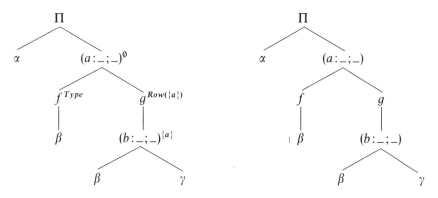

Script Erasure   To any record term, we associate the raw term obtained by erasing all superscripts of symbols. Conversely, for any raw term τ', and any sort ι there is at most one record term whose erasure is τ'. Thus any record term τ of sort ι is completely defined by its erasure τ' and the sort ι. In the rest of the paper we will mostly use this convention. Moreover we usually drop the sort whenever it is implicit from context.

EXAMPLE 3   The erasure of

$$\Pi(a^\emptyset : f^{Type}(g^{Type}) ; (c^{\{a\}} : f^{Type}(\alpha) ; h^{Row(\{a,c\})}))$$

is the raw term

$$\Pi(a : f(g) ; c : f(\alpha) ; h)$$

There is no record term whose erasure would be

$$\Pi(a : f(b : g ; \alpha) ; h)$$

Record Algebra   The permutation and the extraction of fields in record terms will be obtained by equations, of left commutativity and distributivity respectively. Precisely, let E be the set of axioms

• Left commutativity. For any labels a and b and any finite subset of labels L that do not contain a and b,

$$a^L : \alpha ; (b^{L \cup \{a\}} : \beta ; \gamma) = b^L : \beta ; (a^{L \cup \{b\}} : \alpha ; \gamma)$$

• Distributivity. For any symbol f, any label a and any finite subset of labels L that do not contain a,

$$f^{Row(L)}((a^L : \alpha_1 ; \beta_1), \ldots (a^L : \alpha_p ; \beta_p)) = a^L : f^{Type}(\alpha_1, \ldots \alpha_p) ; f^{Row(L \cup \{a\})}(\beta_1, \ldots \beta_p)$$

With the raw notation the equations are written:

• Left commutativity. At any sort $row(L)$, where L does not contain labels a and b:

$$a : \alpha ; (b : \beta ; \gamma) = b : \beta ; (a : \alpha ; \gamma)$$

• Distributivity. At any sort $row(L)$ where L does not contain label a, and for any symbol f:

$$f((a : \alpha_1 ; \beta_1), \ldots (a : \alpha_p ; \beta_p)) = a : f(\alpha_1, \ldots \alpha_p) ; f(\beta_1, \ldots \beta_p)$$

All axioms are regular, that is, the set of variables of both sides of equations are always identical.

EXAMPLE 4   In the term

$$\Pi(a : pre(num) ; c : pre(bool) ; abs)$$

we can replace abs by $b : abs ; abs$ using distributivity, and use left commutativity to end with the term:

$$\Pi(a : pre(num) ; b : abs ; c : pre(bool) ; abs)$$

In the term

$$\Pi(a : pre(\alpha) ; \theta)$$

we can substitute θ by $b : \theta_b ; c : \theta_c ; \varepsilon$ to get

$$\Pi(a : pre(\alpha) ; b : \theta_b ; c : \theta_c ; \varepsilon)$$

which can then be unified with the previous term field by field.

DEFINITION 2   The algebra of record terms is the algebra $\mathscr{T}(\mathscr{S}, \mathscr{V})$ modulo the equational theory E, written $\mathscr{T}(\mathscr{S}, \mathscr{V})/E$.

Unification in the algebra of record terms has been studied in [Rém92b].

THEOREM 1   Unification in the record algebra is decidable and unitary (every solvable unification problem has a principal unifier).

A unification algorithm is given in the appendix.

Instances of Record Terms   The construction of the record algebra is parameterized by the initial set of symbols $\mathscr{C}$, from which the signature $\mathscr{S}$ is deduced. The signature $\mathscr{S}$ may also be restricted by a signature $\mathscr{S}'$ that is compatible with the equations E, that is, a signature $\mathscr{S}'$ such that for all axioms r and all sorts ι of $\mathscr{S}'$,

$$\mathscr{S}' \vdash r^l :: \iota \Leftrightarrow \mathscr{S}' \vdash r^r :: \iota$$

The algebra $(\mathscr{T}/E){\upharpoonright}\mathscr{S}'$ and $(\mathscr{T}{\upharpoonright}\mathscr{S}')/(E{\upharpoonright}\mathscr{S}')$ are then isomorphic, and consequently unification in $(\mathscr{T}{\upharpoonright}\mathscr{S}')/(E{\upharpoonright}\mathscr{S}')$ is decidable and unitary, and solved by the same algorithm as in $\mathscr{T}/E$. The $\mathscr{S}'$-record algebra is the restriction $\mathscr{T}(\mathscr{S}, \mathscr{V}){\upharpoonright}\mathscr{S}'$ of the record algebra by a compatible signature $\mathscr{S}'$.

We now consider a particular instance of record algebra, where fields are distinguished from arbitrary types, and structured as in section 1. The signature $\mathscr{S}'$ distinguishes a constant symbol abs and a unary symbol pre in $\mathscr{C}$, and is defined with two sorts $type$ and $field$:

$$\mathscr{S}' \vdash \Pi :: field \Rightarrow type$$

$$\mathscr{S}' \vdash abs^l :: field \qquad \iota \in \mathscr{K}$$

$$\mathscr{S}' \vdash pre :: type \Rightarrow field$$

$$\mathscr{S}' \vdash f^{Type} :: type^n \Rightarrow type \qquad f \in \mathscr{C}^n \backslash \{abs, pre, \Pi\}$$

$$\mathscr{S}' \vdash (l^L : \_ ; \_) :: field \otimes field \Rightarrow field \qquad l \in \mathscr{L}, L \in \mathscr{P}_{fin}(\mathscr{L} \backslash \{l\})$$

The signature $\mathscr{S}'$ is compatible with the equations of the record algebra. We call *record types* the $\mathscr{S}'$-record algebra.

In fact, record types has a very simple structure. Terms of the sort $Row(L)$ are either of depth 0 (reduced to a variable or a symbol) or are of the form $(a : \tau ; \tau')$. By induction, they are always of the form

$$(a_1 : \tau_1 ; \ldots a_p : \tau_p ; \sigma)$$

where σ is either *abs* or a variable, including the case where p is zero and the term is reduced to σ. Record types are also generated by the pseudo-BNF grammar:

$$\tau ::= \alpha\,|\,\tau \to \tau\,|\,\Pi\rho^{\emptyset} \qquad\qquad\qquad \text{types}$$

$$\rho^L ::= \chi^L\,|\,abs^L\,|\,a:\varphi\,;\rho^{L\cup\{a\}} \qquad a \notin L \qquad \text{rows}$$

$$\varphi ::= \theta\,|\,abs\,|\,pre(\tau) \qquad\qquad\qquad \text{fields}$$

where α, β, γ and δ are type variables, χ, π and ξ are row variables and θ and ε are field variables. We prefer the algebraic approach which is more general.

2.3 Extending the Types of ML with a Sorted Equational Theory

In this section we consider a sorted regular theory $\mathcal{T}/E$ for which unification is decidable and unitary. A regular theory is one whose left and right hand sides of axioms always have the same set of variables. For any term τ of $\mathcal{T}/E$ we write $\mathcal{V}(\tau)$ for the set of its variables. We privilege a sort *Type*.

The addition of a sorted equational theory to the types of ML has been studied in [Rém90, Rém92a]. We recall here the main definitions and results. The language ML that we study is lambda-calculus extended with constants and a *LET* construct in order to mark some of the redexes, namely:

$M ::=$	Terms	M, N
x	Variable	x, y
$\|c$	Constant	c
$\|\lambda x . M$	Abstraction	
$\|MM$	Application	
$\|let\ x = M\ in\ M$	Let binding	

The letter W ranges over finite set of variables. Type schemes are pairs noted $\forall W \cdot \tau$ of a set of variables and a term τ. The symbol $\forall$ is treated as a binder and we consider type schemes equal modulo α-conversion. The sort of a type scheme $\forall W \cdot \tau$ is the sort of τ. Contexts as sequences of assertions, that is, pairs of a term variable and a type. We write $\mathcal{A}$ the set of contexts.

Every constant c comes with a closed type scheme $\forall W \cdot \tau$, written $c : \forall W \cdot \tau$. We write B the collection of all such constant assertions. We define a relation $\vdash$ on $\mathcal{A} \times \text{ML} \times \mathcal{T}$ and parameterized by B as the smallest relation that satisfies the following rules:

$$\frac{x : \forall W \cdot \tau \in A \qquad \mu : W \to \mathscr{T}}{A \vdash_S x : \mu(\tau)} \qquad\qquad \text{Var-Inst}$$

$$\frac{c : \forall W \cdot \tau \in B \qquad \mu : W \to \mathscr{T}}{A \vdash_S c : \mu(\tau)} \qquad\qquad \text{Const-Inst}$$

$$\frac{A[x : \tau] \vdash M : \sigma \qquad \tau \in \mathscr{T}}{A \vdash \lambda x . M : \tau \to \sigma} \qquad\qquad \text{Fun}$$

$$\frac{A \vdash M : \sigma \to \tau \qquad A \vdash N : \sigma}{A \vdash MN : \tau} \qquad\qquad \text{App}$$

$$\frac{A \vdash_S M : \tau \qquad A[x : \forall W \cdot \tau] \vdash_S N : \sigma \qquad W \cap \mathscr{V}(A) = \emptyset}{A \vdash_S let\ x = M\ in\ N : \sigma} \qquad\qquad \text{Let-Gen}$$

$$\frac{A \vdash M : \sigma \qquad \sigma =_E \tau}{A \vdash M : \tau} \qquad\qquad \text{Equal}$$

They are the usual rules for ML except the rule Equal that is added since the equality on types is taken modulo the equations E.

A typing problem is a triple of $\mathscr{A} \times \text{ML} \times \mathscr{T}$ written $A \rhd M : \tau$. The application of a substitution μ to a typing problem $A \rhd M : \tau$ is the typing problem $\mu(A) \rhd M : \mu(\tau)$, where substitution of a context is understood pointwise and only affects the type part of assertions. A solution of a typing problem $A \rhd M : \tau$ is a substitution μ such that $\mu(A) \vdash M : \mu(\tau)$. It is principal if all other solutions are obtained by left composition with μ of an arbitrary solution.

THEOREM 2 (principal typings)   If the sorted theory $\mathscr{T}/E$ is regular and its unification is decidable and unitary, then the relation $\vdash$ admits principal typings, that is, any solvable typing problem has a principal solution.

Moreover, there is an algorithm that given a typing problem computes a principal solution if one exists, or returns failure otherwise.

An algorithm can be obtained by replacing free unification by unification in the algebra of record terms in the core-ML type inference algorithm. A clever algorithm for type inference is described in [Rém92b].

2.4   Typechecking Record Operations

Using the two preceding results, we extend the types of ML with record types assuming given the following basic constants:

Basic constants for ΠML

$\{\ \}:\Pi(abs)$

$\_.a:\Pi(a:pre(\alpha);\theta)\to\alpha$

$\{\_\ with\ a=\_\}:\Pi(a:\theta;\chi)\to\alpha\to\Pi(a:pre(\alpha);\chi)$

There are countably many constants. We write $\{a_1=x_1;\dots a_n=x_n\}$ as syntactic sugar for:

$\{\{a_1=x_1;\dots a_{n-1}=x_{n-1}\}\ with\ a_n=x_n\}$

We illustrate this system by examples in the next section.

The equational theory of record types is regular, and has a decidable and unitary unification. It follows from theorems 2 and 1 that the typing relation of this language admits principal typings, and has a decidable type inference algorithm.

3   Programming with Records

We first show on simple examples how most of the constructions described in the introduction are typed, then we meet the limitations of this system. Some of them can be cured by slightly improving the encoding. Finally, we propose and discuss some further extensions.

3.1   Typing Examples

A typechecking prototype has been implemented in the CAML language. It was used to automatically type all the examples presented here and preceded by the # character. In programs, type variables are printed according to their sort in $\mathscr{S}'$. Letters χ, π and ξ are used for field variables and letters α, β, etc. are used for variables of the sort *type*. We start with simple examples and end with a short program.

Simple record values can be built as follows:

```
#let car = {name = "Toyota"; age = "old"; id = 7866};;
car:
 Π (name:pre (string); id:pre (num); age:pre (string); abs)
#let truck = {name = "Blazer"; id = 6587867567};;
truck:Π (name:pre (string); id:pre (num); abs)
#let person = {name = "Tim"; age = 31; id = 5656787};;
person:
 Π (name:pre (string); id:pre (num); age:pre (num); abs)
```

Each field defined with a value of type τ is significant and typed with *pre*(τ). Other fields are insignificant, and their types are gathered in the template *abs*. The record person can be extended with a new field vehicle:

```
#let driver = {person with vehicle = car};;
driver:
  Π (vehicle:pre (Π (name:pre (string); id:pre (num);
                     age:pre (string); abs));
     name:pre (string); id:pre (num); age:pre (num); abs)
```

This is possible whether this field was previously undefined as above, or defined as in:

```
#let truck_driver = {driver with vehicle = truck};;
truck_driver:
  Π (vehicle:pre (Π (name:pre (string); id:pre (num); abs));
     name:pre (string); id:pre (num); age:pre (num); abs)
```

The concatenation of two records is not provided by this system.

The sole construction for accessing fields is the "dot" operation.

```
#let age x = x.age;;            #let id x = x.id;;
age:Π (age:pre (α); χ) → α      id:Π (id:pre (α); χ) → α
```

The accessed field must be defined with a value of type α, so it has type pre (α), and other fields may or may not be defined; they are described by a template variable χ. The returned value has type α. As any value, age can be sent as an argument to another function:

```
#let car_info field = field car;;
car_info:(Π (name:pre (string); id:pre (num);
             age:pre (string); abs) → α) → α
#car_info age;;
it:string
```

The function equal below takes two records both possessing an id field of the same type, and possibly other fields. For simplicity of examples we assume given a polymorphic equality equal.

```
#let eq x y = equal x.id y.id;;
eq:Π (id:pre (α); χ) → Π (id:pre (α); π) → bool
```

```
#eq car truck;;
it:bool
```

We will show more examples in section 3.3.

3.2 Limitations

There are two sorts of limitations, one is due to the encoding method, the other one results from ML generic polymorphism. The only source of polymorphism in record operations is generic polymorphism. A field defined with a value of type τ in a record object is typed by $pre(\tau)$. Thus, once a field has been defined every function must see it defined. This forbids merging two records with different sets of defined fields. We will use the following function to shorten examples:

```
#let choice x y = if true then x else y;;
choice:α → α → α
```

Typechecking fails with:

```
#choice car truck;;
Typechecking error:collision between pre (string) and abs
```

The age field is undefined in truck but defined in car. This is really a weakness, since the program

```
#(choice car truck).name;;
Typechecking error:collision between pre (string) and abs
```

which should be equivalent to the program

```
#choice car.name truck.name;;
it:string
```

may actually be useful. We will partially solve this problem in section 3.3. A natural generalization of the eq function defined above is to abstract over the field that is used for testing equality

```
#let field_eq field x y = equal (field x) (field y);;
field_eq:(α → β) → α → α → bool
```

It is enough general to test equality on other values than records. We get a function equivalent to the program eq defined in section 3.1 by applying field_eq to the function id.

```
#let id_eq = field_eq id;;
id_eq:Π (id:pre (α); χ) → Π (id:pre (α); χ) → )bool
#id_eq car truck;;
Typechecking error:collision between pre (string) and abs
```

The last example fails. This is not surprising since field is bound by a lambda in
field_eq, and therefore its two instances have the same type, and so have both
arguments x and y. In eq, the arguments x and y are independent since they are two
instances of id. This is nothing else but ML generic polymorphism restriction. We
emphasize that, as record polymorphism is entirely based on generic polymorphism,
the restriction applies drastically to records.

3.3 Flexibility and Improvements

The method for typechecking records is very flexible: the operations on records have
not been fixed at the beginning, but at the very end. They are parameters that can vary
in many ways.

The easiest modification is changing the types of basic constants. For instance,
asserting that $\{\_\ with\ a = \_\}$ comes with type scheme:

$$\{\_\ with\ a = \_\} : \Pi(a:abs;\chi) \to \alpha \to \Pi(a:pre(\alpha);\chi)$$

makes the extension of a record with a new field possible only if the field was previously undefined. This slight change gives exactly the strict version that appears in
both attempts to solve Wand's system [JM88, OB88]. Weakening the type of this
primitive may be interesting in some cases, because the strict construction may be
easier to implement and more efficient.

We can freely change the types of primitives, provided we know how to implement
them correctly. More generally, we can change the operations on records themselves.
Since a defined field may not be dropped implicitly, it would be convenient to add a
primitive removing explicitly a field from a record

$$\_\backslash a : \Pi(a:\theta;\chi) \to \Pi(a:abs;\chi),$$

In fact, the constant $\{\_\ with\ a = \_\}$ is not primitive. It should be replaced by the strict
version:

$$\{\_\ with\ !a = \_\} : \Pi(a:abs;\chi) \to \alpha \to \Pi(a:pre(\alpha);\chi),$$

and the $\_\backslash a$ constant, since the original version is the composition $\{\_\backslash a\ with\ !a = \_\}$.
Our encoding also allows typing a function that renames fields

$$rename^{a \leftarrow b} : \Pi(a:\theta;b:\varepsilon;\chi) \to \Pi(a:abs;b:\theta;\chi)$$

The renamed field may be undefined. In the result, it is no longer accessible. A more primitive function would just exchanges two fields

$$exchange^{a \leftrightarrow b} : \Pi(a:\theta;b:\varepsilon;\chi) \to \Pi(a:\varepsilon;b:\theta;\chi)$$

whether they are defined or not. Then the *rename* constant is simply the composition:

$$(\_\backslash a) \circ exchange^{a \leftrightarrow b}$$

More generally, the decidability of type inference does not depend on the specific signature of the *pre* and *abs* type symbols. The encoding of records can be revised. We are going to illustrate this by presenting another variant for type-checking records.

We suggested that a good type system should allow some polymorphism on records values themselves. We recall the example that failed to type

```
#choice car truck;;
Typechecking error:collision between pre (string) and abs
```

because the age field was defined in car but undefined in truck. We would like the result to have a type with *abs* on this field to guarantee that it will not be accessed, but common, compatible fields should remain accessible. The idea is that a defined field should be seen as undefined whenever needed. From the point of view of types, this would require that a defined field with a value of type τ should be typed with both $pre(\tau)$ and *abs*.

Conjunctive types [Cop80] could possibly solve this problem, but they are undecidable in general. Another attempt is to make *abs* of arity 1 by replacing each use of *abs* by $abs(\alpha)$ where α is a generic variable. However, it is not possible to write $\forall \theta \cdot \theta(\tau)$ where θ ranges over *abs* and *pre*. The only possible solution is to make *abs* and *pre* constant symbols by introducing an infix field symbol "." and write $abs.\alpha$ and $pre.\alpha$ instead of $abs(\alpha)$ and $pre(\alpha)$. It is now possible to write $\forall \varepsilon \cdot (\varepsilon.\tau)$. Formally, the signature $\mathscr{S}'$ is replaced by the signature $\mathscr{S}''$ given below, with a new sort *flag*:

$\mathscr{S}'' \vdash \Pi :: field \Rightarrow type$

$\mathscr{S}'' \vdash abs^l :: flag \qquad l \in \mathscr{K}$

$\mathscr{S}'' \vdash pre^l :: flag \qquad l \in \mathscr{K}$

$\mathscr{S}'' \vdash \, .^l :: flag \otimes type \Rightarrow field \qquad l \in \mathscr{K}$

$\mathscr{S}'' \vdash f^{Type} :: type^{\varrho(f)} \Rightarrow type \qquad f \in \mathscr{C} \backslash \{abs, pre, .\}$

$\mathscr{S}'' \vdash (l^L : \_; \_) :: field \otimes field \Rightarrow field \qquad l \in \mathscr{L}, L \in \mathscr{P}_{fin}(\mathscr{L} \backslash \{l\})$

Record constants now come with the following type schemes:

Basic constants for ΠML′

$\{\ \}: \Pi(abs.\alpha)$

$\_.a: \Pi(a:pre.\alpha;\chi) \to \alpha$

$\{\_\ with\ a = \_\}: \Pi(a:\theta;\chi) \to \alpha \to \Pi(a:\varepsilon.\alpha;\chi)$

It is easy to see that system ΠML′ is more general than system ΠML; any expression typeable in the system ΠML is also typeable in the system ΠML′: replacing in a proof all occurrences of *abs* by *abs*.α and all occurrence of *pre*(τ) by *pre*.τ (where α does not appear in the proof), we obtain a correct proof in ΠML′.

We show the types in the system ΠML′ of some of previous examples. Flag variables are written ε, ζ and η. Building a record creates a polymorphic object, since all fields have a distinct *flag* variable:

```
#let car = {name = "Toyota"; age = "old"; id = 7866};;
car:Π (name:ε.string; id:ζ.num; age:η.string; abs.α)
#let truck = {name = "Blazer"; id = 6587867567};;
truck:Π (name:ε.string; id:ζ.num; abs.α)
```

Now these two records can be merged,

```
#choice car truck;;
it:Π (name:ε.string; id:ζ.num; age:abs.string; abs.α)
```

forgetting the `age` field in `car`. Note that if the presence of field `age` has been forgotten, its type has not: we always remember the types of values that have stayed in fields. Thus, the type system ΠML′ rejects the program:

```
#let person = {name = "Tim"; age = 31; id = 5656787};;
person:Π (name:ε.string; id:ζ.num; age:η.num; abs.α)
#choice person car;;
Typechecking error:collision between num and string
```

This is really a weakness of our system, since both records have common fields `name` and `id`, which might be tested on later. This example would be correct in the explicitly typed language QUEST [Car89]. If we add a new collection of primitives

$\_\backslash a: \Pi(a:\theta;\chi) \to \Pi(a:abs.\alpha;\chi),$

then we can turn around the failure above by explicitly forgetting label age in at least one record

```
#choice (car \ age) person;;
it:Π (age:abs.num; name:ε.string; id:ζ.num; abs.α)
#choice car (person \ age);;
it:Π (age:abs.string; name:ε.string; id:ζ.num; abs.α)
#choice (car \ age) (person \ age);;
it:Π (age:abs.α; name:ε.string; id:ζ.num: abs.β)
```

A more realistic example illustrates the ability to add annotations on data structures and type the presence of these annotations. The example is run into the system ΠML′, where we assume given an infix addition + typed with num → num → num.

```
#type tree (ε) = Leaf of num
#               | Node of {left:pre.tree (ε); right:pre.tree (ε);
#                          annot:ε.num; abs.unit}
#;;
New constructors declared:
Node:Π (left:pre.tree (ε); right:pre.tree (ε); annot:ε.num; abs.unit)
    → tree (ε)
Leaf:num → tree (ε)
```

The variable ε indicates the presence of the annotation annot. For instance this annotation is absent in the structure

```
#let winter = 'Node {left = 'Leaf 1; right = 'Leaf 2};;
winter:tree (abs)
```

The following function annotates a structure.

```
#let rec annotation =
# function
#     Leaf n → 'Leaf n, n
#   | Node {left = r; right = s} →
#       let (r,p) = annotation r in
#       let (s,q) = annotation s in
#           'Node {left = r; right = s; annot = p+q}, p+q;;
annotation:tree (ε) → tree (ζ) * num
```

```
#let annotate x = match annotation x with y,_ → y;;
annotate:tree (ε) → tree (ζ)
```

We use it to annotate the structure winter.

```
#let spring = annotate winter;;
spring:tree (ε)
```

We will read a structure with the following function.

```
#let read = function 'Leaf n → n | 'Node r → r.annot;;
read:tree (pre) → num
```

It can be applied to the value spring, but not to the empty structure winter.

```
#read winter;;                                      #read spring;;
Typechecking error:collision between pre and abs    it:num
```

But the following function may be applied to both winter and spring:

```
#let rec left =                  #left winter;;
# function                       it:num
#    'Leaf n → n
# | 'Node r → left (r.left);;    #left spring;;
left:tree (ε) → num              it:num
```

3.4 Extensions

In this section we describe two possible extensions. The two of them have been implemented in a prototype, but not completely formalized yet.

One important motivation for having records was the encoding of some object oriented features into them. But the usual encoding uses recursive types [Car84, Wan89]. An extension of ML with variant types is easy once we have record types, following the idea of [Rém89], but the extension is interesting essentially if recursive types are allowed.

Thus it would be necessary to extend the results presented here with recursive types. Unification on rational trees without equations is well understood [Hue76, MM82]. In the case of a finite set of labels, the extension of theorem 2 to rational trees is easy. The infinite case uses an equational theory, and unification in the extension of first order equational theory to rational trees has no decidable and unitary algorithm in general, even when the original theory has one. But the simplicity of the record theory lets us conjecture that it can be extended with regular trees.

Another extension, which was sketched in [Rém89], partially solves the restrictions due to ML polymorphism. Becasue subtyping polymorphism goes through lambda abstractions, it could be used to type some of the examples that were wrongly rejected. ML type inference with subtyping polymorphism has been first studied by Mitchell in [Mit84] and later by Mishra and Fuh [FM88, FM89]. The *LET*-case has only been treated in [Jat89]. But as for recursive types, subtyping has never been studied in the presence of an equational theory. Although the general case of merging subtyping with an equational theory is certainly difficult, we believe that subtyping is compatible with the axioms of the algebra of record types. We discuss below the extension with subtyping in the finite case only. The extension in the infinite case would be similar, but it would rely on the previous conjecture.

It is straightforward to extend the results of [FM89] to deal with sorted types. It is thus possible to embed the language ΠML_{fin} into a language with subtypes $\Pi ML_\subset$. In fact, we use the language $\Pi ML'_\subset$ that has the signature of the language $\Pi ML'$ for a technical reason that will appear later. The subtype relation we need is closed structural subtyping. Closed[2] structural subtyping is defined relatively to a set of atomic coercions as the smallest *E*-reflexive (i.e. that contains $=_E$) and transitive relation $\subset$ that contains the atomic coercions and that satisfies the following rules [FM89]:

$$\frac{\sigma \subset \tau \qquad \tau' \subset \sigma'}{\tau \to \tau' \subset \sigma \to \sigma'}$$

$$\frac{\tau_1 \subset \sigma_1, \ldots \tau_p \subset \sigma_p}{f(\tau_1, \ldots \tau_p) \subset f(\sigma_1, \ldots \sigma_p)} \qquad f \in \mathscr{C} \backslash \{\to\}$$

In $\Pi ML'_\subset$, we consider the unique atomic coercion $pre \subset abs$. It says that if a field is defined, it can also be view as undefined. We assign the following types to constants:

Basic constants for $\Pi ML'_\subset$

$\{\ \} : \Pi(abs \, . \, \alpha_1, \ldots abs \, . \, \alpha_l)$

$\_ . \, a : \Pi(\theta_1 \ldots, pre \, . \, \alpha \ldots \theta_l) \to \alpha$

$\{\_ \, with \, a = \_\} : \Pi(\theta_1, \ldots \theta_l) \to \alpha \to \Pi(\theta_1 \ldots, pre \, . \, \alpha, \ldots \theta_l)$

If the types look the same as without subtyping, they are taken modulo subtyping, and are thus more polymorphic. In this system, the program

```
let id_eq = field_eq id;;
```

is typed with:

```
id_eq:{id:pre.α; χ} → {id:pre.α; χ} → bool
```

This allows the application modulo subtyping ed_eq car truck. The field age is implicitly forgotten in truck by the inclusion rules. However, we still fail with the example choice person car. The presence of fields can be forgotten, yet their types cannot, and there is a mismatch between num and string in the old field of both arguments. A solution to this failure is to use the signature $\mathscr{S}'$ instead of $\mathscr{S}''$. However the inclusion relation now contains the assertion $pre(\alpha) \subset abs$ which is not atomic. Such coercions do not define a structural subtyping relation. Type inference with non structural inclusion has not been studied successfully yet and it is surely difficult (the difficulty is emphasized in [Rém89]). The type of primitives for records would be the same as in the system ΠML_{fin}, but modulo the non-structural subtyping relation.

Conclusion

We have described a simple, flexible and efficient solution for extending ML with operations on records allowing some sort of inheritance. The solution uses an extension of ML with a sorted equational theory over types. An immediate improvement is to allow recursive types needed in many applications of records.

The main limitation of our solution is ML polymorphism. In many cases, the problem can be solved by inserting retyping functions. We also propose structural subtyping as a more systematic solution. But it is not clear yet whether we would want such an extension, for it might not be worth the extra cost in type inference.

Acknowledgments

I am grateful for interesting discussions with Peter Buneman, Vol Breazu-Tannen and Carl Gunter, and particularly thankful to Xavier Leroy and Benjamin Pierce whose comments on the presentation of this article were very helpful.

Unification on Record Types

The algorithm is an adaptation of the one given in [Rém92b], which we recommend for a more thorough presentation. It is described by transformations on unificands that keep unchanged the set of solutions. Multi-equations are multi-sets of terms, written $\tau_1 = \ldots \tau_p$, and unificands are systems of multi-equations, that is, multi-sets of multi-equations, with existential quantifiers. Systems of multi-equations are written U. The union of systems of multi-equations (as multi-sets) is written $U \wedge U'$ and $\exists \alpha \cdot U$ is the existential quantification of α in U. Indeed, $\exists$ acts as a binder and systems of multi-equations are taken modulo α-conversion, permutation of consecutive binders, and $\exists \alpha \cdot U$ is assumed equal to U whenever α is not free in U. We also consider both unificands $U \wedge \exists \alpha \cdot U'$ and $\exists \alpha \cdot U \wedge U'$ equal whenever α is not in U. Any unificand can be written $\exists W \cdot U$ where W is a set of variables, and U does not contain any existential.

The algorithm reduces a unificand into a solved unificand in three steps, or fails. The first step is described by rewriting rules of figure 1. Rewriting always terminates. A unificand that cannot be transformed anymore is said completely decomposed if no multi-equation has more than one non-variable term, and the algorithm pursues with the occur check while instantiating the equations by partial solutions as described below, otherwise the unificand is not solvable and the algorithm fails.

We say that a multi-equation e' is inner a multi-equation e if there is at least a variable term of e' that appears in a non-variable term of e, and we write $e' < e$. We also write $U' \not< U$ for

$$\forall e' \in U', \forall e \in U, e' \not< e$$

The system U is independent if $U \not< U$.

The second step applies the rule

$$\text{If } e \wedge U \not< e, \qquad \frac{e \wedge U}{e \wedge \hat{e}(U)} \rightsquigarrow \qquad\qquad\qquad \text{REPLACE}$$

until all possible candidates e have fired the rule once, where $\hat{e}$ is the trivial solution of e that sends all variable terms to the non-variable term if it exists, or to any (but fixed) variable term otherwise. If the resulting system U is *independent* (i.e. $U \not< U$), then the algorithm pursues as described below; otherwise it fails and U is not solvable.

Last step eliminates useless existential quantifiers and singleton multi-equations by repeated applicaton of the rules:

$$\text{If } \alpha \notin e \wedge U, \qquad \frac{\exists \alpha \cdot (\alpha = e \wedge U)}{e \wedge U} \rightsquigarrow \qquad \frac{\{\tau\} \wedge U}{U} \rightsquigarrow \qquad\qquad \text{GARBAGE}$$

This always succeeds, with a system $\exists W \cdot U$ that is still independent. A principal solution of the system is $\hat{U}$, that is, the composition, in any order, of the trivial

$$\text{If } \alpha \in \mathcal{V}(\tau) \wedge \tau \in e \backslash \mathcal{V}, \qquad \frac{U \wedge (\alpha \mapsto \sigma)(e)}{U \wedge \exists \alpha \cdot (e \wedge \alpha = \sigma)} \qquad\qquad \text{GENERALIZE}$$

$$\frac{U \wedge a : \tau ; \tau' = abs = e}{U \wedge \bigwedge \begin{cases} abs = e \\ \tau = abs \\ \tau' = abs \end{cases}} \qquad \frac{U \wedge a : \alpha ; \alpha' = b : \beta ; \beta' = e}{U \wedge \exists \gamma \cdot \bigwedge \begin{cases} b : \beta ; \beta' = e \\ \alpha' = b : \beta ; \gamma \\ \beta' = a : \alpha ; \gamma \end{cases}} \qquad \text{MUTATE}$$

$$\frac{U \wedge f(\tau_1, \ldots \tau_p) = f(\alpha_1, \ldots \alpha_p) = e}{U \wedge \bigwedge \begin{cases} f(\alpha_1, \ldots \alpha_p) = e \\ \tau_i = \alpha_i, \quad i \in [1, p] \end{cases}} \qquad\qquad \text{DECOMPOSE}$$

$$\frac{U \wedge \alpha = e \wedge \alpha = e'}{U \wedge \alpha = e = e'} \qquad\qquad \text{FUSE}$$

Figure 1
Rewriting rules for record-type unification

solutions of its multi-equations. It is defined up to a renaming of variables in W. The soundness and correctness of this algorithm is described in [Rém92b].

The REPLACE step is actually not necessary, and a principal solution can be directly read from a completely decomposed form provided the transitive closure of the inner relation on the system is acyclic (see [Rém92b] for details).

With the signature $\mathcal{S}''$ the only change to the algorithm is the addition of the mutation rules:

$$\frac{a : \tau ; \tau' = pre = e}{\bigwedge \begin{cases} pre = e \\ \tau = pre \\ \tau' = pre \end{cases}} \qquad \frac{a : \alpha ; \beta = \gamma_1 \cdot \gamma_2 = e}{\exists \alpha_1 \alpha_2 \beta_1 \beta_2 \cdot \bigwedge \begin{cases} \gamma_1 \cdot \gamma_2 = e \\ \alpha = \alpha_1 \cdot \alpha_2 \\ \beta = \beta_1 \cdot \beta_2 \\ \gamma_1 = a : \alpha_1 \cdot \beta_1 \\ \gamma_2 = a : \alpha_2 \cdot \beta_2 \end{cases}}$$

Note that in the first mutation rule, all occurrences of *pre* in the conclusion (the right hand side) of the rewriting rule have different sorts and the three equations could not be merged into a multi-equation. They surely will not be merged later since a common constant cannot fire fusion of two equations (only a variable can). As all rules are well sorted, rewriting keeps unificands well sorted.

Notes

1. It can be understood as an "append" on association lists in lisp compared to the "with" operation which should be understood as "cons".

2. In [FM89], the structural subtyping is *open*. With open structural subtyping only some of the atomic coercions are known, but there are potentially many others that can be used (opened) during typechecking of later phrases of the program. Closed subtyping is usually easier than open subtyping.

References

[Ber88]   Bernard Berthomieu. Une implantation de CCS. Technical Report 88367, LAAS, 7, Avenue du Colonnel Roche, 31077 Toulouse, France, décembre 1988.

[Car84]   Luca Cardelli. A semantics of multiple inheritance. In *Semantics of Data Types*, volume 173 of *Lecture Notes in Computer Science*, pages 51–68. Springer Verlag, 1984. Also in Information and Computation, 1988.

[Car86]   Luca Cardelli. Amber. In *Combinators and Functional Programming Languages*, volume 242 of *Lecture Notes in Computer Science*, pages 21–47. Springer Verlag, 1986. Proceedings of the 13th Summer School of the LITP.

[Car89]   Luca Cardelli. Typefull programming. In *IFIP advanced seminar on Formal Methods in Programming Langage Semantics*, Lecture Notes in Computer Science. Springer Verlag, 1989.

[Car91]   Luca Cardelli. Extensible records in a pure calculus of subtyping. Private Communication, 1991.

[CCH$^+$89]   Peter Canning, William Cook, Walter Hill, Walter Olthoff, and John C. Mitchell. F-Bounded polymorphism for object oriented programming. In *The Fourth International Conference on Functional Programming Languages and Computer Architecture*, 1989.

[CH89]   Guy Cousineau and Gérard Huet. *The CAML Primer*. INRIA-Rocquencourt BP 105, F-78 153 Le Chesnay Cedex, France, 1989.

[CM89]   Luca Cardelli and John C. Mitchell. Operations on records. In *Fifth International Conference on Mathematical Foundations of Programming Semantics*, 1989.

[Cop80]   Mario Coppo. An extended polymorphic type system for applicative languages. In *MFCS '80*, volume 88 of *Lecture Notes in Computer Science*, pages 194–204. Springer Verlag, 1980.

[Cur87]   Pavel Curtis. *Constrained Quantification in Polymorphic Type Analysis*. PhD thesis, Cornell, 1987.

[FM88]   You-Chin Fuh and Prateek Mishra. Type inference with subtypes. In *ESOP '88*, volume 300 of *Lecture Notes in Computer Science*, pages 94–114. Springer Verlag, 1988.

[FM89]   You-Chin Fuh and Prateek Mishra. Polymorphic subtype inference: Closing the theory-practice gap. In *TAPSOFT '89*, 1989.

[HMT91]   Robert Harper, Robin Milner, and Mads Tofte. *The definition of Standard ML*. The MIT Press, 1991.

[HP90]   Robert W. Harper and Benjamin C. Pierce. Extensible records without subsumption. Technical Report CMU-CS-90-102, Carnegie Mellon University, Pittsburg, Pensylvania, February 1990.

[Hue76]   Gérard Huet. *Résolution d'équations dans les langages d'ordre 1, 2, . . . , ω*. Thèse de doctorat d'état, Université Paris 7, 1976.

[Jat89]   Lalita A. Jategaonkar. ML with extended pattern matching and subtypes. Master's thesis, MIT, 545 Technology Square, Cambridge, MA 02139, August 89.

[JM88]   Lalita A. Jategaonkar and John C. Mitchell. ML with extended pattern matching and subtypes. In *Proceedings of the 1988 Conference on LISP and Functional Programming*, 1988.

[LC90]   Giuseppe Longo and Luca Cardelli. A semantic basis for QUEST. In *Proceedings of the 1990 Conference on LISP and Functional Programming*, 1990.

[Mil80]   Robin Milner. A calculus of communicating systems. In *Lecture Notes in Computer Science*, volume 230. Springer Verlag, 1980.

[Mit84]   John C. Mitchell. Coercion and type inference. In *Eleventh Annual Symposium on Principles Of Programming Languages*, 1984.

[MM82]   Alberto Martelli and Ugo Montanari. An efficient unification algorithm. *ACM Transactions on Programming Languages and Systems*, 4(2):258–282, 1982.

[OB88]   Atsushi Ohori and Peter Buneman. Type inference in a database langage. In *ACM Conference on LISP and Functional Programming*, pages 174–183, 1988.

[Rém89]   Didier Rémy. Records and variants as a natural extension of ML. In *Sixteenth Annual Symposium on Principles Of Programming Languages*, 1989.

[Rém90]   Didier Rémy. *Algèbres Touffues. Application au Typage Polymorphe des Objects Enregistrements dans les Languages Fonctionnels*. Thèse de doctorat, Université de Paris 7, 1990.

[Rém92a]   Didier Rémy. Extending ML type system with a sorted equational theory. Technical report 1766, INRIA-Rocquencourt BP 105, F-78 153 Le Chesnay Cedex, 1992.

[Rém92b]   Didier Rémy. Syntactic theories and the algebra of record terms. Technical report 1869, INRIA-Rocquencourt BP 105, F-78 153 Le Chesnay Cedex, 1992. To appear.

[Rey88]   John C. Reynolds. Preliminary design of the programming language Forsythe. Technical Report CMU-CS-88-159, Carnegie Mellon University, Pittsburgh, Pennsylvania, June 1988.

[Wan87]   Mitchell Wand. Complete type inference for simple objects. In *Second Symposium on Logic In Computer Science*, 1987.

[Wan89]   Mitchell Wand. Type inference for record concatenation and multiple inheritance. In *Fourth Annual Symposium on Logic In Computer Science*, pages 92–97, 1989.

[Wei89]   Pierre Weis. *The CAML Reference Manual*. BP 105, F-78 153 Le Chesnay Cedex, France, 1989.

4 Type Inference for Objects with Instance Variables and Inheritance

Mitchell Wand

Abstract

We show how to construct a complete type inference system for object systems with protected instance variables, publicly accessible methods, first-class classes, and single inheritance. This is done by extending Rémy's scheme for polymorphic record typing to allow potentially infinite label sets, and interpreting objects in the resulting language.

1 Introduction

Object-Oriented Programming (OOP) has become a popular paradigm because it provides a well-engineered combination of services to the programmer. The activities at work in OOP include a uniform reference principle, information-hiding, inheritance, and distributed definition. By a uniform reference principle, we refer to the use of field selection or message-passing as a generic way of retrieving data from composite structures. By information-hiding, we refer to the typical way in which the internal structure of an object is protected from the outside world: the "instance variables" of an object are manipulable only through the interface of the "methods." Inheritance refers to the manner in which new classes of objects are created as incremental variations of old ones. Distributed definition refers to the syntactic structure of class definitions in certain object systems, in which the definitions of the methods may be textually distributed through a program or system. We have listed these activites to suggest a decreasing order of unanimity: almost every OOP system provides a uniform reference principle, while systems vary widely in their treatment of inheritance and distributed definition.

In [Wand 87], we introduced a language and type system for dealing with record structures. That system addressed only the first of these activities: the use of record structures as a uniform reference principle. In this paper we show how to extend this system to model information-hiding and single inheritance. The resulting system is strongly typed: no well-typed program will even produce a "mthod not found" message. The system is also polymorphic: it requires no type declarations, and procedures will work on inputs of many types whenever possible. The system is also noteworthy in that it allows classes as first-class citizens of the language.

We do this by interpreting the language of classes in the language of records. In this way, the typing rules for the language of records give strong typing for the language of classes as well.

The underlying type system for records is adapted from Rémy [Rémy 89], which gives a clean solution to the difficulties of the system in [Wand 87] and in addition allows the inference of recursive types, which are important in this application. We extend Rémy's system to allow infinite label sets, and show how the unification algorithm can be extended to handle these infinitely-wide trees.

We then establish a protocol for representing classes as records and show how class creation and invocation can be interpreted as syntactic sugar for the corresponding record operations. We also give another version in which classes are insulated from their representation as records.

We conclude with some remarks on structural and name equivalence for types, and discuss related work.

2   Records: Basic Definitions

Records are composite structures with components indexed by a fixed set L of labels. We assume that one can effectively determine whether a given label is present or absent in a record. Therefore, we model records as total functions

$$L \to (V + \{absent\})$$

For the moment, we will assume that L is finite; we will remedy this assumption in Section 4. The basic operations on records are selection, null, and extension.

- Selection along label a, written $(-).a$, selects the a-th component of the record:

$$r.a = r(a)$$

- The null record *null* is the one with no fields: $\lambda a . absent$.

- Record extension is the standard extension of a function by one point:

$$(r \text{ with } a = v) = \lambda b . ((b = a) \Rightarrow v, r(b))$$

We write r **with** $[a_1 = v_1 ; \ldots ; a_k = v_k]$ as an abbreviation for r **with** $[a_1 = v_1] \ldots$ **with** $[a_k = v_k]$.

3   Strong Typing for Records

Our basic approach is to take the type of a record to be the record of the types of its components. Thus the type of a record is a function $L \to (Type + \{absent\})$. This suggests type constructions of the form:

$\rightarrow : Type \times Type \Rightarrow Type$

$\Pi : [L \Rightarrow (Type + \{absent\})] \Rightarrow Type$

Using an observation of Rémy [Rémy 89], we can turn this back into an ordinary algebraic signature by introducing a new kind (called *Field*), and using the signature:

$\rightarrow : Type \times Type \Rightarrow Type$

$\Pi : Field^L \Rightarrow Type$

absent : *Field*

pres : *Type* $\Rightarrow$ *Field*

In this scheme, a field *absent* signifies a field which is absent from the record; a field *pres(t)* indicates a field which is present and has a value of type *t*. Type schemes in which a field may be either presnt or absent can be modelled by using a field variable. Since the definition is inductive, semantics can be assigned to these types in an obvious way. Recursive types can be considered as well. In the final version of this system, we will allow L to be infinite, so that Π becomes an infinitary constructor. For the moment, however, it will suffice to imagine L to be finite.

In addition, we will allow type variables τ_1, τ_2, ..., field variables f_1, f_2, ..., and type constants (but not field constants). A *type* (or *field*) will consist of a well-kinded tree of kind *Type* or *Field*, respectively. These trees will have Π-nodes which branch card(L) ways, with daughter nodes indexed by L. In general, we will also allow trees to be countably deep.

Since L is finite, we will write Π as an ordinary type constructor, of arity card(L). In this system, we can write principal type schemes for the basic record operations:

null : $\Pi(absent, \ldots, absent)$

$(-).a : \Pi(f_1, \ldots, pres(t), \ldots, f_n) \rightarrow t$

$(-)$ **with** $a = (-) : \Pi(f_1, \ldots, f_n) \rightarrow t \rightarrow \Pi(f_1, \ldots, pres(t), \ldots, f_n)$

Here we set $n = \text{card}(L)$, the f_i are field variables, and the modified component of the Π constructors is the one corresponding to the label a.

It is instructive to analyze these typeschemes. The first says that *null* builds a record all of whose fields are absent. The second says that selection takes as input any record whose a field is present, and returns a value of the same type as that a field. The use of field variables allows this type to express the proposition that the other fields may be either present or absent. The last says that extension takes as inputs any record and any value, and returns a record of the same type as the input, except that the a field is guaranteed to be present with type t. These types are consistent with the semantics given earlier. Many other operations have types which are expressible in this language (see [Rémy 89]).

If L is finite, then this is a conventional type system (albeit with a slightly non-standard kind system), to which all the usual results on polymorphic typing apply. In particular, one can infer principal types with or without reflexive (infinitely deep) types and with or without polymorphic values created using the standard **let** construct of ML. We conjecture that other extensions, such as Mitchell's extension to subtyping on ground types [Mitchell 84, see also Wand & O'Keefe 89] or O'Toole and Gifford's quantification schemes [O'Toole & Gifford 89] are easily incorporated.

4   Dealing with Infinite Label Sets

In general it is not enough to typecheck programs with finite L. If one is checking a small module of a very large system, one may not know in advance what labels may be used in the larger system. Similar problems arise if one is incrementally checking a piece of a program in an interactive system. Hence it is necessary to provide for the infinite set of labels which are possible in the language.

When L is infinite, we will need some notation for specifying functions in $Field^L$, which we sometimes call *rows*. We observe that only the labels actually mentioned in the program need be dealt with explicitly; all the other labels can be treated as ellipses. Without loss of generality, let us assume that the labels which actually appear in the program are numbered 1 through n. (We will see later how this assumption may be eliminated). Let ρ, ρ', etc. be a new class of variables called *extension* variables (following [Jategaonkar & Mitchell 88]). We can think of an extension variable as a labelled ellipsis abbreviating an infinite sequence of field variables.

We write

$$\Pi[F_1, \ldots, F_n] \; empty$$

for the product type

$$\Pi(F_1, \ldots, F_n, absent, absent, \ldots)$$

and

$$\Pi[F_1, \ldots, F_n]\rho$$

for the product type

$$\Pi(F_1, \ldots, F_n, f_{\rho, n+1}, f_{\rho, n+2}, \ldots)$$

where the $f_{\rho, i}$ are fresh field variables. We refer to the first n labels as *explicit* labels, and to the others as *implicit*.

In this way we reduce Π from an infinitary constructor to a finitary $n + 1$-ary constructor, with a kind structure given by:

$\rightarrow : Type \times Type \Rightarrow Type$

$\Pi : Field^n \times Extension \Rightarrow Type$

$absent : Field$

$pres : Type \Rightarrow Field$

$empty : Extension$

Note that the kind *Extension* has only extension variables and the constant *empty*, denoting the ellipsis whose components are all *absent*. We then observe:

- All the constants have principal types which are finitely representable in this scheme.
- Any two finitary terms have a unifier if and only if their infinitary translations do, and their most general unifier represent the most general unifier of their translations.

Hence we can deal with unification (and principal types for the language without concatenation) by simply calculating with the representations.

While this development is adequate theoretically to deal with infinite label sets, it is inadequate to deal with the problem that led us to consider infinite label sets in the first place: namely, the problem of incrementally checking a portion of a program, without knowing the entire set of labels needed.

In order to deal with this problem, we observe that it is not necessary for all Π nodes to have exactly the same set of explicit labels. To capture these distinctions, we write a typical Π node as

$$\Pi[a_1 : F_1, \ldots a_k : F_k]\rho$$

to indicate that the explicit labels are $a_1, \ldots, a_k$.

In this language, we can succinctly write the types of the constants:

$null : \Pi[\ ] empty$

$(-).a : \Pi[a : pres(t)]\rho \rightarrow t$

$(-) \text{ with } a = (-) : \Pi[a : f]\rho \rightarrow t \rightarrow \Pi[a : pres(t)]\rho$

The unification algorithm will work if we maintain the following invariants:

• All Π nodes with the same extension variable have the same explicit labels, so that each extension variable has a well-defined domain.

• When two Π nodes are unified, they must have the same explicit labels.

The first invariant is satisfied by the types of the constants as written above, so both invariants are true before unification.

Now, under this invariant, consider unifying two terms T_M and T_N. As we traverse these trees, we may reach corresponding Π nodes with different sets of explicit labels. In order to unify these, we first pad the nodes to give them the same set of explicit labels: let L_M be the set of labels explicit in the first node and L_N the set of labels explicit in the second node. For each label $a \in L_M \backslash L_N$, replace every node in T_N of the form

$$\Pi[a_1 : F_1, \ldots, a_n : F_n]\rho \quad \text{(where } \rho \text{ is the extension variable in the second node)}$$

by

$$\Pi[a_1 : F_1, \ldots, a_n : F_n, a : f_{\rho \cdot a}]\rho$$

and each node of the form

$$\Pi[a_1 : F_1, \ldots, a_n : F_n]\ empty$$

by

$$\Pi[a_1 : F_1, \ldots, a_n : F_n, a : absent]\ empty$$

Pad T_M similarly. We can do such global padding by substituting a construction such as $[a : f_{\rho \cdot a}]\rho_1$ for ρ, where ρ_1 is a fresh extension variable. We can then unify as usual.

Note that the creation of new variables is bounded by the number of new nodes that would be created had we done all the padding at once, by simply choosing to make all the labels in the whole program explicit before unifying. Hence the algorithm still halts, even though new variables are being introduced.

ML code for the algorithm is shown in Appendix A.

This unification algorithm can be adapted for use in a typechecker in a straightforward way. If we use an implementation which returns a substitution, then the substitution can include the substitution for padding the extension variables. This substitution can then be used to update the type hypotheses in the usual way. If we use a congruence-closure style algorithm, then the free type variables in the type hypotheses will share nodes with the variables in the types to be unified, so this updating will be done automatically by the unification algorithm.

The last difficulty to be faced in adapting the usual type inference algorithms to these infinitary trees is the treatment of **let**. The usual treatment of **let** is to create a typescheme by quantifying over all type variables not appearing in the type hypotheses, and then to create new variables for each quantified variable in the typescheme of an identifier [Clément *et al.* 86]. In our system, this might involve quantifying over an infinite number of field variables. But this is not a problem, as one can abbreviate this by quantifying over the corresponding extension variables, and generating new extension variables as needed.

This completes the description of the type inference algorithm for infinite label sets.

5   Modelling Objects

While this typing system seems to handle ordinary record structures well, one needs additional levels of detail to handle more realistic object-oriented systems. Such systems typically provide some level of information-hiding by hiding the "instance variables" of an object from the outside world, manipulating them only through publicly-available procedures called "methods."

We model an object as a record of methods. These methods are usually procedures. They share access to the instance variables that are local to the object. The instance variables are hidden from the rest of the program by scoping. A class is modelled as a procedure which takes values for the instance variables and produces an object. Thus we define

class $(x_1, \ldots, x_n)$
  methods $a_1 = M_1 ; \ldots ; a_k = M_k$ **end**

to be syntactic sugar for the procedure

$\lambda(x_1, \ldots, x_n) . null$ **with**$[a_1 = M_1 ; \ldots ; a_k = M_k]$

which is the constructor function for this class. This constructs a record in which the method names $a_1, \ldots, a_k$ are associated with method bodies $M_1, \ldots, M_k$ respectively. Furthermore, the instance variables $x_1, \ldots, x_n$ are known to the method bodies, but are hidden from the user of this record.

In this model, we do not need an explicit **new** operator, but we will need one later for more sophisticated models; hence we define:

new $C(N_1, \ldots, N_n) \equiv (CN_1 \ldots N_n)$

In this model, class constructors are first-class citizens which may be named. For example, we could define:

let *nil* = **class** ()
    methods
     null? = *true*;
     car = *error*;
     cdr = *error*
    end
  cons = **class** (*a d*)
    methods
     null? = *false*;
     car = *a*;
     cdr = *d*
    end

When we expand this declaration, *nil* gets the principal typescheme

$$() \rightarrow \Pi[null?:pres(\text{bool}), car:pres(\alpha), cdr:pres(\beta)]$$

(where α and β are free type variables) and *cons* gets typescheme

$$\alpha \times \beta \rightarrow \Pi[null?:pres(\text{bool}), car:pres(\alpha), cdr:pres(\beta)]$$

Thus invocations of *nil* or of *cons* yield objects of the same type: a record consisting of *null?*, *car*, and *cdr* methods. The instance variables *a* and *d* are hidden except insofar as they are retrievable through the methods.

In this model, the type of an object is the type of the record of its methods. Thus the type of an object describes its behavior: it tells the names of the methods which are available for that object and the type of each method. If we define

let *map* = $\lambda f\, l$. **if** l. *null?*
     then new *nil*()
     else new *cons*(($f\, l$. *car*), (*map* $f\, l$. *cdr*))

then the principal type of *map* is

$$(\alpha \rightarrow \beta) \rightarrow \tau_\alpha \rightarrow \tau_\beta$$

where τ_a and τ_b satisfy the equations

$$\tau_a = \Pi([null?:pres(\text{bool}), car:pres(\alpha), cdr:pres(\tau_a)]\rho)$$

$$\tau_b = \Pi([null?:pres(\text{bool}), car:pres(\beta), cdr:pres(\tau_b)])$$

Thus we can deduce that *map* takes an object which behaves as a homogeneous list of α's and returns an object which behaves as a homogeneous list of β's (*cf* [Mishra & Reddy 85]).

Things get more complicated if we add **self**. To handle **self**, we modify our modelling protocol, so that a class is associated with a procedure which takes values for the instance variables and produces a procedure from objects to objects. This latter procedure takes as its input a value for **self** and produces the appropriate record of methods. Then **new** can construct an object with the correct binding for **self** by applying the fixed-point combinator to this procedure. With this protocol, we can define **class** and **new** as follows:

$$\textbf{class } (x_1, \ldots, x_n)$$
$$\quad \textbf{methods } a_1 = M_1 ; \ldots ; a_k = M_k \textbf{ end}$$
$$\equiv \lambda \, (x_1, \ldots, x_n) . \lambda \, \textbf{self} . [a_1 = M_1 ; \ldots ; a_k = M_k]$$
$$\quad \textbf{new } C(N_1, \ldots, N_n) \equiv Y(C \, N_1 \ldots N_n)$$

Here we have used the fixed-point combinator on the domain of functions of records to records. This is fine for semantics but is generally not supported in applicative-order languages like Scheme or ML, which compute fixpoints only over procedures; a real implementation would need to simulate this by somewhat cleverer code.

We can obtain type rules for these constructs by expanding them into the language of records and then symbolically working out the resulting type constraints. If we do this, we get the following derived type rules for **class** and **new**:

$$\frac{A, \vec{x} : \vec{\alpha}, \textbf{self} : \sigma \vdash M_j : \tau_j \quad j = 1, \ldots, k}{A \vdash \textbf{class } (\vec{x}) \textbf{ methods } \vec{a}_j = \vec{M}_j \textbf{ end} : \vec{\alpha} \to \sigma \to \Pi[\vec{a} : pres(\vec{\tau})]}$$

$$\frac{A \vdash C : (\alpha_1 \times \cdots \times \alpha_n) \to \sigma \to \sigma \quad A \vdash N_1 : \alpha_1 \ldots A \vdash N_n : \alpha_n}{A \vdash \textbf{new } C(N_1, \ldots, N_n) : \sigma}$$

Here we have used vector notation to indicate a sequence of variables, types, or expressions.

6   Modelling Inheritance

We can now add inheritance to the model in a relatively straightforward way. We introduce the syntax

$$\textbf{class } (x_1, \ldots, x_n)$$
$$\quad \textbf{inherits } P(Q_1, \ldots, Q_p)$$
$$\quad \textbf{methods } a_1 = M_1 ; \ldots ; a_k = M_k \textbf{ end}$$

which signifies a class which is to inherit from class P; the expressions $Q_1, \ldots, Q_p$ determine how to instantiate the instance variables of the parent class. (This protocol for initializing instance variables requires knowledge about the instance variables of the parent class; other protocols can be devised which avoid this drawback, such as that of [Reddy 88], which we discuss in Section 9).

As pointed out by Cook and others [Cook 88, Kamin 88, Reddy 88], we must be careful at this point to make sure that in any instance of this class, **self** in the methods of the parent class is bound to the *entire* object, not just the portion of the object corresponding to the parent class. Thus the parent class acts like a virtual class in Simula. This can be easily achieved through with our modelling protocol:

class $(x_1, \ldots, x_n)$
    inherits $P(Q_1, \ldots, Q_p)$
    methods $a_1 = M_1; \ldots; a_k = M_k$ **end**
$\equiv \lambda(x_1, \ldots, x_n). \lambda$ **self**.
    $(P(Q_1 \ldots Q_p)$ **self**$)$ **with** $[a_1 = M_1; \ldots; a_k = M_k]$

Thus, when the class receives the value for **self**, it creates the record of methods for P, setting the instance variables for P to the values of Q (these may refer to **self**), and setting the value of **self** seen by the methods of P to be the **self** of the entire record. It then extends this record by adding the methods in the daughter class.

The rule for **new** remains as before:

new $C(N_1, \ldots, N_n) \equiv Y(CN_1 \ldots N_n)$

so its typing rule is unchanged.

Expanding the definition of **class** yields the following typing rule:

$$\frac{\begin{array}{c} A, \vec{x} : \vec{\alpha} \vdash \vec{Q} : \vec{\beta} \\ A, \vec{x} : \vec{\alpha}, \textbf{self} : \sigma \vdash P : \vec{\beta} \to \sigma \to \Pi[\vec{l} : \vec{F}]\rho \\ A, \vec{x} : \vec{\alpha}, \textbf{self} : \sigma \vdash \vec{M} : \vec{\tau} \end{array}}{A \vdash \textbf{class } (\vec{x}) \textbf{ inherits } P(\vec{Q}) \textbf{ methods } \vec{a} = \vec{M} : \vec{\alpha} \to \sigma \to \Pi[\vec{a} : \overrightarrow{pres(\tau)}][\vec{l} : \vec{F}]\rho}$$

In the result type, we use updating notation in the metalanguage; the product type in the result is

$$\Pi(\lambda a . a = a_j \Rightarrow pres(\tau_j), a = l_i \Rightarrow F_i, f_{\rho.a})$$

Since we are working with a fixed set of explicit variables at any given time, this can still be expressed in the language of Section 4.

Let us consider an example which shows how this inheritance mechanism works and which also illustrates the kind of deductions which this type system can make.

let $A =$ **class** (a)
   methods $sum = \lambda().(a + \textbf{self}.b())$ **end**
in let $B =$ **class** (a, b)
               inherits $A(a)$
               methods $b = \lambda().b$ **end**
      $C =$ **class** (b)
               inherits $A(5 - b)$
               methods $b = \lambda().b$ **end**
      $D =$ **class** (b)
               inherits $A(5 - b)$
               methods $c = \lambda().b$ **end**
      $E =$ **class** (a, b)
               inherits $B(a, b)$
               methods $b = \lambda().5$ **end**

Here A is a class which cannot be instantiated, since it requires a **self** containing a b method. B and C are two classes which inherit from A in different ways: B inherits by passing its second argument to A as its a instance value, so a call to sum on an instance of B will return the sum of a and b. C, however, passes $5 - b$ to A, so a call to sum on an instance of C will always return 5. The class D cannot be instantiated, since it still does not provide a b method. However, some descendant of D may eventually provide such a method.

Let us see how some of this information is reflected in the types assigned to these classes: A gets type

$$\text{int} \to \Pi[b:pres(\text{int}), sum:f]\rho \to \Pi[b:absent, sum:pres(\text{int})]\rho$$

The result type for A has only a sum method defined, so the label b is mapped to *absent*. A's *self* argument, however, must contain an integer-valued b method, so it is not self-applicable. B gets type

$$\text{int} \times \beta \to \Pi[b:pres(\text{int}), sum:f] \to \Pi[b:pres(\beta), sum:pres(\text{int})]$$

inheriting its *sum* method from A. The type of B matches the type $(\alpha_1 \times \cdots \times \alpha_n) \to \sigma \to \sigma$ needed for **new**, so we can make instances of B. Note that we deduce the fact that the second argument to B is an integer only at the point that we make an instance, not at the point of class definition. This caution is necessary, as demonstrated by class E. Here the definition of the b method in B is overridden, so the second argument to B can be of any type whatsoever. The analyses of the other classes proceed similarly.

It is significant that in this system, classes as well as objects are first-class values. They can be passed to and returned from procedures. For example, one can write

$$\lambda p \cdot \lambda x \cdot \textbf{new } p(x + 1)$$

This is a procedure which, given a class p, returns another procedure which, when called, creates a new instance of p with instance variable one greater than its argument. The type of this program is

$$(\text{int} \to \sigma \to \sigma) \to \text{int} \to \sigma$$

Similarly, one can write procedures which produce new classes:

$$\lambda p \cdot \textbf{class } (x) \textbf{ inherits } p(x + 1)$$

This procedure is similar to the preceding one, except that instead of creating an instance of p, it creates a new class. This new class may then be inherited into other classes. The type of this procedure is

$$(\text{int} \to \sigma \to \Pi\rho) \to (\text{int} \to \sigma \to \Pi\rho)$$

However, passing classes as parameters has the usual problem with quantification in ML-style type systems: any polymorphism in the type of the argument is lost. Thus, it is impossible to write a procedure which takes a class as an argument, and then uses that class as the parent of two different classes. There has been some progress on type inference for polymorphic parameters [Kfoury *et al.* 88], but this remains a difficult open problem.

Multiple inheritance is modellable using records, as well. For example, we could interpret

$\textbf{class } (x_1, \ldots, x_n)$
    $\textbf{inherits } P(Q_1, \ldots, Q_p), P'(Q'_1, \ldots, Q'_q)$
    $\textbf{methods } a_1 = M_1 ; \ldots ; a_k = M_k \textbf{ end}$

as

$$\lambda(x_1, \ldots, x_n) \cdot \lambda \textbf{ self} \cdot (P(Q_1 \ldots Q_p) \textbf{ self}) \| (P'(Q'_1 \ldots Q'_p) \textbf{ self}) \textbf{ with } [a_1 = M_1 ; \ldots ; a_k = M_k]$$

where $\|$ indicates concatenation of records. Unfortunately, concatenation of records (under any reasonably polymorphic treatment of duplicate fields) does not have a principal type in our system. Consider the following example:

$\lambda xy.(x \| y).a + 1$

If we interpret concatenation as overwriting fields to the right, then this should be applicable to any pair of records x and y in which y has an integer a field *or* in which x has an integer a field and y has an absent a field. This may be expressed as having types of the form

$$\Pi\rho \to \Pi[a:pres(\text{int})]\rho' \to \text{int}$$

and

$$\Pi[a:pres(\text{int})]\rho \to \Pi[a:absent]\rho' \to \text{int}$$

This term does not have a principal type in any known system, including [Cardelli 88, Rémy 89]. It is possible, however, to extend the system we have described to generate a finite set of principal types for terms involving concatenation [Wand 89].

7   Opaque Class Systems

Our model of classes is transparent, in that the types are the same as those of the underlying de-sugared terms. It is possible to "forge" an object, since we know its representation. It may be desirable in some languages or implementations to prevent this by keeping the representation of objects hidden, and thus distinct from the representation of records. Such a distinction would be crucial to a system implemented using generic functions, for example.

A simple solution is to make objects unforgeable by using a different type constructor for records and for objects, say by adding a new type constructor

$Record:Field^L \Rightarrow Type$

with separate constructors and selectors. Thus values of object type (that is, of Π type) could be constructed only using **class** and **new**.

It would also be possible to introduce a new constructor

$Class:Type \times Type \times Type \to Type$

so that the type of a **class** expression would be *Class*(type of parameters, type of self, type of object). However, it is not clear what additional purpose this might serve.

8   Intensional and Extensional Types

There has been considerable confusion in the literature over the distinction between *type* and *class*. In this section, we will briefly discuss how our system addresses this issue.

Our view of *type* is structural or extensional. That is, the type of an object is a signature containing the types of its methods. A program which is type-correct in our system will never generate a "method not found" error, because selection on a label is not allowed unless that label is provably present in the record. One object is substitutable for another so long as it has the same type: such a substitution may change the behavior of the program, but it will never cause a "method not found" error.

Other systems use a name-based or intensional view of type. In such systems, each class constitutes a type, and one object is not substitutable for another unless it is of the same class. Such systems must then wrestle with the problem of making this view live compatibly with inheritance.

Why should such a restriction be seen as desirable? An attractive explanation comes from the literature on abstract data types [*e.g.* Hoare 72]. There a class is seen as some data (the representation) along with the set of permissible operations on that data. The reason that the set of operations is crucial is that there may be some invariant (the "concrete invariant") that must be maintained on the representation. For example, in a abstract data type for a histogram, one of the instance variables might always contain the total number of data points in the histogram. This requires an invariant to hold between this instance variable and the instance variable holding the histogram array.

Similarly, one might expect invariant relations to hold between different methods in an object. For example, in our previous example, B and C generate objects of the same type, but if c is an instance of C, then we expect $c \cdot s = 5$ to hold, whereas this is not true of instances of B. If the code which uses these classes depends on such additional properties, then substituting an instance of B for an instance of C will cause the program to become incorrect.

We may hypothesize, then, that the intensional type of a class consists of the extensional or structural type that we have computed plus the invariants that are intended to hold among the instance variables and methods. One can easily sketch the semantics of such a view in a semantics of types that allows arbitrary predicates, such as the PER model [*e.g.*, Mitchell 86], but static analysis of intensional types would require full-blown theorem-proving rather than simple unification. Name equivalence may be regarded as a fail-safe approximation to typing using explicit invariants ("x is an instance of C" always implies "x satisfies C's invariants").

9   Related Work

[Cardelli 88] introduced record models of objects, including subtyping. His system did not deal with records of indefinite width, as in

$\lambda x . x$ **with** $a := (x . a + 1)$

nor did his system attempt to do type inference. [Wand 87] attempted to do type inference for records including record overwriting of this kind; unfortunately the unification algorithm in this paper was incorrect.

[Rémy 89] introduced the notion of fields, which gave an obviously correct treatment of records using the usual notion of unification, thus avoiding the complications of unification in non-free algebras. Rémy treated only finite label sets; one of the contributions of this paper is to extend this work to infinite label sets.[1]

The system we have used focusses on polymorphism in the procedures; Rémy also introduced another system in which the records themselves are polymorphic. This system uses the following signature:

$\rightarrow : Type \times Type \Rightarrow Type$

$\Pi : (Tag \times Type)^L \Rightarrow Type$

$absent : Tag$

$pres : Tag$

In this system, the principal type schemes of the basic operations are given by:

$null : \Pi(absent, t_1, \ldots, absent, t_n)$

$(-) . a : \Pi(f_1, t_1, \ldots, pres, t, \ldots, f_n, f_n) \rightarrow t$

$(-)$ **with** $a = (-) : \Pi(f_1, \ldots, f_n) \rightarrow t \rightarrow \Pi(f_1, \ldots, f', t, \ldots, f_n)$

In this system, a record is regarded as a polymorphic object, in which any field containing a value may be instantiated as either present (for use by selection) or as absent (forgotten). The set of terms typable under this system is incomparable with those typable under the original system. This system seems preferable for some applications, but giving it a plausible semantics remains an open problem.

[Jategaonkar & Mitchell 88] gave a type system for extendible records in ML, including ML patterns and subtyping on ground (*i.e.* name-equivalent) types. [Stansifer 88] also contributed a treatment of type inference for records.

[Reddy 88] gives a semantics for objects as closures which is very close in spirit to ours. He gives a traditional denotational semantics, whereas we give a concrete semantics [Wand 85]: a translation into an underlying lambda-calculus. This gives a direct demonstration that objects really are closures. Furthermore, again following [Wand 85], we obtain finer type information by looking at the type of the resulting terms than is possible by looking just at the denotational semantics: we derive typing rules for the source language by saying that if a source language phrase is well-typed, then its translation must be. By contrast, in a traditional denotational semantics, the translation of a source language phrase is always well-typed.

Reddy's system differs in details from ours. Most interestingly, he avoids problems with initializing instance variables by always initializing them to be new (uninitialized) L-values. The corresponding translation in our system would be something like

class $(x_1, \ldots, x_n)$
    inherits P
    methods $a_1 = M_1; \ldots; a_k = M_k$ **end**
$\equiv \lambda$ **self** . **letvars** $(x_1, \ldots, x_n)$ **in**
    $(P \text{ self})$ **with** $[a_1 = M_1; \ldots; a_k = M_k]$

where **letvars** is a construct which creates and binds n new uninitialized locations. Here each class knows enough to initialize the right number of instance variables. One can do type inference for this translation as well, but one must be suitably careful about polymorphic references [*e.g.* Tofte 87]. Again, one also needs to be careful about the correct implementation of the fixed point operator.

10 Conclusions

We have presented a polymorphic type discipline for a language with objects, including hidden instance variables, methods, single inheritance, and classes as first-class values. This type discipline has decidable principal typing, obtained by interpreting classes and objects in a typed language of records. The type system for records is obtained by extending the system of Rémy by giving an algorithm for infinite label sets.

Acknowledgments

Atsushi Ohori, Luca Cardelli, Pavel Curtis, Mads Tofte, and Chris Haynes all contributed careful readings of [Wand 87]. Conversations with Ryan Stansifer, Patrick

O'Keefe, Dan Friedman, John Mitchell, Lalita Jategaonkar, and Peter Wegner at various times also helped clarify the issues.

Notes

This Material is based on work supported by the National Science Foundation under grants DCR 8605218 and CCR 8811591.

1. An early version of [Rémy 89] remarked that infinite label sets could be treated by "lazily expanding" ellipses, but did not give an algorithm or proof.

References

[Cardelli 88]   Cardelli, L. "A Semantics of Multiple Inheritance," *Information and Computation 76* (1988), 138–164.

[Clément *et al.* 86]   Clément, D., Despeyroux, J., Despeyroux, T., and Kahn, G. "A Simple Applicative Language: Mini-ML" *Proc. 1986 ACM Symp. on Lisp and Functional Programming*, 13–27.

[Cook 88]   Cook, W., "A self-ish model of inheritance," Ph.D. dissertation, Brown University, 1988.

[Hoare 72]   Hoare, C. A. R., "Proving Correctness of Data Representations," *Acta Informatica 1* (1972), 271–281.

[Jategaonkar & Mitchell 88]   Jategaonkar, L. A., and Mitchell, J. C. "ML with Extended Pattern Matching and Subtypes," *Proc. 1988 ACM Conf. on Lisp and Functional Programming*, 198–211.

[Kamin 88]   Kamin, S. "Inheritance in Smalltalk-80: A Denotational Definition," *Conf. Rec. 15th Ann. ACM Symp. on Principles of Programing Languages* (1988), 80–87.

[Kfoury *et al.* 88]   Kfoury, A. J., Tiuryn, J., and Urzycyzn, P. "A Proper Extension of ML with an Effective Type-Assignment" *Conf. Rec. 15th Ann. ACM Symp. on Principles of Programming Languages* (1988), 58–69.

[Mishra & Reddy 85]   Mishra, P., and Reddy, U. S. "Declaration-Free Type Checking" *Conf. Rec. 12th Ann. ACM Symp. on Principles of Programming Languages* (1985), 7–21.

[Mitchell 84]   Mitchell, J. C. "Coercion and Type Inference (summary)," *Conf. Rec. 11th Ann. ACM Symp. on Principles of Programming Languages* (1984), 175–185.

[Mitchell 86]   Mitchell, J. C. "A Type-Inference Approach to Reduction Properties and Semantics of Polymorphic Expressions" *Proc. 1986 ACM Conf. on Lisp and Functional Programming*, 308–319.

[O'Toole & Gifford 89]   O'Toole, J. W., and Gifford, D. K. "Type Reconstruction with First-Class Polymorphic Values," *Proc. SIGPLAN '89 Conf. on Programming Language Design and Implementation*, *SIGPLAN Notices 24*, 7 (July, 1989), 218–226.

[Reddy 88]   Reddy, U. S. "Objects as Closures: Abstract Semantics of Object Oriented Languages" *Proc. ACM Conf. on Lisp and Functional Programming*, (1988) 289–297.

[Rémy 89]   Rémy, D. "Typechecking records and variants in a natural extension of ML," *Conf. Rec. 16th Ann. ACM Symp. on Principles of Programming Languages* (1989), 77–88.

[Stansifer 88]   Stansifer, R. "Type Inference with Subtypes," *Conf. Rec. 15th Ann. ACM Symp. on Principles of Programming Languages* (1988), 88–97.

[Tofte 87]   Tofte, M. "Operational Semantics and Polymorphic Type Inference," Ph.D. dissertation, University of Edinburgh, 1987.

[Wand 85]   Wand, M. "Embedding Type Structure in Semantics" *Conf. Rec. 12th ACM Symp. on Principles of Prog. Lang.* (1985), 1–6.

[Wand 87]   Wand, M. "Complete Type Inference for Simple Objects" *Proc. 2nd IEEE Symposium on Logic in Computer Science* (1987), 37–44.

[Wand 89]   Wand, M. "Type Inference for Record Concatenation and Multiple Inheritance," *Information & Computation* 93 (1991), 1–15. Preliminary version appeared in *Proc. 4th IEEE Symposium on Logic in Computer Science* (1989), 92–97.

[Wand & O'Keefe 89]   Wand, M., and O'Keefe, P. "On the Complexity of Type Inference with Coercion," *Conf. on Functional Programming Languages and Computer Architecture* (London, September, 1989).

Appendix A   ML Code for the Unification Algorithm

The code shown here implements the unification algorithm with recursive types and with on-demand expansion of extension variables.

```
(* Trees include Types, Fields, and Extensions. Kinding restrictions
are not modelled. *)

datatype Tree = var of string * int |
                const of string |
                absent |
                present of Tree |
                arrow of Tree * Tree |
                record of Tree |
                extension of (string * Tree) list * Tree |
                empty ;

fun tvar s = var(s,0);

fun mapappend [] = "" |
    mapappend (x :: y) = (x ^ (mapappend y));

(* Nodes: last component is link to representative for union/find *)

datatype Node = nullnode |
                varnode of string * int * Node ref |
                constnode of string |
                absentnode of Node ref |
                presentnode of Node * Node ref |
                arrownode of Node * Node * Node ref |
                recordnode of Node * Node ref |
                extensionnode of (string * Node) list * Node |
                        (* extension nodes are never
                        equivalenced *)
                emptynode of Node ref;
```

```
exception Link_of_Null of unit;
fun link (nullnode) = raise Link_of_Null {} |
    link (constnode(s)) = ref nullnode |
    link (varnode(s,i,l)) = l |
    link (absentnode(l)) = l |
    link (presentnode(s, l)) = l |
    link (arrownode(n1, n2, x)) = x |
    link (recordnode(_, l)) = l |
    link (extensionnode(_, _)) = ref nullnode |
    link (emptynode(l)) = l;
val gen_num = let
        val count = ref 0
        in fn x => (count := !count + 1 ; !count) end;
fun find n = if !(link n) = nullnode then n else find (!(link n));
fun equiv n n1 =
    let val r = (find n)
        and r1 = (find n1)
    in (link r) := r1 end;
(* simple tables *)
val empty_table = [];
fun add_to_table table sym v = (sym, v) :: table ;
fun lookup x ((y, v)::table) succ fail = if x = y then (succ v) else
                                         lookup x table succ
                                         fail |
    lookup x [] succ fail = fail() ;
(* translate type expression to DAG *)
fun translate (v as var(s,i)) A =
            lookup v A (fn x => (x, A))
                      (fn () => let val n = varnode (s, i, ref
                                                        nullnode)
                            in (n, add_to_table A v n) end ) |
    translate (const(s)) A = (constnode(s), A) |
    translate (absent) A = (absentnode (ref nullnode), A) |
    translate (present(t)) A =
        let val (n, A) = translate t A
        in (presentnode(n, ref nullnode), A) end |
```

```
    translate (arrow(t1, t2)) A =
       let val (n1, A1) = translate t1 A ;
           val (n2, A2) = translate t2 A1
       in (arrownode(n1, n2, ref nullnode), A2) end |
    translate (record(t)) A =
       let val (n, A) = translate t A
       in (recordnode(n, ref nullnode), A) end |
    translate (extendion(1, t)) A =
       let fun loop [] A = ([], A) |
               loop ((s,t)::1) A =
                  let val (n, A1) = translate t A;
                      val (1, A2) = loop 1 A1
                  in ((s,n)::1, A2) end;
           val (n1, A1) = translate t A ;
           val (1, A2) = loop 1 A1
       in (extensionnode(1, n1), A2) end |
    translate (empty) A = (emptynode(ref nullnode), A) ;
(* and back again *)
fun member x (y :: 1) = if x = y then true else member x 1 |
    member x [] = false ;
val untranslate =
    let
        fun loop n seen = (* assumes n is a representative *)
                if member n seen then var("...",0)
                  else case n of
                        varnode(s,i,r) => var(s,i) |
                        constnode(s) => const(s) |
                        absentnode(1) => absent |
                        presentnode(n1,1) => present(loop (find n1)
                                                        (n::seen)) |
                        arrownode(n1, n2, r)=>
                          arrow(loop (find n1) (n::seen),
                                loop (find n2) (n::seen)) |
                        recordnode(t,1) => record(loop (find t)
                                                        (n::seen)) |
                        extensionnode(1,n2) =>
                          extension(map (fn (s,n1)=>(s, loop
                                                        (find n1)
                                                        (n::seen)))
```

```
                                    1,
                          loop (find n2) (n::seen)) |
                    emptynode(_) => empty |
                    nullnode => raise Link_of_Null()
          in (fn n => (loop n [])) end;
fun printn (n: Node) = print ((tree_to_string (untranslate n))^"\n");
fun printsl (sl : string list) = (print "["; (map (fn s => (print s;
    print ", ")) sl); print "]\n"; {});
(* Now we get to the interesting stuff *)
exception Kinding_Failed of Node;
(* get list of explicit labels in a row. Assumes its argument is a
representative *)
fun explicits (extensionnode(pairs, ext)) =
        (map #1 pairs) @ (explicits (find ext)) |
    explicits (varnode(_,_,_)) = [] |
    explicits (n) = raise Kinding_Failed n ;
fun setdiff [] l2 = [] |
    setdiff (x::l1) l2 = if member x l2 then setdiff l1 l2
                                        else x::(setdiff l1 l2);
(* pad t newlabels newext -- pads row t by finding its extension
variable and then unifying it with an extension mapping newlabels to
either fresh variables or to absent. Assumes its argument is a
        representative. Note that extension nodes are never
        equivalenced!
*)
fun pad t newlabels newext =
    let fun loop (extensionnode(_,t)) = loop (find t) |
            loop (n as varnode (_,_,_)) =
                (equiv n (extensionnode
                        (map (fn s => (s, varnode("f", gen_num(),
                                                  ref nullnode)))
                            newlabels,
                         newext))) |
            loop (n as emptynode(_)) =
                (equiv n (extensionnode
                        (map (fn s => (s, varnode("f", gen_num(),
                                                  ref nullnode)))
```

```
                          newlabels,
                     newext));
                   equiv newext (emptynode (ref nullnode))) |
          loop n = (printn n; raise Kinding_Failed n)
     in loop (find t) end;
fun find_field s (extensionnode(pairs, ext)) =
     lookup s pairs (fn f => f) (fn () => find_field s
                                              (find ext)) |
     find_field s (_) = raise Kinding_Failed (nullnode);
```

(* subgoals: takes two rows, assumed to have same explicits, and
generates list of subgoals to be unified *)

(* also assumes that there are no duplicates in the explicits. This
invariant is maintained by this portion of the code. *)

```
fun subgoals r1 r2 =
     let val r1 = find r1 and r2 = find r2;
         val e1 = explicits r1
         in map (fn s => (find_field s r1, find_field s r2)) e1 end;
exception Unify_Failed of Node * Node;

fun unify n1 n2 =
 let val n1 = find n1 and n2 = find n2 in
     if n1 = n2 then {}
     else case (n1, n2) of
         (varnode(_,_,_), n2) => equiv n1 n2 |
         (constnode(s), constnode(t)) => if s = t then {} else raise
                                         Unify_Failed
                                            (n1, n2) |
         (n1, varnode(_,_,_)) => equiv n2 n1 |
         (absentnode(_), absentnode(_)) => equiv n1 n2 |
         (presentnode(t1,_),presentnode(t2,_)) =>
            (equiv n1 n2; unify t1 t2) |
         (arrownode(t1, t2, r), arrownode(u1, u2, s)) =>
            (equiv n1 n2; unify t1 u1; unify t2 u2) |
         (recordnode(t1,_),recordnode(t2,_)) =>
            (equiv n1 n2; unify_row t1 t2) |
         (extensionnode(_,_), _) => (printn n1; raise Kinding_Failed
                                         n1) |
```

```
         (_, extensionnode(_,_)) => (printn n2; raise Kinding_Failed
                                                           n2 )|
         n => raise Unify_Failed (n1, n2)
     end
and unify_row t1 t2 =
     let val exp1 = explicits t1 and exp2 = explicits t2;
         val a = setdiff exp1 exp2 and b = setdiff exp2 exp1
         val r = varnode("r",gen_num(), ref nullnode);
     in (pad t1 b r; pad t2 a r;
         map (fn (n1,n2) => unify n1 n2) (subgoals t1 t2);
         {}) end;
fun unify1 n1 n2 = unify n1 n2
          handle Unify_Failed (n1, n2) => (print ''Unify
                                                     Failed:\n";
                                      printn n1; printn n2;
                                      ()) |
                  Kinding_Failed (n) => (print "Kinding Failed:\n";
                                      printn n; ()) ;
fun testit () =
       let val (n1, A) =
               translate (arrow(tvar "x", arrow(tvar "y", tvar
               "y"))) [];
           val (n2, A) = translate (arrow(tvar "x", tvar "x")) A
       in (unify n1 n2;
           print (tree_to_string (untranslate n1));
           print "\n"; true) end;
fun test2 () =
    let val (n1, A) = translate (arrow(tvar "x", tvar "y")) [];
        val (n2, A)  translate (tvar "x") A
    in (unify n1 n2;
        print (tree_to_string (untranslate n1));
        print "\n"; true) end;
fun make2 () = let
    val (n1, A) = translate
                      (record
                       (extension([("a",present(const "bool"))],
                                 tvar "r1"))) [];
```

```
    val (n2, A) = translate
                      (record
                       (extension([("b",present(const "int"))],
                                  tvar "r2"))) A
      in (n1, n2) end;
fun test3 () = let val (n1, n2) = make2 () in
 (unify1 n1 n2;
      print (tree_to_string (untranslate n1)) ;
      print "\n"; true) end;
```

5 Static Type Inference for Parametric Classes

Atsushi Ohori and Peter Buneman

Abstract

Method inheritance and data abstraction are central features of object-oriented programming that are attained through a hierarchical organization of classes. Recent studies have shown that method inheritance can be supported by an ML style type inference when extended to labeled records. This is based on the observation that a function that selects a field f of a record can be given a polymorphic type that enables it to be applied to any record which contains a field f. Several type systems also provide data abstraction through abstract type declarations. However, these two features have not yet been properly integrated in a statically checked polymorphic type system.

This paper proposes a static type system that achieves this integration in an ML-like polymorphic language by adding a class construct which allows the programmer to build a hierarchy of classes connected by multiple inheritance declarations. Classes can be parameterized by types allowing "generic" definitions. The type correctness of class declarations is statically checked, and a principal scheme is inferred for any type correct program containing methods and objects defined in classes. Moreover, the type system can be extended to include the structures and operations needed for database programming and therefore can serve as a basis of an object-oriented database programming language.

1 Introduction

Code sharing is a term that implies the ability to write one piece of code that can be applied to different kinds of data. What this means in practice depends on what we mean by "kinds of data". In object-oriented languages [GR83] each data element (object) belongs to a unique member of a class hierarchy. The code that is applicable to that object is not only the code that is defined in its own class but also the one defined in its super-classes. As an example, we can define a class *person* with a method *increment_age* that increments a person's age by 1. We may define a subclass, *employee*, of *person* and expect that the same method, *increment_age*, can be applied to instances of the class *employee*.

In contrast, languages such as Ada [IBH+79], CLU [LAB+81], Standard ML [HMT90] and Miranda [Tur85]—to name a few—provide a generic or polymorphic type system that allows code to be refined by instantiating type variables. Moreover,

First appeared in *Proceedings of ACM OOPSLA Conference*, SIGPLAN Notices, Vol 24, Number 10, October 1989, pages 445–456. © The Association for Computing Machinery, Inc., 11 West 42nd Street, New York, New York 10036.

in the type system of ML, a most general polymorphic type-scheme may be inferred for an (untyped) function and the correctness of the application of that function is checked by finding a suitable instantiation of the type variables. For example, in ML, one may define a polymorphic function *reverse* that reverses a list. From a definition of *reverse* that contains no mention of types, the ML type system is able to infer that $list(t) \rightarrow list(t)$ is a most general polymorphic type-scheme of *reverse* where t is a type variable. One may subsequently apply this function to a list of arbitrary type, i.e. a value of any type of the form $list(\tau)$. Through this polymorphic type inference mechanism, ML achieves much of the flexibility of programming without the need to express type information, as in dynamically typed languages, while maintaining most of the advantages—for program correctness and efficiency—of a static type system. A drawback to ML is that it does not combine data abstraction with inheritance in the same sense that object-oriented languages do this. While ML provides data abstraction through abstract data type declarations, it does not allow these to be organized into a class hierarchy.

The purpose of this paper is to develop a static type system that supports both forms of code sharing by combining ML polymorphism and explicit class definitions. In our type system a programmer can define a hierarchy of classes. A class can be parametric and can contain multiple inheritance declarations. The type correctness of such a class definition (including the type consistency of all inherited methods) is statically checked by the type system. Moreover, apart from the type assertions needed in the definition of a class, the type system has a static type inference similar to that available in ML.

We develop such a type system by exploiting a form of type inference for labeled records and labeled disjoint unions originally suggested by Wand [Wan87]. Labeled records and labeled disjoint unions are the structures that one naturally uses to implement a class hierarchy. For example, to implement a subclass in object-oriented languages one usually adds instance variables to those of the parent class; but one can equally well think of this as adding fields to a record type that implements the parent class. We combine a type inference system for these structures with explicit type declarations that represent classes. The main technical contribution is to demonstrate that such a combination is possible. We show that the resulting type system is sound with respect to the underlying type system and that it has a type inference algorithm. These results can be used to develop a programming language that integrates central features of object-oriented programming and those of statically typed polymorphic languages. Moreover, it is also possible to extend the type system to incorporate a number of structures and operations for database programming. The extended type system can serve as a basis for database programming languages, where databases are represented as typed data structures and queries and other database operations are cleanly represented as statically typed polymorphic functions. Parametric classes and polymorphism capture various aspects of object-oriented databases. Based on these results a prototype programming language embodying the type system described in this paper (with the exception of class parameterization) has been implemented at University of Pennsylvania. The "core" of the language, i.e. the language without class construct, was described in [OBBT89]. A more detailed description of the language can be found in [BO90].

Wand [Wan87] observed that method inheritance can be supported in an ML-like strongly typed language by extending ML's type inference mechanism to labeled records and labeled disjoint unions. In this paradigm, classes correspond to record types and inheritance is realized by polymorphic typing of functions on records. For example, if we represent the classes *person* and *employee* by the record types [*Name*:*string*, *Age*:*int*] and [*Name*:*string*, *Age*:*int*, *Salary*:*int*] then the requirement that the method *increment_age* defined on the class *person* should be inherited by *employee* simply means that the type of the function *increment_age* should be a polymorphic type whose instances include not only the type [*Name*:*string*, *Age*:*int*] → [*Nam*:*string*, *Age*:*int*] but also the type [*Name*:*string*, *Age*:*int*, *Salary*:*int*] → [*Name*:*string*, *Age*:*int*, *Salary*:*int*].

Wand's system, however, does not share ML's feature of existence of *principal* typing schemes (see [OB88, Wan88] for an analysis of this issue.) Based on Wand's general observation, [OB88] extended the notion of principal type-schemes to include conditions on type variables. (See also [Sta88, JM88, Rem89, Wan89] for related studies.) This extension allows ML polymorphism to be extended to standard operations on records and variants and also to various database operations such as *join* and *projection*. (See also [Wan89, CM89, HP91, Rem92] for proposals for other operations on records.) For example, the function *increment_age* can be implemented by the following code:

fun *increment_age*(*p*) = **modify**(*p*, *Age*, *p* . *Age* + 1)

where *e.l* selects the *l* field from the record *e*, and **modify**(*p*, *l*, *e*) returns the new record that is same as *p* except that its *l* field is changed to *e*. For this function, the following principal *conditional type-scheme* is inferred:

[(*t*)*Age*:*int*] → [(*t*)*Age*:*int*]

The notation [(*t*)*l*$_1$:τ_1,...,*l*$_n$:τ_n] represents a *conditional type variable* *t*, for which substitutions are restricted to those θ such that $\theta(t)$ is a record type containing the fields *l*$_i$:$\theta(\tau_i)$, $1 \leq i \leq n$. Since both [*Name*:*string*, *Age*:*int*] and [*Name*:*string*, *Age*:

int, Salary: *int*] satisfy the condition, [*Name*: *string*, *Age*: *int*] → [*Name*: *string*, *Age*: *int*] and [*Name*: *string*, *Age*: *int*, *Salary*: *int*] → [*Name*: *string*, *Age*: *int*, *Salary*: *int*] are both instances of the above conditional type-scheme. By this mechanism the function *increment_age* can be safely applied not only to *person* objects but also to *employee* objects.

The type inference method suggested by this example shows an integration of method inheritance and a static type system with ML polymorphism. This approach is not subject to the phenomenon of "loss of type information" associated with type systems based on the subsumption rule [Car88]—the problem observed by Cardelli and Wegner [CW85] (see [BTBO89] for a discussion on this problem). However this approach relies on the structure of record types of objects: inheritance is derived from the polymorphic nature of field selection. We would like to borrow from object-oriented languages the idea that the programmer can control the sharing of methods through an explicitly defined hierarchy of classes and that objects are manipulated only through methods defined in these classes, achieving *data abstraction*.

Galileo [ACO85] integrates inheritance and class hierarchies in a static type system by combining the subtype relation in [Car88] and abstract type declarations. Galileo, however, does not integrate polymorphism or type inference. [JM88] suggests the possibility of using their type inference method to extend ML's abstract data types to support inheritance. Here we provide a formal proposal that achieves the integration of ML style parametric abstract data types and multiple inheritance by extending the type inference method presented in [OB88]. The class declarations we describe can be regarded as a generalization of ML's abstract data types, but there seems to be no immediate connection with the notion of abstract types as existential types in [MP85].

As an example, the class *person* can be implemented by the following class definition:

class *person* = [*Name*: *string*, *Age*: *int*] **with**
   fun *make_person*(*n*, *a*) = [*Name* = *n*, *Age* = *a*]
     : (*string* ∗ *int*) → *persion*;
   fun *name*(*p*) = *p* . *Name* : **sub** → *string*;
   fun *age*(*p*) = *p* . *Age* : **sub** → *int*;
   fun *increment_age*(*p*) = **modify**(*p*, *Age*, *p* . *Age* + 1)
     : **sub** → **sub**;
end

Outside of this definition, the actual structure of objects of the type *person* is hidden and *person* objects can only be manipulated through the explicitly defined set of interface functions (methods). This is enforced by treating classes as if they were base types and the methods as the primitive operations associated with them.

As in Miranda's abstract data types, we require the programmer to specify the type (type-scheme) of each method. The keyword **sub** in the type specifications of methods is a special type variable representing all possible subclasses of the class being defined. It is to be regarded as an assertion by the programmer (which may later prove to be inconsistent with a subclass definition) that a method can be applied to values of any subclass. For example, we may define a subclass

class *employee* = [*Name* : *string*, *Age* : *int*, *Sal* : *int*]
isa *person* **with**
   fun *make_employee*(*n*, *a*) =
       [*Name* = *n*, *Age* = *a*, *Sal* = 0]
     : (*string* ∗ *int*) → *employee*;
   fun *add_salary*(*e*, *s*) = **modify**(*e*, *Sal*, *e* . *Sal* + *s*)
     : (**sub** ∗ *int*) → **sub**;
   fun *salary*(*e*) = *e* . *Sal* : **sub** → *int*
end

which inherits the methods *name*, *age* and *increment_age*, but not *make_person* from the class *person* because there is no **sub** in the type specification of *make_person*. For reasons that will emerge later we have given the complete record type required to implement *employee*, not just the additional fields we need to add to the implementation of *person*. It is possible that for simple record extensions such as these we could invent a syntactic shorthand that is more in line with object-oriented languages. Continuing in the same fashion, we may define classes

class *student* =
  [*Name* : *string*, *Age* : *int*, *Grade* : *real*]
isa *person* **with**
  ⋮
end
class *researchFellow* =
  [*Name* : *string*, *Age* : *int*, *Grade* : *real*, *Sal* : *int*]
isa {*employee*, *student*} **with**
  ⋮
end

The second of these illustrates the use of multiple inheritance.

The type system we are proposing can statically check the type correctness of these class definitions containing multiple inheritance declarations. Moreover, the type system always infers a principal conditional type-scheme for expressions containing methods defined in classes. For example, for the following function

fun $raise\_salary(p) = add\_salary(p, \textbf{div}(salary(p), 10))$

which raises the salary of an object by approximately 10%, the type system infers the following principal conditional type-scheme:

$(t < employee) \rightarrow (t < employee)$

where $(t < employee)$ is a conditional type variable whose instances are restricted to subclasses of *employee*. This function can be applied to objects of any subclass of *employee* and the type correctness of such applications is statically checked.

To demonstrate the use of type parameters, consider how a class for lists might be constructed. We start from a class which defines a "skeletal" structure for lists.

class $pre\_list = (\textbf{rec}\ t\ .\ \langle Empty : unit, List : [Tail : t] \rangle)$
with
   $nil = \langle Empty = (\ ) \rangle : \textbf{sub};$
   fun $tl(x) = \textbf{case}\ x\ \textbf{of}$
                   $\langle Empty = y \rangle \Rightarrow \ldots error \ldots;$
                   $\langle List = z \rangle \Rightarrow z\ .\ Tail;$
          end : $\textbf{sub} \rightarrow \textbf{sub}$
   fun $null(x) = \textbf{case}\ x\ \textbf{of}$
                     $\langle Empty = y \rangle \Rightarrow true;$
                     $\langle List = z \rangle \Rightarrow false;$
          end : $\textbf{sub} \rightarrow bool;$
end

This example shows the use of recursive types ($\textbf{rec}\ t.\tau$) and labeled variant types ($\langle l_1 : \tau_1, \ldots l_n : \tau_n \rangle$) with the associated **case** expressions. By itself, the class *pre_list* is useless for it provides no method for constructing non-empty lists. We may nevertheless derive a useful subclass from it.

class $list(a) =$
  $(\textbf{rec}\ t\ .\ \langle Empty : unit, List : [Head : a, Tail : t] \rangle)$
isa pre_list
with
  fun $cons(h, t) = \langle List = [Head = h, Tail = t] \rangle$
    $: (a * \textbf{sub}) \rightarrow \textbf{sub};$

fun $hd(x) = $ **case** x **of**

$\qquad\qquad \langle Empty = y \rangle \Rightarrow \dots error \dots;$

$\qquad\qquad \langle List = z \rangle \Rightarrow z . Head;$

$\qquad$ **end** : **sub** $\rightarrow a;$

end

which provides the usual polymorphic operations on lists. Separating the definition into two parts may seem pointless here but we may be able to define other useful subclasses of *pre_list*. Moreover, since *a* may itself be a record type, we may be able to define further useful subclasses of *list*. This is something we shall demonstrate in Section 6. The type correctness of these parametric class declarations is also statically checked by the type system and type inference also extends to methods of parametric classes.

In the following sections we define a simple core language and describe type inference for this language. We then extend the core language with class declarations and show that the extended type system is correct with respect to the underlying type system and provide the necessary results to show that there is a type inference algorithm. To simplify the presentation, we omit sets and database operations treated in [OB88]. However, the theory of parametric classes is completely compatible with these structures. We briefly describe the method to extend the type system presented here to sets and database operations in Section 7. We also omit proofs of some of the results. Their detailed proofs as well as the full treatment of sets and database operations can be found in [Oho89b]. In Section 8 we consider the limitations and implementation aspects of our type system. The combination of multiple inheritance with type parameters requires certain restrictions, and some care is needed to make sure of the existence and correctness of the type inference method. Even if some other formulation of classes in a statically typed polymorphic language is preferable to the system proposed here, we believe that similar issues will arise.

2   The Core Language

The set of types (ranged over by τ) of the core language, i.e. the language without class definitions, is given by the following abstract syntax:

$$\tau ::= b | [l : \tau, \dots, l : \tau] | \langle l : \tau, \dots, l : \tau \rangle | \tau \rightarrow \tau | (\textbf{rec } v . \tau(v))$$

where b stands for base types and $(\textbf{rec } v . \tau(v))$ represents recursive types. $\tau(v)$ in $(\textbf{rec } v . \tau(v))$ is a type expression possibly containing the symbol v. In $(\textbf{rec } v . \tau(v))$, $\tau(v)$ must be either a record type, a variant type or a function type. The same restriction will apply to similar notations defined below. Formally, the set of types is defined as the set of *regular trees* [Cou83] constructed from base types and type constructors. The above syntax should be regarded as representations of regular trees. In particular (**rec** $v . \tau(v)$) represents a regular tree that is a unique solution to the equation $v = \tau(v)$. By the restriction of $\tau(v)$, (**rec** $v . \tau(v)$) always denotes a regular tree. For convenience, we assume a set of special labels $\#1, \ldots, \#n, \ldots$ and treat a product type $(\tau_1 * \tau_2 * \cdots * \tau_n)$ as a shorthand for the record type $[\#1 : \tau_1, \ldots, \#n : \tau_n]$.

The set of raw terms (un-checked untyped terms, ranged over by e) is given by the following syntax:

$$e ::= c^\tau \,|\, x \,|\, \mathbf{fn}\ x \Rightarrow e \,|\, e(e) \,|\, [l = e, \ldots, l = e] \,|\, e.l \,|\, \mathbf{modify}(e, l, e) \,|\, \langle l = e \rangle \,|$$

$$\mathbf{case}\ e\ \mathbf{of}\ \langle l = x \rangle \Rightarrow e; \cdots; \langle l = x \rangle \Rightarrow e\ \mathbf{end}$$

where c^τ stands for constants of type τ, x stands for a given set of variables and $\langle l = e \rangle$ stands for injections to variants. We write $\mathbf{fn}\ (x_1, \ldots, x_n) \Rightarrow e$ for the shorthand for $\mathbf{fn}\ x \Rightarrow e'$ where e' is the term obtained form e by substituting x_i with $x . \#i$ ($1 \le i \le n$). Recursion is represented by a fixed point combinator, which is definable in the core language. The following definition of Y given in [Plo75] can be used to define recursive functions under the usual "call-by-value" evaluation:

$$Y = \mathbf{fn}\ f \Rightarrow (\mathbf{fn}\ x \Rightarrow f(\mathbf{fn}\ y \Rightarrow (x(x))(y)))$$
$$(\mathbf{fn}\ x \Rightarrow f(\mathbf{fn}\ y \Rightarrow (x(x))(y)))$$

A recursive function definition of the form $\mathbf{fun}\ f(x) = e$ where f appears in the body e is regarded as a shorthand for $f = Y(\mathbf{fn}\ f \Rightarrow \mathbf{fn}\ x \Rightarrow e)$. ML's *let* polymorphism [Mil78, DM82] is compatible with the type system we will develop in this paper and polymorphic *let* binding can be easily added to the language. Interested readers are referred to [Oho89a] for a formal treatment of adding *let*-expressions in a type system like the one defined in this paper.

An association between a raw term and a type is called a *typing*. A *type assignment* $\mathcal{A}$ is a function from a subset of variables to types. For a given type assignment $\mathcal{A}$, we write $\mathcal{A}\{x : v\}$ for the type assignment $\mathcal{A}'$ such that $dom(\mathcal{A}') = dom(\mathcal{A}) \cup \{x\}$, $\mathcal{A}'(x) = v$, and $\mathcal{A}'(y) = \mathcal{A}(y)$ for all $y \in dom(\mathcal{A})$, $y \ne x$. A typing is then defined as a formula of the form $\mathcal{A} \rhd e : \tau$ that is derivable in the proof system shown in Figure 1. We write $\vdash \mathcal{A} \rhd e : \tau$ if $\mathcal{A} \rhd e : \tau$ is derivable.

In general a raw term has infinitely many typings. One important feature of the ML family of languages is the existence of a type inference algorithm, which is based on the existence of a *principal typing* scheme for any typable raw term. The set of

$$\mathscr{A} \vartriangleright c^b : b \qquad\qquad\qquad\qquad\qquad\qquad\qquad\qquad\qquad \text{(CONST)}$$

$$\mathscr{A} \vartriangleright x : \tau \quad \text{if } \mathscr{A}(x) = \tau \qquad\qquad\qquad\qquad\qquad\qquad \text{(VAR)}$$

$$\frac{\mathscr{A} \vartriangleright e_1 : \tau_1, \ldots, \mathscr{A} \vartriangleright e_n : \tau_n}{\mathscr{A} \vartriangleright [l_1 = e_1, \ldots, l_n = e_n] : [l_1 : \tau_1, \ldots, l_n : \tau_n]} \qquad\qquad \text{(RECORD)}$$

$$\frac{\mathscr{A} \vartriangleright e : \tau}{\mathscr{A} \vartriangleright e . l : \tau'} \quad \text{if } \tau \text{ is a record type containing } l : \tau' \qquad \text{(SELECT)}$$

$$\frac{\mathscr{A} \vartriangleright e_1 : \tau \qquad \mathscr{A} \vartriangleright e_2 : \tau'}{\mathscr{A} \vartriangleright \mathbf{modify}(e_1, l, e_2) : \tau} \quad \text{if } \tau \text{ is a record type containing } l : \tau' \qquad \text{(MODIFY)}$$

$$\frac{\mathscr{A} \vartriangleright e : \tau}{\mathscr{A} \vartriangleright \langle l = e \rangle : \tau'} \quad \text{if } \tau' \text{ is a variant type containing } l : \tau \qquad \text{(VARIANT)}$$

$$\frac{\mathscr{A} \vartriangleright e : \langle l_1 : \tau_1, \ldots, l_n : \tau_n \rangle, \ \mathscr{A}\{x_i : \tau_i\} \vartriangleright e_i : \tau (1 \leq i \leq n)}{\mathscr{A} \vartriangleright \mathbf{case}\ e\ \mathbf{of}\ \langle l_1 = x_1 \rangle \Rightarrow e_1 ; \cdots ; \langle l_n = x_n \rangle \Rightarrow e_n\ \mathbf{end} : \tau} \qquad \text{(CASE)}$$

$$\frac{\mathscr{A} \vartriangleright e_1 : \tau_1 \rightarrow \tau_2 \qquad \mathscr{A} \vartriangleright e_2 : \tau_1}{\mathscr{A} \vartriangleright e_1(e_2) : \tau_2} \qquad\qquad\qquad \text{(APP)}$$

$$\frac{\mathscr{A}\{x : \tau_1\} \vartriangleright e : \tau_2}{\mathscr{A} \vartriangleright \mathbf{fn}\ x \Rightarrow e : \tau_1 \rightarrow \tau_2} \qquad\qquad\qquad\qquad \text{(ABS)}$$

Figure 1
Typing rules for the core language

type-schemes (ranged over by ρ) is the set of regular trees represented by the following syntax:

$$\rho ::= t \,|\, b \,|\, [l : \rho, \ldots, l : \rho] \,|\, \langle l : \rho, \ldots, l : \rho \rangle \,|\, \rho \rightarrow \rho \,|\, (\mathbf{rec}\ v . \rho(v))$$

where t stands for type variables. A substitution θ is a function from type variables to type-schemes such that $\theta(t) \neq t$ for only finitely many t. We write $[\rho_1/t_1, \ldots, \rho_n/t_n]$ for the substitution θ such that $\{t | \theta(t) \neq t\} = \{t_1, \ldots, t_n\}$ and $\theta(t_i) = \rho_i$, $1 \leq i \leq n$. A substitution uniquely extends to type-schemes (and other syntactic structures containing type-schemes). For finite types, this is the unique homomorphic extension of θ. For general regular trees, see [Cou83] for a technical definition. A type-scheme ρ is an *instance* of a type-scheme ρ' if there is a substitution θ such that $\rho = \theta(\rho')$. An instance ρ is *ground* if it is a type. A substitution θ is *ground for* ρ if $\theta(\rho)$ is a type. A *type assignment scheme* Γ is a function from a finite subset of variables to type-schemes. A *typing scheme* is then defined as a formula of the form $\Gamma \vartriangleright e : \rho$ such that all its ground instances are typings. A typing scheme $\Gamma \rhd e : \rho$ is *principal* if for any typing $\mathcal{A} \rhd e : \tau$, $(\mathcal{A} \uparrow^{dom(\Gamma)}, \tau)$ is a ground instance of (Γ, ρ), where $f \uparrow^{X}$ is the function restriction of f to X. A principal typing scheme can be also characterized syntactically as a *most general* typing scheme with respect to an ordering induced by substitutions.

For ML it is well-known ([Mil78, DM82]) that for any typable raw term, there is a principal typing scheme; moreover, there is an algorithm to compute this typing scheme. For example, the ML type inference algorithm computes the following principal typing scheme for the function $id \equiv \mathbf{fn}(x) \Rightarrow x$:

$$\emptyset \rhd id : t \rightarrow t$$

The set of all typings of id is correctly represented by the set of all ground instances of the above typing scheme (with possible weakening of type assignments). By this mechanism, ML achieves static type-checking and polymorphism (when combined with the binding mechanism of *let*). In the above example, the function id can be safely used as a function of any type of the form $\tau \rightarrow \tau$.

In our core language, however, a typable raw term does not necessarily have a principal typing scheme because of the conditions associated with the rules (SELECT), (MODIFY) and (VARIANT). In [OB88] this problem is resolved by extending type-schemes to include conditions on substitutions of type variables. The set of *conditional type-schemes* (ranged over by T) is the set of regular trees represented by the following syntax:

$$T ::= t \mid [(t)l : T, \ldots, l : T] \mid \langle (t)l : T, \ldots, l : T \rangle \mid b \mid [l : T, \ldots, l : T] \mid \langle l : T, \ldots, l : T \rangle \mid T \rightarrow T \mid$$

$$(\mathbf{rec}\ v\ .\ T(v))$$

$[(t)l : T, \ldots, l : T]$ and $\langle (t)l : T, \ldots, l : T \rangle$ are *conditional type variables*. Intuitively, $[(t)l_1 : T_1, \ldots, l_n : T_n]$ and $\langle (t)l_1 : T_1, \ldots, l_n : T_n \rangle$ respectively represent record types and variant types that contain the set of fields $l_1 : T_1$, ..., $l_n : T_n$. This intuition is made precise by the notion of *admissible instances*. For a conditional type-scheme T, the *condition erasure* of T, denoted by $erase(T)$, is the type scheme obtained form T by "erasing" all conditions from conditional type variables, i.e. by replacing all conditional type variables of the form $[(t)\ldots]$ and $\langle (t')\ldots \rangle$ by t and t' respectively. Substitutions are extended to conditional type-schemes as $\theta(T) = \theta(erase(T))$. A ground substitution θ for $[(t)l_1 : T_1, \ldots, l_n : T_n]$ is *admissible* for $[(t)l_1 : T_1, \ldots, l_n : T_n]$ if $\theta(t)$ is a record type containing $l_1 : \theta(T_1)$, ..., $l_n : \theta(T_n)$. Similarly, θ is admissible for $\langle (t)l_1 : T_1, \ldots, l_n : T_n \rangle$ if $\theta(t)$ is a variant type containing $l_1 : \theta(T_1)$, ..., $l_n : \theta(T_n)$. A ground substitution is admissible for a conditional type-scheme T if it is admissible for all conditional type variables in T. A type τ is an *admissible instance* of T if there is an admissible ground substitution θ for T such that $\tau = \theta(T)$. A conditional type-scheme denotes the set of all its admissible instances. For example, the conditional type-scheme

$$[(t)Age:int] \to [(t)Age:int]$$

denotes the set of all types of functions on records containing $Age:int$ field that return a record of the same type.

By using conditional type-schemes, Damas and Milner's result for ML can be extended to our language. A *conditional type assignment scheme* Γ is a function from a finite subset of variables to conditional type-schemes. A *conditional typing scheme* is a formula of the form $\Gamma \rhd e : T$ such that all its admissible instances are typings. We write $\vdash \Gamma \rhd e : T$ if it is a conditional typing scheme. A conditional typing scheme $\vdash \Gamma \rhd e : T$ is *principal* if for any typing $\vdash \mathscr{A} \rhd e : \tau$, $\mathscr{A} \uparrow^{dom(\Gamma)} \rhd e : \tau$ is an admissible instance of $\Gamma \rhd e : T$. As in ML a principal conditional typing scheme of e represents the set of all typings for e.

In [OB88] the following property is shown for a language containing labeled records and a number of structures and operations for databases:

THEOREM 1   For any raw term e, if e has a typing then it has a principal conditional typing scheme. Moreover, there is an algorithm which, given any raw term, computes its principal conditional typing scheme if one exists and reports failure if not.

This result can be easily adapted to our language. The following is an examples of a principal conditional typing scheme:

$$\emptyset \rhd \textbf{fn } x \Rightarrow \textbf{modify}(x, Age, x . Age + 1) : [(t)Age:int] \to [(t)Age:int]$$

This property guarantees that we can statically check the type correctness of any given raw term.

3   Formulation of Classes

In this section, we first present a proof system for class declarations as an extension to the core language. We then show the soundness of the proof system relative to the soundness of the type system of the core language and develop a type inference algorithm for the extended language.

3.1 Proof System for Classes

We assume that there is a given ranked alphabet of *class constructors* (ranged over by c) and a set of *method names* (ranged over by m). A class constructor of arity 0 is a constant (non-parametric) class. The set of types is extended by class constructors:

$$\tau ::= b \mid [l:\tau,\ldots,l:\tau] \mid \langle l:\tau,\ldots,l:\tau\rangle \mid \tau \to \tau \mid c(\tau,\ldots,\tau) \mid (\mathbf{rec}\ v\,.\,\tau(v))$$

The set of raw terms is extended by method names:

$$e ::= m \mid c^\tau \mid \ldots$$

In order to allow parametric class declarations, we extend the set of type-schemes with class constructors:

$$\rho ::= t \mid b \mid [l:\rho,\ldots,l:\rho] \mid \langle l:\rho,\ldots,l:\rho\rangle \mid \rho \to \rho \mid c(\rho,\ldots,\rho) \mid (\mathbf{rec}\ v\,.\,\rho(v))$$

In particular, we call type-schemes of the form $c(\rho_1,\ldots,\rho_k)$ *class-schemes*. We write $c(\bar{t})$ and $c(\bar{\rho})$ for $c(t_1,\ldots,t_k)$ and $c(\rho_1,\ldots,\rho_k)$ where k is the arity of c.

A *class definition D* has the following syntax:

class $c(\bar{t}) = \rho$ **isa** $\{c_1(\overline{\rho_{c_1}}),\ldots,c_n(\overline{\rho_{c_n}})\}$ **with**
   $m_1 = e_1 : M_1;$
          $\vdots$
   $m_n = e_n : M_n;$
end

$c(\bar{t})$ is the class-scheme being defined by this definition. $\bar{t}$ in $c(\bar{t})$ are type parameters, which must contain all the type variables that appear in the class definition. ρ is the implementation type-scheme of the class $c(\bar{t})$, which must not be a type variable. $\{c_1(\overline{\rho_{c_1}}),\ldots,c_n(\overline{\rho_{c_n}})\}$ is the set of immediate super-class schemes from which $c(\bar{t})$ directly inherits methods. We will show below that the subclass relationship is obtained from this immediate **isa** relation by taking the closure under transitivity and instantiation. Note that class definitions allow both *multiple inheritance* and type parameterization. If the set of super-classes is empty then the **isa** declaration is omitted. If the set is a singleton set then we omit the braces { and }. Each m_i is the name of a method implemented by the code e_i. Method names m_i should not appear in any method bodies e_j in the same class definition. This restriction is enforced by the type system defined below. It should be noted however that this restriction does not imply that we disallow (mutually) recursive method definitions, which can be provided by the following syntactic sugar:

rec $m_1 = e_1 : M_1$;

and $\cdots$

$\vdots$

and $m_n = e_n : M_n$;

defined as

$$m_1 = (Y(\mathbf{fn}(x_1, \ldots, x_n) \Rightarrow (e'_1, \ldots, e'_n))) . \#1 : M_1$$

$$\vdots$$

$$m_n = (Y(\mathbf{fn}(x_1, \ldots, x_n) \Rightarrow (e'_1, \ldots, e'_n))) . \#n : M_n$$

where e'_i is the term obtained form e_i by substituting m_i by x_i ($1 \leq i \leq n$). M_i is a *method type* specifying the type of m_i, whose syntax is given below:

$$M ::= \mathbf{sub} \,|\, t \,|\, b \,|\, [l : M, \ldots, l : M] \,|\, \langle l : M, \ldots, l : M \rangle \,|\, M \to M \,|\, c(M, \ldots, M)$$

sub is a distinguished type variable ranging over all subclasses of the class being defined. Note that we restrict method types to be finite types. This is necessary to ensure the decidability of type-checking of class definitions.

A *class context* (or simply *context*) $\mathscr{D}$ is a finite sequence of class definitions:

$$\mathscr{D} ::= \varnothing \,|\, \mathscr{D}; D$$

where $\varnothing$ is the empty sequence.

Class declarations are forms of bindings for which we need some mechanism to resolve naming conflicts, such as visibility rules and explicit name qualifications. Here we ignore this complication and assume that method names and class constructor names are unique in a given context. Like a typing scheme, a class definition containing type variables intuitively represents the set of all its instances. The scope of type variables is the class definition in which they appear.

The special type variable **sub** that appears in method type specifications denotes the set of all possible subclasses that the programmer will declare later. This can be regarded as a form of *bounded quantification* [CW85]. The method type M containing **sub** corresponds to $\forall \mathbf{sub} < c(\bar{t}). M$ where $c(\bar{t})$ is the class being defined. The relation $<$ is the *subclass relation under a context* $\mathscr{D}$, denoted by $\mathscr{D} \vdash c_1(\overline{\rho_1}) < c_2(\overline{\rho_2})$, which is defined as the smallest transitive relation on class schemes containing:

1. $\mathscr{D} \vdash c(\bar{t}) < c(\bar{t})$ if $\mathscr{D}$ contains a class definition of the form **class** $c(\bar{t}) = \rho \cdots$ **end**,

2. $\mathscr{D} \vdash c_1(\overline{t_1}) < c_2(\overline{\rho_2})$ if $\mathscr{D}$ contains a class definition of the form **class** $c_1(\overline{t_1}) = \rho$ **isa** $\{\ldots, c_2(\overline{\rho_2}), \ldots\}$ **with** $\cdots$ **end**,

3. $\mathscr{D} \vdash c_1(\overline{\rho_1}) < c_2(\overline{\rho_2})$ if $\mathscr{D} \vdash c_1(\overline{\rho'_1}) < c_2(\overline{\rho'_2})$ and $(\overline{\rho_1}, \overline{\rho_2})$ is an instance of $(\overline{\rho'_1}, \overline{\rho'_2})$,

The combination of multiple inheritance and type parameterization requires certain conditions on **isa** declarations. A context $\mathscr{D}$ is *coherent* if whenever $\mathscr{D} \vdash c_1(\overline{\rho_1}) < c_2(\overline{\rho_2})$ and $\mathscr{D} \vdash c_1(\overline{\rho_1}) < c_2(\overline{\rho_2'})$, then $\overline{\rho_2} = \overline{\rho_2'}$. We require a context to be coherent. This condition is necessary to develop a type inference algorithm. The following property is easily shown.

LEMMA 1   For a given context $\mathscr{D}$, it is decidable whether $\mathscr{D}$ is coherent or not.

We say that a subclass relation $\mathscr{D} \vdash c_1(\overline{\rho_1}) < c_2(\overline{\rho_2})$ is more general than $\mathscr{D} \vdash c_1(\overline{\rho_1'}) < c_2(\overline{\rho_2'})$ if $(\overline{\rho_1'}, \overline{\rho_2'})$ is an instance of $(\overline{\rho_1}, \overline{\rho_2})$. A subclass relation $\mathscr{D} \vdash c_1(\overline{\rho_1}) < c_2(\overline{\rho_2})$ is *principal* if it is more general than all provable subclass relations between c_1 and c_2.

Under the coherence condition, the subclass relation has the following property:

LEMMA 2   For any coherent context $\mathscr{D}$ and any method names c_1, c_2, if $\mathscr{D} \vdash c_1(\overline{\rho_1}) < c_2(\overline{\rho_2})$ then there is a principal subclass relation $\mathscr{D} \vdash c_1(\overline{t_1}) < c_2(\overline{\rho_2'})$. Moreover, there is an algorithm which, given a coherent context $\mathscr{D}$ and a pair c_1, c_2, returns either $(\overline{t}, \overline{\rho})$ or failure such that if it returns $(\overline{t}, \overline{\rho})$ then $\mathscr{D} \vdash c_1(\overline{t}) < c_2(\overline{\rho})$ is a principal subclass relation between c_1, c_2 otherwise there is no subclass relation between c_1 and c_2.

Note that since the substitution relation is decidable, this result implies that the subclass relation is decidable.

The extended type system has the following forms of judgments:

$\vdash \mathscr{D}$ $\mathscr{D}$ is a well typed class context,

$\vdash \mathscr{D}, \mathscr{A} \rhd e : \tau$ the typing $\mathscr{D}, \mathscr{A} \rhd e : \tau$ is derivable.

The proof systems for these two forms of judgments are defined simultaneously.

Let D be a class definition of the form **class** $c(\overline{t}) = \rho_c \cdots$ **end**. D induces the *tree substitution* ϕ_D on type-schemes. For finite type-schemes, $\phi_D(\rho)$ is defined by induction on the structure of ρ as follows:

$\phi_D(b) = b$

$\phi_D(t) = t$

$\phi_D(f(\rho_1, \ldots, \rho_n)) = f(\phi_D(\rho_1), \ldots, \phi_D(\rho_n))$ for any type constructor f s.t. $f \neq c$

$\phi_D(c(\overline{\rho})) = \rho_c[\phi_D(\overline{\rho})/\overline{t}]$

where $[\phi_D(\overline{\rho})/\overline{t}]$ denotes $[\phi_D(\rho_1)/t_1, \ldots, \phi_D(\rho_k)/t_k]$ (with k the arity of c). Since ρ_c is not a type variable, ϕ_D is a *non-erasing second-order substitution* on trees [Cou83], which extends uniquely to regular trees. See [Cou83] for the technical details. Since regular trees are closed under second-order substitution [Cou83], $\phi_D(\rho)$ is a well defined type-scheme.

The rule for $\vdash \mathscr{D}$ is defined by induction on the length of $\mathscr{D}$:

1. The empty context is a well typed context, i.e. $\vdash \varnothing$.

2. Suppose $\vdash \mathscr{D}$. Let D be the following class definition:

   class $c(\bar{t}) = \rho$ **isa** $\{c_1(\overline{\rho_{c_1}}), \ldots, c_n(\overline{\rho_{c_n}})\}$
   with
   $\quad m_1 = e_1 : M_1;$
   $\quad \vdots$
   $\quad m_n = e_n : M_n$
   end.

   Then $\vdash \mathscr{D}; D$ if the following conditions hold:

   (a) it is coherent,

   (b) if a class name c' appears in some of $\rho, c_1(\overline{\rho_{c_1}}), \ldots, c_n(\overline{\rho_{c_n}})$ then $\mathscr{D}$ contains a definition of the form **class** $c'(\bar{t}') \cdots$ **end**,

   (c) $\vdash \mathscr{D}, \varnothing \rhd e_i : \tau$ for any ground instance τ of $\phi_D(M_i[\rho/\mathbf{sub}])$,

   (d) if $m = e_m : M_m$ is any method defined in some declaration of class $c'(\bar{t}')$ in $\mathscr{D}$ such that $\mathscr{D}; D \vdash c(\bar{t}) < c'(\overline{\rho'})$, then $\vdash \mathscr{D}, \varnothing \rhd e_m : \tau$ for any ground instance τ of $M_m[\overline{\rho'}/\bar{t}', \rho/\mathbf{sub}]$.

We have already discussed the necessity of the condition (a). The necessity of the condition (b) is obvious. The condition (c) states that each method defined in the definition of the class $c(\bar{t})$ is type consistent with its own implementation. Note that since M_i is finite, $\phi_D(M_i[\rho/\mathbf{sub}])$ is effectively computable by the inductive definition of ϕ_D. The condition (d) ensures that all methods of all super-classes that are defined in $\mathscr{D}$ are also applicable to the class $c(\bar{t})$. This is done by checking the type consistency of each method e_m defined in a super-class against the type-scheme obtained from M_m by instantiating its type variables with type-schemes specified in **isa** declaration in the definition of the class $c(\bar{t})$ and replacing the variable **sub** with the implementation type ρ of the class $c(\bar{t})$.

The proof rules for typings are given by extending the proof rules for typings of the core language by the following rule:

$\vdash \mathscr{D}, \mathscr{A} \rhd m : \tau \quad$ if $\vdash \mathscr{D}$ and there is a method $m = e : M$ of a class $c(\bar{t})$ in $\mathscr{D}$ such that τ is an instance of $M[\overline{\rho}/\bar{t}, c'(\bar{t}')/\mathbf{sub}]$ for some $\mathscr{D} \vdash c'(\bar{t}') < c(\overline{\rho})$.   (METHOD)

The well definedness of these two mutually dependent definitions can be checked by indution on the length of $\mathscr{D}$. Since the decidability of judgments of the form $\vdash \mathscr{D}$ will follow from Lemma 1, 2, and the decidability of typing judgments, the decidability of static typechecking of the entire type system is established by the existence of a complete type inference algorithm for typing judgments, which we will develop in Section 5. But first, we establish the soundness of the type system. The following property is useful:

LEMMA 3   If $\vdash \mathscr{D}; D$ and $m = e : M$ is defined in D then m does not appear in the body of any method definition in $\mathscr{D}; D$.

4   Soundness of the Type System

Let $\mathscr{D}$ be a given context and τ be a type. The *exposure of τ under $\mathscr{D}$*, denoted by $expose_{\mathscr{D}}(\tau)$, is the type given by the following inductive definition on the length of $\mathscr{D}$:

1. if $\mathscr{D} = \varnothing$ then $expose_{\mathscr{D}}(\tau) = \tau$,
2. if $\mathscr{D} = \mathscr{D}'; D$ then $expose_{\mathscr{D}}(\tau) = expose_{\mathscr{D}'}(\phi_D(\tau))$.

By the condition (b) of the definition for $\vdash \mathscr{D}$, if $\vdash \mathscr{D}, \mathscr{A} \rhd e : \tau$ then $expose_{\mathscr{D}}(\tau)$ does not contain any class name and therefore a type in the core language. Intuitively, $expose_{\mathscr{D}}(\tau)$ is the type obtained from τ by recursively replacing all its classes by their implementation types. We extend $expose_{\mathscr{D}}$ to syntactic structures containing type-schemes.

The *unfold* of a raw term e under a context $\mathscr{D}$, denoted by $unfold_{\mathscr{D}}(e)$, is the raw term given by the following inductive definition on the length of $\mathscr{D}$:

1. if $\mathscr{D} = \varnothing$ then $unfold_{\mathscr{D}}(e) = e$,

2. if $\mathscr{D} = \mathscr{D}';$ **class** ... **with**
$$m_1 = e_1 : M_1;$$
$$\vdots$$
$$m_n = e_n : M_n$$
   end,

then $unfold_{\mathscr{D}}(e) = unfold_{\mathscr{D}'}(e[e_1/m_1, \ldots, e_n/m_n])$.

By Lemma 3, if $\vdash \mathscr{D}, \mathscr{A} \rhd e : \tau$ then $unfold_{\mathscr{D}}(e)$ does not contain any method name and is therefore a raw term in the core language. $unfold_{\mathscr{D}}(e)$ corresponds to the raw term obtained from e by recursively replacing all method names defined in $\mathscr{D}$ with their implementations. We then have the following theorem.

THEOREM 2   If $\vdash \mathscr{D}, \mathscr{A} \rhd e : \tau$ then $\vdash expose_{\mathscr{D}}(\mathscr{A}) \rhd unfold_{\mathscr{D}}(e) : expose_{\mathscr{D}}(\tau)$ in the core language.

Proof (Sketch)   The proof is by induction on the length of $\mathscr{D}$. The basis is trivial. The induction step is by induction on the structure of e. Cases other than $e = m$ follow directly from the properties of *expose* and *unfold*. The case for $e = m$ is proved by the typing rule (METHOD) and the definitions of *expose*, *unfold*.   ∎

Since the soundness of the core language can be shown by using, for example, the techniques developed in [Tof88], the above theorem establishes the soundness of the type system with parametric classes. In particular, since the type system of the core language prevents all run-time type errors, a type correct program in the extended language cannot produce a run-time type error.

The converse of this theorem, of course, does not hold, but we would not expect it to hold, for one of the advantages of data abstraction is that it allows us to distinguish two methods that may have the same implementation. As an example, suppose $\mathscr{D}$ contains definitions for the classes *car* and *person* whose implementation types coincide and *person* has a method *minor* which determines whether a person is older than 21 or not. By the coincidence of the implementations, $\vdash \emptyset \rhd expose_{\mathscr{D}}(minor(c))$: *bool* for any *car* object c. But $\vdash \mathscr{D}, \mathscr{A} \rhd minor(c) : bool$ is not provable unless we declare (by a sequences of **isa** declarations) that *car* is a subclass of *person*. This prevents illegal use of a method through a coincidence of the implementation schemes.

5   Type Inference for the Extended Language

We next show that there is a static type inference algorithm for the extended language. The set of conditional type-schemes is extended with classes and new conditional type variables:

$$T ::= c(T, \ldots, T) | (t < \{T, \ldots, T\}) | \cdots$$

where $(t < \{T, \ldots, T\})$ stands for new form of conditional type variables, called *bounded type variables*. Intuitively, $(t < \{T_1, \ldots, T_n\})$ represents the set of all instances $\theta(t)$ that are subclasses of all of $\theta(T_1), \ldots, \theta(T_n)$ under a given context $\mathscr{D}$. This intuition is made precise by extending the notion of condition erasure $erase(T)$, substitution instances $\theta(T)$ and the admissibility of substitutions. The condition erasure $erase(T)$ of T is extended to bounded type variables, i.e. *erase* also replaces conditional type variables of the form $(t < \{T_1, \ldots, T_n\})$ by t. The definition of instances is the same as before. The admissibility of substitutions is now defined relative to a context $\mathscr{D}$. A ground substitution θ is *admissible for* $(t < \{T_1, \ldots, T_n\})$ *under a context* $\mathscr{D}$ if $\mathscr{D} \vdash \theta(t) < \theta(T_i)$ for all $1 \leq i \leq n$. Note that for a bounded type variable $(t < \{T_1, \ldots, T_n\})$ to have an admissible substitution, each T_i must be a type-scheme of the form $c(T, \ldots, T)$. The rules for other forms of conditional type variables are the same as before. A ground substitution is admissible for a conditional type-scheme T under a context $\mathscr{D}$ if it is admissible for all conditional types variables in T under $\mathscr{D}$. A type τ is an *admissible instance of* T *under* $\mathscr{D}$ if there is an admissible ground substitution θ for T under $\mathscr{D}$ such that $\tau = \theta(T)$. A conditional type-scheme denotes the set of all its admissible instances under a given context.

The relationship between the provability of conditional typing schemes and typings is similar to the one in the core language except it is now defined relative to a given context $\mathscr{D}$. $\Gamma \rhd e : T$ is a *conditional typing scheme under* $\mathscr{D}$, denoted by $\vdash \mathscr{D}, \Gamma \rhd e : T$, if $\vdash \mathscr{D}, \mathscr{A} \rhd e : \tau$ holds for any admissible instance $\mathscr{A} \rhd e : \tau$ of $\Gamma \rhd e : T$ under $\mathscr{D}$. The definition for *principality* is also the same. We then have the following theorem which is an extension of Theorem 1:

THEOREM 3   For any raw term e, and any well typed context $\mathscr{D}$ if e has a typing under $\mathscr{D}$ then it has a principal conditional typing scheme under $\mathscr{D}$. Moreover, there is an algorithm which, given any raw term and any well typed context $\mathscr{D}$, computes its principal conditional typing scheme under $\mathscr{D}$ if one exists, and reports failure otherwise.

Proof (sketch)   The strategy is based on that used in [OB88]. The algorithm to compute a principal conditional typing scheme is defined in two steps. It first constructs a typing scheme and a set of conditions of the forms $T < T'$ (representing bound conditions), $[(l : T) \in T']$ (representing field inclusion relation on record types) and $\langle (l : T) \in T' \rangle$ (representing field inclusion relation on variant types). The algorithm then reduces the set of conditions to conditional type-schemes. For a condition of the from $T < T'$, the reduction is done by producing a most general substitution θ such that $\mathscr{D} \vdash \theta(T) < \theta(T')$. This is possible because of the property shown in Lemma 2. The reduction of conditions of the forms $[(l : T) \in T']$ and $\langle (l : T) \in T \rangle$ is done by producing a substitution θ and a set of conditional types of the form $[(t)l : T, \ldots]$ and $\langle (t)l : T, \ldots \rangle$.   ∎

6   Further Examples

In Section 1, we defined the classes *person* and *employee*. The sequence of the two definitions is indeed a type correct class context in our type system. Figure 2 shows an

```
-> class person = [Name:string,Age:int]
   with ... end;
>> class person with
       make_person : (string*int) -> person
       name : ('a < person) -> string
       age : ('a < person) -> int
       increment_age : ('a < person) -> ('a < person)
-> class employee = [Name:string,Age:int,Sal:int]
   with ... end;
>> class employee is a person with
       make_employee : (string*int) -> employee
       add_salary : (('a < employee)*int) -> ('a < employee)
       salary : ('a < employee) -> int
   inherited methods:
       name : ('a < person) -> string
       age : ('a < person) -> int
       increment_age : ('a < person) -> ('a < person)
-> val joe = make_person("Joe",21);
>> val joe = _ : person
-> val helen = make_employee("Helen",31)
>> val helen = _ : employee
-> age(joe);
>> 21 : int
-> val helen = increment_age(helen);
>> val helen = _ : employee
-> age(helen);
>> 32 : int
```

Figure 2
A simple interactive session with classes

interactive session involving these class definitions in our prototype implementation, whose syntax mostly follows that of ML. $->$ is input prompt followed by user input. $>>$ is output prefix followed by the system output. ($'a <$ person) and ($'a <$ employee) are bounded type variables. As seen in the example, the system displays the set of all inherited methods for each type correct class definition.

Let us look briefly at some further examples of how type parameterization can interact with inheritance. At the end of Section 1 we defined a polymorphic list class *list(a)*. We could immediately use this by implicit instantiation of *a*. For example, the function

fun *sum(l)* = **if** *null(l)* **then** 0
                            else *hd(l)* + *sum(tl(l))*

will be given the type *list(int)* → *int*, as would happen in ML. However we can instantiate the type variable *a* in other ways. For example, we could construct a class

class *genintlist(b)* =
  (**rec** *t* . ⟨*Empty* : *unit*,
            List : [*Head* : [*Ival* : *int*, *Cont* : *b*],
                      Tail : *t*]⟩)
isa *list*([*Ival* : *int*, *Cont* : *b*])
with
  $\vdots$
end

which could be used, say, as the implementation type for a "bag" of values of type *b*. In this case all the methods of *pre_list* and *list* are inherited. However, we might also attempt to create a subclass of *list* with the following declaration in which we directly extend the record type of the *List* variant of the implementation:

class *genintlist(b)* =
  (**rec** *t* . ⟨*Empty* : *unit*,
            List : [*Head* : *int*, *Cont* : *b*, *Tail* : *t*]⟩)
isa *list(int)*
with
  $\vdots$
end

In this class, all the methods of *pre_list* could be inherited but the method *cons* of *list(a)* cannot be inherited because the implementation type of *genintlist(b)* is incompatible with any of the possible types of *cons*. In this case, the type checker reports an error.

7 Extension for Database Programming

The type system described so far can be further extended to incorporate the structures and operations necessary for databases. Indeed, the core type system of [OB88] on which this paper is based includes set data types and a number of database operations. This extension together with the mechanism of parametric classes presented here makes the language appropriate as the basis of an object-oriented database programming language. Here we briefly describe the extension. For the detailed type inference system and its relevance to database programming, see respectively [OB88, BO90].

Since sets and most database operations require decidable equality on terms, they cannot be introduced on arbitrary terms. For this reason, we identify subsets of terms and types as what we call *description terms* and *description types*. Description types are those that do not contain function types (outside the scope of a reference type). Description types are a generalization of ML's *eqtypes* and also have available a number of useful database operations such as *join* and *projection*.

It is not difficult to introduce a set type constructor on description types. The crucial step toward a satisfactory integration of databases and a polymorphic type system is to introduce database operations that are powerful enough to manipulate complex database objects. One important operation common in databases is to *join* two records of consistent information. For example $[Name = "Joe", Age = 21]$ and $[Name = "Joe", Sal = 30,000]$ join to form $[Name = "Joe", Age = 21, Sal = 30,000]$. This can be regarded as a form of record concatenation [Wan89, HP91, Rem91], but can be generalized to arbitrary complex description terms to form natural join of complex database objects. In [BJO91, Oho90], we have achieved this by exploiting *information orderings* $\sqsubseteq$ and $\ll$ respectively on description terms and description types. $d_1 \sqsubseteq d_2$ represents our intuition that d_2 is a better description than d_2 and $\delta_1 \ll \delta_2$ denotes the fact that the structure represented by δ_2 is "more informative" than that represented by δ_1. Here is a simple example of $\ll$.

$$\{[Name : [Fn : string, Ln : string], Age : int]\}$$
$$\ll \{[Name : [Fn : string, Mi : char, Ln : string],$$
$$Age : int, Salary : int]\}$$

where $\{\_\}$ is the set type constructor. The natural join is then regarded as the operator which "combines" two consistent descriptions and is generalized to arbitrary description terms (even those involving cyclic definitions) as:

$$\textbf{join}(d_1, d_2) = d_1 \sqcup_\sqsubseteq d_2$$

with the following polymorphic type:

$$\mathbf{join} : (\delta_1 * \delta_2) \to \delta_1 \sqcup_\ll \delta_2$$

Figure 3 shows an example of the generalized natural join of complex values. Other database operations can also be defined using the orderings.

It should be noted that the ordering on types, although somewhat similar to that used in [Car88], is in no sense a part of record polymorphism. In particular, it has no connection to the notion of structural subtyping. We introduced the orderings only to represent *join* and other database operations. This should be apparent from the fact that we have already incorporated field selection and other operations as polymorphic operations without having to make use of subtyping.

To integrate sets, *join* and other database operations in the type system, the necessary extensions are a new class of type variables that ranges only over description types, and new forms of conditions on type variables that capture polymorphic nature of database operations. In the case of *join*, the necessary condition is of the form $\sigma = jointype(\sigma_1, \sigma_2)$. It was shown in [OB88] that these extensions preserve the existence of principal conditional typing schemes and the extended system still has a complete type inference algorithm. Since our mechanism of parametric classes relies only on the existence of a type inference algorithm, the entire language can be extended to database structures. Using operations on sets and *join*, database queries including SQL like expressions of the form

select $\cdots$ **from** $\cdots$ **where** $\cdots$

can be defined and freely combined with class structures. This achieves a proper integration of object-oriented programming and database programming in a static type system.

```
join({[Name=[Last="Ludford"], Children={"Jeremy", "Christopher"}],
      [Name=[Last="Gurman"], Children={"Adam", "Benjamin"}]},
     {[Name=[First="Bridget", Last="Ludford"],
       Address=[Street="33 Cleveden Dr", City="Glasgow"]],
      [Name=[First="Wilfred", Last="Anderson"],
       Address=[Street="13 Princes St", City="Edinburgh"]]})
   ={[Name=[First="Bridget", Last="Ludford"],
      Children={"Jeremy","Christopher"},
      Address=[Street="33 Cleveden Dr", City="Glasgow"]]}
```

Figure 3
An example of higher-order join

For example, the classes *student* and *employee* we have defined earlier can be used to construct a database containing sets of types {*student*} and {*employee*}. For such a database, queries can be easily defined as polymorphic functions as shown in the following example:

fun *wealthy S* = **select** *name*(*x*)
           from *x* ∈ *S*
           where *salary*(*x*) > 100000
  : {(*t* < *employee*)} → {*string*}
fun *good_students S* = **select** *name*(*x*)
              from *x* ∈ *S*
              where *grade*(*x*) > 3.7
  : {(*t* < *student*)} − > {*string*}
fun *good_fellows S* =
  intersection(*wealthy*(*S*), *good_students*(*S*))
    : {(*t* < {*student*, *employee*})} − > {*string*}

Moreover, by representing *object identity* by reference types as implemented in Standard ML, the type system can capture various aspects of object-oriented databases.

8   Limitations and Implementation

First, we should point out that the language we have proposed differs in some fundamental ways from object-oriented languages in the Smalltalk tradition. A static type system does not fit well with *late binding*—a feature of many object-oriented languages. One reason to have late binding seems to be to implement *overriding* of methods. It is possible that some form of overloading could be added to the language to support this.

One limitation in our type system is the restriction we imposed on inheritance declarations in connection with type parameters. We required that if a class $c(t_1, \ldots, t_k)$ is a subclass of both $c'(\tau_1, \ldots, \tau_j)$ and $c'(\tau'_1, \ldots, \tau'_j)$ then $\tau_i = \tau'_i$ for all $1 \le i \le j$. This is necessary to preserve the existence of principal conditional typing schemes for all typable raw terms. This disallows certain type consistent declarations such as:

class $C_1(t) = \tau$ **with**
    fun $m(x) = m(x) : \mathbf{sub} \to t$
end

class $C_2 = \tau'$ **isa** $\{C_1(int), C_1(bool)\}$ **with**
$$c = e : C_2$$
$$\vdots$$
end

which is type consistent in any implementation types τ, τ' but creates a problem that terms like $m(c)$ do not have a principal conditional typing scheme. However, we believe that the condition is satisfied by virtually all ordinary class declarations. Note that in the above example the result type of the method m is the free type variable t without any dependency of its domain type **sub**, which reflects the property that the method m does not terminate on any input. The authors could not construct any natural example that is type consistent but that does not satisfy this coherence condition.

We have only allowed a single **sub** variable. This restricts the expressiveness of method types. For example, we may want to define a method $older$ which compares any two objects of any subclasses of $person$. One possible definition of $older$ in the definition of a class $person$ is

$$older = \mathbf{fn}\,(x, y) \Rightarrow x.Age > y.Age : (\mathbf{sub} * \mathbf{sub}) \to bool$$

The type system infers the following conditional type-scheme for $older$

$$((t < person) * (t < person)) \to bool$$

But this type-scheme requires $older$ to be applied to a pair of objects of the *same* type. This problem can be solved by introducing multiple **sub** variables. Since possible subclasses of a given class is always finite, it is not hard to extend our formal type system to allow multiple **sub** variables and to show that the extension preserves the soundness of the type system and the existence of a complete type inference algorithm. As we will note below, however, such extension makes it more difficult to implement the type inference algorithm.

From a practical perspective, our type system does not immediately yield an efficient implementation. To typecheck a new class definition, the type system requires the typechecking of the raw terms that correspond to new methods defined in the class, and also the consistency checking of all methods of all super-classes already defined against the implementation type of the new class. A naive way to do this would involve recursively unfolding definitions of methods and repeated type-checking of the resulting raw terms in the type system of the core language, which will be prohibitively expensive when the class hierarchy becomes large. Fortunately, this problem can be avoided using the existence of a principal conditional typing scheme for any typable raw term in the extended language. One strategy is to *save* the principal conditional typing scheme of a method when it is first defined. Typechecking of new methods involving this method name can be done by using the saved principal typing scheme of the method. The type consistency of this method against implementation types of newly defined subclasses can be determined by checking whether the required method types are instances of the saved principal conditional type-scheme or not. These techniques eliminate both recursive unfolding and repeated type-checking of method bodies. Since checking whether a method type is an instance of a given principal conditional type-scheme or not can be done efficiently, this strategy yields an efficient implementation of static type-checking of class hierarchies. This strategy, however, relaies on the fact that the type system only allows a single **sub** variable. An efficient implementation strategy for a type system with multiple **sub** variables remains to be investigated.

9   Conclusion

We have presented a type inference system for classes that supports inheritance and parametricity in a statically typed language similar to ML. This achieves a proper integration of object-oriented programming and ML style polymorphic typing. Moreover, the type system can be further extended to include the structures and operations needed for database systems, and can therefore serve as a basis of object-oriented databases.

Some further syntactic sugaring may be appropriate, and we need to investigate scoping rules and overloading to bring our system into line with conventional object-oriented languages. It is also possible that there may be some integration between what we have proposed and the system of modules for Standard ML [Mac86] and its refinement [MMM91].

Another interesting question is a semantics of class definitions. A definition of a class determines a subset of types that are compatible with the set of methods (i.e. the set of raw lambda terms that implement the methods). This suggests that a class definition could be regarded as a form of existential type $\exists \mathbf{sub} : K . (M_1 * \ldots * M_n)$ where K denotes the subset of types that are compatible to the set of methods and $M_1, \ldots, M_n$ are the types of the methods defined in the class definition. This is a form of *bounded existential types* introduced in [CW85] but differs from theirs in that the kind K reflects directly the implementations of methods. Semantics of such types should explain not only the functionality of the set of methods (as is done in [MP85]) but also the structure of a kind K determined by a set of raw lambda terms.

Acknowledgment

We would like to thank Anthony Kosky for his helpful comments on a draft of this paper. In particular, he pointed out the limitation of single **sub** variable mentioned above.

Note

This research was supported in part by grants NSF IRI86-10617, ARO DAA6-29-84-k-0061 and ONR NOOO-14-88-K-0634.

References

[ACO85]   A. Albano, L. Cardelli, and R. Orsini. Galileo: A strongly typed, interactive conceptual language. *ACM Transactions on Database Systems*, 10(2):230–260, 1985.

[BJO91]   P. Buneman, A. Jung, and A. Ohori. Using powerdomains to generalize relational databases. *Theoretical Computer Science*, 91(1):23–56, 1991.

[BO90]   P. Buneman and A. Ohori. Polymorphism and type inference in database programming. Technical report, Universities of Glasgow and Pennsylvania, 1990. To appear in *ACM Transaction on Database Systems*.

[BTBO89]   V. Breazu-Tannen, P. Buneman, and A. Ohori. Can object-oriented databases be statically typed? In *Proc. 2nd International Workshop on Database Programming Languages*, pages 226–237, 1989. Morgan Kaufmann Publishers.

[Car88]   L. Cardelli. A semantics of multiple inheritance. *Information and Computation*, 76:138–164, 1988. (Special issue devoted to Symp. on Semantics of Data Types, 1984).

[CM89]   L. Cardelli and J. Mitchell. Operations on records. In *Proc. Mathematical Foundation of Programming Semantics, Lecture Notes in Computer Science 442*, pages 22–52, 1989.

[Cou83]   B. Courcelle. Fundamental properties of infinite trees. *Theoretical Computer Science*, 25:95–169, 1983.

[CW85]   L. Cardelli and P. Wegner. On understanding types, data abstraction, and polymorphism. *Computing Surveys*, 17(4):471–522, 1985.

[DM82]   L. Damas and R. Milner. Principal type-schemes for functional programs. In *Proc. ACM Symp. on Principles of Programming Languages*, pages 207–212, 1982.

[GR83]   A. Goldberg and D. Robson. *Smalltalk-80: the language and its implementation*. Addison-Wesley, 1983.

[HMT90]   R. Milner, M. Tofte, and R. Harper. *The definition of Standard ML*. MIT Press. 1990.

[HP91]   R. Harper and B. Pierce. A record calculus based on symmetric concatenation. In *Proc. ACM Symp. on Principles of Programming Languages*, pages 131–142, 1991. Extended version available as Carnegie Mellon Technical Report CMU-CS-90-157.

[IBH+79]   J. H. Ichbiah, J. G. P. Barnes, J. C. Heliard, B. Krieg-Bruckner, O. Roubine, and B. A. Wichmann. Rationale of the design of the programming language Ada. *SIGPLAN Notices*, 14(6), 1979.

[JM88]   L. A. Jategaonkar and J. C. Mitchell. ML with extended pattern matching and subtypes. In *Proc. ACM Conf. on LISP and Functional Programming*, pages 198–211, 1988.

[LAB+81]   Barbara Liskov, Russell Atkinson, Toby Bloom, Eliot Moss, J. Craig Schaffert, Robert Scheifler, and Alan Snyder. *CLU Reference Manual, Lecture Notes in Computer Science 114*. Springer-Verlag, 1981.

[Mac86]   D. B. MacQueen. Using dependent types to express modular structure. In *Proc. ACM Symp. on Principles of Programming Languages*, pages 277–286, 1986.

[Mil78]   R. Milner. A theory of type polymorphism in programming. *Journal of Computer and System Sciences*, 17:348–375, 1978.

[MMM91]   J. Mitchell, S. Meldal, and N. Madhav. An extension of Standard ML modules with subtyping and inheritance. In *Proc. ACM Symp. on Principles of Programming Languages*, pages 270–278, 1991.

[MP85]   J. C. Mitchell and G. D. Plotkin. Abstract types have existential types. *ACM Transaction on Programming Languages and Systems*, 10(3):470–520, 1988.

[OB88]   A. Ohori and P. Buneman. Type inference in a database programming language. In *Proc. ACM Conf. on LISP and Functional Programming*, pages 174–183, 1988.

[OBBT89]   A. Ohori, P. Buneman, and V. Breazu-Tannen. Database programming in Machiavelli—a polymorphic language with static type inference. In *Proc. ACM SIGMOD Conference*, pages 46–57, 1989.

[Oho89a]   A. Ohori. A simple semantics for ML polymorphism. In *Proc. ACM Conf. on Functional Programming Languages and Computer Architecture*, pages 281–292, 1989.

[Oho89b]   A. Ohori. *A Study of Types, Semantics and Languages for Databases and Object-oriented Programming*. PhD thesis, University of Pennsylvania, 1989.

[Oho90]   A. Ohori. Semantics of types for database objects. *Theoretical Computer Science*, 76:53–91, 1990.

[Plo75]   G. Plotkin. Call-by-name, call-by-value, and the λ-calculus. *Theoretical Computer Science*, 1:125–159, 1975.

[Rem89]   D. Rémy. Typechecking records and variants in a natural extension of ML. In *Proc. ACM Symp. on Principles of Programming Languages*, pages 242–249, 1989.

[Rem92]   D. Rémy. Typing record concatenation for free. In Proc. ACM Symp. on Principles of Programming Languages, pages 166–176, 1992.

[Sta88]   R. Stansifer. Type inference with subtypes. In *Proc. ACM Symp. on Principles of Programming Languages*, pages 88–97, 1988.

[Tof88]   M. Tofte. *Operational Semantics and Polymorphic Type Inference*. PhD thesis, Department of Computer Science, University of Edinburgh, 1988.

[Tur85]   D. A. Turner. Miranda: A non-strict functional language with polymorphic types. In *Functional Programming Languages and Computer Architecture, Lecture Notes in Computer Science 201*, pages 1–16. Springer-Verlag, 1985.

[Wan87]   M. Wand. Complete type inference for simple objects. In *Proc. Symp. on Logic in Computer Science*, pages 37–44, 1987.

[Wan88]   M. Wand. Corrigendum: Complete type inference for simple object. In *Proc. Symp. on Logic in Computer Science*, 1988.

[Wan89]   M. Wand. Type inference for records concatenation and simple objects. In *Proc. Symp. on Logic in Computer Science*, pages 92–97, 1989.

III COHERENCE

6 A Modest Model of Records, Inheritance, and Bounded Quantification

Kim B. Bruce and Giuseppe Longo

1 Introduction

Over the last several years there has been growing interest in object-oriented languages in the programming languages community, and this interest has spread to other technical communities such as those in software engineering and data base. (*Note.* In this paper we consider object-oriented languages to be those which include support for inheritance on subtypes.) Simula 67 (Birtwistle *et al.*, 1973) and Smalltalk (Goldberg and Robson, 1983) in their various incarnations represent the earliest work on object-oriented languages. More recently other languages have been developed including C++ (Stroustrup, 1986) and VBase (Andrews and Harris, 1986) (both based on C), Flavors (Weinreb and Moon, 1981) and LOOPS (Bobrow and Stefik, 1982) (extensions of LISP), OWL (Schaffert *et al.*, 1986) (based on Clu), and Eiffel (Meyer, 1988).

Cardelli (1988) (an earlier version of which appeared in 1984) developed one of the earliest formal approaches to inheritance, introducing both the syntax and semantics of an extension of the classical typed lambda calculus supporting inheritance. Building on some earlier work on type containment by Mitchell (1988), Cardelli and Wegner (1985) (from now on CW, 1985) presented an extension of the second-order lambda calculus supporting inheritance. This language supported both parametric and subtype (inheritance) polymorphism by means of bounded quantification. We will use the notation introduced by CW (1985), including their name for the language, Bounded Fun.

The formal definition of subtype, based on the notion of inheritance, is based on the intuition that if a function may be applied to an argument of type τ then it should make sense to apply it (in some natural way) to an argument of type σ, for $\sigma \leq \tau$. In particular, suppose that σ and τ are record types, and that σ contains all of the same fields as τ (each with the same type as the corresponding field in τ), with possibly some extra fields. Then $\sigma \leq \tau$, since any function which can be applied to an argument of type τ only depends on the fact that the argument has particular fields which appear in τ. Having extra fields causes no difficulty, so conceptually it makes sense to apply this function to elements of type σ as well. The point now is to give a precise mathematical meaning to this, in particular in the context of higher order languages.

First appeared in *Information and Computation* 87(1990), pages 196–240. © Academic Press, Inc., 1 East First Street, Duluth, MN 55802.

In Bounded Fun, we use **fun** $(x : \sigma)$. **e** to denote a function which takes an argument of type σ, **all t . e** to denote a function which takes a type parameter, and **all t $\leq$ τ . e** to denote a function which takes a type parameter which is restricted to be a subtype of τ. The following example will give the flavor of the language.

Let τ be a record type with (at least) fields "elts" and "$<$," where "elts" has type "Array of t" and "$<$" has type $t \times t \to$ bool, for some type t. Let fun$(u : \tau)$. e be a term which, when given input $u : \tau$, sorts the array in the field "elts" and leaves the output unchanged in the other fields. This program may work on all "sortable" records; that is, on all records which contain (at least) the fields "elts" and "$<$." Formally, let

sortable_rec(t) = (elts : Array of t, $<$: $t \times t \to$ Bool).

Then fun$(u : \tau)$. e would work on any $u : \tau$ provided that $\tau \leq$ sortable_rec(t), for some t. The following polymorphic function will perform a sort on any "sortable" record:

sort = all t . all $s \leq$ sortable_rec(t) . fun$(u : s)$. e.

If we wish to apply sort to a record u_0 of record type

σ = (elts : Array of Int, $<$: Int $\times$ Int $\to$ Bool, ...),

we simply write sort[Int][σ](u_0). Thus one can imagine writing quite powerful and expressive programs in this extension of the typed λ-calculus (although, see Section 6), where functions can be applied to elements, to types, and even to restricted collections of types (see CW, 1985, for further examples). Languages in which these type parameters may be omitted may be understood as abbreviations of Bounded Fun. Thus the results in this paper can be seen to be quite general.

Mitchell (1988) was primarily concerned with type inference in a similar language, while (CW, 1985) is an exposition of various extensions of the lambda calculus, including those supporting polymorphism and inheritance. In both Cardelli (1988) and CW (1985), the authors suggest that the semantics of these languages may be understood in terms of the ideal model developed by MacQueen, Plotkin, and Sethi (1984). In these models, types are interpreted as ideals in a cpo (complete partial order) which is rich enough to model all of the data types of the model. These ideal models were originally developed to model languages like ML. Ideal models are models of the untyped lambda calculus with an associated type inference scheme to infer possible types for terms. Unfortunately these models are not sound for the typed lambda calculus (and extensions) because of the failure of weak extensionality (see Bruce *et al.*, 1990 for further discussion). Also, they do not give meaning to either polymorphic application (applying a term to a type) or second-order terms.

This paper originated in an attempt to formulate a sound model for Bounded Fun. Bruce and Wegner (1990) present an abstract model of inheritance based on algebraic models. Our definition of a model for Bounded Fun integrates those ideas with the model definition for the second-order lambda calculus given in Bruce *et al.* (1990). In particular, this new definition models the notion of subtype by the existence of a "natural coercer" from the type to a supertype. Thus if an expression, e, of type $A \leq B$ is used in a context where an element of type B is expected, the meaning of e in type A can be coerced to an element of type B. Given the general definition, the principal aim of this paper is to provide a concrete model for Bounded Fun. This model is based on the per (partial equivalence relation) model for the second-order lambda calculus. (*Note.* The sets involved in these models are sometimes called *Modest* sets and are the objects of the category **M** below.)

These models have a long and complex history involving successive inventions (and reinventions) of concepts by Troëlstra (1972), Girard (1972), and most recently by Moggi (1986). Subsequently important contributions have been made by Mitchell (1986), Breazu-Tannen and Coquand (1987), and others. More recent work investigating the connection of this work to category theory and intuitionism includes Hyland (1988), Hyland *et al.* (1990), Hyland and Pitts (1987), Carboni *et al.* (1987), Pitts (1987), Longo (1988), and Longo and Moggi (1991).

In this new model, types are interpreted as partial equivalence relations (relations which are symmetric and transitive, but not necessarily reflexive) over ω. The set of elements of a type, A, is the set of equivalence classes of A, $Q(A) = \{\{n\}_A | nAn\}$, where $\{n\}_A = \{m | mAn\}$.

In object-oriented programming languages, subtypes usually arise in two principal ways:

(i) The elements of a subtype form a subset of the supertype.

(ii) In record types, the subtype has all of the fields of the supertype, with possibly more fields.

Note that when these are combined, more complex combinations are possible.

These two aspects of subtypes are captured easily by partial equivalence relations (pers). If fewer elements are desired, simply throw away some equivalence classes (it is a *partial* equivalence relation, after all). In case (ii), the argument is a bit more· subtle. If $A \leq B$ because it has more fields, then A can make finer distictions than B (since element of A contain more information than elements of B). This can be modelled by making the per for A a refinement of B. Thus if m and n are related according to A, they must be related according to B. Conversely, if m is distinguishable from n in B, then it is still distinguishable in A. Nevertheless, we may have m unrelated to n via A, but related according to the more limited information available to B.

Amazingly, both of these notions (of throwing away equivalence classes and taking refinements of partial equivalence relations) correspond to the per of the subtype being a subset of the per of the supertype. That is, we will define $A \leq B$ iff $A \subseteq B$ (when each is looked at as a set of ordered pairs). Note, however, that since the elements of types A and B are equivalence classes, it will typically *not* be the case that the set of elements of type A is a subset of the set of elements of type B. In particular, this will fail when A is a proper refinement of B. The "natural coercer" from A to B referred to earlier is the natural map which takes the element $\{n\}_A$ of type A to $\{n\}_B$ of type B, where $\{n\}_A$ is the equivalence class of n in A.

In the earlier presentations of the per models, polymorphic types were presented as intersections of their instantiations. E.g., $[\![\forall t . t \to t]\!]\eta = \bigcap_{A \in \text{Type}} (A \to A)$. Following the category theoretic approach mentioned above, a more natural interpretation as "indexed products" may be given, which turns out to be isomorphic to the intersection interpretation. In terms of the previous example, one has

$$[\![\forall t . t \to t]\!]\eta = \left[\prod_{A \in \text{Type}} (A \to A) \right]_{\mathbf{M}} \cong \bigcap_{A \in \text{type}} (A \to A),$$

for $[\prod_{A \in \text{Type}} (A \to A)]_{\mathbf{M}}$ as defined in Section 5 (see Longo and Moggi, 1991, for details and category theoretic justifications). Also records are interpreted by "indexed products," since they may be viewed as dependent types (Section 3). By this, the approach we propose unifies the mathematical understanding of polymorphic, dependent, and record types.

The key point with the semantics below is its simplicity and its "set-theoretic" flavor. Indeed, we can give a very simple interpretation of records and inheritance for a polymorphic language, since we (implicitly) work in (a model of) intuitionistic set theory. The model, Hyland's Effective Topos, is hidden in the background of our elementary treatment but gives it structural significance and the ultimate motivation (see Pitts, 1987; Longo and Moggi, 1991).

The paper begins with a brief introduction to the typed lambda calculus with records and subtypes in Section 2. This language is a slight simplification of that given in Cardelli (1988). In Section 3 we show informally how to construct a model of this language from partial equivalence relations. It is our hope that this informal introduction will provide the reader with a solid intuition on which to base the study of the more complex language, Bounded Fun.

In Section 4 we begin by presenting the syntax and semantics of Minimal Bounded Fun. Minimal Bounded Fun is essentially a weakening of the usual Bounded Fun by dropping the "subsumption" rule from the type inference system. We then introduce an extension of the language obtained by adding a constant, **convert**, and appropriate rules to ensure that this constant is interpreted as a well-behaved coercion function. Technical results about terms with the same "erasures" in this language allow us to use models of this richer language to interpret Bounded Fun. In Section 5 we introduce ω-sets and show how to construct a model for Bounded Fun by using the ω-sets to interpret kinds, and modest sets (pers) to model the types of the language. In Section 6 we discuss problems with Bounded Fun that have appeared as a result of examining this model and possible directions for future work to improve the language. Section 7 provides a summary of the paper and places it within the context of other recent work.

2   The Typed Lambda Calculus with Records and Subtypes

In this section we present an informal overview of the typed lambda calculus with records and subtypes. We presume that the reader is familiar with the syntax and semantics of the classical typed lambda calculus. As a brief reminder, we note that we will write fun $(x:\sigma).\,e$ for the function with body e and formal parameter x of type σ. (ee') will denote function application as usual. We write $e:\tau$ to indicate that e has type τ. The material in this section is adapted from CW (1985).

We begin by introducing record types.

2.1   DEFINITION   Let L be a set of labels or identifiers.

(i) $(I_1:A_1,\ldots,I_n:A_n)$ is a **record type** if $A_1,\ldots,A_n$ are types and $I_1,\ldots,I_n$ are in L;

(ii) $(I_1=a_1,\ldots,I_n=a_n):(I_1:A_1,\ldots,I_n:A_n)$ if $a_1:A_1,\ldots,$ and $a_n:A_n$.

For example:

$car\_type = (make:string, model:string, year:int)$

is a record type and

$my\_car = (make=Fiat, model=Panda, year=1986)$

is a record of type car_type.

Thus a record type is a finite set of associations of identifiers (corresponding to the fields of the record) with types. Its elements are functions from the set of (component) identifiers to types such that each identifier is sent to an element of the corresponding type. More formally,

$f \in \llbracket (I_1 : A_1, \ldots, I_n : A_n) \rrbracket \eta$ iff for all $1 \leq i \leq n,$ $f(\llbracket I_i \rrbracket \eta) \in \llbracket A_i \rrbracket \eta.$

For example, the interpretation $\llbracket my\_car \rrbracket \eta$ of the record my_car above is the function, f, such that

$f(\llbracket \text{make} \rrbracket \eta) = \llbracket \text{Fiat} \rrbracket \eta \in \llbracket \text{String} \rrbracket \eta,$

$f(\llbracket \text{model} \rrbracket \eta) = \llbracket \text{Panda} \rrbracket \eta \in \llbracket \text{String} \rrbracket \eta,$

$f(\llbracket \text{year} \rrbracket \eta) = \llbracket 1986 \rrbracket \eta \in \llbracket \text{Int} \rrbracket \eta.$

As mentioned in the Introduction, subtypes are used in object-oriented programming languages such as Smalltalk, $C++$, Owl, etc., as a way of allowing subtypes to inherit operations from their supertypes (see Bruce and Wegner, 1987, for a more complete discussion of inheritance in terms of behavioral compatibility).

In this context, we will characterize $A \leq B$ by the existence of a "natural" coercion function which takes elements of A to elements of B. Thus if $\text{coerce}_{A,B}$ is such a coercion function and $f : B \to C$, then f can be applied to an element a of A by computing $f(\text{coerce}_{A,B}(a))$. In the modest model in this paper, $\text{coerce}_{A,B}$ will be a very natural (although not necessarily injective) function (see Section 3 and Remark 5.2.2). Depending on the language design, one can make these coercion functions part of the language (requiring them to appear explicitly in computations) or let a type-checker infer them where necessary. Whichever way is chosen, one may use the system given below to infer type inclusions.

2.2   DEFINITION   An inequality of the form $\sigma \leq \tau$, where σ, τ are type expressions, is said to be a **type constraint**. If, moreover, t is a type variable then we say $t \leq \tau$ is a **simple type constraint** which declares t. If $t \leq \tau$ is included in a set C of simple type constraints then we say t is **declared** in C. A **type constraint system** is defined as follows:

(i)   The empty set is a type constraint system.

(ii)   If C is a type constraint system and $t \leq \tau$ is a simple type constraint such that t is not declared in C and such that every free variable in τ is declared in C, then $C \cup \{t \leq \tau\}$ is a type constraint system.[1]

Define type constraint derivations of the form $C \vdash \sigma \leq \tau$, for C a type constraint system and σ, τ type expressions, from the following set of axioms and rules:

Type Constraint Axioms

$$C \cup \{t \leq \tau\} \vdash t \leq \tau$$

$$C \vdash \tau \leq \tau$$

Type Constraint Rules

$$\frac{C \vdash \rho \leq \sigma, C \vdash \sigma \leq \tau}{C \vdash \rho \leq \tau}$$

$$\frac{C \vdash \sigma' \leq \sigma, C \vdash \tau \leq \tau'}{C \vdash \sigma \to \tau \leq \sigma' \to \tau'}$$

$$\frac{\text{For all } 1 \leq j \leq m, C \vdash \sigma_j \leq \tau_j}{C \vdash (I_1 : \sigma_1, \ldots, I_m : \sigma_m, \ldots, I_n : \sigma_n) \leq (I_1 : \tau_1, \ldots, I_m : \tau_m)} \quad \text{for } m \leq n.$$

The type assignment axioms for this language are only slightly more complex than for the simple typed lambda calculus. In this section we will work in a language where the coercion from a subtype to a type is handled implicitly. In the higher order case discussed later, we will handle this explicitly. A syntactic type assignment, A, is a finite set of the form

$$A = \{x_1 : \tau_1, \ldots, x_n : \tau_n\}$$

with no variable x_i appearing more than once in A. Define type assignment derivations of the form $C, A \vdash e : \sigma$, for C a type constraint system, A a syntactic type assignment, e a term of the typed lambda calculus, and σ a type, from the following set of axioms and rules:

Type Assignment Axioms

$$C, A \cup \{x : \tau\} \vdash x : \tau$$

$$C, A \vdash c^\tau : \tau \quad \text{(where } c^\tau \text{ is a typed constant of type } \tau\text{)}.$$

Type Assignment Rules

$$\frac{C, A \cup \{x : \sigma\} \vdash e : \tau}{C, A \vdash \text{fun}(x : \sigma). e : \sigma \to \tau}$$

$$\frac{C, A \vdash e : \sigma \to \tau, C, A \vdash e' : \sigma}{C, A \vdash (ee') : \tau}$$

$$\frac{C, A \vdash e_i : \tau_i \quad \text{for } i = 1, \ldots, n}{C, A \vdash (I_1 = e_1, \ldots, I_n = e_n) : (I_1 : \tau_1, \ldots, I_n : \tau_n)}$$

$$\frac{C, A \vdash e : (I_1 : \tau_1, \ldots, I_n : \tau_n)}{C, A \vdash e . I_i : \tau_i} \quad \text{for } i = 1, \ldots, n. \tag{rec}$$

The legal terms of the language with respect to a collection of simple type constraints C and syntactic type assignment A are those terms e of the language for which there is a type expression τ such that $C, A \vdash e : \tau$. We will only provide a semantics for the legal terms (with respect to some C, A).

The rules above will form the first order core of the language Minimal Bounded Fun (see Section 4.3). That language will be extended into two relevant languages, for the purposes of our discussion. They will differ in the formal description of a crucial phenomenon: how to consider a term with a given type as a member of a larger type (this is related to the notions of subtype and inheritance in object-oriented languages). Indeed, Bounded Fun formalizes this aspect by extending Minimal Bounded Fun by the following **subsumption** rule:

$$\frac{C, A \vdash e : \sigma, \, C \vdash \sigma \leq \tau}{C, A \vdash e : \tau} . \tag{sub}$$

The natural coercion functions discussed above allow one to create models in which the rule (sub) above is sound in a weak sense, i.e., by coercing the meaning of e from an element of the type σ to an element of type τ (see Sections 3 and 5). These will be the models of Coerced Bounded Fun, the other extension of Minimal Bounded Fun, where (sub) is replaced by a formal description of this weak sense, via coercions. It will be important to note that this "natural" coercer need not be exactly the identity function. We will see this in the **PER** model discussed below, where this coercer is derived naturally from the identity function, but is not itself the identity (or even injective). However, by this understanding of (sub), it will be also possible to give meaning to (sub) in the stronger (or literal) sense, as described at the end of Section 4.

We note here that Reynolds (1980) seems to be the earliest author to consider the use of non-injective maps to model coercions in computer science. He used these coercions to examine the use of implicit conversions and generic (overloaded) operators from a category-theoretic point of view. He argues that these implicit conversions should behave as homomorphisms with respect to generic operators. Bruce and Wegner (1990) introduce a similar use of coercions to model subtype and inheritance in providing an algebraic model of subtypes and inheritance. This latter paper provided the starting point for the approach in this paper.

3 PER Models

In this section we present the fundamental ideas behind a semantics of the language described in Section 2. The point of this section is to introduce the use of pers as a model of the type structure of a language, with special emphasis on how pers can be used to model subtypes. Since this section is primarily intended to provide an intuitive introduction to the ideas used in more complex settings later in the paper, no attempt is made to carefully specify the formal semantics of terms here. This is done in great detail in Sections 4 and 5.

Let $(\omega, \cdot)$ be Kleene's applicative structure, i.e., $n \cdot p$ is the nth partial recursive function applied to p. Recall that A is a per on ω iff A is a symmetric and transitive binary relation on ω. If A is a per, let $\text{dom}(A) = \{n \,|\, nAn\}$. Notice that A is a (total) equivalence relation on $\text{dom}(A)$. For $n \in \text{dom}(A)$, let $\{n\}_A$ be the equivalence class of n with respect to A. Let $Q(A) = \{\{n\}_A \,|\, n \in \text{dom}(A)\}$, the **quotient set** of ω with respect to A.

3.1 DEFINITION   The category **PER** (of partial equivalence relations on ω) has as

objects: $A \in$ **PER** iff A is a symmetric and transitive relation on ω.

morphisms: $f \in$ **PER**$[A, B]$ iff $f : Q(A) \to Q(B)$ and

$$\exists n \forall p (pAp \Rightarrow f(\{p\}_A) = \{n \cdot p\}_B).$$

Morphisms in **PER** are "computable" in the sense that they are fully described by partial recursive functions which are total on the domain of the source relation. A is a **discrete** per if for all $n \in \text{dom}(A)$, $\{n\}_A$ is the singleton set $\{n\}$.

The types of our model will be partial equivalence relations. If A is a type (per) then the set of elements of type A is given by $Q(A)$. That is, the elements of a type A are equivalence classes with respect to A.

In order to interpret types correctly we must indicate how to interpret arrow and record types.

Function Spaces   Let A, B, be pers. Define $A \to B$ to be the per such that:

$$\forall m, n, m(A \to B)n \Leftrightarrow \forall p, q(pAq \Rightarrow m \cdot pBn \cdot q).$$

If $n \in \text{dom}(A \to B)$, $\{n\}_{(A \to B)} \in Q(A \to B)$ "represents" a function f from $Q(A)$ to $Q(B)$ such that for all $\{p\}_A \in Q(A)$, $f(\{p\}_A) = \{n \cdot p\}_B$. That is, n represents a function on ω which preserves equivalence classes of A.

Record Spaces   Let $D = \{d_j \,|\, j \in J\}$ be a set of natural numbers indexed by elements of a set J. By a slight abuse of notation, we will also use D to denote the discrete per with domain D. Let C_j, for $j \in J$, be objects of PER. Define then

$$m\left[\prod_D C_j\right]n \Leftrightarrow \forall j \in J \quad (m \cdot d_j)C_j(n \cdot d_j).$$

As for function spaces, if $n \in \text{dom}([\prod_D C_j])$, $\{n\}_A$ "represents" a function f from D to $\bigcup_{j \in J} Q(C_j)$ such that for all $d_j \in D$, $f(d_j) = \{n \cdot d_j\}_{C_j}$. Note that since D, as a per, is discrete, the above definition can be taken as a simple generalization of the definition for function spaces (more on this in Section 5.2).

3.2 *Remark* $\text{Dom}[\prod_D C_j] = \bigcap_{j \in J}\{n|(n \cdot d_j)C_j(n \cdot d_j)\} = \{n|\forall j \in J \ (n \cdot d_j)C_j(n \cdot d_j)\}$
$= \{n|\forall j \in J \ (n \cdot d_j) \in \text{dom}(C_j)\}$.

The arrow types are interpreted over **PER** by function spaces, as usual. For record types, let $D = \{d_j | j \in J\}$ be the interpretation of the labels in $L' = \{l_j | j \in J\}$. Then, given a record type $A = (l_1 : A_1, \ldots, l_k : A_k)$, such that the interpretation of each A_j in **PER** is C_j, define the interpretation of A to be $[\prod_D C_j]$ (see Section 5 to understand this as a dependent or indexed product).

The subtype relation is interpreted as follows.

3.3 DEFINITION   Given objects B and C in **PER**, define $B \leq C$ by $B \subseteq C$ as sets of ordered pairs. I.e., for all m, n, if mBn then mCn.

Equivalently, $B \leq C$ iff for all $n \in \text{dom}(B)$, $\{n\}_B \subseteq \{n\}_C$. In other words, the partial partition of ω given by B is "finer" than the partial partition given by C. It is interesting to note that even though subtype is defined in terms of subset of pers represented as ordered pairs, the set of elements of the subtype B is *not* a subset of the set of elements of the supertype C. In particular, if $\{n\}_B \in Q(B)$, then the "natural" coercer from B to C mentioned in Section 2 takes $\{n\}_B$ to $\{n\}_C$, where, as noted above, $\{n\}_B \subseteq \{n\}_C$. Clearly, $\{n\}_C$ is unique; thus, one may define $\text{coerce}_{BC}: B \to C$ by

$$\text{coerce}_{B,C}(\{n\}_B) = \{n\}_C.$$

Notice that $\text{coerce}_{B,C}$ is actually a morphism in **PER**, as it is computed by any index (program) for the identity function. This fact makes it "natural" as a non-injective "embedding."

In the Introduction we provided some intuition as to why this definition of subtype is very natural. We need now to prove that the inference rules in Section 2 are sound with respect to this interpretation. The following theorem takes care of the non-trivial type constraint rules, in particular for function spaces and records (the last of which would fail if records were interpreted as ordinary products).

3.4 THEOREM

(i) $C' \le C$ and $E \le E'$ imply $C \to E \le C' \to E'$.

(ii) If $D' = \{d_i | i \in I\} \subseteq D = \{d_j | j \in J\}$, such that $\forall i \in I$, $C_i \le C'_i$, then

$$\left[\prod_D C_j \right] \le \left[\prod_{D'} C'_i \right].$$

Proof

(i) $\forall m$, n, $m(C \to E)n \Leftrightarrow \forall p,q(pCq \Rightarrow (m \cdot p)E(n \cdot q)) \Rightarrow \forall p,q(pC'q \Rightarrow (m \cdot p)E'(n \cdot q)) \Leftrightarrow m(C' \to E')n$.

(ii) $m[\prod_D C_j]n \Leftrightarrow \forall j \in J(m \cdot d_j)C_j(n \cdot d_j) \Rightarrow \forall i \in I(m \cdot d_i)C'_i(n \cdot d_i) \Leftrightarrow m[\prod_{D'} C'_i]n$. ■

The result also follows from Theorem 5.2.3 in Section 5.

One may also give a formal definition of the meaning of terms and show that the type assignment axioms and rules are sound. As for the rules, note that (sub) is not quite sound as it is. One has to use coercions, i.e., $b : B \le C$ implies, for $b = \{n\}_B$, $\text{coerce}_{BC}(\{n\}_B) = \{n\}_C$ which is an element of type C.

As for the other rules, they are interpreted as in the usual quotient-set semantics of typed λ-calculus. Details will be given in Sections 4 and 6. Briefly, $e \cdot e' : \tau$ is described as the application of two equivalence classes, $\{n\}_{B \to C}$ and $\{m\}_B$, say, by setting

$$\{n\}_{B \to C} \cdot \{m\}_B = \{n \cdot m\}_C.$$

Fun $(x : \sigma) . e : \sigma \to \tau$ is interpreted as a morphism between the two types, or, more precisely, as the equivalence class of indices of its computations.

Now that we have completed an informal survey of the per-based semantics of this first-order typed language, in the next section we begin a more formal and complete examination of the syntax and semantics of the more complex language Bounded Fun.

4   Syntax and Semantics of Bounded Fun

In this section we develop the formal syntax and semantics of the language Bounded Fun described in CW (1985). Bounded Fun is an extension of the second-order lambda calculus (itself invented independently by Girard, 1972, and Reynolds, 1974), which supports subtypes and inheritance. Readers are referred to CW (1985) for examples of the expressibility of that language. The language defined here is modified slightly from the presentation in CW (1985). The definition of the models of this language is based on that for the second-order lambda calculus given in Bruce *et al.* (1990). The presentation, thus, has an elementary set-theoretic flavor, which avoids the difficulties (and depth) of the categorical approaches at the price of some technicalities. We believe that this may be more appealing to most computer scientists. For informative categorical approaches, based on relevant categorical structures, one should consult the work of Seely (1986) and Moggi (see Asperti and Longo, 1989).

In Sections 4.1 and 4.2 we develop the syntax and semantics of the language without the rule (sub) introduced in Section 2. We will call this language Minimal Bounded Fun. In Section 4.3 we introduce an extension of the language with a constant **convert** and axioms and rules which govern its behavior. We call this language Coerced Bounded Fun. Finally, we introduce the semantics of the usual Bounded Fun (i.e., Minimal Bounded Fun with the added rule (sub)) by relating it to that of Coerced Bounded Fun.

4.1   The Syntax of Minimal Bounded Fun

We begin with a description of the language. As noted above, the only difference between the language introduced in this section and usual Bounded Fun is the omission of the type inference rule (sub). In Section 4.3, we return to the original system.

We note that the definitions of kind expressions and constructor expressions are mutually recursive, since type expressions (a subset of the constructor expressions) appear in kind expressions. We use the notation $e[a/v]$ to denote the expression formed by replacing all free occurrences of v in e by a (where the names of bound variables of e are changed where necessary to avoid capturing free variables of a). The formal definition is left as an exercise to the reader.

Kind Expressions   In the following the reader should think of T as representing the collection of all types, and for each type τ, $T_{\leq}\tau$ as the set of all types less than or equal to τ. Let L be a countable collection of labels, $\{I_1, I_2, \ldots\}$, and for each $s \subseteq \omega$, let $L_s = \{I_j | j \in s\}$. Other kind expressions will denote other classes of higher order objects such as functions from one kind to another and functions from types to kinds.

The set of all **kind expressions**, κ, is defined as follows:

$$\kappa ::= T \,|\, T_{\leq}\tau \,|\, L_s \,|\, \kappa_1 \Rightarrow \kappa_2 \left| \prod_{t:T} \kappa, \right.$$

where T and $T_{\leq}$ are special symbols, τ is a type expression (the definition of type expressions is given below), t is a constructor variable of kind T (i.e., a type variable—see below), and $s \subseteq \omega$.

Constructor Expressions   Constructor expressions are used to build objects of various kinds. The most commonly used constructor expressions are those which are used to construct new types from other types or functions on types. Examples are given after the definition.

Let $\mathscr{C}_{cst}$ be a collection of constructor constant symbols, with associated kinds, and $\mathscr{V}_{cst}$ be an infinite collection of constructor variable symbols, with associated kinds. Read $\mu : \kappa$ as μ is a constructor expression of kind κ. The **constructor expressions** (with their associated kinds) are defined as follows:

(i) $c^\kappa : \kappa$ for $c^\kappa \in \mathscr{C}_{cst}$, $v^\kappa : \kappa$ for $v^\kappa \in \mathscr{V}_{cst}$.

(ii)   If $\mu : \kappa \Rightarrow \kappa'$, $v : \kappa$ then $(\mu v) : \kappa'$.

(iii)   If $\mu : \prod_{t:T} \kappa$, $\rho : T$ then $(\mu\rho) : \kappa[\rho/t]$.

(iv)   If $\mu : \kappa'$ then $\lambda v^\kappa . \mu : \kappa \Rightarrow \kappa'$, if v^κ does not occur free in κ'.

(v)   If $\mu : \kappa$ then $\pi t . \mu : \prod_{t:T} \kappa$, if $t \in \mathscr{V}_{cst}$, $t : T$.

(vi)   If $j \in s \subseteq \omega$ then $I_j : L_s$.

We will say that $\tau : T$ is a **type expression**. We will assume that there are an infinite number of constant constructor symbols in our language. These must include:

(i) $\rightarrow : T \Rightarrow (T \Rightarrow T)$ (written in infix style).

(ii) $\forall : (T \Rightarrow T) \Rightarrow T$, and $\forall_\le : \prod_{t:T} ((T_\le t \Rightarrow T) \Rightarrow T)$.

(Note that we will usually write $\forall t . \sigma$, rather than $\forall (\lambda t^T . \sigma)$, and $\forall t \le \tau . \sigma$, rather than $(\forall_\le \tau)(\lambda t^{T_{\le \tau}} . \sigma)$.)

(iii)   For each finite $s \subseteq \omega$, a constructor, $R_s : (L_s \Rightarrow T) \Rightarrow T$.

If $L_s = \{J_1, \ldots, J_n\}$ and $F : L_s \Rightarrow T$, where for each J_i, $F(J_i) = \tau_i$, then $R_s F$ will usually be written $(J_1 : \tau_1, \ldots, J_n : \tau_n)$, as in Section 2.

Although we have not specified it here, we presume that there is a mechanism in the language to specify all functions in $L_s \Rightarrow T$ for each finite $s \subseteq \omega$. For example, if $L_s = \{J_1, \ldots, J_n\}$ there might be a constructor constant $F_s : T \Rightarrow T \Rightarrow \cdots \Rightarrow T$ (where T occurs $n + 1$ times) such that $F_s \tau_1 \cdots \tau_n$ denotes the function which takes each J_k to τ_k.

If C is a collection of simple type constraints, then we can derive other type constraints using the axioms and rules in Section 2 plus the following rules:

Type Constraint Rules

$$\frac{C \vdash \sigma' \leq \sigma, \, C \cup \{t \leq \sigma'\} \vdash \tau \leq \tau' \quad \text{for } t \text{ not free in } C}{C \vdash \forall t \leq \sigma . \tau \leq \forall t \leq \sigma' . \tau'}$$

$$\frac{C \vdash \tau \leq \tau' \quad \text{for } t \text{ not free in } C}{C \vdash \forall t . \tau \leq \forall t . \tau'}.$$

Note that these are relatively straightforward generalizations of the rules for function spaces given in Section 2.

Terms We begin our description of the terms of the language by first defining pre-terms. These are expressions which may not be typeable, and hence not all of these will be meaningful in our models. Let $\mathscr{V}_{\text{term}}$ be an infinite collection of variables and $\mathscr{C}_{\text{term}}$ be a set of constants, each of the constants having a fixed closed type.

4.1.1   DEFINITION   The set **PreTerm** of pre-terms is defined by:

$$e ::= c \,|\, x \,|\, \text{fun}(x : \sigma) . e \,|\, (ee') \,|\, \text{all } t^T . e \,|\, \text{all } t^{T \leq \tau} . e \,|\, e[\sigma] \,|\, (J_1 = e_1, \ldots, J_n = e_n) \,|\, e . I,$$

where $c \in \mathscr{C}_{\text{term}}$, $x \in \mathscr{V}_{\text{term}}$, σ, τ are type expressions, and $J_1, \ldots, J_n, I$ are identifiers from L.

For simplicity we will abbreviate terms of the form all $t^T . e$ by dropping the superscript on the type variable: all $t . e$, and we abbreviate terms of the form all $t^{T \leq \tau} . e$ by dropping the superscript and writing the type constraint more explicitly: all $(t \leq \tau) . e$.

In order to determine whether pre-terms are type-correct, we must first assign types to the free variables occurring in terms. Let A be a syntactic type assignment. The type assignment axioms and rules for Minimal Bounded Fun are as in Section 2 plus the following:

Type Assignment Rules

$$\frac{C \cup \{t \leq \sigma\}, A \vdash e : \tau \quad \text{for } t \text{ not free in } A \text{ or } C}{C, A \vdash \text{all}(t \leq \sigma) . e : \forall t \leq \sigma . \tau}$$

$$\frac{C, A \vdash e : \tau \quad \text{for } t \text{ not free in } A \text{ or } C}{C, A \vdash \text{all } t . e : \forall t . \tau}$$

$$\frac{C, A \vdash e : \forall t \leq \sigma' . \tau, \, C \vdash \sigma \leq \sigma'}{C, A \vdash e[\sigma] : \tau[\sigma/t]}$$

$$\frac{C, A \vdash e : \forall t . \tau}{C, A \vdash e[\sigma] : \tau[\sigma/t]}.$$

We write $C, A \vdash_m e : \sigma$ for type inference in Minimal Bounded Fun. We say that a pre-term e is a **term** of Minimal Bounded Fun with respect to C, A if there is a type expression σ such that $C, A \vdash_m e : \sigma$. We indicate the existence of such a σ by writing $e \in MBF_{C,A}$.

The conversion axioms and rules which correspond to the operational semantics of the language are variants of the usual (α) and (β) axioms with associated rules for the typed lambda calculus. Readers who are familiar with the second-order lambda calculus, will have no trouble writing down the appropriate variants here. (Note that there is one version of each of (α) and (β) for each of the three variable binding operations). It is also easy to formulate appropriate versions of the (η) axiom for this language (this axiom guarantees that each of the kinds of functions is extensional). The model given Section 5 will also satisfy all of the (η) axioms.

4.2   The Semantics of Minimal Bounded Fun

Our definition of models for Minimal Bounded Fun is based on that of the environment models for the second-order lambda calculus given in Bruce *et al.* (1990). The main conceptual addition necessary for Minimal Bounded Fun is a partial ordering on types which satisfies the types constraint rules. Elements of record types are interpreted as functions from the field labels to elements of the corresponding types (as in Section 2), while (bounded) polymorphic functions are interpreted as functions from (bounded sets of) types to elements of the corresponding types.

Since the material in the next two sections is rather technical, the reader is strongly urged simply to skim these sections of the paper on a first reading. Section 5 should be mainly understandable with only a cursory knowledge of this section on the definition of formal models.

The semantic structures for our higher order objects, the constructor expressions, are based on the definition of models for the simple typed lambda calculus in which the kind expressions replace type expressions and the constructor expressions replace typed terms.

A **kind frame** $Kind$ for a set C_{cst} of constructor constants is a tuple

$$Kind = \left\langle \text{Kinds}, \{\text{Kind}^k | k \in \text{Kinds}\}, \{\Phi_{k,k'} | k, k' \in \text{Kinds}\}, \right.$$

$$\left. \{\Phi_f | f \in \text{Type} \rightarrow \text{Kinds}\}, I_{Kind}, \Rightarrow, \prod_{\mathbf{T}}, \leq \right\rangle,$$

where $\langle \{\text{Kind}^k | k \in \text{Kinds}\}, \{\Phi_{k,k'} | k, k' \in \in \text{Kinds}\}, I_{Kind} \rangle$ is essentially a model of the typed lambda calculus, with

(1) Kinds, a set closed under $\Rightarrow$, and $\prod_T f$ for $f \in$ Type $\to$ Kinds,

(2) Each Kind^k represents the set of all constructors with kind k,

(3) Each $\Phi_{k,k'} : \mathrm{Kind}^{k \Rightarrow k'} \to (\mathrm{Kind}^k \to \mathrm{Kind}^{k'})$ is an injection which allows each element of Kind$^{k \Rightarrow k'}$ to be interpreted as a function,

(4) For $f \in$ Type $\to$ Kinds, $\Phi_f : \mathrm{Kind}^{\prod_T f} \to (\prod_{a \in \mathrm{Type}} f(a))$ is an injection which allows each element of Kind$^{\prod_T f}$ to be interpreted as a function,

(5) I_{Kind} is a function giving the denotation of constructor and kind constants. Let T abbreviate $I_{Kind}(T)$ and Type abbreviate Kind^T. Let $T_\leq :$ Type $\to$ Kinds be defined so that for $b \in$ Type, $k = T_\leq b$ implies that Kind$^k = \{a \in \mathrm{Type} | a \leq b\}$ (such a k must exist for each b by (7) below). For $a \in$ Type, let Type$^{\leq a}$ abbreviate Kind$^{T_\leq a}$. Let $L_s = I_{Kind}(L_s)$.

(6) $\leq$ is a partial ordering on Type which satisfies:

(i) If $a' \leq a$ and $b \leq b'$ then $a \to b \leq a' \to b'$.

(ii) If $F : \mathrm{Kind}^{L_s \Rightarrow T}$, $G : \mathrm{Kind}^{L_r \Rightarrow T}$, where $r \subseteq s$, and for all $j \in r$,

$$\Phi_{L_s, T}(F)(j) \leq \Phi_{L_r, T}(G)(j), \quad \text{then } R_s F \leq R_r G.$$

(iii) If $F \in \mathrm{Kinds}^{(T_\leq n) \Rightarrow T}$, $G \in \mathrm{Kind}^{(T_\leq b') \Rightarrow T}$ such that $b' \leq b$ and for all $a \leq b'$,

$$\Phi_{T_\leq b, T}(F)(a) \leq \Phi_{T_\leq b', T}(G)(a), \quad \text{then } \forall_\leq(b)(F) \leq \forall_\leq(b')(G).$$

(iv) If $F \in \mathrm{Kind}^{T \Rightarrow T}$, $G \in \mathrm{Kind}^{T \Rightarrow T}$ such that for all $a \in$ Type,

$$\Phi_{T, T}(F)(a) \leq \Phi_{T, T}(G)(a), \quad \text{then } \forall F \leq \forall G.$$

(7) For each $b \in$ Type there is a $k \in$ Kinds such that Kind$^k = \{a \in \mathrm{Type} | a \leq b\}$.

Interpretations of constructor expressions are as for the simply typed lambda calculus. Let η be an environment which assigns constructor variables to elements of corresponding kinds in $\bigcup_{k \in \mathrm{Kinds}} \mathrm{Kind}^k$. $\eta[a/v]$ is defined as that environment which is identical to η except that it takes the value a on v. We define the meaning of kind expressions as

$[\![T]\!]\eta = T$,

$[\![T_\leq \tau]\!]\eta = T_\leq([\![\tau]\!]\eta)$,

$[\![L_s]\!]\eta = L_s$,

$[\![\kappa_1 \Rightarrow \kappa_2]\!]\eta = [\![\kappa_1]\!]\eta \Rightarrow [\![\kappa_2]\!]\eta$,

$\left[\!\left[\prod_{t:T} \kappa\right]\!\right]\eta = \prod_T (\lambda a \in T. \mathrm{Kind}^{[\![\kappa]\!]\eta[a/t]})$, and the meaning of constructor expressions as

$$\llbracket v^\kappa \rrbracket \eta = \eta(v^\kappa),$$

$$\llbracket c^\kappa \rrbracket \eta = I_{Kind}(c^\kappa), \; \llbracket I_j \rrbracket \eta = I_{Kind}(I_j)$$

$$\llbracket \mu v \rrbracket \eta = \Phi_{k,k'}(\llbracket \mu \rrbracket \eta)\llbracket v \rrbracket \eta \quad \text{for} \quad \mu : \kappa \Rightarrow \kappa', \, k = \llbracket \kappa \rrbracket \eta, \, k' = \llbracket \kappa' \rrbracket \eta,$$

$$\llbracket \mu \rho \rrbracket \eta = \Phi_f(\llbracket \mu \rrbracket \eta)\llbracket \rho \rrbracket \eta, \quad \text{where} \quad f(a) = \llbracket \kappa \rrbracket \eta[a/t] \quad \text{for} \quad a \in Type, \, \mu : \prod_{t:T} \kappa, \, \rho : T$$

$$\llbracket \lambda v^\kappa . \mu \rrbracket \eta = \Phi_{k,k'^{-1}}(f), \quad \text{where} \quad f(a) = \llbracket \mu \rrbracket \eta[a/v^\kappa] \text{ for all}$$

$a \in Kind^k, \mu : \kappa', k = \llbracket \kappa \rrbracket \eta, k' = \llbracket \kappa' \rrbracket \eta,$

$$\llbracket \pi t . \mu \rrbracket \eta = \Phi_{f^{-1}}(g), \quad \text{where} \quad g(a) = \llbracket \mu \rrbracket \eta[a/t] \quad \text{for all } a \in Type, \, \mu : \kappa, \text{ and for}$$

$a \in Type, f(a) = \llbracket \kappa \rrbracket \eta[a/t].$

Notice that I_{Kind} must give meanings to $\rightarrow$, $\forall$, $\forall_\le$, and R_s for each $s \subseteq \omega$. For notational simplicity we use the same symbol for these syntactic objects and their meanings. We say that an environment η is **well-kinded** with respect to *Kind* if for each constructor variable, v^κ, $\eta(v^\kappa) \in Kind^{\llbracket \kappa \rrbracket \eta}$. A **kind model** for $\mathscr{C}_{cst}$ is a kind frame for $\mathscr{C}_{cst}$ in which every constructor expression has a meaning with respect to all well-kinded environments.

Environment models for Minimal Bounded Fun will be defined using kind structures to interpret kinds and constructors, with added domains to interpret the terms.

4.2.2 DEFINITION A frame F for Minimal Bounded Fun with constants from $\mathscr{C}_{cst}$ and $\mathscr{C}_{term}$ is a tuple

$$F = \langle Kind, Dom, \{\Phi_{a,b}\}, \{\Phi_F\}, \{\Phi_{F,b}\} \rangle$$

which satisfies conditions (i) through (vi) below:

(i) $Kind = \langle Kinds, \{Kind^k | k \in Kinds\}, \{\Phi_{k,k'} \in Kinds\}, \{\Phi_f | f \in Type \rightarrow Kinds\}, I_{Kind}, \Rightarrow, \prod_T, \le \rangle$ is a kind model for $\mathscr{C}_{cst}$,

(ii) $Dom = \langle \{Dom^a | a \in Type\}, I_{Dom} \rangle$, where $I_{Dom} : \mathscr{C}_{term} \rightarrow \bigcup_{a \in Type} Dom^a$ such that for each $c^\tau \in \mathscr{C}_{term}$, $I_{Dom}(c^\tau) \in Dom^{\llbracket \tau \rrbracket \eta}$,

(iii) For each $a, b \in Type$, there is a set $[Dom^a \rightarrow Dom^b]$ of functions from Dom^a to Dom^b with $\Phi_{a,b} : Dom^{a \rightarrow b} \rightarrow [Dom^a \rightarrow Dom^b]$ a bijection.

(iv) For each $F \in Kind^{T \Rightarrow T}$ and $F = \Phi_{T,T}(F)$, there is a subset $[\prod_{a \in Type} Dom^{F(a)}] \subseteq \prod_{a \in Type} Dom^{F(a)}$ with $\Phi_F : Dom^{\forall F} \rightarrow [\prod_{a \in Type} Dom^{F(a)}]$ a bijection. Here $\forall = \Phi_{T \Rightarrow T, T}(\forall)$.

(v) For each $b \in Type$ and $F \in \text{Kind}^{(T_{\leq b} \Rightarrow T)}$ and $F = \Phi_{T_{\leq b}, T}(F)$, there is a subset
$[\prod_{a \in Type^{\leq b}} \text{Dom}^{F(a)}] \subseteq \prod_{a \in Type^{\leq b}} \text{Dom}^{F(a)}$ with $\Phi_{F,b} : \text{Dom}^{\forall_{\leq b} F} \rightarrow [\prod_{a \in Type^{\leq b}}$
$\text{Dom}^{F(a)}]$ a bijection. Here $\forall_{\leq b} = \Phi_{T \Rightarrow T, T}(\forall_{\leq b})$.

(vi) For each $F \in \text{Kind}^{L_s \Rightarrow T}$ and $F = \Phi_{L_s, T}(F)$, there is a subset $[\prod_{i \in L_s} \text{Dom}^{F(i)}] \subseteq$
$\prod_{i \in L_s} \text{Dom}^{F(i)}$ with $\Phi_F : \text{Dom}^{R_s F} \rightarrow [\prod_{i \in L_s} \text{Dom}^{F(i)}]$ a bijection. Here $R_s = \Phi_{L_s \Rightarrow T, T}(R_s)$.

Condition (iii) states that $\text{Dom}^{a \rightarrow b}$ must "represent" some set $[\text{Dom}^a \rightarrow \text{Dom}^b]$ of
functions from Dom^a to Dom^b. Similarly, conditions (iv), (v), and (vi) specify that the
other complex domains must represent some appropriate collections of functions.
Note in particular that by our abbreviations, (vi) implies that $(J_1 : \tau_1, \ldots, J_n : \tau_n)$
represents a collection of functions, g, such that for $1 \leq i \leq n$, $g(I_{Kind}(J_i)) \in \text{Dom}^{[\tau_i]\eta}$.
(*We offer a note of reassurance to the reader who has made it this far. The rest of the
section is rather straightforward.*)

Frames have exactly the right structure to define the meaning of terms of Minimal
Bounded Fun. Let A be a syntactic type assignment. Let η be an environment
mapping $\mathcal{V}_{cst}$ to elements of the appropriate kinds, and $\mathcal{V}_{term}$ to elements of
$\bigcup_{a \in Type} \text{Dom}^a$. We say that η *satisfies* C, A, written $\eta \models C, A$, if $\eta(x) \in [A(x)]\eta$ for
each variable $x \in \text{dom}(A)$, and $\eta(t) \leq [\tau]\eta$ for each $t \leq \tau$ in C.

4.2.3 DEFINITION Let F be a second-order functional domain for Minimal Bounded
Fun, let A be a syntactic type assignment, and C a collection of simple type constraints. If $\eta \models C, A$ then the meanings of terms of Minimal Bounded Fun can be
defined inductively on the derivation of typings as follows:

$[C, A \vdash_m x : \tau]\eta = \eta(x)$,

$[C, A \vdash_m c^\tau : \tau]\eta = I_{Dom}(c^\tau)$,

$[C, A \vdash_m (ee') : \tau]\eta = (\Phi_{a,b}[C, A \vdash_m e : \sigma \rightarrow \tau]\eta)[C, A \vdash_m e' : \sigma]\eta$,

where $[\sigma]\eta = a$ and $[\tau]\eta = b$,

$[C, A \vdash_m \text{fun}(x : \sigma).e : \sigma \rightarrow \tau]\eta = \Phi_{a,b}^{-1}g$,

where $g(d) = [C, A \cup \{x : \sigma\} \vdash_m e : \tau]\eta[d/x]$ for all $d \in \text{Dom}^a$,

$[\sigma]\eta = a$, and $[\tau]\eta = b$,

$[C, A \vdash_m e.J_i : \tau_i]\eta = \Phi_F([C, A \vdash_m e : (J_1 : \tau_1, \ldots, J_n : \tau_n)]\eta)([J_i]\eta)$,

where $F \in \text{Kind}^{L_s \Rightarrow T}$ such that for $1 \leq i \leq n$, $\Phi_{L_s, T}(F)([J_i]\eta) = [\tau_i]\eta$,

$[\![C, A \vdash_m (J_1 = e_1, \ldots, J_n = e_n) : (J_1 : \tau_1, \ldots, J_n : \tau_n)]\!]\eta = \Phi_F^{-1} g$ where $F \in \text{Kind}^{L_s \Rightarrow T}$

such that for $1 \leq i \leq n$, $\Phi_{L_s, T}(F)([\![J_i]\!]\eta) = [\![\tau_i]\!]\eta$ and $g([\![J_i]\!]\eta) = [\![C, A \vdash_m e_i : \tau_i]\!]\eta$,

$[\![C, A \vdash_m e[\sigma] : \tau[\sigma/t]]\!]\eta = (\Phi_{F,b}[\![C, A \vdash_m e : \forall t \leq \sigma'.\tau]\!]\eta)([\![\sigma]\!]\eta)$, where

$F = [\![\lambda t^{T \leq \sigma'}.\tau]\!]\eta$ and $b = [\![\sigma']\!]\eta$,

$[\![C, A \vdash_m e[\sigma] : \tau[\sigma/t]]\!]\eta$

$= (\Phi_F[\![C, A \vdash_m e : \forall t.\tau]\!]\eta)([\![\sigma]\!]\eta)$,   where $F = [\![\lambda t.\tau]\!]\eta$,

$[\![C, A \vdash_m \text{all } (t \leq \sigma).e : \forall t \leq \sigma.\tau]\!]\eta = \Phi_{F,b}^{-1} g$, where $g(a)$

$= [\![C \cup \{t \leq \sigma\}, A \vdash_m e : \tau]\!]\eta[a/t]$ for all $a \in Type^{\leq b}$ and $F = [\![\lambda t \leq \sigma.\tau]\!]\eta$,

where $b = [\![\sigma]\!]\eta$.

$[\![C, A \vdash_m \text{all } t.e : \forall t.\tau]\!]\eta = \Phi_F^{-1} g$,

where $g(a) = [\![C, A \vdash_m e : \tau]\!]\eta[a/t]$ for all $a \in Type$ and $F = [\![\lambda t.\tau]\!]\eta$.

As the reader no doubt suspects, the semantics given in Definition 4.2.3 is independent of the particular derivation of the typing. This explains why we did not annotate terms with derivations. The following lemma, which corresponds to Lemmas 2 and 8 of Bruce *et al.* (1990), shows that the above definition is well defined. If μ, ν are constructor expressions, we write $\vdash_{con} \mu = \nu$, if the equality is provable in a proof system in which versions of the usual (α), (β), and (η) axioms and corresponding congruence rules are given for the constructor expressions.

4.2.4 LEMMA Suppose Δ_1, Δ_2 are derivations of typings C, $A \vdash_m e : \sigma$ and C, $B \vdash_m e : \tau$, respectively, and η is an environment such that:

(1) for every x free in e, $\vdash_{con} A(x) = B(x)$, and

(2) $\eta \models C, A$ and $\eta \models C, B$.

Then

(3) $\vdash_{con} \sigma = \tau$, and

(4) $[\![C, A \vdash_m e : \sigma]\!]\eta = [\![C, A \vdash_m e : \tau]\!]\eta$ (where the first term is evaluated with respect to the typing derivation Δ_1, and the second with respect to Δ_2).

When we begin with $\sigma = \tau$, we get the desired result. The proof is virtually identical to those given for Lemmas 2 and 8 in Bruce *et al.* (1988). The reader is referred to that paper for more details.

4.2.5 DEFINITION   A frame F for Minimal Bounded Fun is a model of Minimal Bounded Fun if, for all $\eta \models C, A$ and all e such that $C, A \vdash_m e : \sigma$, $[\![C, A \vdash_m e : \sigma]\!]\eta$ is defined.

It is easy to verify that every model, F, of Bounded Fun satisfies the type constraint and type assignment rules. In particular, if $\eta \models C, A$ and $C, A \vdash_m e : \tau$, then $[\![C, A \vdash_m e : \tau]\!]\eta \in \text{Dom}^{[\![\tau]\!]\eta}$. The proofs are only minor variants of the similar rules for the second-order lambda calculus in Bruce *et al.* (1990). Similarly, it is easy to verify the conversion rules (e.g., the variants of (α) and (β)).

4.3   The Semantics of the Original Bounded Fun

In this section we will provide the semantics of the original Cardelli and Wegner system with the type inference rule (sub). We will see that this introduces much greater complexity to the semantics. This complexity arises since there may be several quite distinct type derivations for the same expression. In particular there may be several distinct typing derivations which result in the assignment of the same type expression to a term. Lemma 4.2.4 becomes much more difficult to prove in the presence of rule (sub).

We choose to approach this problem indirectly by first introducing the polymorphic constant **convert**, which is used to coerce elements from subtypes to supertypes. After introducing appropriate axioms and rules to govern the behavior of this constant, we show that any typing derivation of a term in the Cardelli and Wegner system corresponds to a typing derivation of a coerced term in our system (which does not include the type inference rule (sub)). Moreover, the "erasure" of this coerced term yields the original term. Finally we show that the meaning of all coerced terms with the same "erasure" cohere in a way to be made precise later, allowing us to define the meaning of terms in the original system.

Since in Sections 4.1 and 4.2 we have omitted rule (sub) which states that the set of types of a term is closed under supertypes, it is useful to add the new polymorphic constant:

convert : $\forall t . \forall s \leq t . s \to t$.

The function of **convert** is to transform a value of type s to type t for $s \leq t$. This constant will allow us to define more flexible record selectors as follows. If I is an identifier then we can define

select_I : $\forall t . \forall s \leq (I : t) . s \to t$

by

select_I = all t . all $(s \leq (I : t))$. fun$(x : s)$. **convert** $[I : t][s]x$.

Thus one can select components of elements which are subtypes of record types.

Note that if $C, A \vdash e:\sigma$, and $C \vdash \sigma \leq \tau$, then $C, A \vdash$ **convert** $[\tau][\sigma]e:\tau$. However, we note here that it does *not* necessarily follow that for an environment η,

$$[\![C, A \vdash e:\sigma]\!]\eta = [\![C, A \vdash \textbf{convert} \ [\tau][\sigma]e:\tau]\!]\eta.$$

In particular, it does *not* follow that if $C \vdash \sigma \leq \tau$, then $[\![\sigma]\!]\eta \subseteq [\![\tau]\!]\eta$. Thus **convert** will typically have a real semantic effect.

We will now extend Minimal Bounded Fun to include the constant **convert** as well as axioms and rules to ensure that it behaves properly.

4.3.1   DEFINITION   Define Coerced Bounded Fun to be the extension of Minimal Bounded Fun obtained by adding the constant, **convert**, with type $\forall t . \forall s \leq t . s \rightarrow t$, to the language and adding the following axioms and rules:

$$\textbf{convert} \ [\sigma][\sigma] = \text{fun} \ (x:\sigma).x \tag{E1}$$

$$\frac{C \vdash \sigma \leq \tau, C \vdash \tau \leq \rho}{C, A \vdash (\textbf{convert} \ [\rho][\tau]) \circ (\textbf{convert} \ [\tau][\sigma]) = \textbf{convert} \ [\rho][\sigma]} \tag{E2}$$

$$\frac{C \vdash \sigma' \leq \sigma, \tau \leq \tau', C, A \vdash e:\sigma \rightarrow \tau}{\left(\begin{array}{l} C, A \vdash \textbf{convert} \ [\sigma' \rightarrow \tau'][\sigma \rightarrow \tau]e \\ \quad = \text{fun} \ (x:\sigma').\textbf{convert} \ [\tau'][\tau](e(\textbf{convert} \ [\sigma][\sigma']x)) \end{array}\right)} \tag{E3}$$

$$\frac{C \vdash \sigma' \leq \sigma, C \cup \{t \leq \sigma'\} \vdash \tau \leq \tau', C, A \vdash e:\forall t \leq \sigma . \tau}{\left(\begin{array}{l} C, A \vdash \textbf{convert} \ [\forall t \leq \sigma' . \tau'][\forall t \leq \sigma . \tau]e \\ \quad = \text{all} \ (t \leq \sigma').\textbf{convert} \ [\tau'][\tau](e[t]) \end{array}\right)} \tag{E4}$$

$$\frac{C \vdash \sigma' \leq \sigma, C, A \vdash e:\forall t . \tau}{C, A \vdash \textbf{convert} \ [\forall t . \tau'][\forall t . \tau]e = \text{all} \ t . \textbf{convert} \ [\tau'][\tau](e[t])} \tag{E5}$$

$$\frac{C \vdash \rho \leq \sigma \rightarrow \tau, \sigma' \leq \sigma, C, A \vdash e:\rho, e':\sigma'}{\left(\begin{array}{l} C, A \vdash (\textbf{convert} \ [\sigma \rightarrow \tau][\rho]e)(\textbf{convert} \ [\sigma][\sigma']e') \\ \quad = (\textbf{convert} \ [\sigma' \rightarrow \tau][\rho]e)e' \end{array}\right)} \tag{E6}$$

$$\frac{\left(\begin{array}{l} C \vdash \rho \leq (\forall t \leq \beta . \pi), \rho \leq (\forall t \leq \beta' . \pi'), \\ \quad \sigma \leq \beta, \sigma \leq \beta', \pi[\sigma/t] \leq \pi'[\sigma/t], C, A \vdash e:\rho \end{array}\right)}{\left(\begin{array}{l} C, A \vdash (\textbf{convert} \ [\forall t \leq \beta' . \pi'][\rho]e)[\sigma] \\ \quad = \textbf{convert} \ [\pi'[\sigma/t]][\pi[\sigma/t]]((\textbf{convert} \ [\forall t \leq \beta . \pi][\rho]e)[\sigma]) \end{array}\right)} \tag{E7}$$

$$\frac{C \vdash \rho \leq \forall t . \pi, \rho \leq \forall t . \pi', \pi[\sigma/t] \leq \pi'[\sigma/t], C, A \vdash e:\rho}{\left(\begin{array}{l} C, A \vdash (\textbf{convert} \ [\forall t . \pi'][\rho]e)[\sigma] \\ \quad = \textbf{convert} \ [\pi'[\sigma/t]][\pi[\sigma/t]]((\textbf{convert} \ [\forall t . \pi][\rho]e)[\sigma]) \end{array}\right)} \tag{E8}$$

$$\frac{C \vdash \rho_i \leq \sigma_i, C, A \vdash e_i : \rho_i, \text{ for } 1 \leq i \leq k \leq n}{\left(\begin{array}{l} C, A \vdash (\textbf{convert } [(J_1 : \sigma_1, \ldots, J_k : \sigma_k)][(J_1 : \rho_1, \ldots, J_n : \rho_n)](J_1 = e_1, \ldots, J_n = e_n)) \\ \quad = (J_1 = \textbf{convert } [\sigma_1][\rho_1]e_1, \ldots, J_k = \textbf{convert } [\sigma_k][\rho_k]e_k) \end{array}\right)} \quad (E9)$$

$$\frac{C \vdash \rho \leq \sigma, C, A \vdash e : (I : \rho)}{C, A \vdash (\textbf{convert } [\sigma][\rho]e . I) = (\textbf{convert } [(I : \sigma)][(I : \rho)]e) . I} \quad (E10)$$

$$\frac{C \vdash \rho \leq (J_1 : \sigma_1, \ldots, J_n : \sigma_n), C, A \vdash e : \rho}{C, A \vdash (\textbf{convert } [(J_1 : \sigma_1, \ldots, J_n : \sigma_n)][\rho]e) . J_k = (\textbf{convert } [(J_k : \sigma_k)][\rho]e) . J_k} \quad (E11)$$

The above axioms and rules were chosen to ensure that **convert** behaves essentially as a homomorphism (i.e., making certain diagrams commute). We do not know if these are minimal axioms for this system and would hope that (E7) and (E8) in particular could be simplified. These axioms and rules will be used in the proof of Theorem 4.3.7.

As Coerced Bounded Fun extends Minimal Bounded Fun by the constant **convert** specified by the above axioms and rules, a model for Coerced Bounded Fun is a model for Minimal Bounded Fun which has an interpretation for **convert** which satisfies its properties. The meanings of terms is as given for Minimal Bounded Fun. Note that since we have only added conversion rules rather than type inference rules, Lemma 4.2.4 still holds. We write $C, A \vdash_c e = e'$, and $C, A \vdash_c e : \sigma$ for proofs of equality and type inference in this language. Note if e is a term which contains no occurrence of **convert**, then $C, A \vdash_c e : \sigma$ iff $C, A \vdash_m e : \sigma$.

We next extend Minimal Bounded Fun in another direction: Bounded Fun is obtained from Minimal Bounded Fun by adding the subsumption rule (sub) of Section 2.

4.3.2 DEFINITION Let Bounded Fun be the system whose language, type inference, and proof system is the same as Minimal Bounded Fun, but whose type inference rules also includes the subsumption rule:

$$\frac{C \vdash \sigma \leq \tau, C, A \vdash e : \sigma}{C, A \vdash e : \tau}. \quad (\text{sub})$$

We write $C, A \vdash_{bf} e = e'$, and $C, A \vdash_{bf} e : \sigma$ for proofs of equality and type inference in this language to distinguish it from the minimal and coerced systems. We write $e \in BF_{C,A}$ if there is a σ such that $C, A \vdash_{bf} e : \sigma$.

An added difficulty in interpreting this system is that terms typically have meanings of several types. Moreover, there may be several proofs that a term has a particular type. For example, if $C \vdash \sigma \leq \tau, C, A \vdash e : \tau \to \rho$, and $C, A \vdash e' : \sigma$ then one can show that $C, A \vdash ee' : \rho$ by first inferring $C \vdash \tau \rightarrow \rho \leq \sigma \rightarrow \rho$, and then $C, A \vdash e : \sigma \rightarrow \rho$ by the subsumption rule, and finally using the rule for typing function application. Alternatively, one could infer $C, A \vdash e' : \tau$ by subsumption and then using the rule for typing function applications. Since the meaning of terms is defined by induction on the proof of typing, it is not at all clear that the meaning obtained through these different proofs are the same.

The original version of this paper, Bruce and Longo (1988), did not explicitly address this question. In Breazu-Tannen *et al.* (1991), this is taken care of by translating terms of Bounded Fun into terms of the second-order lambda calculus and then showing that all possible translations were provably equal. We subsequently decided to approach the problem in a somewhat different fashion, replacing conditions on models that appeared in the previous version of this paper by the explicit axioms on **convert** given in Definition 4.3.1 above. (We note that because of the uniformity of the coercion functions used in the specific model given in Section 5, it is obvious that all possible meanings of a term in the same type are equal.) In what follows, we show that this approach guarantees that the interpretation of a term in a particular type is independent of the proof that it has that type.

We will interpret terms of Bounded Fun as abbreviations of certain terms of Coerced Bounded Fun. We say a term of Coerced Bounded Fun is **translatable** if all occurrences of the constant **convert** appear in subterms of the form **convert** $[\sigma][\tau]e$, where σ and τ are type expressions and e is a translatable term of Coerced Bounded Fun. (This is equivalent to treating **convert** as a new term-building operator which takes three arguments, two types and the third a term. We choose this alternative approach so that we can use the model definition given in Section 4.2 without having to redo all the work in that section.)

4.3.3   DEFINITION   Let e be a translatable term of Coerced Bounded Fun. Define e_{abbrev} to be the term of Bounded Fun defined inductively as follows:

(i)   If e is a variable or constant, let $e_{\text{abbrev}} = e$.

(ii) $(ee')_{\text{abbrev}} = e'_{\text{abbrev}}$, if e is of the form **convert** $[\sigma][\tau]$,
        $= (e_{\text{abbrev}} e'_{\text{abbrev}})$, otherwise.

(iii) $(\text{fun } (x : \sigma) . e)_{\text{abbrev}} = \text{fun } (x : \sigma) . e_{\text{abbrev}}$.

(iv) $(\text{all } (t \leq \sigma) . e)_{\text{abbrev}} = \text{all } (t \leq \sigma) . e_{\text{abbrev}}$.

(vi) $(\text{all } t . e)_{\text{abbrev}} = \text{all } t . e_{\text{abbrev}}$.

(vii) $(J_1 = e_1, \ldots, J_n = e_n)_{\text{abbrev}} = (J_1 = e_{1 \text{ abbrev}}, \ldots, J_n = e_{n \text{ abbrev}})$.

(viii) $(e . J)_{\text{abbrev}} = e_{\text{abbrev}} . J$.

Thus e_{abbrev} is obtained from a translatable term e by replacing all subterms of the form **convert** $[\sigma][\tau]e'$. We say that a term e of Coerced Bounded Fun is a **fattening** of a term e' of Bounded Fun if it is translatable and $e_{abbrev} = e'$.

We now show the close connection between derivations of terms in the Coerced and usual Bounded Fun.

4.3.4 LEMMA   Let e be a translatable expression of Coerced Bounded Fun. Then, if $C, A \vdash_c e : \sigma$, one has C, $A \vdash_{bf} e_{abbrev} : \sigma$.

Proof   By induction on the complexity of the proof that $C, A \vdash_c e : \sigma$. Recall that the type inference rules of Bounded Fun contain all of those from Coerced Bounded Fun. Most of the proof is completely routine. The only interesting part is for the application rule. Suppose $C, A \vdash_c e : \sigma \to \tau$ and $C, A \vdash_c e' : \sigma$, yielding the result that $C, A \vdash_c (ee') : \tau$. Then by induction, $C, A \vdash_{bf} e_{abbrev} : \sigma \to \tau$ and $C, A \vdash_{bf} e'_{abbrev} : \sigma$.

(a) If e is of the form **convert** $[\tau][\sigma]$, then $(ee')_{abbrev} = e'_{abbrev}$ and $C \vdash \sigma \le \tau$. Thus by (sub), $C, A \vdash_{bf} e'_{abbrev} : \tau$, and $C, A \vdash_{bf} (ee')_{abbrev} : \tau$.

(b) Otherwise $(ee')_{abbrev} = (e_{abbrev} e'_{abbrev})$. Hence the result follows from the application rule. ∎

Interestingly, one can go the other direction as well.

4.3.5 LEMMA   Let e be a formula of Bounded Fun. If $C, A \vdash_{bf} e : \sigma$ then there is a translation term e' of Coerced Bounded Fun such that e' is a fattening of e and $C, A \vdash_c e' : \sigma$.

Proof e' is defined by induction on the length of the proof of $C, A \vdash_{bf} e : \sigma$. All steps but the one corresponding to the rule (sub) are trivial. Thus we present only the step for (sub) here. Suppose that $C, A \vdash_{bf} e : \sigma$ and hence by induction there is a translatable e'' such that e'' is a fattening of e and $C, A \vdash_c e'' : \sigma$. Suppose now that $C \vdash \sigma \le \tau$, and hence by (sub), $C, A \vdash_{bf} e : \tau$. Then let $e' = $ **convert** $[\tau][\sigma]e''$. Clearly e' is translatable, $e'_{abbrev} = e''_{abbrev} = e$, and $C, A \vdash_c e' : \tau$, as desired. ∎

Our goal is to provide a meaning for a term e of Bounded Fun by first constructing a translatable term e' of Coerced Bounded Fun as in Lemma 4.3.5, and then giving e the same meaning as e'. In order to show that this is well defined, we must show that all such terms of Coerced Bounded Fun have the same meaning. In fact, we will prove something stronger than this. In particular, if a term e of Bounded Fun can be given types σ and τ where $\sigma \le \tau$, then the meaning in type σ can be coerced (using **convert**) into the meaning in type τ. In order to prove the key theorem we use the following lemma due to Curien and Ghelli.

4.3.6 LEMMA (Curien and Ghelli, 1990) For all C, A, and $e \in BF_{C,A}$ there is a (provably) minimum type τ such that $C, A \vdash_{\text{bf}} e : \tau$. I.e., if $C, A \vdash_{\text{bf}} e : \tau'$, then $C \vdash \tau \leq \tau'$.

The following theorem shows that all fattenings of a term $e \in BF_{C,A}$ "cohere" nicely.

4.3.7 THEOREM For all C, A, and $e \in BF_{C,A}$, if τ is a minimum type for e with respect to C, A, then there is a fattening e' of e such that

(1) $C, A \vdash_{c} e' : \tau$, and

(2) For all fattenings e'' of e, if $C, A \vdash_{c} e'' : \tau'$, then

$C, A \vdash_{c}$ **convert** $[\tau'][\tau]e' = e''$.

Proof The proof is by induction on the structure of terms. In view of Lemma 4.3.5 we only need to prove (2), with respect to the term e' in (1).

(i) $e = x$. Let $e' = x$ and let τ be the minimum type for x as in Lemma 4.3.6. If e'' is a fattening of x, then $e'' = $ **convert** $[\tau'][\tau]x$ for some τ', and we are done. (Here and later, we implicitly use the transitivity of **convert**, i.e., rule (E2).)

(ii) $e = c$, for c a constant. Similar to above.

(iii) $e = (fk)$. Let τ be the minimum type for e, ρ be the minimum type for f, and π the minimum type for k, as in Lemma 4.3.6. By Lemma 4.3.5, the derivation that e has type τ leads to a term e' of Coerced Bounded Fun, which is a fattening of e such that $C, A \vdash_{c} e' : \tau$. By the definition of the fattening of a term, $C, A \vdash_{c} e' = $ convert $[\tau][\tau'](f''k'')$, where f'' and k'' are fattenings of f and k, respectively. Since τ is minimal, $\tau' = \tau$ and $C, A \vdash_{c} e' = (f''k'')$ (by (E1) and β-reduction). Therefore $C, A \vdash_{c} f'' : \pi' \to \tau$ and $C, A \vdash_{c} k'' : \pi'$ for some π' such that $C \vdash \pi \leq \pi'$ (the inequality follows by the minimality of π). By induction, $C, A \vdash_{c} f'' = $ **convert** $[\pi' \to \tau][\rho]f'$ and $C, A \vdash_{c} k'' = $ **convert** $[\pi'][\pi]k'$ for some f' and k' fattenings of f and k, respectively. Therefore,

$$C, A \vdash_{c} e' = (\textbf{convert } [\pi' \to \tau][\rho]f')(\textbf{convert } [\pi'][\pi]k')$$

$$= (\textbf{convert } [\pi \to \tau][\rho]f')k' \quad \text{by (E6),} \tag{$\ddagger$}$$

Suppose e'' is a fattening of e such that $C, A \vdash_{c} e'' : \tau''$. Again by the definition of fattening, $C, A \vdash_{c} e'' = $ **convert** $[\tau''][\tau'](f''k'')$, where f'' and k'' are fattenings of f and k, respectively. Let $C, A \vdash_{c} f'' : \pi'' \to \tau'$ and $C, A \vdash_{c} k'' : \pi''$ for some π'' such that $C \vdash \pi \leq \pi''$ (again the inequality follows by the minimality of π). Note that $C \vdash \tau \leq \tau'$ by Lemmas 4.3.4 and 4.3.6. By induction, $C, A \vdash_{c} f'' = $ **convert** $[\pi'' \to \tau'][\rho]f'$ and $C, A \vdash_{c} k'' = $ **convert** $[\pi''][\pi]k'$. Thus

$$C, A \vdash_c (f'' k'') = (\textbf{convert } [\pi'' \to \tau'][\rho] f')(\textbf{convert } [\pi''][\pi] k')$$

$$= (\textbf{convert } [\pi \to \tau'][\rho] f') k' \quad \text{by (E6),}$$

$$= (\textbf{convert } [\pi \to \tau'][\pi \to \tau](\textbf{convert } [\pi \to \tau][\rho] f')) k' \quad \text{by (E2),}$$

$$= \textbf{convert } [\tau'][\tau]((\textbf{convert } [\pi \to \tau][\rho] f') k') \quad \text{by (E3) and (E1),}$$

$$= \textbf{convert } [\tau'][\tau] e'. \quad \text{by (\ddag).}$$

Therefore,

$$C, A \vdash_c e'' = \textbf{convert } [\tau''][\tau'](f'' k'')$$

$$= \textbf{convert } [\tau''][\tau'](\textbf{convert } [\tau'][\tau] e') \quad \text{by above,}$$

$$= \textbf{convert } [\tau''][\tau] e'. \quad \text{by (E2).}$$

(iv) $e = \text{fun } (x : \sigma) . f$. Let τ be the minimum type for e, and let e' be the term of Coerced Bounded Fun which is a fattening of e and such that $C, A \vdash_c e' : \tau$. As in the previous case, $C, A \vdash_c e' = \textbf{convert } [\tau][\tau'](\text{fun } (x : \sigma) . f')$, where f' is a fattening of f. As before $\tau = \tau'$, so $\tau = \sigma \to \pi$ for some π, and $C, A \vdash_c e' = \text{fun } (x : \sigma) . f'$. Note that π is minimal for f with respect to $C, A \cup \{x : \sigma\}$ (otherwise τ would not be the minimum type for e).

   Suppose e'' is a fattening of e such that $C, A \vdash_c e'' : \tau''$. Again by the definition of fattening, $C, A \vdash_c e'' = \textbf{convert } [\tau''][\tau'](\text{fun } (x : \sigma) . f'')$, where f'' is a fattening of f. By induction, $C, A \vdash_c f'' = \textbf{convert } [\pi''][\pi] f'$ for some π''. Thus,

$$C, A \vdash_c e'' = \textbf{convert } [\tau''][\tau'](\text{fun } (x : \sigma) . f'')$$

$$= \textbf{convert } [\tau''][\tau'](\text{fun } (x : \sigma) . (\textbf{convert } [\pi''][\pi] f'))$$

$$= \textbf{convert } [\tau''][\tau'](\textbf{convert } [\sigma \to \pi''][\sigma \to \pi](\text{fun } (x : \sigma) . f')) \quad \text{by (E3)}$$

$$= \textbf{convert } [\tau''][\sigma \to \pi](\text{fun } (x : \sigma) . f') \quad \text{by (E2)}$$

$$\text{since } \tau' \text{ must equal } \sigma \to \pi'' \text{ for this to be typed,}$$

$$= \textbf{convert } [\tau''][\sigma \to \pi] e' \quad \text{by definition of } e'.$$

(v) $e = f[\sigma]$. Let τ be the minimum type for e and ρ be the minimum type for f, as in Lemma 4.3.6. As before we get a term e' of Coerced Bounded Fun, which is a fattening of e and such that $C, A \vdash_c e' : \tau$. By the definition of fattening, $C, A \vdash_c e' = \textbf{convert } [\tau][\tau'](f''[\sigma])$, where f'' is a fattening of f. Since τ is minimal, $\tau' = \tau$ and $C, A \vdash_c e' = f''[\sigma]$ (by (E1) and β-reduction). Here we get two cases, either (a) $C, A \vdash_c f'' : \forall t \leq \beta . \pi$, or (b) $C, A \vdash_c f'' : \forall t . \pi$ for some β, π. We investigate these in turn.

(a) Suppose $C, A \vdash_c f'' : \forall t \leq \beta . \pi$ for some β, π. Therefore $\tau = \pi[\sigma/t]$. By induction, $C, A \vdash_c f'' = \textbf{convert } [\forall t \leq \beta . \pi][\rho] f'$, where f' is a fattening of f. Therefore,

$$C, A \vdash_c e' = (\textbf{convert } [\forall t \leq \beta . \pi][\rho] f')[\sigma]. \tag{$\ddagger\ddagger$}$$

Also $C \vdash \sigma \leq \beta$, since the term is typeable.

Suppose e'' is a fattening of e such that $C, A \vdash_c e'' : \tau''$. Again by the definition of fattening, $C, A \vdash_c e'' = \textbf{convert } [\tau''][\tau'](f''[\sigma])$, where f'' is fattening of f. Let $C, A \vdash_c f'' : \forall t \leq \beta' . \pi'$. Thus $C \vdash \sigma \leq \beta$ and $C \vdash \pi[\sigma/t] \leq \pi'[\sigma/t]$ (again the inequality follows by the minimality of τ). Note that $C \vdash \tau \leq \tau'$ by Lemmas 4.3.4 and 4.3.6. By induction, $C, A \vdash_c f'' = \textbf{convert } [\forall t \leq \beta' . \pi'][\rho] f'$. Thus,

$$C, A \vdash_c f''[\sigma] = (\textbf{convert } [\forall t \leq \beta' . \pi'][\rho] f')[\sigma]$$

$$= \textbf{convert } [\pi'[\sigma/t]][\pi[\sigma/t]](\textbf{convert } [\forall t \leq \beta . \pi][\rho] f')[\sigma])$$

by (E7)

$$= \textbf{convert } [\pi'[\sigma/t]][\pi[\sigma/t]] e'. \quad \text{by } (\ddagger\ddagger).$$

The rest of this case is carried through exactly like case (iii).

(b) is similar to (a), using (E8) rather than (E7).

(vi)–(vii) on terms of the form all $(t \leq \sigma) . e$ and all $t . e$ are similar to (iv) using (E4) and (E5) rather than (E3).

(viii) $e = f . I$. Let τ be the minimum type for e, and σ be the minimum type for f, as in Lemma 4.3.6. As before we get a term e' of Coerced Bounded Fun, which is a fattening of e and such that $C, A \vdash_c e' : \tau$. As with previous cases, $C, A \vdash_c e' = f'' . I$, where f'' is a fattening of f. Therefore $C, A \vdash_c f'' : (J_1 : \rho_1, \ldots, J_n : \rho_n)$, where $I = J_k$ and $\tau = \rho_k$ for some k. By induction, $C, A \vdash_c f'' = \textbf{convert } [(J_1 : \rho_1, \ldots, J_n : \rho_n)][\sigma] f'$ for some f' a fattening of f. But note that by (E11) $C, A \vdash_c (\textbf{convert } [(J_1 : \rho_1, \ldots, J_n : \rho_n)][\sigma] f') . I = (\textbf{convert } [(I : \tau)][\sigma] f') . I$. Therefore for simplicity, we take $e' = (\textbf{convert } [(I : \tau)][\sigma] f') . I$.

Suppose e'' is a fattening of e such that $C, A \vdash_c e'' : \tau''$. As with previous cases, $C, A \vdash_c e'' = \textbf{convert } [\tau''][\tau'](f'' . I)$, where f'' is a fattening of f. Suppose $C, A \vdash_c f'' : (J_1'' : \rho_1'', \ldots, J_n'' : \rho_n'')$, where again $I = J_k''$ and $\tau' = \rho_k''$ for some k. By the minimality of τ, $\tau \leq \tau'$. By induction, $C, A \vdash_c f'' = \textbf{convert } [(J_1'' : \rho_1'', \ldots, J_n'' : \rho_n'')][\sigma] f'$. Thus,

$C, A \vdash_c f'' . I$

$\qquad = (\textbf{convert} \ [(J_1'' : \rho_1'', \ldots, J_n'' : \rho_n'')][\sigma]f') . I$

$\qquad = (\textbf{convert} \ [(I : \tau')][\sigma]f') . I \quad \text{by (E11)},$

$\qquad = (\textbf{convert} \ [(I : \tau')][(I : \tau)](\textbf{convert} \ [(I : \tau)][\sigma]f')) . I \quad \text{by (E2)},$

$\qquad = \textbf{convert} \ [\tau'][\tau]((\textbf{convert} \ [(I : \tau)][\sigma]f') . I) \quad \text{by (E10)},$

$\qquad = \textbf{convert} \ [\tau'][\tau]e'.$

The proof is completed as in the previous cases.

(ix) $e = (J_1 = e_1, \ldots, J = e_n)$. This case is straightforward (using (E9)) and is omitted here. ■

4.3.8   COROLLARY   Let $e \in BF_{C,A}$.

(1) If e_1 and e_2 are fattenings of e and τ is a type such that $C, A \vdash_c e_1 : \tau$, and $C, A \vdash_c e_2 : \tau$, then $C, A \vdash_c e_1 = e_2$.

(2) If e_1 and e_2 are fattenings of e such that $C, A \vdash_c e_1 : \sigma$, and $C, A \vdash_c e_2 : \tau$, where $C \vdash \sigma \leq \tau$, then $C, A \vdash_c \textbf{convert} \ [\tau][\sigma]e_1 = e_2$.

Proof

(1) Let τ' be a minimal type for e with respect to C, A and let e' be a fattening of e guaranteed in Theorem 4.3.7. Therefore $C, A \vdash_c e_1 = \textbf{convert} \ [\tau][\tau']e'$ and $C, A \vdash_c e_2 = \textbf{convert} \ [\tau][\tau']e'$. Therefore, $C, A \vdash_c e_1 = e_2$.

(2) Similar. ■

We can now define the meaning of terms in Bounded Fun. Recall that a model F of Coerced Bounded Fun is a model of Minimal Bounded Fun which has an interpretation for the constant **convert** which satisfies the axioms and rules in 4.3.1.

4.3.9   DEFINITION   Let F be a model of Coerced Bounded Fun. We define the interpretation of terms of Bounded Fun in F as follows. Let A be a syntactic type assignment and C a collection of simple type constraints. If $\eta \models C, A$ then if $e \in BF_{C,A}$ and $C, A \vdash_{bf} e : \tau$, define $[\![C, A \vdash_{bf} e : \tau]\!]\eta = [\![C, A \vdash_c e' : \tau]\!]\eta$, where e' is a fattening of e such that $C, A \vdash_c e' : \tau$.

We must of course ensure that this definition makes sense, but this follows easily from the previous results in this section. By Lemma 4.3.5, for each e as in the definition there is an appropriate translatable e' in Coerced Bounded Fun. By Corollary

4.3.8, part 1, and the soundness of F (as a model of Coerced Bounded Fun), it does not matter which such e' we choose. This establishes the soundness of the subsumption rule and that the semantics of terms in (the original) Bounded Fun is well defined.

Note also that by Corollary 4.3.8, part 2, if $C, A \vdash_c e_1 : \sigma$, and $C, A \vdash_c e_2 : \tau$, where $C \vdash \sigma \leq \tau$, then $[\![C, A \vdash_{bf} e : \sigma]\!] \eta$ can be obtained by coercing $[\![C, A \vdash_{bf} e : \sigma]\!] \eta$ from $[\![\sigma]\!] \eta$ to $[\![\tau]\!] \eta$ using the interpretation of **convert**.

In the next section we will construct an explicit model of Bounded Fun from partial equivalence relations. We will see that while the interpretation of **convert** will be a non-trivial polymorphic function, it will be defined in a very simple way which will enable us to verify (E1) through (E8) rather trivially.

5   The Modest Model of Bounded Fun

5.1   Modest and ω-Sets

In this section we show how to construct a model of Bounded Fun from a generalization of the category **PER**. This will be done by using some ideas of Eugenio Moggi, leading to the "small completeness" or closure under suitable products of the category **PER**. The approach in this subsection is more completely developed in Longo and Moggi (1988) (see also Rosolini, 1986; Hyland, 1988; Hyland *et al.* (1990); Hyland and Pitts, 1987; Carboni *et al.* 1987; Ehrhard, 1988; etc., for related category-theoretic work and Asperti and Longo, 1991, for the categorical background).

The point is that we need a frame (or "global" category) where also T, the collection of all types, is an object, so that we can interpret "universal quantification" over T. Recall, for this purpose, that these structures originated in (higher types or) generalized computatility. An early and elegant approach was proposed by Malcev, in the early fifties, with the category **EN** of numbered sets, whose objects are pairs (A, e_A), where A is a countable set and $e_A : \omega \to A$ is an "enumeration" or total onto map. Morphisms are functions $f : A \to B$ such that, for some recursive f', $f \circ e_A = e_B \circ f'$. Clearly any numbered set induces exactly one **equivalence relation**, e.r., on ω (a total one!) by $n A m$ iff $e_A(n) = e_A(m)$, while lots of numbered sets induce the same e.r. (see the *Out* map below). The idea is to define a category which includes both **PER** and **EN** as full subcategories. For this, one may just take the category **M** in 5.1.1 of countable (*modest*) sets A, with a **partial** enumeration $f_A : \omega \to A$. As partial maps are just single-valued relations in $\omega \times A$, we write $n f_A a$ for $f_A(n) = a$.

5.1.1   DEFINITION   The category **M** (of modest sets) has as

objects. $(A, f_A) \in \mathbf{M}$ iff A is a set and $f_A : \omega \to A$ is a partial onto map;

morphisms. $f \in \mathbf{M}[A, B]$ iff $f : A \to B$ and $\exists n, \forall a \in A, \forall p f_A a, (n \cdot p) f_B f(a)$.

M is not yet our "global" category. To define it, just drop the condition that the f_A relations are single-valued (we then call them "$\vdash_A$" relations or **realizability relations**, and we may omit the indices). That is, define:

5.1.2   DEFINITION   The category ω-**Set** has as

objects. $(A, \vdash_A) \in \omega$-**Set** iff A is a set, $\vdash_A \subseteq \omega \times A$ and $\forall a \in A, \exists p \vdash_A a$;

morphisms. $f \in \omega$-**Set** $[(A, \vdash_A), (B, \vdash_B)]$ iff $f : A \to B$ and $\exists n, \forall a \in A, \forall p \vdash_A a, n \cdot p \vdash_B f(a)$ (notation: $n \vdash_{A \to B} f$).

It is obvious that **M** is a full subcategory of ω-**Set**. Moreover, **PER** may be fully and faithfully embedded in **M** (and ω-**Set**). For every per, A, define the ω-set $\mathrm{In}(A) = (Q(A), \in_A)$, where $Q(A)$ is the set of equivalence classes of A and $\in_A$ is the usual membership relation restricted to $\omega \times Q(A)$. Clearly, $\mathrm{In}(A)$ is a modest set, since A is a per and, hence, the elements of $Q(A)$ are disjoint (nonempty) subsets of ω, i.e., $\in_A$ is single valued. Therefore, *In* defines an embedding from **PER** into **M**. Conversely, for every modest set, $(X, \vdash)$, we define a per $\mathrm{Out}(X)$, by

$$n \, \mathrm{Out}(X) \, m \Leftrightarrow \exists a \in X \quad \text{such that } n \vdash a \quad \text{and} \quad m \vdash a.$$

In conclusion, (In, Out) is an equivalence between the categories **PER** and **M**, which extends to an isomorphism between pers and ω-sets of the form $(Q(A), \in_A)$. Thus, even if **M** is not a small category, it is "essentially small" as it is equivalent to a small one. It is convenient to define it, as in categories one usually works "up to isomorphisms."

We are now going to use a strong closure property of the category **M** (and, by isomorphisms, of **PER**). As already mentioned, one crucial point in the interpretation of Bounded Fun as a higher order language is the meaning of the universal quantifier. We are going to interpret it as an "indexed product" in the category ω-**Set**. Recall that $\prod_{a \in A} g(a)$ is the set of functions, f, such that for all $a \in A$, $f(a) \in g(a)$.

5.1.3   DEFINITION   Let $(A, \vdash_A) \in \omega$-**Set**   and $g : A \to \omega$-**Set**. Define the ω-set $([\prod_{a \in A} g(a)], \vdash_{\prod, g})$ by

(1) $f \in [\prod_{a \in A} g(a)]$ iff $f \in \prod_{a \in A} g(a)$ and $\exists n, \forall a \in A, \forall p \vdash_A a, n \cdot p \vdash_{g(a)} f(a)$,

(2) $n \vdash_{\prod, g} f$ iff $\forall a \in A, \forall p \vdash_A a, n \cdot p \vdash_{g(a)} f(a)$.

Observe that if $g: A \to \omega$-**Set** is a constant function, $g(a) = (B, \vdash_B)$ for all $a \in A$, say, then $(\llbracket \prod_{a \in A} g(a) \rrbracket, \vdash_{\prod, g}) = (B^A, \vdash_{A \to B})$, the object representing ω-**Set** $[A, B]$ in ω-**Set**, where $\eta \vdash_{A \to B} f$ iff $\forall a \in A$, $\forall p \vdash_A a$, $n \cdot p \vdash_B f(a)$. Indeed, **M** and ω-**Set** are CCCs.

One can directly obtain a product in **PER**, when the range of g is restricted to **M**. (Note that this restriction is needed in order to obtain a well-defined per.)

5.1.4   DEFINITION   Let $(A, \vdash_A) \in \omega$-**Set** and $g: A \to$ **M**. Let $\llbracket \prod_{\alpha \in A} g(a) \rrbracket_{\mathbf{PER}} \in$ **PER** be defined by

$$n \left[\prod_{a \in A} g(a) \right]_{\mathbf{PER}} m \quad \text{iff } \forall a \in A, \forall p, q \vdash_A a, n \cdot p \, (\mathrm{Out}(g(a))) \, m \cdot q.$$

The products defined in 5.1.3 and 5.1.4 are isomorphic for $g: A \to$ **M**.

5.1.5   THEOREM   Let $(A, \vdash_A) \in \omega$-**Set** and $g: A \to$ **M**. Then $(\llbracket \prod_{a \in A} g(a) \rrbracket, \vdash_{\prod, g})$ is in **M** and is isomorphic to $\mathrm{In}(\llbracket \prod_{a \in A} g(a) \rrbracket_{\mathbf{PER}})$.

Proof   Let $\vdash_{\prod, g}$ be defined as in 5.1.3. We first prove that $\vdash_{\prod, g}$ is a single-valued relation. Assume that $n \vdash_{\prod, g} f$ and $n \vdash_{\prod, g} h$. We show that $\forall a \in A$, $f(a) = h(a)$ and, thus, that $f = h$. By definition $\forall a \in A$, $\forall p \vdash_A a$, $n \cdot p \vdash_{g(a)} f(a)$ and $n \cdot p \vdash_{g(a)} h(a)$, and thus $f(a) = h(a)$ since, for all a, $\vdash_{g(a)}$ is single valued (and any a in A is realized by some natural number). The isomorphism is given by $J(f) = \{n | n \vdash_{\prod, g} f\}$; thus the range of J is a collection of disjoint sets in ω (equivalence classes). J and its inverse are realized by the (indices for the) identity function.   ∎

In conclusion, a product of pers indexed by an arbitrary ω-set A, in the sense of 5.1.3, when $g: A \to$ **M**, is an object of **PER**, to within isomorphism.

As should be clear by now, types are interpreted by the objects of **PER**, or, roughly, T is interpreted by **PER**. We take a further step though, and interpret T as an object of ω-**Set**, by turning the entire category **PER** into an ω-set. Indeed (the collection of objects of) **PER** is a set. Consider then

$$\mathbf{M_0} = (\mathbf{PER}, \vdash_{\mathbf{PER}}) \in \omega\text{-}\mathbf{Set}, \quad \text{where } \vdash_{\mathbf{PER}} = \omega \times \mathbf{PER},$$

i.e., $\forall n$, $\forall A \in$ **PER**, $n \vdash_{\mathbf{PER}} A$. Thus we look at **PER** as a full subcategory of ω-**Set**, via *In*, and as an object too. Clearly, $\mathbf{M_0}$ is an ω-set, but it is not modest (**PER** could not be turned into a modest set, for cardinality reasons). Indeed, we never required T to be a type.

Thus, by 5.1.5, **PER** is equivalent to the subcategory **M** of ω-**Set** closed by products indexed by any object in ω-**Set**, including, of course, the object $\mathbf{M_0}$ representing **PER** itself. This strong closure property of **PER** will give the mathematical meaning over

Kleene's $(\omega, \cdot)$ of the impredicative definition of second order types. (To be precise, though, more non-trivial work needs to be done. Namely, one has to prove that $\mathbf{M_0}$ is the object component of an internal category of ω-**Set** and the product is the right adjoint of the diagonal functor, which makes all of this categorically sound, see Longo and Moggi, 1991 and Asperti and Longo, 1991).

5.2 Subtypes and Inheritance

We are now in the position to investigate subtypes in **PER**. As before, ω-**Set** is used as an (essential) tool.

5.2.1 DEFINITION   Let $(A, \vdash_A)$, $(B, \vdash_B) \in \omega$-**Set**. Define

$$(A, \vdash_A) \leq (B, \vdash_B) \quad \text{iff } \forall a \in A, \qquad \exists b \in B, \qquad \forall n (n \vdash_A a \Rightarrow n \vdash_B b).$$

Let $\iota : A \to B$ be a choice function such that if $\iota(a) = b$ then $\forall n \, (n \vdash_A a \Rightarrow n \vdash_B b)$. (Note that as there is not necessarily a unique such b for every a, ι has to choose one.)

5.2.2 *Remark*   This can be seen to be a straightforward generalization of the definition of subtype given in Section 2 as follows. By the (In, Out) correspondence between **PER** and **M** given after Definition 5.1.2, one has, for $(A, \vdash_A)$, $(B, \vdash_B) \in \mathbf{M}$,

Out$(A) \leq$ Out(B) in **PER**   iff $(A, \vdash_A) \leq (B, \vdash_B)$ in ω-**Set**.

Conversely, for A, $B \in$ **PER**, $A \leq B$ iff $\forall n, m \, (n \, A \, m \Rightarrow n \, B \, m)$ iff In$(A) \leq$ In(B), or, viewing A and B as sets of ordered pairs, In$(A) \leq$ In(B) iff $A \subseteq B$ (cf. Definition 3.3). Thus the definition of $\leq$ is preserved in the correspondence between **PER** and ω-**Set** via **M**. Moreover, take A, $B \in$ **PER** such that $A \leq B$, then the translation to ω-sets results in $\iota : Q(A) \to Q(B)$ such that $\iota(\{n\}_A) = \{n\}_B$. In this case, it is easy to see that ι is *uniquely* defined. Note that ι, the coercion morphism, is computed by all the indices of the identity function.

In the sequel, for technical convenience, we prefer to work in **PER**, rather than **M**, when unambiguous. For example, instead of a map $g : A \to \mathbf{M}$ we directly consider the map $G =$ Out $\circ \, g : A \to$ **PER**, if helpful, or, also, we identify, **PER** with In(**PER**). By this we avoid too many *In*'s and *Out*'s.

5.2.3 THEOREM   Let $(A, \vdash_A)$, $(A', \vdash_{A'}) \in \omega$-**Set** and let $G : A \to$ **PER**, $G' : A' \to$ **PER**. Assume that $A' \leq A$ via $\iota : A' \to A$ and that $\forall a' \in A'$, $G(\iota(a')) \leq G'(a')$. Then

$$\left[\prod_{a \in A} G(a) \right]_{\mathbf{PER}} \leq \left[\prod_{a' \in A'} G'(a') \right]_{\mathbf{PER}}.$$

Proof   Assume that $n[\prod_{a \in A} G(a)]_{\mathbf{PER}} m$ or, equivalently, that

$$\forall a \in A, \qquad \forall p, q \vdash_A a, \qquad (n \cdot p)\, G(a)\, (m \cdot q). \qquad (*)$$

We need to prove that $\forall a' \in A'$, $\forall p, q \vdash_{A'} a'$, $(n \cdot p)G'(a')(m \cdot q)$. Observe that, by the definition of $A' \leq A$ via ι, one has

$$\forall a' \in A', \qquad p \vdash_{A'} a' \Rightarrow p \vdash_A \iota(a'). \qquad (\ddagger)$$

Thus, by $(\ddagger)$, $(*)$, and the hypothesis on G and G',

$$a' \in A' \quad \text{and} \quad p, q \vdash_{A'} a'$$

$$\Rightarrow p, q \vdash_A \iota(a'))$$

$$\Rightarrow (n \cdot p)\, G\, (\iota(a'))(m \cdot q).$$

$$\Rightarrow (n \cdot p)\, G'\, (a')(m \cdot q). \quad \blacksquare$$

The simplicity of 5.2.3 is due to the merits of the "set-theoretic flavor" of the model. However, it is an important "structural" result of the present paper, as it shows that very general products preserve subtypes. For example, the usual inclusion of records, formalized in Bounded Fun, is realized in this model by 5.2.3, by taking A and A' in **PER** (as in Theorem 3.4(ii)). Similarly for general first- and second-order bounded quantifications, which all turn out to be handled similarly, i.e., by the same notion of product (indexed by different objects). In the next subsection, we use this property to construct a model for Bounded Fun.

5.3   Construction of the Model

Using the properties developed in the previous two sections, it is relatively straightforward (though a bit lengthy) to show how to construct a model of Extended Bounded Fun. Kinds are interpreted as elements of ω-**Set** (in particular, T by $\mathbf{M_0} = (\mathbf{PER}, \vdash_{\mathbf{PER}})$). The interpretation of **convert** will be a function *coerce*, such that for $A \leq B$, one has *coerce* $B\, A(\{n\}_A) = \{n\}_B$ for nAn, as already pointed out. The effect of *coerce* $B\, A$ is simply to forget some structural information (captured in the partial equivalence relation A), which is no longer relevant in the supertype B. Indeed, the per A is "finer" than B (in the case of record types, this gives meaning to "A has more fields than B").

We proceed by identifying the parts of the model according to the definitions given in Section 4.2. For the sake of simplicity, we keep considering **PER** both as a category (indeed, a full subcategory of ω-**Set**) and as a set (indeed, the set component in the ω-set, $\mathbf{M_0} = (\mathbf{PER}, \vdash_{\mathbf{PER}})$).

1. Let Type = **PER** and $\mathbf{T} = \mathbf{M_0} = (\mathbf{PER}, \vdash_{\mathbf{PER}})$, where $\vdash_{\mathbf{PER}} = \omega \times$ Type.

2. Define $\leq$ on Type by $A \leq B$ iff $A \subseteq B$ (when looked at as a set of ordered pairs), as in Section 3.

3. For B a per, let Type$^{\leq B} = \{A \in$ Type$|A \leq B\}$ and $\mathbf{T}^{\leq B} = ($Type$^{\leq B}, \vdash_{T^{\leq B}})$, where for all $A \leq B$ and for all n, $n \vdash_{T^{\leq B}} A$.

4. For $S \subseteq \omega$, let $\mathbf{D_s} = (s, \vdash_s)$, where for $n \in s$, $\{m|m \vdash_s n\} = \{n\}$. $\mathbf{D_s}$ is an ω-set corresponding to the discrete per on s.

5. Define *Kinds* to be the least subset of ω-set containing $\{\mathbf{T}\} \cup \{\mathbf{T}^{\leq \mathbf{B}}|B$ a per$\} \cup \{\mathbf{D_s}|s \subseteq \omega\}$ and closed under products over **T** (i.e., if f: Type $\to$ *Kinds*, then $([\prod_{a \in \mathbf{T}} f(a)], \vdash_{\prod,f}) \in$ *Kinds*) and function spaces (i.e., if **K**, **K**$' \in$ *Kinds* then so is $(\omega$-Set$[\mathbf{K}, \mathbf{K}'], \vdash_{\mathbf{K} \to \mathbf{K}'}))$.

6. a. Let $I_{Kind}(\mathbf{T}) = \mathbf{T}$ and $I_{Kind}(L_s) = \mathbf{D_s}$.

    b. If $\mathbf{K} = (K, \vdash)$ is a kind, then let Kind$^{\mathbf{K}} = K$ (e.g., Kind$^{\mathbf{T}} =$ Type).

    c. Let the interpretation of $\Rightarrow$ be $\Rightarrow$, where $(\mathbf{K} \Rightarrow \mathbf{K}') = (\omega$-Set$[\mathbf{K}, \mathbf{K}'], \vdash_{\mathbf{K} \to \mathbf{K}'})$.

    d. Similarly, for f: Type $\to$ *Kinds*, the interpretation of $\prod_{\mathbf{T}} f$ is $\prod_{\mathbf{T}} f = ([\prod_{a \in \mathbf{T}} f(a)], \vdash_{\prod,f})$.

    e. $\Phi_{\mathbf{K}, \mathbf{K}'}$ is the identity on Kind$^{\mathbf{K} \Rightarrow \mathbf{K}'}$. Similarly, Φ_f is the identity of Kind$^{\prod_{\mathbf{T}} f}$.

    f. Let the interpretation of $T_\leq$ be G, where for all pers B, $G(B) =$ **Type**$^{\leq \mathbf{B}}$.

    g. For each $s \subseteq \omega$, let $I_{Kind}(R_s) = \prod_s$, where if $F \in$ Kind$^{\mathbf{D_s} \Rightarrow \mathbf{Type}}$, $\prod_s(F) = [\prod_{a \in \mathbf{D_s}} F(a)]_{\mathbf{PER}}$.

    h. $I_{Kind}(\to)$ is defined on Type as in Section 3,

    i. $I_{Kind}(\forall) = \prod$, where if $F \in \omega$-Set$[\mathbf{T}, \mathbf{T}]$, $\prod(F) = [\prod_{t \in \text{Type}} F(t)]_{\mathbf{PER}}$.

    j. $I_{Kind}(\forall_\leq) = \prod_\leq$, where if $B \in$ Type, $F \in \omega$-Set$[\mathbf{T}^{\leq \mathbf{B}}, \mathbf{T}]$, $\prod_\leq(B)(F) = [\prod_{t \in \text{Type}^{\leq B}} F(t)]_{\mathbf{PER}}$.

7. We can then show that **Kind** = $\langle$Kinds, $\{$Kind$^k|k \in$ Kinds$\}$, $\{\Phi_{k,k'}|k, k' \in$ Kinds$\}$, $\{\Phi_f|f \in$ Type $\to$ Kinds$\}$, I_{Kind}, $\Rightarrow$, $\prod_{\mathbf{T}}$, $\leq \rangle$ is a kind structure.

8. To define a frame, make the following definitions:

    a. For $B \in$ Type, let Dom$^B = Q(B)$,

    b. $\Phi_{A,B}(\{n\}_{A \to B}) = f \in Q(A) \to Q(B)$, where $f(\{p\}_A = \{n \cdot p\}_B$,

    c. For $F = \omega$-Set$[\mathbf{T}, \mathbf{T}]$ and $\prod(F) = [\prod_{t \in \text{Type}} F(t)]_{\mathbf{PER}}$, let $\Phi_F(\{n\}_{\prod(F)}) = g \in \prod_{t \in \text{Type}} Q(F(t))$, such that for all $B \in$ Type, $g(B) = \{n \cdot 0\}_{F(B)}$.

    d. For $F \in \omega$-Set$[\mathbf{T}^{\leq \mathbf{B}}, \mathbf{T}]$ and $\prod_\leq(B)(F) = [\prod_{t \in \text{Type}^{\leq B}} F(t)]_{\mathbf{PER}}$, let $\Phi_{F,B}(\{n\}_{\prod_\leq(B)(F)}) = g \in \prod_{t \in \text{Type}^{\leq B}} Q(F(t))$, such that, for $C \leq B$, $g(C) = \{n \cdot 0\}_{F(C)}$.

(*Note*. The choice of "$n \cdot 0$" in points c and d above is justified by 5.3.1 below.)

Note that by Theorem 5.2.3, the inequality on types satisfies all of the properties required for a kind structure in Definition 4.2.1. It can be shown that this frame is indeed a model of Minimal Bounded Fun by showing that all terms have an interpretation in the model. This proof is based on the fact that the partial recursive functions are represented in $(\omega, \cdot)$ by the indices. Indeed, nothing else is required for the entire model construction. Thus, all above (and below) can be proved starting with **any** (possibly partial) combinatory algebra or model of Curry's combinators k and s. (Besides their computational power, k (and s) explicitly appear in 5.3.1 (and in Longo and Moggi, 1991)). In a sense, $(\omega, \cdot)$ is the "least" applicative structure one may start with, since any $(p)CA$ contains (a representation of) the natural numbers.

This structure is also a model of Extended Bounded Fun where the interpretation of **convert** is given by an equivalence class (with respect to type $[\![\forall t . \forall s \leq t . s \to t]\!]\eta$ for any legal environment, η) which contains the number p with the property that for all $m, n, p \cdot m \cdot n$ gives the index of an identity function on the natural numbers. (In terms of Curry's combinator, k, take $p = k \cdot (k \cdot i)$, where i is an index of the identity function.) The equivalence class of any such p will do. (*The reader may wish to test his/her understanding of the above model and Definition* 4.2.3 *by verifying that any such p gives an element with the right properties.*) By the above definition, if $A \leq B$ then $[\![\textbf{convert } t\ s]\!]\eta[B/t, A/s] = \{i\}_{A \to B}$ for i an index of the identity function. Thus the interpretation of **convert** t s does not change the representative of the partial equivalence class to which it is applied, only the partial equivalence relation with respect to which its equivalence class is formed. As a result it is completely trivial to verify that the axioms and rules, (E1) through (E8), of Explicit Bounded Fun are sound in this model. Thus by Definition 4.3.9 and the remarks that follow it, the structure defined above is a model of Bounded Fun. Note that the function coerce$_{A, B}$ introduced in Section 2 is simply $[\![\textbf{convert } t\ s]\!]\eta[B/t, A/s]$.

We note here that, using the machinery developed above on general products, it would be rather simple to extend the model to dependent products. That is, we could interpret types of the form $\forall x : \sigma . \tau$, where σ and τ are type expressions. These would be interpreted as pers of the form $[\![\prod_{a \in A} G(a)]\!]_{\textbf{PER}}$, for A the interpretation of σ, and G the interpretation of $\lambda x : \sigma . \tau$, following 5.1.4. Of course, the syntax should include type constraint and type assignment rules to take care of these new constructs. This requires some work only because, when types may contain terms, the equational theory of types must be thoroughly described, as in Martin-Löf's approaches (see Coquand and Huet, 1985; Hyland and Pitts, 1987, Longo and Moggi, 1991 for the blending of first- and second-order in impredicative approaches).

We may finally relate the construction above to the interpretation of types suggested by Girard (1972) and Troelstra (1973) for system **F** and *II* order arithmetic.

Following their work, we have interpreted types as partial equivalence relations, i.e., as objects of **PER**. Moreover, we interpreted T by $\mathbf{M_0} = (\mathbf{PER}, \vdash_{\mathbf{PER}})$ in ω-**Set**, in order to have a "frame" where also the second order "$\forall$" could be understood as a product.

For the first-order predicative case or dependent types, it is easy to check that Troelstra's interpretation of types coincides with ours (cf. 5.1.4 and Troelstra, 1973, Section 4). As for the more challenging case, i.e., when quantification is over T, Girard and Troelstra suggested that $\forall t : T. \tau$ be interpreted as

$$n\,([\![\forall t : T.\tau]\!]\eta)\,m \quad \text{iff for all } A \in \mathbf{PER},\, n\,([\![\tau]\!]\eta[A/t])\,m. \tag{Inter}$$

$$\text{iff } n\left(\bigcap_{A \in \mathbf{PER}} [\![\tau]\!]\eta[A/t]\right)m.$$

This interpretation was proved to be sound by interpreting typed terms *after erasing all of the type information from them*. Surprisingly enough, Moggi (1986) hinted that the intersection over **PER** is indeed a product, within Hyland's Effective Topos. Proofs, in various settings, were then suggested by Rosolini and Scott, Hyland and Freyd, Curien and Longo (see Rosolini, 1986; Hyland, 1988; Longo, 1988). Theorem 5.3.1 below says that the intersection is isomorphic to a product when working in ω-**Set** as the frame category.

5.3.1   THEOREM   Let $(A, \vdash_A) \in \omega$-**Set** be such that $\vdash_A = \omega \times A$ and let $G : A \to \mathbf{PER}$. Then $[\![\prod_{a \in A} G(a)]\!]_{\mathbf{PER}} \cong \bigcap_{a \in A} G(a)$ in **PER**.

Proof (Longo and Moggi, 1988)   Set $S = \bigcap_{a \in A} G(a)$ and $\prod = [\![\prod_{a \in A} G(a)]\!]_{\mathbf{PER}}$. Define $Iso \in \mathbf{PER}[S, \prod]$ as follows: Let k be such that, for all $n, m, k \cdot n \cdot m = n$. Then, for $n \in \mathrm{dom}(S)$, define

$$Iso(\{n\}_S) = \{k \cdot n\}_{\prod}.$$

Notice that $k \cdot n \in \mathrm{dom}(\prod)$, since $\forall a \in A, nG(a)n$ and, hence,

$$\forall a \in A, \qquad \forall m, q \in \omega, \qquad k \cdot n \cdot m\, G(a)\, k \cdot n \cdot q, \quad \text{as } \vdash_A = \omega \times A.$$

It is easy to see that the value of $Iso(c)$ is independent of the representative of the equivalence class. Clearly, $k \vdash Iso$.

To show Iso is injective, suppose that $m, n \in \mathrm{dom}(S)$ and that $\{n\}_S \neq \{m\}_S$. Therefore there is an $a \in A$ such that **not** $m\,G(a)\,n$. Therefore, **not** $k \cdot n \cdot 0\,G(a)\,k \cdot m \cdot 0$, and thus **not** $k \cdot n \prod k \cdot m$. Hence $Iso(\{n\}_S) \neq Iso(\{m\}_S)$, so Iso is injective.

It only remains to show that Iso is surjective and that its inverse is realized by some natural number. Let $m \prod m$. By definition,

$$\forall a \in A, \qquad \forall u, q \in \omega, \qquad m \cdot u\, G(a)\, m \cdot q, \quad \text{since } \vdash_A = \omega \times A. \qquad\qquad (*)$$

Take $n = m \cdot 0$. Then $\forall a \in A$, $n\, G(a)\, n$. We claim that $Iso(\{n\}_S) = \{k \cdot n\}_\Pi = \{m\}_\Pi$. For this, it is sufficient to show that $m \prod (k \cdot n)$. But by $(*)$, one has

$$\forall a \in A, \qquad \forall u, \qquad m \cdot u\, G(a)\, m \cdot 0.$$

Thus, since for all q, $k \cdot n \cdot q = n = m \cdot 0$,

$$\forall a \in A, \qquad \forall u, q, \qquad m \cdot u\, G(a)\, k \cdot n \cdot q,$$

so $m \prod (k \cdot n)$. Finally, take p such that for all m, $p \cdot m = m \cdot 0$. Clearly p realizes Iso^{-1}. ∎

Notice that in the proof above for $(A, \vdash_A) = \mathbf{M_0}$, if $c = \{n\}_S$, then $\Phi_G(Iso(c))(a) = \{n\}_{G(a)}$, see also 8c above. Indeed, when universally quantified types are interpreted as intersections, elements of these types are equivalence classes in the intersections, such as c. Then $\Phi_G(Iso(c))(a)$ tells us how to apply c to (the interpretation of) a type a (and suggested by 8c and d above). In conclusion, Theorem 5.3.1 is needed if one wants to show that the Girard-Troelstra interpretation of second-order types as intersection yields a model in the sense above (or as in Seely, 1987; see Hyland, 1988; Asperti and Longo, 1991; Meseguer, 1989). Indeed, it shows that their suggested model may be turned into a satisfactory interpretation with no need to erase types from terms. However, while types have the same interpretation, terms need to be interpreted differently, thus preserving their intended meaning as (typed) polymorphic programs.

Remark   In the notation above, $\Phi_G(Iso(c))(a) = \{n\}_{G(a)}$ is the definition of "polymorphic" application in Moggi's electronic mail message of February 1986, which suggested the various proofs of this simple but surprising fact. The result is relevant also for two more reasons that we have no space to discuss here. First, it gives an immediate understanding on how, under the assumptions in 5.3.1, the intersection of partial equivalence relations is (isomorphic to) their indexed product in Hyland's topos-theoretic model, **Eff**, of IZF (see Hyland, 1988; Longo and Moggi, 1991; Ehrhard, 1988; and Asperti and Longo, 1991, where the adjointness properties of this product are discussed). Second, it suggests an interesting foundational analysis, as the proof is based on the Uniformity Principle (UP, or the contrapositive of König's lemma), which is independent of IZF, but valid in **Eff**. The use of UP is implicit in the proof above, but the interested reader may recover it in the proof of the "surjectivity" of *Iso* (see Rosolini, 1986 or Longo, 1988, for explicit discussions).

6   Problems with Bounded Fun and Future Work

While the Modest model described above provides a sound interpretation of the language, the model indicates some difficulties with the language. The following lemma provides an indication that Bounded Fun is either too strong or too weak (it is debatable which it is) to express important operations that would be expected in an object-oriented language.

6.1   LEMMA   Let σ be a type expression and η be an environment for the Modest model described above. Then $[\![\forall t \leq \sigma . t \to t]\!]\eta$ contains only the interpretation of all $(t \leq \sigma). \lambda x : t . x$, the restriction of the polymorphic identity function.

Proof   Let h be in the domain of the per, $\prod = [\![\forall t \leq \sigma . t \to t]\!]\eta$, and let $B = [\![\sigma]\!]\eta$. We claim that h acts as the polymorphic identity for all types $\leq B$. Now let m be in the dom(B) and let $C_m = \{(m, m)\}$, representing the type with only one element, $\{m\}_B$. Thus $C_m \leq B$. By definition of the semantics of bounded quantification, $h \cdot n (C_m \to C_m) h \cdot n$ for all n (actually, 8c–d gives $h \cdot 0 (C_m \to C_m) h \cdot 0$; but this is the same by the definition of $\vdash_{PER}$ in $\mathbf{M_0}$). Then, by the definition of $\to$ on pers, it follows that for all p, q, if $p C_m q$ then $(h \cdot n \cdot p) C_m (h \cdot n \cdot q)$. Since C_m only contains (m, m) this implies that $(h \cdot n \cdot m) C_m (h \cdot n \cdot m)$. But this can only happen if for all n, $h \cdot n \cdot m = m$.

Since we can repeat this for all $m \in$ dom(B), it follows that for all n, $h \cdot n$ is the identity function on dom(B); namely, $h = k \cdot i$, for an index i of the identity function on dom(B). Thus for all $C \leq B$, and for all n, $\{h \cdot n\}_{C \to C} = \{i\}_{C \to C}$ represents the identity function on the type C. Thus $\{h\}_A = [\![$ all $(t \leq \sigma). \lambda x : t . x]\!]\eta$ since our model is extensional.   ∎

This lemma shows that the Modest model contains no functions which can be used for polymorphic record updates. That is, suppose we wish to define:

simple_update_$I : \forall t \leq (I : \text{Integer}). t \to t$

which is intended to apply some uniform (polymorphic) operation to record component I, while leaving the other portions of the record alone. Unfortunately, by the above lemma, the only such operation which is in the model (and hence is definable) is the (bounded) polymorphic identity function. (On the other hand, there are many functions with type $\forall t \leq (I : \text{integer}). t \to (I : \text{Integer}).$)

We can try to provide a somewhat more complex solution by deciding that rather than depending on a fixed update function, we might better supply the update_I function with another (polymorphic) function which is defined only on subtypes of the type of the I-component. For example:

update_$I : \forall s . \forall t \leq \{I : s\} . (\forall u \leq s . u \to u) \to (t \to t)$.

Unfortunately, we run into the same problem here, since the type $(\forall u \leq s . u \to u)$ contains only the (bounded) polymorphic identity function.

It seems that the best we could do is to extend the type expressions by adding the expression $t . I$ if $t \leq \{I : s\}$ for some type s. This expression would denote the type of the I-component of the type t. We could then write:

weaker_update_$I : \forall s . \forall t \leq \{I : s\} . (t . I \to t . I) \to (t \to t)$.

Thus weaker_update_I takes a function which takes an argument of the same type as that of the I-component of and returns an element of the same type. However, such a term does not provide as much parametric polymorphism since the functions supplied which operate on the various $t . I$'s need not have any connection to any other.

The fact that this model does not contain many polymorphic functions (at least in the types of the form $\forall t \leq \sigma . t \to t$), points out serious weaknesses in the expressibility of Bounded Fun. Since our model is sound, any term of these types which was expressible would have to be represented in the model. Since they are not represented, they must not be expressible.

What is the problem? In a sense there are too many subtypes. The key to the proof of the above lemma was the fact that for every element of a type, that type has a subtype which contains only that element. As a result, since the polymorphic functions were required to take elements of any subtype back to that subtype, all elements had to be fixed, or in other words the polymorphic function had to behave as the identity.

A possible solution to this problem is to restrict the notion of subtype to only "object-oriented" subtype. After all, it is the "subset" types which seem to be causing us problems. While such a restriction might rule out subtypes such as char $\leq$ string, integer $\leq$ real, etc., it is not entirely clear that these are desirable subtypes. Efforts are underway by several researchers to revise the language and create richer models (e.g., see Cardelli and Longo, 1989). A promising alternative approach is to add a new construct to the language denoting extensions to record types. See Wand (1989) and Jategaonkar and Mitchell (1988) for variants on this approach.

There is another more radical approach to the problem, which is to separate the notions of subtype and inheritance. Several authors (e.g., Liskov, 1988; Snyder, 1986) have argued recently that object-oriented programming involves (at least) two quite different notions: code reuse, and inheritance of representation. Code reuse depends on having functions of the same name and the same (parameterized) functionality in various types. For instance, the code from a quicksort can be applied to any type which supports a binary Boolean-valued operation on the type. (Of course, whether it

behaves properly or even terminates depends on the meaning of these operations.)
Thus code reuse (at least in the sense of object-oriented programming) depends only
on the interface of the operations associated with the type (i.e., the signatures of the
operations defined on the type). The semantics of these operations is irrelevant for
type-checking. On the other hand, many uses of object-oriented programming depend
on objects of a subtype inheriting the methods of a supertype (although it is not
atypical to redefine the inherited operations).

In order to support this view of object-oriented programming, we would expect to
throw away rule (sub), for type checking (the authors have always been uncomfortable
with this rule anyway). When looking at types or modules, it is necessary only to
look at the signature of the operations supported. We would then define $\sigma \leq \tau$ iff σ
supports the same (names of) operations as τ. However, objects of type σ cannot be
treated as objects of type τ. Subtyping thus becomes purely syntactic, having no
semantic consequences.

The notions of subtype and inheritance supported by most object-oriented languages include a combination of these syntactic and semantic properties. Elements of
subtypes inherit operations whenever possible and convenient, but languages also
allow the user to redefine operations whenever desired (without affecting the relation
of subtype). In these languages (e.g., Smalltalk), the representation of a subtype is
inherited from the supertype, but there is no compelling reason for this. The abstract
types of Smalltalk fit into this view quite easily. These ideas remain to be worked
out in detail, but we have hopes of providing a complete semantic specification of a
language supporting these ideas.

7 Summary and Relation to Other Work

In this paper we have given a formal semantics for the language Bounded Fun from
CW, (1985), which supports both parametric and subtype polymorphism. (Subtype
polymorphism is based on inheritance and might also be called structural polymorphism.) We have also shown how to use partial equivalence relations to model inheritance in this language, which supports the notion of subtype and record types. (Our
language actually differs from theirs in some minor ways.) A generalization of partial
equivalence relations, known as ω-sets, were used in combination with modest sets
(pers) to provide the first known model of Bounded Fun (with explicit polymorphism). The connections with previous work on the semantics of explicit parametric
polymorphism, based on the Girard-Troelstra interpretation (e.g., Mitchell, 1986),
is given by noting that the semantics of polymorphic types presented here (via

dependent products) is isomorphic to that given by the intersection interpretation of polymorphism.

Bainbridge *et al.* (1990) introduced the subcategory of **PER, I**, which contains the same objects as **PER**, but whose morphisms consist only of these from **PER** which are witnessed by an index of the identity function. These morphisms consist of exactly those functions of the form *coerce BA*, where $A \leq B$ according to the definition in this paper. They show that every morphism in **PER** can be decomposed into an isomorphism followed by a morphism from **I** followed by another isomorphism, a very simple but surprising property of **PER**. The results in this paper were discovered independently of those results, which were not meant to understand subtyping and inheritance.

We note here that an alternative model, according to the definition in Bruce *et al.* (1990), could be constructed using a subcategory of ω-sets, called multi-modest sets, **MM**. Its objects have the property that if A is a multi-modest set and $a, b \in A$ such that $n \vdash_A a$ and $n \vdash_A b$, then $\{n | n \vdash_A a\} = \{n | n \vdash_A b\}$. Notice that object $\mathbf{M_0}$ of ω-**Set**, which internally represents **PER** and is given at the end of Section 5.1, is a multi-modest set. However, category-theoretical problems in embedding **M** as an internal category and constructing a right adjoint of the diagonal function led us to drop **MM** in favor of ω-**Set**. Indeed, while the ω-**Set** construction leads to a model in the sense of Seely (1986) (see Longo and Moggi, 1988, and Asperti and Longo, 1989, for details), this does not seem possible when using **MM**.

An entirely different model of Bounded Fun, based on the "interval semantics," is given in Martini (1988). Martini's model does not interpret dependent types and, thus, uses a different method to support record types. It does, however, interpret recursive definitions of functions. Following our work, Amadio (1988) investigates a variant of the modest model which interprets both records and recursive definitions of functions.

An important issue is whether one can consistently extend Bounded Fun with "arbitrary" recursive definitions of data types (i.e., find a model for such extensions). Breazu-Tannen *et al.* (1991) have recently produced a technique for using arbitrary models of the second-order lambda calculus as models of Bounded Fun by encoding bounded quantification using explicit coercers. Their technique involves translating formulas of Bounded Fun into formulas of the second-order lambda calculus. Their translation is somewhat more complex than ours, resulting in translations of types as well as terms of Bounded Fun. However, since their translation allows them to interpret Bounded Fun in an arbitrary model of the second-order lambda calculus, they can interpret Bounded Fun in a model which provides solutions to recursive domain equations. We do not know how their translation into a second-order model based on **PER** relates to our model of Bounded Fun. As a matter of fact, further interesting variants of this model have been used in Amadio (1989) to interpret extensions of Bounded Fun which allow recursively defined types. Moreover, Amadio (1989) gives several informative ways to solve domain equations on his categories of pers and confirms by this the richness and flexibility of the **PER** based models (or, perhaps, the relevance of the underlying Effective Topos for understanding polymorphism and more).

Finally, we note with interest the recent paper of Canning *et al.* (1989) which introduces an extension of Bounded Fun in which the expression τ in the formula all $(t \leq \tau) . e$ may contain t as a free variable. As demonstrated in the cited paper, this provides added expressibility in the language, capturing more programs of interest to the object-oriented community. Interestingly, the **PER** semantics presented in this paper appear to also provide a sound semantic model for this new construct.

Acknowledgments

Longo thanks his (former) students Eugenio Moggi, Andrea Asperti, and Roberto Amadio for several instructive discussions and for the recent joint work, as stimulating as the previous common experiences. With P. L. Curien, he had a chance to discuss Moggi's understanding of "products-as-intersections." Dana Scott convinced us in several lectures and discussions of the relevance of the various categories of Modest Sets for the purposes of semantics. Thanks also to Luca Cardelli and Peter Wegner for stimulating our interest in subtypes and inheritance. The lemma in Section 6 arose as a result of a discussion with John Mitchell at a workshop in "Category Theory and Semantics" at Carnegie-Mellon University in the spring of 1988. Special thanks to Breazu-Tannen *et al.* (1991), who pointed out some serious omissions related to the coherence of terms in Coerced Bounded Fun in an earlier version of this paper.

Notes

An earlier version of this paper appeared in the Proceedings of the Third Annual Symposium on Logic in Computer Science, 1988. Partially supported by NATO Civil Alliance Grant #RG.86/0129 for international collaboration in research, "The semantics of types in programming languages."

Kim B. Bruce was partially supported by NSF Grant DCR8603890 and a grant from Williams College.

Giuseppe Longo's work has been made possible also by the generous hospitality of the Computer Science Dept., Carnegie-Mellon University, while teaching there during the academic year 1987/88.

1. Note that we must assume our language has at least one type constant, since otherwise the empty set will be the only type constraint system.

References

Amadio, R. (1988), A fixed point extension of the second-order lambda-calculus: Observable equivalences and models, *in* "Proceeding, L.I.C.S. 88, Edinburgh," pp. 51–60.

Amadio, R. (1989), "Recursion over Realizability Structures," Report, Dip. Informatica, Pisa.

Amadio, R. (1989a), Proof theoretic properties of a theory of inheritance, in preparation, Dip. Informatica, Pisa.

Andrews, T., and Harris, C. (1987), Combining language and database advances in an object-oriented development environment, Proceeding of OOPSLA '87, *SIGPLAN Notices* **22**, No. 12, 430–440.

Asperti, A., and Longo, G. (1991), Categories, types, and structures: An introduction to category theory for the working computer scientist, MIT Press.

Bainbridge, E. S., Freyd, P. J., Scedrov, A., and Scott, P. J. (1990), Functorial polymorphism; *Theoret. Comput. Sci.* **70**, 35–64.

Birtwistle, G., Dahl, O. J., Myrhaug, B., and Nygaard, K. (1973), "Simula Begin," Studentliteratur, Lund, and Auerback, New York.

Bobrow, D. G., and Stefik, M. J. (1982), "Loops: An Object-Oriented Programming System for Interlisp," Xerox PARC.

Breazu-Tannen, V., and Coquand, T. (1987), Extensional models for polymorphism, *Theoret. Comput. Scie.* **59**, 85–114.

Breazu-Tannen, V., Coquand, T., Gunter, C., and Scedrov, A. (1991), Inheritance and explicit coercion, *Inform. and Comput.* **93**, 172–221.

Bruce, K., and Meyer, A. (1984), A completeness theorem for second-order polymorhic lambda calculus, *in* "Proceedings, International Symposium on the Semantics of Data Types" (Kahn, MacQueen, and Plotkin, Eds.), Lect. Notes in Comput. Sci., Vol. 173, pp. 131–144, Springer-Verlag, New/York/Berlin.

Bruce, K., Meyer, A., and Mitchell, J. (1990), The semantics of second order lambda-calculus, *Inform. and Comput.* **85**, 76–134.

Bruce, K., and Wegner, P. (1990), "An Algebraic Model of Subtype and Inherence," Brown University Technical Report CS-87-21; *in* "Advances in Database Programming Language," ed. F. Bancilhon and P. Buneman, Addison-Wesley, pp. 75–96.

Canning, P., Cook, W., Hill, W., Mitchell, J., and Olthoff, W. (1989), "*F*-bounded quantification for Object-Oriented Programming," in *Functional Programming and Computer Architecture*, pp. 273–280, ACM.

Carboni, A., Freyd, P., and Scedrov, A. (1987), A categorical approach to realizability and polymorphic types, *in* "Proceedings, 3d Symposium on Mathematical Foundations of Programming Language Semantics" Main, Mislove, and Schmidt, Eds.), pp. 23–42, Lect. Notes in Comput. Sci., Vol. 198, Springer-Verlag, New York/Berlin.

Cardelli, L. (1988), A semantics of multiple inheritance, *Inform. and Comput.* **76**, 138–164. preliminary version appeared in "Proceedings of International Symposium on the Semantics of Data Types" (Kahn, MacQueen, and Plotkin, Eds.), Lect. Notes in Comput. Sci., Vol. 173, pp. 51–67, Springer-Verlag, New York/Berlin.

Cardelli, L., and Longo, G. (1991), "A Semantic Basis for **Quest**," *J. Funct. Prog.,* **1**, 417–458.

Cardelli, L., and Wegner, P. (1985), On understanding types, data abstraction, and polymorphism, *ACM Comput. Surveys* **17**, 47–522.

Coquand, T., and Huet, G. (1985), "Constructions: A Higher Order Proof System for Mechanizing Mathematics," Report 401, INRIA, presented at EUROCAL 85.

Curien, P.-L., and Ghelli, G. (1992), Coherence of subsumption, minimum typing and type-checking in $F_{\leq}$, *Math. Struct. in Comput. Sci.,* **2**, 55–91.

Ehrhard, T. (1988), A categorical semantics of constructions, *in* "Proceedings of L.I.C.S. '88, Edinburgh, pp. 264–273.

Girard, J. (1972), "Interprétation fonctionelle et élimination des coupures dans l'arithmetic d'ordre supérieur," Thèse de Doctorat d'Etat, Paris.

Goldberg, A., and Robson, D. (1983), "Smalltalk-80: The Language and Its Implementation," Addison-Wesley, Reading, MA.

Hyland, M. (1982), The effective Topos, in "The L.E.J. Brouwer Centary Symposium" (Troelstra and Van Dalen, Eds.), pp. 165–216, North-Holland, Amsterdam.

Hyland, M. (1988), A small complete category, in "Ann. Pure Appl. Logic," Vol. 40, pp. 93–133, North-Holland, Amsterdam.

Hyland, M., and Pitts, A. (1987), The theory of Constructions: Categorical semantics and topos-theoretic models, Boulder, Amer. Math. Soc. Notes.

Hyand, M., Robinson, E., and Rosolini, P. (1990), The discrete objects in the effective topos, *Proc. London Math. Soc. (3)* **60**, 1–36.

Jategaonkar, L., and Mitchell, J. (1988), ML with extended pattern matching and subtypes, in "Proceedings, 1988 ACM Conference on the LISP and Functional Programming," pp. 198–211.

Liskov, B. (1988), Data abstraction and hierarchy, Addendum, "Proceedings of OOPSLA '87," *SIGPLAN Notices* **23**, No. 5, 17–34.

Longo, G. (1988), On Church's formal theory of functions and functionals, Ann. Pure Appl. Logic **40**, 93–133, North-Holland, Amsterdam.

Longo, G. (1988a), From type structures to type theories, Lecture Notes for a graduate course at Carnegie-Mellon University, 1987/88.

Longo, G., and Moggi, E. (1991), Constructive natural deduction and its ω-set interpretation, *Math. Struct. in Comput. Sci.*, **1**, 215–254.

MacQueen, D., Plotkin, G., and Sethi, R. (1984), An ideal model for recursive polymorphic types, in "Proceedings, 11th ACM Symposium on the Principles of Programming Languages," pp. 165–174.

Martini, S. (1988), "Modelli non estensionali del polimorfismo in programmazione funzionale," Tesi di Dottorato, Pisa, forthcoming.

Meseguer, J. (1989), Relating models of polymorphism, in "Proceedings, 16th ACM Symposium on the Principles of Programming Languages," pp. 228–241.

Meyer, A., Mitchell, J., Moggi, E., and Statman, R. (1987), Empty types in polymorphic lambda calculus, in "Proceedings of POPL '87," pp. 253–262.

Meyer, B. (1988), "Object-oriented Software Construction," Prentice-Hall, New York.

Mitchell, J. C. (1984), Semantic models for second-order lambda calculus, in "Proceedings, 25th IEEE Sympos. on Foundations of Computer Science," pp. 289–299.

Mitchell, J. C. (1984a), Coercion and type inference, "Proceedings, 11th ACM Symposium on the Principles of Programming Languages," pp. 175–185.

Mitchell, J. C. (1986), A type-inference approach to reduction properties and semantics of polymorphic expressions, in "Proceedings, ACM Conference on LISP and Functional Programming Boston." pp. 308–319.

Mitchell, J. C. (1988), Polymorphic type inference and containment, *Inform. and Comput.* **76**, 211–249. (An earlier version appeared in "Symposium on Semantics of Data Types" (Kahn, MacQueen, Plotkin, Eds.), Lect. Notes in Comput. Sci., Vol. 173, pp. 257–278, Springer-Verlag, New York/Berlin).

Moggi, E. (1986), Message on "Types electronic-mailing list," January, 1986.

Pitts, A. (1987), Polymorphism is set theoretic, constructively., in "Symposium on Category Theory and Comput. Sci., Edinburgh" (Pitts *et al.*, Eds.), Lect. Notes in Comput. Sci., Vol. 283, Springer-Verlag, New York/Berlin.

Reynolds, J. C. (1974), Towards a theory of type structure, in "Paris Colloquium on Programming," Lect. Notes in Comput. Sci., Vol. 19, pp. 408–425, Springer-Verlag, New York/Berlin.

Reynolds, J. C. (1980), Using category theory to design implicit conversions and generic operators, *in* "Semantics Directed Compiler Generation," Lect. Notes in Comput. Sci., Vol. 94, pp. 211–258, Springer-Verlag, New York/Berlin.

Reynolds, J. C. (1984), Polymorphism is not set-theoretic, *in* "Symposium on Semantics of Data Types" (Kahn, MacQueen, and Plotkin, Eds.), Lect. Notes in Comput. Sci., Vol. 173, pp. 145–156, Springer-Verlag, New York/Berlin.

Rosolini, G. (1986), "About Modest Sets," notes for a talk delivered in Pisa.

Seely, R. A. G. (1986), "Categorical semantics for higher order polymorphic lambda calculus," *J. Symbolic Logic* **52**, 969–989.

Shaffert, C., Cooper, T., Bullis, B., Kilian, M., and Wilpolt, C. (1986), An introduction to Trellis/Owl, *in* "Proceedings of OOPSLA '86," *SIGPLAN Notices*, **21**, No. 11, 9–16.

Snyder, A. (1986), Encapsulation and inheritance in object-oriented programming languages, *in "Proceedings* of OOPSLA '86," *SIGPLAN Notices* **21**, No. 11, 38–45.

Stroustrup, B. (1986), "The $C++$ Programming Language," Addison-Wesley, Menlo Park, CA.

Troelstra, A. S. (1973), Notes in intuitionistic second order arithmetic, "Cambridge Summer School in Mathematicial Logic," Lect. Notes in Math., Vol. 337, pp. 171–203, Springer-Verlag, New York/Berlin.

Wand, M. (1989), Type inference for record concatenation and multiple inheritance, *in* "Proceedings, Fourth Annual Symposium on Logic in Computer Science," pp. 92–97.

Weinreb, D., and Moon, D. (1981). "Lisp Machine Manual, Chapter 20: Objects, Message-Passing, and Flavors," Symbolics Inc., Cambridge, MA.

7 Inheritance as Implicit Coercion

Val Breazu-Tannen, Thierry Coquand, Carl A. Gunter, and Andre Scedrov

Abstract

We present a method for providing semantic interpretations for languages with a type system featuring *inheritance* polymorphism. Our approach is illustrated on an extension of the language Fun of Cardelli and Wegner, which we interpret via a translation into an extended polymorphic lambda calculus. Our goal is to interpret inheritances in Fun via *coercion functions* which are definable in the target of the translation. Existing techniques in the theory of semantic domains can be then used to interpret the extended polymorphic lambda calculus, thus providing many models for the original language. This technique makes it possible to model a rich type discipline which includes parametric polymorphism and recursive types as well as inheritance. A central difficulty in providing interpretations for explicit type disciplines featuring inheritance in the sense discussed in this paper arises from the fact that programs can type-check in more than one way. Since interpretations follow the type-checking derivations, *coherence* theorems are required: that is, one must prove that the meaning of a program does not depend on the way it was type-checked. Proofs of such theorems for our proposed interpretation are the basic technical results of this paper. Interestingly, proving coherence in the presence of recursive types, variants, and abstract types forced us to reexamine fundamental equational properties that arise in proof theory (in the form of commutative reductions) and domain theory (in the form of strict vs. non-strict functions).

1 Introduction

In this paper we discuss an approach to the semantics of a particular form of inheritance which has been promoted by John Reynolds and Luca Cardelli. This inheritance system is based on the idea that one may axiomatize a relation $\leq$ between type expressions in such a way that whenever the *inheritance judgement* $s \leq t$ is provable for type expressions s and t, then an expression of type s can be "considered as" an expression of type t. This property is expressed by the *inheritance* rule (sometimes also called the *subsumption* rule), which states that if an expression e is of type s and $s \leq t$, then e also has type t. The consequence of the inclusion of this form of typing rule are significant from a semantic point of view. It is our goal in this paper to look carefully at what we consider to be a robust and intuitive approach to systems which have this form of inheritance and examine in some detail the semantic implications of the inclusion of inheritance judgements and the inheritance rule in a type discipline.

First appeared in *Information and Computation* 93(1991), pages 172–221. © Academic Press, Inc., 1 East First Street, Duluth, MN 55802.

Several attempts have been made recently to express some of the distinctive features of object-oriented programming, principally *inheritance*, in the framework of a rich type discipline which can accommodate strong static type-checking. This endeavor searches for a language that offers some of the flexibility of object-oriented programming (Goldberg and Robson, 1983) while maintaining the reliability, and sometimes increased efficiency of programs which type-check at compile-time (see (Breazu-Tannen, Buneman, and Gunter, 1988) for a related comparison).

A type system introduced in Reynolds (1980) captured some basic intuitions about inheritance relations between familiar type expressions built from records, variants (sums), and higher types. A language which exploited this form of type discipline was developed by Cardelli (1984, 1988a) where the first attempt was made to describe a rigorous form of mathematical semantics for such a system. His approach uses ideals and it is shown that the type discipline is consistent with the semantics in the sense that type-checking is shown to "prevent type errors." Subsequent work has aimed at combining inheritance with richer type disciplines, in particular featuring *parametric polymorphism*. One direction of research (Wand, 1987; Jategaonkar and Mitchell, 1988; Ohori and Buneman, 1988; Stansifer, 1988) has investigated expressing inheritance and type inference mechanisms, similarly to the way in which parametric polymorphism is expressed in ML-like languages. Another direction of research investigates the expression of inheritance through explicit subtyping mechanisms which are part of the type-checking systems, as in Cardelli and Wegner's language Fun (Cardelli and Wagner, 1985) and further work (Cardelli, 1988b, 1989a, Cardelli and Mitchell, 1989). Cardelli and Wegner sketch a model for Fun based on ideals. An extensional model for Fun was subsequently described by Bruce and Longo (1988). Their model interprets inheritances as identity relations between partial equivalence relations (PER's). Another model of Fun, using the interval interpretation of Cartwright (1985), has been given by Martini (1988). In Martini's semantics, inheritance is interpreted as a form of inclusion between intervals. This model also includes a general recursion operator for functions (but not types).

In this paper we present a novel approach to the problem of developing a simple mathematical semantics for languages which feature inheritance in the sense of Reynolds and Cardelli. The form of semantics that we propose will take a significant departure from the characteristic shared by the semantics mentioned above. We will not attempt to model inheritance as a binary relation on a family of types. In particular, our interpretation will not use anything like an inclusion relation between types. Instead, we interpret the inheritance relation between type *expressions* as indicating a certain coercion which remains implicit in instances in which the inheritance is used in type-checking. We show how these coercions can be made explicit using *definable* terms of a calculus without inheritance, and thus depart from the "relational" interpretation of the inheritance concept. Using this idea, we are able to show how many of the models of polymorphism and recursive types which have no relevant concept of type inclusion, can nevertheless be seen as models for a calculus with inheritance.

We illustrate our approach on the language Fun of Cardelli and Wegner extended with recursive types but the kind of results we obtain are non-trivial for any calculus that combines inheritance, parametric polymorphism, and recursive types. The method we propose proceeds first with a translation of Fun into an extended polymorphic lambda calculus with recursive types. As we mentioned above, this translation interprets inheritances in Fun as *coercion functions* already *definable* in the extended polymorphic lambda calculus. Then, we can use existing techniques for modeling polymorphism and recursion (such as those described in Amadio, Bruce, and Longo, 1986; Girard, 1986; Coquand, Gunter, and Winskel, 1987, 1989) to interpret the extended polymorphic lambda calculus, thus providing models for the original language with inheritance. This method achieves simultaneous modeling of parametric polymorphism, recursive types, and inheritance. In the process, the paradigm "inheritance as definable coercion" proves itself remarkably robust, which makes us confident that it will apply to a large class of rich type disciplines with inheritance.

The paper is divided into seven sections. Following this introduction, the second section provides some general examples and motivation to prepare the reader for the technical details in the subsequent sections. The third section discusses how our semantics applies to a calculus **SOURCE** which has inheritance, exponentials, records, generics, and recursive types. We show how this is translated into a calculus **TARGET** without inheritance and state our results about the coherence of the translation. We hope that the results in this simpler setting will help the reader get an idea of what our program is before we proceed to a more interesting calculus in the remainder of the paper. The fourth section is devoted to developing a translation for an expanded calculus which adds variants. Fundamental equational properties of variants lead us to develop a target language which has a *type of coercions*. The fifth section, which contains the difficult technical results of the paper, shows that our translation is coherent. In the sixth section we discuss mathematical models for the full calculus. Since most of the work has already been done, we are able to produce many models using standard domain-theoretic techniques. The concluding section makes some remarks about what we feel has been achieved and what new challenges still need to be confronted.

2 Inheritance as Implicit Coercion

A simple analogy will help explain our translation-based technique. Consider how the ordinary *untyped* λ-calculus is interpreted semantically in such sources as Scott (1980), Meyer (1982), Koymans (1982), and Barendregt (1984). One begins by postulating the existence of a semantic domain D and a pair of arrows $\Phi : D \to (D \to D)$ and $\Psi : (D \to D) \to D$ such that $\Phi \circ \Psi$ is the identity on $D \to D$. Certain conditions are required of $D \to D$ to insure that "enough" functions are present. To interpret an untyped λ-term, one defines a translation $M \mapsto M^*$ on terms which takes an untyped term M and creates a typed term M^*. This operation is defined by induction:

- for a variable, $x^* \equiv x : D$,
- for an application, $M(N)^* \equiv \Phi(M^*)(N^*)$, and
- for an abstraction, $(\lambda x . M)^* \equiv \Psi(\lambda x : D . M^*)$

(where we use $\equiv$ for syntactic equality of expressions). For example, the familiar term

$$\lambda f . (\lambda x . f(xx))(\lambda x . f(xx))$$

translates to

$$\Psi(\lambda f : D . \Phi(\Psi(\lambda x : D . \Phi(f)(\Phi(x)(x))))(\Psi(\lambda x : D . \Phi(f)(\Phi(x)(x))))).$$

The fact that the latter term is unreadable is perhaps an indication of why we use the former term *in which the semantic coercions are implicit*. Nevertheless, this translation provides us with the desired semantics for the untyped term since we have converted that term into a term in a calculus which we know how to interpret. Of course, this assumes that we really do know how to provide a semantics for the typed calculus supplemented with triples such as D, Φ, Ψ. Moreover, there are some equations we must check to show that the translation is sound. But, at the end of the day, we have a simple, intuitive explanation of the interpretation of untyped λ-terms based on our understanding of a certain simply typed λ-theory. In this paper we show how a similar technique may be used to provide an intuitive interpretation for inheritance, even in the presence of parametric polymorphism and type recursion. As mentioned earlier, our interpretation is carried out by translating the full calculus into a calculus without inheritance (the *target* calculus) whose semantics we already understand. However, our idea differs significantly from the interpretation of the untyped λ-calculus as described above in at least one important respect: typically, the coercions (such as Φ and Ψ above) which we introduce will be *definable* in the target calculus. Hence our target calculus needs to be an extension of the ordinary polymorphic λ-calculus with records, variants, abstract types, and recursive types. But it need not have any inheritance.

From this lead, we may now propose a way to explain the semantics of an expression in a language with inheritance. Our semantics interprets typing judgements, i.e., assertions $\Gamma \vdash e : s$ that expression e has type s in context Γ. Ordinarily such a judgement is assigned a semantics inductively in the proof of the judgement using the typing rules. However, the system we are considering may also include instances of the *inheritance* rule which says that if e has type s and s is a subtype of t, then e has type t. How are we to relate the interpretation of the type expressions s and t so that the meaning of e can be viewed as living in both places? Our proposal: the proof that s is a subtype of t generates a *coercion* P from s into t. The inheritance (subsumption) rule is interpreted by the application of the coercion P to the interpretation of e as an element of s. It will be seen below that this technique can be made to work very smoothly since the language we are interpreting may have a familiar *inheritance-free* fragment in which coercions such as P can be defined. In effect, we can therefore "project" the language onto an inheritance-free fragment of itself.

For further illustration, let us now look at an example which combines parametric polymorphism and inheritance. In the polymorphic λ-calculus, it is possible to form expressions in which there are abstractions over *type variables*. For example, the term $e \equiv \Lambda a . \lambda x : a . x$ is an operator which takes a type s as an argument and returns the identity function $\lambda x : s . x$ on that type as a value. The type of e *is* indicated by the expression $\forall a . a \to a$. Semantically, one may think of the meaning of this expression as an indexed product where a ranges over all types. Although this explanation is a bit too simple as it stands, it does help with the basic intuition. If one wishes to make an abstraction over the *subtypes* of a given type, one may use the concept of a *bounded quantification* (Cardelli and Wegner, 1985). Consider, for example, the term

$$e' \equiv \Lambda a \leq \{l : s\} . \lambda x : a . (x . l),$$

where $\{l : s\}$ is a *record* expression which has one field. labelled l, with type s. The expression e' denotes an operator which takes a subtype t of $\{l : s\}$ (we write $t \leq \{l : s\}$) and returns as value a function from t to s. (The reader should not confuse a, a type variable, with t, a type expression.) Intuitively, a subtype of $\{l : s\}$ is a record which has an l field whose type is a subtype of s. The type of e' is indicated by the expression $u' \equiv \forall a \leq \{l : s\} . a \to s$. How should we think of this type semantically? Taking an analogy with the intuitive semantics of polymorphic quantification, we want to think of the meaning of u' as some kind of indexed product. But indexed over what? In this paper we argue that one may get an intuitive semantics of bounded quantification by thinking of a type expression such as u' as a family of types *indexed over coercions* (i.e, *certain functions*) *from a type a into the type s*.

To support this intuition we must explain the meaning of the application $e'(t)$ of the expression e' to a type expression t which is a subtype of $\{l:s\}$. The key fact is this: given type expressions v and w and a proof that v is a subtype of w, there is a canonical coercion from v into w. Hence, the application $e'(t)$ has, as its meaning, the element of $t \rightarrow s$ obtained by applying the meaning of e'—which is an element of an indexed product —to the canonical coercion from t to $\{l:s\}$. This leads us to consider u' as the type

$$\forall a . (a \rightarrowtail \{l:s\}) \rightarrow a \rightarrow s,$$

where $a \rightarrowtail \{l:s\}$ is a "type of coercions." In category-theoretic jargon: the meaning of a bounded quantification with bound v will be an adjoint to a fibration over the *slice category* over v. This follows the analogy with models of polymorphism which are based on adjoints to fibrations over the category of all domains (as in Coquand, Gunter, and Winskel, 1989, for example).

Although we believe that the translation just illustrated is intuitive, we need to show that it is *coherent*. In other words, we must show that the semantic function is well defined. The need for coherence comes from the fact that a typing judgement may have many different derivations. In general, it is customary to present the semantics of typed lambda calculi as a map defined inductively on type-checking derivations. Such a method would therefore assign a meaning to each derivation tree. We do believe, though, that the *language* consists of the derivable typing judgements, rather than of the derivation trees. For many calculi, such as the simply typed or the polymorphic lambda calculus, there is at most one derivation for any typing judgement. Therefore, in such calculi, giving meaning to derivations is the same as giving meaning to derivable judgements. But for other calculi, such as Martin-Löf's Intuitionistic Type Theory (ITT) (Martin-Löf, 1984) (see Salvesen, 1988), the Calculus of Constructions (Coquand and Huet, 1988) (see Streicher, 1988), and—of immediate concern to us—Cardelli and Wegner's Fun, this is not so, and one must prove that derivations yielding the same judgement are given the same meaning. This idea has also appeared in the context of category theory and our use of the term "coherence" is partially inspired by its use there, where it means the uniqueness of certain canonical morphisms (see, e.g., Kelly and MacLane, 1971, and MacLane and Pare, 1985). Although we have not attempted a rigorous connection in this paper, the possibility of unifying coherence results for a variety of different calculi offers an interesting direction of investigation. In the case of Fun, we show the coherence of our semantic approach by proving that *translations of any two derivations of the same typing judgement are equated in the target calculus.*

Hence, the coherence of a given translation is a property of the equational theory of the target calculus. When the target calculus is the polymorphic lambda calculus extended with records and recursive types, the standard axiomatization of its equational theory is sufficient for the coherence theorem. But when we add variants, the standard axiomatization of these features, while sufficient for coherence, clashes with the standard axiomatization of recursive types, yielding an inconsistent theory (see Lawvere, 1969, and Huwig and Poigné, 1989, for variants, that is, coproducts). The solution lies in two observations: (1) the (too) strong axioms are only needed for "coercion terms," and (2) in the various models we examined these coercion terms have special interpretations (such as *strict*, or *linear* maps), so special in fact that they satisfy the corresponding restrictions of the strong axioms! Correspondingly, one has to restrict the domains over which "coercion variables" can range, which leads naturally to the type of coercions mentioned above.

3   Translation for a Fragment of the Calculus

For pedagogic reasons, we begin by considering a language whose type structure features function spaces (exponentials), record types, bounded generic types (an inheritance-generalized form of universal polymorphism), recursive types, and, of course, inheritance. In the next section we will enrich this calculus by the addition of variants. As we have mentioned before, this leads to some (interesting) complications which we avoid by restricting ourselves to the simpler calculus of this section. Since the calculus in the next section is stronger, we omit details for the proofs of results in this section. They resemble the proofs for the calculus with variants, but the calculations are simpler. Rather than generate four different names for the calculi which we shall consider in this section and the next we simply refer to the calculus with inheritance as **SOURCE** and the inheritance-free calculus into which it is translated as **TARGET**. The fragment of the calculus which we consider in this section is fully described in the appendices to the paper.

We provide semantics to **SOURCE** via a *translation* into a language for which several well-understood semantics already exist. This "target" language, which we shall call **TARGET**, is an extension with record and recursive types of the Girard-Reynolds polymorphic lambda calculus (see Coquand, Gunter, and Winskel, 1987, for the semantics of **TARGET**). Therefore, **SOURCE** extends with inheritance and bounded generics **TARGET**, which is in turn an extension of what Girard calls **System F** in Girard (1986). Our translation takes derivations of inheritance and typing judgements in **SOURCE** into derivations of typing judgements in **TARGET**. We translate the inheritance judgements of **SOURCE** into definable terms of **TARGET** which can be thought of as *canonical explicit coercions*. Bounded generics translate into usual generics, but of "higher" type, which take an additional argument which can be thought of as an *arbitrary coercion*.

In arguing that this translation yields a semantics for **SOURCE**, we encounter, as mentioned in the introduction, an important complication: as we shall see, in **SOURCE** as well as in Fun, there may be *several* distinct derivations of the *same* typing judgement (or inheritance judgement, for that matter). We consider, however, the *language* to consist of the derivable typing judgements, rather than of the derivation trees. This distinction can be ignored in System **F** or **TARGET**, where there is at most one derivation for any typing judgements, so giving meaning to derivations is the same as giving meaning to derivable judgements. But for **SOURCE** and Fun, this is not so, and one must show that derivations yielding the same judgement are given the same meaning. This meaning is then defined to be the meaning of the judgement. This crucial problem was overlooked by publications on the semantics of inheritance prior to Breazu-Tannen *et al.* (1989).

We solve the problem as follows. It turns out that our translation takes syntactically distinct derivations of the same **SOURCE** judgement into syntactically distinct derivations in **TARGET**. But we give an *equational axiomatization* as an integral part of **TARGET**, and we show that our translation takes derivations of the same **SOURCE** judgement into derivations of *provably equal* judgements in **TARGET**. By this *coherence* result, *any* model of **TARGET**, being also a model of its equational theory, will provide a well-defined semantics for the derivable judgements of **SOURCE**.

The Source Calculus

For notation, we will follow the spirit of Fun (Cardelli and Wegner, 1985) making precise only the differences. The type expressions include type variables a and a distinguished constant *Top*. If s and t are type expressions, then $s \rightarrow t$ is the type of functions from s to t. If $s_1, \ldots, s_n$ are type expressions, and $l_1, \ldots, l_n$ is a collection of distinct *labels*, then $\{l_1 : s_1, \ldots, l_n : s_n\}$ is a *record* type expression. We make the syntactic assumption that the order of the labels is irrelevant. If s and t are type expressions then $\forall a \leq s . t$ is a *bounded quantification* which binds free occurrences of the variable a in the type expression t (but not in s). Similarly, $\mu a . t$ is a *recursive* type expression in which the type variable a is bound in the type expression t. Intuitively, $\mu a . t$ is the solution of the equation $a = t$. We will use $[s/a]t$ for substitution. The *raw terms* of the language include (term) variables x, applications $d(e)$, and lambda abstractions $\lambda x : t . e$. An expression $\{l_1 = e_1, \ldots, l_n = e_n\}$ is called a record with *fields* $l_1, \ldots, l_n$ and the expression $e . l$ is the *selection* of the field l. Again, we assume that the order of the fields of a record is irrelevant, but the labels must all be distinct. We also have bounded type abstraction $\Lambda a \leq t \,.\, e$ and the corresponding application $e(t)$. To form terms of recursive type $\mu a \,.\, t$ we have *intro* expressions $\mathtt{intro}[\mu a \,.\, t]e$ and they are eliminated from the recursion by *elim* expressions $\mathtt{elim}\ e$. See Appendix A to find a grammar for the type expressions and raw terms of the fragment.

Raw terms are type-checked by deriving *typing judgments*, of the form $\Gamma \vdash e : t$, where Γ is a context. *Contexts* are defined recursively as follows: $\varnothing$ is a context; if Γ is a context which does not declare a, and the free variables of t are declared in Γ, then $\Gamma, a \leq t$ is a context; if Γ is a context which does not declare x, and the free variables of t are declared in Γ, then $\Gamma, x : t$ is a context. The proof system for deriving typing judgments is the relevant fragment of the corresponding proof system for Fun (see Cardelli and Wegner, 1985, pp. 519–520) enriched with two type-checking rules for the introduction and elimination of recursive types (Coquand, Gunter, and Winskel, 1987). A complete list of these proof rules is in Appendix A under the heading **Fragment**.

Among these proof rules, the following two illustrate the effect of inheritance on type-checking:

$$\frac{\Gamma \vdash e : s \quad \hat{\Gamma} \vdash s \leq t}{\Gamma \vdash e : t} \tag{INH}$$

$$\frac{\Gamma \vdash e : \forall a \leq s \,.\, t \quad \hat{\Gamma} \vdash r \leq s}{\Gamma \vdash e(r) : [r/a]t}. \tag{B-SPEC}$$

They make use of *inheritance judgments* which have the form $C \vdash s \leq t$, where C is an inheritance context. *Inheritance contexts* are contexts in which only declarations of the form $a \leq t$ appear. If Γ is a context, we denote by $\hat{\Gamma}$ the inheritance context obtained from Γ by erasing the declarations of the form $x : t$. The proof system for deriving inheritance judgments is, with the exception of one rule, the same as the relevant fragment of the corresponding proof system for Fun (see Cardelli and Wegner, 1985, p. 519). In this paper we do not attempt to enrich it with any rule deriving inheritances *between* recursive types. A discussion of this issue appears in our conclusions. The Appendix contains a complete list of these proof rules too.

In comparison with Fun, we would like to strengthen the rule deriving inheritances between bounded generics, and we are able to do so for some of our results. Where Fun had just

$$\frac{C, a \leq t \vdash u \leq v}{C \vdash \forall a \leq t \,.\, u \leq \forall a \leq t \,.\, v} \tag{W-FORALL}$$

we will consider

$$\frac{C \vdash s \leq t \quad C, a \leq s \vdash u \leq v}{C \vdash \forall a \leq t . u \leq \forall a \leq s . v}. \tag{FORALL}$$

This makes the system strictly stronger, allowing more inheritances to be derived, and thus more terms to be type-checked.

Originally, we believed that coherence could be proved for a system that includes variants and the stronger rule (FORALL) (Breazu-Tannen *et al.*, 1989). In dealing with the case construct for variant types, however, our coherence proof uses an order-theoretic property (see Lemma 11) which fails for the stronger system for deriving inheritances that uses (FORALL) (for a counterexample, see Giorgio Ghelli's dissertation (1990)). Thus, we prove the coherence of the translation of variants (Theorem 13) only for the weaker system with (W-FORALL). Note, however, that we prove coherence in the presence of (FORALL) for the system without variants (Theorem 4) and for the system for deriving inheritances between types, including variant types (Lemma 9).

Remark Decidability of type-checking in the stronger system is a nontrivial question. The question whether an algorithm of Luca Cardelli will decide the provability of judgements in this calculus has only recently been settled by Ghelli (1990).

The salient feature of bringing inheritance into a type system is that (in given contexts) terms will *not* have a unique type any more. For example, due to the rule

$$C \vdash t \leq Top \tag{TOP}$$

where the free variables of t are declared in C, by [INH], all terms that type-check with some type will also type-check with type *Top*. This makes it possible to define ordinary generics as syntactic sugar: $\forall a . t =^{\text{def}} \forall a \leq Top . t$.

The proof system for **SOURCE**, while quite intuitive, allows for the following complication: there may be more than one derivation of the same typing judgement. In fact, we only need record types (RECD), [VAR], [SEL], and [INH] (see Appendix) to provide such an example: in the context $x : \{l_1 : Top, l_2 : Top\}$, we can either directly derive by [SEL] $x . l_1 : Top$, or derive by [VAR] $x : \{l_1 : Top, l_2 : Top\}$, then by (RECD) and [INH] $x : \{l_1 : Top\}$, and finally by [SEL] $x . l_1 : Top$. In view of this, for any semantics given by "induction on the rules," one needs to prove that derivations of the same judgment have the same meaning.

The Target Calculus

As mentioned before, **TARGET** is the Girard-Reynolds polymorphic lambda calculus, enriched record and recursive types (Coquand, Gunter, and Winskel, 1987, 1989;

Breazu-Tannen and Coquand, 1988). Here, we present it as a simplification of **SOURCE**. Types are given by

$$a \mid s \rightarrow t \mid \forall a \,.\, t \mid \{l_1 : s_1, \ldots, l_n : s_n\} \mid \mu a \,.\, t$$

and terms by

$$x \mid M(N) \mid \lambda x : t \,.\, M \mid \Lambda a \,.\, M \mid$$

$$M(t) \mid \{l_1 = M_1, \ldots, l_n = M_n\} \mid M \,.\, l \mid \texttt{intro}[\mu a \,.\, t] M \mid \texttt{elim}\, M.$$

For $n = 0$ we get the *empty record type* $\mathbf{1} =^{\mathrm{def}} \{\ \}$ and the *empty record*, for which we will keep the notation $\{\ \}$. *Typing contexts* are the obvious simplification of contexts in which only typing judgements occur (there is no inheritance relation in **TARGET**). The rules for deriving typing judgements in the fragment of **TARGET** discussed in this section can be found in Appendix B. The following is a well-known fact:

PROPOSITION 1   In **TARGET**, derivations of typing judgements are unique.

Proof   All the "elimination" rules, [APPL], [SEL], [SPEC], and [R-ELIM], are "cut" rules, in the sense that there is information in the premises that does not appear in the conclusion. Consequently, they should in principle cause problems for the uniqueness of derivations. However, the lost information is always in the type part, and types "should" be unique. This suggests the strengthening of the induction hypothesis, which then passes trivially through these "cut" rules.

One proves therefore that for any two derivations Δ_1 and Δ_2, if Δ_1 ends in $\Upsilon \vdash M : t_1$ and Δ_2 ends in $\Upsilon \vdash M : t_2$, then $\Delta_1 \equiv \Delta_2$ (in particular, $t_1 \equiv t_2$).

The proof can be done straightforwardly by induction either on the maximum of the heights of Δ_1 and Δ_2, or on the sum of those heights, or even on the structure of M (with a bit of reformulation).   ∎

A technical point: it turns out that type decorations are unnecessary on "elimination" constructs, but they are in fact necessary on some "introduction" constructs, such as lambda abstraction and the recursive type construct $\texttt{intro}[\ ]$. Later on, with the addition of variants in Section 4, we will find that we need to differ with Cardelli and Wegner (1985) and decorate with types the constructs that "inject" into variant types (see Appendix B).

Equations are derived by a proof system (see Coquand, Gunter, and Winskel, 1987, 1989; Breazu-Tannen and Coquand, 1988) which contains rules such as reflexivity, symmetry, transitivity, congruence with respect to function application, closure under functional abstraction (ξ), congruence with respect to application to types, and closure with respect to type abstraction (type ξ). There are also the {BETA} and {ETA} rules for both functional and type abstraction, rules saying that `intro[ ]` and `elim` are inverse to each other, as well as

$$\{l_1 = M_1, \ldots, l_n = M_n\} . l_i = M_i, \qquad\qquad \{\text{RECD-BETA}\}$$

where $n \geq 1$, and

$$\{l_1 = M . l_1, \ldots, l_n = M . l_n\} = M, \qquad\qquad \{\text{RECD-ETA}\}$$

where $M : \{l_1 : s_1, \ldots, l_n : s_n\}$. The last rule gives, for $n = 0$, the equation $\{ \ \} = M$ which makes **1** into a terminator. Under our interpretation, the type *Top* will be nothing like a "universal domain" which can be used to interpret *Type : Type* (Coquand, Gunter, and Winskel, 1989; Gunter and Jung, 1990). On the contrary, it will be interpreted as a one point domain in the models we list below!

The Translation

For any **SOURCE** `item` we will denote by `item*` its translation into **TARGET**. We begin with the types. Note the translation of bounded generics and of *Top*.

$$a* \stackrel{\text{def}}{=} a$$

$$Top* \stackrel{\text{def}}{=} \mathbf{1}$$

$$(s \to t)* \stackrel{\text{def}}{=} s* \to t*$$

$$\{l_1 : s_1, \ldots, l_n : s_n\}* \stackrel{\text{def}}{=} \{l_1 : s_1^*, \ldots, l_n : s_n^*\}$$

$$(\forall a \leq s.t)* \stackrel{\text{def}}{=} \forall a . (a \to s*) \to t*$$

$$(\mu a . t)* \stackrel{\text{def}}{=} \mu a . t*.$$

One shows immediately that $([s/t]t)* \equiv [s*/a]t*$. We extend this to contexts and inheritance contexts, which translate into just typing contexts in **TARGET**.

$$\varnothing* \stackrel{\text{def}}{=} \varnothing$$

$$(\Gamma, a \leq t)* \stackrel{\text{def}}{=} \Gamma*, a, f : a \to t*$$

$$\varnothing* \stackrel{\text{def}}{=} \varnothing$$

$$(C, a \leq t)* \stackrel{\text{def}}{=} C*, a, f : a \to t*$$

$$(\Gamma, x : t)* \stackrel{\text{def}}{=} \Gamma*, x : t*,$$

where f is a *fresh* variable for each a.

Next we will describe how we translate the derivations of judgments of **SOURCE**. The translation is defined by recursion on the structure of the derivation trees. Since these are freely generated by the derivation rules, it is sufficient to provide for each derivation rule of **SOURCE** a corresponding rule on trees of **TARGET** judgments. It will be a lemma (Lemma 2 to be precise) that these corresponding rules are *directly derivable* in **TARGET**; therefore the translation takes derivations in **SOURCE** into derivations in **TARGET**.

A **SOURCE** derivation yielding an inheritance judgment $C \vdash s \leq t$ is translated as a tree of **TARGET** judgments yielding $C^* \vdash P : s^* \to t^*$. We present three of the rules here; the full list for the fragment appears in Appendix C. The coercion into *Top* is simply the constant map:

$$C^* \vdash \lambda x : t^* . \{\ \} : t^* \to \mathbf{1}. \qquad\qquad (\text{TOP})^*$$

To see how coercion works on types, assume that we are given a coercion $P : s \to t$ from s into t and a coercion $Q : u \to v$ from u into v. Then it is possible to coerce a function $f : t \to u$ into a function from s to t as follows. Given an argument of type s, coerce it (using P) into an argument of type t. Apply the function f to get a value of type u. Now coerce this value in u into a value in v by applying Q. This describes a function of the desired type. More formally, we translate the (ARROW) rule by

$$\frac{C^* \vdash P : s^* \to t^* \quad C^* \vdash Q : u^* \to v^*}{C^* \vdash R : (t^* \to u^*) \to (s^* \to v^*)}, \qquad\qquad (\text{ARROW})^*$$

where $R =^{\text{def}} \lambda z : t^* \to u^* . P ; z ; Q$. (We use ; as shorthand for *composition*. For example, $P ; z ; Q$ above stands for $\lambda x : s^* . Q(z(P(x)))$, where x is fresh.) Now, to translate the rule (FORALL) which describes the inheritance relation for the bounded quantification we view the quantification as ranging over a type together with a coercion from that type into the bound

$$\frac{C^* \vdash P : s^* \to t^* \quad C, a, f : a \to s^* \vdash Q : u^* \to v^*}{C^* \vdash R : (\forall a . (a \to t^*) \to u^*) \to (\forall a . (a \to s^*) \to v^*)}, \qquad\qquad (\text{FORALL})^*$$

where $R =^{\text{def}} \lambda z : (\forall a . (a \to t^*) \to u^*) . \Lambda a . \lambda f : a \to s^* . Q(z(a)(f ; P))$.

Now, a **SOURCE** derivation yielding an typing judgment $\Gamma \vdash e : t$ is translated as a tree of **TARGET** judgments yielding $\Gamma^* \vdash M : t^*$. For example, the inheritance rule is translated by simply making the inheritance coercion "explicit":

$$\frac{\Gamma^* \vdash M : s^* \quad \hat{\Gamma}^* \vdash P : s^* \to t^*}{\Gamma^* \vdash P(M) : t^*} \qquad\qquad [\text{INH}]^*$$

The specialization of a bounded quantification is more subtle. The variable is instantiated by substituting the type expression to which the abstraction is applied, but then the coercion from the argument type to the bound type must be passed as an argument to the resulting function:

$$\frac{\Gamma^* \vdash M : \forall a.(a \to s^*) \to t^* \quad \hat{\Gamma}^* \vdash P : r^* \to s^*}{\Gamma^* \vdash M(r^*)(P) : [r^*/a]t^*}. \qquad\qquad \text{[B-SPEC]}^*$$

The remaining rules for translating the fragment are given in Appendix C. It is possible to check that the translated rules are derivable in the target language:

LEMMA 2   The rules (TOP)*–(TRANS)* and [VAR]*–[INH]* are directly derivable in **TARGET**.

Coherence of the Translation

For any derivation Δ in **SOURCE**, let Δ^* be the **TARGET** derivation into which it is translated. The central result about *inheritance* judgments says that, given a judgment $s \leq t$ and a pair of proofs Δ_1 and Δ_2 of this judgment, the coercions induced by these two proofs are provably equal in the equational theory of **TARGET**. More formally, we have the following:

LEMMA 3 (Coherence of the translation of inheritance)   Let Δ_1 and Δ_2 be two **SOURCE** derivations of the same inheritance judgment, $C \vdash s \leq t$. Let Δ_1^*, Δ_2^* yield (coercion) terms P_1, P_2. Then $P_1 = P_2$ is provable in **TARGET**.

The central result about *typing* judgments says that, given a judgment $e : t$ and a pair of proofs Δ_1 and Δ_2 of this judgment, the translations of these proofs end in sequents (translations of $e : t$) which are provably equal in the equational theory of **TARGET**; i.e., we have

THEOREM 4 (Coherence)   Let Δ_1 and Δ_2 be two **SOURCE** derivations yielding the same typing judgment, $\Gamma \vdash e : t$. Let Δ_1^*, Δ_2^* yield terms M_1, M_2. Then $M_1 = M_2$ is provable in **TARGET**.

The proofs of the lemma and theorem are almost as difficult as the ones we shall give for the corresponding results in the full language. Since the proofs of these results for the fragment follow similar lines to the proofs for the full language we omit the proofs of Lemma 3 and Theorem 4 in favor of the proofs of Lemma 9 and Theorem 13 below.

4   Between Incoherence and Inconsistency: Adding Variants

The calculus described so far does not deal with a crucial type constructor: variants. In particular, it is very useful to have a combination of variant types with recursive types. On the other hand, the combination of these operators in the same calculus is also problematic, especially for the equational theory. The situation is familiar from both domain theory and proof theory. In this section we propose an approach which will suffice to prove the coherence theorem which we need to show that our semantic function is well-defined.

We extend the type formation rules of **SOURCE** by adding *variant* type expressions $[l_1 : t_1, \ldots, l_n : t_n]$, where $n \geq 1$. We also extend the term formation rule by the formation of variant terms $[l_1 : t_1, \ldots, l_i = e, \ldots, l_n : t_n]$ and the *case statement*

case e of $l_1 \Rightarrow f_1, \ldots, l_n \Rightarrow f_n$.

The inheritance judgement derivation rules are extended correspondingly with the rule

$$\frac{C \vdash s_1 \leq t_1 \cdots C \vdash s_p \leq t_p}{C \vdash [l_1 : s_1, \ldots, l_p : s_p] \leq [l_1 : t_1, \ldots, l_p : t_p, \ldots, l_q : t_q]}. \qquad \text{(VART)}$$

Note the "duality" between this rule and the inheritance rule (RECD) for records (see Appendix A). While a record subtype has more fields, a variant subtype has fewer variations (summands).

As before, we intend to translate this calculus into a calculus without inheritance and, naturally, we extend **TARGET** with variants (see Appendix B). Note how the syntax of variant injections differs from Cardelli and Wegner (1985). This is in order for the resulting system to enjoy the property of having unique type derivations: the proof of Proposition 1 extends immediately to the variant constructs. Most importantly, we must extend the equational theory of **TARGET** in a manner that insures the coherence of our translation. It is here that we encounter an interesting problem which readers who know domain theory will find familiar. The following two axioms hold in a variety of models:

case $\text{inj}_{l_i}(M_i)$ of $l_1 \Rightarrow F_1, \ldots, l_n \Rightarrow F_n = F_i(M_i),$ $\qquad\qquad$ {VART-BETA}

where $F_1 : t_1 \rightarrow t, \ldots, F_n : t \rightarrow t, M_i : t_i$ and inj_{l_i} is shorthand for $\lambda x : t_i . [l_1 : t_1, \ldots, l_i = x, \ldots, l_n : t_n]$;

case M of $l_1 \Rightarrow \text{inj}_{l_1}, \ldots, l_n \Rightarrow \text{inj}_{l_n} = M,$ $\qquad\qquad$ {VART-ETA} where $M : [l_1 : t_1, \ldots, l_n : t_n]$. Unfortunately, these two axioms do not suffice to prove all the identifications required by the coherence of our translation!

To see the problem, we start with an example. In **SOURCE**, suppose that $t \le s$ is derivable in the context $\hat{\Gamma}$, and that we have a derivation Δ of $\Gamma \vdash e : [l_1 : t_1, l_2 : t_2]$ and derivations Δ_i of $\Gamma \vdash f_i : t_i \to t$, $i = 1, 2$. Consider then the following two **SOURCE** derivations of the typing judgement $\Gamma \vdash \mathsf{case}\ e\ \mathsf{of}\ l_1 \Rightarrow f_1, l_2 \Rightarrow f_2 : s$.

1. By $\Delta, \Delta_1, \Delta_2$ and the rule [CASE], one deduces $\Gamma \vdash \mathsf{case}\ e\ \mathsf{of}\ l_1 \Rightarrow f_1, l_2 \Rightarrow f_2 : t$. Since $\hat{\Gamma} \vdash t \le s$ by hypothesis, one infers by inheritance $\Gamma \vdash \mathsf{case}\ e\ \mathsf{of}\ l_1 \Rightarrow f_1, l_2 \Rightarrow f_2 : s$.

2. From $\hat{\Gamma} \vdash t \le s$ we can deduce $\hat{\Gamma} \vdash (t_i \to t) \le (t_i \to s)$. Hence, by inheritance form Δ_i, one deduces $\Gamma \vdash f_i : t_i \to s$. Then, from Δ and by the rule [CASE], one deduces $\Gamma \vdash \mathsf{case}\ e\ \mathsf{of}\ l_1 \Rightarrow f_1, l_2 \Rightarrow f_2 : s$.

The coherence property requires that these two derivations have provably equal translations. With the obvious translation for the variant type constructor and the rules [VART] and [CASE] (see Appendix C) and with the translation of the rules [INH], (ARROW), and (REFL) as in Section 3, this comes down to the identity

$$P(\mathsf{case}\ M\ \mathsf{of}\ l_1 \Rightarrow F_1, l_2 \Rightarrow F_2) = \mathsf{case}\ M\ \mathsf{of}\ l_1 \Rightarrow (F_1 ; P), l_2 \Rightarrow (F_2 ; P),$$

where $P : t^* \to s^*$ is a "coercion term," $M : [l_1 : t_1^*, l_2 : t_2^*]$, $F_i : t_i^* \to t^*$, $i = 1, 2$. Thus, we are tempted to postulate

$$P(\mathsf{case}\ M\ \mathsf{of}\ l_1 \Rightarrow F_1, \ldots, l_n \Rightarrow F_n) = \mathsf{case}\ M\ \mathsf{of}\ l_1 \Rightarrow F_1 ; P, \ldots, l_n \Rightarrow F_n ; P,$$
$$\{\text{VART-CRN?}\}$$

where $M : [l_1 : t_1, \ldots, l_n : t_n]$, $F_1 : t_1 \to t, \ldots, F_n : t_n \to t$, $P : t \to s$. This equation follows from the equation that axiomatizes variants analogously to coproducts,

$$Q(M) = \mathsf{case}\ M\ \mathsf{of}\ l_1 \Rightarrow (\mathsf{inj}_{l_1} ; Q), \ldots, l_n \Rightarrow (\mathsf{inj}_{l_n} ; Q), \qquad \{\text{VART-COP?}\}$$

where $M : [l_1 : t_1, \ldots, l_n : t_n]$, $Q : [l_1 : t_1, \ldots, l_n : t_n] \to t$. More precisely, it is possible to check that the system {VART-BETA} + {VART-COP} is equivalent to {VART-BETA} + {VART-CRN} + {VART-ETA}. However, it is known (Lawvere, 1969, Huwig and Poigné, 1989a) that {VART-BETA} + {VART-COP} is inconsistent with the existence of fixed-points. In fact, this may be refined:

PROPOSITION 5   The system {VART-BETA} + {VART-CRN} is (equationally) inconsistent with the existence of fixed-points.

Proof The "categorical" equation {VART-COP} may be thought of as an "induction" principle on a sum: it reduces the proof of an equation $P(M) = Q(M)$, $M : [l_1 : t_1, l_2 : t_2]$, to the proofs of $P(\text{inj}_{l_1}(x)) = Q(\text{inj}_{l_1}(x))$ for $x : t_1$ and $P(\text{inj}_{l_2}(x)) = Q(\text{inj}_{l_2}(x))$ for $x : t_2$. Indeed, we have $P(M) = \text{case } M \text{ of } l_1 \Rightarrow \lambda x . P(\text{inj}_{l_1}(x)), l_2 \Rightarrow \lambda x . P(\text{inj}_{l_2}(x))$ and $Q(M) = \text{case } M \text{ of } l_1 \Rightarrow \lambda x . Q(\text{inj}_{l_1}(x)), l_2 \Rightarrow \lambda x . Q(\text{inj}_{l_2}(x))$. Given a type t, it is possible to define a "negation-like" operation on $[l_1 : t, l_2 : t]$ by $\text{neg}(M) = \text{case } M \text{ of } l_1 \Rightarrow \lambda x . \text{inj}_{l_2}(x), l_2 \Rightarrow \lambda x . \text{inj}_{l_1}(x)$. Given $x, y : t$, it is easy enough to define an operation $f(M, N) : t$, for $M, N : [l_1 : t, l_2 : t]$ in such a way that $f(\text{inj}_{l_1}(u), \text{inj}_{l_1}(u)) = f(\text{inj}_{l_2}(v), \text{inj}_{l_2}(v)) = x$, and $f(\text{inj}_{l_1}(u), \text{inj}_{l_2}(v)) = f(\text{inj}_{l_2}(v), \text{inj}_{l_1}(u)) = y$. We deduce then from the "induction principle" that $f(M, M) = x$ and $f(M, \text{neg}(M)) = y$, identically for $M : [l_1 : t, l_2 : t]$; hence the (equational) inconsistency when we have a fixed-point combinator.

The fact that we can use instead of {VART-COP?} + {VART-BETA} the weaker system {VART-BETA} + {VART-CRN?} comes simply from the fact that we can "relativise" this reasoning to the elements of $[l_1 : t, l_2 : t]$ of the form $\text{case } M \text{ of } \text{inj}_{l_1}, \text{inj}_{l_2}$, elements that satisfy the equation {VART-ETA}. ∎

Thus, a naive approach gives us an unattractive choice between incoherence and inconsistency! We are saved from this by the observation that, at least in the example above, we do not seem to need the "full" us of {VART-CRN} but only those instances in which P is a term coming out of a translation of an inheritance judgment, i.e., a "coercion term." Such terms are much simpler than general terms. In particular, we note that in models based on continuous maps, such terms denote *strict* maps, and in models based on stable maps, they denote *linear* maps. Appropriate constructions for interpreting variants can be given in both cases, such that {VART-CRN} is sound, as long as P ranges only over strict (or linear) maps.

Maintaining the same philosophy to our approach as in Section 3 we will try to *abstractly* embody in **TARGET** a sufficient amount of formalism to insure the provable coherence of our translation. Thus. the previous discussion of variants leads us to introduce a new type constructor $s \rightarrowtail t$, the type of "coercions" from s to t. Consequently, the coercion assumptions $a \leq t$ that occur in inheritance contexts must translate to variables ranging over types of coercions $f : a \rightarrowtail t^*$. As a consequence, the translation of bounded quantification must change:

$$(\forall a \leq s . t)^* \stackrel{\text{def}}{=} \forall a . ((a \rightarrowtail s^*) \rightarrow t^*).$$

In order to express the correct versions of {VART-CRN}, we introduce a family of constants in **TARGET**,

$$\iota_{s,t} : (s \rightarrowtail t) \rightarrow (s \rightarrow t),$$

called *coercion-coercion combinators*. With this, we have

$$\iota(P)(\mathtt{case}\ M\ \mathtt{of}\ l_1 \Rightarrow F_1, \ldots, l_n \Rightarrow F_n) = \mathtt{case}\ M\ 1\ \mathtt{of}\ l_1 \Rightarrow F_1; \iota(P), \ldots, l_n \Leftarrow F_n; \iota(P),$$
$$\{\text{VART-CRN}\}$$

where $M : [l_1 : t_1, \ldots, l_n : t_n]$, $F_1 : t_1 \to t, \ldots, F_n : t_n \to t$, $P : t \circ\!\!\rightarrow s$ (the complete list is in Appendix B).

In order to translate all inheritance judgements into coercion terms, we add a special set of constants (coercion combinators) that "compute" the translations of the rules for deriving inheritance judgements. To prove coherence, we axiomatize the behavior of the ι-images of these combinators. For example, the coercion combinator for the rule (ARROW) takes a pair of coercions as arguments and yields a new coercion as value:

$$\mathtt{arrow}[s, t, u, v] : (s \circ\!\!\rightarrow t) \to (u \circ\!\!\rightarrow v) \to ((t \to u) \circ\!\!\rightarrow (s \to v)).$$

Since (ARROW) is a rule *scheme*, we naturally have a *family* of such combinators, indexed by types. To simplify the notation, these types will be omitted whenever possible. The equational property of the $\mathtt{arrow}$ combinator is given in terms of the coercion coercer,

$$\iota(\mathtt{arrow}(P)(Q)) = \lambda z : t \to u . (\iota(P)); z ; (\iota(Q)),$$

where $P : s \circ\!\!\rightarrow t$, $Q : u \circ\!\!\rightarrow v$. For the rule (TRANS), we introduce

$$\mathtt{trans}[r, s, t] : (r \circ\!\!\rightarrow s) \to (s \circ\!\!\rightarrow t) \to (r \circ\!\!\rightarrow t)$$

which, of course, behaves like composition, modulo the coercion coercer,

$$\iota(\mathtt{trans}(P)(Q)) = \iota(P); \iota(Q),$$

where $P : t \circ\!\!\rightarrow s$, $Q : s \circ\!\!\rightarrow t$. The combinator for the rule (FORALL) is the most involved,

$$\mathtt{forall}[s, t, a, u, v] : (s \circ\!\!\rightarrow t) \to \forall a . ((a \circ\!\!\rightarrow s) \to (u \circ\!\!\rightarrow v))$$
$$\to (\forall a . ((a \circ\!\!\rightarrow t) \to u) \circ\!\!\rightarrow \forall a . ((a \circ\!\!\rightarrow s) \to v)),$$

with the equational axiomatization

$$\iota(\mathtt{forall}(P)(W)) = \lambda z : (\forall a . (a \circ\!\!\rightarrow t) \to u) . \Lambda a .$$
$$\lambda f : a \circ\!\!\rightarrow s . \iota(W(a)(f))(z(a)(\mathtt{trans}(f)(P))),$$

where $P : s \circ\!\!\rightarrow t$, $W : \forall a . (a \circ\!\!\rightarrow s) \to (u \circ\!\!\rightarrow v)$. Of course, we have gone to the extra inconvenience of introducing the type of coercions in order to provide a satisfactory account of variants. These require a scheme of combinators having the types

$$\texttt{vart}[s_1,\ldots,s_p,t_{p+1},\ldots,t_q]:(s_1 \rightsquigarrow t_1) \rightarrow \cdots \rightarrow (s_p \rightsquigarrow t_p)$$

$$\rightarrow ([l_1:s_1,\ldots,l_p:s_p] \rightsquigarrow [l_1:t_1,\ldots,l_p:t_p,\ldots,l_q:t_q]).$$

And it is now possible to assert a consistent equation for these combinators,

$$\iota(\texttt{vart}(R_1)\cdots(R_p)) = \lambda w:[l_1:s_1,\ldots,l_p:s_p].$$

$$\texttt{case } w \texttt{ of } l_1 \Rightarrow \iota(R_1); \texttt{inj}_{l_1},\ldots,l_p \Rightarrow \iota(R_p); \texttt{inj}_{l_p},$$

where $R_1:s_1 \rightsquigarrow t_1,\ldots,R_p:s_p \rightsquigarrow t_p$. In order to prove the equalities between terms of coercion type one uses the rule

$$\frac{\iota(P) = \iota(Q)}{P = Q} \qquad\qquad \{\text{IOTA-INJ}\}$$

which asserts that ι is an injection. In fact, all of the models we give below will interpret ι as an inclusion. It is natural to ask whether the coercion coercer ι could have been omitted from the calculus in favor of a rule

$$\frac{P:s \rightsquigarrow t}{P:s \rightarrow t}.$$

This would have the unfortunate consequence that a typing judgement $e:s$ would no longer uniquely encode its proof and the coherence question would therefore arise again! The other combinators and their equational properties are described in Appendix B.

We are now ready to explain how to translate our full language **SOURCE** (complete with variants) into the language **TARGET** (with the coercion coercer and combinators). For starters, the inheritance judgement for the function space is simply translated using the $\texttt{arrow}$ combinator:

$$\frac{C^* \vdash P:s^* \rightsquigarrow t^* \quad C^* \vdash Q:u^* \rightsquigarrow v^*}{C^* \vdash \texttt{arrow}(P)(Q):(t^* \rightarrow u^*) \rightsquigarrow (s^* \rightarrow v^*)} \qquad \text{(ARROW)}^*$$

The translation of an inheritance between quantified types takes the induced coercion and a polymorphic function as its arguments:

$$\frac{C^* \vdash P:s^* \rightsquigarrow t^* \quad C^*,a,f:a \rightsquigarrow s^* \vdash Q:u^* \rightsquigarrow v^*}{C^* \vdash \texttt{forall}(P)(\Lambda a.\lambda f:a \rightsquigarrow s^*.Q):\forall a.((a \rightsquigarrow t^*) \rightarrow u^*) \rightsquigarrow \forall a.((a \rightsquigarrow s^*) \rightarrow v^*)}.$$

$$\text{(FORALL)}^*$$

Other inheritance judgements are similarly translated. The real work is being done by equational properties of the combinators.

The proofs of typing judgements are translated in a manner quite similar to how they were translated in the fragment. For example,

$$\frac{\Gamma^* \vdash M : \forall a \, . \, ((a \rightsquigarrow s^*) \to t^*) \quad \hat{\Gamma}^* \vdash P : r^* \rightsquigarrow s^*}{\Gamma^* \vdash M(r^*)(P) : [r^*/a]t^*} \qquad \text{[B-SPEC]}^*$$

is affected only by indicating that the map into the bound must be a coercion. The inheritance rule is translated by

$$\frac{\Gamma^* \vdash M : s^* \quad \hat{\Gamma}^* \vdash P : s^* \rightsquigarrow t^*}{\Gamma^* \vdash \imath(P)(M) : t^*}, \qquad \text{[INH]}^*$$

since a coercion cannot be applied until it is made into a function by an application of the coercion coercer. The full description of the translation of the full language is given in Appendix C. We now turn to the proof of the central technical results of the paper.

5   Coherence of the Translation for the Full Calculus

In this section we prove first the coherence of the translation of inheritance judgements. This result is then used to show the coherence of the translation of typing judgements.

The main cause for having distinct derivations of the same inheritance judgements is the rule (TRANS). Our strategy is to show that the use of (TRANS) can be coherently postponed to the end of derivations (Lemma 6), and then to prove the coherence of the translation of (TRANS)- postponed derivations (Lemma 8).

We introduce some convenient notations for the rest of this section. For any derivation Δ in **SOURCE**, let Δ^* be the **TARGET** derivation into which it is translated. We write $C \vdash r_0 \le \cdots \le r_n$ instead of $C \vdash r_0 \le r_1, \ldots, C \vdash r_{n-1} \le r_n$. The composition of coercions given by $\mathtt{trans}$ occurs so often that we write $P \odot Q$ instead of $\mathtt{trans}(P)(Q)$. It is easy to see, making essential use of the rule $\{\text{IOTA-INJ}\}$, that $\odot$ is provably *associative*. We take advantage of this to unclutter the notation. We also write I instead of $\mathtt{refl}$. Again it is easy to see that I is provably an identity for $\odot$; that is, $I \odot M = M \odot I = M$ is provable in **TARGET**.

LEMMA 6   For any **SOURCE** derivation Δ yielding the inheritance judgment $C \vdash s \le t$, there exist types $r_0, \ldots, r_n$ such that $s \equiv r_0, r_n \equiv t$, and (TRANS)-free derivations $\Delta_1, \ldots, \Delta_n$ yielding respectively

$$C \vdash r_0 \le \cdots \le r_n.$$

Moreover, if the translations $\Delta^*, \Delta_1^*, \ldots, \Delta_n^*$ yield respectively the (coercion) terms $C^* \vdash P : s^* \multimap t^*$, $C^* \vdash P_1 : r_0^* \multimap r_1^*, \ldots, C^* \vdash P_n : r_{n-1}^* \multimap r_n^*$ then

$$C^* \vdash P = P_1 \odot \cdots \odot P_n$$

is provable in **Target**.

Proof By induction on the height of the derivation Δ. The base is trivial since derivations consisting of instances of (TOP), (VAR), or (REFL) are already (TRANS)-free. We present the more interesting cases of the induction step.

Suppose Δ ends with an application of (ARROW). By the induction hypothesis there are (TRANS)-free derivations for

$$s \equiv r_0 \leq \cdots \leq r_m \equiv t \quad \text{and} \quad u \equiv w_0 \leq \cdots \leq w_n \equiv v$$

(for simplicity, we omit the context). From these, using (REFL) and (ARROW) we get (TRANS)-free derivations for

$$t \to u \equiv r_m \to u \leq \cdots \leq r_0 \to u \equiv s \to w_0 \leq \cdots \leq s \to w_n \equiv s \to v.$$

(This is not most economical: one can get a derivation requiring only $\max(m, n)$, rather than $m + n$, steps of (TRANS) at the end.) Proving the equality of the corresponding translations uses the associativity of $\odot$ and the fact that I acts like an identity, as well as

$$\mathtt{arrow}(P)(Q) \odot \mathtt{arrow}(R)(S) = \mathtt{arrow}(R \odot P)(Q \odot S) \tag{1}$$

which can be verified, in view of {IOTA-INJ}, by applying ι to both sides, resulting in a simple {BETA}-conversion.

Suppose Δ ends with an application of (FORALL). By the induction hypothesis there are (TRANS)-free derivations for

$$C \vdash s \equiv r_0 \leq \cdots \leq r_m \equiv t \quad \text{and} \quad C, a \leq s \vdash u \equiv w_0 \leq \cdots \leq w_n \equiv v.$$

From these, using (REFL) and (FORALL) we get (TRANS)-free derivations for

$$C \vdash \forall a \leq t . u \equiv \forall a \leq r_m . u \leq \cdots \forall a \leq r_0 . u \equiv \forall a \leq s . u$$

$$\equiv \forall a \leq s . w_0 \leq \cdots \leq \forall a \leq s . w_n \equiv \forall a \leq s . v.$$

Proving the equality of the corresponding translations uses

$$\mathtt{forall}(P)(\Lambda a . \lambda f : a \multimap s . Q) \odot \mathtt{forall}(R)(\Lambda a . \lambda g : a \multimap t . S)$$

$$= \mathtt{forall}(R \odot P)(\Lambda a . \lambda g : a \multimap t . [g \odot R/f] Q \odot S) \tag{2}$$

and can be verified by applying ι to both sides.

Suppose Δ ends with an application of (VART). By the induction hypothesis there are (TRANS)-free derivations for

$$s_1 \equiv r_0^1 \leq \cdots \leq r_{n_1}^1 = t_1$$

$$\vdots$$

$$s_p \equiv r_0^p \leq \cdots \leq r_{n_p}^p \equiv t_p$$

(for simplicity, we omit the context). From these, using (REFL) and (VART) we get (TRANS)-free derivations for

$$[l_1 : s_1, \ldots, l_p : s_p] \equiv [l_1 : r_0^1, \ldots, l_p : s_p] \leq \cdots \leq [l_1 : r_{n_1}^1, \ldots, l_p : s_p]$$

$$\leq \cdots \leq [l_1 : r_{n_1}^1, \ldots, l_p : r_0^p]$$

$$\leq \cdots \leq [l_1 : r_{n_1}^1, \ldots, l_p : r_{n_p}^p] \equiv [l_1 : t_1, \ldots, l_p : t_p]$$

$$\leq [l_1 : t_1, \ldots, l_p : t_p, \ldots, l_q : t_q].$$

Proving the equality of the corresponding translations uses

$$\mathtt{vart}(P_1) \cdots (P_p) \odot \mathtt{vart}(Q_1) \cdots (Q_q)$$

$$= \mathtt{vart}(P_1 \odot Q_1) \cdots (P_p \odot Q_p) \qquad (p \leq q). \tag{3}$$

To verify this, let L be the left hand side of the equation, R the right hand side and let w be a fresh variable. By extensionality (or {ETA} and {XI}) and by {IOTA-INJ}, it is sufficient to show $\iota(L)(w) = \iota(R)(w)$. By {VART-COP}, this follows from

$$\mathtt{case}\ w\ \mathtt{of}\ l_1 \Rightarrow (\mathtt{inj}_{l_1}; \iota(L)), \ldots, l_p \Rightarrow (\mathtt{inj}_{l_p}; \iota(L))$$

$$= \mathtt{case}\ w\ \mathtt{of}\ l_1 \Rightarrow (\mathtt{inj}_{l_1}; \iota(R)), \ldots, l_p \Rightarrow (\mathtt{inj}_{l_p}; \iota(R))$$

which is readily verified.

When Δ ends with (TRANS), we just concatenate the chains of (TRANS)-free derivations and the equality of the translations is an immediate consequence of the associativity of $\odot$. ■

The following is used to handle one of the cases in Lemma 8 below.

LEMMA 7   For any two (TRANS)-free derivations, Δ yielding $C \vdash s \leq t$ and Θ yielding $C, a \leq t \vdash u \leq v$, there exist types $r_0, \ldots, r_n$ such that $u \equiv r_0, r_n \equiv v$, and (TRANS)-free derivations $\Sigma_1, \ldots, \Sigma_n$ yielding respectively $C, a \leq s \vdash r_0 \leq \cdots \leq r_n$, such that $\max(\mathrm{height}(\Sigma_1), \ldots, \mathrm{height}(\Sigma_n)) \leq \max(\mathrm{height}(\Delta), \mathrm{height}(\Theta))$. Moreover, if the translations $\Delta^*, \Theta^*, \Sigma_1^*, \ldots, \Sigma_n^*$ yield respectively the (coercion) terms $C^* \vdash P : s^* \hookrightarrow t^*$,

$C^*, a, g : a \multimap t^* \vdash Q : u^* \multimap v^* C^*, a, f : a \multimap s^* \vdash R_1 : r_0^* \multimap r_1^*, \ldots, C^*, a, f : a \multimap$
$s^* \vdash R_n : r_{n-1}^* \multimap r_n^*$ then

$$C^*, a, f : a \multimap s^* \vdash R_1 \odot \cdots \odot R_n = [f \odot P/g] Q$$

is provable in **TARGET**.

Proof   By induction on the height of Θ.   ∎

LEMMA 8   Let $\Delta_1, \ldots, \Delta_m$ be (TRANS)-free derivations in **SOURCE** yielding respectively $C \vdash s_0 \leq \cdots \leq s_m$ and $\Theta_1, \ldots, \Theta_n$ be (TRANS)-free derivations yielding respectively $C \vdash t_0 \leq \cdots \leq t_n$. Let the translations $\Delta_1^*, \ldots, \Delta_m^*, \Theta_1^*, \ldots, \Theta_n^*$ yield respectively the (coercion) terms

$$C^* \vdash P_1 : s_0^* \multimap s_1^*, \ldots, C^* \vdash P_m : s_{m-1}^* \multimap s_m^*,$$

$$C^* \vdash Q_1 : t_0^* \multimap t_1^*, \ldots, C^* \vdash Q_n : t_{n-1}^* \multimap t_n^*.$$

If $s_0 \equiv t_0$ and $s_m \equiv t_n$ then

$$C^* \vdash P_1 \odot \cdots \odot P_m = Q_1 \odot \cdots \odot Q_n$$

is provable in **TARGET**.

Proof   We begin with the following remarks:

• If one of $s_0, \ldots, s_m, t_0, \ldots, t_n$, is *Top* then the desired equality holds. Indeed, then $s_m \equiv Top \equiv t_n$ and the equality follows from the identity

$$P = \mathtt{top} \tag{4}$$

which is verified by applying ι to both sides (recall that **1** is a terminator).

• Those derivations among $\Delta_1, \ldots, \Delta_m, \Theta_1, \ldots, \Theta_n$ which consist entirely of one application of (REFL) can be eliminated without loss of generality. Indeed, the corresponding coercion term is I which acts as an identity for $\odot$.

• If none of the derivations among $\Delta_1, \ldots, \Delta_m, \Theta_1, \ldots, \Theta_n$ consists of just (TOP), then those derivations which consist of just (VAR) can also be eliminated without loss of generality. Indeed, once we have eliminated the (REFL)'s, the (VAR)'s must form an initial segment of both $\Delta_1, \ldots, \Delta_m$ and $\Theta_1, \ldots, \Theta_n$ because whenever $s \leq a$ is derivable, s must also be a type variable. Let us say that $s_0 \equiv a_0, \ldots, s_{p-1} \equiv a_{p-1}$ ($p \leq m$), where $\Delta_1, \ldots, \Delta_p$ are *all* the derivations consisting of just (VAR), and also that $t_0 \equiv b_0, \ldots, t_{q-1} \equiv b_{q-1}$ ($q \leq n$), where $\Theta_1, \ldots, \Theta_q$ are all the derivations consisting of just (VAR). Then, $a_0 \leq a_1, \ldots, a_{p-1} \leq s_p$, as well as $b_0 \leq b_1, \ldots, b_{q-1} \leq t_q$, must all occur in

C. But $a_0 \equiv s_0 \equiv t_0 \equiv b_0$ so by the uniqueness of declarations in contexts, $a_1 \equiv b_1, \ldots,$ etc. Suppose $p < q$. Then, $s_p \equiv b_p$ is a variable. Since Δ_{p+1} cannot be just a (REFL) or a (TOP) it must be a (VAR), contradicting the maximality of p. Thus $p = q$ and $s_p \equiv t_q$ and the (VAR)'s can be eliminated.

We proceed to prove the lemma by induction on the maximum of the heights of the derivations $\Delta_1, \ldots, \Delta_m, \Theta_1, \ldots, \Theta_n$. The basis of the induction is an immediate consequence of the remarks above.

For the induction step in the view of the remarks above, we can assume without loss of generality that none of the derivations is just a (TOP), (VAR), or (REFL). Consequently, $\Delta_1, \ldots, \Delta_m, \Theta_1, \ldots, \Theta_n$ must all end with the same rule, depending on the type construction used in $s_0 \equiv t_0$.

If all derivations end in (ARROW), the desired equality follows from the induction hypothesis, the associativity of $\odot$, and Eq. (1). Similarly for (VART) using Eq. (3). The desired equality in the case (FORALL) follows from the induction hypothesis using Lemma 7, from the associativity of $\odot$, and from Eq. (2). The remaining cases are straight-forward. ∎

This gives us the coherence of the translation of inheritance judgments. To state it we need some terminology. We say that two **SOURCE** derivations which yield the same judgment are *congruent* if their translations in **TARGET** yield provably equal terms. We will write $\Delta_1 \cong \Delta_2$ for congruence of derivations. It is easy to check that $\cong$ *is* in fact a congruence with respect to the operations on derivations induced by the rules.

LEMMA 9 (Coherence of the translation of inheritance) If Δ_1 and Δ_2 are two **SOURCE** derivations yielding the same inheritance judgment then $\Delta_1 \cong \Delta_2$ (their translations yield provably equal terms in **TARGET**).

Proof Immediate consequence of Lemmas 6 and 8. ∎

Before we turn to the coherence of the translation of typing judgments, we note a few facts about inheritance judgments that follow from Lemma 6 and that will be invoked subsequently. These facts are closely related to the remarks opening the proof of Lemma 8.

Remark 10 If $C \vdash s \leq t$ is derivable, $s \equiv a$, a type variable, and $t \not\equiv a$ then

• if $t \equiv b$, also a type variable, there must exist type variables $a_0, \ldots, a_n$, $n \geq 1$ such that $a \equiv a_0$, $b \equiv a_n$, and $a_{i-1} \leq a_i \in C$, $i = 1, \ldots, n$;

- if t is not a type variable, there must exist type variables $a_0, \ldots, a_n$, $n \geq 0$ and a type u such that $a \equiv a_0$, $a_{i-1} \leq a_i \in C$, $i = 1, \ldots, n$, $a_n \leq u \in C$, and $C \vdash u \leq t$ (of course, this is trivial when $t \equiv Top$).

If $C \vdash s \leq t$ is derivable, and s is not a type variable, then t cannot be a type variable, and if moreover $t \not\equiv Top$, then s and t must both have the "same" outermost type constructor (as detailed exhaustively below) and

- if $s \equiv s_1 \rightarrow s_2$ and $t \equiv t_1 \rightarrow t_2$ then $C \vdash t_1 \leq s_1$ and $C \vdash s_2 \leq t_2$;
- if $s \equiv \{l_1 : s_1, \ldots, l_q : s_q\}$ and $t \equiv \{l_1 : t_1, \ldots, l_p : t_p\}$ then $p \leq q$ and $C \vdash s_1 \leq t_1, \ldots,$ $C \vdash s_p \leq t_p$;
- if $s \equiv \forall a \leq s_1 . s_2$ and $t \equiv \forall a \leq t_1 . t_2$ then $C \vdash t_1 \leq s_1$ and $C, a \leq t_1 \vdash s_2 \leq t_2$;
- if s and t are both recursive types then they must be identical;
- if $s \equiv [l_1 : s_1, \ldots, l_p : s_p]$ and $t \equiv [l_1 : t_1, \ldots, l_q : t_q]$ then $p \leq q$ and $C \vdash s_1 \leq t_1, \ldots,$ $C \vdash s_p \leq t_p$.

We turn now to the coherence of the translation of typing judgments, which is the central technical result of the paper. As explained in Section 3, we weaken the system by replacing the rule (FORALL) with (W-FORALL) (see Appendix A). With this, we have the following order-theoretic property about the inheritance judgments, which fails in the presence of (FORALL). The property asserts the existence of conditional greatest lower bounds and of least upper bounds.

LEMMA 11   Replace (FORALL) with (W-FORALL). Let C be an inheritance context and let t_1, t_2 be types.

1. If there is an r with $C \vdash r \leq t_i$ $(i = 1, 2)$, then there exists a type $t_1 \sqcap t_2$ such that

- $C \vdash t_1 \sqcap t_2 \leq t_i$ $(i = 1, 2)$ and
- for any s such that $C \vdash s \leq t_i$ $(i = 1, 2)$ we have $C \vdash s \leq t_1 \sqcap t_2$.

2. There is a type $t_1 \sqcup t_2$ such that

- $C \vdash t_i \leq t_1 \sqcup t_2$ $(i = 1, 2)$ and
- for any s such that $C \vdash t_i \leq s$ $(i = 1, 2)$ we have $C \vdash t_1 \sqcup t_2 \leq s$.

Proof   Because of the contravariance property of the first argument of the function space operator manifest in the rule (ARROW), we will prove items 1 and 2 simultaneously. In view of Lemma 6, it is sufficient to work with proofs where all instances of (TRANS) appear at the end. Since moreover any two types have a common upper bound, *Top*, the statement of the lemma is equivalent to the following formulation:

For any $\Delta_1,\ldots,\Delta_m$, (TRANS)-free derivations in **SOURCE** yielding respectively $C \vdash u_0 \leq \cdots \leq u_m$ and any $\Theta_1,\ldots,\Theta_n$, (TRANS)-free derivations yielding respectively $C \vdash v_0 \leq \cdots \leq v_n$,

1. if $u_0 \equiv v_0$, and let $t_1 \equiv u_m$ and $t_2 \equiv v_n$, then there is a type $t_1 \sqcap t_2$ having the properties in item 1 of the lemma:

2. if $u_m \equiv v_n$, and let $t_1 \equiv u_0$ and $t_2 \equiv v_0$, then there is a type $t_1 \sqcup t_2$ having the properties in item 2 of the lemma.

This is shown by induction on the maximum of m, n and of the heights of $\Delta_1,\ldots,$ $\Delta_m, \Theta_1,\ldots,\Theta_n$. To be able to apply the induction hypothesis, a case analysis is performed, depending on the structure of t_1 and t_2. We will only look at a few illustrative cases. The facts listed in Remark 10 and the reasoning that produced these facts as well as the remarks opening the proof of Lemma 8 are used throughout.

For example, if t_1 is a type variable in item 1, then u_i is also a type variable for each i, and $u_{i-1} \leq u_i \in C$, $i = 1,\ldots,m$. Then one of $C \vdash u_0 \leq \cdots \leq u_m$ or $C \vdash v_0 \leq \cdots \leq v_n$ must be an initial segment of the other, so t_1 and t_2 are comparable and $t_1 \sqcap t_2$ can be taken as the smaller among them. For item 2, if t_1 is a type variable, then $u_0 \leq u_1 \in C$ and, by the induction hypothesis (m decreases), $t_1 \sqcup t_2$ can be taken to be $u_1 \sqcup t_2$.

As another example, suppose that in item 1 t_1 has the form $\forall a \leq s . r_1$. If $u_0 \equiv v_0$ is a type variable, then $u_0 \leq u_1 \in C$ and $v_0 \leq v_1 \in C$ hence $u_1 \equiv v_1$ and we can apply the induction hypothesis by eliminating Δ_1, Θ_1. Assume that $u_0 \equiv v_0$ is not a type variable. By Remark 10 (simplified to take into account the weakening of (FORALL)), it must have the form $\forall a \leq s . r$. Again by Remark 10 t_2 is either *Top* or has the form $\forall a \leq s . r_2$. If $t_2 \equiv Top$ then $t_1 \sqcap t_2$ can be taken to be t_1. Otherwise, there are (TRANS)-free derivations $\Delta'_1,\ldots,\Delta'_m$ yielding $C, a \leq s \vdash u'_0 \leq \cdots \leq u'_m$ and $\Theta'_1,\ldots,\Theta'_n$ yielding respectively $C, a \leq u \vdash v'_0 \leq \cdots \leq v'_n$, where $u'_0 \equiv v'_0$ and $u'_m = r_1$ and $v'_n \equiv r_2$, and where each of these derivations has strictly smaller height than the corresponding one among $\Delta_1,\ldots,\Delta_m, \Theta_1,\ldots,\Theta_n$. By the induction hypothesis we get a type $r_1 \sqcap r_2$, and we can then take $t_1 \sqcap t_2$ to be $\forall a \leq s . r_1 \sqcap r_2$. This calculation makes clear where our proof breaks down if we were to use the more general rule (FORALL) instead of (W-FORALL). Indeed, if the bounds on the type variables were allowed to differ, as in the more general case, we would be unable to apply the induction hypothesis since the two contexts would differ between the Θ's and the Δ's.

We omit the remaining cases, which use similar ideas.   ∎

We use this property in the proof of Lemma 12, which is a slightly stronger result than the actual coherence of the translation of typing judgements. Of course, the strengthening is exploited in a proof by induction. First we introduce a definition and more convenient notations. For derivations yielding typing judgements we define the *essential height* which is computed as the usual height, with the proviso that [INH] and the rules yielding inheritance judgments do *not* increase it. We also use a special notation for describing "composition" of derivations via the rules. We explain this notation through two examples. If Σ yields $\Gamma \vdash e : s$ and Θ yields $\hat{\Gamma} \vdash s \leq t$, then $[INH]\langle \Sigma, \Theta \rangle$ yields $\Gamma \vdash e : t$. If Δ yields $\Gamma, x : s \vdash e : t$ then $[ABS]\langle \Delta \rangle$ yields $\Gamma \vdash \lambda x : s . e : s \to t$.

In preparation for the proof of the next lemma, we have two remarks.

• We have the congruence

$$[INH]\langle [INH]\langle \Sigma, \Theta_1 \rangle, \Theta_2 \rangle \cong [INH]\langle \Sigma, (TRANS)\langle \Theta_1, \Theta_2 \rangle \rangle.$$

This follows from the fact that $\iota(Q)(\iota(P)(M)) = \iota(P \odot Q)(M)$ which is immediately verified.

• Any **SOURCE** derivation is congruent to a derivation of the form $[INH]\langle \Delta, \Theta \rangle$ where Δ does *not* end with an application of the [INH] rule. This follows from the previous remark and, in the case when the original derivation did not end in [INH], from

$$\Delta \cong [INH]\langle \Delta, (REFL) \rangle$$

which in turn follows from $M = \iota(I)(M)$.

LEMMA 12   Replace (FORALL) with (W-FORALL). For any two **SOURCE** derivations, Δ_i yielding $\Gamma \vdash e : t_i$ ($i = 1, 2$), there exist a type s, a derivation Σ yielding $\Gamma \vdash e : s$, and two derivations Θ_i yielding $\hat{\Gamma} \vdash s \leq t_i$ ($i = 1, 2$), such that

$$\Delta_i \cong [INH]\langle \Sigma, \Theta_i \rangle \qquad (i = 1, 2).$$

Proof   By induction on the maximum of the essential heights of Δ_1, Δ_2. In view of the previous remarks, it is sufficient to prove the statement of the lemma assuming that neither Δ_1 nor Δ_2 ends in [INH] (but we retain the actual statement of the lemma in the induction hypothesis). For such derivations, Δ_1 and Δ_2 must end with the same rule (which rule depends on the structure of e). We do a case analysis according to this last rule, and we include here only the cases which we believe are important for the understanding of the result (even if their treatment is straightforward) as well as some cases which are particularly complex. We will call the type s, whose existence is the essence of the result, the *common type*.

Rule [VAR]   It must be the case that $t_1 \equiv t_2 \equiv r$ where $x : r$ occurs in Γ. Consequently, the treatment of this rule is trivial: take the common type to be r, $\Sigma \equiv$ [VAR], and $\Theta_1 \equiv \Theta_2 \equiv$ (REFL).

The introduction rules are quite simple and we illustrate them with the rule [ABS]. Suppose that $\Delta_i \equiv [\text{ABS}]\langle\Delta_i'\rangle$ and that Δ_i yields $\Gamma \vdash \lambda x:s.e:s \to t_i$ (s is the same since it appears in the term), thus Δ_i' yields $\Gamma, x:s \vdash e:t_i$ ($i = 1, 2$). Apply the induction hypothesis to Δ_1', Δ_2' to obtain r, Σ', Θ_1', Θ_2'. Also by the induction hypothesis,

$$\Delta_i \cong [\text{ABS}]\langle[\text{INH}]\langle\Sigma', \Theta_i'\rangle\rangle \qquad (i = 1, 2).$$

We claim that the right hand side is congruent to

$$[\text{INH}]\langle[\text{ABS}]\langle\Sigma'\rangle, (\text{ARROW})\langle(\text{REFL}), \Theta_i'\rangle\rangle.$$

This implies that the statement of the lemma holds for Δ_1, Δ_2, with common type $s \to r$, with $\Sigma \equiv [\text{ABS}]\langle\Sigma'\rangle$, and with $\Theta_i \equiv (\text{ARROW})\langle(\text{REFL}), \Theta_i'\rangle$ ($i = 1, 2$). The congruence claim follows from

$$\lambda x:s.\iota(P)(M) = \iota(\texttt{arrow}(I)(P))(\lambda x:s.M)$$

which is readily verified.

Rule [B-SPEC]   To simplify the notation, we omit the contexts. Suppose that $\Delta_i \equiv [\text{B-SPEC}]\langle\Delta_i', \Xi_i\rangle$ and that Δ_i yields $e(r):[r/a]t_i$ (r is the same since it appears in the term and we can take the bound variable to be the same without loss of generality), thus Δ_i' yields $e:\forall a \le s_i.t_i$ and Ξ_i yields $r \le s_i$ ($i = 1, 2$). Apply the induction hypothesis to Δ_1', Δ_2' to obtain w, Σ', Θ_1', Θ_2'. Also by the induction hypothesis,

$$\Delta_i \cong [\text{B-SPEC}]\langle[\text{INH}]\langle\Sigma', \Theta_i'\rangle, \Xi_i\rangle \qquad (i = 1, 2). \tag{5}$$

Since $w \le \forall a \le s_i.t_i$ ($i = 1, 2$) it follows from Remark 10 (simplified to take into account the weakening of (FORALL)) that there must exist types u, v such that $s_i \equiv u$, $a \le s_i \vdash v \le t_i$ ($i = 1, 2$) and $w \le \forall a \le u.v$ are derivable. It follows that $r \le u$, and, by Lemma 6 and by iterated Lemma 7, that $a \le r \vdash v \le t_i$ ($i = 1, 2$) are derivable. Next, we will use the following sublemma:

SUBLEMMA   For any derivation Δ yielding $C, a \le r \vdash s \le t$ there exists a derivation Σ yielding $C \vdash [r/a]s \le [r/a]t$ such that, if the translations Δ^*, Σ^* yield respectively

$$C^*, a, f:a \rightsquigarrow r^* \vdash P:s^* \rightsquigarrow t^*, \qquad C^* \vdash Q:[r^*/a]s^* \rightsquigarrow [r^*/a]t^*,$$

then

$$C^* \vdash Q = (\Lambda a.\lambda f:a \rightsquigarrow r^*.P)(r^*)(I)$$

is provable in **TARGET**.

The sublemma is proved by induction on the height of Δ and is omitted. The sublemma allows us to obtain $[r/a]v \leq [r/a]t_i$ from $a \leq r \vdash v \leq t_i$ $(i = 1, 2)$. Let Θ_i be some derivation of $[r/a]v \leq [r/a]t_i$ $(i = 1, 2)$. Let Ξ be some derivation of $r \leq u$. Let Ω be some derivation of $w \leq \forall a \leq u \, . \, v$. One can readily verify that the right hand side of (5) is congruent to

$$[INH]\langle[B\text{-}SPEC]\langle[INH]\langle\Sigma', \Omega\rangle, \Xi\rangle, \Theta_i\rangle.$$

This implies that the statement of the lemma holds for Δ_1, Δ_2, with common type $[r/a]v$, with $\Sigma \equiv [B\text{-}SPEC]\langle[INH]\langle\Sigma', \Omega\rangle, \Xi\rangle$, and with Θ_i being just Θ_i $(i = 1, 2)$. (*Note*. There is no difficulty in dealing with (FORALL) instead of (W-FORALL) here: $s_i \equiv u$ would be simply replaced by $s_i \leq u$.)

Rule [R-ELIM]   Suppose that $\Delta_i \equiv [R\text{-}ELIM]\langle\Delta_i'\rangle$ and that Δ_i yields $\Gamma \vdash \text{elim}\, e:$ $[\mu a_i \, . \, t_i/a_i]t_i$, thus Δ_i' yields $\Gamma \vdash e : \mu a_i \, . \, t_i$ $(i = 1, 2)$. Apply the induction hypothesis to Δ_1', Δ_2' obtaining s', Σ', Θ_1', Θ_2'. Also by the induction hypothesis,

$$\Delta_i \cong [R\text{-}ELIM]\langle[INH]\langle\Sigma', \Theta_i'\rangle\rangle \qquad (i = 1, 2).$$

Since $s' \leq \mu a_i \, . \, t_i$ $(i = 1, 2)$ are derivable, it follows from Remark 10 that there must exist a, t such that $\mu a_i \, . \, t_i \equiv \mu a \, . \, t$ $(i = 1, 2)$ and $s' \leq \mu a \, . \, t$ are derivable. Let Θ' be any derivation of $s' \leq \mu a \, . \, t$. Since by Lemma 9, $\Theta_1' \cong \Theta_2' \cong \Theta'$, the statement of the lemma holds with common type $[\mu a \, . \, t/a]t$, with $\Sigma \equiv [R\text{-}ELIM]\langle[INH]\langle\Sigma', \Theta'\rangle\rangle$, and with $\Theta_i \equiv (REFL)$ $(i = 1, 2)$.

Rule [CASE]   Again, to simplify the notation we omit the contexts. Suppose that $\Delta_i \equiv [CASE]\langle\Delta_i', \Delta_{1i}', \ldots, \Delta_{ni}'\rangle$ and that Δ_i yields $\text{case}\, e\, \text{of}\, l_1 \Rightarrow f_1, \ldots, l_n \Rightarrow f_n : t_i$, thus Δ_i' yields $e : [l_1 : t_{1i}, \ldots, l_n : t_{ni}]$, and Δ_{ji}' yields $f_j : t_{ji} \rightarrow t_i$ $(j = 1, \ldots, n)$ $(i = 1, 2)$. Apply the induction hypothesis to Δ_1', Δ_2' to obtain s, Σ', Θ_1', Θ_2'. Also apply the induction hypothesis to Δ_{j1}', Δ_{j2}' to obtain s_j, Σ_j', Θ_{j1}', Θ_{j2}' $(j = 1, \ldots, n)$. By the induction hypothesis,

$$\Delta_i \cong [CASE\langle[INH]\langle\Sigma', \Theta_i'\rangle,$$

$$[INH]\langle\Sigma_1', \Theta_{1i}'\rangle, \ldots, [INH]\langle\Sigma_n', \Theta_{ni}'\rangle\rangle \qquad (i = 1, 2). \tag{6}$$

Since $s \leq [l_1 : t_{1i}, \ldots, l_n : t_{ni}]$ $(i = 1, 2)$ are derivable, it follows again from Remark 10 that there must exist $m \leq n$ and types $r_1, \ldots, r_m$ such that $r_1 \leq t_{1i}, \ldots, r_m \leq t_{mi}$ $(i = 1, 2)$ and $s \leq [l_1 : r_1, \ldots, l_m : r_m]$ are derivable. Again similarly, for each $j = 1, \ldots, n$, since $s_j \leq t_{ji} \rightarrow t_i$ $(i = 1, 2)$ are derivable, there must exist u_j, v_j such that $t_{ji} \leq u_j$ and $v_j \leq t_i$ $(i = 1, 2)$ as well as $s_j \leq u_j \rightarrow v_j$ are derivable. Thus, we can derive $r_j \leq t_{ji} \leq u_j$ $(j = 1, \ldots, n)$ $(i = 1, 2)$. However, the fact that the v_j's may be distinct causes a problem when we want to apply [CASE]. This is resolved by Lemma 11. Since $n \geq 1$, there exists a common lower bound of t_1 and t_2 (say v_1), hence $v \equiv t_1 \sqcap t_2$ exists and we can derive $v_j \leq v \leq t_i$ ($j = 1, \ldots, n$) ($i = 1, 2$). We conclude that there exists a derivation Θ'' of $s \leq [l_1 : u_1, \ldots, l_n : u_n]$, that there exist derivations Θ''_j of $s_j \leq u_j \to v$ ($j = 1, \ldots, n$), and that there exist derivations Θ_i of $v \leq t_i$ ($i = 1, 2$). With these, we claim that the right hand side of (6) is congruent to

$$[\text{IHN}] \langle [\text{CASE}] \langle [\text{INH}] \langle \Sigma', \Theta'' \rangle, [\text{INH}] \langle \Sigma'_1, \Theta''_1 \rangle, \ldots, [\text{INH}] \langle \Sigma'_n, \Theta''_n \rangle \rangle, \Theta_i \rangle.$$

This implies that the statement of the lemma holds for Δ_1, Δ_2, with common type v, with $\Sigma \equiv [\text{CASE}] \langle [\text{INH}] \langle \Sigma', \Theta'' \rangle, [\text{INH}] \langle \Sigma'_1, \Theta''_1 \rangle, \ldots, [\text{INH}] \langle \Sigma'_n, \Theta''_n \rangle \rangle$, and with Θ_i being just Θ_i ($i = 1, 2$).

To prove the congruence claim we introduce notations for certain derivations of inheritance judgements whose existence we have established. For each $j = 1, \ldots, n$, $i = 1, 2$, let Ξ_{ji} be sme derivation for $t_{ji} \leq u_j$. Then (ARROW) $\langle \Xi_{ji}, \Theta_i \rangle$ is a derivation for $u_j \to v \leq t_{ji} \to t_i$. By Lemma 9 we have

$$\Theta'_{ji} \cong (\text{TRANS}) \langle \Theta''_j, (\text{ARROW}) \langle \Xi_{ji}, \Theta_i \rangle \rangle \tag{7}$$

Let Ξ be some derivation of $s \leq [l_1 : r_1, \ldots, l_m : r_m]$. For each $j = 1, \ldots, m$, $i = 1, 2$, let Ω_{ji} be some derivation for $r_j \leq t_{ji}$. By Lemma 9 we have

$$\Theta'_i \cong (\text{TRANS}) \langle \Xi, (\text{VART}) \langle \Omega_{1i}, \ldots, \Omega_{mi} \rangle \rangle \tag{8}$$

and

$$\Theta'' \cong (\text{TRANS}) \langle \Xi, (\text{TRANS}) \langle (\text{VART}) \langle \Omega_{1i}, \ldots, \Omega_{mi} \rangle, \langle \text{VART}) (\Xi_{1i}, \ldots, \Xi_{ni} \rangle \rangle \rangle. \tag{9}$$

With these, the congruence claim follows from

case $\iota(P \odot \text{vart}(Q_1) \cdots (Q_m))(M)$ of $l_1 \Rightarrow$

$\quad \iota(R_1 \odot \text{arrow}(S_1)(T))(F_1), \ldots, l_n \Rightarrow \iota(R_n \odot \text{arrow}(S_n(T))(F_n)$

$\quad = \iota(T)(\text{case } \iota(P \odot \text{vart}(Q_1) \cdots (Q_m) \odot \text{vart}(S_1) \cdots (S_n))(M)$

$\qquad \text{of } l_1 \Rightarrow \iota(R_1)(F_1), \ldots, l_n \Rightarrow \iota(R_n)(F_n)).$

By Eq. (3) and {VART-CRN} the right hand side equals

case $\iota(P \odot \text{vart}(Q_1 \odot S_1) \cdots (Q_m \odot S_m))(M)$

$\quad \text{of } l_1 \Rightarrow \iota(R_1)(F_1); \iota(T), \ldots, l_n \Rightarrow \iota(R_n)(F_n); \iota(T)$

and the equality is readily verified. ∎

THEOREM 13 (Coherence)   Replace (FORALL) with (W-FORALL). If Δ_1 and Δ_2 are two **SOURCE** derivations yielding the same typing judgement then $\Delta_1 \cong \Delta_2$ (their translations yield provably equal terms in **TARGET**).

Proof   Take $t_1 \equiv t_2$ in Lemma 12. By Lemma 9, $\Theta_1 \cong \Theta_2$. It follows that $\Delta_1 \cong \Delta_2$.   ∎

6   Models

So far we have not actually given a model for the language **SOURCE**. In this section we correct this omission. However, it is a central point of this paper that there is *basically nothing new that we need to do in this section*, since calculi satisfying the equational theory of **TARGET** have been thoroughly studied in the literature on the semantics of type systems. Domain-theoretic semantics suggests natural candidates for a special class of maps with the properties needed to interpret the operators $\to$ and $\hookrightarrow$.

The domain-theoretic interpretations that we have examined so far are summarized in the following table. The necessary properties for all but the last row can be found in Coquand and Erhard (1987) and Hyland and Pitts (1989), Coquand, Gunter, and Winskel (1989), Amadio, Bruce, and Longo (1986), Coquand, Gunter, and Winskel (1987), and Girard (1987), respectively. The properties needed for the last row can be checked in a manner similar to Girard (1987).

Types	Terms	Coercions	Variants
Algebraic lattices		bistrict maps	sep sum of lattices
Scott domains	continuous maps	strict maps	separated sums
Finitary projections			separated sums
dI domains		strict stable maps	
Coherent spaces	stable maps	linear maps	$!A \oplus !B$
dI domains			

By a bistrict map of lattices we mean a continuous map which preserves both bottom and top elements. A separated sum of lattices L and M is the disjoint sum of L and M together with new top and bottom elements. Note that the category of Scott domains (finitary projections, respectively) and strict maps does have finite coproducts, given by coalesced sums of domains, and this implies that the required equation

$$P(\text{case } M \text{ of } l_1 \Rightarrow F_1, \ldots, l_n \Rightarrow F_n) = \text{case } M \text{ of } l_1 \Rightarrow F_1; P, \ldots, l_n \Rightarrow F_n; P$$

$$\{\text{VART-CRN?}\}$$

holds if P is a strict map (in fact, a separated sum of domains A and B is just the coalesced sum of the lifted domains $A_\perp$ and $B_\perp$). Furthermore, it may be checked that strictness is preserved by the formation of coercion maps from given ones according to the coercion rules given in Section 3 and at the beginning of this section. This model satisfies also $\{\text{VART-BETA}\} + \{\text{VART-ETA}\}$. An important property used in the case of Scott domains (finitary projections, respectively) is that the continuous maps from C to D are in one-to-one correspondence with the strict maps from $C_\perp$ to D. Analogous remarks hold for stable maps and linear maps, with $!C$ instead of $C_\perp$ (see Girard, 1989, Chapt. 8).

From a category-theoretic point of view, the main point is that we are dealing with *two categories*, one a reflective subcategory of the other; i.e., the inclusion functor has a left adjoint. The subcategory contains all objects of the larger category. While the larger category is cartesian closed, the reflective subcategory (in which our coercions live) does have coproducts.

From a proof-theoretic point of view, it is interesting to note that our solution is similar to the treatment of proof-theoretic commutation rules for disjunction (see Troelstra, 1973, 4.1.3, on p. 279 for a presentation of commutation rules). The so-called commutation rules for sums in proof theory are closely related to the equations $\{\text{VART-CRN?}\}$, where P is an "evaluation" map (see the Appendix B of Girard, 1988).

7 Conclusions and Directions for Further Investigation

The development of calculi for the representation of inheritance polymorphism and the semantics of such calculi are a growing and dynamic area of research investigation in programming languages. We expect that the calculi considered in this paper are only a small sample of what is yet to be developed; In this section we will speculate on a few of the most important directions for further development which will play a significant role in future work of the authors of this paper in particular and the research community in general.

Partial Equivalence Relations

Much of the research on the semantics of the system which we have considered has been based on the use of PERs as described by Bruce and Longo (1988). It is therefore worthwhile to compare the approach in this paper to this alternative approach. There is an evident means of carrying out a technical comparison: since the PER model interprets the calculus **TARGET**, it also interprets **SOURCE** via our translation. But the semantics in Bruce and Longo (1988) gives the interpretation (without recursion) directly using PERs. Could these two interpretations be the same? For a certain fragment of **SOURCE** (including recursion but not bounded quantification), Cardone has recently answered the question in the affirmative for his form of semantics (Cardone, 1989) (where coherence is not an issue because the interpretation of a judgment $e:s$ is given as the equivalence class, in s, of the interpretation of the erasure of e—hence the meaning is not defined inductively on a derivation). For the full calculus the answer is still unknown as this paper is being written. Amadio's thesis contains some results about the relationship between explicit coercions and PER inclusion (Amadio, 1991b).

Equational Theory

The reader has probably noted that we have never offered an equational theory for **SOURCE**, only one for **TARGET**. At the current time, the proper equational theory for **SOURCE** is still a subject of active research. However, our translation does suggest an equational theory. One can prove that two terms of **SOURCE** are equal by showing that their translations are equivalent in the equational theory for **TARGET**. Any of the models we have proposed will satisfy the resulting equational theory. (Whether this is also true of the interpretation of Bruce and Longo (1988) may follow if this interpretation is the same as ours.) Since our translation is computable, it follows that this reflected equational theory for **SOURCE** is recursively enumerable; it is natural to ask for a reasonable axiomatization of this theory. Note, for example, if $e = e':s$ holds in **SOURCE** and $s \leq t$, then $e = e':t$ also holds in the reflected theory. There are probably many similarly interesting derived equational rules.

Recursion

Any attempt to provide a model for a calculus which combines inheritance and recursion must deal with the seemingly contradictory semantic characteristics of inheritance and recursion at higher types. Ordinarily, the rule for inheritance between exponentials (function spaces) is given as

$$\frac{u \leq s \quad t \leq v}{s \to t \leq u \to v},$$

where s, t, u, v are type expressions and $\leq$ is the relation of inheritance (reading $s \leq t$ as "s inherits from t"). Note, in particular, the *contra* variance in the first argument of the $\rightarrow$ operator. In contrast, semantic domains which solve recursive domain equations such as $D = D \rightarrow D$ are generally constructed using a technique—adjoint pairs to be precise—which make it possible to "order" types using a concept of approximation based on the rule

$$\frac{\phi : s \rightarrow u \quad \psi : t \rightarrow v}{\phi \rightarrow \psi : (s \rightarrow t) \rightarrow (u \rightarrow v)},$$

where $\phi = \langle \phi^L, \phi^R \rangle$ and $\psi = \langle \psi^L, \psi^R \rangle$ are adjoint pairs and $\phi \rightarrow \psi$ is the adjoint pair $\langle \lambda f . \psi^L \circ f \circ \phi^R, \lambda f . \psi^R \circ f \circ \phi^L \rangle$. Note, for this case, the *covariance* in the first argument of the $\rightarrow$ operator. Because of this difference, models such as the PER interpretation of Bruce and Longo (1988), which provides a semantics for inheritance and parametric polymorphism, do not evidently extend to a semantics for recursive types. To provide for recursive types under this interpretation Coppo (1985) and Coppo and Zacchi (1985) utilize an appeal to the structure of the underlying universal domain. which is itself an inverse limit which solves a recursive equation. Amadio (1989, 1991a) and Cardone (1989) have explored this approach in considerable detail. There has also been progress on understanding the solution of recursive equations over domains internally to the PER model which should provide further insights (Freyd, 1990; Freyd *et al.*, 1990). On the other hand, models such as those of Girard (1986) and Coquand, Gunter, and Winskel (1987, 1989), which handle parametric polymorphism and recursive types, do not provide an evident interpretation for inheritance. It has been the purpose of this paper to resolve this problem by an appeal to the paradigm of "inheritance as implicit coercion." However, this leaves open the question of how recursive types can be treated with this technique if one is to include a more powerful set of rules for deriving inheritance judgements between recursive types.

One complicating problem is to decide exactly what form of inheritance between recursive types is desired. For example, it seems very reasonable that if s is a subtype of t then the type of lists of s's should be a subtype of lists of t's. This is not actually derivable in the inheritance system described in this paper since there are no rules for inheritance between recursive types. But care must be taken: if s is a subtype of t then is the solution of the equations $a = a \rightarrow s$ be a subtype of the solution of $a = a \rightarrow t$? There are several possible approaches to answering this question. The PER interpretation provides a good guide: we can ask whether the solutions of these two equations have the desired relation in the PER model. Concerning the coercions approach we are forced to ask whether there is any intuitive coercion between these two types. If there is, we have not seen it! It is reasonable to conjecture that inheritance relations derived using the following rule will be acceptable,

$$\frac{C, a \leq Top \vdash s \leq t}{C \vdash \mu a . s \leq \mu a . t},$$ (REC)

where types s and t have only *positive* occurrences of the variable a. Unfortunately, this misses many interesting inheritance relations that one would like to settle. Discussions of this problem will appear in several future publications on this subject. A rather satisfactory treatment using coercions has been described in Breazu-Tannen, Gunter, and Scedrov (1989) using the "Amber rule" of Cardelli (1986).

Operational Semantics

Despite its importance there is virtually no literature on theoretical issues concerning the operational semantics of languages with inheritance polymorphism. In particular, at the time we are writing there are no published discussions of the relationship (if any!) of the denotational models which have been studied to the intended operational semantics of a programming language based on the models. In fact, the operational semantics of no existing "practical" programming language is based on the kind of semantics discussed in this or any of the other papers on the semantics of Fun. This is because there is a divergence between the "traditional" style of semantics for the λ-calculus and the way the evaluation mechanisms of modern functional programming languages actually work. In particular, no functional programming language in common use evaluates past a lambda abstraction. Hence the identification of the constantly divergent function with the divergent element will cause the denotational semantics to fail to be computationally adequate with respect to the evaluation. Another related problem concerns the use of the β-rule and call-by-value evaluation. Many of the functional programming languages now in use evaluate all actual function parameters. This evaluation strategy immediately causes the full β-rule to fail. For example the application of a constant function to a divergent argument will diverge in general. Semantically, this means that terms of higher type must be interpreted as *strict* functions. In a subsequent paper (Breazu-Tannen, Gunter, and Scedrov, 1990), three of the authors of the current document have explored the operational semantics of inheritance with a coercion semantics in a call-by-value setting. The results there are intuitively pleasing, but there is much more that needs to be done. This direction of investigation offers several opportunities for practical applications of the specification and implementation of compilers and interpreters for new languages with inheritance.

Existentials

We have omitted discussion of existentials in this paper. We believe that the coherence results we have described will extend to a suitable interpretation of the existential types using the equational theory for weak sums, but did not choose to involve ourselves in additional cases that this would mean for our proofs.

Order-Sorted Algebra

The use of coercions in a first-order setting has been investigated in work (Goguen, Jonannaud, and Meseguer, 1985; Goguen and Meseguer, unpublished). In particular, the implementation of OBJ2 utilized a form of "inheritance as implicit coercion" approach. Related work by Bruce and Wegner appears in (Bruce and Wegner, 1990).

Abstract Coherence

Since there are many different calculi for which a coherence theorem is interesting, it is very useful to have a more abstract theory from which special instances of coherence can be derived, thus making coherence a more routine part of a semantic theory for an inheritance calculus such as the one we have discussed. We mentioned earlier that coherence was an issue in category theory and this might provide a framework for a more general theory. (However, the results on coherence in the category theory literature are insufficient for the results of this paper so further extensions will be needed). Using rewriting techniques, Curien and Ghelli (1990) have developed a type-theoretic approach to the abstract coherence problem for $F_\leq$ which is a subsystem of **SOURCE** featuring only function and bounded generic types. It would be interesting to see this technique extended to all of **SOURCE**, especially in view of the complications we encountered with variants.

Subtyping of Bounded Quantification

Our main coherence result was proved for a weaker version of the system, one that uses the rule (W-FORALL) instead of (FORALL) (see Appendix A). We believe that this is only a technical restriction that arose from our particular proof, and that coherence holds for the stronger system. A proof would however require a way to circumvent the usage of Lemma 11 in the treatment of the [CASE] rule in Lemma 12, since Lemma 11 fails when (FORALL) is postulated (for a counterexample, see Giorgio Ghelli's dissertation (Ghelli, 1990). Perhaps greatest lower bounds and least upper bounds can be replaced by some canonical choice of lower and upper bounds, a choice that may result from the derivation of the typing judgement itself.

Record Update

For practical applications of calculi such as Fun, a particularly important problem concerns the semantics of "record update." The idea is this: given a function $f : s \to t$ and a record e with a field l of type s, we would like to modify or update the l field of e

by replacing $e.l$ by $f(e.l)$ *without losing or modifying any of the other fields of e.* The development of calculi which can deal with this form of polymorphism and the ways in which Fun and related languages can be used to represent similar techniques are an object of considerable current investigation. One recent effort in this direction is (Cardelli and Mitchell, 1991), but several other efforts are under way. Despite its importance we have not explored this issue in this paper since the discussion about it is very unsettled and it will merit independent treatment at a later date.

We believe that the "inheritance as implicit coercion" method is quite robust. For example, it easily extends to accommodate "constant" inheritances between base types, such as $int \leq real$, as long as coherence conditions similar to the ones arising in the proofs of the relevant lemmas in this paper hold between the constant coercions which interpret these inheritances. Moreover, we expect that our methods will extend to the functional part of Quest (Cardelli, 1989) and to the language described in (Cardelli and Mitchell, 1991), using the techniques of Coquand (1988) and Lamarche (1988). Current work on inheritance and subtyping such as Cook, Hill, and Canning (1990) and Mitchell (1990) will provide new challenges. We *do not claim* that every interesting aspect of inheritance can necessarily be handled in this way. However, our treatment, by showing that inheritance can be uniformly eliminated in favor of definable coercion, provides a challenge to formalisms which purport to introduce inheritance as a fundamentally new concept. Moreover, our basic approach to the semantics of inheritance should provide a useful contrast with other approaches.

Appendix A: The Language SOURCE

Type Expression

Fragment

$a \,|\, Top \,|\, s \to t \,|\, \{l_1 : s_1, \ldots, l_m : s_m\} \,|\, \forall a \leq s.t \,|\, \mu a.t$

Variants

$|\, [l_1 : t_1, \ldots, l_n : t_n],$

where a ranges over type variables, $m, n \geq 1$, and, in $\forall a \leq s.t$, a cannot be free in s. We use $[s/a]t$ for substitution.

Raw Terms

Fragment

$x \,|\, d(e) \,|\, \lambda x : t.e \,|\, \{l_1 = e_1, \ldots, l_m = e_m\} \,|\, e.l \,|\, \Lambda a \leq t.e \,|\, e(t) \,|\, \texttt{into}[\mu a.t]e \,|\, \texttt{elim}\, e$

Variants

$|[l_1:t_1,\ldots,l_i=e,\ldots,l_n:t_n]|$ case e of $l_1 \Rightarrow f_1,\ldots,l_n \Rightarrow f_n$,

where x ranges over (term) variables and $m, n \geq 1$. (Note the type decorations on variant "injections"; this is necessary for the uniqueness of type derivations in the inheritance-less system and it differs from Cardelli and Wegner (1985).)

Raw terms are type-checked by deriving *typing judgments* of the form $\Gamma \vdash e:t$, where Γ is a context. *Contexts* are defined recursively as follows: $\varnothing$ is a context; if Γ is a context which does not declare a, and the free variables of t are declared in Γ, then $\Gamma, a \leq t$ is a context; if Γ is a context which does not declare x, and the free variables of t are declared in Γ, then $\Gamma, x:t$ is a context. The proof system for deriving typing judgments makes use of *inheritance judgments* which have the form $C \vdash s \leq t$, where C is an inheritance context. *Inheritance contexts* are contexts in which only declarations of the form $a \leq t$ appear. If Γ is a context, we denoted by $\hat{\Gamma}$ the inheritance context obtained from Γ by erasing the declarations of the form $x:t$.

Rules for Deriving Inheritance Judgments

Fragment

$$C \vdash t \leq Top, \tag{TOP}$$

where the free variables of t are declared in C;

$$C_1, a \leq t, C_2 \vdash a \leq t \tag{VAR}$$

$$\frac{C \vdash s \leq t \quad C \vdash u \leq v}{C \vdash t \to u \leq s \to v} \tag{ARROW}$$

$$\frac{C \vdash s_1 \leq t_1 \cdots C \vdash s_p \leq t_p}{C \vdash \{l_1:s_1,\ldots,l_p:s_p,\ldots,l_q:s_q\} \leq \{l_1:t_1,\ldots,l_p:t_p\}} \tag{RECD}$$

$$\frac{C \vdash s \leq t \quad C, a \leq s \vdash u \leq v}{C \vdash \forall a \leq t.u \leq \forall a \leq s.v}. \tag{FORALL}$$

For Lemmas 11 and 12 and for Theorem 13, this is replaced with the weaker

$$\frac{C, a \leq t \vdash u \leq v}{C \vdash \forall a \leq t.u \leq \forall a \leq t.v} \tag{W-FORALL}$$

$$C \vdash t \leq t, \tag{REFL}$$

where the free variables of t are declared in C,

$$\frac{C \vdash r \leq s \quad C \vdash s \leq t}{C \vdash r \leq t}. \tag{TRANS}$$

Variants

$$\frac{C \vdash s_1 \leq t_1 \cdots C \vdash s_p \leq t_p}{C \vdash [l_1:s_1,\ldots,l_p:s_p] \leq [l_1:t_1,\ldots,l_p:t_p,\ldots,l_q:t_q]}. \tag{VART}$$

Rules for Deriving Typing Judgments

Fragment

$$\Gamma_1, x:t, \Gamma_2 \vdash x:t \tag{VAR}$$

$$\frac{\Gamma, x:s \vdash e:t}{\Gamma \vdash \lambda x:s.e:s \to t} \tag{ABS}$$

$$\frac{\Gamma \vdash d:s \to t \quad \Gamma \vdash e:s}{\Gamma \vdash d(e):t} \tag{APPL}$$

$$\frac{\Gamma \vdash e_1:t_1 \cdots \Gamma \vdash e_m:t_m}{\Gamma \vdash \{l_1 = e_1,\ldots,l_m = e_m\}:\{l_1:t_1,\ldots,l_m:t_m\}} \tag{RECD}$$

$$\frac{\Gamma \vdash e:\{l_1:t_1,\ldots,l_m:t_m\}}{\Gamma \vdash e.l_i:t_i} \tag{SEL}$$

$$\frac{\Gamma, a \leq s \vdash e:t}{\Gamma \vdash \Lambda a \leq s.e:\forall a \leq s.t} \tag{B-GEN}$$

$$\frac{\Gamma \vdash e:\forall a \leq s.t \quad \hat{\Gamma} \vdash r \leq s}{\Gamma \vdash e(r):[r/a]t} \tag{B-SPEC}$$

$$\frac{\Gamma \vdash e:[\mu a.t/a]t}{\Gamma \vdash \mathtt{intro}[\mu a.t]e:\mu a.t} \tag{R-INTRO}$$

$$\frac{\Gamma \vdash e:\mu a.t}{\Gamma \vdash \mathtt{elim}\, e:[\mu a.t/a]t} \tag{R-ELIM}$$

$$\frac{\Gamma \vdash e:s \quad \hat{\Gamma} \vdash s \leq t}{\Gamma \vdash e:t} \tag{INH}$$

Variants

$$\frac{\Gamma \vdash e : t_i}{\Gamma \vdash [l_1 : t_1, \ldots, l_i = e, \ldots, l_n : t_n] : [l_1 : t_1, \ldots, l_i : t_i, \ldots, l_n : t_n]} \qquad \text{[VART]}$$

$$\frac{\Gamma \vdash e : [l_1 : t_1, \ldots, l_n : t_n] \quad \Gamma \vdash f_1 : t_1 \to t \cdots \Gamma \vdash f_n : t_n \to t}{\Gamma \vdash \text{case } e \text{ of } l_1 \Rightarrow f_1, \ldots, l_n \Rightarrow f_n : t} . \qquad \text{[CASE]}$$

Appendix B: The Language TARGET

Type Expressions

Fragment

$a \mid s \to t \mid \{l_1 : s_1, \ldots, l_m : s_m\} \mid \forall a . t \mid \mu a . t$

Variants

$\mid [l_1 : t_1, \ldots, l_n : t_n]$

Coercion Space

$\mid s \rightarrowtail t,$

where a ranges over type variables and $n \geq 1$. For $m = 0$ we get the *empty record type* $\mathbf{1} =^{\text{def}} \{ \ \}$.

Raw Terms

Fragment

$x \mid M(N) \mid \lambda x : t . M \mid \{l_1 = M_1, \ldots, l_m = M_m\}$

$\mid M . l \mid \Lambda a . M \mid M(t) \mid \texttt{intro}[\mu a . t] M \mid \texttt{elim } M$

Variants:

$\mid [l_1 : t_1, \ldots, l_i = M, \ldots, l_n : t_n] \mid \texttt{case } M \text{ of } l_1 \Rightarrow F_1, \ldots, l_n \Rightarrow F_n$

Coercion-Coercion Combinator:

$\mid t_{s,t}$

Coercion Combinators:

$\mid \texttt{top}[t] \mid \texttt{arrow}[s, t, u, v] \mid \texttt{recd}[s_1, \ldots, s_q, t_1, \ldots, t_p] \mid \texttt{forall}[s, t, a, u, v] \mid$

$\texttt{vart}[s_1, \ldots, s_p, t_1, \ldots, t_q] \mid \texttt{refl}[t] \mid \texttt{trans}[r, s, t],$

where x ranges over (term) variables and $n \geq 1$. For $m = 0$ we get the *empty record*, for which we will keep the notation $\{\ \}$. We will usually omit the cumbersome type tags on the coercion (-coercion) combinators. We use $[N/x]M$ for substitution.

Typing judgments have the form $\Upsilon \vdash M : t$, where Υ is a typing context. *Typing contexts* are defined recursively as follows: $\varnothing$ is a context; if Υ is a context which does not declare a, then Υ, a is a typing context; if Υ is a context which does not declare x, and the free variables of t are declared in Υ, then $\Upsilon, x : t$ is a typing context.

Rules for Deriving Typing Judgments

Fragment

Same as in Appendix A: [VAR], [ABS], [APPL], [RECD] (in particular, for $n = 0$, $\Upsilon \vdash \{\ \} : \mathbf{1}$), [SEL].

$$\frac{\Upsilon, a \vdash M : t}{\Upsilon \vdash \Lambda a . M : \forall a . t} \qquad \text{[GEN]}$$

$$\frac{\Upsilon \vdash M : \forall a . t}{\Upsilon \vdash M(s) : [s/a]t} \qquad \text{[SPEC]}$$

Same as in Appendix A: [R-INTRO], [R-ELIM].

Variants

Same as in Appendix A: [VART], [CASE].

Coercion (-Coercion) Combinators

We omit the typing contexts to simplify the notation:

$\iota_{s,t} : (s \rightsquigarrow t) \rightarrow (s \rightarrow t)$

$\mathtt{top}[t] : t \rightsquigarrow \mathbf{1}$

$\mathtt{arrow}[s,t,u,v] : (s \rightsquigarrow t) \rightarrow (u \rightsquigarrow v) \rightarrow ((t \rightarrow u) \rightsquigarrow (s \rightarrow v))$

$\mathtt{recd}[s_1,\ldots,s_q,t_1,\ldots,t_p] : (s_1 \rightsquigarrow t_1) \rightarrow \cdots \rightarrow (s_p \rightsquigarrow t_p)$

$\quad \rightarrow (\{l_1 : s_1,\ldots,l_p : s_p,\ldots,l_q : s_q\} \rightsquigarrow \{l_1 : t_1,\ldots,l_p : t_p\})$

$\mathtt{forall}[s,t,a,u,v] : (s \rightsquigarrow t) \rightarrow \forall a . ((a \rightsquigarrow s) \rightarrow (u \rightsquigarrow v))$

$\quad \rightarrow (\forall a . ((a \rightsquigarrow t) \rightarrow u) \rightsquigarrow \forall a . ((a \rightsquigarrow s) \rightarrow v))$

$$\mathtt{vart}[s_1,\ldots,s_p,t_1,\ldots,t_q]:(s_1 \multimap t_1) \to \cdots \to (s_p \multimap t_p)$$

$$\to ([l_1:s_1,\ldots,l_p:s_p] \multimap [l_1:t_1,\ldots,l_p:t_p,\ldots,l_q:t_q])$$

$$\mathtt{refl}[t]:t \multimap t$$

$$\mathtt{trans}[r,s,t]:(r \multimap s) \to (s \multimap t) \to (r \multimap t).$$

Equational Theory

Technically, equational judgments should all contain a typing context under which both terms in the equation typecheck with the same type (Breazu-Tannen and Coquand, 1988; Coquand, Gunter, and Winskel, 1987, 1989). To simplify the notation, we will in most cases omit these contexts.

Fragment

We omit the simple rules for reflexivity, symmetry, transitivity, and congruence with respect to function application, record formation, field selection, application to types, recursive type introduction, and recursive type elimination.

$$\frac{\Upsilon, x:s \vdash M = N}{\Upsilon \vdash \lambda x:s.\,M = \lambda x:s.\,N} \qquad\qquad\qquad \{\mathrm{XI}\}$$

$$\frac{\Upsilon, a \vdash M = N}{\Upsilon \vdash \Lambda a.\,M = \Lambda a.\,N} \qquad\qquad\qquad \{\text{Type-XI}\}$$

$$(\lambda x:s.\,M)(N) = [N/x]M, \qquad\qquad\qquad \{\mathrm{BETA}\}$$

where $N:s$.

$$\lambda x:s.\,M(x) = M, \qquad\qquad\qquad \{\mathrm{ETA}\}$$

where $M:s \to t$ and x not free in M.

$$\{l_1 = M_1,\ldots,l_m = M_m\}.l_i = M_i, \qquad\qquad \{\text{RECD-BETA}\}$$

where $m \geq 1$, $M_1:t_1,\ldots,M_m:t_m$.

$$\{l_1 = M.l_1,\ldots,l_m = M.l_m\} = M, \qquad\qquad \{\text{RECD-ETA}\}$$

where $M:\{l_1:t_1,\ldots,l_m:t_m\}$. For $m = 0$, this rules gives $\{\ \} = M$, which makes **1** into a terminator.

$$(\Lambda a.\,M)(r) = [r/a]M \qquad\qquad\qquad \{\text{FORALL-BETA}\}$$

$$\Lambda a.\,M(a) = M, \qquad\qquad\qquad \{\text{FORALL-ETA}\}$$

where $M : \forall a . t$ and a not free in M.

$$\texttt{elim}(\texttt{intro}[\mu a . t] M) = M, \qquad\qquad\qquad \{\text{R-BETA}\}$$

where $M : \mu a . t$.

$$\texttt{intro}[\mu a . t](\texttt{elim}\, M) = M, \qquad\qquad\qquad \{\text{R-ETA}\}$$

where $M : [\mu a . t / a] t$.

Variants

We omit the simple rules for congruence with respect to variant formation, and for case analysis.

$$\texttt{case}\ \texttt{inj}_{l_i}(M_i)\ \texttt{of}\ l_1 \Rightarrow F_1, \ldots, l_n \Rightarrow F_n = F_i(M_i), \qquad \{\text{VART-BETA}\}$$

where $F_1 : t_1 \to t, \ldots, F_n : t_n \to t$, $M_i : t_i$ and $\texttt{inj}_{l_i}$ is shorthand for $\lambda x : t_i . [l_1 : t_1, \ldots, l_i = x, \ldots, l_n : t_n]$.

$$\texttt{case}\ M\ \texttt{of}\ l_1 \Rightarrow \texttt{inj}_{l_1}, \ldots, l_n \Rightarrow \texttt{inj}_{l_n} = M, \qquad \{\text{VART-ETA}\}$$

where $M : [l_1 : t_1, \ldots, l_n : t_n]$.

$$\iota(P)(\texttt{case}\ M\ \texttt{of}\ l_1 \Rightarrow F_1, \ldots, l_n \Rightarrow F_n) = \texttt{case}\ M\ \texttt{of}\ l_1 \Rightarrow F_1 ; \iota(P), \ldots, l_n \Rightarrow F_n ; \iota(P),$$
$$\{\text{VART-CRN}\}$$

where $M : [l_1 : t_1, \ldots, l_n : t_n]$, $F_1 : t_1 \to t, \ldots, F_n : t_n \to t$, $P : t \rightsquigarrow s$. Alternatively, we could require, instead of $\{\text{VART-ETA}\} + \{\text{VART-CRN}\}$,

$$\iota(Q)(M) = \texttt{case}\ M\ \texttt{of}\ l_1 \Rightarrow (\texttt{inj}_{l_1} ; \iota(Q)), \ldots, l_n \Rightarrow (\texttt{inj}_{l_n} ; \iota(Q)), \qquad \{\text{VART-COP}\}$$

where $M : [l_1 : t_1, \ldots, l_n : t_n]$, $Q : [l_1 : t_1, \ldots, l_n : t_n] \rightsquigarrow t$.

Coercion (-Coercion) Combinators

$$\iota(\texttt{top}) = \lambda x : t . \{\ \}$$

$$\iota(\texttt{arrow}(P)(Q)) = \lambda z : t \to u . (\iota(P)) ; z ; (\iota(Q)),$$

where $P : s \rightsquigarrow t$, $Q : u \rightsquigarrow v$.

$$\iota(\texttt{recd}(R_1) \cdots (R_p))$$

$$= \lambda w : \{l_1 : s_1, \ldots, l_p : s_p, \ldots, l_q : s_q\} . \{l_1 : \iota(R_1)(w . l_1), \ldots, l_p : \iota(R_p)(w . l_p)\},$$

where $R_1 : s_1 \rightsquigarrow t_1, \ldots, R_p : s_p \rightsquigarrow t_p$.

$\iota(\texttt{forall}(P)(W))$

$\quad = \lambda z : (\forall a.(a \rightarrowtail t) \rightarrow u).\Lambda a.\lambda f : a \rightarrowtail s.\iota(W(a)(f))(z(a)(\texttt{trans}(f)(P))),$

where $P : s \rightarrowtail t,\ W : \forall a.(a \rightarrowtail s) \rightarrow (u \rightarrowtail v).$

$\iota(\texttt{vart}(R_1)\cdots(R_p))$

$\quad = \lambda w : [l_1 : s_1, \ldots, l_p : s_p].\texttt{case } w \texttt{ of } l_1 \Rightarrow \iota(R_1); \texttt{inj}_{l_1}, \ldots, l_p \Rightarrow \iota(R_p); \texttt{inj}_{lp},$

where $R_1 : s_1 \rightarrowtail t_1, \ldots, R_p : s_p \rightarrowtail t_p.$

$\iota(\texttt{refl}) = \lambda x : t.x$

$\iota(\texttt{trans}(P)(Q)) = \iota(P); \iota(Q),$

where $P : r \rightarrowtail s,\ Q : s \rightarrowtail t.$

$$\frac{\iota(P) = \iota(Q)}{P = Q}. \qquad\qquad\qquad\qquad\qquad\qquad\qquad \{\text{IOTA-INJ}\}$$

Appendix C: The Translation

We present first the remaining of the translation of the fragment discussed in Section 3.

$$C_1^*, a, f : a \rightarrow t^*, C_2^* \vdash f : a \rightarrow t^* \qquad\qquad\qquad\qquad\qquad (\text{VAR})^*$$

$$\frac{C^* \vdash P_1 : s_1^* \rightarrow t_1^* \cdots C^* \vdash P_p : s_p^* \rightarrow t_p^*}{C^* \vdash R : \{l_1 : s_1^*, \ldots, l_p : s_p^*, \ldots, l_q : s_q^*\} \rightarrow \{l_1 : t_1^*, \ldots, l_p : t_p^*\}}, \qquad (\text{RECD})^*$$

where $R =^{\text{def}} \lambda w : \{l_1 : s_1^*, \ldots, l_p : s_p^*, \ldots, l_q : s_q^*\}.\{l_1 : P_1(w.l_1), \ldots, l_p : P_p(w.l_p)\}.$

$$C^* \vdash \lambda x : t^*.x : t^* \rightarrow t^*, \qquad\qquad\qquad\qquad\qquad\qquad (\text{REFL})^*$$

where the free variables of t^* are declared in C^*.

$$\frac{C^* \vdash P : r^* \rightarrow s^* \quad C^* \vdash Q : s^* \rightarrow t^*}{C^* \vdash P; Q : r^* \rightarrow t^*}. \qquad\qquad\qquad\qquad (\text{TRANS})^*$$

The rules [VAR], [ABS], [APPL], [RECD], [SEL], [R-INTRO], and [R-ELIM] are translated straightforwardly; see below. Here is the translation of the only other rule left (the translations of the other rules appears in Section 3):

$$\frac{\Gamma^*, a, f : a \rightarrow s^* \vdash M : t^*}{\Gamma^* \vdash \Lambda a.\lambda f : a \rightarrow s^*.M : \forall a.((a \rightarrow s^*) \rightarrow t^*)}. \qquad\qquad [\text{B-GEN}]$$

In the following, we present the translation for the full calculus. As before, for any **SOURCE** item we will denote by `item*` its translation into **TARGET**. We begin with the types (note the translation of bounded generics and of *Top*):

$$a* \overset{\text{def}}{=} a$$

$$Top* \overset{\text{def}}{=} \mathbf{1}$$

$$(s \to t)* \overset{\text{def}}{=} s* \to t*$$

$$\{l_1 : s_1, \ldots, l_m : s_m\} \overset{\text{def}}{=} \{l_1 : s_1^*, \ldots, l_m : s_m^*\}$$

$$(\forall a \le s \,.\, t)* \overset{\text{def}}{=} \forall a \,.\, ((a \rightarrowtail s*) \to t*)$$

$$(\mu a \,.\, t)* \overset{\text{def}}{=} \mu a \,.\, t*$$

$$[l_1 : s_1, \ldots, l_n : s_n]* \overset{\text{def}}{=} [l_1 : s_1^*, \ldots, l_n : s_n^*].$$

One sees immediately that $([s/a]t)* \equiv [s*/a]t*$. We extend this to contexts and inheritance contexts, which translate into just typing contexts in **TARGET**:

$$\varnothing* \overset{\text{def}}{=} \varnothing$$

$$(\Gamma, a \le t)* \overset{\text{def}}{=} \Gamma*, a, f : a \rightarrowtail t*$$

$$(\Gamma, x : t)* \overset{\text{def}}{=} \Gamma*, x : t*$$

$$\varnothing* \overset{\text{def}}{=} \varnothing$$

$$(C, a \le t)* \overset{\text{def}}{=} C*, a, f : a \rightarrowtail t*,$$

where f is a *fresh* variable for each (a, f).

Next we describe how we translate the derivations of judgments of **SOURCE**. The translation is defined by recursion on the structure of the derivation trees. Since these are freely generated by the derivation rules, it is sufficient to provide for each derivation rule of **SOURCE** a corresponding rule on trees of **TARGET** judgments. One then checks that these corresponding rules are *directly derivable* in **TARGET** (Lemma 14 below), therefore the translation takes derivations in **SOURCE** into derivations in **TARGET**.

A **SOURCE** derivation yielding an inheritance judgment $C \vdash s \le t$ is translated as a tree of **TARGET** judgments $C* \vdash P : s* \rightarrowtail t*$. Here are the **TARGET** rules that correspond to the rules for deriving inheritance judgments in **SOURCE**:

$$C* \vdash \text{top} : t* \rightarrowtail \mathbf{1} \qquad\qquad\qquad\qquad\qquad\qquad (\text{TOP})*$$

$$C_1^*, a, f : a \rightarrowtail t*, C_2^* \vdash f : a \rightarrowtail t* \qquad\qquad\qquad\qquad (\text{VAR})*$$

$$\frac{C^* \vdash P : s^* \multimap t^* \quad C^* \vdash Q : u^* \multimap v^*}{C^* \vdash \mathtt{arrow}(P)(Q) : (t^* \to u^*) \multimap (s^* \to v^*)} \qquad \text{(ARROW)*}$$

$$\frac{C^* \vdash P_1 : s_1^* \multimap t_1^* \cdots C^* \vdash P_p : s_p^* \multimap t_p^*}{C^* \vdash \mathtt{recd}(P_1) \cdots (P_p) : \{l_1 : s_1^*, \ldots, l_p : s_p^*, \ldots, l_q : s_q^*\} \multimap \{l_1 : t_1^*, \ldots, l_p : t_p^*\}} \qquad \text{(RECD)*}$$

$$\frac{C^* \vdash P : s^* \multimap t^* \quad C^*, a, f : a \multimap s^* \vdash Q : u^* \multimap v^*}{C^* \vdash \mathtt{forall}(P)(\Lambda a . \lambda f : a \multimap s^* . Q) : \forall a . ((a \multimap t^*) \to u^*) \multimap \forall a . ((a \multimap s^*) \to v^*)} $$
$$\text{(FORALL)*}$$

$$\frac{C^* \vdash P_1 : s_1^* \multimap t_1^* \cdots C^* \vdash P_p : s_p^* \multimap t_p^*}{C^* \vdash \mathtt{vart}(P_1) \cdots (P_p) : [l_1 : s_1^*, \ldots, l_p : s_p^*] \multimap [l_1 : t_1^*, \ldots, l_p : t_p^*, \ldots, l_q : t_q^*]} \qquad \text{(VART)*}$$

$$C^* \vdash \mathtt{refl} : t^* \multimap t^*, \qquad \text{(REFL)*}$$

where the free variables of t^* are declared in C^*.

$$\frac{C^* \vdash P : r^* \multimap s^* \quad C^* \vdash Q : s^* \multimap t^*}{C^* \vdash \mathtt{trans}(P)(Q) : r^* \multimap t^*}. \qquad \text{(TRANS)*}$$

A **SOURCE** derivation yielding a typing judgment $\Gamma \vdash e : t$ is translated as a tree of **TARGET** judgments yielding $\Gamma^* \vdash M : t^*$. Here are the **Target** rules that correspond to the rules for deriving typing judgments in **SOURCE**.

The rules [VAR], [ABS], [APPL], [RECD], [SEL], [R-INTRO], [R-ELIM], [VART], and [CASE] all have direct correspondents in **TARGET** so their translation is straightforward. We illustrate it with two examples:

$$\Gamma_1^*, x : t^*, \Gamma_2^* \vdash x : t^* \qquad \text{[VAR]*}$$

$$\frac{\Gamma^*, x : s^* \vdash M : t^*}{\Gamma^* \vdash \lambda x : s^* . M : s^* \to t^*}. \qquad \text{[ABS]*}$$

Here is the translation of the other three rules:

$$\frac{\Gamma^*, a, f : a \multimap s^* \vdash M : t^*}{\Gamma^* \vdash \Lambda a . \lambda f : a \multimap s^* . M : \forall a . ((a \multimap s^*) \to t^*)} \qquad \text{[B-GEN]*}$$

$$\frac{\Gamma^* \vdash M : \forall a . ((a \multimap s^*) \to t^*) \quad \hat{\Gamma}^* \vdash P : r^* \multimap s^*}{\Gamma^* \vdash M(r^*)(P) : [r^*/a] t^*} \qquad \text{[B-SPEC]*}$$

$$\frac{\Gamma^* \vdash M : s^* \quad \hat{\Gamma}^* \vdash P : s^* \multimap t^*}{\Gamma^* \vdash \iota(P)(M) : t^*}. \qquad \text{[INH]*}$$

LEMMA 14 The rules (TOP)*–(TRANS)* and [VAR]*–[INH]* are directly derivable in **TARGET**. ∎

8 Acknowledgments

Breazu-Tannen's research was partially supported by ARO Grant DAAG29-84-K-0061 and ONR Grant NOOO14-88-K-0634. Many of the results of this paper were obtained during Coquand's visit to the University of Pennsylvania, partially sponsored by Scedrov's funds from the Natural Sciences Association. Gunter's research was partially supported by ARO Grant DAAG29-84-K-0061 and ONR Grant NOOO14-88-K-0557. Scedrov's research was partially supported by NSF Grant CCR-87-05596, by ONR Grant NOOO14-88-K-0635, and by the 1987 Young Faculty Award from the Natural Sciences Association of the University of Pennsylvania.

References

Amadio, R., Bruce, K. B., and Longo, G. (1986), The finitary projection model for second order lambda calculus and solutions to higher order domain equations, in "Logic in Computer Science" (A. Meyer. Ed.), pp. 122–130, IEEE Comput. Soc. Press, Washington, DC.

Amadio, R. (1989), "Recursion over Realizability Structures," Research Report TR 1/89, University of Pisa.

Amadio, R. (1991a), Recursion over realizability structures, *Inform. and Comput.* **91**, 55–85.

Amadio. R. (1991b), "Recursion and Subtyping in Lambda Calculi," Ph.D. thesis, University of Pisa.

Barendregt (1984), "The Lambda Calculus: Its Syntax and Semantics," Studies in Logic and the Foundations of Mathematics, Vol. 103, revised edition, Elsevier, Amsterdam/New York.

Breazu-Tannen, V., Buneman, P., and Gunter, C. A. (1988), Typed functional programming for the rapid development of reliable software, in "Productivity: Progress, Prospects and Payoff" (J. E. Gaffney, Ed.), pp. 115–125, Assoc. Comput. Mach., New York.

Breazu-Tannen, V., and Coquand, T. (1988), Extensional models for polymorphsim, *Theoret. Computer Sci.* **59**, 85–114.

Breazu-Tannen, V., Coquand, T., Gunter, C. A., and Scedrov, A. (1989), Inheritance and explict coercion (preliminary report), in "Logic in Computer Science" (R. Parikh. Ed.), pp. 112–134, IEEE Comput. Soc. Press, Washington, DC.

Breazu-Tannen, V., Gunter, C., and Scedrov, A. (1989), "Denotational Semantics for Subtyping between Recursive Types," Research Report MS-CIS-89-63/Logic and Computation 12, Department of Computer and Information Science. Univ. of Pennsylvania.

Breazu-Tannen, V., Gunter, C., and Scedrov, A. (1990). Computing with coercions. in "Lisp and Functional Programming" (M. Wand, Ed.), pp. 44–60, Assoc. Comput. Mach., New York.

Bruce, K. B., and Longo, G. (1988), A modest model of records, inheritance and bounded quantificatlon, in "Logic in Computer Science" (Y. Gurevich, Ed.), pp. 38–50, IEEE Comput. Soc. Press, Washington, DC.

Bruce, K., and Wegner, P. (1990), An algebraic model of subtype and inheritance. in "Advances in Database Programming Languages" (F. Bancilhon and P. Buneman, Eds.), pp. 75–96, ACM Press and Addison-Wesley, New York.

Cardelli, L. (1984), A semantics of multiple inheritance, in "Semantics of Data Types" (G. Kahn, D. B. MacQueen. and G. D. Plotkin. Eds.), pp. 51–67, Lecture Notes in Computer Science, Vol. 173, Springer-Verlag, Berlin/New York.

Cardelli, L. (1986), Amber, in "Combinators and Functional Programming Languages" (G. Cousineau, P.-L. Curien, and B. Robinet, Eds.), pp. 21–47, Lecture Notes in Computer Science. Vol. 242, Springer-Verlag, Berlin/New York.

Cardelli, L. (1988a), A semantics of multiple inheritance, *Inform. and Comput.* **76**, 138–164.

Cardelli, L. (1988b), Structural subtyping and the notion of power type, *in* "Symposium on Principles of Programming Languages" (J. Ferrante and P. Mager. Eds.), pp. 70–79, Assoc. Comput. Mach., New York.

Cardelli, L. (1989a), "Typeful Programming," Research Report 45, DEC Systems, Palo Alto, CA.

Cardelli, L., and Mitchell, J. (1991), Operations on records, *Math. Structures in Comput. Sci.* **1**, 3–48.

Cardelli, L., and Wegner, P. (1985), On understanding types. data abstraction and polymorphism, *ACM Comput. Surveys* **17**(4), 471–522.

Cardone, F. (1989). Relational semantics for recursive types and bounded quantification. *in* "International Colloquium on Automata. Languages and Programs" (G. Ausiello, M. Dezani-Ciancaglini, and S. Ronchi Della Rocca, Eds.), pp. 164–178. Lecture Notes in Computer Science, Vol. 372. Springer-Verlag, Berlin/New York.

Cartwright, R. (1985), Types as intervals, *in* "Symposium on Principles of Programming Languages" (B. K. Reid. Ed.), Assoc. Comput. Mach., New York.

Cook, W. R., Hill, W. L., and Canning, P. S. (1990). Inheritance is not subtyping. *in* "Principles of Programming Languages" (P. Hudak, Ed.), pp. 125–135. Assoc. Comput. Mach., New York.

Coppo, M. (1985), A completeness theorem for recursively defined types, *in* "International Colloquium on Automata, Languages and Programs" (W. Brauer, Ed.), pp. 120–129, Lecture Notes in Computer Science, Vol. 194, Springer-Verlag, Berlin/New York.

Coppo, M., and Zacchi, M. (1986), Type inference and logical relations, *in* "Symposium on Logic in Computer Science" (A. Meyer, Ed.), pp. 218–226. Assoc. Comput. Mach., New York.

Coquand, T. (1988), Categories of embeddings. *in* "Logic in Computer Science" (Y. Gurevich, Ed.), pp. 256–263, IEEE Comput. Soc. Press, Washington, DC.

Coquand, T., and Ehrhard, T. (1987), An equational presentation of higher-order logic, *in* "Category Theory and Computer Science" (D. H. Pitt, A. Poigné, and D. E. Rydeheard, Eds.), pp. 40–56, Lecture Notes in Computer Science, Vol. 283, Springer-Verlag, Berlin/New York.

Coquand, T., Gunter, C. A., and Winskel G. (1987), DI-domains as a model of polymorphism, *in* "Mathematical Foundations of Programming Language Semantics" (M. Main, A. Melton, M. Mislove, and D. Schmidt, Eds.), pp. 344–363, Lecture Notes in Computer Science, Vol. 298, Springer-Verlag, Berlin/New York.

Coquand, T., Gunter, C. A., and Winskel, G. (1989), Domain theoretic models of polymorphism, *Inform. and Comput.* **81**, 123–167.

Coquand, T., and Huet, G. (1988), The calculus of constructions, *Inform. and Comput.* **76**, 95–120.

Curien, P.-L., and Ghelli, G. (1990), Coherence of subsumption, *in* "Proceedings CAAP'90, LNCS 431." [Full version to appear in "Mathematical Strucures in Computer Science."]

Freyd, P. (1990), Recursive types reduced to inductive types, *in* "Logic in Computer Science" (J. C. Mitchell, Ed.), pp. 498–507, IEEE Comput. Soc. Press, Washington, DC.

Freyd, P., Mulry, P., Rosolini, G., and Scott, D. S. (1990), Extensional PERs, *in* "Logic in Computer Science" (J. C. Mitchell, Ed.), pp. 346–365, IEEE Computer Society Press, Washington, DC.

Ghelli, G. (1990), "Proof-Theoretic Studies about a Minimal Type System Integrating Inclusion and Parametric Polymorphism," Ph.D. thesis, University of Pisa.

Girard, J. Y. (1986), The system F of variable types: Fifteen years later, *Theoret. Comput. Sci.* **45**, 159–192.

Girard, J. Y. (1987), Linear logic, *Theoret. Comput. Sci.* **50**, 1–102.

Girard, J. Y. (1988), Normal functors, power series, and λ-calculus, *Ann. Pur Appl. Logic* **37**, 129–177.

Girard, J. Y., Lafont, Y., and Taylor, P. (1989), "Proofs and Types," Cambridge Univ. Press, London/New York.

Goguen, J. A., Jouannaud, J.-P., and Meseguer, J. (1985), Operational semantics for order-sorted algebra, *in* "International Colloquium on Automata, Languages and Programs" (W. Brauer, Ed.), pp. 221–231, Lecture Notes in Computer Science, Vol. 194, Springer-Verlag, Berlin/New York.

Goguen, J. A., and Meseguer, J. (unpublished manuscript), Order-sorted algebra. I. Equational deduction for multiple inheritance, overloading, exceptions and partial operations.

Goldberg, A., and Robson, D. (1983), "Smalltalk-80: The Language and Its Implementation," Addison-Wesley, Reading, MA.

Gunter, C. A., and Jung, A. (1990), Coherence and consistency in domains (extended outline), *J. Pure Appl. Algebra* **63**, 49–66.

Huwig, H., and Poigné, A. (1989), A note on inconsistencies caused by fixpoints in a cartesian closed category, *Theoret. Comput. Sci.*, to appear.

Hyland, J. M. E., and Pitts, A. (1989), The theory of constructions: Categorical semantics and topos-theoretic models, *in* "Categories in Computer Science and Logic" (J. W. Gray and A. Scedrov, Eds.), pp. 137–199, Contemporary Math., Vol. 92, Amer. Math. Soc. Providence, RI.

Jategaonkar, L., and Mitchell, J. C. (1988), ML with extended pattern matching and subtypes, *in* "Symposium on LISP and Functional Programming" (R. Cartwright, Ed.), pp. 198–211, Assoc. Comput. Mach., New York.

Kelly, G. M., and MacLane, S. (1971), Coherence in closed categories, *J. Pure Appl. Algebra* **1**, 97–140. Erratum, *J. Pure Appl. Algebra* **2**, 219.

Koymans, C. (1982), Models of the lambda calculus. *Inform. and Control* **52**, 306–332.

Lamarche, F. (1988), "Modelling Polymorphism with Categories," Ph.D. thesis, McGill University.

Lawvere, F. W. (1969), Diagonal arguments and cartesian closed categories, *in* "Category Theory, Homology Theory, and Their Applications II," pp. 134–145, Lecture Notes in Mathematics, Vol. 92, Springer-Verlag, Berlin New York.

MacLane, S., and Pare, R. (1985), Coherence for bicategories and indexed categories, *J. Pure Appl. Algebra* **37**, 59–80.

Martin-Löf, P. (1984), "Intuitionistic Type Theory," Studies in Proof Theory, Bibliopolis, Italy.

Martini, S. (1988), Bounded quantifiers have interval models, *in* "Symposium on LISP and Functional Programming" (R. Cartwright, Ed.), pp. 164–173, Assoc. Comput. Mach., NY.

Meyer, A. R. (1982), What is a model of the lambda calculus?, *Inform. and Control* **52**, 87–122.

Mitchell, J. (1990), Toward a typed foundation for method specialization and inheritance, *in* "Principles of Programming Languages" (P. Hudak, Ed.), pp. 109–124, Assoc. Comput. Mach., New York.

Ohori, A., and Buneman, P. (1988), Type inference in a database programming language, *in* "Symposium on LISP and Functional Programming" (J. Cartwright, Ed.), pp. 174–183, Assoc. Comput. Mach., New York.

Reynolds, J. C. (1980), Using category theory to design implicit conversions and generic operators, *in* "Semantics-Directed Compiler Generation" (N. D. Jones, Ed.), pp. 211–258, Lecture Notes in Computer Science, Vol. 94, Springer-Verlag, Berlin/New York.

Salvesen, A. (1988), Polymorphism and monomorphism in Martin-Löf's type theory, Technical Report, Norwegian Computing Center, P.b. 114, Blindern, 0316 Oslo 3, Norway, December 1988.

Scott, D. S. (1980), Relating theories of the lambda calculus, *in* "To H. B. Curry: Essays on Combinatory Logic, Lambda Calculus and Formalism" (J. R. Hindley, Ed.), pp. 403–450, Academic Press, New York.

Stansifer, R. (1988), Type inference with subtypes, *in* "Symposium on Principles of Programming Languages" (J. Ferrante and P. Mager, Eds.), pp. 88–97, Assoc. Comput. Mach., New York.

Streicher, T. (1988), "Correctness and Completeness of a Categorical Semantics of the Calculus of Constructions," Ph.D. thesis, Passau University.

Troelstra, A. S. (1973), "Metamathematical Investigations of Intuitionistic Arithmetic and Analysis," Lecture Notes in Mathematics, Vol. 344, Springer-Verlag, Berlin/New York.

Wand, M. (1987), Complete type inference for simple objects, *in* "Symposium on Logic in Computer Science" (D. Gries, Ed.), pp. 37–46. IEEE Comput. Soc. Press, Washington, DC.

8 Coherence of Subsumption, Minimum Typing and Type-Checking in $F_\leq$

Pierre-Louis Curien and Giorgio Ghelli

Abstract

A subtyping relation $\leq$ between types is often accompanied by a typing rule, called subsumption: if a term a has type T and $T \leq U$, then a has type U. In presence of subsumption, a well-typed term does not codify its proof of well typing. Since a semantic interpretation is most naturally defined by induction on the structure of typing proofs, a problem of coherence arises: different typing proofs of the same term must have related meanings. We propose a proof-theoretical, rewriting approach to this problem. We focus on $F_\leq$, a second-order lambda calculus with bounded quantification, which is rich enough to make the problem interesting. We define a normalizing rewriting system on proofs, which transforms different proofs of the same typing judgement into a unique normal proof, with the further property that all the normal proofs assigning different types to a given term in a given environment differ only by a final application of the subsumption rule. This rewriting system is not defined on the proofs themselves but on the terms of auxiliary type system, in which the terms carry complete information about their typing proof. This technique gives us three different results:

- Any semantic interpretation is coherent if and only if our rewriting rules are satisfied as equations.

- We obtain a proof of the existence of a minimum type for each term in a given environment.

- From an analysis of the shape of normal form proofs, we obtain a deterministic type-checking algorithm, which is sound and complete by construction.

1 Introduction

In many typed calculi, only well-typed terms can be assigned a reasonable semantics. Thus the semantics of a term is often defined not by induction on its structure, but by induction on the structure of a typing proof. In this context, if typing rules are non-deterministic, i.e. if a single term can be proved well-typed in many different ways, then the following problems arise:

- Semantic coherence: the problem of proving that different semantic interpretations of the same term, corresponding to different typing proofs, are equal or at least equivalent in some sense.

- Most general typing: the problem of proving that a most general type can be assigned to each well-typed term. In this paper we study subtyping, and in this context most general means minimum with respect to the subtyping relation.

First appeared in *Mathematical Structures in Computer Science* 2 (1992), pages 55–91. © Cambridge University Press, 40 West 20th Street, New York, NY, 10011-4211.

• Soundness and completeness of type-checking: the problem of finding a deterministic type-checking algorithm which is sound and complete with respect to the typing rules, and which returns the most general type. Soundness and completeness ensure that the algorithm is a semi-decision procedure.

Observe that these three problems seem (or at least have been often considered) unrelated. We approach them in a unified way, and exploit the approach in the context of the language $F_{\leq}$, a second-order λ-calculus with bounded quantification, which derives from the language Fun of Cardelli and Wegner (1985). $F_{\leq}$ is also the second-order core of the language Quest of Cardelli (Cardelli and Longo, 1991). We refer to these papers for motivation about subtyping disciplines. The most basic examples of subtypes are usually given using records (e.g. 'car' as a subtype of 'vehicle'); it is interesting to note that records are not primitive in $F_{\leq}$, but can be faithfully encoded in $F_{\leq}$ (see section 2.2, and Cardelli and Longo 1991).

We are aware of the following existing solutions to these problems:

• Semantic coherence has been solved in Bruce and Longo (1990) (hereafter referred to as BL) in the context of the PER interpretation of Fun (see section 7 of this paper for a very brief account). Bruce and Longo define an auxiliary language called Minimal Bounded Fun, and interpret Fun via this language. They exploit the minimum type result proved here. An early concern can also be found in Oles (1982), in the context of a functor category semantics of coercive simply typed λ-calculi.

• In Breazu-Tannen et al. (1993) (hereafter referred to as BCGS), coherence is proved for a special syntactic interpretation of $F_{\leq}$ in F.

• A deterministic type-checking algorithm for *Fun* has been established by Cardelli (Cardelli, personal communication), and the authors of BCGS told us that they had a proof of soundness and completeness of this algorithm (Gunter, personal communication).

• Existence of a minimum typing for a simpler system where only unbounded quantification is allowed, has been proved in Amadio (1989). Existence of a minimum type in the language Fun (and $F_{\leq}$) was an open problem.

In this paper we solve all the three problems together. We give five sufficient conditions to be satisfied by a rewriting system on typing proofs which ensure at the same time the reduction of coherence to the satisfaction of a set of equations, and the existence of a minimum type for each term in a given environment. These conditions are independent of any specific model.

Then we define a specific rewriting system on the typing proofs of $F_\leq$, which satisfies our five conditions. Weak normalization is one of the conditions. By studying the form of normal form proofs, we then define a deterministic type system for $F_\leq$ which specifies a sound and complete type-checking algorithm for $F_\leq$.

For a convenient formalization of our manipulations on proofs, the rewriting system is not defined directly on proofs, but on the terms of a more explicit system, which is defined by enriching the terms of the original system, so as to keep a complete trace of typing proofs. An explicit system of this kind was already present in BL, but was not pushed there to the point where an explicit term completely codifies a proof (see the end of section 2.3).

Here is a brief outline of the organization of the paper. In section 2, the type system of $F_\leq$ is defined, together with our enriched type system. We also briefly discuss the expressivity of $F_\leq$. In section 3, we abstractly state our five conditions for an unspecified proof reduction system, and we derive the coherence and type minimality properties from the five conditions. In section 4, the proof rewriting system is defined, and some of its properties are studied. In section 5, the desired properties are proved. In section 6, we derive a type-checking algorithm from the analysis of normal form proofs. In section 7, we show how the interpretations of BCGS and BL fit in our framework. In section 8, some conclusions are drawn.

2 Syntax and Type Rules of the Two Languages

We define $F_\leq$ in section 2.1. We pause in section 2.2 to discuss the expressivity of $F_\leq$. The explicit version of $F_\leq$ is described in section 2.3, and the two systems are related in section 2.4. In section 2.5, we prove some elementary properties of the explicit system. In section 2.6, we investigate the shape of well-typed explicit terms.

2.1 The Systems $F_\leq$

The types and expressions of $F_\leq$ are defined as follows:

$A ::= t\,|\,\text{Top}\,|\,A \rightarrow A\,|\,\forall t \leq A \,.\, A$

$a ::= x\,|\,\text{top}\,|\,\lambda x : A \,.\, a\,|\,a(a)\,|\,\Lambda t \leq A \,.\, a\,|\,a\{A\}$

where:

- t ranges over type variables, x over expression variables;
- $\lambda x : A \,.\, a$ is the usual typed lambda-abstraction;
- $a(b)$ is function application;

- $\Lambda t \leq A . a$ is the second-order abstraction of the expression a with respect to the type variable t (only the subtypes of the bound A can be accepted as parameters of the resulting function);

- Top is a supertype of all types, so that an unbounded second-order lambda abstraction can be written as $\Lambda t \leq \text{Top} . a$;

- top is the 'canonical' element of type Top (in the equational theory considered in Curien and Ghelli (1991), all well-typed terms are equal (to top), when considered as terms of type Top);

- $a\{A\}$ is the application of a second-order function to a type;

- $A \rightarrow B$ is the type of a first order abstraction $\lambda x : A . a$ where a has type B;

- $\forall t \leq A . B$ is the type of a function $\Lambda t \leq A . a$, where B is the type of a, generally depending on t.

The constants $\forall$, λ and Λ bind their variable in their second argument, and terms are considered up to α-conversion, as usual. Terms are typed w.r.t. environments, which specify the types of ordinary variables, and the bounds of type variables.

To improve readability of the rules, we adopt some conventions about meta-variables:

Γ	environments
a, b, f	expressions (f used mostly for functions)
x, y, z	expression variables
A, B, C, T, U, V	type expressions
t, u, v	type variables

The typing and subtyping relations are specified via the following judgments:

Γ env	Γ is a well-formed environment
$\Gamma \vdash A$ type	A is a type
$\Gamma \vdash A \leq B$	A is a subtype of B
$\Gamma \vdash a : A$	a is an expression of type A

The full listing of the typing rules of $F_{\leq}$ can be found in appendix A; we list here only the most important rules which make it differ from system F.

Types

$$\frac{\Gamma \vdash A \text{ type} \quad \Gamma, t \leq A \vdash B \text{ type}}{\Gamma \vdash \forall t \leq A . B \text{ type}} \qquad (\forall \text{ Form})$$

Subtypes

$$\frac{\Gamma, t \le A, \Gamma' \text{ env}}{\Gamma, t \le A, \Gamma' \vdash t \le A} \qquad\qquad (\text{Var } \le)$$

$$\frac{\Gamma \vdash A \text{ type}}{\Gamma \vdash A \le \text{Top}} \qquad\qquad (\text{Top } \le)$$

$$\frac{\Gamma \vdash A \le A' \quad \Gamma \vdash B \le B'}{\Gamma \vdash A' \to B \le A \to B'} \qquad\qquad (\to \le)$$

$$\frac{\Gamma \vdash A \le A' \quad \Gamma, t \le A \vdash B \le B'}{\Gamma \vdash \forall t \le A'.B \le \forall t \le A.B'} \qquad\qquad (\forall \le)$$

$$\frac{\Gamma \vdash A \text{ type}}{\Gamma \vdash A \le A} \qquad\qquad (\text{Id } \le)$$

$$\frac{\Gamma \vdash A \le B \quad \Gamma \vdash B \le C}{\Gamma \vdash A \le C} \qquad\qquad (\text{Trans } \le)$$

Expressions

$$\frac{\Gamma \text{ env}}{\Gamma \vdash \text{top} : \text{Top}} \qquad\qquad (\text{Top})$$

$$\frac{\Gamma, t \le A \vdash b : B}{\Gamma \vdash \Lambda t \le A.b : \forall t \le A.B} \qquad\qquad (\forall \text{ Intro})$$

$$\frac{\Gamma \vdash f : \forall t \le A.B \quad \Gamma \vdash A' \le A}{\Gamma \vdash f\{A'\} : B[t \leftarrow A']} \qquad\qquad (\forall \text{ Elim})$$

$$\frac{\Gamma \vdash a : A \quad \Gamma \vdash A \le B}{\Gamma \vdash a : B} \qquad\qquad (\text{Subsump})$$

The subtyping rules are either basic (constraint $t \le A$ fetched in the environment, or $A \le$ Top) or higher-order (with the usual contravariance-covariance feature). The typing rules for environments and expressions are those of F, with the exception of the $\forall$ rules, and of the rule Subsump, which introduces non-determinism in typing: the same typing judgement can be proved in different ways, and different types can be assigned to a given expression in a given environment.

The representation adopted for environments (which we borrowed from Luca Cardelli) deserves some comments. The rules to form environments are the following:

Environments

$$(\ ) \ \mathrm{env} \qquad\qquad\qquad\qquad\qquad\qquad\qquad\qquad\qquad (\varnothing \ \mathrm{env})$$

$$\frac{\Gamma \ \mathrm{env} \quad \Gamma \vdash A \ \mathrm{type} \quad t \notin \Gamma^1}{\Gamma, t \le A \ \mathrm{env}} \qquad\qquad\qquad (\le \mathrm{env})$$

$$\frac{\Gamma \ \mathrm{env} \quad \Gamma \vdash A \ \mathrm{type} \quad x \notin \Gamma}{\Gamma, x : A \ \mathrm{env}} \qquad\qquad\qquad (: \mathrm{env})$$

Thus environments are sequences of *mixed* declarations of typed ordinary variables and bounded type variables. Moreover, we adopt the convention that a variable is declared *at most once* in an environment (there is no loss of generality, thanks to α-conversion). This allows us to get rid of the usual side condition in the rule $\forall$ Intro. Specifically, the side condition says: in the premise $\Gamma, t \le A \vdash b : B$ of $\forall$ Intro, if $\Gamma = \Gamma', x : B', \Gamma''$, then t cannot appear freely in B'. One may show that if the premise is true, then $\Gamma' \vdash B'$ type must be provable, and that each free variable of B' must be declared in Γ'. Thus there should be a declaration $t \le A'$ in Γ', contradicting the convention.

This type system is inspired by the type system defined in BL for a kernel of the language Fun of Cardelli and Wegner (1985). $F_\le$ differs from BL-Fun as follows:

- BL-Fun has no Top type;

- records are primitive in BL-Fun, while thanks to Top they can be encoded in $F_\le$;

- BL-Fun has both bounded and unbounded quantified types, and has no rules to compare them.

Some authors have also studied an intermediate system Fbq where the type Top is not defined, but where bounded and unbounded quantified types can be compared (see Ghelli 1990). In the original type-system Fun, only quantified types with the same bound could be compared, while the subtyping rule for quantified types in the second-order fragment of Quest is the same as in $F_\le$. Finally, let us mention that Fun and Quest have recursive types and values, which are not considered here.

$F_\le$ is just a pure type system, i.e. a theory of typing and subtyping judgements, without any associated equational or rewriting theory. Different theories can be associated with $F_\le$. In Ghelli (1990), it is proved that $\beta\eta$ reduction (first- and second-order) is strongly terminating on $F_\le$, as on system F. $\beta\eta$ reduction is not confluent on $F_\le$, but in the same work, a confluent extension for $\beta\eta$ is defined for the weaker system Fbq. In Curien and Ghelli (1991), an extension of $\beta\eta$ with a rule equating all terms of type Top is considered, and a weakly normalizing and confluent rewriting system is defined for this theory. In Cardelli *et al.* (1991), a still richer equatorial theory, called $F_{<:}$, is defined; $F_{<:}$ seems difficult to express in terms of a rewriting system, but is quite powerful. The results reported here are independent of any specific choice of an equational theory.

Hereafter we shall often refer to the type system introduced in this section as the *original* system (as opposed to the explicit system, introduced in section 2.3).

2.2 The Expressivity of $F_\le$

Before proceeding further with $F_\le$, we want to pause and show that, although limited, this language can express interesting type inclusions. The power of second-order λ-calculus is to provide encodings for simple data types, e.g. the booleans. We show how the bounded quantification feature can be used to encode subtypes of the type of booleans, namely: the type containing only true, the type containing only false and the empty type. We briefly sketch how records can be encoded in $F_\le$. Variants can be encoded in terms of records, and bounded existential quantification in terms of bounded universal quantification, along the lines of the known encodings of union and existential quantification in higher-order intuitionistic logic.

Let us consider the usual encoding of booleans in system $F : \forall t \,.\, t \to t \to t$. If we read $\forall t \ldots$ as $\forall t \le \mathrm{Top} \ldots$, then this type TF of booleans has exactly four subtypes in $F_\le$ (the example is due to Cardelli):

- $TF \equiv \forall t \le \mathrm{Top} \,.\, t \to t \to t$ (the booleans)
- $F \equiv \forall t \le \mathrm{Top} \,.\, \mathrm{Top} \to t \to t$ (just false)
- $T \equiv \forall t \le \mathrm{Top} \,.\, t \to \mathrm{Top} \to t$ (just true)
- $\perp \equiv \forall t \le \mathrm{Top} \,.\, \mathrm{Top} \to \mathrm{Top} \to t$ (an empty type)

One can prove the following inclusions: $\perp \le T$, $\perp \le F$, $T \le TF$ and $F \le TF$, as summarized in the picture below:

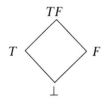

Moreover, there is no term of type $\perp$, and only one β normal form of type T:

$$\mathrm{true}_T = \Lambda t \le \mathrm{Top} \,.\, \lambda x : t \,.\, \lambda y : \mathrm{Top} \,.\, x.$$

In TF we find the following β normal forms:

- true_T again (by subsumption),
- $\text{true}_{TF} = \Lambda t \leq \text{Top} . \lambda x : t . \lambda y : t . x$,
- $\text{false}_F = \Lambda t \leq \text{Top} . \lambda x : \text{Top} . \lambda y : t . y$,
- $\text{false}_{TF} = \Lambda t \leq \text{Top} . \lambda x : t . \lambda y : t . y$.

If we consider true_T and true_{TF} (and similarly false_T and false_{TF}) as equal terms of type TF, the four subtypes of TF in $F_\leq$ codify exactly the four subsets of the set {true, false}. Actually any reasonable version of $\beta\eta$ equivalence should identify, say true_T and true_{TF}, as discussed in Cardelli *et al.* (1991), Ghelli (1990), and Curien and Ghelli (1991). Using the notion of reduction defined in Curien and Ghelli (1991), true_T is not even a normal form of type TF, as it reduces to true_{TF}.

We now briefly hint at the encoding of records. We first transfer to $F_\leq$, the encoding of products in F:

$$A \times B = \forall t \leq \text{Top} . (A \rightarrow B \rightarrow t) \rightarrow t$$

$$\langle a, b \rangle : A \times B = \Lambda t \leq \text{Top} . \lambda(e : A \rightarrow B \rightarrow t) . e(a)(b) : \forall t \leq \text{Top} . (A \rightarrow B \rightarrow t) \rightarrow t$$

$$\textbf{fst}(\text{pair} : A \times B) : A = \text{pair} \{A\} (\lambda x : A . \lambda y : B . x)$$

$$\textbf{snd} (\text{pair} : A \times B) : B = \text{pair} \{B\} (\lambda x : A . \lambda y : B . y).$$

This encoding of pairs satisfies:

$$\frac{\Gamma \vdash T' \leq T \quad \Gamma \vdash U' \leq U}{\Gamma \vdash T' \times U' \leq T \times U}. \qquad\qquad (\text{Pair} \leq)$$

We use the following notations for records and record types:

$$\text{rcd}(1_1 := v_1, \dots, 1_n := v_n) : \text{Rcd}(1_1 : T_1, \dots, 1_n : T_n)$$
$$\text{rcd}_{i \in I}(1_i := v_i) \qquad\qquad : \text{Rcd}_{i \in I}(1_i : T_i)$$
$$\text{rcd}_{i \in I}(1_i := v_i) . 1_i \qquad\qquad : T_i.$$

Record types obey the following subtyping and reduction rules:

$$\frac{\forall i \in I \quad \Gamma \vdash T_i \leq U_i \qquad \forall j \in J \quad \Gamma \vdash T_j \text{ type}}{\Gamma \vdash \text{Rcd}_{i \in I \cup J}(1_i : T_i) \leq \text{Rcd}_{i \in I}(1_i : U_i)} \qquad (\text{Rcd} \leq)$$

$$\text{rcd}_{i \in I}(1_i := a_i) . 1_j > a_j \quad \text{for } j \in I \qquad\qquad (\text{Rcd} \beta)$$

Rule Rcd $\leq$ states that a record type with more fields is a subtype of a record type with less fields (provided that the types associated in the subtype with the common labels are subtypes of those associated with the same labels in the supertype).

The key observation leading to an encoding of record types in $F_\leq$ is the following one. Call *tuple types* right-associated product types terminating with Top, like

$A \times (\ldots \times (Z \times \text{Top})\ldots)$ which we denote as $A \otimes \cdots \otimes Z$

for any $n, m \geq 0$, they enjoy the following property:

$$\frac{\forall i \in 1 \ldots n \quad \Gamma \vdash T_i \leq U_i \quad \forall j \in 1 \ldots m \quad \Gamma \vdash T_{n+j} \quad \text{type}}{\Gamma \vdash T \otimes \cdots \otimes T_{n+m} \leq U_1 \otimes \cdots \otimes U_n} \qquad (\text{Tuple} \leq)$$

(i.e. $\Gamma \vdash T_1 \times (\ldots \times (T_n \times (T_{n+1} \times (\ldots(T_{n+m} \times \text{Top})\ldots)))\ldots) \leq U_1 \times (\ldots \times (U_n \times \text{Top})\ldots))$.

This happens because the first n factors of the first product are subtypes of the first n factors of the second product, and the $(n + 1)$th factor of the first product, $(T_{n+1} \times (\ldots \times (T_{n+m} \times \text{Top})\ldots))$, is a subtype of the $(n + 1)$th factor of the second product, which is Top.

If we now want to encode records instead of tuples, we may identify labels with integers, without loss of generality. For each finite set of labels $L \subseteq \omega$, and for each indexed family $\{A_i\}_{i \in L}$ of types, the record type $\text{Rcd}_{i \in L}(i : A_i)$ can be encoded as follows:

$\text{Rcd}_{i \in L}(i : A_i) = ?_L A_1 \otimes \cdots \otimes ?_L A_{\max L}$ where $?_L A_i$ is A_i if $i \in L$, and Top otherwise.

A record of this type can be encoded as

$\text{rcd}_{i \in L}(i := a_i) = \langle ?_L a_1 \langle \ldots, \langle ?_L a_{\max L}, \text{top} \rangle \ldots \rangle\rangle$

where $?a_i$ is a_i if $i \in L$, and top otherwise.

The dot selection is obtained as follows:

$\_.i = \text{fst} \circ \text{snd}^{i-1}$ (where $\text{fst} = \lambda x . \mathbf{fst}(x)$, $\text{snd} = \lambda x . \mathbf{snd}(x)$).

It is easy to check that this encoding satisfies Rcd $\leq$ and Rcd β (see Ghelli (1990) for details).

Finally, we sketch how variants and bounded existential quantifications can be encoded.

Existential Quantification

$\exists t \leq T . U = \forall z \leq \text{Top} . (\forall t \leq T . U \to z) \to z$

(**open** $e : \exists t \leq T . U$ **as** $x\{s\}$ **in** e') : $V = e\{V\}(\Lambda s \leq T . \lambda x : U[t \leftarrow s] . e')$

pack $[t \leq T = A'$ **in** $U]e = \Lambda z \leq \mathrm{Top} . \lambda f : \forall t \leq T . U \rightarrow z . f\{A'\}e$

Variants

$\mathbf{Var}_{i \in L}(1_i : T_i) = \forall z \leq \mathrm{Top} . \mathrm{Rcd}_{i \in L}(1_i : T_i \rightarrow z) \rightarrow z$

case v **of** $(1_i \Rightarrow f_i)_{i \in I} = v\{T\}\mathrm{rcd}_{i \in L}(1_i := f_i)$ (T is the type of f_i's)

$\mathbf{var}[1_k = a_k] : \mathbf{Var}_{i \in L}(1_i : T_i) = \Lambda z \leq \mathrm{Top} . \lambda(r : \mathrm{Rcd}_{i \in L}(1_i : T_i \rightarrow z)) . (r . 1_k)(a_k).$

The corresponding typing, subtyping and reduction rules are derivable via this translation; this is shown in detail in Ghelli (1990).

2.3   The Explicit System

The explicit system $cF_\leq$ codifies the typing and subtyping proofs of $F_\leq$. It has one more sort, the sort of *coercions* (coercions are introduced to codify subtyping proofs):

$A ::= t \mid \mathrm{Top} \mid A \rightarrow A \mid \forall t \leq A . A$

$a ::= x \mid \mathrm{top} \mid \lambda x : A . a \mid a(a) \mid \Lambda t \leq A . a \mid a\{A, c\} \mid c \langle a \rangle$

$c ::= t_A \mid \mathrm{Top}_A \mid c \rightarrow c \mid \forall t \leq c . c \mid \mathrm{Id}_A \mid c \cdot c.$

The expressions of the explicit system will be often called 'c'-expressions ('c' for coercions), to distinguish them from the expressions of the original system $F_\leq$. We shall use c-terms for c-expressions and coercions.

c-expressions are defined like expressions in the original system, with the exception of $c\langle a \rangle$ and $a\{A, c\}$. In $cF_\leq$, the subsumption rule is no longer valid: when A is a subtype of B, a term a of type A can be mapped into the type B by applying to it a coercion c proving $A \leq B$; coercion application is denoted $c\langle a \rangle$. When an expression a of type $\forall t \leq A . B$ is applied to a subtype A' of A, it needs a further parameter: a coercion c proving $A' \leq A$; the application is denoted by $a\{A', c\}$.

Types in $cF_\leq$ are identical to the types of the original system. Indexes in the coercions t_A, Top_A and Id_A will be sometimes omitted. Note that the same variable names are used as type variables and as coercion variables; the context will determine which sort is meant. The coercions of the form $c \rightarrow d$ ($\forall t \leq c . d$) are called $\rightarrow (\forall)$ coercions.

We list only the typing rules which differ from the original system: the subtyping rules, the subsumption rule and $\forall$ Elim. In the c-system, subtyping judgements have the form:

$\Gamma \vdash C : A \leq B.$

These are the new meta-variable conventions:

c, d, e coercions.

t, u, v coercion variables

Subtypes

$$\frac{\Gamma, t \leq A, \Gamma' \text{ env}}{\Gamma, t \leq A, \Gamma' \vdash t_A : t \leq A} \qquad\qquad (\text{Var} \leq)$$

$$\frac{\Gamma \vdash A \text{ type}}{\Gamma \vdash \text{Top}_A : A \leq \text{Top}} \qquad\qquad (\text{Top} \leq)$$

$$\frac{\Gamma \vdash c : A \leq A' \quad \Gamma \vdash d : B \leq B'}{\Gamma \vdash c \to d : A' \to B \leq A \to B'} \qquad\qquad (\to \leq)$$

$$\frac{\Gamma \vdash c : A \leq A' \quad \Gamma, t \leq A \vdash d : B \leq B'}{\Gamma \vdash \forall t \leq c . d : \forall t \leq A' . B \leq \forall t \leq A . B'} \qquad\qquad (\forall \leq)$$

$$\frac{\Gamma \vdash A \text{ type}}{\Gamma \vdash \text{Id}_A : A \leq A} \qquad\qquad (\text{Id} \leq)$$

$$\frac{\Gamma \vdash c : A \leq B \quad \Gamma \vdash d : B \leq C}{\Gamma \vdash d \cdot c : A \leq C} \qquad\qquad (\text{Trans} \leq)$$

Terms

$$\frac{\Gamma \vdash a : A \quad \Gamma \vdash c : A \leq B}{\Gamma \vdash c \langle a \rangle : B} \qquad\qquad (\text{Coerce})$$

$$\frac{\Gamma \vdash f : \forall t \leq A . B \quad \Gamma \vdash c : A' \leq A}{\Gamma \vdash f \{A', c\} : B[t \leftarrow A']} \qquad\qquad (\forall \text{ Elim})$$

In the sequel we will denote, when useful, the entailment relation of the explicit system with $\vdash_C$, to distinguish it from the entailment relation $\vdash$ of the original system.

The design of the explicit system has been guided by the *terms-as-proofs* paradigm, which views type system as a system to prove *propositions* which are codified by the types, and in which the terms codify the *proofs* of these propositions. In the original system, the way in which judgements like $A \leq B$ are proved, and the point where a subsumption is applied, are not recorded. In the explicit system *Minimal Bounded Fun* of BL, there exists a unique coercion c_{AB} for all the proofs of any provable subtyping

$A \leq B$. These coercions keep track of the points where subsumptions are applied, but the proofs of subtypings are not recorded in the terms. In our explicit system, both pieces of information are encoded in the c-terms.

2.4   Relation between the Two Systems

There is a one-to-one correspondence between proofs in the two systems; since there is also a one-to-one correspondence between terms and proofs in the explicit system, the *terms* of $cF_{\leq}$ are isomorphic to the *proofs* of $F_{\leq}$. To be more precise, we can define a forgetful function Erase which erases *coercion* subterms:

$\mathrm{Erase}(c\langle a \rangle) = \mathrm{Erase}(a)$

$\mathrm{Erase}(a\{A, c\}) = \mathrm{Erase}(a)\{A\}$

$\mathrm{Erase}(a(b)) = \mathrm{Erase}(a)(\mathrm{Erase}(b))$

$\mathrm{Erase}(\lambda x : A . b) = \lambda x : A . \mathrm{Erase}(b)$

$\mathrm{Erase}(\Lambda t \leq A . b) = \Lambda t \leq A . \mathrm{Erase}(b)$

$\mathrm{Erase}(\Gamma \vdash_c a : A) = \Gamma \vdash \mathrm{Erase}(a) : A$

$\mathrm{Erase}(\Gamma \vdash_c c : A \leq B) = \Gamma \vdash A \leq B$.

Erase can be extended to proof trees: if Π_c is a proof of a judgement in the explicit system, then Erase (Π_c) is the proof obtained by applying Erase to all the judgements in the tree Π_c.

PROPOSITION 2.1   Erase maps explicit proofs to proofs in $F_{\leq}$, and is a bijection.

Proof Hint   Elementary induction on the rules.   ∎

We shall later refer to Erase(a) as the coercion erasure of a, in contrast to a more drastic erasure of both coercions and types, which will be used in section 5.

2.5   Some Syntactic Properties

First we state in which precise sense the explicit system is deterministic.

PROPOSITION 2.2   In a fixed environment, any term in the explicit system admits at most one typing proof and, a fortiori, at most one type.

By the determinism of the explicit type system, if, say $\Gamma \vdash_c a : A$ and a' is an occurrence of a subterm of a, then Γ, a and a' uniquely determine an environment Γ' and a type A' s.t. $\Gamma' \vdash_c a' : A'$ appears in the typing proof of $\Gamma \vdash_c a : A$. For instance, if

$\Gamma \vdash_C \Lambda t \leq A \,.\, b : \forall t \leq A \,.\, B$, then the occurrence of b in $\Lambda t \leq A \,.\, b$ is associated with the judgement $\Gamma, t \leq A \vdash_C b : B$. The following replacement property holds (we only state it for typing judgements):

LEMMA 2.3 (Replacement.)   If $\Gamma \vdash_C a : A$, and if b is a subterm of a with associated judgement $\Gamma' \vdash_C b : B$, if b' satisfies $\Gamma' \vdash_C b' : B$, and if $a_{b'}$ is defined as a where the subterm b has been replaced by b', then also $\Gamma \vdash_C a_{b'} : A$.

Proof   Obvious, by the previous proposition, and noticing that only the conclusions of subproofs matter when combining subproofs in an inference rule.   ■

The following lemma shows that typing behaves well w.r.t. (two specific forms of) substitution.

LEMMA 2.4 (Substitution.)   The following two forms of substitution properties hold:

$$\Gamma, t \leq B, \Gamma' \vdash_C c : T \leq U, \quad \Gamma \vdash_C d : A \leq B$$

$$\Rightarrow \Gamma, \Gamma'[t \leftarrow A] \vdash_C c[t_B \leftarrow d, t \leftarrow A] : T[t \leftarrow A] \leq U[t \leftarrow A] \tag{1}$$

where $\Gamma'[t \leftarrow A] \equiv t_1 \leq B_1[t \leftarrow A], \ldots, t_n \leq B_n[t \leftarrow A]$ when $\Gamma' \equiv t_1 \leq B_1, \ldots, t_n \leq B_n$. (A type variable t can be substituted by a type A satisfying its constraint $t \leq B$, provided that the coercion t_B which proved $t \leq B$ is substituted by a proof d of $A \leq B$.)

$$\Gamma, t \leq B, \Gamma' \vdash_C c : T \leq U, \quad \Gamma, t \leq A \vdash_C d : t \leq B \Rightarrow \Gamma, t \leq A, \Gamma' \vdash_C c[t_B \leftarrow d] : T \leq U \tag{2}$$

(an assumption $t \leq B$ can be strengthened into $t \leq A$, provided that the coercion t_B which proved $t \leq B$ is changed to a coercion d proving $t \leq B$ in the new context).

Proof   By induction on the structure of c. We only detail the case Var $\leq$, i.e. c is a coercion variable. We have two subcases:

(a) If $c = t_B$ the properties can be rewritten as:

    (1) $\Gamma, t \leq B, \Gamma' \vdash_C t_B : t \leq B, \Gamma \vdash_C d : A \leq B \Rightarrow \Gamma, \Gamma'[t \leftarrow A] \vdash_C d : A \leq B[t \leftarrow A]$

    (2) $\Gamma, t \leq B, \Gamma' \vdash_C t_B : t \leq B, \Gamma, t \leq A \vdash_C d : t \leq B \Rightarrow \Gamma, t \leq A, \Gamma' \vdash_C d : t \leq B$.

In both implications the thesis follows by weakening[2] from the second hypothesis; in the first statement, note that t cannot occur free in B, as B was the bound of t in the hypothesis.

(b) If $c = u_U$, where u is a type variable different from t, then the properties can be rewritten as:

(1) $\Gamma, t \leq B, \Gamma' \vdash_c u : u \leq U, \Gamma \vdash_c d : A \leq B \Rightarrow \Gamma, \Gamma'[t \leftarrow A] \vdash_c u : u \leq U[t \leftarrow A]$

(2) $\Gamma, t \leq B, \Gamma' \vdash_c u : u \leq U, \Gamma, t \leq A \vdash_c d : t \leq B \Rightarrow \Gamma, t \leq A, \Gamma' \vdash_c u : u \leq U.$

In both cases the conclusion is an application of Var $\leq$ to u. The variable u can be declared either in Γ or in Γ'; the second implication is obvious in both cases. For the first implication, if u is declared in Γ, then t cannot occur free in its bound U, and if u is bounded by U in Γ, then it is bounded by $U[t \leftarrow A]$ in $\Gamma'[t \leftarrow A]$.   ∎

2.6   The Shape of Well-Typed Terms

In this subsection, we describe what well-formed coercions and provable subtypings 'look like'. More formally, we define a sublanguage of the language of 'raw' coercions defined in section 2.3, generating all the well-type coercions.

We consider here coercions as words, that is modulo associativity of the composition. We do not give the grammar of the well-shaped coercions, but rather present an automaton that generates them.

Our automaton is depicted in figure 1. We draw a node for each of the four syntactic forms of types (variable, $\rightarrow$, $\forall$ and Top), and an arrow from a node A to a node B, labelled r, for each rule r, different from Trans $\leq$, allowing the proof that a type with form A is a subtype of a type with form B. So, for every proof that a type of form A is a subtype of a type of form B there exists a path in the picture, going from

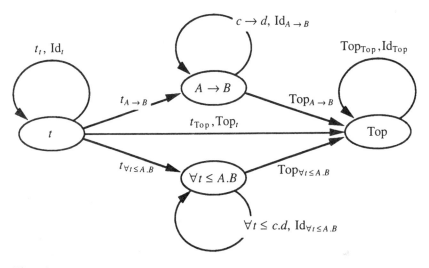

Figure 1
The classes of subtyping that can be proved and the corresponding coercions

A to B, labelled by the outermost structure of the corresponding coercion. More precisely, if a coercion proving a subtyping $A \le B$, seen as a word, has the form $c_n \cdot \ldots \cdot c_1$, then there is a path labelled $a_1 \ldots a_n$ between the nodes corresponding to A and B, such that each c_i can be obtained instantiating the coercion metavariables in a_i.

Let us exemplify what can be deduced observing the automaton. One easily checks that no path can connect the nodes $A \to B$ and $\forall t \le A . B$ of the automaton. If $c : A \to B \le A' \to B'$ then c is a composition of $c \to d$ coercions intermixed with $\mathrm{Id}_{T \to U}$ coercions. The set of coercions of this form can be codified by the regular expression $(c \to d | \mathrm{Id}_{T \to U})^+$. Similar regular expressions can be written down for the other type constructors.

3   Coherence Conditions

By the correspondence stated in section 2.4, proof transformation in $F_\le$ can be investigated as term rewriting in the explicit system. We shall define a rewriting system, called a *coerce reduction system*, in the next section. First we concentrate on the properties we want this system to satisfy. We outline the properties before we actually define our reduction system, because these properties constitute the guidelines of a general methodology to prove coherence and type minimality properties, which we believe is largely independent of the specific system examined.

3.1   The Conditions

We require the following five conditions:

Notation: $A < B$ stands for $A \le B$ and A different from B.

Fact 1 (Erasure invariance): both sides of each reduction rule have the same coercion erasure.

Fact 2 (Subject reduction): if a type can be assigned in an environment to a c-term a, and a reduces to b, then the same type can be assigned in the same environment to b.

Fact 3 (Weak termination): for each well typed c-term, there exists a reduction sequence which transforms it into a normal form.

Fact 4 (Uniqueness of subtyping normal forms): if c and c' are coercions in normal form proving the same subtyping in the same environment, then c and c' are identical.

To state our last property, we need the following notion: a c-expression a which is not of the form $c \langle b \rangle$ is called *head coercion free*.

Fact 5 (Quasi-uniqueness of c-expression normal forms): if a, a' are c-expressions in coerce normal form and have the same erasure, and if $\Gamma \vdash_c a : A$ and $\Gamma \vdash_c a' : A'$, then there exists a head coercion free term a'', having type A'' in Γ, such that:

(a) either $A'' \equiv A$ and $a \equiv a''$, or $A'' < A$ and $a \equiv c\langle a'' \rangle$ (for some coercion c);

(b) either $A'' \equiv A'$ and $a' \equiv a'$, or $A'' < A'$ and $a' \equiv c\langle a'' \rangle$ (for some coercion c).

In other words a and a' are equal modulo the deletion of an uppermost coercion application.

Remark a'' in fact 5 is unique and completely determined by a (or a') alone. Define the uppermost coercion erasure of a c-expression as:

$UE(a) = b$ if $a \equiv c\langle b \rangle$ for some c, $UE(a) = a$ otherwise.

Then a'' is $UE(a)$. In fact if $a \equiv c\langle b \rangle$ for some c, then a'' must be equal to b, as a'' is head coercion free; if a has not the form $c\langle b \rangle$, then a'' must be equal to a.

3.2 Coherence and Minimal Typing

The coherence and minimal-type properties are directly derived from facts 1–5. For our last problem, type-checking, we shall have to enter into the specific details of the rewriting system (we thus delay this study until section 6).

THEOREM 3.1 (Coherence.) If Π' and Π'' are two proofs of the same judgement $\Gamma \vdash a : A$ in the original system, and a' and a'' are the associated terms in the explicit calculus, then a' and a'' are equal modulo the coerce rules.

Proof Suppose that Π' and Π'' are proofs of the same judgement $\Gamma \vdash a : A$ in the original system. By Proposition 2.1, there exist two expressions a' and a'' in the explicit language whose typing proofs correspond to Π' and Π'', whose erasure is a, and which have type A in the explicit system. By fact 3, a' and a'' can be reduced to normal c-expressions b' and b''. By fact 1, the erasure of b' and b'' is still a, and by fact 2, their type is still A. By fact 5, there exists a term b with type A'' such that one of the following alternatives holds:

(1) if $A'' < A$, then b' and b'' have the form $c'\langle b \rangle$ and $c''\langle b \rangle$, where both c' and c'' are normal form coercions which prove the same subtype relation $A'' \leq A$. By fact 4, c' and c'' are identical too.

(2) if $A'' \equiv A$, we get directly $b' \equiv b'' \equiv b$.

In both cases, b' and b'' are identical. This proves that a' and a'' are equal modulo the coerce rules. ∎

The theorem guarantees that if a semantic interpretation of $F_\leq$ satisfies the coerce rules, i.e. gives the same meaning to equivalent proofs, then it also gives the same meaning to all the different proofs of a given judgement. In other words, the meaning of a judgement is intrinsic and does not depend on its proof. Hence, proving coherence of an interpretation is reduced to proving the satisfaction of the equations underlying the coerce rules.

Notice that in the statement of theorem 3.1, a' and a'' are not only provably equal, they also have a common normal form. Using this remark, we get the confluence property as an immediate corollary:

COROLLARY 3.2   The coerce reduction system is confluent.

Proof   We first show that all the normal forms of a given c-term a coincide. Suppose that a', a'' are two normal forms of a. Then they have the same type by fact 2. So we can apply theorem 3.1 in the strong form just stated: a' and a'' have a common normal form. Being already normal forms, a' and a'' coincide. Confluence follows then by fact 3: if there are two derivations from a to a', a'', then each can be prolongated to normal forms of a' and a'', thus of a; therefore these normal forms coincide, and the confluence diagram is completed.   ∎

NB. This does not show however that all reduction sequences terminate (strong termination). We believe that this property also holds in the system defined in section 4, but it is certainly harder to prove, and is not needed in this paper.

The existence of a minimum typing also follows from facts 1–5.

THEOREM 3.2 (Minimality.)   For each term a which can be assigned a type A in an environment Γ in the original type system, there exists a minimum type M such that:

$$\Gamma \vdash a : M, \text{ and, for all } B, \Gamma \vdash a : B \text{ implies } \Gamma \vdash M \leq B.$$

Proof   Let Π be a proof of $\Gamma \vdash a : A$. Let a' be the corresponding c-expression; by proposition 2.1, we have $\Gamma \vdash_c a' : A$. By facts 3, 2, 1, a' can be reduced to a normal form c-expression b' whose type in the explicit system is still A and whose erasure is still a. By fact 5, b' has form $c\langle b\rangle$ or b, where b is a head coercion free normal c-expression whose type M is a subtype of A. As the erasure of b is still a, $\Gamma \vdash a : M$ holds, by proposition 2.1. By the remark following fact 5, the c-expression b (and *a fortiori* its type M) obtained from Π as above does not depend on the specific proof Π, but only on the term a typed by the proof. This means that for each type B and for each proof of a judgement $\Gamma \vdash a : B$, the preceding construction gives always the same type $M \leq B$, from which the thesis follows.   ∎

4 The Rewriting System

In this section we define a reduction system on the terms of the explicit calculus presented in section 2.3. In section 4.1, the system is defined, while in section 4.2 some of its general properties are shown. In the next section we shall prove that facts 1–5 of section 3.1 hold.

4.1 The Reduction System

We are interested in relating proofs, i.e. *typed* terms of the explicit calculus. Thus the equations underlying our rewrite rules should have the general form

$$\Gamma \vdash a = b : A.$$

We shall not carry the environments around in the reduction rules, though. Type indexes in atomic coercions (Top_T, Id_T and t_T) are enough to rebuild the information needed for the proofs. In the rules IdL, IdR, Top and $\forall$, we assume that the subtyping proved by c is $\Gamma \vdash c : A \leq B$. Our reduction system is defined by the following three sets of rules, called the *coerce reduction rules*:

Coercion Rules

I

$$(c \cdot d) \cdot e > c \cdot (d \cdot e) \tag{Ass}$$

$$\text{Id}_B \cdot c > c \tag{IdL}$$

$$c \cdot \text{Id}_A > c \tag{IdR}$$

$$\text{Id}_A \rightarrow \text{Id}_B > \text{Id}_{A \rightarrow B} \tag{Id $\rightarrow$}$$

$$\forall t \leq \text{Id}_A . \text{Id}_B > \text{Id}_{\forall t \leq A . B} \tag{Id $\forall$}$$

$$\text{Top}_B \cdot c > \text{Top}_A \tag{Top}$$

$$t_{\text{Top}} > \text{Top}_t \tag{Var Top}$$

$$\text{Top}_{\text{Top}} > \text{Id}_{\text{Top}} \tag{Top Id}$$

II

$$(c \rightarrow d) \cdot (c' \rightarrow d') > (c' \cdot c) \rightarrow (d \cdot d') \tag{$\rightarrow'$}$$

$$(c \rightarrow d) \cdot ((c' \rightarrow d') \cdot e) > ((c' \cdot c) \rightarrow (d \cdot d')) \cdot e \tag{$\rightarrow''$}$$

$$\forall t \leq c . d \cdot \forall t \leq c' \cdot d' > \forall t \leq c' \cdot c . d \cdot (d'[t_B \leftarrow c \cdot t_A]) \tag{$\forall'$)^3}$$

$$\forall t \leq c . d \cdot (\forall t \leq c' . d' \cdot e) > (\forall t \leq c' \cdot c . d \cdot (d'[t_B \leftarrow c \cdot t_A])) \cdot e \tag{$\forall''$}$$

Expression Rules

III

$$\mathrm{Id}\langle a \rangle > a \tag{Id}$$

$$((c \to d)\langle a \rangle)b > d\langle a(c\langle b \rangle)\rangle \tag{App'}$$

$$((c \to d) \cdot e \langle a \rangle)b > d\langle e\langle a \rangle(c\langle b \rangle)\rangle \tag{App''}$$

$$((\forall t \leq c . d)\langle f \rangle)\{A, e\} > d[t \leftarrow A][t_B \leftarrow e]\langle f\{A, c \cdot e\}\rangle \qquad e : A \leq B \tag{App2'}$$

$$((\forall t \leq c . d) \cdot c'\langle f \rangle)\{A, e\} > d[t \leftarrow A][t_B \leftarrow e]\langle (c'\langle f \rangle)\{A, c \cdot e\}\rangle \qquad e : A \leq B \tag{App2''}$$

$$\lambda x : A . c\langle b \rangle > (\mathrm{Id}_A \to c)\langle \lambda x : A . b \rangle \tag{λ}$$

$$\Lambda t \leq A . c\langle b \rangle > (\forall t \leq \mathrm{Id}_A . c)\langle \Lambda t \leq A . b \rangle \tag{Λ}$$

$$c\langle d\langle a \rangle\rangle > (c \cdot d)\langle a \rangle \tag{Comp}$$

The coercion rules simplify subtyping proofs; they are divided in two groups. The rules of the first group perform the most obvious sort of cleaning. In particular, the three monoid laws Ass, IdL and IdR allow us to view compositions of coercions as words of coercions. The second group of rules is more sophisticated. It describes a *cut elimination* process: the rule Trans $\leq$ is pushed towards the leaves of the proof.

The expression rules simplify typing proofs by changing the way of applying subsumption:

• the rules App, App2, λ and Λ are designed to delay the application of subsumption as far as possible, to get the minimum type (the equational redundancy of App(λ) and App2(Λ) is unessential and would even have disappeared if we had taken as basic the view of coercions-as-words);

• the Id rule eliminates a useless subsumption;

• Comp transforms multiple coercion application to single composed coercion application. This can trigger a new process of subtyping proof simplification, as it creates a new coercion composition.

It is worth noting that we could have defined different reduction systems, with different normal forms, enjoying properties 1 to 5. Namely the structural rule Ass could have been reversed (or ignored). Also the rules Id $\rightarrow$ and Id $\forall$ could have been reversed (this would fit with logical presentations where axioms $A \vdash A$ are given on atoms only). We feel that these are minor variants.

According to the direction we have given in the Ass rule, we will follow the notational convention that in a non-parenthesized sequence of compositions the '$\cdot$' operator associates to the right.

4.2 The Shape of Coerce Normal Forms

In section 2.6, we analysed how well-typed c-terms are shaped. The condition that a c-term is in normal form further constrains its shape. The following analysis stems directly from section 2.6. We shall also use the fact that the context determines how variable coercions can be composed, for which we introduce a notation:

Notation   Given an environment Γ containing $t \leq A$, we set $A = \Gamma(t)$; $\Gamma^*(t)$ is the minimum supertype of t which is not a variable and is defined by:

$\Gamma^*(t) = \Gamma(t)$ if $\Gamma(t)$ is not a variable

$\Gamma^*(t) = \Delta^*(\Gamma(t))$ if $\Gamma(t)$ is a variable and $\Gamma = \Delta, t \leq \Gamma(t), \Delta'$.

Since Δ is shorter than Γ, the definition is well founded. Also the length of coercions, with respect to the uppermost Trans $\leq$ compositions '$\cdot$', will play a role in the sequel; this measure is defined formally by:

$\text{length}(t) = \text{length}(\text{Top}) = \text{length}(\text{Id}) = \text{length}(c \rightarrow d) = \text{length}(\forall t \leq c . d) = 1$

$\text{length}(c \cdot d) = \text{length}(c) + \text{length}(d)$

PROPOSITION 4.1   If $c : A \leq A$ is in normal form, then $c \equiv \text{Id}_A$. Coercions in normal form which prove strict inclusions $A < B$ can only have the following forms, according to the structure of the types they relate (see figure 2):

(1) if $c : t < u$, then c is a composition of variables, which is determined in a unique way by the environment.

(2) If $c : A \rightarrow B < A' \rightarrow B'$ then c is an $\rightarrow$ coercion.

(3) If $c : \forall t \leq A . B < \forall t \leq A' . B'$ then c is a $\forall$ coercion.

(4) If $c : t < A \rightarrow B$ then c is a composition of variables, which is determined a unique way by the environment, composed with a coercion of class (2) if $\Gamma^*(t) \neq A \rightarrow B$.

(5) If $c : t < \forall t \leq A . B$ then c is a composition of variables, which is determined in a unique way by the environment, composed with a coercion of class (3) if $\Gamma^*(t) \neq \forall t \leq A . B$.

(6) If $c: A < \text{Top}$ then c is Top_A.

Proof By a simple analysis of the paths allowed by the automaton of section 2.6. The only delicate point is to check the first part of the statement, but this follows from lemma 4.2. ■

Lemma 4.1 says, in brief, that the only kind of coercion composition allowed in normal form coercions is a subword of $(c \to d) \cdot u_{A \to B} \cdot t_u \cdot \ldots \cdot t'_{u'}$ or of $(\forall t \leq c \cdot d) \cdot u_{\forall t \leq A \cdot B} \cdot t_u \cdot \ldots \cdot t'_{u'}$.

The next lemma is needed to complete the proof of proposition 4.1, but it has also an interest of its own, since it shows that the type inclusion relation is antisymmetric (hence is an order relation).

LEMMA 4.2   if $\Gamma \vdash c: A \leq A'$ and $\Gamma \vdash d: A' \leq A$, with c and d normal form coercions, then $A \equiv A'$ and $c \equiv d \equiv \text{Id}_A$.

Proof By an easy checking on the automaton of section 2.6, we can have $A \leq B$ and $B \leq A$ only if A and B belong to the same syntactic class. The case where they are both variables or both Top is easy. If $A \equiv T \to U$, and $A' \equiv T' \to U'$, proposition 4.1 allows two possibilities: $c \equiv \text{Id}_A$ or $c \equiv c' \to c''$ (the same is true for d):

(1) $c \equiv c' \to c''$, $d \equiv d' \to d''$. We have $\Gamma \vdash c': T' \leq T$, $\Gamma \vdash d': T \leq T'$, $\Gamma \vdash c'': U \leq U'$, $\Gamma \vdash d'': U' \leq U$. By induction hypothesis we have $c' \equiv d' \equiv \text{Id}_T$ and $c'' \equiv d'' \equiv \text{Id}_U$, which is impossible in a normal form coercion, by $\text{Id} \to$.

(2) $c \equiv \text{Id}_A$. Since $c: A \leq A'$, then $A \equiv A'$, hence $T \equiv T'$ and $U \equiv U'$. If d is equal to $d' \to d''$, then induction applies to d' and d'', since, say $\Gamma \vdash d': T \leq T'$ and $T \equiv T'$ immediately imply $\Gamma \vdash d': T' \leq T$. This entails $d \equiv \text{Id}_T \to \text{Id}_U$, which is impossible by rule $\text{Id} \to$. Then also $d = \text{Id}_A$.

(3) $d \equiv \text{Id}_A$: this case is similar to case (2).

The bounded quantification case is handled similarly. ■

Figure 2 depicts the normal form coercions. Figure 2(a) has been obtained by removing t_{Top} and Top_{Top} edges from figure 1 (reduction rules Var Top and Top Id) and by splitting all states into two disconnected initial and final states, since it represents the normal form coercions of length one. Figure 2(b) has been obtained by removing from figure 2(a) the Top coercions, which cannot be left-composed with other coercions (rule Top), the Id coercions (rules IdL and IdR), and by unwinding the $c \to d$ and the $\forall t \leq c \cdot d$ coercions, which cannot be composed with coercions of the same form (rules of group II); any other coercion composition is allowed in normal form coercions.

(a)

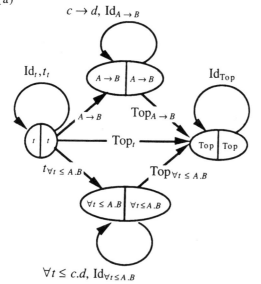

(b)

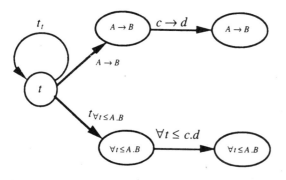

Figure 2
(a) One-step normal form coercions. (b) Composed normal form coercions.

Next we describe the shape of the normal forms of c-expressions.

PROPOSITION 4.3 c-expressions in coerce normal form (normal form for short) have the following form:

(1) top;

(2) $c\langle x\rangle$;

(3) $c\langle \lambda x:A.a\rangle$;

(4) $c\langle \Lambda t\le A.a\rangle$;

(5) $c\langle (t^*\langle a\rangle)(c'\langle b\rangle)\rangle$;

(6) $c\langle (t^*\langle a\rangle)\{A,c''\}\rangle$.

Where:

- the coercion applications of c, c' and t^* are optional;

- c, c', c'' are in normal form;

- t^* is the composition of variables proving $t \le \Gamma^*(t)$ where t is the type of a (hence t^* is absent if the type of a is not a type variable);

- a and b are c-expressions in head coercion free normal form.

Proof Easy checking by induction on the structure of the coercion erasure. Case (1) is settled thanks to proposition 4.1. ∎

The two following more specific lemmas, which can be skipped at first reading, will be needed in the proof of weak termination (5.3).

LEMMA 4.4 Expressions in I + III normal form have the following form:

(1) top;

(2) $c\langle x\rangle$;

(3) $c\langle \lambda x:A.a\rangle$;

(4) $c\langle \Lambda t\le A.a\rangle$;

(5) $c\langle (t^*\langle a\rangle)(c'\langle b\rangle)\rangle$;

(6) $c\langle (t^*\langle a\rangle)\{A,c''\}\rangle$.

Where:

- the coercion applications of c, c' and t^* are optional;

- c, c', c'' are in I normal form;

- t^* is the composition of variables proving $t \leq \Gamma^*(t)$ where t is the type of a;
- a and b are c-expressions in head coercion free I + III normal form.

Proof The lemma is proved like proposition 4.3. The case (1) is settled thanks to proposition 4.1 and corollary 4.6. ■

LEMMA 4.5   If a coercion c reduces to Id, then all the leaves of c are themselves Id or Top_{Top}.

Proof The thesis will follow from the following claim: if c reduces to c' and all the leaves of c' are themselves Id or Top_{Top}, then c enjoys the same property. To see this suppose that t_A or Top_C, with $C \neq \text{Top}$, occurs in c. No rule other than Top can get rid of such a leave. The only case to consider is thus: c reduces to c' by Top, and the 'bad' leaf occurs below d in Top rule redex $\text{Top}_B \cdot d$. This redex can only be reduced to Top_{Top} by the hypothesis on c', which entails $\Gamma \vdash d : \text{Top} \leq B$. As we can easily check on the automaton of 2.6, this forces $B \equiv \text{Top}$ and $d \in (\text{Id}_{\text{Top}} | \text{Top}_{\text{Top}})^+$. Thus all the leaves below d are 'good': contradiction. ■

COROLLARY 4.6   If a coercion c reduces to Id, then it can be reduced to Id using only the rules of group I.

Proof Since all the leaves of c are either Id or Top_{Top}, c can be reduced to Id in two phases. First apply Top Id until all the leaves are Id. Then, by using IdL, Id $\rightarrow$ and Id $\forall$, all the subcoercions with form $\text{Id} \cdot \text{Id}$, $\text{Id} \rightarrow \text{Id}$ and $\forall t \leq \text{Id}.\text{Id}$ can be reduced to Id. We have used only the rules of group I. ■

5   Proof of the Coherence Conditions

In this section we prove that our rewriting system enjoys the properties stated in section 3. The five following subsections are devoted to the five properties.

5.1   Erasure Preserving

Fact 1 can be easily checked rule by rule.

5.2   Subject Reduction

By the replacement property (lemma 2.3), it is enough to check:

$$\forall \Gamma, A: \quad \Gamma \vdash_c \text{lhs} : A \Rightarrow \Gamma \vdash_c \text{rhs} : A$$

for each instance lhs > rhs of any reduction rule. This is routine for most rules with the notable exceptions of the $\forall$ and App2 rules, for which we give details. Let us consider the left hand side of $\forall'$:

$$\Gamma \vdash (\forall t \le c.d) \cdot (\forall t \le c'.d') : \forall t \le C.T \le \forall t \le A.V.$$

We must prove that the right-hand side $\forall t \le c' \cdot c.d \cdot (d'[t \leftarrow c \cdot t])$ proves the same subtyping in the same environment Γ. The determinism of deduction rules in the explicit system allows decomposing the last steps of the proof codified by the left-hand side:

$$\frac{\dfrac{\mathbf{\Gamma \vdash c' : B \le C} \quad \mathbf{\Gamma, t \le B \vdash d' : T \le U}}{\Gamma \vdash \forall t \le c'.d' : \forall t \le C.T \le \forall t \le B.U} \quad \dfrac{\mathbf{\Gamma \vdash c : A \le B} \quad \mathbf{\Gamma, t \le A \vdash d : U \le V}}{\Gamma \vdash \forall t \le c.d : \forall t \le B.U \le \forall t \le A.V}}{\Gamma \vdash (\forall t \le c.d) \cdot (\forall t \le c'.d') : \forall t \le C.T \le \forall t \le A.V}.$$

In particular, the four boldface judgements are provable in the system $\vdash_C$. Using the second form of the substitution lemma, we can recombine these judgements in another way:

$$\text{(lemma)}^5 \frac{\mathbf{\Gamma, t \le B \vdash d' : T \le U} \quad \dfrac{\Gamma, t \le A \vdash t_A : t \le A \quad \mathbf{\Gamma, t \le A \vdash c : A \le B}}{\Gamma, t \le A \vdash c \cdot t_A : t \le B}}{\Gamma, t \le A \vdash d'[t_B \leftarrow c \cdot t_A] : T \le U} \quad (\Pi)$$

$$(\Pi)$$

$$\frac{\dfrac{\mathbf{\Gamma \vdash c : A \le B} \quad \mathbf{\Gamma \vdash c' : B \le C}}{\Gamma \vdash c' \cdot c : A \le C} \quad \dfrac{\Gamma, t \le A \vdash d'[t_B \leftarrow c \cdot t_A] : T \le U \quad \mathbf{\Gamma, t \le A \vdash d : U \le V}}{\Gamma, t \le A \vdash d \cdot d'[t_B \leftarrow c \cdot t_A] : T \le V}}{\Gamma \vdash \forall t \le c' \cdot c.d \cdot d'[t_B \leftarrow c \cdot t_A] : \forall t \le C.T \le \forall t \le A.V}.$$

Subject reduction for the App2 rules can be proved in the same way, using now the first form of the substitution lemma. We present the decomposition and the recomposition with no further remarks.

Left-hand side of App2':

$$\Gamma \vdash ((\forall t \le c.d)\langle f \rangle)\{A, e\} : B'[t \leftarrow A].$$

Proof decomposition:

$$\frac{\dfrac{\mathbf{\Gamma \vdash f : \forall t \le A''.B''} \quad \dfrac{\mathbf{\Gamma \vdash c : A' \le A''} \quad \mathbf{\Gamma, t \le A' \vdash d : B'' \le B'}}{\Gamma \vdash \forall t \le c.d : \forall t \le A''.B'' \le \forall t \le A'.B'}}{\Gamma \vdash ((\forall t \le c.d)\langle f \rangle) : \forall (t \le A').B'} \quad \mathbf{\Gamma \vdash e : A \le A'}}{\Gamma \vdash ((\forall t \le c.d)\langle f \rangle)\{A, e\} : B'[t \leftarrow A]}.$$

Proof recomposition:

$$\frac{\dfrac{\mathbf{\Gamma \vdash f : \forall t \le A''.B''} \quad \dfrac{\mathbf{\Gamma \vdash e : A \le A'} \quad \mathbf{\Gamma \vdash c : A' \le A''}}{\Gamma \vdash c \cdot e : A \le A''}}{\Gamma \vdash f\{A, c \cdot e\} : B''[t \leftarrow A]} \quad \dfrac{\mathbf{\Gamma, t \le A' \vdash d : B'' \le B'} \quad \mathbf{\Gamma \vdash e : A \le A'}}{\Gamma \vdash d[t \leftarrow A][t_{A'} \leftarrow e] : B''[t \leftarrow A] \le B''[t \leftarrow A]}}{\Gamma \vdash d[t \leftarrow A][t_{A'} \leftarrow e]\langle f\{A, c \cdot e\}\rangle : B'[t \leftarrow A]}.$$

5.3   Weak Normalization

The usual way of proving a normalization property of a system is by means of a well-founded 'complexity measure' associated with each term of the system, which each reduction step strictly reduces. In our case, we will have to overcome a problem given by the ∀ rules:

$$\forall t \leq c . d \cdot \forall t \leq c' . d' \; > \; \forall t \leq c' \cdot c . d \cdot (d'[t \leftarrow c \cdot t]). \qquad\qquad \forall'$$

In these rules, the subterm d' of the left-hand side is expanded to a subterm $d'[t \leftarrow c \cdot t]$ in the right-hand side. This means that any complexity measure based on the size of terms is potentially increased by an application of a ∀ rule. Furthermore, while · elimination is the aim of our technique, this reduction adds a · operator for each instance of the variable t in d'. This problem had a large influence in our proof strategy.

To manage the complexity of all reduction rules, we divide our reduction strategy in two phases. In the first phase we apply only the rules of the groups I and III, in any order. The termination of this phase is proved in section 5.3.1. In the second phase we apply only the rules of the groups I and II with an innermost strategy. We prove in section 5.3.2 that these rules cannot create III-redexes, and in section 5.3.3 that this second phase stops. This completes the plan of the proof of weak termination. Before we detail these phases, let us remark that group I is strongly terminating (Ass pushes parentheses to the right, and the other rules strictly decrease the size of the coercion[6]).

5.3.1   Termination of Phase I

In phase I, we apply the rules of groups I and III in any order, until a normal form is reached. We exhibit a well-founded measure for proving termination of this phase. Consider the coercion erasure of a c-expression (section 2.4), which by fact 1 is a reduction invariant. We can associate with each node (i.e. occurrence) of this erasure the sequence of coercions which are applied at the corresponding node in the full c-expression. Then we associate with each node the sum of the sizes of these coercions, plus two times the length of the sequence (this addend is needed only to ensure that Comp decreases the global measure too). The measure of the whole expression is the tuple of the integers associated with the nodes of the erasure of the expression, visited in a left-depth-first order. Actually what matters is that a son of an abstraction node or a left son of an application node is visited before its father, and before its right brother in the case of an application. These tuples are ordered lexicographically. For an example, look at the following picture which presents a measure of the complexity of a term (I + III reduction).

Term to be measured (the erasure is underlined):

$\mathrm{Id}\langle(\underline{\lambda x:A}\,.\,\mathrm{Id}\langle t\cdot u\langle\underline{a}\rangle\rangle)(((c\to d)\cdot\mathrm{Id}\langle c'\to d'\langle\underline{f}\rangle\rangle)(\underline{b}))\rangle.$

Its erasure:

$(\lambda x\,.\,a)(fb).$

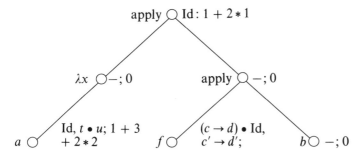

The syntactic tree of the term. At the left of each node is the corresponding syntactic operator, and at the right the list of the associated coercions, followed by the integer measure of the list.

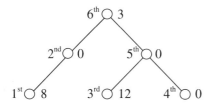

The nodes of the tree labelled with their depth-first visit position (at the left) and with their coercion measure (right):

The resulting tuple:

$\langle 8, 0, 12, 0, 0, 3\rangle.$

Group III rules strictly decrease the measure. *Comp* affects the measure only locally: it decreases the complexity at the concerned node of the erasure by 1 (specifically it augments the sum of sizes by 1, but decreases the length by 1). The other rules of group III decrease either the size or the number of the coercions applied to a node, and possibly increase the number of the coercions applied to the father or to the right brother of the same node.

For the rules of group I, which are terminating, it is enough to check that they do not increase the measure. The rules of group I can affect the measure only locally: except Ass, they all decrease the integer associated with the corresponding node of the erasure. I reductions can also occur in type applications, since a coercion c is present in say $f\{A, c\}$, but this does not affect the measure. This proves termination of phase I.

5.3.2 No III-Redexes Are Created in Phase 2 Since during phase 2 only I + II normalization is performed, in order to prove that phases 1 + 2 stop only on I + II + III normal forms, we must show that if phase 2 starts with a term in I + III normal form, then it does not create any new III-redex. We prove this claim rule by rule, by looking at the shape of I + III normal forms as described in lemma 4.4.

Comp: While in phase 1 the rules of group III move coercions from one node of the coercion erasure of the expression to another node, in phase 2 coercions are simplified 'where they are' without moving them around the erasure of the expression; this immediately entails that no Comp redex can be created in phase 2.

Id: Recall that, by corollary 4.6, any I normal form coercion different from Id cannot be reduced to Id; this entails that no Id redex can be created in phase 2.

App: At the end of phase 1, any coercion applied to the left-hand side of an application is a composition of coercion variables (cases 4, 5 of lemma 4.4). Such a composition is a normal form which cannot be modified by phase 2. The same reasoning applies to the App2 rules. Thus no App or App2 redexes are created in phase 2.

λ, Λ: At the end of phase 1 no body of an abstraction can have a coercion applied to it (cases 2, 3 of lemma 4.4), and phase 2 cannot modify this situation. Thus no λ or Λ redexes are created in phase 2.

5.3.3 Termination of Phase 2 Recall that in phase 2 we only use the rules of groups I and II, and apply them in an innermost way, i.e. we never simplify a redex containing a subterm which is a redex too.

The termination of phase 2 is the hardest part of our proof. First we define the *intermediate type* of a coercion composition $d \cdot e$, where $e : A \leq B$ and $d : B \leq C$, as the type B. Then we define the complexity measure of a c-expression a as the multiset[7] of the sizes of the intermediate types of all the II redexes of a, considered modulo Ass, IdL and IdR. We work modulo Ass, because some ways of associating compositions may hide a II redex, like in the following example:

$$(c \to d) \cdot (((c' \to d') \cdot t) \cdot u).$$

As in phase 1, since group I is strongly terminating, we need only to check

- that the application of I rules does not increase the measure,
- that the application of II rules strictly decreases the measure.

Suppose for example that Id $\to$ is applied in a context of shape $c \cdot (\mathrm{Id}_A \to \mathrm{Id}_B) \cdot e$, resulting in $c \cdot e$. We distinguish subcases corresponding to the various ways in which the $\cdot$'s can be roots of II redexes. If c and e are $\to$ coercions, two occurrences of $A \to B$ are replaced by one occurrence of $A \to B$. If only one of c, e is an $\to$ coercion, then one occurrence of $A \to B$ disappears from the multiset. If neither c nor e is an $\to$ coercion, the measure does not change. The situation with the other rules of group I is no more complicated.

Consider now a $\forall'$ redex $(\forall t \le c \cdot d) \cdot (\forall t \le c' \cdot d')$ with intermediate type $\forall t \le B \cdot U$ (refer to the proof trees in section 5.2). We have to analyse which new intermediate types could be added to the measure after reduction. Recall that the right-hand side is $\forall t \le c' \cdot c \cdot d' [t_B \leftarrow c \cdot t_A]$. Thanks to the innermost strategy chosen, c does not contain any II redex, and so $c \cdot t_A$ does not either, as II redexes cannot have a variable as an argument of $\cdot$. So no existing redexes can be duplicated. The only possible new redexes are $c' \cdot c, d \cdot d' [t_B \leftarrow c \cdot t_A]$, and subterms $k \cdot t_B$ of d' which after the substitution become $k \cdot c \cdot t_A$ (the root of the redex is the first $\cdot$). The intermediate types of these possible redexes are B, U and B respectively, whose size is smaller than the size of $\forall t \le B \cdot U$. Redexes with form $k \cdot (\forall t \le c \cdot d) \cdot (\forall t \le c' \cdot d')$, exterior to the left-hand side, are still redexes with the same associated type after the reduction. The types associated with any other exterior redex do not change, by lemma 2.3. So a $\forall'$ reduction drops a $\forall t \le B \cdot U$ from the complexity multiset of a c-term and introduces, at most, some B and U types, so that the global complexity of the term decreases.

The proof that the other three rules of group II also strictly reduce the complexity of the reduced term proceeds in the same way. This completes our proof of weak termination.

5.4 Uniqueness of the Normal Form Subtyping Proofs

Fact 4 follows immediately from proposition 4.1, which leaves no choice, as is easily checked formally by induction on the size of a coercion in normal form.

5.5 Quasi-Uniqueness of the Normal Forms of c-Terms with the Same Erasure

In our system, fact 5 can be equivalently stated as: if a, a' are c-terms in coerce normal form and have the same erasure, and if there exists an environment Γ such that $\Gamma \vdash_c a : A$ and $\Gamma \vdash_c a' : A'$, then $UE(a) \equiv UE(a')$; in other words the uppermost coercion erasure of a well-typed c-expression is uniquely determined by its coercion erasure. We showed in the remark that if fact 5 holds, so does the restatement. Now suppose that $UE(a) \equiv UE(a')$. We claim that this common uppermost erasure a'' satisfies the conditions of (old) fact 5, say condition (a). Call A'' the type associated with a''.

Condition (a): if $a'' \equiv a$ then $A'' \equiv A$; if $a \equiv c\langle a'' \rangle$, then we have $A'' < A$, as, by lemma 4.2, the only coercion in normal form proving $A \leq A$ is Id, and $\text{Id}\langle a \rangle$ is not in normal form.

Now we prove this version of fact 5, by induction on the structure of the uppermost erasure of a and a'. We shall proceed by cases on the form of the uppermost erasures:

$$UE(a) ::= x \,|\, \text{top} \,|\, \lambda x : A . b \,|\, \Lambda t \leq A . b \,|\, f(b) \,|\, f\{A, c\}$$

$$UE(a') ::= x \,|\, \text{top} \,|\, \lambda x : A . b' \,|\, \Lambda t \leq A . b' \,|\, f'(b') \,|\, f'\{A, c'\}.$$

The case $c\langle a \rangle$ is impossible by the definition of uppermost erasure and the fact that a, a' are normal forms. Since a and a' have the same coercion erasure, their uppermost erasures fall in the same syntactic class. Also the corresponding occurrences of types and variables are equal, as they are equal in the equal coercion erasures; for this reason we use the same letter A/x to denote corresponding occurrences of types/variables in the above 'grammar'.

We can apply the induction hypothesis to the pair of non-type and non-variable corresponding subterms (e.g. b and b', or f and f'), since they still have the same erasure and are typed in the same environment. To be precise, the subterms are typable exactly in the Γ environment where the two terms are typed, with the only exception of the b/b' subterms of λ and Λ abstractions, which are both typed in the $\Gamma, x : A/t \leq A$ environment.

Now consider the five possible forms of the uppermost erasures of a and a':

(1) $UE(a/a') \equiv x$, top: immediate.

(2) $UE(a) \equiv \lambda x : A . b$, $UE(a') \equiv \lambda x : A . b'$. The uppermost erasures of b and b' are equal by induction hypothesis. But b and b' cannot have form $c\langle b'' \rangle$ as otherwise $\lambda x : A . b/b'$ would be a λ redex: so $b \equiv UE(b)$ and $b' \equiv UE(b')$, from which $b \equiv b'$ and $\lambda x : A . b \equiv \lambda x : A . b'$ follow.

(3) $UE(a) \equiv \Lambda t \leq A . b$, $UE(a') \equiv \Lambda t \leq A . b'$. Same reasoning as in case 2.

(4) $UE(a) \equiv f(b)$, $UE(a') \equiv f'(b')$. Fix an environment Γ in which both expressions are typed. f has type $A \to B$, for some A and B. There are two subcases:

(i) If the type of $UE(f)$ is a type variable t, we know from proposition 4.3, case (4), that $f \equiv c\langle UE(f)\rangle$ where c is a composition of variables $t_n \cdot \ldots \cdot t_1$ which is entirely determined by Γ and t, proving $t \leq \Gamma^*(t)$. But the same path is forced from $UE(f') \equiv UE(f)$ to f'. Thus $f' \equiv (t_n \cdot \ldots \cdot t_1)\langle UE(f)\rangle \equiv f$.

(ii) If the type of $UE(f)$ is $A \to B$ then no variable coercion t can be applied to $UE(f') \equiv UE(f)$. This forces $f \equiv UE(f)$, and, for the same reason, $f' \equiv UE(f)$.

So in any case f and f' are equal, and *a fortiori* have the same type $A \to B$. This implies that also b and b' have the same type A. By induction hypothesis (using the old version of fact 5), they have the same uppermost erasure b''. If b'' has a type A'' such that $A'' < A$, then b and b' have the form $c\langle b''\rangle$ and $c'\langle b''\rangle$, and by fact 4, c and c' are equal. If b'' has type A, then b and b' are both equal to b''. In any case, b and b' are equal. Summing up, we have $UE(a) \equiv f(b) \equiv f'(b') \equiv UE(a')$.

(5) $UE(a) \equiv f\{A, c\}$, $UE(a') \equiv f'\{A, c'\}$. Reasoning as in case (4), we get that f and f' are equal and have the same type $\forall t \leq T. U$. Then c and c' are normal form coercions proving the same subtyping $A \leq T$, and so they are equal too, thanks to fact 4.

6 Proof Rewriting and Type-Checking

In this section we present a type-checking algorithm for the system $F_\leq$, which is sound and complete, and which stems directly from the analysis of the typing proofs in normal form.

6.1 The Algorithm

The type-checking problem we consider is the following: given an environment Γ and a raw expression[8] a, if there exists a type T such that $\Gamma \vdash a: T$, find the minimum one.

We specify this type-checking algorithm through a set of derived typing rules of $F_\leq$ (this approach leads to an easy soundness and completeness proof). The rules are presented below. The reader will notice that we did not 'create' the rules, but that they simply mirror the normal form analysis carried out in propositions 4.1 and 4.3. The execution strategy and the flow of information are detailed below.

Subtypes

$$\frac{\Gamma \vdash A \text{ type}}{\Gamma \vdash A \leq A} \qquad\qquad\qquad (\text{Alg Id} \leq)$$

$$\frac{\Gamma \vdash A \text{ type}}{\Gamma \vdash A \le \text{Top}} \qquad \text{(Alg Top } \le \text{)}$$

$$\frac{\Gamma, t \le A, \Gamma' \text{ env}}{\Gamma, t \le A, \Gamma' \vdash t \le A} \qquad \text{(Alg Var } \le \text{)}$$

$$\frac{\Gamma \vdash \Gamma(t) \le C}{\Gamma \vdash t \le C} \qquad \text{(Alg Trans } \le \text{)}$$

$$\frac{\Gamma \vdash A \le A' \quad \Gamma \vdash B \le B'}{\Gamma \vdash A' \to B \le A \to B'} \qquad \text{(Alg } \to \, \le \text{)}$$

$$\frac{\Gamma \vdash A \le A' \quad \Gamma, t \le A \vdash B \le B'}{\Gamma \vdash \forall t \le A'. B \le \forall t \le A. B'}. \qquad \text{(Alg } \forall \, \le \text{)}$$

Notation When $\Gamma \vdash t \le A$ has been proved only with Alg Var $\le$ and Alg Trans $\le$, we shall write $\Gamma \vdash t \ll A$. This is to emphasize a different flow of information, as will be explained below.

Expressions

$$\frac{\Gamma, x:A, \Gamma \text{ env}}{\Gamma, x:A, \Gamma' \vdash x:A} \qquad \text{(Alg Var)}$$

$$\frac{\Gamma, x:A, \Gamma' \text{ env}}{\Gamma, x:A, \Gamma' \vdash x:A} \qquad \text{(Alg Top)}$$

$$\frac{\Gamma, x:A \vdash b:B}{\Gamma \vdash \lambda x:A. b:A \to B} \qquad \text{(Alg Abs)}$$

$$\frac{\Gamma \vdash f:A \to B \quad \Gamma \vdash a:A' \quad \Gamma \vdash A' \le A}{\Gamma \vdash f(a):B} \qquad \text{(Alg App)}$$

$$\frac{\Gamma \vdash f:t \quad \Gamma \vdash t \ll A \to B \quad \Gamma \vdash a:A' \quad \Gamma \vdash A' \le A}{\Gamma \vdash f(a):B} \qquad \text{(Alg App')}$$

$$\frac{\Gamma, t \le A \vdash b:B}{\Gamma \vdash \Lambda t \le A. b:\forall t \le A. B} \qquad \text{(Alg Abs2)}$$

$$\frac{\Gamma \vdash f:\forall t \le A. B \quad \Gamma \vdash A' \le A}{\Gamma \vdash f\{A'\}:B[t \leftarrow A']} \qquad \text{(Alg App2)}$$

$$\frac{\Gamma \vdash f:u \quad \Gamma \vdash u \ll \forall t \le A. B \quad \Gamma \vdash A' \le A}{\Gamma \vdash f\{A'\}:B[t \leftarrow A']}. \qquad \text{(Alg App2')}$$

These rules define a type system which will be proved equivalent to the type system of $F_\leq$ in section 6.2. We shall use $\vdash_{\text{Alg}}$ (e.g. $\Gamma \vdash_{\text{Alg}} a : A$) to mean that an $F_\leq$ judgement has been proved by only using these rules.

We first explain how to get an algorithm out of the $\vdash_{\text{Alg}}$ rules. They form an almost deterministic set of rules. The duplication of the Alg App rules gives the false impression that they may conflict, but it will be clear from the more detailed explanations below that the first common premise of, say Alg App and Alg App′ will be first 'executed', and will determine a subsequent deterministic branching. The only non-determinism concerns the first three subtyping rules. They have to be applied on a first-match basis (this is to reflect the rules Top Id and Var Top). There is no backtracking to be considered, since these three rules are 'axioms'.

Let us be more specific about the algorithmic interpretation of the rules (with the first-match discipline). The rules actually specify three algorithms:

• an algorithm which, given an environment and a raw expression, either fails or returns a type; let us call it $\Gamma \vdash_{\text{Alg}} a : ?$.

• An algorithm which, given an environment and a pair of types, either fails or returns 'success'; let us call it $\Gamma \vdash_{\text{Alg}} A \leq B$.

• An algorithm which, given an environment and a type variable, either fails or returns a type; let us call it $\Gamma \vdash_{\text{Alg}} t \ll ?$.

Notation If the algorithm $\Gamma \vdash_{\text{Alg}} a : ?$ terminates and gives A as result, we write $\Gamma \vdash_{\text{Alg}} a \rhd A$.

In all these cases, failure means one of the following alternatives:

• looping forever,

• finding a judgement which cannot be matched with any rule,

• obtaining an answer which does not have the required structure (this concerns the first premise of the Alg App rules, and the second premise of the Alg App′ rules).

These three algorithms are defined mutually recursively by the reduction rules, ordered as they are. Each rule specifies how to transform the problem in the conclusion into the subproblems in the premises. The input parameters, i.e. the variables which are bound when the conclusion is instantiated, are not syntactically distinguished from the output variables, i.e. the variables carrying the results of the computations, according to the logic programming style. But the reader can verify inductively that if in the head (the conclusion) of each rule all the input parameters (as fixed in the paragraph above) are instantiated, then the input parameters of the first premise are instantiated, and when the output of the first premise is computed then all the input parameters of the second premise are instantiated too, and so on. This means that the logical variables are used only for pattern-matching, and so these rules specify a functional program.

6.2   Correctness and Completeness of the Algorithm

Here is how we formulate soundness and completeness of the type-checking algorithm. We shall say that the algorithm is sound if $\Gamma \vdash_{\mathrm{Alg}} a \rhd A \Rightarrow \Gamma \vdash a : A$, and that it is complete if the reverse implication holds. Soundness and completeness of the algorithm, which we shall prove now, imply that it is a semi-decision procedure for the type-checking problem.

We shall actually link three kinds of judgements: $\Gamma \vdash a : A$, $\Gamma \vdash_{\mathrm{Alg}} a : A$, and $\Gamma \vdash_{\mathrm{Alg}} a \rhd A$. We shall prove:

$$\Gamma \vdash a : A \ (A \text{ minimum}) \Rightarrow \Gamma \vdash_{\mathrm{Alg}} a \rhd A \Rightarrow \Gamma \vdash_{\mathrm{Alg}} a : A \Rightarrow \Gamma \vdash a : A \ (A \text{ minimum}).$$

In order to make the link with the coerce reduction system precise, we need a $cF_\leq$ version of the $\vdash_{\mathrm{Alg}}$ rules, i.e. a translation from proofs of, say $\Gamma \vdash_{\mathrm{Alg}} a : A$, to an expression of the $cF_\leq$ system. Here are the interesting cases:

Subtypes

$$\frac{\Gamma \vdash c : \Gamma(t) \leq C}{\Gamma \vdash c \cdot t : t \leq C}. \qquad\qquad\qquad\qquad (c \,\mathrm{Alg}\,\mathrm{Trans} \leq)$$

Expressions

$$\frac{\Gamma \vdash f : A \to B \quad \Gamma \vdash a : A' \quad \Gamma \vdash c : A' \leq A}{\Gamma \vdash f(c\langle a \rangle) : B} \qquad\qquad (c \,\mathrm{Alg}\,\mathrm{App})$$

$$\frac{\Gamma \vdash f : t \quad \Gamma \vdash d : t \ll A \to B \quad \Gamma \vdash c : A' \quad \Gamma \vdash c : A' \leq A}{\Gamma \vdash (d\langle f \rangle)(c\langle a \rangle) : B} \qquad\qquad (c \,\mathrm{Alg}\,\mathrm{App}')$$

$$\frac{\Gamma \vdash f : \forall t \leq A . B \quad \Gamma \vdash c : A' \leq A}{\Gamma \vdash f\{A', c\} : B[t \leftarrow A']} \qquad\qquad (c \,\mathrm{Alg}\,\mathrm{App2})$$

$$\frac{\Gamma \vdash f : u \quad \Gamma \vdash d : u \ll \forall t \leq A . B \quad \Gamma \vdash c : A' \leq A}{\Gamma \vdash (d\langle f \rangle)\{A', c\} : B[t \leftarrow A']}. \qquad\qquad (c \,\mathrm{Alg}\,\mathrm{App2}')$$

PROPOSITION 6.1 (Soundness and completeness.)   For each term a and environment Γ of $F_\leq$, $\Gamma \vdash_{\mathrm{Alg}} a \rhd A$ iff $\Gamma \vdash_{\mathrm{Alg}} a : A$, iff $\Gamma \vdash a : A'$ for some type A'; moreover A is the minimum type of a in environment Γ.

Proof We follow the circular path indicated at the beginning of the subsection:

(1) $\Gamma \vdash a : A$, A minimum $\Rightarrow \Gamma \vdash_{\text{Alg}} a \rhd A$: by fact 5, the thesis follows from the following claim: any *c*-expression in head coercion free normal form *b* encodes an execution of the $\vdash_{\text{Alg}}$ algorithm (modulo Ass). The claim is almost immediate, by induction on the length of *b*, because the derived rules exactly reproduce the cases of propositions 4.3 and 4.1 (for instance Alg App or Alg App′ for proposition 4.3, case (5), Alg Trans $\leq$ and Alg Var $\leq$ for proposition 4.1, cases (4) and (5)). Notice however that Alg Trans $\leq$ forces association of compositions '·' to the left, which does not fit with the convention taken for Ass, whence 'modulo Ass' in the claim.

(2) $\Gamma \vdash_{\text{Alg}} a \rhd A \Rightarrow \Gamma \vdash_{\text{Alg}} a : A$: This is obvious: $\Gamma \vdash_{\text{Alg}} a \rhd A$ can be viewed as a judgement $\Gamma \vdash_{\text{Alg}} a : A$ proved with the first-match strategy.

(3) $\Gamma \vdash_{\text{Alg}} a : A \Rightarrow \Gamma \vdash a : A$, A minimum: The implication $\Gamma \vdash_{\text{Alg}} a : A \Rightarrow \Gamma \vdash a : A$ follows from the fact that the $\vdash_{\text{Alg}}$ rules are derived rules, which may be checked easily, rule by rule. The fact that A is minimum follows from the determinism of the algorithm, and the rest of the proof: indeed, if A is not minimum, let A' be the minimum type for Γ, *a*. By implication (1) we get $\Gamma \vdash_{\text{Alg}} a \rhd A'$, hence by determinism, $A \equiv A'$: contradiction. This concludes the proof. ∎

Remark The proof in fact establishes a bijection between the $\vdash_{\text{Alg}}$ proofs and the head coercion free normal forms of the explicit system.

As a consequence of the correctness and completeness of this algorithm, we obtain that the $\vdash_{\text{Alg}}$ algorithm provides a semi-decision procedure for the type-checking and subtyping problems: if the input terms is typable or the input subtyping is provable, the algorithm will stop with the minimum type of the term or with the answer 'yes'. But this does not prove that the algorithm always stops when applied to non-typable expressions or non-related types. Actually, a recent result shows that there are terms which can make this algorithm loop forever, (Ghelli, 1991). Even more recently, the non-decidability of these problems has been established (Pierce, 1991).

7 Examples of Models

In this section we show how the investigations of BCGS and BL can be accommodated in our formalism. We provide the necessary definitions, but the interested reader will have to refer to those papers for motivations and details.

The BCGS interpretation fits particularly well in our framework. The basic idea underlying it is to get rid of type inclusions by mapping $F_\leq$ into F_1, a slight extension of the second order λ-calculus F of Girard–Reynolds with a terminal type 1. The calculus considered in BCGS has records. We extract here what is relevant to $F_\le$. Here is the syntax of F_1:

$$A ::= t \,|\, 1 \,|\, A \to A \,|\, \forall t \,.\, A$$

$$a ::= x \,|\, ! \,|\, \lambda x : A \,.\, a \,|\, a(a) \,|\, \Lambda t \,.\, a \,|\, a\{A\}.$$

The main difference with $F_\le$ is that quantification is not bounded. 1 and ! are to be matched with Top and top. We list only the typing rules which differ from those of $F_\le$:

Environments

$$\frac{\Gamma \text{ env}}{\Gamma, t \text{ env}}$$
(Type env)

Types

$$\frac{\Gamma \text{ env}}{\Gamma \vdash 1 \text{ type}}$$
(1 Form)

$$\frac{\Gamma \vdash A \text{ type} \quad \Gamma, t \vdash B \text{ type}}{\Gamma \vdash \forall t \,.\, B \text{ type}}$$
(∀ Form)

Terms

$$\frac{\Gamma \text{ env}}{\Gamma \vdash ! : 1}$$
(1 Intro)

$$\frac{\Gamma, t \vdash b : B}{\Gamma \vdash \Lambda t \,.\, b : \forall t \,.\, B}$$
(∀ Intro)

$$\frac{\Gamma \vdash f : \forall t \,.\, B \quad \Gamma \vdash A' \text{ type}}{\Gamma \vdash f\{A'\} : B[t \leftarrow A']}.$$
(∀ Elim)

The theory consists of (both kinds of) β, η, and a special rule for 1:

$$a = ! \quad (\text{if } \Gamma \vdash a : 1).$$
(Terminal)

Notice that in F_1, as happens in $F_\le$, equations are defined between typing judgements rather than terms (see Curien and DiCosmo (1991) for details).

The authors of BCGS define a translation, denoted here by *, from proofs of $F_\le$ to F_1 (so they define also a translation from $cF_\le$ to F_1; we will sometimes switch to this second point of view). The basic ideas underlying the translation from $F_\le$ to F_1 are the following:

- A subtyping proof $c : A \le B$ is translated by a term $c^* : A^* \to B^*$, and a subsumption application $c\langle a\rangle$ is translated by function application $c^*(a^*)$.

- A constraint $t \le A$ in the environment is replaced by two variable declarations: t, and $x : t \to A^*$, where x is a fresh variable, playing the role of a coercion variable.

- A bounded quantified type $\forall t \le A . B$ is transformed into $\forall t . (t \to A^*) \to B^*$.

Formally, the translation is as follows. A judgement J of $F_\le$ is translated to a judgement J^* of F_1:

Translation of Environments

$(\ )^* = (\ )$

$(\Gamma, t \le A)^* = \Gamma^*, t, x : t \to A^*$ x not declared in Γ^*

$(\Gamma, x : A)^* = \Gamma^*, x : A^*.$

Translation of Types

$t^* = t$

$\mathrm{Top}^* = 1$

$(A \to B)^* = A^* \to B^*.$

$(\forall t \le A . B)^* = \forall t . (t \to A^*) \to B^*.$

The following shortened translation of terms will probably help reading the detailed one:

Notation $M; N$ stands for $\lambda x : N(Mx)$.

Translation of Subtyping Proofs

$t^* = x$

$(\mathrm{Top}_A)^* = \lambda z : A^* .\, !$

$(c_{AA'} \to d_{BB'})^* = \lambda z : A'^* \to B^* . c^* ; z ; d^*$

$(\forall t \le c_{AA'} . d_{BB'})^* = \lambda z : (\forall t . (t \to A'^*) \to B^*) . \Lambda t . \lambda x : t \to A . d^*(z\{t\}(x ; c^*))$

$(\mathrm{Id}_A)^* = \lambda x : A^* . x$

$(d \cdot c)^* = c^* ; d^*.$

Translation of Expressions

$$x^* = x$$

$$(\lambda x : A . b)^* = \lambda x : A^* . b^*$$

$$f(a)^* = f^*(a^*)$$

$$(\Lambda t \leq A . b)^* = \Lambda t . \lambda x : t \to A^* . b^*$$

$$f\{A', c\}^* = f^*\{A'^*\}(c^*)$$

$$c\langle a \rangle^* = c^*(a^*).$$

Translation of Coercions (full)[9]

$$\frac{(\Gamma, t \leq A, \Gamma')^* = \Delta, t, x : t \to A^*, \Delta' \equiv \Delta''}{(\Gamma, t \leq A, \Gamma' \vdash t : t \leq A)^* = \Delta'' \vdash x : t \to A^*}$$

$$\frac{(\Gamma)^* = \Delta}{(\Gamma \vdash \mathrm{Top}_A : A \leq \mathrm{Top})^* = \Delta \vdash \lambda z : A^* . ! : A^* \to \mathrm{Top}}$$

$$\frac{(\Gamma \vdash c : A \leq A')^* = \Delta \vdash P : A^* \to A'^* \quad (\Gamma \vdash d : B \leq B')^* = \Delta \vdash Q : B^* \to B'^*}{(\Gamma \vdash c \to d : A' \to B \leq A \to B')^* = \Delta \vdash \lambda z : A'^* \to B^* . P ; z ; Q : (A'^* \to B^*) \to (A^* \to B'^*)}$$

$$\frac{(\Gamma \vdash c : A \leq A')^* = \Delta \vdash P : A^* \to A'^* \quad (\Gamma, t \leq A \vdash d : B \leq B')^* = \Delta, t, x : t \to A^* \vdash Q : B^* \to B'^*}{(\Gamma \vdash \forall t \leq c . d : (\forall t \leq A' . B) \leq (\forall t \leq A . B'))^* = \Delta \vdash R : (\forall t . (t \to A'^*) \to B^*) \to (\forall t . (t \to A^*) \to B'^*)}$$

where $R = \lambda z : \forall t . (t \to A'^*) \to B^* . \Lambda t . \lambda x : t \to A^* . Q(z\{t\}(x ; P))$.

$$\frac{(\Gamma)^* = \Delta}{(\Gamma \vdash \mathrm{Id}_A : A \leq A)^* = \Delta \vdash \lambda x : A^* . x : A^* \to A^*}$$

$$\frac{(\Gamma \vdash c : A \leq B)^* = \Delta \vdash P : A^* \to B^* \quad (\Gamma \vdash d : B \leq C)^* = \Delta \vdash Q : B^* \to C^*}{(\Gamma \vdash d \cdot c : A \leq C)^* = \Delta \vdash P ; Q : A^* \to C^*} .$$

Translation of Expressions (full)

$$\frac{(\Gamma, x : A, \Gamma')^* = \Delta, x : A^*, \Delta' \equiv \Delta''}{(\Gamma, x : A, \Gamma' \vdash x : A)^* = \Delta'' \vdash x : A^*}$$

$$\frac{(\Gamma, x : A \vdash b : B)^* = \Delta, x : A^* \vdash N : B^*}{(\Gamma \vdash \lambda x : A . b : A \to B)^* = \Delta \vdash \lambda x : A^* . N : A^* \to B^*}$$

$$\frac{(\Gamma \vdash f : A \to B)^* = \Delta \vdash M : A^* \to B^* \quad (\Gamma \vdash a : A)^* = \Delta \vdash N : A^*}{(\Gamma \vdash f(a) : B)^* = \Delta \vdash M(N) : B^*}$$

$$\frac{(\Gamma, t \leq A \vdash b : B)^* = \Delta,\, t,\, x : t \to A^* \vdash N : B^*}{(\Gamma \vdash \Lambda t \leq A \,.\, b : \forall t \leq A \,.\, B)^* = \Delta \vdash \Lambda t \,.\, \lambda x : t \to A^* \,.\, N : \forall t \,.\, (t \to A^*) \to B^*}$$

$$\frac{(\Gamma \vdash f : \forall t \leq A \,.\, B)^* = \Delta \vdash M : \forall t \,.\, (t \to A^*) \to B^* \quad (\Gamma \vdash c : A' \leq A)^* = \Delta \vdash P : A'^* \to A^*}{(\Gamma \vdash f\{A',c\} : B[t \leftarrow A'])^* = \Delta \vdash M\{A'^*\}(P) : B^*[t \leftarrow A'^*]}$$

$$\frac{(\Gamma \vdash a : A)^* = \Delta \vdash M : A^* \quad (\Gamma \vdash c : A \leq B)^* = \Delta \vdash P : A^* \to B^*}{(\Gamma \vdash c\langle a\rangle : B)^* = \Delta \vdash P(M) : B^*} \, .$$

We shall need the following substitution property (proof omitted):

(*) $\quad (d[t \leftarrow e])^* = d^*[x \leftarrow e^*]$ (where x is as in the translation of $\Gamma, t \leq A$ above).

We now rapidly check the satisfaction of the equations underlying (most of) the coerce rules:

- Ass, IdL, IdR: Easy checking (composition is coded by ... composition in the CCC of λ-terms (cf, Curien (1986) or Lambek and Scott (1986)). Notice however that η is needed for the Id laws.[10]

- Id $\to$: $(\mathrm{Id}_A \to \mathrm{Id}_B)^* = \lambda z \,.\, (\lambda x \,.\, x); z; (\lambda x \,.\, x) =_\beta \lambda z y \,.\, z y =_\eta \lambda z \,.\, z$, and similarly for Id $\forall$ using η for type application.

- Top : $(\mathrm{Top}_B \cdot c)^* = \lambda z \,.\, (\lambda x \,.\, !)(c^*(z)) =_\beta \lambda z \,.\, ! = (\mathrm{Top}_A)^*$.

- Var Top, Top Id: By Terminal.

- $\forall'$: $(\forall t \leq c \cdot d \,.\, \forall t \leq c' \,.\, d')^*$
$= (\lambda z \,.\, \Lambda t \,.\, \lambda x \,.\, d'^*(z\{t\}(x; c'^*))); (\lambda z \,.\, \Lambda t \,.\, \lambda x \,.\, d^*(z\{t\}\,(x; c^*)))$
$= \lambda z \,.\, \Lambda t \,.\, \lambda x \,.\, d^*((\Lambda t' \,.\, \lambda x \,.\, d'^*(z\{t'\}(x; c'^*)))\{\,t\}(x; c^*))$
$= \lambda z \,.\, \Lambda t \,.\, \lambda x \,.\, d^*(d'^*\,[x \leftarrow x; c^*](z\{t\}(x; c^*; c'^*)))$
$=_* (\forall t \leq c' \cdot c \,.\, d \cdot (d'[t \leftarrow c \cdot t]))^*$.

- Id, Comp: Obvious.

- App2' : $(((\forall t \leq c \,.\, d)\langle f\rangle)\{A, e\})^* = (\lambda z \,.\, \Lambda t \,.\, \lambda x \,.\, d^*(z\{t\}(x; c^*)))f^*\{A^*\}(e^*)$
$= d^*[x \leftarrow e^*](f^*\{A^*\}(e^*; c^*)) =_* (d[t \leftarrow e]\langle f\{A, c \cdot e\}\rangle)^*$.

- Λ : $((\forall t \leq \mathrm{Id}_A \,.\, c)\langle \Lambda t \leq A \,.\, b\rangle)^* = (\lambda z \,.\, \Lambda t \,.\, \lambda x \,.\, c^*(z\{t\}(x; (\lambda x \,.\, x))))(\Lambda t \,.\, \lambda x \,.\, b^*)$
$= (\lambda z \,.\, \Lambda t \,.\, \lambda x \,.\, c^*(z\{t\}(x)))(\Lambda t \,.\, \lambda x \,.\, b^*) = \Lambda t \,.\, \lambda x \,.\, c^*((\Lambda t \,.\, \lambda x \,.\, b^*)\{t\}(x))$
$= (\Lambda t \leq A \,.\, c\langle b\rangle)^*$.

Now we pass to the BL interpretation. The translation of our equations is not so immediate here, because the authors of BL manage to have a direct interpretation of $\Gamma \vdash A \leq A'$, which uses only information on A, A'. Thus, while the interpretation of terms is defined by induction on typing proofs, the interpretation of a subtyping proof depends only on the proved judgement.

Let us recall briefly that a partial equivalence relation A (p.e.r.) is a symmetric and transitive relation on a set X. A is thus an equivalence relation on a subset of X. One writes X/A for the quotient, and $[n]_A$ for the equivalence class of n. In BL, an order relation on p.e.r.'s over a given set is defined as follows:

$A \leq A'$ iff for all m, n $A(m, n)$ implies $A'(m, n)$.

There is a map $c_{A, A'}$ which is canonically associated with such a pair of p.e.r.'s: the map which sends the A equivalence class of n to the A' equivalence class of n (for any n):

$c_{A, A'}([n]_A) = [n]_{A'}$.

This is a map in the category of p.e.r.'s.[11]

We can now give brief hints about the BL interpretation.

Types   A type with free variables is interpreted in a (semantic) environment ρ which instantiates both kinds of variables, respecting the syntactic constraints $t \leq A$ in the syntactic environment. For example $[\![t]\!] = \rho(t)$, $[\![\text{Top}]\!]$ is the p.e.r. Top s.t. $\text{Top}(m, n)$ holds for any m, n. The function space implements the idea that two integers are equivalent if, when viewed as indexes of partial recursive functions, they map equivalent integers to equivalent integers. The bounded quantification is interpreted as an infinite intersection of p.e.r.'s.

Coercions   Coercions are *not* interpreted by induction on their structure, but directly using their type. All that needs to be done is to check that the inclusions implied by the subtyping rules of $F_\leq$ hold in the model. The coercion rules (groups I and II) are then trivially verified, since both sides of any equation are by definition interpreted by the same arrow $c_{A, A'}$, which is canonically defined, using only information taken in A and A'.

Expressions   Since the information about the proofs of subtyping is irrelevant, the actual set of equations which has to be checked to prove coherence is:

$$(c_{A' \to B, B \to B'}\langle a \rangle) b = c_{B, B'}\langle a(c_{A, A'}\langle b \rangle) \rangle \tag{App}$$

$$(c_{\forall t \leq A' . B, \forall t \leq A . B'}\langle f \rangle)\{C\} = c_{B[t \leftarrow C], B'[t \leftarrow C]}\langle f\{C\} \rangle \tag{App2}$$

$$\lambda x : A . c_{B, B'}\langle b \rangle = c_{A \to B, A \to B'}\langle \lambda x : A . b \rangle \tag{λ}$$

$$\Lambda t \leq A . c_{B, B'}\langle b \rangle = c_{\forall t \leq A . B, \forall t \leq A . B'}\langle \Lambda t \leq A . b \rangle \tag{Λ}$$

$$c_{A, A} = \text{Id}_A \tag{Id}$$

$$c_{B, C} \cdot c_{A, B} = (c \cdot d)_{A, C}. \tag{Comp}$$

These equations appear in this form in BL, to which we refer for more details.

8 Conclusions and Directions for Future Work

We have treated in a unified way three problems which address quite different issues: semantic (coherence), type-theoretic (minimum typing), operational (type checking). Our main tool has been the definition of a confluent and normalizing rewriting system on proofs, and we found it convenient to codify such proofs as terms of an auxiliary language which respects the terms-as-proofs paradigm.

We believe that the analysis of normal form proofs is a basic instrument for further proof-theoretic studies about subtyping. It has been used with this aim in Ghelli (1990) and in Curien and Ghelli (1991); in Cardelli *et al.* (1991), it is underlying the proof of conservativity of typing judgements in $F_\le$ over typing judgements in F.

The applicability of this approach to richer systems should be investigated: systems with recursive definitions, with multiple bounds on variables and with lower bounded quantifications offer many interesting open problems. An extension to systems with records and variants is much easier, and does not seem to raise any new problem. Coherence has been recently examined for intersection types in Reynolds (1991).

Our approach should also apply to systems like dependent types or the theory of constructions, which have a similar non-determinism of typing proofs (the role of Subsump is played by the retyping rule which allows the derivation of $a:B$ from $a:A$ and $A = B$).

More abstractly, we believe that our language of coercions is a guide to an abstract definition of categorical models of typed λ-calculi with inheritance. For simple types, they should be defined as cartesian closed categories with a distinguished collection of coercion arrows, closed under certain operations.

Acknowledgements

We thank Luca Cardelli for many discussions about inheritance, and for providing examples of the expressivity of $F_\le$. Carl Gunter made some suggestions about subtyping algorithms. Giuseppe Longo, Val Breazu-Tannen, Thierry Coquand and Andre Scedrov made constructive comments on a very preliminary e-mail skeleton of this work.

Appendix A. The System $F_\le$

Syntax

$A ::= t \,|\, \text{Top} \,|\, A \to A \,|\, \forall t \le A \,.\, A$

$a ::= x \,|\, \text{top} \,|\, \lambda x : A \,.\, a \,|\, a(a) \,|\, \Lambda t \le A \,.\, a \,|\, a\{A\}.$

Typing Rules

Environments.   (Sequences whose individual components have the form $x : A$ or t.)

$$(\,) \, \text{env} \qquad\qquad\qquad\qquad\qquad\qquad\qquad\qquad (\varnothing \, \text{env})$$

$$\frac{\Gamma \, \text{env} \quad \Gamma \vdash A \, \text{type} \quad t \notin \Gamma}{\Gamma, t \leq A \, \text{env}} \qquad\qquad (\leq \text{env})$$

$$\frac{\Gamma \, \text{env} \quad \Gamma \vdash A \, \text{type} \quad x \notin \Gamma}{\Gamma, x : A \, \text{env}} \qquad\qquad (: \text{env})$$

Types

$$\frac{\Gamma, t \leq A, \Gamma' \, \text{env}}{\Gamma, t \leq A, \Gamma' \vdash t \, \text{type}} \qquad\qquad (\text{Var Form})$$

$$\frac{\Gamma \vdash A \, \text{type} \quad \Gamma \vdash B \, \text{type}}{\Gamma \vdash A \rightarrow B \, \text{type}} \qquad\qquad (\rightarrow \text{Form})$$

$$\frac{\Gamma \, \text{env}}{\Gamma \vdash \text{Top type}} \qquad\qquad (\text{Top Form})$$

$$\frac{\Gamma, t \leq A \vdash B \, \text{type}}{\Gamma \vdash \forall t \leq A . B \, \text{type}} \qquad\qquad (\forall \, \text{Form})$$

Subtypes

$$\frac{\Gamma, t \leq A, \Gamma' \, \text{env}}{\Gamma, t \leq A, \Gamma' \vdash t \leq A} \qquad\qquad (\text{Var} \leq)$$

$$\frac{\Gamma \vdash A \leq A' \quad \Gamma \vdash B \leq B'}{\Gamma \vdash A' \rightarrow B \leq A \rightarrow B'} \qquad\qquad (\rightarrow \leq)$$

$$\frac{\Gamma \vdash A \, \text{type}}{\Gamma \vdash A \leq A} \qquad\qquad (\text{Id} \leq)$$

$$\frac{\Gamma \vdash A \, \text{type}}{\Gamma \vdash A \leq \text{Top}} \qquad\qquad (\text{Top} \leq)$$

$$\frac{\Gamma \vdash A \leq A' \quad \Gamma, t \leq A \vdash B \leq B'}{\Gamma \vdash \forall t \leq A' . B \leq \forall t \leq A . B'} \qquad\qquad (\forall \leq)$$

$$\frac{\Gamma \vdash A \leq B \quad \Gamma \vdash B \leq C}{\Gamma \vdash A \leq C} \qquad\qquad (\text{Trans} \leq)$$

Expressions

$$\frac{\Gamma, x : A, \Gamma' \text{ env}}{\Gamma, x : A, \Gamma' \vdash x : A} \qquad\qquad \text{(Var)}$$

$$\frac{\Gamma, x : A \vdash b : B}{\Gamma \vdash \lambda x : A . b : A \to B} \qquad\qquad (\to \text{Intro})$$

$$\frac{\Gamma, t \leq A \vdash b : B}{\Gamma \vdash \Lambda t \leq A . b : \forall t \leq A . B} \qquad\qquad (\forall \text{Intro})$$

$$\frac{\Gamma \vdash a : A \quad \Gamma \vdash A \leq B}{\Gamma \vdash a : B} \qquad\qquad \text{(Subsump)}$$

$$\frac{\Gamma \text{ env}}{\Gamma \vdash \text{top} : \text{Top}} \qquad\qquad \text{(Top)}$$

$$\frac{\Gamma \vdash f : A \to B \quad \Gamma \vdash a : A}{\Gamma \vdash f(a) : B} \qquad\qquad (\to \text{Elim})$$

$$\frac{\Gamma \vdash f : \forall t \leq A . B \quad \Gamma \vdash A' \leq A}{\Gamma \vdash f\{A'\} : B[t \leftarrow A']} \qquad\qquad (\forall \text{Elim})$$

Appendix B. The System $cF_\leq$

Syntax

$A ::= t \,|\, \text{Top} \,|\, A \to A \,|\, \forall t \leq A . A$

$a ::= x \,|\, \text{top} \,|\, \lambda x : A . a \,|\, a(a) \,|\, \Lambda t \leq A . a \,|\, a\{A, c\} \,|\, c\langle a\rangle$

$c ::= t_A \,|\, \text{Top}_A \,|\, c \to c \,|\, \forall t \leq c . c \,|\, \text{Id}_A \,|\, c \cdot c.$

Typing Rules   (We list only those distinct from the corresponding ones in $F_\leq$.)

Subtypes

$$\frac{\Gamma, t \leq A, \Gamma' \text{ env}}{\Gamma, t \leq A, \Gamma' \vdash t_A : t \leq A} \qquad\qquad (\text{Var} \leq)$$

$$\frac{\Gamma \vdash c : A \leq A' \quad \Gamma \vdash d : B \leq B'}{\Gamma \vdash c \to d : A' \to B \leq A \to B'} \qquad\qquad (\to \leq)$$

$$\frac{\Gamma \vdash A \text{ type}}{\Gamma \vdash \text{Id}_A : A \leq A} \qquad\qquad (\text{Id} \leq)$$

$$\frac{\Gamma \vdash A \text{ type}}{\Gamma \vdash \text{top}_A : A \leq \text{Top}} \tag{Top $\leq$}$$

$$\frac{\Gamma \vdash c : A \leq A' \quad \Gamma, t \leq A \vdash d : B \leq B'}{\Gamma \vdash \forall t \leq c . d : \forall t \leq A' . B \leq \forall t \leq A . B'} \tag{$\forall \leq$}$$

$$\frac{\Gamma \vdash c : A \leq B \quad \Gamma \vdash d : B \leq C}{\Gamma \vdash d \cdot c : A \leq C} \tag{Trans $\leq$}$$

Terms

$$\frac{\Gamma \vdash a : A \quad \Gamma \vdash c : A \leq B}{\Gamma \vdash c \langle a \rangle : B} \tag{Coerce}$$

$$\frac{\Gamma \vdash f : \forall t \leq A . B \quad \Gamma \vdash c : A' \leq A}{\Gamma \vdash f\{A', c\} : B[t \leftarrow A']} \tag{$\forall$ Elim}$$

Rewrite System

Coercion Rules

I

$$(c \cdot d) \cdot e > c \cdot (d \cdot e) \tag{Ass}$$

$$\text{Id}_B \cdot c > c \qquad c : A \leq B \tag{IdL}$$

$$c \cdot \text{Id}_A > c \qquad c : A \leq B \tag{IdR}$$

$$\text{Id}_A \rightarrow \text{Id}_B > \text{Id}_{A \rightarrow B} \tag{Id $\rightarrow$}$$

$$\forall t \leq \text{Id}_A . \text{Id}_B > \text{Id}_{\forall t \leq A . B} \tag{Id $\forall$}$$

$$\text{Top}_B \cdot c > \text{Top}_A \qquad c : A \leq B \tag{Top}$$

$$t_{\text{Top}} > \text{Top}_t \tag{Var Top}$$

$$\text{Top}_{\text{Top}} > \text{Id}_{\text{Top}} \tag{Top Id}$$

II

$$(c \rightarrow d) \cdot (c' \rightarrow d') > (c' \cdot c) \rightarrow (d \cdot d') \tag{$\rightarrow'$}$$

$$(c \rightarrow d) \cdot ((c' \rightarrow d') \cdot e) > ((c' \cdot c) \rightarrow (d \cdot d')) \cdot e \tag{$\rightarrow''$}$$

$$\forall t \leq c . d \cdot \forall t \leq c' . d' > \forall t \leq c' \cdot c . d \cdot (d'[t_B \leftarrow c \cdot t_A]) \qquad c : A \leq B \tag{$\forall'$}$$

$$\forall t \leq c . d \cdot (\forall t \leq c' . d' \cdot e) > (\forall t \leq c' \cdot c . d \cdot (d'[t_B \leftarrow c \cdot t_A])) \cdot e \qquad c : A \leq B \tag{$\forall''$}$$

Expression Rules

III

$$\text{Id}\langle a \rangle > a \tag{Id}$$

$$((c \to d)\langle a \rangle)b > d\langle a(c\langle b \rangle) \rangle \tag{App'}$$

$$((c \to d) \cdot e \langle a \rangle)b > b\langle e\langle a \rangle(c\langle b \rangle) \rangle \tag{App''}$$

$$((\forall t \leq c \,.\, d)\langle f \rangle)\{A, e\} > d[t \leftarrow A][t_B \leftarrow e]\langle f\{A, c \cdot e\} \rangle \qquad e : A \leq B \tag{App2'}$$

$$((\forall t \leq c \,.\, d) \cdot c'\langle f \rangle)\{A, e\} > d[t \leftarrow A][t_B \leftarrow e]\langle (c'\langle f \rangle)\{A, c \cdot e\} \rangle \qquad e : A \leq B \tag{App2''}$$

$$\lambda x : A \,.\, c\langle b \rangle > (\text{Id}_A \to c)\langle \lambda x : A \,.\, b \rangle \tag{λ}$$

$$\Lambda t \leq A \,.\, c\langle b \rangle > (\forall t \leq \text{Id}_A \,.\, c)\langle \Lambda t \leq A \,.\, b \rangle \tag{Λ}$$

$$c\langle d\langle a \rangle \rangle > (c \cdot d)\langle a \rangle \tag{Comp}$$

Notes

This work was carried out while the first author was visiting DEC SRC, Palo Alto. The work of the second author was carried out with the partial support of EEC Esprit Basic Research Action 3070 FIDE and of Italian CNR Progetto Finalizzato Sistemi Informatici e Calcolo Parallelo.

1. By $t \notin \Gamma$ ($x \notin \Gamma$), we mean: $t(x)$ is not declared in Γ.

2. Weakening means adding assumptions about fresh variables to the environment, which does not invalidate any proved judgement. Formally ($\Gamma \vdash_c c : A \leq B$ and Γ, Γ' env) $\Rightarrow \Gamma, \Gamma' \vdash_c c : A \leq B$, provided that no variable bound in Γ is bound in Γ'.

3. There is no loss of generality in assuming that the two coercions have the same bound variable t, thanks to α-conversion.

4. This follows from $\Gamma \vdash c : A \leq B$ by weakening.

5. This is not a deduction in the system, but an application of the substitution lemma.

6. The size of a term (a coercion in particular) is the number of nodes of its syntactic tree.

7. A multiset of integers A is smaller than a multiset B if B can be obtained dropping some integers from A and substituting any of them with a multiset of smaller numbers; for example $\{5, 4, 2\} > \{5, 3, 3, 1, 2\}$.

8. A raw expression is a term which is syntactically correct but not necessarily typable.

9. These rules should be read bottom up, like we did for the type checking rules in section 6.

10. This is however inessential. One could have translated $\Gamma \vdash c : A \leq A'$ into $\Gamma^*, A^* \vdash c^* : A'^*$ instead of $\Gamma^* \vdash c^* : A^* \to A'^*$, and this gets rid of the need for η. But the translation is then slightly heavier.

11. If A, B are p.e.r.'s in ω (natural numbers, equipped with Kleene application, denoted by $\_\{\_\}$), an arrow $f : A \to B$ is a function (in SET) from ω/A to ω/B for which there exists m (called a code for f) s.t. for all p, q, if $A(p, q)$, then $m\{p\}$ and $m\{q\}$ are defined and $B(m\{p\}, m\{q\})$. The codes for $c_{A, A'}$ are the codes for the identity function.

References

Amadio, R. (1989) Formal theories of inheritance for typed functional languages. *Technical Report*, Dipartimento di Informatica, Università di Pisa, Pisa, Italy.

Breazu-Tannen, V., Coquand, T., Gunter, C. and Scedrov, A. (1993) Inheritance as implicit coercion. *Information and Computation* **93**(1). Also in this volume.

Bruce, K. B. and Longo, G. (1990) A modest model of records, inheritance and bounded quantification. *Information & Computation* **87**(1/2) 196–240. Also in this volume.

Cardelli, L. and Longo, G. (1991) A semantic basis for Quest. *Journal of Functional Programming* **1**(4).

Cardelli, L., Martini, S., Mitchell, J. C. and Scedrov, A. (1991) An extension of system F with subtyping. *Proc. Conf. on Theoretical Aspects of Computer Software, Sendai, Springer-Verlag, Berlin, Lecture Notes in Computer Science*. 526. To appear in *Information and Computation*.

Cardelli, L. and Wegner, P. (1985) On understanding types, data abstraction and polymorphism. *ACM Computing Surveys* **17**(4).

Curien, P.-L. (1986) *Categorical Combinators, Sequential Algorithms and Functional Programming*. Pitman.

Curien, P.-L. and Di Cosmo, R. (1991) Confluence in the typed λ-calculus extended with surjective pairing and a terminal type. *Proc. ICALP 91, Springer Lecture Notes in Computer Science*. 510.

Curien, P.-L. and Ghelli, G. (1991) Subtyping + extensionality: confluence of $\beta\eta\, top_\leq$ in $F_\leq$. *Proc. Conf. on Theoretical Aspects of Computer Software, Sendai, Japan, Springer-Verlag, Berlin, Lecture Notes in Computer Science*. 526.

Ghelli, G. (1993) Divergence of $F_\leq$ type checking. Technical Report TR/5/93, Dipartimento di Informatica, Università di Pisa. To appear in *Theoretical Computer Science*.

——— (1991) On the decidability of type checking for Fun. Unpublished note. Dipartimento di Informatica, Università di Pisa, Pisa, Italy.

Lambek, J. and Scott, P. J. (1986) *Introduction to Higher-Order Categorical Logic*. Cambridge University Press.

Oles, F. J. (1982) A category theoretic approach to the semantics of programming languages. Syracuse University.

Pierce, B. (1993) Bounded quantification is undecidable. To appear in *Information & Computation*. Also in this volume.

Reynolds, J. (1991) The coherence of languages with intersection types. *Int. Conf. on Theoretical Aspects of Computer Software, Sendai, Japan, September 91, Springer Lecture Notes in Computer Science*. 526.

IV RECORD CALCULI

9 Operations on Records

Luca Cardelli and John C. Mitchell

Abstract

We define a simple collection of operations for creating and manipulating record structures, where records are intended as finite associations of values to labels. A second-order type system over these operations supports both subtyping and polymorphism. We provide typechecking algorithms and limited semantic models.

Our approach unifies and extends previous notions of records, bounded quantification, record extension, and parametrization by row-variables. The general aim is to provide foundations for concepts found in object-oriented languages, within a framework based on typed lambda-calculus.

1 Introduction

Object-oriented programming is based on record structures (called *objects*) intended as named collections of values (*attributes*) and functions (*methods*). Collections of objects form *classes*. A *subclass* relation is defined on classes with the intention that methods work 'appropriately' on all members belonging to the subclasses of a given class. This property is important in softward engineering because it permits after-the-fact extensions of systems by subclasses, without requiring modificatons to the systems themselves.

The first object-oriented language, Simula67, and most of the more recent ones (see references) are typed by using simple extensions of the type rules for Pascal-like languages. These extensions mainly involve a notion of *subtyping*. In addition to subtyping, we are interested here in more powerful type systems that smoothly incorporate *parametric polymorphism*.

Type systems for record structures have recently received much attention. They provide foundations for typing in object-oriented languages, database languages, and their extensions. In Cardelli (1988) the basic notions of record types, a intended here, were defined in the context of a first-order type system for fixed-size records. Then Wand (1987) introduced the concept of *row-variables* while trying to solve the type inference problem for records; this led to a system with extensible records and limited second-order typing. His system was later refined and shown to have principal types in Jategaonkar and Mitchell (1988), Rémy (1989), and again in Wand (1989). The

First appeared in *Mathematical Structures in Computer Science* 1 (1991), pages 3–48. © Cambridge University Press, 40 West 20th Street, New York, NY 10011-4211.

resulting system provides a flexible integration of record types and Milner-style type inference (Milner, 1978).

Meanwhile Cardelli and Wegner (1985) defined a full second-order extension of the system with fixed-size records, based on techniques from Mitchell (1984). In that system, a program can work polymorphically over all the subtypes B of a given record type A, and it can preserve the 'unknown' fields (the ones in B but not in A) of record parameters from input to output. However, some natural functions are not expressible. For example, by the nature of fixed-size records there is no way to add a field to a record and preserve all its unknown fields. Less obviously, a function that updates a record field, in the purely applicative sense of making a modified copy of it, is forced to remove all the unknown fields from the result. Imperative update also requires a careful typing analysis.

In this paper we describe a second-order type system that incorporates extensible records and solves the problem of expressing the natural functions mentioned above. We believe this second-order approach makes the presentation of record types more natural. The general idea is to extend a standard second-order (or even higher-order) type system with a notion of subtyping at all types. Record types are then introduced as specialized type constructions with some specialized subtyping rules. These new constructions interact well with the rest of the system. For example, row-variables fall out naturally from second-order type variables, and contravariance of function spaces and universal quantifiers mixes well with record subtyping.

In moving to second-order typing we give up the principal type property of weaker type systems, in exchange for some additional expressiveness. But most importantly for us, we gain some perspective on the space of possible operations on records and record types, unencumbered (at least temporarily) by questions about type inference. Since it is not clear yet where the bounds of expressiveness may lie, this perspective should prove useful for comparisons and further understanding.

The first part of the paper is informal and introduces the main concepts and problems by means of examples. Then we formalize our intuitions by a collection of type rules. We give a normalization procedure for record types, and we show soundness of the rules with respect to a simple semantics for the pure calculus of records. Finally, we discuss applications and extensions of the basic calculus.

2   Informal Development

Before looking at a formal system, we describe informally the desired operations on records and we justify the rules that are expected to hold. The final formal system is rather subtle, so these explanations should be useful in understanding it.

We also give simple examples of how records and their operations can be used in the context of object-oriented languages.

2.1 Record Values

A *record value* is intended to represent, in some intuitive semantic sense, a finite map from labels to values where the values may belong to different types. Syntactically, a record value is a collection of *fields*, where each field is a labeled value. To capture the notion of a map, the labels in a given record must be distinct. Hence the labels can be used to identify the fields, and the fields can be taken to be unordered. This is the notation we use:

$\langle \rangle$ the empty record.

$\langle x = 3, y = true \rangle$ a record with two fields, labeled x and y, equivalent to
                         $\langle y = true, x = 3 \rangle$.

There are three basic operations on record values.

- *Extension* $\langle r|x = a \rangle$; adds a field of label x and value a to a record r, provided a field of label x is not already present. (This condition will be enforced statically.) We write $\langle r|x = a|y = b \rangle$ for $\langle \langle r|x = a \rangle|y = b \rangle$.

- *Restriction* $r \backslash x$; removes the field of label x, if any, from the record r. We write $r \backslash xy$ for $r \backslash x \backslash y$.

- *Extraction* $r . x$; extracts the value corresponding to the label x from the record r, provided a field having that label is present. (This condition will be enforced statically.)

We have chosen these three operations because they seem to be the fundamental constituents of more complex operations. An alternative, considered in Wand (1987), would be to replace extension and restriction by a single operation that either modifies or adds a field of label x, depending on whether another field of label x is already present. In our system, the extension operation is not required to check whether a new field is already present in a record: its absence is guaranteed statically. The restriction operation has the task of removing unwanted fields and fulfilling that guarantee. This separation of tasks has advantages for efficiency, and for static error detection since fields cannot be overwritten unintentionally by extension alone. Based on a comparison between the systems of Wand (1987) and Jategaonkar and Mitchell (1988), it also seems possible that a reasonable fragment of our language will have a practical type inference algorithm.

Here are some simple examples. The symbol $\leftrightarrow$ (value equivalence) means that two expressions denote the same value:

$$\langle\langle\ \rangle|x = 3\rangle \leftrightarrow \langle x = 3\rangle \qquad\qquad\qquad \text{extension}$$

$$\langle\langle x = 3\rangle|y = true\rangle \leftrightarrow \langle x = 3, y = true\rangle$$

$$\langle x = 3, y = true\rangle\backslash y \leftrightarrow \langle x = 3\rangle \qquad\qquad \text{restriction (cancelling } y)$$

$$\langle x = 3, y = true\rangle\backslash z \leftrightarrow \langle x = 3, y = true\rangle \qquad\qquad \text{(no effect)}$$

$$\langle x = 3, y = true\rangle.x \leftrightarrow 3 \qquad\qquad\qquad \text{extraction}$$

$$\langle\langle x = 3\rangle|x = 4\rangle \qquad\qquad\qquad\qquad \text{invalid extension}$$

$$\langle x = 3\rangle.y \qquad\qquad\qquad\qquad\qquad \text{invalid extraction.}$$

Some useful derived operators can be defined in terms of the ones above.

- *Renaming* $r[x \leftarrow y] =_{\text{def}} \langle r\backslash x|y = r.x\rangle$: changes the name of a record field.
- *Overriding* $\langle r \leftarrow x = a\rangle =_{\text{def}} \langle r\backslash x|x = a\rangle$: if x is present in r, overriding replaces its value with one of a possibly unrelated type, otherwise extends r (cf. Wand, 1989). Given adequate type restrictions, this can be seen as an updating operator, or a method overriding operator. We write $\langle r \leftarrow x = a \leftarrow y = b\rangle$ for $\langle\langle r \leftarrow x = a\rangle \leftarrow y = b\rangle$.

Obviously, all records can be constructed from the empty record using extension operations. In fact, in the formal preentation of the calculus, we regard the syntax for a record of many fields as an abbreviation for iterated extensions of the empty record, e.g.:

$$\langle x = 3\rangle =_{\text{def}} \langle\langle\ \rangle|x = 3\rangle$$

$$\langle x = 3, y = true\rangle =_{\text{def}} \langle\langle\langle\ \rangle|x = 3\rangle|y = true\rangle.$$

This definition allows us to express the fundamental properties of records in terms of combinations of simple operators of fixed arity, as opposed to n-ary operators. Hence, we never have to use schemas with ellipses, such as $\langle x_1 = a_1, \ldots, x_n = a_n\rangle$, in our formal treatment.

Since $r\backslash x \leftrightarrow r$ whenever r lacks a field of label x, we can formulate the definition above using any of the following expressions:

$$\langle\langle\ \rangle|x = 3|y = true\rangle \leftrightarrow \langle\langle\langle\ \rangle\backslash x|x = 3\rangle\backslash y|y = true\rangle$$

$$\leftrightarrow \langle\langle\ \rangle \leftarrow x = 3 \leftarrow y = true\rangle.$$

The latter forms match better a similar definition for record types, given in the next section.

2.2   Record Types

In describing operations on record values we made positive assumptions of the form 'a field of label x *must* occur in record r' and negative assumptions of the form 'a field of label x *must not* occur in record r'.

These constraints will be verified statically by embedding them in a type system, hence *record types* will convey both positive and negative information. Positive information describes the fields that members of a record type *must* have. (Members may have additional fields.) Negative information describes the fields the members of that type *must not* have. (Members may lack additional fields.)

Note that both positive and negative information expresses constraints, hence increasing either kind of information will lead to smaller sets of values. The smallest amount of informaton is expressed by the record type with no fields, $\langle\!\langle\,\rangle\!\rangle$, which therefore denotes the collection of all records, since all records have at least no fields and lack at least no fields. This type is called the *total* record type.

$\langle\!\langle\,\rangle\!\rangle$	the type of all records. Contains, e.g.: $\langle\,\rangle$, $\langle x = 3\rangle$.
$\langle\!\langle\,\rangle\!\rangle\backslash x$	the type of all records which lack fields of label x. E.g.: $\langle\,\rangle$, $\langle y = true\rangle$, but not $\langle x = 3\rangle$.
$\langle\!\langle x : Int, y : Bool\rangle\!\rangle$	the type of all records which have *at least* fields of labels x and y, with values of types *Int* and *Bool*. E.g.: $\langle x = 3, y = true\rangle$, $\langle x = 3, y = true, z = \text{'str'}\rangle$, but not $\langle x = 3, y = 4\rangle$, $\langle x = 3\rangle$.
$\langle\!\langle x : Int\rangle\!\rangle\backslash y$	the type of all records which have *at least* a field of label x and type *Int*, and no field of label y. E.g. $\langle x = 3, z = \text{'str'}\rangle$, but not $\langle x = 3, y = true\rangle$.

Hence a record type is characterized by a finite collection of (*positive*) *type fields* (i.e. labeled types) and *negative type fields* (i.e. labels).[1] We often simply say 'fields' for 'type fields'. The positive fields must have distinct labels and are unordered. Negative fields are also unordered. We have assumed so far that types are normalized so that positive and negative labels are distinct, otherwise positive and negative fields may cancel, as described shortly.

As with record values, we have three basic operations on record types.

• *Extension* $\langle\!\langle R | x : A\rangle\!\rangle$: this type denotes the collection obtained from R by adding x fields with values in A in all possible ways (provided that none of the elements of R has x fields). More precisely, this is the collection of those records $\langle r | x = a\rangle$ such that r is in R and a is in A, provided that a positive type field x is not already present in R. (This condition will be enforced statically.) We sometimes write $\langle\!\langle R | x : A | y : B\rangle\!\rangle$ for $\langle\!\langle\langle\!\langle R | x : A\rangle\!\rangle | y : B\rangle\!\rangle$.

- *Restriction* $R \backslash x$: this type denotes the collection obtained from R by removing the field x (if any) from all its elements. More precisely, this is the collection of those records $r \backslash x$ such that r is in R. We write $R \backslash xy$ for $R \backslash x \backslash y$.

- *Extraction* $R . x$: this type denotes the type associated with label x in R, provided R has such a positive field. (This condition will be enforced statically.)

Again, derived operators can be defined in terms of the ones above.

- *Renaming* $R[x \leftarrow y] =_{\text{def}} \langle\!\langle R \backslash x | y = R . x \rangle\!\rangle$: changes the name of a record type field.
- *Overriding* $\langle\!\langle R \leftarrow x : A \rangle\!\rangle =_{\text{def}} \langle\!\langle R \backslash x | x : A \rangle\!\rangle$: if a type field x is present in R, overriding replaces it with a field x of type A, otherwise extends R. Given adequate type restrictions, this can be used to override a method type in a class signature (i.e. record type) with a more specialized one, to produce a subclass signature.

The crucial formal difference between these operators on types and the similar ones on values is that type restrictions do not cancel as easily, for example: $\langle\!\langle \rangle\!\rangle \backslash y \neq \langle\!\langle \rangle\!\rangle$, $\langle\!\langle x : A \rangle\!\rangle \backslash y \neq \langle\!\langle x : A \rangle\!\rangle$, etc., since $\langle\!\langle \rangle\!\rangle \backslash y$ is a smaller set than $\langle\!\langle \rangle\!\rangle$. As a consequence, one must always make a type restriction before making a type extension, as can be seen in the examples below, because the extension operator needs proof that the extension label is missing. The symbol $\leftrightarrow$ (type equivalence) means also that two type expressions denote the same type.

$$\langle\!\langle \langle\!\langle \rangle\!\rangle \backslash x | x : Int \rangle\!\rangle \leftrightarrow \langle\!\langle x : Int \rangle\!\rangle \qquad \text{extension}$$

$$\langle\!\langle \langle\!\langle x : Int \rangle\!\rangle \backslash y | y : Bool \rangle\!\rangle \leftrightarrow \langle\!\langle x : Int, y : Bool \rangle\!\rangle$$

$$\langle\!\langle x : Int, y : Bool \rangle\!\rangle \backslash y \leftrightarrow \langle\!\langle x : Int \rangle\!\rangle \backslash y \qquad \text{restriction (cancelling } y\text{)}$$

$$\langle\!\langle x : Int, y : Bool \rangle\!\rangle \backslash z \leftrightarrow \langle\!\langle x : Int, y : Bool \rangle\!\rangle \backslash z \qquad \text{(no effect on } x, y\text{)}$$

$$\langle\!\langle x : Int, y : Bool \rangle\!\rangle . x \leftrightarrow Int \qquad \text{extraction}$$

$$\langle\!\langle \langle\!\langle \rangle\!\rangle | x : Int \rangle\!\rangle \qquad \text{invalid extension}$$

$$\langle\!\langle \langle\!\langle x : Int \rangle\!\rangle | x : Int \rangle\!\rangle \qquad \text{invalid extension}$$

$$\langle\!\langle x : Int \rangle\!\rangle . y \qquad \text{invalid extraction.}$$

It helps to read these examples in terms of the collections they represent. For example, the first example for restriction says that if we take the collection of records that have x and y (and possibly more) fields, and remove the y field from all the elements in the collection, then we obtain the collection of records that have an x field (and possibly more fields) but no y field. In particular, we do not obtain the collection of records that have x and possibly more fields, because those would include y.

The way positive and negative information is formally manipulated is easier to understand if we regard record types as abbreviations, as we did for record values, e.g.:

$$\langle x:Int\rangle =_{\text{def}} \langle\langle\ \rangle\backslash x | x:Int\rangle$$

$$\langle x:Int, y:Bool\rangle =_{\text{def}} \langle\langle\langle\ \rangle\backslash x | x:Int\rangle\backslash y | y:Bool\rangle.$$

Then, when considering $\langle y:Bool\rangle\backslash y$ we actually have the expansion $\langle\langle\ \rangle\backslash y | y:Bool\rangle\backslash y$. If we allow the outside positive and negative y labels to cancel, we are still left with $\langle\ \rangle\backslash y$. In other words, the inner y restriction reminds us that y fields have been eliminated.

Remark   It is deceptive to think that every record in $\langle R | x:A\rangle$ has at least the fields of some record in R (i.e. that $\langle R | x:A\rangle$ has 'more type fields' than R), since $\langle R | x:A\rangle$ is not necessarily contained in R. For example, if $R = \langle\ \rangle\backslash x$ the two collections are incomparable.

Based on this example, one might then think that $\langle R\backslash x | x:A\rangle$ has more type fields than R, and this is indeed true for $R = \langle\ \rangle$. However, in general this fails; for example $R = \langle\ \rangle\backslash x$ makes the collections incomparable, and $R = \langle\langle\ \rangle\backslash x | x:A\rangle$ causes the two collections to have the same fields.

It is also deceptive to think that $R\backslash x$ has fewer type fields than R, since R is in general not contained in $R\backslash x$. This containment is true for $R = \langle\ \rangle\backslash x$, but false for $R = \langle\ \rangle$ where the opposite is true, and $R = \langle\langle\ \rangle\backslash x | x:A\rangle$ makes the two collections incomparable.

These observations might appear to conflict with our previous assertion that positive and negative information always makes things smaller. The assertion is true for normalized record types, but not for arbitrary applications of operators which may later cancel out. We shall study the normalization process in a later section.

2.3   Record Value Variables

Now that we have a first understanding of record types, we can introduce record value variables which are declared to have some record type. For example, $r:\langle\ \rangle\backslash y$ means that r must not have a field y, and $r:\langle x:A\rangle$ means that r must have a field x of type A. The well-formed record expressions can now be formulated more precisely:

$\langle r | x = a\rangle$ where $r:\langle\ \rangle\backslash x$

$r\backslash x$ where $r:\langle\ \rangle$

$r.x$ where $r:\langle x:A\rangle$ for some A.

Record value variables can now be used to write function abstractions. Here we have a function that increments a field of a record, and adds another field to it:

let $f(r: \langle\!\langle x : Int \rangle\!\rangle \backslash y): \langle\!\langle x : Int, y : Int \rangle\!\rangle = \langle r \leftarrow x = r \, . \, x + 1 | y = 0 \rangle.$

This function requires an argument with a field x and no field y; it has type:

$f : \langle\!\langle x : Int \rangle\!\rangle \backslash y \rightarrow \langle\!\langle x : Int, y : Int \rangle\!\rangle$

and can be used as follows:

$f(\langle x = 3 \rangle) \leftrightarrow \langle x = 4, y = 0 \rangle : \langle\!\langle x : Int, y : Int \rangle\!\rangle$

$f(\langle x = 3, z = true \rangle) \leftrightarrow \langle x = 4, y = 0, z = true \rangle : \langle\!\langle x : Int, y : Int \rangle\!\rangle.$

The first application uses the non-trivial fact that $\langle x = 3 \rangle : \langle\!\langle x : Int \rangle\!\rangle \backslash y$. We could also have matched the parameter type precisely by $f(\langle x = 3 \rangle \backslash y)$, which is of course equivalent. The second application is noticeable for several reasons. First, it uses the non-trivial fact that $\langle x = 3, z = true \rangle : \langle\!\langle x : Int \rangle\!\rangle \backslash y$. Second, the 'extra' field z is preserved in the result value, because of the way f is defined. Third, the 'extra' field z is not preserved in the result type, because f has a fixed result type; we shall come back to this problem.

Remark   An alternative syntactic notation, along the lines of Jategaonkar and Mitchell (1988), could use pattern matching of record parameters:

let $f(\langle rr \backslash y | x = rx \rangle): \langle\!\langle x : Int, y : Inst \rangle\!\rangle = \langle rr | x = rx + 1 | y = 0 \rangle.$

Here the actual parameter must match the shape of a record with a field x and a collection of remaining components that lack y. The variables rr and rx are bound to the appropriate components and then used in the body of f, where rr acquires the assumption that it does not contain either x or y fields. There are some non-trivial details to pattern matching in the presence of subtyping. Since our main objective is to illustrate the fundamental ideas, we choose the simpler syntax.

2.4   Record Type Variables

In the previous section we introduced record value variables, and we used record types to impose restrictions on the values which could be bound to such variables. Now we want to introduce record type variables in order to write programs that are polymorphic over a collection of record types. We similarly need to express restrictions on the admissible types that these variables can be found to; these restrictions are written as subtype specifications.

To write subtype specifications, we use a predicate $A <: B$ meaning that A is a *subtype* of B: in other words, every value of A is also a value of B. The typing rule based on this condition is called *subsumption*, and will play a central role in the formal system.

Using subtype assumptions, we can better formulate the restrictions on the record type operators:

$\langle\!\langle R | x : A \rangle\!\rangle$ where $R <: \langle\!\langle\ \rangle\!\rangle \backslash x$

$R \backslash x$ where $R <: \langle\!\langle\ \rangle\!\rangle$

$R . x$ where $R <: \langle\!\langle x : A \rangle\!\rangle$ for some A.

We may now write a polymorphic version of the function f of the previous section:

let $f(R <: \langle\!\langle x : Int \rangle\!\rangle \backslash y)(r : R) : \langle\!\langle R | y : Int \rangle\!\rangle = \langle r \leftarrow x = r . x + 1 | y = 0 \rangle.$

This function expects first a type parameter R which must be a subtype of $\langle\!\langle x : Int \rangle\!\rangle \backslash y$, and then an actual value parameter of type R. An example application is:

$f(\langle\!\langle x : Int, z : Bool \rangle\!\rangle \backslash y)(\langle x = 3, z = true \rangle)$

$\quad \leftrightarrow \langle x = 4, y = 0, z = true \rangle : \langle\!\langle x : Int, y : Int, z : Bool \rangle\!\rangle.$

First, note that R is bound to $\langle\!\langle x : Int, z : Bool \rangle\!\rangle \backslash y$, which is a subtype of $\langle\!\langle x : Int \rangle\!\rangle \backslash y$ as required. Second, $\langle x = 3, z = true \rangle$ has type $\langle\!\langle x : Int, z : Bool \rangle\!\rangle \backslash y$ as required. Third, the result type, obtained by instantiating R, is $\langle\!\langle \langle\!\langle x : Int, z : Bool \rangle\!\rangle \backslash y | y : Int \rangle\!\rangle$, which is the same as $\langle\!\langle x : Int, y : Int, z : Bool \rangle\!\rangle$ by definition. Finally, note that the 'extra' field z has not been forgotten in the result type this time, because all the '*extra*' fields are carried over from input to output type by the type variable R. This is the advantage of writing f in polymorphic style.

What is the type of f then? We cannot write this type with simple function arrows, because we have a free variable R to bind. Moreover, we want to mark the precise location where this binding occurs, because this permits more types to be expressed. Hence, we use an explicit *bounded universal quantifier*:

$f : \forall (R <: \langle\!\langle x : Int \rangle\!\rangle \backslash y) R \rightarrow \langle\!\langle R | y : Int \rangle\!\rangle.$

This reads rather naturally: 'for all types R which are subtypes of $\langle\!\langle x : Int \rangle\!\rangle \backslash y$, f is a function from R to $\langle\!\langle R | y : Int \rangle\!\rangle$'. (The scope of a quantifier extends to the right as much as possible.)

Remark Notice that we have freedom in the typing of the polymorphic function f; for example, we could have chosen the typing:

$$let\ f(R <: \langle\!\langle\ \rangle\!\rangle\backslash xy)(r: \langle\!\langle R|x: Int \rangle\!\rangle): \langle\!\langle R|x: Int|y: Int \rangle\!\rangle = \langle r \leftarrow x = r.x + 1|y = 0 \rangle$$

$$f(\langle\!\langle z: Bool \rangle\!\rangle\backslash xy)(\langle x = 3, z = true \rangle): \langle\!\langle x: Int, y: Int, z: Bool \rangle\!\rangle.$$

This typing turns out to be incomparable with the previous one; in general we do not seem to have a 'best' way of typing an expression. However, we have not studied this aspect of the system carefully.

2.5 Subtype Hierarchies

Our operations on record types and record values make it easy to define new types and values by *reusing* previously defined types and values.

For example, we want to express the subtype hierarchy shown in the diagram below, where various entities can have a combination of coordinates x and y, radius r, and color c.

First, we could define each type independently:

let Point $= \langle\!\langle x: Real, y: Real \rangle\!\rangle$

let Color Point $= \langle\!\langle x: Real, y: Real, c: Color \rangle\!\rangle$

let Disc $= \langle\!\langle x: Real, y: Real, r: Real \rangle\!\rangle$

let Color Disc $= \langle\!\langle x: Real, y: Real, r: Real, c: Color \rangle\!\rangle.$

But these explicit definitions do not scale up easily to large hierarchies; it is much more convenient to define each type in terms of previous ones, e.g.:

let Point $= \langle\!\langle x: Real, y: Real \rangle\!\rangle$

let Color Point $= \langle\!\langle Point \leftarrow c: Color \rangle\!\rangle$

let Disc $= \langle\!\langle Point \leftarrow r: Real \rangle\!\rangle$

let Color Disc $= \langle\!\langle Color Point \leftarrow r: Real \rangle\!\rangle.$

Note that $\langle\!\langle Point|c: Color \rangle\!\rangle$ would not be well-formed here, since members of *Point* may have a c label. In section 4.3 we shall examine another way of defining this hierarchy, for example deriving *Point* from *Color Point* by 'retracting' the c field.

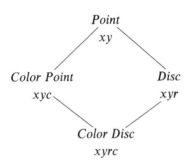

Similarly, record values can be defined by reusing available values:

let p: *Point* = $\langle x = 3, y = 4 \rangle$

let cp: *Color Point* = $\langle p \leftarrow c: green \rangle$

let cd: *Color Disc* = $\langle cp \leftarrow r = 1 \rangle$

let d: *Disc* = $cd \backslash c$.

We should notice here that the subtyping relation depends only on the structure of the types, and not on how the types are named or constructed. Similarly, record values belong to record types uniquely based on their structure, independently of how they are declared or constructed.

Another observation, which we already made in a more abstract context, is that *Point*\r < : *Point* since *Point* does not contain *r*, but *Point*\y is incomparable with *Point* since *Point* requires *y* : *Int* while *Point*\y forbids it.

2.6 The Update Problem

The type system for records we have described in the previous sections was initially motivated by a single example which involves typing an update function. Here updating is intended in the functional sense of creating a copy of a record with a modified field, but the discussion is also relevant to imperative updating.

The problem is to define a function that updates a field of a record and returns the new record; the type of this function should be such that when an argument of the function has a subtype of the expected input type, the result has a related subtype. That is, no type information regarding additional fields should be lost in updating. (We have already seen that bounded quantification can be useful in this respect.)

It is pretty clear what the body of such a function should look like; for example for an input *r* and a boolean field *b* which has to be negated, we would write:

$\langle r \leftarrow b = not(r.b) \rangle$ (an abbreviation for $\langle r \backslash b | b = not(r.b) \rangle$).

The overriding operator here preserves the additional fields of r.

One might expect the following typing, which seems to preserve subtype information as desired:

$let\ update(R <: \langle\!\langle b: Bool \rangle\!\rangle)(r: R): R = \langle r \leftarrow b = not(r.b) \rangle.$

In words, we expect *update* to be a function from R to R, for any subtype R of $\langle\!\langle b: Bool \rangle\!\rangle$. But this typing is not derivable from our rules, and, worse, it is semantically unsound. To see this, assume we have a type *True* $<: Bool$ with unique element *true*, as follows:[2]

$true: True <: Bool$

$not: Bool \rightarrow Bool$ (alternatively, $not: \forall(A <: Bool)A \rightarrow Bool$)

$update(\langle\!\langle b: True \rangle\!\rangle)(\langle b = true \rangle) \leftrightarrow \langle b = false \rangle: \langle\!\langle b: True \rangle\!\rangle.$

This use of *update* produces an obviously incorrect result type. In general, a function with result type R has a fixed range; it cannot restrict its output to an arbitrary subtype of R, even when this subtype is given as a parameter.

To avoid this problem, we must update the result type as well as the result. The correct typing comes naturally from typechecking the body of *update* according to the rules for each construct involved; note how the shape of the result type matches the shape of the body of the function:

$let\ update(R <: \langle\!\langle b: Bool \rangle\!\rangle)(r: R): \langle R \leftarrow b: Bool \rangle = \langle r \leftarrow b = not(r.b) \rangle$

$update(\langle\!\langle b: True \rangle\!\rangle)(\langle b = true \rangle)$

$\quad \leftrightarrow \langle b = false \rangle: (\langle\!\langle\!\langle b: True \rangle\!\rangle \leftarrow b: Bool \rangle \leftrightarrow \langle\!\langle b: Bool \rangle\!\rangle).$

The outcome is that the overriding operator on types, which involves manipulation of negative information, is necessary to express the type of update functions. Bounded quantification by itself is not sufficient.

The type $\forall(B <: A) B \rightarrow B$ turns out to contain only the identity function on A in many natural semantic models, such as Bruce and Longo (1988). For example take $A = Int$ and let the subranges $[n..m]$ be subtypes of *Int*. Then any function of type $\forall(B <: Int) B \rightarrow B$ can be instantiated to $[n..n] \rightarrow [n..n]$, hence it must be the identity on $[n..n]$ for any n, and hence the identity over all of *Int*.

A further complication manifests itself when updating acts deep in a structure, because then we have to preserve type information with subtyping occurring at multiple levels. Here is the body of a function that negates the $s.a.b$ field of a record s of type $\langle\!\langle a : \langle\!\langle b : Bool \rangle\!\rangle \rangle\!\rangle$:

$$\langle s \leftarrow a = \langle s.a \leftarrow b = not(s.a.b) \rangle \rangle.$$

The following is a correct typing which does not lose information on subtypes (simpler typings would). Here we need to introduce an additional type parameter in order to use two type variables in the result type and to avoid two possible ways of losing type information:

$$let\ deepUpdate(R <: \langle\!\langle b : Bool \rangle\!\rangle)(S <: \langle\!\langle a : R \rangle\!\rangle)(s : S) : \langle\!\langle S \leftarrow a : \langle\!\langle R \leftarrow b : Bool \rangle\!\rangle \rangle\!\rangle$$

$$= \langle s \leftarrow a = \langle s.a \leftarrow b = not(s.a.b) \rangle \rangle.$$

Of course this is rather clumsy; we need one additional type parameter for each additional depth level of updating. Fortunately, we can avoid the extra type parameters by using *extraction* types $S.a$. Again, the following typing comes naturally from typechecking the body of *deepUpdate* according to the rules for each construct:

$$let\ deepUpdate(S <: \langle\!\langle a : \langle\!\langle b : Bool \rangle\!\rangle \rangle\!\rangle)(s : S) : \langle\!\langle S \leftarrow a : \langle\!\langle S.a \leftarrow b : Bool \rangle\!\rangle \rangle\!\rangle$$

$$= \langle s \leftarrow a = \langle s.a \leftarrow b = not(s.a.b) \rangle \rangle.$$

The output type is still complex (it could be inferred) but the input is more natural. Here is a use of this function:

$$deepUpdate(\langle\!\langle a : \langle\!\langle b : True, c : C \rangle\!\rangle, d : D \rangle\!\rangle)(\langle a = \langle b = true, c = v \rangle, d = w \rangle$$

$$\leftrightarrow \langle a = \langle b = false, c = v \rangle, d = w \rangle : \langle\!\langle a : \langle\!\langle b : Bool, c : C \rangle\!\rangle, d : D \rangle\!\rangle.$$

Here we have provided an argument type that is a subtype of $\langle\!\langle a : \langle\!\langle b : Bool \rangle\!\rangle \rangle\!\rangle$ in 'all possible ways'.

Finally, we should remark that the complexity of the update problem seems to manifest itself only in the functional case, while simpler solutions are available in the imperative case. Simpler type systems for records, such as the one in Cardelli and Wegner (1985), may be adequate for imperative languages when properly extended with imperative constructs, as sketched below.

The imperative updating operator := has the additional constraint that the new record should have the same type as the old record, since intuitively updating is done 'in place'. This requirement produces something very similar to the typing we have initially shown to be unsound. Here assignable fields are identified by *var*:

$$let\ update(R <: \langle\!\langle var\ b : Bool \rangle\!\rangle)(r : R) : R = r.b := not(r.b).$$

Soundness is then recovered by requiring that assignable fields be both covariant and contravariant. Hence, *True* $<: Bool$ does not imply $\langle var\ b : True \rangle <: \langle var\ b : Bool \rangle$, thereby blocking the counterexamples to soundness.

Imperative update, with the natural requirement of not changing the type of a record, leads to simpler typing. However, this approach does not completely solve the problem we have discussed in this section. Imperative update alone does not provide the functionality of polymorphically extending existing records; when this is added, all the problems discussed above about functional update resurface.

3   Formal Development

Now that we have acquired some intuitions, we can discuss the formal type inference rules in detail. We first define judgment forms and environment structures. Then we look at inference rules individually, and we analyze their properties. Finally, we provide a set-theoretical semantics for the pure calculus of records.

3.1   Judgments and Inferences

A *judgment* is an inductively defined predicate between environments, value terms, and type terms. The following judgments are used in formalizing our system:

$\vdash E\ env$ E is an environment

$E \vdash A\ type$ A is a type

$E \vdash A <: B$ A is a subtype of B

$E \vdash a : A$ a has type A

$E \vdash A \leftrightarrow B$ equivalent types

$E \vdash a \leftrightarrow b : A$ equivalent values of type A.

The formal system is given by a set of *inference rules* below, each expressed as a finite set of *antecedent* judgments and side conditions (above a horizontal line) and a single *conclusion* judgment (below the line). Most inference rules are actually *rule schemas*, where meta-variables must be instantiated to obtain concrete inferences. For typographical reasons, we write the side conditions for these schemas as part of the antecedent.

3.2   Environments

An environment E is a finite sequence of: (a) unconstrained type variables; (b) type variables constrained to be subtypes of a given type; and (c) value variables associated with their type.

We use $dom(E)$ for the set of type and value variables defined in an environment.

$$\overline{\vdash \varnothing \; env} \qquad\qquad\qquad\qquad\qquad\qquad\qquad\qquad (\text{ENV1})$$

$$\frac{X \notin dom(E)}{\vdash E, X \; env} \qquad\qquad\qquad\qquad\qquad\qquad\qquad (\text{ENV2})$$

$$\frac{E \vdash A \; type \qquad X \notin dom(E)}{\vdash E, X <: A \; env} \qquad\qquad\qquad\qquad (\text{ENV3})$$

$$\frac{E \vdash A \; type \qquad x \notin dom(E)}{\vdash E, x : A \; env} . \qquad\qquad\qquad\qquad (\text{ENV4})$$

Hence, a legal environment is obtained by starting with the empty environment $\varnothing$ and extending it with a finite set of *assumptions* for type and value variables. Note that the assumptions involve distinct variables; we could perhaps allow multiple assumptions (e.g. $\varnothing, X <: A, X <: B$) but this would push us into the more general discipline of *conjunctive types*.

Assumptions about variables can then be extracted from well-formed environments:

$$\frac{\vdash E, X, E' \; env}{E, X, E' \vdash X \; type} \qquad\qquad\qquad\qquad\qquad (\text{VAR1})$$

$$\frac{\vdash E, X <: A, E' \; env}{E, X <: A, E' \vdash X \; type} \qquad\qquad\qquad\qquad (\text{VAR2})$$

$$\frac{\vdash E, X <: A, E' \; env}{E, X <: A, E' \vdash X <: A} \qquad\qquad\qquad\qquad (\text{VAR3})$$

$$\frac{\vdash E, x : A, E' \; env}{E, x : A, E' \vdash x : A} . \qquad\qquad\qquad\qquad (\text{VAR4})$$

All legal inferences take place in (well-formed) environments. All judgments are recursively defined in terms of other judgments. For example, above we have used the typing judgment $E \vdash A \; type$ constructing environments; vice versa, well-formed environments are involved in constructing types.

We now consider the remaining judgments in turn.

3.3 Record Type Formation

The following collection of rules determines when record types are well-formed. There is some interdependence between this section and the following ones, since equivalence rules have assumptions that involve subtyping, which is discussed later. Fortunately, these assumptions are fairly simple, so a full understanding of the subtype relation is not required at this point.

$$\frac{\vdash E \; env}{E \vdash \langle \rangle \; type} \tag{F1}$$

$$\frac{E \vdash R <: \langle \rangle \backslash x \qquad E \vdash A \; type}{E \vdash \langle R | x : A \rangle \; type} \tag{F2}$$

$$\frac{E \vdash R <: \langle \rangle}{E \vdash R \backslash x \; type} \tag{F3}$$

$$\frac{E \vdash R <: \langle S | x : A \rangle <: \langle \rangle}{E \vdash R \, . \, x \; type}. \tag{F4}$$

As shown above, and already discussed informally, the legal record types are: the type of all records, $\langle \rangle$; a record type variable X (because of (VAR2) in the previous section); an extension $\langle R | x : A \rangle$ of a record type R, provided R does not have x; and a restriction $R \backslash x$ of a record type R. Moreover, extracting a component $R . x$ of a record type R that has a label x, produces a legal type.

In general, if R does not have x, then R will be a subtype of the type $\langle \rangle \backslash x$ of all records without x. This explains the hypothesis of rule (F2). In rule (F4) we use $R <: \langle S | x : A \rangle$ to guarantee that every record in R has an x field.

3.4 Record Type Equivalence

When are two record types equivalent? We discuss here the formal rules for answering such a question. Type equivalence, as a relation, is reflexive (over well-formed expressions), symmetric, and transitive; it is denoted by the symbol $\leftrightarrow$. Substituting two equivalent types in a third type should produce an equivalent result; this is called the *congruence* property, and requires a number of rules to be fully formalized (these are listed in section 3.7). We now consider, by cases, the equivalence of extended, restricted and extracted record types.

Two extended record types are equivalent if we can reorder their fields to make them identical (or, recursively, equivalent). This simple fact is expressed by the following rule. A number of applications of this rule, and of the congruence property, may be necessary to adequately reorder the fields of a record type.

$$\frac{E \vdash R <: \langle \rangle \backslash xy \qquad E \vdash A, B \; type \qquad x \neq y}{E \vdash \langle \langle R | x : A \rangle | y : B \rangle \leftrightarrow \langle \langle R | y : B \rangle | x : A \rangle}. \tag{TE1}$$

Similarly, we can reorder restrictions. Moreover, a double restriction $R \backslash xx$ reduces to $R \backslash x$. This fact is expressed in slightly more general form below, since the assumption that R does not have x is sufficient to deduce that $R \backslash x$ is the same as R:

$$\frac{E \vdash R <: \langle\!\langle \; \rangle\!\rangle \backslash x}{E \vdash R \backslash x \leftrightarrow R} \tag{TE2}$$

$$\frac{E \vdash R <: \langle\!\langle \; \rangle\!\rangle}{E \vdash R \backslash xy \leftrightarrow R \backslash yx}. \tag{TE3}$$

The most interesting rules concern the distribution of restriction over extension. An outside restriction and inner extension of the same variable can cancel each other. Otherwise, a restriction can be pushed inside or outside of an extension of a different variable.

$$\frac{E \vdash R <: \langle\!\langle \; \rangle\!\rangle \backslash x \qquad E \vdash A \; type}{E \vdash \langle\!\langle R | x : A \rangle\!\rangle \backslash x \leftrightarrow R} \tag{TE5}$$

$$\frac{E \vdash R <: \langle\!\langle \; \rangle\!\rangle \backslash x \qquad E \vdash A \; type \qquad x \neq y}{E \vdash \langle\!\langle R | x : A \rangle\!\rangle \backslash y \leftrightarrow \langle\!\langle R \backslash y | x : A \rangle\!\rangle}. \tag{TE6}$$

Note however that in a situation like $\langle\!\langle R \backslash x | x : A \rangle\!\rangle$ no cancellation or swap can occur. The inner restriction may be needed to guarantee that the extension is sensible, and so neither is redundant.

Finally, a record extraction is equivalent to the extracted type:

$$\frac{E \vdash R <: \langle\!\langle \; \rangle\!\rangle \backslash x \qquad E \vdash A \; type}{E \vdash \langle\!\langle R | x : A \rangle\!\rangle . x \leftrightarrow A} \tag{TE7}$$

$$\frac{E \vdash R <: \langle\!\langle S | y : B \rangle\!\rangle \backslash x <: \langle\!\langle \; \rangle\!\rangle \qquad E \vdash A \; type \qquad x \neq y}{E \vdash \langle\!\langle R | x : A \rangle\!\rangle . y \leftrightarrow R . y} \tag{TE8}$$

$$\frac{E \vdash R <: \langle\!\langle S | y : B \rangle\!\rangle <: \langle\!\langle \; \rangle\!\rangle \qquad x \neq y}{E \vdash R \backslash x . y \leftrightarrow R . y}. \tag{TE4}$$

These equivalence rules can be given a direction and interpreted as rewrite rules producing a normal form for record types: normalization is investigated in a later section.

3.5 Record Subtyping

We have seen that subtyping is central to the notion of abstracting over record type variables, and we have intuitively justified some of the valid subtype assertions. In this section we take a more rigorous look at the subtype relation.

Subtyping should at least be a pre-order: a reflexive and transitive relation. Given a substitutive type equivalence relation $\leftrightarrow$, such as the one discussed in the previous section, we require:

$$\frac{E \vdash A \leftrightarrow B}{E \vdash A <: B} \tag{G1}$$

$$\frac{E \vdash A <: B \qquad E \vdash B <: C}{E \vdash A <: C}. \tag{G2}$$

Reflexivity is a special case of (G1).

It would be natural to require subtyping to be anti-symmetric, hence obtaining a partial order. A reasonable semantics of subtyping will in fact construct such a partial order. However, it might be too strong to require anti-symmetry as a type rule. In some systems anti-symmetry may introduce obscure ways of proving type equivalence, while in other systems it may be provable from the other rules. Moreover, anti-symmetry does not seem very useful for typechecking, hence we do not include it.

The basic intuition about subtyping is that it behaves much like the subset relation; this is expressed by the *subsumption* rule, which claims that if $A <: B$ and a is an element of A, then a is also an element of B.

$$\frac{E \vdash a:A \qquad E \vdash A <: B}{E \vdash a:B}. \tag{G3}$$

We feel strongly that subsumption should be included in the type system, since this rule gives object-oriented programming much of its flavor. One should not be satisfied, for programming purposes, with emulating subsumption by explicit coercions. The latter technique is interesting and adequate for providing semantics to a language with subsumption (Breazu-Tannen *et al.*, 1989; Curien & Ghelli, 1989), but even then it would seem more satisfactory to exhibit a model that satisfies subsumption directly.

Combining (G1) and (G3) we obtain another standard type rule:

$$\frac{E \vdash a:A \qquad E \vdash A \leftrightarrow B}{E \vdash a:B}.$$

This rule is normally taken as primitive, but here it is derived.

We are now ready to talk about subtyping between record types. It helps if we break this problem into pieces and ask what are the subtypes of: (1) the total record type $\langle \rangle$, (2) an extended record type $\langle R | x : A \rangle$, (3) a restricted record type $R \backslash x$, and (4) a record type extraction $R . x$.

Case (1)   Every record type should be a subtype of the total record type. Hence, we have three subcases: (1a) the total record type is of course a subtype of itself, and this is simply a consequence of (G1); (1b) any well-formed extended record type is a subtype of $\langle\!\langle\,\rangle\!\rangle$; and (1c) any well-formed restricted record type is a subtype of $\langle\!\langle\,\rangle\!\rangle$. Hence we have the following rules corresponding to (1b) and (1c) respectively:

$$\frac{E \vdash R <: \langle\!\langle\,\rangle\!\rangle\backslash x \qquad E \vdash A\ type}{E \vdash \langle\!\langle R | x : A \rangle\!\rangle <: \langle\!\langle\,\rangle\!\rangle} \tag{s1}$$

$$\frac{E \vdash R <: \langle\!\langle\,\rangle\!\rangle}{E \vdash R\backslash x <: \langle\!\langle\,\rangle\!\rangle}. \tag{s2}$$

Case (2)   A subtype of an extended record type will be another extended record type, provided all respective components are in the subtype relation:

$$\frac{E \vdash R <: S <: \langle\!\langle\,\rangle\!\rangle\backslash x \qquad E \vdash A <: B}{E \vdash \langle\!\langle R | x : A \rangle\!\rangle <: \langle\!\langle S | x : B \rangle\!\rangle}. \tag{s3}$$

The condition $A <: B$ says that we can produce a subtype by weakening the type of a given field. The condition $R <: S$ tells us that we can produce a subtype either: (a) by weakening other fields inductively, because of (s3) itself; or (b) by requiring the presence of additional components, because of (s1); or (c) by requiring the absence of additional components, for example y, because from (s2) we are able to derive $\langle\!\langle\,\rangle\!\rangle\backslash yx <: \langle\!\langle\,\rangle\!\rangle\backslash x$.

Case (3)   The subtype rule for restricted types is semantically straightforward: if every r in R occurs in S, then every $r\backslash x$ in $R\backslash x$ occurs in $S\backslash x$:

$$\frac{E \vdash R <: S <: \langle\!\langle\,\rangle\!\rangle}{E \vdash R\backslash x <: S\backslash x}. \tag{s4}$$

Remark   Although this rule looks innocent, it hides some interesting subtlety in its assumption. Let us analyze $R <: S$ by cases.

The cases when R and S are themselves restrictions (either of x or of some other variable) are straightforward. Similarly simple are the cases when R and S are matching extensions, both of them either containing or not containing an x field.

Suppose however that R has a positive x field and S does not, for example $R = \langle\!\langle T | x : A \rangle\!\rangle$ and $S = T$. In that case, if we had $R <: S$ we would erroneously conclude that $R\backslash x = \langle\!\langle T | x : A \rangle\!\rangle\backslash x \leftrightarrow T <: T\backslash x = S\backslash x$ (which is false for $T = \langle\!\langle\,\rangle\!\rangle$).

Fortunately there was a flaw in this argument; the assumption for (s4) requires $R = \langle\!\langle T | x : A \rangle\!\rangle <: T = S$, but this is false (for $T = \langle\!\langle\,\rangle\!\rangle\backslash x$). Note also that taking $R = \langle\!\langle T\backslash x | x : A \rangle\!\rangle$ and $S = T$ leads to a similar contradiction for $T = \langle\!\langle\,\rangle\!\rangle\backslash x$.

A legal instance of the assumption is $R = \langle\!\langle\,\rangle\backslash x | x : A\rangle <: \langle\,\rangle = S$, from which we conclude that $R\backslash x = \langle\!\langle\,\rangle\backslash x : A\rangle\backslash x \leftrightarrow \langle\,\rangle\backslash x <: \langle\,\rangle\backslash x = S\backslash x$, which is correct.

Case (4) We have to consider the subtypes of record type extractions; that is situations of the form $R.x <: T.x$, or more generally $R.x <: A$ under an assumption $R <: \langle S | x : B\rangle$. If R can be converted to the form $R = \langle R' | x : A\rangle$, then the extraction $R.x$ simplifies and no special rule is required to deduce $R.x <: A$. But if R is a type variable, for example, the following rule is necessary:

$$\frac{E \vdash R <: \langle S | x : A\rangle <: \langle\,\rangle}{E \vdash R.x <: A}. \tag{s5}$$

This says that if R has an x field of type A, then $R.x$ is a subtype of A (and possibly equal to A).

Finally, there is another subtyping rule that we must consider. If every record r in R has an x field, then any such r is described also by the type $\langle R\backslash x | x : R.x\rangle$, since $r\backslash x$ is described by $R\backslash x$ and the x field of r is described by $R.x$. Therefore we have the following inclusion:

$$\frac{E \vdash R <: \langle S | x : A\rangle <: \langle\,\rangle}{E \vdash R <: \langle R\backslash x | x : R.x\rangle}. \tag{s6}$$

The inverse inclusion is not necessarily valid, although it might seem natural to require it as we shall see later.

The rule (s6) can be used in the following derivation, which provides a 'symmetrical' version of (s5) as a derived rule:

$$
\begin{array}{ll}
 & E \vdash R <: S <: \langle T | x : A\rangle <: \langle\,\rangle \\
(\text{s6}) & \overline{E \vdash S <: \langle S\backslash x | x : S.x\rangle} \\
(\text{G2}) & \overline{E \vdash R <: \langle S\backslash x | x : S.x\rangle} \\
(\text{s5}) & \overline{E \vdash R.x <: S.x.}
\end{array}
$$

In the absence of (s6), the derived rule above would have to be taken as primitive, replacing (s5).

3.6 Record Typing and Equivalence

Now that we have seen the rules for type equivalence and subtyping, the rules for record values follow rather naturally. The only subtle point is about the empty record. We must be able to assign it a type which lacks any given set of labels. This is obtained by repeatedly applying the following two rules:

$$\frac{\vdash E \; env}{E \vdash \langle\rangle\backslash x_1 \ldots x_n : \langle\rangle} \tag{I1}$$

$$\frac{E \vdash \langle\rangle\backslash x_1 \ldots x_n : R <: \langle\rangle}{E \vdash \langle\rangle\backslash x_1 \ldots x_n : R\backslash x}. \tag{I2}$$

The remaining constructions on record values are typed by the corresponding constructions on record types, given the appropriate assumptions:

$$\frac{E \vdash r : R <: \langle\rangle\backslash x \qquad E \vdash a : A}{E \vdash \langle r | x = a\rangle : \langle\!\langle R | x : A\rangle\!\rangle} \tag{I3}$$

$$\frac{E \vdash r : R <: \langle\rangle}{E \vdash r\backslash x : R\backslash x} \tag{E1}$$

$$\frac{E \vdash r : \langle\!\langle R | x : A\rangle\!\rangle <: \langle\rangle}{E \vdash r . x : A}. \tag{E2}$$

As we did in the previous section, we can use the rule (s6) to derive a 'symmetrical' version of (I2):

$$
\begin{array}{ll}
& E \vdash r : R <: \langle\!\langle S | x : A\rangle\!\rangle <: \langle\rangle \\
\text{(s6)} & \overline{E \vdash R <: \langle\!\langle R\backslash x | x : R . x\rangle\!\rangle} \\
\text{(G3)} & \overline{E \vdash r : \langle\!\langle R\backslash x | x : R . x\rangle\!\rangle} \\
\text{(E2)} & \overline{E \vdash r . x : R . x.}
\end{array}
$$

Finally, we have to examine the rules for record value equivalence. These rules are formally very similar to the ones already discussed for record type equivalence; record extensions can be permuted, record components can be extracted, and restrictions can be permuted and pushed inside extensions, sometimes cancelling each other.

The main formal difference between these and the rules for types is that we equate $\langle\rangle\backslash x \leftrightarrow \langle\rangle$. Hence, restriction can always be completely eliminated from variable-free records.

Because of the formal similarity we omit a detailed discussion; the complete set of rules for our type system follows in the next section.

3.7 Type Rules

We can now summarize and complete the rules for record types and values, along with selected auxiliary rules. These rules are designed to be immersed in a second-order λ-calculus with bounded quantification (see Cardelli and Wegner, 1985), and possibly with recursive values and types.

We only list the names of the rules that have already been discussed.

3.7.1 Environments

$$(\text{ENV}1)\ldots(\text{ENV}4),\ (\text{VAR}1)\ldots(\text{VAR}4).$$

3.7.2 General Properties of $<:$ and $\leftrightarrow$

$$(\text{G}1)\ldots(\text{G}3)$$

$$\frac{E \vdash A \leftrightarrow B}{E \vdash B \leftrightarrow A} \tag{G4}$$

$$\frac{E \vdash A \leftrightarrow B \qquad E \vdash B \leftrightarrow C}{E \vdash A \leftrightarrow C} \tag{G5}$$

$$\frac{E \vdash a \leftrightarrow b : A}{E \vdash b \leftrightarrow a : A} \tag{G6}$$

$$\frac{E \vdash a \leftrightarrow b : A \qquad E \vdash b \leftrightarrow c : A}{E \vdash a \leftrightarrow c : A}. \tag{G7}$$

3.7.3 Formation

$$(\text{F}1)\ldots(\text{F}4).$$

3.7.4 Subtyping

$$(\text{S}1)\ldots(\text{S}6).$$

3.7.5 Introduction/Elimination

$$(\text{I}1)\ldots(\text{I}3),\ (\text{E}1),\ (\text{E}2).$$

3.7.6 Type Congruence

$$\frac{\vdash E\ env}{E \vdash \langle\,\rangle \leftrightarrow \langle\,\rangle} \tag{TC1}$$

$$\frac{E \vdash X\ type}{E \vdash X \leftrightarrow X} \tag{TC2}$$

$$\frac{E \vdash R \leftrightarrow S <: \langle\,\rangle \backslash x \qquad E \vdash A \leftrightarrow B}{E \vdash \langle R | x : A \rangle \leftrightarrow \langle S | x : B \rangle} \tag{TC3}$$

$$\frac{E \vdash R \leftrightarrow S <: \langle\!\langle \; \rangle\!\rangle}{E \vdash R\backslash x \leftrightarrow S\backslash x} \tag{TC4}$$

$$\frac{E \vdash R \leftrightarrow S <: \langle\!\langle T|x:A \rangle\!\rangle <: \langle\!\langle \; \rangle\!\rangle}{E \vdash R.x \leftrightarrow S.x}. \tag{TC5}$$

3.7.7 Type Equivalence

$$(\text{TE}1)\dots(\text{TE}8).$$

3.7.8 Value Congruence

$$\frac{\vdash E \; env}{E \vdash \langle \; \rangle \leftrightarrow \langle \; \rangle : \langle\!\langle \; \rangle\!\rangle} \tag{VC1a}$$

$$\frac{E \vdash x:A}{E \vdash x \leftrightarrow x:A} \tag{VC2}$$

$$\frac{E \vdash r \leftrightarrow s:R <: \langle\!\langle \; \rangle\!\rangle\backslash x \qquad E \vdash a \leftrightarrow b:A}{E \vdash \langle r|x=a \rangle \leftrightarrow \langle s|x=b \rangle : \langle\!\langle R|x:A \rangle\!\rangle} \tag{VC3}$$

$$\frac{E \vdash r \leftrightarrow s:R <: \langle\!\langle \; \rangle\!\rangle}{E \vdash r\backslash x \leftrightarrow s\backslash x:R\backslash x} \tag{VC4}$$

$$\frac{E \vdash r \leftrightarrow s:R <: \langle\!\langle S|x:A \rangle\!\rangle <: \langle\!\langle \; \rangle\!\rangle}{E \vdash r.x \leftrightarrow s.x:R.x}. \tag{VC5}$$

3.7.9 Value Equivalence

$$\frac{E \vdash r:R <: \langle\!\langle \; \rangle\!\rangle\backslash xy \qquad E \vdash a:A \qquad E \vdash b:B \qquad x \neq y}{E \vdash \langle\langle r|x=a \rangle|y=b \rangle \leftrightarrow \langle\langle r|y=b \rangle|x=a \rangle : \langle\!\langle\!\langle R|x:A \rangle\!\rangle|y:B \rangle\!\rangle} \tag{VE1}$$

$$\frac{\vdash E \; env}{E \vdash \langle \; \rangle\backslash x \leftrightarrow \langle \; \rangle : \langle\!\langle \; \rangle\!\rangle} \tag{VE2}$$

$$\frac{E \vdash r:R <: \langle\!\langle \; \rangle\!\rangle\backslash x}{E \vdash r\backslash x \leftrightarrow r:R} \tag{VE3}$$

$$\frac{E \vdash r:R <: \langle\!\langle \; \rangle\!\rangle}{E \vdash r\backslash xy \leftrightarrow r\backslash yx:R\backslash xy} \tag{VE4}$$

$$\frac{E \vdash r:\langle\!\langle R|x:A \rangle\!\rangle <: \langle\!\langle \; \rangle\!\rangle \qquad x \neq y}{E \vdash r\backslash y.x \leftrightarrow r.x:A} \tag{VE5}$$

$$\frac{E \vdash r:R <: \langle\!\langle\,\rangle\!\rangle \backslash x \qquad E \vdash a:A}{E \vdash \langle r | x = a \rangle \backslash x \leftrightarrow r:A} \tag{VE6}$$

$$\frac{E \vdash r:R <: \langle\!\langle\,\rangle\!\rangle \backslash x \qquad E \vdash a:A \qquad x \neq y}{E \vdash \langle r | x = a \rangle \backslash y \leftrightarrow \langle r \backslash y | x = a \rangle : \langle\!\langle R | x:A \rangle\!\rangle \backslash y} \tag{VE7}$$

$$\frac{E \vdash r:R <: \langle\!\langle\,\rangle\!\rangle \backslash x \qquad E \vdash a:A}{E \vdash \langle r | x = a \rangle . x \leftrightarrow a:A} \tag{VE8}$$

$$\frac{E \vdash r:\langle\!\langle R | y:B \rangle\!\rangle \backslash x <: \langle\!\langle\,\rangle\!\rangle \qquad E \vdash a:A \qquad x \neq y}{E \vdash \langle r | x = a \rangle . y \leftrightarrow r . y:B} \tag{VE9}$$

$$\frac{E \vdash r:R <: \langle\!\langle S | x . A \rangle\!\rangle <: \langle\!\langle\,\rangle\!\rangle}{E \vdash r \leftrightarrow \langle r \backslash x | x = r . x \rangle : R} \,. \tag{VE10}$$

3.7.10 Special Rules In the following sections we discuss the rules (VC1b) and (TE9) below; these are valid only with respect to particular semantic interpretations.

$$\frac{E \vdash r:\langle\!\langle\,\rangle\!\rangle \qquad E \vdash s:\langle\!\langle\,\rangle\!\rangle}{E \vdash r \leftrightarrow S:\langle\!\langle\,\rangle\!\rangle} \tag{VC1b}$$

$$\frac{E \vdash R <: \langle\!\langle S | x:A \rangle\!\rangle <: \langle\!\langle\,\rangle\!\rangle}{E \vdash R \leftrightarrow \langle\!\langle R \backslash x | x:R . x \rangle\!\rangle} \,. \tag{TE9}$$

In presence of (TE9), the rule (S6) is redundant, and the rules (TC5) and (VC5) are implied by the simpler (TC5b) and (VC5b) below.

$$\frac{E \vdash R \leftrightarrow \langle\!\langle S | x:A \rangle\!\rangle <: \langle\!\langle\,\rangle\!\rangle}{E \vdash R . x \leftrightarrow A} \tag{TC5b}$$

$$\frac{E \vdash r \leftrightarrow s:\langle\!\langle R | x:A \rangle\!\rangle <: \langle\!\langle\,\rangle\!\rangle}{E \vdash r . x \leftrightarrow s . x:A} \,. \tag{VC5b}$$

3.7.11 Properties

LEMMA 3.7.1

(1) If $E \vdash A$ *type*, then $\vdash E$ *env.*
(2) If $E \vdash A <: B$, then $\vdash E$ *env.*

Proof Simple simultaneous induction on derivations, with (F1) as the base case. ∎

LEMMA 3.7.2

(1) If $E \vdash A \leftrightarrow B$, then $E \vdash A$ *type* and $E \vdash B$ *type.*

(2) If $E \vdash A <: B$, then $E \vdash A$ *type* and $E \vdash B$ *type*.

Proof Show (1) and (2) simultaneously by induction on derivations. The hardest case is (TE1). The next hardest is (TE8). All the others are substantially simpler. We prove (TE1) below and leave the remaining cases to the reader.

To prove (1) for (TE1), we assume $E \vdash R <: \langle\!\langle\,\rangle\!\rangle\backslash xy$ and $E \vdash A, B$ type. Using (s2) and (s4) we may derive $E \vdash \langle\!\langle\,\rangle\!\rangle\backslash xy <: \langle\!\langle\,\rangle\!\rangle\backslash x$ and so by transitivity and (F2) we have $E \vdash \langle\!\langle R|x:A\rangle\!\rangle$ *type*. The next goal is to show that $\langle\!\langle R|x:A\rangle\!\rangle$ is a subtype of $\langle\!\langle\,\rangle\!\rangle\backslash y$. Using (s2) and (s4) we have $E \vdash R <: \langle\!\langle\,\rangle\!\rangle\backslash y$ by transitivity, and so by (TE2), $E \vdash R\backslash y \leftrightarrow R$. The type congruence rules give $E \vdash \langle\!\langle R|x:A\rangle\!\rangle \leftrightarrow \langle\!\langle R\backslash y|x:A\rangle\!\rangle$. By (TE6) and transitivity we now have $E \vdash \langle\!\langle R|x:A\rangle\!\rangle \leftrightarrow \langle\!\langle R|x:A\rangle\!\rangle\backslash y$. From (s1) and the original hypotheses, it is easy to show $E \vdash \langle\!\langle R|x:A\rangle\!\rangle <: \langle\!\langle\,\rangle\!\rangle$ and so by (s4), $E \vdash \langle\!\langle R|x:A\rangle\!\rangle\backslash y <: \langle\!\langle\,\rangle\!\rangle\backslash y$. This allows us to derive $E \vdash \langle\!\langle R|x:A\rangle\!\rangle <: \langle\!\langle\,\rangle\!\rangle\backslash y$, from which we may finally obtain $E \vdash \langle\!\langle\langle\!\langle R|x:A\rangle\!\rangle|y:B\rangle\!\rangle$ *type*.

The proof of $E \vdash \langle\!\langle\langle\!\langle R|y:B\rangle\!\rangle|x:A\rangle\!\rangle$ *type* is similar. ■

3.7.12 Sample Derivations We show the main steps of some derivations that can be carried out in this system, assuming rules for typing basic constants.

The first example simply builds a record of two fields, with its natural type.

(I1) $\overline{\langle\,\rangle : \langle\!\langle\,\rangle\!\rangle}$

(E1) $\overline{\langle\,\rangle\backslash x : \langle\!\langle\,\rangle\!\rangle\backslash x}$ (CONST) $\overline{3 : Int}$

(I3) $\overline{\langle\langle\,\rangle\backslash x|x = 3\rangle : \langle\!\langle\langle\!\langle\,\rangle\!\rangle\backslash x|x : Int\rangle\!\rangle}$

(E1) $\overline{\langle\langle\,\rangle\backslash x|x = 3\rangle\backslash y : \langle\!\langle\langle\!\langle\,\rangle\!\rangle\backslash x|x : Int\rangle\!\rangle\backslash y}$ (CONST) $true : Bool$

(I3) $\overline{\langle\langle\langle\,\rangle\backslash x|x = 3\rangle\backslash y|y = true\rangle : \langle\!\langle\langle\!\langle\langle\!\langle\,\rangle\!\rangle\backslash x|x : Int\rangle\!\rangle\backslash y|y : Bool\rangle\!\rangle}$

(DEF) $\langle x = 3, y = true\rangle : \langle\!\langle x : Int, y : Bool\rangle\!\rangle$.

Next, we derive a non-trivial type inclusion. To construct record types of different lengths on the two sides of $<:$, we start with the basic asymmetry of (s1) and we build up symmetrically from there (there is no more direct way).

(G1) $\overline{\langle\!\langle\,\rangle\!\rangle <: \langle\!\langle\,\rangle\!\rangle}$

(s4) $\overline{\langle\!\langle\,\rangle\!\rangle\backslash x <: \langle\!\langle\,\rangle\!\rangle\backslash x}$

(s1) $\overline{\langle\!\langle\langle\!\langle\,\rangle\!\rangle\backslash x|x : Int\rangle\!\rangle <: \langle\!\langle\,\rangle\!\rangle}$

(s4) $\overline{\langle\!\langle\langle\!\langle\,\rangle\!\rangle\backslash x|x : Int\rangle\!\rangle\backslash y <: \langle\!\langle\,\rangle\!\rangle\backslash y}$ (G1) $\overline{Bool <: Bool}$

(s3) $\overline{\langle\!\langle\langle\!\langle\langle\!\langle\,\rangle\!\rangle\backslash x|x : Int\rangle\!\rangle\backslash y|y : Bool\rangle\!\rangle <: \langle\!\langle\langle\!\langle\,\rangle\!\rangle\backslash y|y : Bool\rangle\!\rangle}$

(DEF) $\langle\!\langle x : Int, y : Bool\rangle\!\rangle <: \langle\!\langle y : Bool\rangle\!\rangle$.

Now we show that a given record lacks a given label. This time the key rule is (I2). Some type equivalence rules are used to rearrange the type into a standard form.

$$(\text{I}1) \quad \dfrac{}{\langle\,\rangle : \langle\,\rangle}$$

$$(\text{I}2) \quad \dfrac{\langle\,\rangle : \langle\,\rangle\backslash y \quad (\text{s}2) \quad \overline{\langle\,\rangle\backslash y <: \langle\,\rangle}}{}$$

$$(\text{E}1) \quad \dfrac{\langle\,\rangle\backslash x : \langle\,\rangle\backslash y\backslash x \quad (\text{s}4) \quad \overline{\langle\,\rangle\backslash y\backslash x <: \langle\,\rangle\backslash x} \quad (\text{CONST}) \quad \overline{3 : Int}}{}$$

$$(\text{I}3) \quad \dfrac{\langle\langle\,\rangle\backslash x | x = 3\rangle : \langle\!\langle\,\rangle\backslash y\backslash x | x : Int\rangle}{}$$

$$(\text{TE}3, \text{TC}3, \text{G}1, \text{G}3) \quad \dfrac{\langle\langle\,\rangle\backslash x | x = 3\rangle : \langle\!\langle\,\rangle\backslash x\backslash y | x : Int\rangle}{}$$

$$(\text{TE}6, \text{G}1, \text{G}3) \quad \dfrac{\langle\langle\,\rangle\backslash x | x = 3\rangle : \langle\!\langle\,\rangle\backslash x | x : Int\rangle\backslash y}{}$$

$$(\text{DEF}) \quad \langle x = 3\rangle : \langle x : Int\rangle\backslash y.$$

Finally, we show that by removing a label we obtain a subtype. The basic asymmetry here is provided by (s2).

$$(\text{G}1) \quad \dfrac{}{\langle\,\rangle <: \langle\,\rangle}$$

$$(\text{s}2) \quad \dfrac{}{\langle\,\rangle\backslash y <: \langle\,\rangle}$$

$$(\text{s}4) \quad \dfrac{\langle\,\rangle\backslash y\backslash x <: \langle\,\rangle\backslash x \quad (\text{G}1) \quad \overline{Int <: Int}}{}$$

$$(\text{s}3) \quad \dfrac{\langle\!\langle\,\rangle\backslash y\backslash x | x : Int\rangle <: \langle\!\langle\,\rangle\backslash x | x : Int\rangle}{}$$

$$(\text{TE}3, \text{TC}2, \text{G}1, \text{G}2) \quad \dfrac{\langle\!\langle\,\rangle\backslash x\backslash y | x : Int\rangle <: \langle\!\langle\,\rangle\backslash x | x : Int\rangle}{}$$

$$(\text{TE}6, \text{G}1, \text{G}2) \quad \dfrac{\langle\!\langle\,\rangle\backslash x | x : Int\rangle\backslash y <: \langle\!\langle\,\rangle\backslash x | x : Int\rangle}{}$$

$$(\text{DEF}) \quad \langle x : Int\rangle\backslash y : \langle x : Int\rangle.$$

3.8 Semantics of the Pure Calculus of Records

Our stated intent is to define a second-order type system for record structures. However, models of such a system are rather complex, and outside the scope of this paper.

In this section we provide a simple set-theoretical model of the pure calculus of records, without any additional functional or polymorphic structure. The intent here is to show the plausibility of the inference rules for records, by proving their soundness with respect to a natural model.

This model is natural because it embodies the strong set-theoretical intuitions of subtyping seen as a subset relation, and of records seen as finite tuples. Although this model does not extend to more complex language features, it exhibits the kind of simple-minded but (usually) sound reasoning that guides the design and implementation of object-oriented languages.

3.8.1 Syntax We start with the language implied by the type rules of section 3.7. Since no basic non-record values are expressible in this calculus, we must make some arbitrary choices to get started. To this end, we will consider an extension of the pure calculus with any collection G_1, G_2, ... of basic (ground) type symbols and an arbitrary collection of subtype relations $G_i <: G_j$ between them. To incorporate these new symbols into the calculus, we add the following two rules (which preserve lemmas 3.7.1 and 3.7.2):

$$\frac{\vdash E\ env}{E \vdash G_i\ type} \qquad \frac{\vdash E\ env}{E \vdash G_i <: G_j} \quad \text{(as appropriate)}.$$

For simplicity, we do not introduce value constants; instead we work with environments containing assumptions of the form $k : G_i$.

We will now construct a model of the extended calculus.

3.8.2 Semantic Domains In the following, we rely largely on context to distinguish between syntactic expressions and semantic expressions, and we often identify terms with their denotations.

We start by choosing some fixed set of labels L, and a collection of sets $\mathcal{G}_1$, $\mathcal{G}_2$, ... corresponding to the type symbols G_1, G_2, ... such that $\mathcal{G}_i \subseteq \mathcal{G}_j$ if $G_i <: G_j$ is a subtyping axiom.

For simplicity, we assume that no element of any $\mathcal{G}_i$ is a finite partial function on L (i.e. a record, as we shall see shortly). This assumption is useful when we define the subtype relations of sections 3.9 and 3.10.

Since $\langle \rangle$ serves as a type of all records, we will need some value space closed under record formation. This property may be accomplished by regarding records as finite functions from L to values, and using *ranked* values with rank $< \omega$. We use $A \rightarrow_{\text{fin}} B$ for the set of partial functions from A to B with finite domain, $f(x)\uparrow$ to indicate that the partial function f is undefined at x, and $f(x)\downarrow$ to indicate that f is defined at x.

Define set $\mathcal{R}_i$ of records of rank i, and set $\mathcal{V}_i$ of values of rank i, as follows:

$$\mathcal{V}_0 = \bigcup_j \mathcal{G}_j \qquad \mathcal{V}_{i+1} = \mathcal{R}_i \cup \mathcal{V}_i$$
$$\mathcal{R}_0 = L \rightarrow_{\text{fin}} \mathcal{V}_0 \qquad \mathcal{R}_{i+1} = L \rightarrow_{\text{fin}} \mathcal{V}_{i+1}$$
$$\mathcal{R} = \bigcup_{i < \omega} \mathcal{R}_i \qquad \text{the set of } records$$
$$\mathcal{V} = \bigcup_{i < \omega} \mathcal{V}_i \qquad \text{the set of } values.$$

The essential properties of this construction are summarized by the relationship:

$$\mathcal{R} = (L \rightarrow_{\text{fin}} \mathcal{V}) \subseteq \mathcal{V}.$$

It is clear by construction that $\mathcal{R}_i \subseteq \mathcal{V}_{i+1}$ and so $\mathcal{R} \subseteq \mathcal{V}$. To see that $\mathcal{R} = L \rightarrow_{\text{fin}} \mathcal{V}$, we first show that $L \rightarrow_{\text{fin}} \mathcal{V} \subseteq \mathcal{R}$. If $r \in L \rightarrow_{\text{fin}} \mathcal{V}$, then since $dom(r)$ is finite there is some i with $range(r) \subseteq \mathcal{V}_i$; hence $r \in \mathcal{R}_i \subseteq \mathcal{R}$. The converse follows from the fact that if $r \in \mathcal{R}$, then $r \in \mathcal{R}_i = (L \rightarrow_{\text{fin}} \mathcal{V}_i) \subseteq L \rightarrow_{\text{fin}} \mathcal{V}$.

We now summarize the notation used to describe the semantic interpretation of syntactic constants and operators:

$$\varnothing = \lambda y \in L. \uparrow$$

$$r - x =_{\text{def}} \lambda y \in L. \, if \; y = x \; then \uparrow else \; r(y) \quad \text{provided } r \in \mathcal{R} \text{ and } x \in L.$$

$$r[x = a] =_{\text{def}} \lambda y \in L. \, if \; y = x \; then \; a \; else \; r(y) \quad \text{provided } r \in \mathcal{R}, \, x \in L, \, a \in \mathcal{V}, \text{ and} \\ x \notin dom(r).$$

$r(x)$ is well-defined, provided $r \in \mathcal{R}$, $x \in L$, and $x \in dom(r)$.

LEMMA 3.8.1

(1) The empty record $\varnothing$ is an element of $\mathcal{R}$.

(2) For any $r \in \mathcal{R}$ we have $r - x \in \mathcal{R}$.

(3) If $r \in \mathcal{R}$ is not defined on x, then for any $a \in \mathcal{V}$ we have $r[x = a] \in \mathcal{R}$.

(4) If $r \in \mathcal{R}$ is defined on x, then $r(x) \in \mathcal{V}$.

Proof

(1) The empty function is a finite function.

(2) If $r \in \mathcal{R}$ then $r - x$ remains a finite partial function in $\mathcal{R}$.

(3) Suppose $r \in \mathcal{R}$ with $x \notin dom(r)$, and $a \in \mathcal{V}$. Then $r[x = a]$ is well-defined (is a function) and belongs to $\mathcal{R}$.

(4) If $r \in \mathcal{R} = L \rightarrow_{\text{fin}} \mathcal{V}$ and $r(x)$ is defined then $r(x) \in \mathcal{V}$. ∎

3.8.3 Types and Type Operations Types are interpreted as subsets of our global value set; hence we have a type of all values, and a type of all records. Subtyping is interpreted as set inclusion.

We introduce the following notation for operations on record types:

$$R - x =_{\text{def}} \{r - x | r \in R\} \quad \text{if } R \subseteq \mathcal{R}.$$

$$R[x:A] =_{\text{def}} \{r[x = a] | r \in R, a \in A\} \quad \text{if } R \subseteq \mathcal{R} - x \; (R \text{ undefined on } x) \text{ and } A \subseteq \mathcal{V}.$$

$$R(x) =_{\text{def}} \{r(x) | r \in R\} \text{ if } R \subseteq S[x:A] \text{ for some } S \subseteq \mathcal{R} \text{ and } A \subseteq \mathcal{V}.$$

LEMMA 3.8.2   Under the conditions stated above, the sets $R - x$ and $R[x:A]$ are subsets of $\mathscr{R}$, and the sets $R(x)$ are subsets of $\mathscr{V}$.

Proof

(1) If $R \subseteq \mathscr{R}$, then $R - x = \{r - x | r \in R\} \subseteq \mathscr{R}$, by 3.8.1.

(2) If $R \subseteq \mathscr{R} - x$, then R is a set of functions $r \in L \rightarrow_{\text{fin}} \mathscr{V}$ with $x \notin dom(r)$. Hence for any $A \subseteq \mathscr{V}$, $R[x:A] = \{r[x = a] | r \in R, a \in A\} \subseteq \mathscr{R}$, by 3.8.1.

(3) If $R \subseteq S[x:A]$, then for any $r \in R$, $r \in S[x:A] = \{s[x = a] | s \in S, a \in A\}$; so that $r(x) \in A$. Hence $R(x) = \{r(x) | r \in R\} \subseteq A \subseteq \mathscr{V}$. ∎

3.8.4   Interpretation of Judgments   An *assignment* ρ is a partial map from type variables to subsets of $\mathscr{V}$, and from ordinary variables to elements of $\mathscr{V}$. We say that an assignment ρ *satisfies* an environment E if the following conditions are satisfied:

If X in E, then $\rho(X) \subseteq \mathscr{V}$

If $X <: A$ in E, then $\rho(X) \subseteq A_\rho \subseteq \mathscr{V}$

If $x:A$ in E, then $\rho(x) \in A_\rho \subseteq \mathscr{V}$

where A_ρ is the type defined by A under the assignment ρ. Similarly, we indicate by a_ρ the value of a term a under an assignment ρ for its free variables.

The judgments of our system are interpreted as follows.

$\vdash E \; env \approx$ for every initial segment E', $X <: A$ or E', $x:A$ of E, if ρ satisfies E' then $A_\rho \subseteq \mathscr{V}$.

$E \vdash A \; type \approx A_\rho \subseteq \mathscr{V}$, for every ρ satisfying E.

$E \vdash A <: B \approx A_\rho \subseteq B_\rho \subseteq \mathscr{V}$, for every ρ satisfying E.

$E \vdash A \leftrightarrow B \approx A_\rho = B_\rho \subseteq \mathscr{V}$, for every ρ satisfying E.

$E \vdash a:A \approx a_\rho \in A_\rho \subseteq \mathscr{V}$, for every ρ satisfying E.

$E \vdash a \leftrightarrow b:A \approx a_\rho = b_\rho \in A_\rho \subseteq \mathscr{V}$, for every ρ satisfying E.

Type and value expressions are interpreted using:

$\langle\!\langle \; \rangle\!\rangle \approx \mathscr{R}$

$R \backslash x \approx R - x$

$\langle\!\langle R | x:A \rangle\!\rangle \approx R[x:A]$

$$R \cdot x \approx R(x)$$

$$\langle \, \rangle \approx \varnothing$$

$$r \backslash x \approx r - x$$

$$\langle r | x = a \rangle \approx r[x = a]$$

$$r \cdot x \approx r(x).$$

3.8.5 Soundness   Finally, we can show that this semantics satisfies the type rules. More precisely, we consider the system *S1* consisting of all the rules listed in section 3.7, except for the special rules (vc1b) and (TE9)

THEOREM 3.8.3 (soundness)   The inference rules of system *S1* are sound with respect to the interpretation of judgments given in this section.

Proof   See appendix.   ■

3.9   A Construction Giving $R = \langle\!\langle R \backslash x | x : R \cdot x \rangle\!\rangle$

The type equivalence rule below seems very natural semantically. It also simplifies the types associated with the override operation, and has application to extensional models studied in the next section.

$$\frac{E \vdash R <: \langle\!\langle S | x : A \rangle\!\rangle <: \langle \, \rangle}{E \vdash R \leftrightarrow \langle\!\langle R \backslash x | x : R \cdot x \rangle\!\rangle} . \tag{TE9}$$

In the simple model described in section 3.8, it is easy to see that if $R \subseteq \langle\!\langle x : A \rangle\!\rangle$, then, as required by (s6):

$$R \subseteq \langle\!\langle R \backslash x x : R \cdot x \rangle\!\rangle.$$

The reason is that every record r in R has an x component $r(x) \in R(x)$, and remaining components $r - x$ in $R - x$. However, it is not necessarily true that every combination of $r - x$ from $R - x$ and $r(x)$ from $R(x)$ occur together in a single record in R. For example, the set of records:

$$R = \{\langle x = 1, y = true \rangle, \langle x = 0, y = false \rangle\}$$

is clearly a subset of $\langle\!\langle x : Int \rangle\!\rangle$. However, $R \neq \langle\!\langle R \backslash x | x : R \cdot x \rangle\!\rangle$ since the records $\langle x = 1, y = false \rangle$ and $\langle x = 0, y = true \rangle$ do not appear in R. In category-theoretic terms, the equation $R = \langle\!\langle R \backslash x | x : R \cdot x \rangle\!\rangle$ says that R is the product of $R \backslash x$ and $R \cdot x$.

In this section we present a variant of the construction of section 3.8 in which rule (TE9) is sound. Since we are ultimately interested in polymorphism and bounded quantification, we construct a model with $R = \langle\!\langle R \backslash x | x : R . x \rangle\!\rangle$ for every semantic type R with $R . x$ defined. The construction uses the same collection of values as before, but allows only certain subsets of $\mathscr{V}$ as types. In this way we eliminate sets of records which violate (TE9).

We use a value space satisfying:

$$\mathscr{R} = (L \rightarrow_{\text{fin}} \mathscr{V}) \subseteq \mathscr{V}$$

constructed as in section 3.8. Then for each natural number i, we define the collection $\mathscr{T}_i$ of subsets of $\mathscr{V}$ which we wish to consider types of stage i. At the first stage, we may select any subsets of $\mathscr{V}$, provided we include the given ground types $\mathscr{G}_j$. For definiteness, let us take:

$$\mathscr{T}_0 = \{\mathscr{G}_1, \mathscr{G}_2, \ldots\}.$$

We now define record types over preceding types. At each stage we take all record types defined by a finite set of labeled component types, and a finite set of absent labels. Each component type must belong to the preceding stage.

This construction may be clarified using an auxiliary definition. Suppose $P : L \rightarrow_{\text{fin}} \mathscr{T}_i$ is a finite partial function from labels to types at stage i, and $N \subseteq_{\text{fin}} L$ is a finite set of labels disjoint from the domain of P. Then the set $\mathscr{R}^{P,N}$ of records with components present according to P and components absent according to N is defined by:

$$\mathscr{R}^{P,N} = \{r \in \mathscr{R} | \forall x \in L . (P(x) \downarrow \supset r(x) \in P(x)) \wedge (x \in N \supset r(x) \uparrow)\}.$$

We define the set of record types at stage $i + 1$ to be the set of all $\mathscr{R}^{P,N}$ for suitable 'present' function P and 'absent' set N:

$$\mathscr{T}_{i+1} = \{\mathscr{R}^{P,N} | P : L \rightarrow_{\text{fin}} \mathscr{T}_i \wedge N \subseteq_{\text{fin}} L \wedge dom(P) \cap N = \varnothing\} \cup \mathscr{T}_i.$$

Note that $\mathscr{R} = \mathscr{R}^{\varnothing, \varnothing}$ belongs to every $\mathscr{T}_{i+1}$.

The collection $\mathscr{T}$ of all types is defined by:

$$\mathscr{T} = \bigcup_{i < \omega} \mathscr{T}_i.$$

As we have defined $\mathscr{T}$, the set $\mathscr{V}$ of all values is not a type. However, it is possible to include $\mathscr{V}$ in $\mathscr{T}_0$ if desired.

It is natural to consider any set of records $\mathscr{R}^{P,N}$ with $P : L \rightarrow_{\text{fin}} \mathscr{T}$ and $N \subseteq_{\text{fin}} L$, as a 'record type' over $\mathscr{V}$. Define $\mathscr{RT}$ to be the collection of all record types:

$$\mathscr{RT} =_{\text{def}} \{\mathscr{R}^{P,N} | P : L \rightarrow_{\text{fin}} \mathscr{T}, N \subseteq_{\text{fin}} L, \quad \text{and} \quad dom(P) \cap N = \varnothing\}.$$

Note that $\mathscr{R}^{\varnothing,\,\varnothing} = \bigcup \mathscr{R}\mathscr{T}$, so $\mathscr{R}\mathscr{T}$ has a maximal element. We may show that $\mathscr{T}$ is precisely the union of $\mathscr{T}_0$ and the record types over $\mathscr{V}$; that is $\mathscr{T} = \mathscr{T}_0 \cup \mathscr{R}\mathscr{T}$.

LEMMA 3.9.1 If $P: L \rightarrow_{\text{fin}} \mathscr{T}$ and $N \subseteq_{\text{fin}} L$ with $dom(P) \cap N = \varnothing$, then $\mathscr{R}^{P,\,N} \in \mathscr{T}$. That is, $\mathscr{R}\mathscr{T} \subseteq \mathscr{T}$.

Proof Suppose $P: L \rightarrow_{\text{fin}} \mathscr{T}$ and $N \subseteq_{\text{fin}} L$. Since the domain of P is finite, there is some i with $P: L \rightarrow_{\text{fin}} \mathscr{T}_i$. Hence, $\mathscr{R}^{P,\,N} \in \mathscr{T}_{i+1} \subseteq \mathscr{T}$. ∎

In this model we will interpret all judgments as before, except that type variables and type expressions must denote elements of $\mathscr{T}$. Since we consider only elements of $\mathscr{T}$ as types, we define the relation $A \subseteq B$ (*A semantic subtype of B*) as:

$$A \subseteq: B \quad \text{iff} \quad A \subseteq B \quad \text{and} \quad A, B \in \mathscr{T}.$$

By the simplifying assumption in section 3.9 that no ground type contains records, we know that every subtype of $\mathscr{R}$ will be an element of $\mathscr{R}\mathscr{T}$. If we had not made this assumption, then we might have some subtype of $\mathscr{R}$ which 'accidentally' could cause (TE9) to fail.

We may show that for any non-empty $R \in \mathscr{R}\mathscr{T}$, a function P and set N with $R = \mathscr{R}^{P,\,N}$ are determined uniquely.

LEMMA 3.9.2 Let $R \in \mathscr{R}\mathscr{T}$ be non-empty. Then $R = \mathscr{R}^{P,\,N}$ where:

$$dom(P) = \{x \in L \,|\, \forall r \in R \,.\, r(x) \downarrow\},$$

$$N = \{x \in L \,|\, \forall r \in R \,.\, r(x) \uparrow\}, \quad \text{and}$$

$$P(x) = R(x) \quad \text{for all} \quad x \in dom(P).$$

Proof Suppose $R \in \mathscr{R}\mathscr{T}$ is non-empty and let $r_0 \in R$.
We know that $R = \mathscr{R}^{P,\,N}$ for some P, N.

(1) By construction of $\mathscr{R}^{P,\,N}$ we have $\forall r \in R \,.\, dom(P) \subseteq dom(r)$. Moreover, if $\forall r \in R \,.\, r(x) \downarrow$, then $x \in dom(P)$, since $x \notin dom(P)$ implies $r_0 - x \in R$ and $(r_0 - x)(x) \uparrow$. Consider the function f defined by:

$$f(x) = r_0(x) \quad \text{if} \quad \forall r \in R \,.\, r(x) \downarrow, \quad \text{and} \uparrow \text{otherwise}.$$

This function belongs to R, and $dom(f) = \{x \in L \,|\, \forall r \in R \,.\, r(x) \downarrow\} \subseteq dom(P)$. Hence $dom(P) = dom(f) = \{x \in L \,|\, \forall r \in R \,.\, r(x) \downarrow\}$.

(2) By construction of $\mathscr{R}^{P,\,N}$ we have $\forall r \in R \,.\, N \subseteq \uparrow(r) =_{\text{def}} \{x \in L \,|\, r(x) \uparrow\}$. Moreover, if $\forall r \in R \,.\, r(x) \uparrow$, then $x \in N$ (since $x \notin N$ implies either $r_0(x) \downarrow$ or $(r_0[x = a])(x) \downarrow$ for an appropriately chosen $r_0[x = a] \in R$). Choose r_x from $R_x =_{\text{def}} \{r \in R \,|\, r(x) \downarrow\}$ whenever

$R_x \neq \varnothing$, and define:

$g(x) = \uparrow$ if $\forall r \in R \, . \, r(x) \uparrow$, and $r_x(x)$ otherwise.

This function belongs to R and $\uparrow(g) = \{x \in L | \forall r \in R \, . \, r(x) \uparrow\} \subseteq N$. Hence, $N = \uparrow(g) = \{x \in L | \forall r \in R \, . \, r(x) \uparrow\}$.

(3) Assume $x \in dom(P)$.

$$R(x) = \mathscr{R}^{P,N}(x) = \{r(x) | r \in \mathscr{R}, \forall y \in L \, . \, r(y) \in P(y)\} \quad (\text{since } x \notin N)$$

$$= \{r(x) | r \in \mathscr{R}, r(x) \in P(x)\} = \{a \in \mathscr{V} | a \in P(x)\} = P(x). \quad \blacksquare$$

This allows us to write each non-empty record type $R \in \mathscr{R}\mathscr{T}$ as $\mathscr{R}^{P,N}$ without ambiguity. The lemma also demonstrates that whenever $R(x)$ is defined, $R(x) = \mathscr{R}^{P,N}(x) = P(x) \in \mathscr{T}$ is a type.

It is now straightforward to show that the record types are closed under restriction $(R - x)$ and extension $(R[x:B])$:

LEMMA 3.9.3   If $R = \mathscr{R}^{P,N}$ is any record type, then $R - x = \mathscr{R}^{P',N'}$, where

$P' = P - \{\langle x \mapsto P(x)\rangle\}$ if $P(x) \downarrow$, and P otherwise.

$N' = N \cup \{x\}$.

Proof   Straightforward. $\blacksquare$

LEMMA 3.9.4   If $R = \mathscr{R}^{P,N}$ with $x \in N$, and $B \in \mathscr{T}$, then $R[x:B] = \mathscr{R}^{P',N'}$, with:

$P' = P \cup \{\langle x \mapsto B\rangle\}$

$N' = N - \{x\}$.

Proof   By definition, $R[x:B] = \{r[x = b] | r \in R, b \in B\}$. It is easy to check that every $r[x = b]$ belongs to $\mathscr{R}^{P',N'}$ and conversely. $\blacksquare$

The semantic subtyping relation on record types $R \subseteq: R'$ is now determined by the present and absent information.

LEMMA 3.9.5

$\mathscr{R}^{P,N} \subseteq: \mathscr{R}^{P',N'}$ iff

$\forall x \in dom(P') \, . \, P(x) \downarrow \wedge P(x) \subseteq: P'(x)$

$N' \subseteq N$.

Proof Assume $\mathscr{R}^{P,N} \subseteq: \mathscr{R}^{P',N'}$. It is easy to check that $N' \subseteq N$ by the definition of $\mathscr{R}^{P,N}$. Similarly, if $P'(x)\downarrow$ then we must have $P(x)\downarrow \wedge P(x) \subseteq P'(x)$. By definition $P(x)$ and $P'(x)$ are types. The converse is straightforward. ∎

Since the point of this model construction is to give $R = (R - x)[x:R(x)]$ for every record type R with $R(x)\downarrow$, we must also prove this equation. Given the preceding lemmas, the proof is almost immediate.

LEMMA 3.9.6 Let $R \in \mathscr{R}\mathscr{T}$ be a record type with $r(x)\downarrow$ for all $r \in R$. Then $R = (R - x)[x:R(x)]$.

Proof We know $R = \mathscr{R}^{P,N}$ for some finite function P and finite set N. By preceding lemmas, we also have:

$$R - x = \mathscr{R}^{P',N'}$$

$$(R - x)[x:R(x)] = \mathscr{R}^{P'',N''}$$

with $P' = P - \{\langle x \mapsto R(x)\rangle\}$, $N' = N \cup \{x\}$ and $P'' = P' \cup \{\langle x \mapsto R(x)\rangle\}$, $N'' = N' - \{x\}$.

Since $P'' = P$ and $N'' = N$, it follows that $R = (R - x)[x:R(x)]$. ∎

Finally, we have the soundness theorem. System *S2* is system *S1* of theorem 3.8.3 plus the rule (RE9).

THEOREM 3.9.7 (soundness) The inference rules of system *S2* are sound with respect to the interpretation of judgments given above.

Proof See appendix. ∎

3.10 An Extensional Model Construction

The following inference rule gives us an extensional equality between records:

$$\frac{E \vdash r:\langle\rangle \qquad E \vdash s:\langle\rangle}{E \vdash r \leftrightarrow s:\langle\rangle}. \tag{vc1b}$$

The intuitive reason for adopting this rule is that if r and s both belong to $\langle\rangle$, then r and s are indistinguishable. In fact, assume r and s differ at some label x. We cannot use $r.x$ or $s.x$ to distinguish them since neither is well-typed; if we use $r\backslash x$ or $s\backslash x$ then we simply remove the difference.

In addition to giving us more equations between records of type $\langle\rangle$, rule (vc1b) implies the following extensionality property: for any $r, s:\langle x_1:A_1,\ldots,x_k:A_k\rangle$, we have $r \leftrightarrow s : \langle x_1 : A_1, \ldots, x_k : A_k \rangle$ iff $r . x_i \leftrightarrow s . x_i : A_i$ for $i = 1 \ldots k$. The straightforward proof of this uses $r \backslash x_1 \ldots x_k \leftrightarrow s \backslash x_1 \ldots x_k : \langle \, \rangle$ and the value congruence rules.

Recall that in the previous models a record type was simply a set of records, and equality of records was independent of the type. Therefore, any two distinct records would be unequal to elements of $\langle \, \rangle$, causing (vc1b) to fail.

In this section, we will construct a model of the pure record calculus satisfying (TE9) and (vc1b). It will be clear from the construction that (TE9) is essential; we do not know how to construct an extensional model satisfying (vc1b) without requiring that record types satisfy $R = \langle R \backslash x | x : R . x \rangle$. The main use of (TE9) lies in showing that if R is a record type with extensional equality, then both $R - x$ and $R(x)$, then defined, are extensional record types.

We begin with a value space $\mathscr{V}$ satisfying:

$$\mathscr{R} = (L \rightarrow_{\text{fin}} \mathscr{V}) \subseteq \mathscr{V}$$

constructed as in section 3.8, and define types as certain *partial equivalence relations* (abbreviated *PER*'s) over $\mathscr{V}$ (see Longo and Moggi, 1988). A PER is a binary relation which is symmetric and transitive, but not necessarily reflexive. An element of a type is defined as an equivalence class of values in the PER.

Subtyping is based on set containment of partial equivalence relations, as in Bruce and Longo (1988), except that we consider only certain PER's as types.

The type of all records $\langle \, \rangle$ is interpreted by the PER $\mathscr{R} \times \mathscr{R}$. This type has only one element since there is a single equivalence class in $\mathscr{R} \times \mathscr{R}$: while $\langle \, \rangle$ contains all records, all records are equivalent in $\langle \, \rangle$ (hence (vc1b) holds).

The three operations on record types are defined as follows:

- If R is a PER on $\mathscr{R}$ with $r(x)\uparrow$ for every record rRr, and A is a PER on $\mathscr{V}$, then $R[x : A]$ is the relation on $\mathscr{R}$ given by:

$$r \, R[x : A] \, s \quad \text{iff} \quad r - x \, R \, s - x \quad \text{and} \quad r(x) \, A \, s(x).$$

In writing $r(x) \, A \, s(x)$ we imply that $r(x)\downarrow$ and $s(x)\downarrow$.

- If R is a PER on $\mathscr{R}$, we define the relation $R - x$ by:

$$R - x =_{\text{def}} \{ \langle r - x, s - x \rangle | rRs \}.$$

- If R is a PER on $\mathscr{R}$, with $r(x)\downarrow$ whenever rRr, we define the relation $R(x)$ by:

$$R(x) =_{\text{def}} \{ \langle r(x), s(x) \rangle | rRs \}.$$

It is easy to show that under the hypotheses above, $R[x : A]$ is a partial equivalence relation on $\mathscr{R}$. However, $R - x$ and $R(x)$ are not necessarily transitive. This will not cause any problems, as it turns out, since by restricting the class of record types to some collection satisfying (TE9), $R - x$ and $R(x)$ are guaranteed to be types (and hence PER's).

The types over $\mathscr{V}$ will be defined in stages, as before. We begin with some collection:

$$\mathscr{T}_0 = \{\mathscr{E}_1, \mathscr{E}_2, \ldots\}$$

of partial equivalence relations over $\mathscr{V}$ that do not relate any records to themselves. A typical choice would be to begin with the identity relations on the ground types $\mathscr{G}_1$, $\mathscr{G}_2, \ldots$.

Given any finite partial map P from L to PER's over $\mathscr{V}$ and a set $N \subseteq_{\text{fin}} L$ disjoint from the domain of P, we define the PER $\mathscr{R}^{P,N}$ over $\mathscr{R}$ by:

$$r\mathscr{R}^{P,N}s \quad \text{iff} \quad \forall x \in L.(P(x)\downarrow \supset r(x)P(x)s(x)) \wedge (x \in N \supset r(x)\uparrow \wedge s(x)\uparrow).$$

Note that similarity to $\mathscr{R}^{P,N}$ for subsets of $\mathscr{V}$; if we represent a subset $S \subseteq \mathscr{V}$ by the PER $(S \times S) \subseteq (\mathscr{V} \times \mathscr{V})$, the two definitions coincide. It is easy to see that if each $P(x)$ is a PER, then so is $\mathscr{R}^{P,N}$.

Following the earlier definition of record types in stages, we define:

$$\mathscr{T}_{i+1} = \{\mathscr{R}^{P,N} | P : L \rightarrow_{\text{fin}} \mathscr{T}_i \wedge N \subseteq_{\text{fin}} L \wedge dom(P) \cap N = \varnothing\} \cup \mathscr{T}_i$$

and let:

$$\mathscr{T} = \bigcup_{i<\omega} \mathscr{T}_i.$$

This construction has much the same character as the previous non-extensional one, although we have the added complication of establishing that $R - x$ and $R(x)$ (when defined) are PER's whenever $R \in \mathscr{T}$. Since every $R \in \mathscr{T}$ is easily seen to be a PER, we will do this by showing $R - x \in \mathscr{T}$ and $R(x) \in \mathscr{T}$.

It is easy to prove lemma 3.9.1 for this model, showing that we need not consider stages of the construction in later arguments.

LEMMA 3.10.1   If $P : L \rightarrow_{\text{fin}} \mathscr{T}$ and $N \subseteq_{\text{fin}} L$ with $dom(P) \cap N = \varnothing$, then $\mathscr{R}^{P,N} \in \mathscr{T}$. Define the collection of all record types by $\mathscr{R}\mathscr{T} = \{\mathscr{R}^{P,N}\}$.

Subtyping is interpreted as before, with:

$$A \subseteq: B \quad \text{iff} \quad A \subseteq B \quad \text{and} \quad A, B \in \mathscr{T}.$$

We now use present functions and absent sets to show that for every $R \in \mathscr{R}\mathscr{T}$, we have $R - x \in \mathscr{T}$ and $R(x) \in \mathscr{T}$ if $r(x)\downarrow$ for every rRr.

LEMMA 3.10.2   If $R \in \mathscr{R}\mathscr{T}$, then $R - x \in \mathscr{T}$. If $R \in \mathscr{R}\mathscr{T}$ with $r(x) \downarrow$ whenever rRr, then $R(x) \in \mathscr{T}$.

Proof   The lemma is trivial if $R = \varnothing$, hence we assume $R \neq \varnothing$.

(1) Let $R = \mathscr{R}^{P,N}$. Then $R - x = \mathscr{R}^{P',N'}$ with $P' = P - \{\langle x \mapsto P(x)\rangle\}$ and $N' = N \cup \{x\}$. To see this, suppose $r\, R - x\, s$. Then there must be records $r', s' \in \mathscr{R}$ with $r'Rs'$ and $r = r' - x, s = s' - x$. Since $P'(y) \downarrow \,\supset r(y)P(y)s(y)$ and $y \in N' \supset r(y)\uparrow \wedge\, s(y)\uparrow$, it follows that $r\mathscr{R}^{P',N'}s$.

To show the converse, we assume $r\mathscr{R}^{P',N'}s$ and note that since $R \neq \varnothing$, there must be some $b \in \mathscr{V}$ with $bP(x)b$. It is easy to see that $r[x = b]\, R\, s[x = b]$, and so $r\, R - x\, s$.

(2) We now assume $r(x) \downarrow$ whenever rRr. Since $R = \mathscr{R}^{P,N}$, we have $P(x) \in \mathscr{T}$. It remains to show that $R(x) = P(x)$. If $aR(x)b$, then there exist r and s with rRs and $a = r(x), b = s(x)$. By definition of $\mathscr{R}^{P,N}$ it follows that $aP(x)b$.

For the converse, we assume $aP(x)b$; since $R \neq \varnothing$, there exist r and s with $r\mathscr{R}^{P,N}s$ and $r(x) = a, s(x) = b$. Hence $aR(x)b$.   ■

LEMMA 3.10.3   If $R \in \mathscr{R}\mathscr{T}$ with $r(x)\uparrow$ whenever rRr, and $B \in \mathscr{T}$, then $R[x:B] \in \mathscr{T}$.

Proof   The lemma is trivial if $R = \varnothing$. Otherwise, we let $R = \mathscr{R}^{P,N}$ and show that $R[x:B] = \mathscr{R}^{P',N'}$ with $P' = P \cup \{\langle x \mapsto B\rangle\}$ and $N' = N - \{x\}$.

This is straightforward.   ■

It is now an easy matter to show analogs of lemma 3.9.2 and lemma 3.9.6. These conclude the basic properties of the construction. System *S3* is system *S1* of theorem 3.8.3 plus the rules (TE9) and (VC1b).

THEOREM 3.10.4 (soundness)   The inference rules of system *S3* are sound for the PER model construction.

Proof   See appendix.   ■

3.11   The Update Operator

Extensional models are useful to characterize a natural form of record update, here denoted by $r.x:-a$ for functional update. The discussion is also relevant to the typing of imperative update, $r.x := a$, although our models do not directly capture side-effects.

The functional update operator cannot be introduced by a simple definition. We want:

$$r.x:-a =_{\text{def}} \langle r\backslash x | x = a\rangle$$

but only provided that $r.x$ exists, and that $r.x:-a$ does not modify the type of the x field. Sufficient assumptions are that $r:R <:\langle\,\rangle$ and $a:R.x$; then we can derive the following typing:

(E1) $\dfrac{E \vdash r:R <:\langle\,\rangle}{E \vdash r\backslash x:R\backslash x} \qquad E \vdash a:R.x$

(I1) $\dfrac{}{E \vdash \langle r\backslash x | x = a \rangle : \langle\!\langle R\backslash x | x:R.x \rangle\!\rangle}$

(DEF) $E \vdash r.x:-a:\langle\!\langle R\backslash x | x:R.x \rangle\!\rangle.$

This is not quite satisfactory, because we would expect the result type to be R, meaning that the type of a record is not modified by updating one of its fields (with a value of the correct type).

Fortunately, by using (TE9) ($\langle\!\langle R\backslash x | x:R.x \rangle\!\rangle \leftrightarrow R$) we can derive the expected type rule:

$$\frac{E \vdash r:R <:\langle\,\rangle \qquad E \vdash a:R.x}{E \vdash r.x:-a:R}. \tag{UPD}$$

This seems to be a compelling reason for adopting (TE9), because of its impact on such an important operator as updating.

Note that the (UPD) rule is very strong; it applies even when R is a variable. From it we can derive a perhaps more natural but less general rule:

$$\frac{E \vdash r:\langle\!\langle R | x:A \rangle\!\rangle <:\langle\,\rangle \qquad E \vdash a:A}{E \vdash r.x:-a:\langle\!\langle R | x:A \rangle\!\rangle}. \tag{UPD$'$}$$

Remark Here we might be tempted to weaken the assumption to $E \vdash a:A' <:A$, and strength the conclusion to $E \vdash r.x:-a:\langle\!\langle R | x:A' \rangle\!\rangle$. This is valid but undesirable, since we might then be unable to update the x field again with its original contents.

The strong (UPD) rule would not be expressible without $R.x$ types; the following apparently natural variation is unsound:

$$\frac{E \vdash r:R <:\langle\!\langle S | x:A \rangle\!\rangle \qquad E \vdash a:A}{E \vdash r.x:-a:R}.$$

For example, take $A = Bool$, $R = \langle\!\langle x:True \rangle\!\rangle$, and $r = \langle x = true \rangle$; then from $r.x:Bool$ and $false:Bool$ we can derive $r.x:-false:\langle\!\langle x:True \rangle\!\rangle$.

3.12 Normalization and Decidability

Even though the basic ideas behind the record calculus are relatively simple, the formal system has quite a few rules. As a consequence, it is not easy to see, by inspection, how we could determine whether a supposed type A is well-formed, or whether a record expression has type R.

In this section, we show that all of the basic properties of the calculus are decidable, using relatively natural algorithms. In the process, we show that every type expression has a unique normal form (modulo permuting the order of fields) and every typable record expression has a *principal type* in each suitable environment.

The first properties we consider are deciding whether a supposed environment E in well-formed and whether a given A is a well-formed type expression in E. A quick glance at the formation rules shows that in order to determine whether a type is well-formed we must be able to decide the following apparently simple properties; assuming $E \vdash R\ type$ is derivable, we want to know whether $E \vdash R <: \langle\!\langle\ \rangle\!\rangle \backslash x$ and whether there exist S and A such that $E \vdash R <: \langle\!\langle S | x : A \rangle\!\rangle$. Therefore, we consider these first. Once we develop a simple method for these, it is easy to check whether a type or environment is well-formed.

For each drivable $E \vdash R\ type$, we define a labeled tree $Tree(E \vdash R\ type)$ with:

edges: labeled by field names

vertices: labeled by finite sets of field names.

If v is a vertex in $Tree(E \vdash R\ type)$, we call the finite set of field names at v the *absent set at v*.

Intuitively, if $p = x_1 x_2 \ldots x_k$ is a path from the root of $Tree(E \vdash R\ type)$ and $N = \{y_1, y_2, \ldots, y_l\}$ is the absent set of the vertex designated by this path, then:

$$E \vdash (..(R.x_1).x_1\ldots).x_k\ type$$

$$E \vdash (..(R.x_1).x_2\ldots).x_k <: \langle\!\langle\ \rangle\!\rangle \backslash y_1 y_2 \ldots y_l.$$

A convenient notational shorthand is to write $R.p$ for $(..(R.x_1).x_2\ldots).x_k$, where p is the path $p = x_1 x_2 \ldots x_k$. If $p = \varepsilon$ is the empty path, then we may write $R.\varepsilon$ for R. If e is an edge leading from the root of a tree to the root of some subtree, we call e a *root edge*.

We define $Tree(E \vdash R\ type)$ by induction on the length of E. If E has length 0 then R must be the type constant $\langle\!\langle\ \rangle\!\rangle$. In this case, we define:

$Tree(\varnothing \vdash \langle\!\langle\ \rangle\!\rangle\ type) =$ single node with empty absent set.

For context $E = E', X <: A$ we use induction on the form of type expressions:

$Tree(E \vdash Y\ type) = Tree(E' \vdash Y\ type)$ for $Y \neq X$.

$Tree(E \vdash X\ type) = Tree(E' \vdash A\ type)$.

$Tree(E \vdash \langle\!\langle S | x : B \rangle\!\rangle \ type)$ is obtained from $T = Tree(E \vdash S \ type)$ and $T' = Tree(E \vdash B \ type)$ by making T' a subtree of the root of T along a root edge labeled x, and removing x from the absent set of the root of T (if there).

$Tree(E \vdash S \backslash x \ type)$ is obtained from $Tree(E \vdash S \ type)$ by deleting the subtree along the root edge labeled x (if there), and adding x to the absent set of the root.

$Tree(E \vdash S . x \ type)$ is the subtree of $Tree(E \vdash S \ type)$ located along the root edge labeled x.

For context $E = E', X$ the definition of $Tree(E \vdash R \ type)$ is the same as above, except for the following case:

$Tree(E, X \vdash X \ type)$ = empty tree.

For context $E = E', x : A$ we let:

$Tree(E \vdash R \ type) = Tree(E' \vdash R \ type)$.

This concludes the definition.

In the clauses defining $Tree(E \vdash \langle\!\langle S | x : B \rangle\!\rangle \ type)$ and $Tree(E \vdash S . x \ type)$, we have assumed certain properties of $Tree(E \vdash S \ type)$. These are justified by the following lemma.

LEMMA 3.12.1   Suppose $E \vdash R \ type$ and let $T = Tree(E \vdash R \ type)$.

(1) If p is a path in T, then $E \vdash R . p \ type$.

(2) If x is in the absent set of T at position p, then $E \vdash R . p <: \langle\!\langle \ \rangle\!\rangle \backslash x$.

Proof   Induction on the derivation of T.

Case $\varnothing \vdash \langle\!\langle \ \rangle\!\rangle \ type$. Trivial.

Cases $E', X <: A \vdash Y \ type$ and $E', X \vdash Y \ type$ with $Y \neq X$. By induction hypothesis and the property that if $E \vdash J$ for any judgment J, and $E, E' \ env$, then $E, E' \vdash J$.

Case $E', X <: A \vdash X \ type$. By the induction hypothesis $E' \vdash A . p \ type$ and $E' \vdash A . p <: \langle\!\langle \ \rangle\!\rangle \backslash x$. The conclusion follows by repeated use of (F4) and (s6), and transitivity of $<:$.

Case $E', X \vdash X \ type$. Vacuous.

Cases $E', X <: A \vdash \langle\!\langle S | y : B \rangle\!\rangle \ type$ and $E', X \vdash \langle\!\langle S | y : B \rangle\!\rangle \ type$.

Case $p = \varepsilon$. (1) is trivial. (2) by ind. hyp. $E \vdash S <: \langle\!\langle \ \rangle\!\rangle \backslash x$ for x in the absent set of $T(x \neq y)$. Hence, $E \vdash \langle\!\langle S | y : B \rangle\!\rangle <: \langle\!\langle \ \rangle\!\rangle \backslash x$.

Case $p = yp'$. Use (TE7) and ind. hyp. for $E \vdash B$ *type*.

Otherwise. Use (TE8) and ind. hyp. for $E \vdash R$ *type*.

Case $E', X <: A \vdash S \backslash y$ *type* and $E', X \vdash S \backslash y$ *type*.

Case $p = \varepsilon$. Two subcases:

Case $x = y$. Since $E \vdash S \backslash y$ *type* must follow from (F3), we must have $E \vdash S <: \langle\!\langle \rangle\!\rangle$. The result follows by (S4).

Case $x \neq y$. Then x must be in the absent set for $Tree(E \vdash S\ type)$ and so $E \vdash S <: \langle\!\langle \rangle\!\rangle \backslash x$. By (S4), $E \vdash S \backslash y <: \langle\!\langle \rangle\!\rangle \backslash xy$, and we know that $\langle\!\langle \rangle\!\rangle \backslash xy <: \langle\!\langle \rangle\!\rangle \backslash x$.

Case $p \neq \varepsilon$. Then p must be a path in $Tree(E \vdash S\ type)$ not beginning with y. It follows from the ind. hyp. that $E \vdash S <: \langle\!\langle T|z : A \rangle\!\rangle$ for $z \neq y$ the first symbol of p. By (TE4), we have $E \vdash S . z \leftrightarrow S \backslash y . z$, and the lemma follows by the congruence rules.

Cases $E', X <: A \vdash S . y$ *type* and $E', X \vdash S . y$ *type*. Straightforward from ind. hyp.

Case $E', x : A \vdash R$ *type*. By ind. hyp. ∎

The preceding lemma shows that the path and absent information provided by $Tree(E \vdash R\ type)$ is 'sound' with respect to the proof rules of the calculus. Since the proof rules are sound with respect to our semantics, it follows that the assertions of the form $E \vdash R <: \langle\!\langle \rangle\!\rangle \backslash x$ and $\exists S, A . E \vdash R <: \langle\!\langle S|x : A \rangle\!\rangle$ determined from $Tree(E \vdash R\ type)$ are semantically sound.

We may also show that the assertions are semantically complete. It follows from the preceding lemma that the proof rules are also semantically complete for deducing assertions of the form: (1) $E \vdash R <: \langle\!\langle \rangle\!\rangle \backslash x$, and (2) if there exists S and A with $R <: \langle\!\langle S|x : A \rangle\!\rangle$ in every assignment satisfying E, then $E \vdash R <: \langle\!\langle S'|x : A' \rangle\!\rangle$ for some S' and A'.

LEMMA 3.12.2   Suppose $E \vdash R$ *type* and let $T = Tree(E \vdash R\ type)$.

There is a semantic model $\mathcal{M}$ and assignment ρ such that:

(1) If p is a sequence of labels which is not a path in T, then there is some record r *in* R_ρ with $r . p$ undefined.

(2) If p is a path in T with x absent from every record in $(R . p)_\rho$, then x is in the absent set of T at the vertex located at p.

Proof   We may use the model constructed in section 3.8 using a single ground type $\mathcal{G} = \mathbf{N}$, for example. For each environment E, we define an assignment ρ_E such that whenever $E \vdash R$ *type*, there is some $r \in R$ with $r . p \downarrow$ iff p is a path in $Tree(E \vdash R\ type)$. (This is straightforward.) It is easy to verify that for any vertex v in any $Tree(E \vdash R\ type)$, if x is in the absent set at v, then there is no child along any edge labeled x.

This and (1) imply part (2) of the lemma. ∎

By constructing trees of absent sets, it is relatively easy to decide whether a purported environment or type expression is well-formed. The basic idea is simply to check whether $\vdash E$ *env* or $E \vdash R$ *type* by reading the environment and formation rules backwards. This gives us mutually recursive procedures which rely on $Tree(E \vdash R\ type)$ in checking the hypotheses of (F2) and (F4).

THEOREM 3.12.3   Given environment E and expression A, there are mutually recursive procedures which decide whether $\vdash E$ *env* and $E \vdash A$ *type*.

The next problems to consider are, given well-formed types $E \vdash A$ *type* and $E \vdash B$ *type*, whether $E \vdash A \leftrightarrow B$ or $E \vdash A <: B$. Since type equality may be used to prove subtyping assertions, both depend on our choice of type equality rules. For definiteness, let us assume we have (TE9). Similar results seem to hold without (TE9), but we have not checked the details.

If $E \vdash R$ *type*, then it is evident that by directing type equality rules, we may rewrite R to one of the following 'normal' forms:

1. $\langle \rangle$

2. X (a type variable)

3. $((..(R_0 . x_1)...).x_i)\backslash y_1 ... y_j$ where R_0 is either $\langle \rangle$ or a type variable.

4. $\langle R_0 \backslash x_1 ... x_i | y_1 : A_1 ... y_j : A_j \rangle$ where, considering $T = Tree(E \vdash R\ type)$:

- R_0 is either $\langle \rangle$ or a type variable;

- $y_1 ... y_j$ are exactly the labels on the root edges of T;

- $\{y_1 ... y_j\} \subseteq \{x_1 ... x_i\}$;

- $\{x_1 ... x_i\} - \{y_1 ... y_j\}$ is the absent set at the root of T;

- $A_1 ... A_j$ are also in normal form.

In the semantics of section 3.9, the meaning of a type expression of form (4) is a record type $\mathscr{R}^{P,N}$, where $N = \{x_1 ... x_i\} - \{y_1 ... y_j\}$, $dom(P) = \{y_1 ... y_j\}$ and $P(y_n)$ is the meaning of A_n. Since we may construct models in which no type is empty, and assignments in which each type variable denotes a different type, we may show that two type expressions are provably and semantically equal iff they have the same normal forms, modulo differences in the order of field names and component types. By lemma 3.9.5, we may also see that, semantically:

$\langle R_0 \backslash x_1 ... x_i | y_1 : A_1 ... y_j : A_j \rangle \subseteq: \langle S_0 \backslash u_1 ... u_k | v_1 : B_1 ... v_l : B_l \rangle$ iff

- $(\{u_1 ... u_k\} - \{v_1 ... v_l\}) \subseteq (\{x_1 ... x_i\} - \{y_1 ... y_j\})$

- $\{v_1 \dots v_l\} \subseteq \{y_1 \dots y_j\}$
- if $v_m = y_n$ then $A_m \subseteq B_n$.

This property allows us to decide semantic subtyping by normalizing type expressions, comparing outer-most forms, and recursively examining corresponding component types. Since all of the steps of the algorithms correspond to derivations in the proof system, completeness of the proof rules (for type equality or subtyping assertions) follows.

THEOREM 3.12.4   Given $E \vdash A$ *type* and $E \vdash B$ *type*, there are straightforward algorithms to determine whether $E \vdash A \leftrightarrow B$ or $E \vdash A <: B$. Moreover, the proof rules are semantically complete for deducing type equality and subtype assertions.

The final algorithmic problem is, given $E \vdash R$ *type* and an expression r, determine whether $E \vdash r : R$.

Since we can decide whether one type is a subtype of another, it suffices to compute a minimal type S with $E \vdash r : S$ and check whether $E \vdash S <: R$.

However, most record expressions do not have a minimal type. This stems from the fact that for any sequence $x_1 \dots x_k$ of labels, we have $\langle \rangle : \langle\!\langle \rangle\!\rangle \backslash x_1 \dots x_k$, and we can always obtain a smaller type by adding more labels. To get around this problem, we use *type schemas* that contain sequence variables. We show that each typable record expression r has a scheme S such that every type for r is a supertype of some instance of S. This allows us to test whether a record expression has any given type. We use l, $l_1, \dots$ for sequence variables in schemas.

If S is any scheme with sequence variable l, then we say $E \vdash S$ *type* if $E \vdash S'$ *type* for every S' obtained by replacing l with a sequence of labels (including the empty sequence). If $E \vdash S$ *type*, then a useful algorithm is $MakeAbsent(x, S)$ which attempts to compute a substitution instance S' (possibly containing sequence variables) such that $E \vdash S' <: \langle\!\langle \rangle\!\rangle \backslash x$. If such an instance exists, $MakeAbsent(x, S)$ returns the smallest one. If no instance exists, the algorithm *fails*. (Algorithm $MakeAbsent$ uses an extension of $Tree(E \vdash R$ *type*) to schemas; details are straightforward and omitted.)

Using $MakeAbsent$, we may compute a *principal type schema* $PTS(E, r)$, for any well-formed environment E and expression r, as follows:

$PTS(E, \langle \rangle) = \langle\!\langle \rangle\!\rangle \backslash l$ (where l is a fresh sequence variable)

$PTS(E, x) = E(x)$

$PTS(E, r . x) = PTS(E, r) . x$ if defined, else fail

$PTS(E, r \backslash x) = PTS(E, r) \backslash x$

$PTS(E, \langle r | x = a \rangle) = \langle\!\langle MakeAbsent(x, PTS(E, r)) | x : PTS(E, a) \rangle\!\rangle.$

THEOREM 3.12.5 Given $\vdash E$ *env* and an expression r, if $E \vdash r : R$ then $PTS(E, r)$ succeeds, producing S with $E \vdash S' <: R$ for some instance S' of S. Otherwise, $PTS(E, r)$ fails. Furthermore, given $S = PTS(E, r)$ and $E \vdash R$ *type*, it is easy to compute the smallest instance S' of S such that if any instance is a subtype of R, then $E \vdash S' <: R$.

This concludes our investigation of decidability properties. We leave extensions of these properties to functions and polymorphism for further work.

4 Applications and Extensions

One might ask why we should go to the trouble of defining the subtle extension and restriction operators, instead of adopting the override operator as a primitive, as in Wand (1989). In particular, our explicit handling of negative information seems to introduce much complexity.

One answer is that negative information seems necessary to a proper understanding of the override operator. For example, the notion of *absent fields* is critical to Rémy's account of overriding in Rémy (1989). Hence, it seems worthwhile to investigate negative informaton as formalized by a separate operator.

A more pragmatic answer is that overriding really performs two different actions in different situations; it either extends a record or updates it. From a methodological point of view, a single override operator is rather undesirable because it may silently destroy information. A separate extension operator is preferable, because a type error occurs if we attempt to use it to destroy an existing field. A separate update operator is also preferable, because normally we do not want to update a field with a value of a totally different type.

Hence, in a programming language we would probably want to replace the override operator by two separate operators: one for extension, which we have, and one for updating, discussed in section 3.11. The restriction operator could still be used when we really intend to delete a field.

Admittedly, restriction is still ambiguous, because it may or may not remove a field, depending on whether the field is actually present. It is however possible to define a safe restriction operator which produces a type error if the restricted field is not present. Unfortunately, we could not find a way of completely eliminating the need for general restriction (at least on types); this operator seems necessary to express crucial well-formedness conditions.

This said, we are now ready to investigate some useful derived operators.

4.1 The Override Operator

The override operator $\langle r \leftarrow x = a \rangle =_{\text{def}} \langle r \backslash x | x = a \rangle$ is certainly very natural, in fact we have used it almost exclusively in our examples. The derived type rules for this operator, described below, are also very simple, especially if we consider the subsystem with only overriding and extraction. The rules mixing overriding with restriction are still rather interesting.

We recall the definition of the override operartor:

$$\langle r \leftarrow x = a \rangle =_{\text{def}} \langle r \backslash x | x = a \rangle$$

$$\langle\!\langle R \leftarrow x : A \rangle\!\rangle =_{\text{def}} \langle\!\langle R \backslash x | x : A \rangle\!\rangle.$$

The following rules are all simply derivable from the rules for our basic operators (we assume (TE9)); with these, extension need not be a primitive.

Formation

$$\frac{E \vdash R <: \langle\,\rangle \qquad E \vdash A \; type}{E \vdash \langle\!\langle R \leftarrow x : A \rangle\!\rangle \; type} \qquad \frac{E \vdash R <: \langle\!\langle S \leftarrow x : A \rangle\!\rangle <: \langle\,\rangle}{E \vdash R.x \; type}.$$

Subtyping

$$\frac{E \vdash R <: \langle\,\rangle \qquad E \vdash A \; type}{E \vdash \langle\!\langle R \leftarrow x : A \rangle\!\rangle <: \langle\,\rangle} \qquad \frac{E \vdash R <: S <: \langle\,\rangle \qquad E \vdash A <: B}{E \vdash \langle\!\langle R \leftarrow x : A \rangle\!\rangle <: \langle\!\langle S \leftarrow x : B \rangle\!\rangle}$$

$$\frac{E \vdash R <: \langle\!\langle S \leftarrow x : A \rangle\!\rangle <: \langle\,\rangle}{E \vdash R.x <: A} \qquad \frac{E \vdash R <: \langle\!\langle S \leftarrow x : A \rangle\!\rangle <: \langle\,\rangle}{E \vdash R <: \langle\!\langle R \leftarrow x : R.x \rangle\!\rangle}.$$

Introduction/Elimination

$$\frac{E \vdash r : R <: \langle\,\rangle \qquad E \vdash a : A}{E \vdash \langle r \leftarrow x = a \rangle : \langle\!\langle R \leftarrow x : A \rangle\!\rangle} \qquad \frac{E \vdash r : \langle\!\langle R \leftarrow x : A \rangle\!\rangle <: \langle\,\rangle}{E \vdash r.x : A}.$$

Type Congruence

$$\frac{E \vdash R \leftrightarrow S <: \langle\,\rangle \qquad E \vdash A \leftrightarrow B}{E \vdash \langle\!\langle R \leftarrow x : A \rangle\!\rangle \leftrightarrow \langle\!\langle S \leftarrow x : B \rangle\!\rangle} \qquad \frac{E \vdash R \leftrightarrow \langle\!\langle S \leftarrow x : A \rangle\!\rangle <: \langle\,\rangle}{E \vdash R.x \leftrightarrow A}.$$

Type Equivalence

$$\frac{E \vdash R <: \langle\,\rangle \qquad E \vdash A, B \; type \qquad x \neq y}{E \vdash \langle\!\langle \langle\!\langle R \leftarrow x : A \rangle\!\rangle \leftarrow y : B \rangle\!\rangle \leftrightarrow \langle\!\langle \langle\!\langle R \leftarrow y : B \rangle\!\rangle \leftarrow x : A \rangle\!\rangle}$$

$$\frac{E \vdash R <: \langle\!\langle S \leftarrow x:A \rangle\!\rangle <: \langle\!\langle \rangle\!\rangle}{E \vdash R \leftrightarrow \langle\!\langle R \leftarrow x:R.x \rangle\!\rangle}$$

$$\frac{E \vdash R <: \langle\!\langle \rangle\!\rangle \qquad E \vdash A \ type}{E \vdash \langle\!\langle R \leftarrow x:A \rangle\!\rangle \backslash x \leftrightarrow R \backslash x} \qquad \frac{E \vdash R <: \langle\!\langle \rangle\!\rangle \qquad E \vdash A \ type \qquad x \neq y}{E \vdash \langle\!\langle R \leftarrow x:A \rangle\!\rangle \backslash y \leftrightarrow \langle\!\langle R \backslash y \leftarrow x:A \rangle\!\rangle}$$

$$\frac{E \vdash R <: \langle\!\langle \rangle\!\rangle \qquad E \vdash A \ type}{E \vdash \langle\!\langle R \leftarrow x:A \rangle\!\rangle . x \leftrightarrow A}$$

$$\frac{E \vdash R <: \langle\!\langle S \leftarrow y:B \rangle\!\rangle <: \langle\!\langle \rangle\!\rangle \qquad E \vdash A \ type \qquad x \neq y}{E \vdash \langle\!\langle R \leftarrow x:A \rangle\!\rangle . y \leftrightarrow R.y} .$$

Value Congruence

$$\frac{E \vdash r \leftrightarrow s:R <: \langle\!\langle \rangle\!\rangle \qquad E \vdash a \leftrightarrow b:A}{E \vdash \langle r \leftarrow x=a \rangle \leftrightarrow \langle s \leftarrow x=b \rangle : \langle\!\langle R \leftarrow x:A \rangle\!\rangle} \qquad \frac{E \vdash r \leftrightarrow s: \langle\!\langle R \leftarrow x:A \rangle\!\rangle <: \langle\!\langle \rangle\!\rangle}{E \vdash r.x \leftrightarrow s.x:A} .$$

Value Equivalence

$$\frac{E \vdash r:R <: \langle\!\langle \rangle\!\rangle \qquad E \vdash a:A \qquad E \vdash b:B \qquad x \neq y}{E \vdash \langle\langle r \leftarrow x=a \rangle \leftarrow y=b \rangle \leftrightarrow \langle\langle r \leftarrow y=b \rangle \leftarrow x=a \rangle : \langle\!\langle \langle\!\langle R \leftarrow x:A \rangle\!\rangle \leftarrow y:B \rangle\!\rangle}$$

$$\frac{E \vdash r:R <: \langle\!\langle \rangle\!\rangle \qquad E \vdash a:A}{E \vdash \langle r \leftarrow x=a \rangle \backslash x \leftrightarrow r \backslash x:R \backslash x}$$

$$\frac{E \vdash r:R <: \langle\!\langle \rangle\!\rangle \qquad E \vdash a:A \qquad x \neq y}{E \vdash \langle r \leftarrow x=a \rangle \backslash y \leftrightarrow \langle r \backslash y \leftarrow x=a \rangle : \langle\!\langle R \leftarrow x:A \rangle\!\rangle \backslash y}$$

$$\frac{E \vdash r:R <: \langle\!\langle \rangle\!\rangle \qquad E \vdash a:A}{E \vdash \langle r \leftarrow x=a \rangle . x \leftrightarrow a:A}$$

$$\frac{E \vdash r: \langle\!\langle R \leftarrow y:B \rangle\!\rangle <: \langle\!\langle \rangle\!\rangle \qquad E \vdash a:A \qquad x \neq y}{E \vdash \langle r \leftarrow x=a \rangle . y \leftrightarrow r.y:B}$$

$$\frac{E \vdash r: \langle\!\langle R \leftarrow x:A \rangle\!\rangle <: \langle\!\langle \rangle\!\rangle \qquad x \neq y}{E \vdash r \backslash y.x \leftrightarrow r.x:A} \qquad \frac{E \vdash r:R <: \langle\!\langle S \leftarrow x:A \rangle\!\rangle <: \langle\!\langle \rangle\!\rangle}{E \vdash r \leftrightarrow \langle r \leftarrow x=r.x \rangle :R} .$$

4.2 The Rename Operator

We may consider a *rename* operator, that shows another interesting use of $R.x$ types.

$$r[x \leftarrow y] =_{\text{def}} \langle r\backslash x | y = r.x \rangle$$

$$R[x \leftarrow y] =_{\text{def}} \langle\!\langle R\backslash x | y : R.x \rangle\!\rangle.$$

The rules for this operator are easily derived. The only interesting questions are whether renaming with an identical variable produces an equivalent value or type:

$$r[x \leftarrow x] \leftrightarrow r \quad ?$$

$$R[x \leftarrow x] \leftrightarrow R \quad ?$$

These equivalences are derivable for arbitrary r and R, by using:

$$\frac{E \vdash r : R <: \langle\!\langle S | x : A \rangle\!\rangle <: \langle\!\langle\,\rangle\!\rangle}{E \vdash r \leftrightarrow \langle r\backslash x | x = r.x \rangle : R} \tag{VE10}$$

$$\frac{E \vdash R <: \langle\!\langle S | x : A \rangle\!\rangle <: \langle\!\langle\,\rangle\!\rangle}{E \vdash R \leftrightarrow \langle\!\langle R\backslash x | x : R.x \rangle\!\rangle}. \tag{TE9}$$

Recall that (VE10) is satisfied in all our models, but (TE9) only holds in the latter two. These are similar to the *surjective pairing* rules in λ-calculus. An alternative, not involving surjective pairing, is to axiomatize the renaming operators independently.

4.3 The Retraction Operator: Forgetting Information

We have seen that even negative information should be considered as 'additional' information. So, one might ask whether there is any way to *retract* information, both positive and negative. This would seem to be more a convenience than a necessity, since one could avoid introducing information in the first place, rather than retracting it later. However, it is still interesting to investigate the possibilities.

We have not been able to formulate operators that independently retract positive and negative information, but we can describe an operator that retracts all information about a given label in a type. This operator works purely on type information; there is no corresponding operator on values.

The *retraction* operator, $R \sim x$, means 'forget everything about x in record type R'; the following rules enforce the cancellation of all the x information in R.

Formation/Subtyping

$$\frac{E \vdash R <: \langle\!\langle\,\rangle\!\rangle}{E \vdash R \sim x \; type} \qquad \frac{E \vdash R <: S <: \langle\!\langle\,\rangle\!\rangle}{E \vdash R \sim x <: S \sim x} \qquad \frac{E \vdash R <: \langle\!\langle\,\rangle\!\rangle}{E \vdash R <: R \sim x}.$$

Type Equivalence

$$\frac{\vdash E\ env}{E \vdash \langle\rangle \sim x \leftrightarrow \langle\rangle} \qquad \frac{E \vdash R <: \langle\rangle}{E \vdash R \sim xx \leftrightarrow R \sim x} \qquad \frac{E \vdash R <: \langle\rangle}{E \vdash R \sim xy \leftrightarrow R \sim yx}$$

$$\frac{E \vdash R <: \langle\rangle}{E \vdash R\backslash x \sim x \leftrightarrow R \sim x} \qquad \frac{E \vdash R <: \langle\rangle \qquad x \neq y}{E \vdash R\backslash x \sim y \leftrightarrow R \sim y\backslash x}$$

$$\frac{E \vdash R <: \langle\rangle\backslash x \qquad E \vdash A\ type}{E \vdash \langle R|x:A\rangle \sim x \leftrightarrow R \sim x} \qquad \frac{E \vdash R <: \langle\rangle\backslash x \qquad E \vdash A\ type \qquad x \neq y}{E \vdash \langle R|x:A\rangle \sim y \leftrightarrow \langle R \sim y|x:A\rangle}.$$

The main consequences for values involve the rule $R <: R \sim x$ together with the subsumption rule: if $r:R$, then we are allowed to forget some information about r and conclude $r:R \sim x$.

Here are some interesting inferences:

$$\frac{\dfrac{E \vdash R <: \langle\rangle}{E \vdash R \sim x <: \langle\rangle \sim x}}{E \vdash R \sim x <: \langle\rangle} \qquad \frac{E \vdash r:R \qquad \dfrac{E \vdash R <: \langle\rangle}{E \vdash R <: R \sim x}}{E \vdash r:R \sim x}$$

$$\frac{\dfrac{E \vdash r:R}{E \vdash r\backslash x:R\backslash x}}{E \vdash r\backslash x:R \sim x} \qquad \frac{\dfrac{E \vdash r:R <: \langle\rangle\backslash x \qquad E \vdash a:A}{E \vdash \langle r|x=a\rangle:\langle R|x:A\rangle}}{E \vdash \langle r|x=a\rangle:R \sim x.}$$

The conclusion $r\backslash x:R \sim x$ above seems to say that restriction on values can be seen as a retraction operator, as well as a restriction operator.

Going back to a previous example from section 2.5, we can see the usefulness of the retraction operator for defining hierarchies in 'inverse' order:

let ColorDisc $= \langle x:Real, y:Real, r:Real, c:Color\rangle$
let ColorPoint $= ColorDisc \sim r$
let Disc $= ColorDisc \sim c$
let Point $= ColorPoint \sim c$.

Note that the restriction operator would not produce the desired results.

4.4   The Concatenation Operator

Concatenation is a prime candidate for a primitive operator for a calculus of records. Unfortunately this operator is very difficult to handle; so difficult that we have instead chosen extension and restriction as our primitive notions. Here we discuss the main problems.

Type hierarchies are naturally expressed by a concatenation operator $R\|S$ on types; for example we would like to define:

let ColorDisc = ColorPoint$\|$Disc.

Given a corresponding operator of values, $r\|s$ of type $R\|S$ for $r:R$ and $s:S$, we would like to guarantee that if we can derive $r\|s:R\|S$ then there is a successful and unambiguous way to execute $r\|s$ at run-time.

Under these conditions, we can see that concatenation is in fundamental conflict with the subsumption rule. Consider the function:

let f1$(X <: \langle\!\langle x:Int \rangle\!\rangle)(Y <: \langle\!\langle y:Bool \rangle\!\rangle)(r:X)(s:Y):X\|Y = r\|s$
$f1(\langle\!\langle x:Int,z:Int \rangle\!\rangle)(\langle\!\langle y:Bool,z:Bool \rangle\!\rangle)(\langle x = 3, z = 4 \rangle)(\langle x = 3, z = true \rangle) \leftrightarrow ?:?$

There is no explicit conflict in the definition of *f1*, so it should typecheck. But when *f1* is used as above, we have to decide which z field to produce, both in the result type and in the result value. A popular choice is to have $X\|Y$ perform a left-to-right (or right-to-left) overriding of common fields; similarly for $r\|s$ at run-time. However, run-time overriding can run into difficulties:

let f2$(r:\langle\!\langle x:Int \rangle\!\rangle)(s:\langle\!\langle y:Bool \rangle\!\rangle):\langle\!\langle x:Int, y:Bool \rangle\!\rangle = r\|s$
$f2(\langle x = 3, y = 4 \rangle)(\langle y = true, x = false \rangle) \leftrightarrow ?$

Let us assume here that, whatever definition we give to $\|$, it satisfies the equation: $\langle\!\langle x:Int \rangle\!\rangle \| \langle\!\langle y:Bool \rangle\!\rangle = \langle\!\langle x:Int, y:Bool \rangle\!\rangle$; then *f2* is well-typed. Could we use run-time overriding in the invocation of *f2* above? According to the result type of *f2*, the left x should override the right x, while the right y should override the left y, so monodirectional overriding will not work.

An option here is to give a run-time error, but this seems to defeat the purpose of typechecking $r\|s$. Another option might be to compile special code for $r\|s$, according to the types of r and s, so as to pick the x field from r and the y field from s, and to do overriding on the additional fields (to deal with the polymorphic case, below). This idea however runs into further difficulties:

$f1(\langle\!\langle x:Int, y:Int, z:Int \rangle\!\rangle)(\langle\!\langle y:Bool, x:Bool, z:Bool \rangle\!\rangle)$
$\quad (\langle x = 3, y = 4, z = 4 \rangle)(\langle y = true, x = false, z = true \rangle) \leftrightarrow ?:?$

If $X\|Y$ is computed by overriding, here, we get the wrong result. Making $X\|Y$ compatible with the behavior of $r\|s$ above, would require violating some basic rules, such as the beta-conversion rules for type parameters.

Because of all these difficulties, we should now feel compelled to define $R\|S$ only when R and S are disjoint: that is when any field present in an element of R is absent from every element of S, and vice versa. Unfortunately, there is no way to axiomatize this notion without drastically changing our type system: any two record types R and S have a nonempty intersection, and an element of this intersection can be exhibited via the subsumption rule.

5   Conclusions

We have investigated a theory of record operations in presence of type variables and subtyping. The intent is to embed this record calculus in a polymorphic λ-calculus, thus providing a full second-order theory of record structures and their types. Although we have not investigated the type inference problem for this calculus, we have provided typechecking and subtyping algorithms. We have also presented several models of the basic record calculus; a full second-order model is left for future work.

The result is a very flexible system for typing programs that manipulate records. In particular, polymorphism and subtyping are incorporated in full generality. We expect that this theory will be useful in analyzing fundamental aspects of object-oriented programming.

Acknowledgements

We would like to acknowledge G. Longo and E. Moggi, for several clarifying discussions.

Appendix

This appendix contains soundness proofs for the semantic interpretations given in the paper.

Semantics of the Pure Calculus of Records

System $S1$ consists of all the rules listed in section 3.7, except for the special rules (VC1b) and (TE9).

THEOREM 3.8.3 (soundness)   The inference rules of systems $S1$ are sound with respect to the interpretation of judgments given in section 3.8.

Proof   By induction on the length of the derivation of the judgments.

Environments

(ENV1). Vacuously true.

(ENV2). Vacuously true.

(ENV3). By hypothesis, $E \vdash A$ *type* and so $A_\rho \subseteq \mathscr{V}$ for any ρ satisfyig E. Moreover, E is well-formed by lemma 3.7.1, hence $E, X <: A$ is also well-formed.

(ENV4). Similar to (ENV3).

Variables

(VAR1). If ρ satisfies E, X, E', then by definition $\rho(X) \subseteq \mathscr{V}$.

(VAR2). If $\vdash E, X <: A, E'$ *env*, then for any ρ satisfying E we have $A_\rho \subseteq \mathscr{V}$. Thus any ρ satisfying $E, X <: A, E'$ must yield $\rho(X) \subseteq A_\rho \subseteq \mathscr{V}$.

(VAR3). Similar to (VAR2)

(VAR4). If $\vdash E, x : A, E'$ *env*, then for any ρ satisfying E we have $\rho(x) \in A_\rho \subseteq \mathscr{V}$. Thus any ρ satisfying $E, x : A, E'$ must yield $\rho(x) \in A_\rho \subseteq \mathscr{V}$.

General

(G1). If, for every ρ satisfying E, $A_\rho = B_\rho \subseteq \mathscr{V}$ then $A_\rho \subseteq B_\rho$.

(G2). By transitivity of subset.

(G3). If, for every ρ satisfying E, $a_\rho \in A_\rho$ and $A_\rho \subseteq B_\rho$ then $a_\rho \in B_\rho$.

(G4). By symmetry of equality.

(G5). By transitivity of equality.

(G6). If, for every ρ satisfying E, $a_\rho = b_\rho \in A_\rho$ then $b_\rho = a_\rho \in A_\rho$.

(G7). If, for every ρ satisfying E, $a_\rho = b_\rho \in A_\rho$ and $b_\rho = c_\rho \in A_\rho$ then $a_\rho = c_\rho \in A_\rho$.

Formation

(F1). $\mathscr{R} \subseteq \mathscr{V}$.

(F2). If, for every ρ satisfying E, $R_\rho \subseteq \mathscr{R} - x$ and $A_\rho \subseteq \mathscr{V}$ then $R_\rho[x : A_\rho] \subseteq \mathscr{R} \subseteq \mathscr{V}$, by lemma 3.8.2.

(F3). If $R_\rho \subseteq \mathscr{R}$, then $R_\rho - x \subseteq \mathscr{R} \subseteq \mathscr{V}$, by lemma 3.8.2.

(F4). If $R_\rho \subseteq S_\rho[x : A_\rho] \subseteq \mathscr{R}$, then $A_\rho \subseteq \mathscr{V}$; hence $R_\rho(x) \subseteq \mathscr{V}$ by lemma 3.8.2.

Subtyping

(S1). If, for every ρ satisfying E, $R_\rho \subseteq \mathscr{R} - x$, then R_ρ is a set of finite functions $r \in L \to_{\text{fin}} \mathscr{V}$ with $x \notin dom(r)$, For each such r, and any $a \in A_\rho \subseteq \mathscr{V}$, we have $r[x = a] \in L \to_{\text{fin}} \mathscr{V}$. Thus $R_\rho[x : A_\rho] \subseteq \mathscr{R}$.

(s2). If $R_\rho \subseteq \mathcal{R}$, then $R_\rho - x \subseteq R_\rho \subseteq \mathcal{R}$.

(s3). Suppose $R_\rho \subseteq S_\rho \subseteq \mathcal{R} - x$ and $A_\rho \subseteq B_\rho \subseteq \mathcal{V}$. Let $r \in R_\rho[x : A_\rho]$. This means $\exists s \in R_\rho$ with $r = s[x = a]$. Since $s \in S_\rho$ and $A_\rho \subseteq B_\rho$, we have $s[x = a] \in S_\rho[x : B_\rho]$. Hence $R_\rho[x : A_\rho] \subseteq S_\rho[x : B_\rho]$.

(s4). Suppose $R_\rho \subseteq S_\rho \subseteq \mathcal{R}$. If $r' \in R_\rho - x$, then $r' = r - x$ for some $r \in R_\rho$. Since $r \in S_\rho$, it follows that $r' = r - x \in S_\rho - x$.

(s5). Suppose $R_\rho \subseteq S_\rho[x : A_\rho] \subseteq \mathcal{R}$, then for any $r \in R_\rho$, $r \in S_\rho[x : A_\rho] = \{s[x = a] | s \in S_\rho, a \in A_\rho\}$; so that $r(x) \in A_\rho$. Hence $R_\rho(x) = \{r(x) | r \in R_\rho\} \subseteq A_\rho$.

(s6). Suppose $R_\rho \subseteq S_\rho[x : A_\rho] \subseteq \mathcal{R}$, then for any $r \in R_\rho$, $r \in S_\rho[x : A]$, so that $r = s[x = a]$ for some $s \in S_\rho$ and $a \in A_\rho$. We have $a = r(x) \in R_\rho(x)$, and $s = r - x \in R_\rho - x$, hence $r = (r - x)[x = r(x)] \in (R_\rho - x)[x : R_\rho(x)]$. It follows that $R_\rho \subseteq (R_\rho - x)[x : R_\rho(x)]$.

Introduction

(i1). $\varnothing \in \mathcal{R} \subseteq \mathcal{V}$.

(i2). If, for every ρ satisfying E, the empty function $\varnothing \in R_\rho \subseteq \mathcal{R}$, then $\varnothing = \varnothing - x_1 \ldots x_n \in R_\rho - y \subseteq \mathcal{R}$.

(i3). If $r_\rho \in R_\rho$ with $x \notin dom(r_\rho)$ and $a_\rho \in A_\rho$, then $r_\rho[x = a_\rho]$ is well-defined, by lemma 3.8.1, and belongs to $R_\rho[x : A_\rho] \subseteq \mathcal{R}$, by lemma 3.8.2.

Elimination

(e1). If, for every ρ satisfying E, $r_\rho \in R_\rho \subseteq \mathcal{R}$, then $x \notin dom(r_\rho - x)$. Hence $r_\rho - x \in R_\rho - x \subseteq \mathcal{R}$, by lemma 3.8.2.

(e2). If $r_\rho \in R_\rho[x : A_\rho] \subseteq \mathcal{R}$, then $A_\rho \subseteq \mathcal{V}$, and r_ρ is a record with $r_\rho(x) \in A_\rho$.

Type Congruence

(tc1). $\mathcal{R} = \mathcal{R} \subseteq \mathcal{V}$.

(tc2). For every ρ satisfying E, $X_\rho = X_\rho \subseteq \mathcal{V}$.

(tc3). Suppose $R_\rho = S_\rho$, $S_\rho \subseteq \mathcal{R} - x$, and $A_\rho = B_\rho \subseteq \mathcal{V}$. Then $R_\rho[x : A_\rho] = S_\rho[x : B_\rho] \subseteq \mathcal{R} \subseteq \mathcal{V}$.

(tc4). Suppoe $R_\rho = S_\rho \subseteq \mathcal{R}$, then $R_\rho - x = S_\rho - x \subseteq \mathcal{R} \subseteq \mathcal{V}$.

(tc5). Suppose $R_\rho = S_\rho \subseteq T_\rho[x : A_\rho] \subseteq \mathcal{R}$. Then both R_ρ and S_ρ are sets of functions r with $x \notin dom(r)$. Hence $R_\rho(x) = \{r(x) | r \in R_\rho\} = \{r(x) | r \in S_\rho\} = S_\rho(x) \subseteq \mathcal{V}$.

Type Equivalence

(TE1). Suppose, for every ρ satisfying E, $R_\rho \subseteq (\mathscr{R} - x) - y$, A_ρ, $B_\rho \subseteq \mathscr{V}$, and x, $y \in L$. For each $r \in R_\rho$, x, $y \notin dom(r)$. Then, $R_\rho[x:A_\rho][y:B_\rho] = \{s[y = b]|s \in \{r[x = a]|r \in R_\rho, a \in A_\rho\}, b \in B_\rho\} = \{r[x = a][y = b]|r \in R_\rho, a \in A_\rho, b \in B_\rho\} = \{r[y = b][x = a]|r \in R_\rho, b \in B_\rho, a \in A_\rho\} = \{s[x = a]|s \in \{r[y = b]|r \in R_\rho, b \in B_\rho\}, a \in A_\rho\} = R_\rho[y:B_\rho][x:A_\rho] \subseteq \mathscr{R} \subseteq \mathscr{V}$.

(TE2). If $R_\rho \subseteq \mathscr{R} - x$, then R_ρ is a set of r with $x \notin dom(r)$. Hence $R_\rho - x = R_\rho$.

(TE3). If $R_\rho \subseteq \mathscr{R}$ then $(R_\rho - x) - y = (R_\rho - y) - x$.

(TE4). Suppose $R_\rho \subseteq S_\rho[y:B_\rho] \subseteq \mathscr{R}$ and $x \neq y$. For each $r \in R_\rho$, $y \notin dom(r)$. Then, $(R_\rho - x)(y) = \{s(y)|s \in \{r - x|r \in R_\rho\}\} = \{(r - x)(y)|r \in R_\rho\} = \{r(y)|r \in R_\rho\} = R_\rho(y) \subseteq \mathscr{V}$.

(TE5). Suppose $R_\rho \subseteq \mathscr{R} - x$ and $A_\rho \subseteq \mathscr{V}$. Then $R_\rho[x:A_\rho] = \{r[x = a]|r \in R_\rho, a \in A_\rho\}$. So $(R_\rho[x:A_\rho]) - x = \{r|r \in R_\rho\} = R_\rho$.

(TE6). Suppose $R_\rho \subseteq \mathscr{R} - x$, $A_\rho \subseteq \mathscr{V}$, and $x \neq y$. Then, $(R_\rho[x:A_\rho]) - y = \{(r[x = a]) - y|r \in R_\rho, a \in A_\rho\} = \{(r - y)[x = a]|r \in R_\rho, a \in A_\rho\} = (R_\rho - y)[x:A_\rho] \subseteq \mathscr{R} \subseteq \mathscr{V}$.

(TE7). Suppose $R_\rho \subseteq \mathscr{R} - x$ and $A_\rho \subseteq \mathscr{V}$. Then $R_\rho[x:A_\rho] = \{r[x = a]|r \in R_\rho, a \in A_\rho\}$. Hence $(R_\rho[x:A_\rho])(x) = (\{r[x = a]\}(x)|r \in R_\rho, a \in A_\rho\} = A_\rho \subseteq \mathscr{V}$.

(TE8). Suppose $R_\rho \subseteq S_\rho[y:B_\rho] - x \subseteq \mathscr{R}$, $A_\rho \subseteq \mathscr{V}$, and $x \neq y$. Then, $(R_\rho[x:A_\rho])(y) = \{(r[x = a])(y)|r \in R_\rho, a \in A_\rho\} = \{r(y)|r \in R_\rho\} = R_\rho(y) \subseteq \mathscr{V}$.

Value Congruence

(TC1). $\varnothing = \varnothing \subseteq \mathscr{R}$.

(TC2). If, for every ρ satisfying E, $\rho(x) \in A_\rho \subseteq \mathscr{V}$, then $\rho(x) = \rho(x) \in A_\rho$.

(TC3). Suppose $r_\rho = s_\rho \in R_\rho \subseteq \mathscr{R} - x$ and $a_\rho = b_\rho \in A_\rho \subseteq \mathscr{V}$. Then $x \notin dom(r_\rho) \cup dom(s_\rho)$. Hence $r_\rho[x = a_\rho] = s_\rho[x = b_\rho] \in R_\rho[x:A_\rho] \subseteq \mathscr{R}$, by case (I3).

(TC4). Suppose $r_\rho = s_\rho \in R_\rho \subseteq \mathscr{R}$. Then $r_\rho - x = s_\rho - x \in R_\rho - x \subseteq \mathscr{R}$, by case (E1).

(TC5). Suppose $r_\rho = s_\rho \in R_\rho \subseteq S_\rho[x:A_\rho] \subseteq \mathscr{R}$. Then $R_\rho \subseteq (R_\rho - x)[x:R_\rho(x)]$ (by case (S6)), and $r_\rho, s_\rho \in (R_\rho - x)[x:R_\rho(x)]$. Hence, by case (E2), $r_\rho(x) = s_\rho(x) \in R_\rho(x) \subseteq \mathscr{V}$.

Value Equivalence

(VE1). Suppose, for every ρ satisfying E, $r_\rho \in R_\rho \subseteq \mathscr{R} - x - y$, $a_\rho \in A_\rho \subseteq \mathscr{V}$, $b_\rho \in B_\rho \subseteq \mathscr{V}$, and $x \neq y$. Then, x, $y \notin dom(r_\rho)$, and $r_\rho[x = a_\rho][y = b_\rho] = r_\rho[y = b_\rho][x = a_\rho] \in R_\rho[x:A_\rho][y:B_\rho] \subseteq \mathscr{R}$.

(VE2). $\varnothing - x = \varnothing \in \mathscr{R}$.

(VE3). Suppose $r_\rho \in R_\rho \subseteq \mathscr{R} - x$. Since $x \notin dom(r_\rho)$, $r_\rho - x = r_\rho$.

(VE4). Suppose $r_\rho \in R_\rho \subseteq \mathscr{R}$. $(r_\rho - x) - y = (r_\rho - y) - x \in (R_\rho - x) - y \subseteq \mathscr{R}$.

(VE5). Suppose $r_\rho \in R_\rho[x:A_\rho] \subseteq \mathscr{R}$ and $x \neq y$. Then $x \in dom(r_\rho)$ and $r_\rho - y.x = r_\rho.x \in A_\rho \subseteq \mathscr{V}$.

(VE6). Suppose $r_\rho \in R_\rho \subseteq \mathscr{R} - x$ and $a_\rho \in A_\rho \subseteq \mathscr{V}$. Then $x \notin dom(r_\rho)$ and $r_\rho[x = a_\rho] - x = r_\rho$.

(VE7). Suppose $r_\rho \in R_\rho \subseteq \mathscr{R} - x$, $a_\rho \in A_\rho \subseteq \mathscr{V}$ and $x \neq y$. Then $x \notin dom(r_\rho)$ and $(r_\rho[x = a_\rho]) - y = (r_\rho - y)[x = a_\rho] \in (R_\rho[x:A_\rho]) - y \subseteq \mathscr{R}$.

(VE8). Suppose $r_\rho \in R_\rho \subseteq \mathscr{R} - x$, and $a_\rho \in A_\rho \subseteq \mathscr{V}$. Then $x \notin dom(r_\rho)$ and $(r_\rho[x = a_\rho])(x) = a_\rho$.

(VE9). Suppose $r_\rho \in R_\rho[y:B_\rho] - x \subseteq \mathscr{R}$, $a_\rho \in A_\rho \subseteq \mathscr{V}$ and $x \neq y$. Then $B_\rho \subseteq \mathscr{V}$, $x \notin dom(r_\rho)$, $y \in dom(r_\rho)$, and $(r_\rho[x = a_\rho])(y) = r_\rho(y) \in B_\rho$.

(VE10). Suppose $r_\rho \in R_\rho \subseteq S_\rho[x:A_\rho] \subseteq \mathscr{R}$. Then $r_\rho \in S_\rho[x:A_\rho]$, so that $r_\rho = s[x = a]$ for some $s \in S_\rho$ and $a \in A_\rho$. We have $a = r_\rho(x) \in R_\rho(x)$, and $s = r_\rho - x \in R_\rho - x$, hence $r_\rho = (r_\rho - x)[x = r_\rho(x)]$, which is well-formed (is a member of $(R_\rho - x)[x:R_\rho(x)]$). ∎

A Construction Giving $R = \langle\!\langle R \backslash x | x : R . x \rangle\!\rangle$

System $S2$ is system $S1$ of theorem 3.8.3 plus the rule (TE9).

THEOREM 3.9.7 (soundness)   The inference rules of system $S2$ are sound with respect to the interpretation of judgments given in section 3.9.

Proof   The proof follows the general pattern of theorem 3.8.3. The main new properties that are needed are proved as lemmas in section 3.9.

In particular, (TE9) follows from lemma 3.9.6. The formaton rules come from lemmas 3.9.2, 3.9.3, 3.9.4 and 3.9.5. ∎

An Extensional Model Construction

System $S3$ is system $S1$ of theorem 3.8.3 plus the rules (TE9) and (VC1b).

THEOREM 3.10.4 (soundness)   The inference rules of system $S3$ are sound for the PER model construction given in section 3.10.

Proof   The proof follows the general pattern of theorem 3.8.3, using the lemmas proved in section 3.10. ∎

Notes

First appeared in *Mathematical Structures in Computer Science* 1 (1991), pages 3–48. © Cambridge University Press, 40 West 20th Street, New York, NY 10011-4211.

1. In this section we consider only *ground* record types, i.e. those containing no record type variables.

2. Although the singleton type *True* may seem artificial, this argument can be reformulated with any proper inclusion between two types.

References

Breazu-Tannen, V., Coquand, T., Gunter, C. and Scedrov, A. (1989) Inheritance and explicit coercion. *Proc. Fourth IEEE Symp. on Logic in Computer Science*, pp. 112–129.

Bruce, K. B. and Longo, G. (1988) A modest model of records, inheritance and bounded quantification. *Proc. Third IEEE Symp. on Logic in Computer Science*, pp. 38–50.

Bruce, K. B. Meyer, A. R. and Mitchell, J. C. (1990) The semantics of second order lambda calculus. *Informat. Computat.* Vol. 85, No. 1, pp. 76–134.

Cardelli, L. (1988) A semantics of multiple inheritance. In *Information and Computation* 76 138–164. (First appeared in *Semantics of Data Types*, eds G. Kahn, D. B. MacQueen and G. Plotkin. *Springer Lecture Notes in Computer Science* 173, Springer-Verlag, 1984.)

Cardelli, L., Donahue, J., Glassman, L., Jordan, M., Kalsow, B. and Nelson, G. (1989) Modula-3 report (revised). Research Report no. 52, DEC Systems Research Center.

Cardelli, L. and Wegner, P. (1985) On understanding types, data abstraction and polymorphism. *Comput. Surv.* 17(4) 471–522.

Curien, P.-L. and Ghelli, G. (1991) Coherence of subsumption. *Math. Struct. Comp. Sci.*, to appear.

Dahl, O. and Nygaard, K. (1966) Simula, an Algol-based simulation language. *Commun. ACM* 9 671–678.

Girard, J.-Y. (1971) Une extension de l'interprétation de Gödel à l'analyse, et son application à l'élimination des coupures dans l'analyse et la théorie des types. *Proc. Second Scandinavian Logic Symposium*, ed. J. E. Fenstad. North-Holland, pp. 63–92.

——— (1972) Interprétation fonctionelle et élimination des coupures dans l'arithmétique d'ordre supérieur. Thèse de doctorat d'état, University of Paris.

Jategaonkar, L. A. and Mitchell, J. C. (1988) ML with extended pattern matching and subtypes. *Proc. ACM Conf. on Lisp and Functional Programming*, pp. 198–211.

Longo, G. and Moggi, E. (1988) Constructive natural deduction and its 'ω-set' interpretation. Report CMU-CS-88-131, CMU, Dept. of Computer Science, *Math. Struct. Comput. Sci.* 1 (2) to appear.

Meyer, B. (1988) *Object-oriented Software Construction*. Prentice-Hall.

Milner, R. (1978) A theory of type polymorphism in programming. *J. Comput. Sys. Sci.* 17 348–375.

Mitchell, J. C. (1984) Coercion and type inference. *Proc. 11th ACM Symp. on Principles of Programming Languages*, pp. 175–185.

Mitchell, J. C. (1986) A type inference approach to reduction properties and semantics of polymorphic expressions. *Proc. Symp. on Lisp and Functional Programming*, pp. 308–319. (Revised version in *Logic Foundations of Functional Programming*, ed. G. Huet, Addison-Wesley, 1989, pp. 195–212.)

——— (1990) Type systems for programming languages. In: *Handbook of Theoretical Computer Science*, Volume B, eds J. van Leeuwen *et al.*, North-Holland, pp. 365–458.

Ohori, A., Buneman, P. and Breazu-Tannen, V. (1988) database programming in Machiavelli—a polymorphic language with static type inference. Report MS-CIS-88-103, University of Pennsylvania, Computer and Information Science Department.

Ohori, A. and Buneman, P. (1988) Type inference in a Database programming language. *Proc. ACM Conf. on LISP and Functional Programming*, pp. 174–183.

Rémy, D. (1989) Typechecking records and variants in a natural extension of ML. *Proc. 16th ACM Symp. on Principles of Programming Languages*, pp. 77–88.

Reynolds, J. C. (1974) Towards a theory of type structure. In: *Colloquium sur la Programmation. Springer Lecture Notes in Computer Science* **19**, pp. 408–423.

Schaffert, C., Cooper, T., Bullis, B., Kilian, M. and Wilpolt, C. (1986) An introduction to Trellis/Owl. *Proc. ACM Conf. Object-Oriented Programming Systems, Languages and Applications*, pp. 9–16.

Stroustrup, B. (1986) *The C++ Programming Language*. Addison-Wesley.

Wand, M. (1987) Complete type inference for simple objects. *Proc. Second IEEE Symp. on Logic in Computer Science*, pp. 37–44.

Wand, M. (1989) Type inference for record concatenation and multiple inheritance. *Proc. Fourth IEEE Symp. on Logic in Computer Science*, pp. 92–97.

10 Typing Record Concatenation for Free

Didier Rémy

Abstract

We show that any functional language with record extension possesses record concatenation for free. We exhibit a translation from the latter into the former. We obtain a type system for a language with record concatenation by composing the translation with typechecking in a language with record extension. We apply this method to a version of ML with record extension and obtain an extension of ML with either asymmetric or symmetric concatenation. The latter extension is simple, flexible and has a very efficient type inference algorithm in practice. Concatenation together with removal of fields needs one more construct than extension of records. It can be added to the version of ML with record extension. However, many typed languages with records cannot type such a construct. The method still applies to them, producing type systems for record concatenation without removal of fields. Object systems also benefit from the encoding which shows that multiple inheritance does not actually require the concatenation of records but only their extension.

Introduction

Dictionaries are an important data abstraction in programming languages. They are basically partial functions from keys to values. A simple implementation of dictionaries is the *association list*, commonly called *A-list*. A-lists are lists of pairs, the first component being the key to access the value of the second component. The usual *cons* and *append* operations provide facilities for extending the domain of an A-list and merging two A-lists into one defined on the union of the domains of the input lists, respectively. Access to a given key may fail when the key is not in the domain of the A-list, which cannot be checked statically. Records are a highly restricted form of A-lists. Keys may no longer be any values, but belong to a distinguished set of atomic values, called labels. All fields of a record must be specified at creation time. These restrictions make it possible to perform static checks on accesses to record fields.

Then, an important goal in typechecking records, was to allow a record with many fields to be used instead of a records with fewer fields. This was first suggested by Cardelli in the language Amber [Car86] using inclusion on monomorphic types.

Later, Wand [Wan87] used polymorphism instead of a specific inclusion relation on types. He also re-imported the *cons* operation of A-lists which became the

First appeared in *Nineteenth Annual Symposium on Principles of Programming Languages*, 1992, pages 166–176. © The Association for Computing Machinery, Inc. 11 West 42nd Street New York, New York 10036.

extension of records with new fields. Originally, this construction was free (existing fields could be redefined), but strict versions (existing fields could not be redefined) have been proposed [OB88, JM88] to avoid typechecking difficulties. Note that *cons* on A-lists naturally implements free extension.

Record extension quickly became popular, but many languages still only provide the strict version [JM88, Oho90, HP90a]. Finally Wand re-imported the *append* of A-lists, calling it record concatenation. An important motivation for this is the encoding of multiple inheritance [Wan89] in object oriented languages.

Record concatenation is still considered a challenge, since it is either very restricted [HP90a] or leads to combinatorial explosion of typechecking [Wan88]. We propose a general approach to concatenation. In fact we claim that concatenation comes for free once record extension is provided. We justify this assertion by presenting an encoding of the latter into the former. The interest of the encoding is to provide a type system for record concatenation by composing the coding with a type system for record extension.

We introduce the translation in an untyped framework in section 1. In section 2, we apply it to an extension of ML for record extension. In the last section we briefly illustrate the encoding on a few other languages.

1   Encoding of Concatenation

In this section we describe how concatenation can be encoded with extension. The language with record extension, L, is an extension of the untyped λ calculus plus distinguished constructs for record expressions:

$$
\begin{array}{ll}
M ::= x & \text{variable} \\
\quad | \ \lambda x . M & \text{abstraction} \\
\quad | \ M\,M & \text{application} \\
\quad | \ \{\ \} & \text{empty record} \\
\quad | \ \{M \text{ with } a = M\} & \text{record extension} \\
\quad | \ M . a & \text{record access}
\end{array}
$$

The semantics of records is the usual one. Informally, they are partial functions from labels to values. The empty record is defined nowhere. Accessing a field of a record is applying the record to that field. It produces an error if the accessed field is not defined. The *free* extension of a record with a new field defines or redefines that field with the new value. The *strict* extension does the same if the field was undefined, but produces an error otherwise. In an untyped language the free extension is preferred since the more well typed programs, the better.

The *concatenation* (or *merge*) operator ‖ takes two records and returns a new record composed of all fields defined in any of its arguments. There are different semantics given to the merge, when both records define the same field: symmetric concatenation rejects this case [HP90b] while *asymmetric* concatenation takes the value from the last record [Wan89]. We will not consider *recursive* concatenation that would compute the concatenation of common fields by recursively concatenating their values.

The language with record concatenation, $L^{\parallel}$ is

$$M ::= x \mid \lambda x . M \mid M M \mid \{\ \} \mid \{a = M\} \mid M \parallel M \mid M . a$$

The language is an extension of L with a construct for concatenation, but record extension has been replaced by one-field records that are more primitive in the presence of concatenation, since[1]:

$$\{M \text{ with } a = N\} \equiv M \parallel \{a = N\}$$

Reading this equality from right to left is also interesting: it means that one-field concatenation can be written with record extension only. It gives the expected semantics of asymmetric concatenation when the extension is free and the semantics of symmetric concatenation when the extension is strict. We are going to generalize this to a translation from the language $L^{\parallel}$ to the language L.

1.1 The Untyped Translation

The following translation works for both asymmetric and symmetric concatenation. We arbitrarily choose asymmetric concatenation.

The extension of fields provides the one-field concatenation operation:

$$\lambda r . (r \parallel \{a = M\}) = \lambda r . \{r \text{ with } a = M\},$$

which we write $\{a = M\}^{\dagger}$. In fact, we can compute $r \parallel s$ whenever we know exactly the fields of s, since

$$r \parallel \{a_1 = M_1 ; \dots a_n = M_n\} \equiv \{\dots \{r \text{ with } a_1 = M_1\} \dots \text{ with } a_n = M_n\}.$$

This equivalence could also have been deduced from the decomposition of s into one-field concatenations

$$(\dots (r \parallel \{a_1 = M_1\}) \dots \parallel \{a_n = M_n\}),$$

which is also the composition

$$(\{a_n = M_n\}^{\dagger} \circ \dots \{a_1 = M_1\}^{\dagger}) r.$$

We write

$$\{a_1 = M_1; \ldots a_n = M_n\}^\dagger$$

for the abstraction of the previous expression over r. More generally we define the transformation $\dagger$ on record expressions, called *record abstraction*, by:

$$\{\ \}^\dagger \equiv \lambda u . u$$

$$\{a = M\}^\dagger \equiv \lambda u . \{u \text{ with } a = M^\dagger\}$$

$$(M \parallel N)^\dagger \equiv N^\dagger \circ M^\dagger$$

Since any record expression can be decomposed into a combination of the three previous forms, the transformation is defined for all records. It satisfies the property

$$r^\dagger = \lambda u . (u \parallel r).$$

Thus r is equal to $r^\dagger \{\ \}$. If we transform all record expressions in a program, then we have to replace the access $r . a$ by $(r^\dagger \{\ \}) . a$. Actually, it is enough to apply r to a record r' that does not contain the a field and read the field from the result $(r\, r') . a$. In a typed language this solution will leave more flexibility for the type of r. Other constructs of the language simply propagate the translation. Thus the translation is completed by

$$(M . a)^\dagger \equiv (M^\dagger \{\ \}) . a$$

$$(\lambda x . M)^\dagger \equiv \lambda x . M^\dagger$$

$$(M\, N)^\dagger \equiv M^\dagger N^\dagger$$

$$x^\dagger \equiv x$$

The translation works quite well in an untyped framework. However, the encoding is not injective, for instance it identifies the empty record with the identity function. In the next section we adapt the translation to a typed framework.

1.2 The Tagged Translation

In this section we improve the translation so that the encoding becomes injective. The main motivation is to prepare the use of the encoding to get a typed version of $L^\parallel$ by pulling back the typing rules of a typed version of L. The well typed programs of $L^\parallel$ will be the reverse image of the well typed programs of L. The translation should be injective on well typed programs. A solution is to tag the encoding of records, so that they become tagged abstractions, distinct from other abstractions.

In fact we replace L by $L^{\text{Tag, Untag}}$, that is L plus two constants Tag and Untag used to tag and untag values. The only reduction involving Tag or Untag is that Untag (Tag M) reduces to M. Tag and Untag can be thought as the unique constructor and the unique destructor of an abstract data type, respectively. In SML [HMT91] they could be defined as:

```
abstype (α, β) tagged = Tagged of α → β with
  val Tag = fn x ⇒ Tagged x
  val Untag = fn Tagged x ⇒ x
end;
```

Their role is to certify that some functional values are in fact record abstractions, Tag stamps them and Untag reads and removes the stamps. Obviously, these constants are not accessible in $L^{\|}$, i.e. they are introduced during the translation only.

Syntactically the existence of Tag and Untag is not a question, but semantically a model of a calculus with record extension might not possess such constants. On the opposite, finding a particular model in which the constants Tag and Untag exist might be as difficult as finding a direct model for concatenation. Anyhow, we limit our use of the encoding to syntactic issues.

The tagged translation is:

$$\{\ \}^{\dagger} \equiv \text{Tag}(\lambda u.\, u)$$

$$\{a = M\}^{\dagger} \equiv \text{Tag}(\lambda u.\, \{u \text{ with } a = M^{\dagger}\})$$

$$(M \,\|\, N)^{\dagger} \equiv \text{Tag}(\lambda u.\, \text{Untag}(N^{\dagger}(\text{Untag } M^{\dagger} u)))$$

$$(M.a)^{\dagger} \equiv ((\text{Untag } M)\{\ \}).a$$

It does not modify other constructs:

$$(\lambda x.M)^{\dagger} \equiv \lambda x.M^{\dagger}$$

$$(M\,N)^{\dagger} \equiv M^{\dagger} N^{\dagger}$$

$$x^{\dagger} \equiv x$$

We would like to show a property such as: starting with a calculus of record extension, we can translate any program of a calculus with record concatenation into the first calculus enriched with constants Tag and Untag using the translation above, and thereby get—in some sense—an equivalent program.

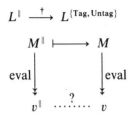

$$L^{\parallel} \xrightarrow{\dagger} L^{\{\text{Tag, Untag}\}}$$

$$M^{\parallel} \longmapsto M$$

Without any such result, the translation † is no more than a good intuition to understanding record concatenation. In the next section it helps finding a type system for a language with concatenation $L^{\parallel}$ from a typed language with extension L, by translating $L^{\parallel}$ programs and then typing them in L.

1.3   Concatenation with Removal of Fields

We omitted one construction in the language L: the restriction of fields. We extend both languages L and $L^{\parallel}$ with record restriction:

$$M ::= \ldots \mid M\backslash a$$

Record restriction takes a record and removes the corresponding field from its domain. As for extension of fields, restriction of fields can be free or strict. We consider free restriction here. The question is obviously the extension of the transformation † to restriction of fields.

The guide line is to keep the equality

$$(M\backslash a)^{\dagger} = \lambda u . u \parallel (M\backslash a)$$

true, since it was true before the introduction of restriction of fields. Actually this equality is needed since it is the basis of the translation of the extraction of fields.

Unfortunately, the attempt

$$(M\backslash a)^{\dagger} = \lambda u . (M^{\dagger}u)\backslash a$$

does not work: the record $u \parallel (M\backslash a)$ is not equal to $(M^{\dagger}u)\backslash a$, since if the record u provides an a field, this field is defined in the left expression but it is undefined in the right expression. In fact $u \parallel (M\backslash a)$ is equal to $M^{\dagger}u$ on all fields but a. On the a field it is undefined if u is, or defined with the value of the a field of u otherwise. This operation cannot be written in the language L; we need another construct,

$$\{M \text{ but } a \text{ from } N\},$$

called *combining*. From two records M and N, it defines one that behaves exactly as M on all fields but a, and as N on the a field. This primitive is stronger than $(\_ \backslash a)$ which could be defined as $\{\_ \text{ but } a \text{ from } \{\ \}\}$.

Now, the translation of $(M \backslash a)$ can be defined by

$$(M \backslash a)^\dagger \equiv \lambda u . \{M^\dagger u \text{ but } a \text{ from } u\}$$

Its tagged version is:

$$(M \backslash a)^\dagger \equiv \text{Tag}(\lambda . \{\text{Untag}(M^\dagger u) \text{ but } a \text{ from } u\})$$

We call L^+ the language L extended with the combining construct. This construct has never been introduced in the literature before. If the language L is typed, it may be the case that the combining primitive cannot be assigned a correct and decent type in the type system of L and L^+ might not be a trivial extension of L or even not exist.

The combining construct is not in $L^\|$ and there is no easy way to provide it in an extension of $L^\|$. Therefore L but not L^+ is a sub-language of $L^\|$.

2 Application to a Natural Extension of ML

In this section we apply the translation where L is a version of ML with record extension, and we get a language with record concatenation. We first review the language Π taken from [Rém90, Rém92c] for record extension. Then we describe in detail two versions of the typed language $\Pi^\|$ obtained by pulling back the typing rules of Π. Last, we discuss the system $\Pi^\|$ on its own, and compare it with other existing systems with concatenation.

2.1 An Extension of ML for Records

The language, called Π, is taken from [Rém90, Rém92c]. It is an extension of ML, where the language of types has been enriched with record types in such a way that record operations can be introduced as primitive functions rather than built in constructs. The main properties are described in [Rém92c] and proved in [Rem90, Rém92b, Rém92a]. The following summary should be sufficient for understanding the next sections. The reader is referred to [Rém92c] for a more thorough presentation.

Let $\mathscr{L}$ be a finite set of labels. We write a, b and c for labels and L for finite subsets of labels. The language of types is informally described by the following grammar (a formal description using sorts can be found in [Rém92c]):

$$\tau ::= \alpha \,|\, \tau \to \tau \,|\, \Pi(\rho^\emptyset) \qquad\qquad\qquad \text{types}$$

$$\rho^L ::= \chi^L \,|\, \text{abs}^L \,|\, a : \varphi \,;\, \rho^{L \cup \{a\}} \qquad a \notin L \quad \text{rows defining all labels but those in } L$$

$$\varphi ::= \theta \,|\, \text{abs} \,|\, \text{pre}(\tau) \qquad\qquad\qquad \text{fields}$$

where α, β, γ and δ are type variables, χ, π and ξ are row variables and θ and ε are field variables.

Intuitively, a row with superscript L describes all fields but those in L, and tells for each of them whether it is present with a value of type τ (positive information $\text{pre}(\tau)$) or absent (negative information abs). A *template* row is either abs or a row variable. It always describes an infinite set of fields. The superscripts in row expressions L are finite sets of labels. Their main role is to prevent fields from being defined twice: the type

$$\Pi(a : \theta \,;\, (a : \varepsilon \,;\, \chi^L))$$

cannot be written for any L. Similarly, all occurrences of the same row variable should be preceded by the same set of labels (possibly in a different order). The type

$$\Pi(a : \theta \,;\, \chi^L) \to \Pi(\chi^L).$$

cannot be written either, since the row variable χ cannot be both in the syntactic class of rows not defining label a and the syntactic class of rows defining all labels. The superscripts are part of the syntax, but we shall omit them whenever they are obvious from context. We write $a : \alpha \,;\, b : \beta \,;\, \gamma$ for $a : \alpha \,;\, (b : \beta \,;\, \gamma)$.

EXAMPLE 1   The following is a well-formed type:

$$\alpha \to \Pi(a : \text{pre}(\alpha) \,;\, b : \text{pre}(\text{num}) \,;\, \text{abs})$$

Types are equal modulo the following equations:

• left commutativity, to reorder fields:

$$(a : \theta \,;\, b : \varepsilon \,;\, \chi) = (b : \varepsilon \,;\, a : \theta \,;\, \chi)$$

• distributivity, to access absent fields:

$$\text{abs} = (a : \text{abs} \,;\, \text{abs})$$

EXAMPLE 2   The record types $\Pi(a : \text{pre}(\alpha) \,;\, \text{abs})$ and $\Pi(b : \text{abs} \,;\, a : \text{pre}(\alpha) \,;\, \text{abs})$ are equal.

Any field defined by a template can be extracted from it using substitution if the template is a variable or distributivity if it is abs.

EXAMPLE 3   In $\Pi(a:\text{pre}(\alpha);\text{abs})$, the template is abs; its superscript is $\{a\}$. To read the b field, we replace abs by $(b:\text{abs};\text{abs})$. The original type becomes $\Pi(a:\text{pre}(\alpha);b:\text{abs};\text{abs})$, and the new template has superscript $\{a,b\}$.

In $\Pi(a:\text{pre}(\alpha);\chi)$, the χ variable can be substituted by $b:\varepsilon;\pi$. The type becomes

$$\Pi(a:\text{pre}(\alpha);b:\varepsilon;\pi)$$

and π is the new template.

The language of expressions is the core ML language.

$$M ::= x\,|\,c\,|\,\lambda x\,.\,M\,|\,M\,M\,|\,\text{let } x = M \text{ in } M$$

where the constants c include the following primitives operating on records, with their types:

Primitives for Record Extension (Π)

$\{\ \}:\Pi(\text{abs})$

$\_\,.\,a:\Pi(a:\text{pre}(\alpha);\chi)\to\alpha$

$\{\_\text{ with }a=\_\}:\Pi(a:\text{abs};\chi)\to\alpha\to\Pi(a:\text{pre}(\alpha);\chi)$

$\_\backslash a:\Pi(a:\theta;\chi)\to\Pi(a:\text{abs};\chi)$

The extension on a field $\{\_\text{ with }a=\_\}$ is strict: a field can only be added to a record r that does not already possess this field. But the restriction of a field $\_\backslash a$ is free: it can be applied to a record which does not have field a. Free extension with a field b is achieved by restriction of field b followed by strict extension with field b. That is, it is the composition:

$$(\_\backslash a)\circ(\{\_\text{ with }a=\_\}):\Pi(a:\theta;\chi)\to\alpha\to\Pi(a:\text{pre}(\alpha);\chi)$$

that we abbreviate $\{\_\text{ with }!a=\_\}$. In the simplest language, the restriction of fields would not be provided, and the extension would be given whether strict or free.

Typing rules are the same as those of ML but where type equality is taken modulo the equations. As in ML, any typeable expression possesses a principal type. We show a few examples extracted from [Rém92c] and run on a CAML prototype.

Records are built all at once as in

```
#let car = {name = "Toyota"; age = "old";
  registration = 7866};;
car:Π (name:pre (string); registration:pre (num);
        age:pre (string); abs)
```

or from previous records by removing or adding fields:

```
#let truck =
  {car \ age with name = "Blazer"; registration = 65867567};;
truck:Π (name:pre (string); registration:pre (num);
         age:abs; abs)
```

Fields are accessed as usual with the "dot" operation.

```
#let registration x = x.registration;;
registration:Π (registration:pre (α); χ) → α
```

Here, the field registration must be defined with a value of type α, so the field registration has type pre (α), and other fields may or may not be defined; they are grouped in the template variable χ. The return value has type α. The function eq below takes two records possessing at least a registration field of the same type[2]:

```
#let eq x y = equal (registration x) (registration y);;
eq:Π (registration:pre (α); χ) → Π
   (registration:pre (α); π) → bool
#eq car truck;;
it:bool
```

The identifier "it" is bound to the last toplevel phrase (the prototype types the expressions but it does not evaluate them). The two records car and truck do not have the same set of fields, but both can still be passed to the function registration.

2.2   An Extension of ML with Record Concatenation

The language Π described in section 2.1 can easily be extended with a combining primitive

$$\{\_ \text{ but } a \text{ from } \_\} : \Pi(a:\theta;\chi) \to \Pi(a:\varepsilon;\pi) \to \Pi(a:\varepsilon;\chi)$$

The extended language is referred to as Π^+. We apply the transformation † with Π as L. We first consider the strict version of Π^+, then we show a few examples and we treat the free version of Π^+ at the end.

Symmetric Concatenation   We encode the language $\Pi^{\|}$ with symmetric concatenation into the version of Π^+ with strict extension. We introduce a new type symbol $\{\_ \Rightarrow \_\}$ of arity two, and we assume given the two constants:

$\mathrm{Tag} : (\Pi(\chi) \to \Pi(\pi)) \to \{\chi \Rightarrow \pi\},$

$\mathrm{Untag} : \{\chi \Rightarrow \pi\} \to (\Pi(\chi) \to \Pi(\pi)).$

They are private to the translation.

A program is typable in $\Pi^{\parallel}$ if and only if its translation is typable in $\Pi^{\mathrm{Tag, Untag}}$ (Π extended with Tag and Untag). However, composing the translation with type-checking in $\Pi^{\mathrm{Tag, Untag}}$ is the same as typechecking in $\Pi^{\parallel}$ with the following types for primitives:

Primitives for Symmetric Concatenation ($\Pi^{\parallel}$)

$\{ \ \} : \{\chi \Rightarrow \chi\}$

$\_\,.\,a : \{a : \mathrm{abs}; \chi \Rightarrow a : \mathrm{pre}(\alpha); \pi\} \to \alpha$

$\{a = \_\} : \alpha \to \{a : \mathrm{abs}; \chi \Rightarrow a : \mathrm{pre}(\alpha); \chi\}$

$\backslash a : \{a : \theta; \chi \Rightarrow a : \varepsilon; \pi\} \to \{a : \theta'; \chi \Rightarrow a : \theta'; \pi\}$

$\parallel : \{\chi \Rightarrow \pi\} \to \{\pi \Rightarrow \xi\} \to \{\chi \Rightarrow \xi\}$

Thus the translation can be avoided.

When typing directly in $\Pi^{\parallel}$ with the rules above, all record types are written with $\{\_ \Rightarrow \_\}$ and the type symbol Π can be removed; the grammar for types becomes

$\tau ::= \alpha \mid \tau \to \tau \mid \{\rho^{\emptyset} \Rightarrow \rho^{\emptyset}\}$

The type $\{\chi \Rightarrow \pi\}$ should be read "I am a record which given any input row of fields χ returns the output row π." The types for the primitives above can be read with the following intuition:

• The empty record returns the input row unchanged.

• As remarked above (section 1), we encoded the extraction of field a in M as the extraction of field a in the application of M to any record that does not contain the a field. Otherwise we would have got the weaker type:

$\_\,.\,a : \{\mathrm{abs} \Rightarrow a : \mathrm{pre}(\alpha); \chi\} \to \alpha$

Thus, the extraction of the a field of r takes a record r which, given any row where a is absent, produces a row where a is defined with some value v. The result $r\,.\,a$ is this value v.

• A one-field record extends the input row, defining one more field (that should not be previously defined).

- The removal of field a from a record M returns a record that acts as M except on the field a where it acts as the empty record.
- Finally, concatenation composes its arguments.

It is easy to see that any program in Π is also a program in $\Pi^{\parallel}$. First, define the extension primitive by:

$$\{M \text{ with } a = N\} \equiv M \parallel \{a = N\}$$

It has type:

$$\{\chi \Rightarrow a : \text{abs} ; \pi\} \to \alpha \to \{\chi \Rightarrow a : \text{pre}(\alpha) ; \pi\}$$

Check that all the following typing assertions are correct in $\Pi^{\parallel}$:

$$\{\ \} : \{\text{abs} \Rightarrow \text{abs}\}$$

$$\_. a : \{\text{abs} \Rightarrow a : \text{pre}(\alpha) ; \pi\} \to \alpha$$

$$\{\_ \text{ with } a = \_\} : \{\text{abs} \Rightarrow a : \text{abs} ; \pi\} \to \alpha \to \{\text{abs} \Rightarrow a : \text{pre}(\alpha) ; \pi\}$$

$$\_\backslash a : \{\text{abs} \Rightarrow a : \varepsilon ; \pi\} \to \{\text{abs} \Rightarrow a : \text{abs} ; \pi\}$$

Last, abbreviate $(\text{abs} \Rightarrow \rho)$ as (ρ) to conclude that $\Pi^{\parallel}$ possesses all the primitives of Π with all types that Π can assign to them. The rest of the language Π is core ML and is also in $\Pi^{\parallel}$.

Examples We show a few examples processed by a prototype written in CAML [CH89, Wei89]. The type inference engine is exactly the one of Π; only the primitives have changed. The syntax is similar to CAML syntax.

The type of a one-field record says that the record cannot be merged with another record that also defines this field:

```
#let a = {a = 1};;
a:{a:abs; χ ⇒ a:pre (num); χ}
```

Two records r and s can be merged if they do not define common fields. For instance, r can be merged on the left with $\{a = 1\}$ if its output row on a is absent.

```
#let left r = r ‖ {a = 1};;
left:{χ ⇒ a:abs; π} → {χ ⇒ a:pre (num); π}
```

The resulting record modifies its input row as r but on field a which is added. Similarly, s can be merged on the right with a if the input field a is present (with the adequate type).

```
#let right s = {a = 1} ‖ s;;
right:{a:pre (num); χ ⇒ π} → {a:abs; χ ⇒ π}
```

In particular, s cannot define an a field, otherwise its input field a would be absent.

Non overwriting of fields is guaranteed on the left by negative information (absent field) at a positive row occurrence, and on the right by positive information (present field) at a positive row occurrence. Some symmetry is preserved! However writing r ‖ s instead of s ‖ r in a program sometime matters: one might typecheck while the other does not, though none of the programs would overwrite fields. If both typecheck, the type of the result will be the same (provided all fields are symmetric).

Here are a few more examples:

```
#let foo = fun r s → (r ‖ s).a;;
foo:{a:abs; χ ⇒ π} → {π ⇒ a:pre (α); ξ} → α
```

This shows the functionality of concatenation on both sides. The result shall have an a field, but what argument will provide it is not specified yet.

```
#let gee = foo {b = 1};;
gee:{b:pre (num); a:abs; χ ⇒ a:pre (α); π} → α
```

Now r must define the a field.

```
#gee a;;
it:num
```

Asymmetric Concatenation The system Π may also provide free extension, with the following primitive:

$$\{\_ \text{ with } !a = \_\} : \Pi(a:\theta;\chi) \to \alpha \to \Pi(a:\text{pre}(\alpha);\chi)$$

This will make concatenation asymmetric:

$$\{!a = \_\} : \alpha \to \{a:\theta;\chi \Rightarrow a:\text{pre}(\alpha);\chi\}$$

For instance, the following example is typeable:

```
#let ab = (fun r → {!a = 1} ‖ r) {!a = true; !b = 1};;
ab:{a:χ; b:π; ξ ⇒ a:pre (bool); b:pre (num); ξ}
```

This shows that asymmetric fields can be redefined with values of possibly incompatible types.

The choice between strict and free extension is encoded in the extension primitive, but the choice between asymmetric and symmetric concatenation is not encoded in the concatenation primitive which is always the composition. It is not concatenation which is symmetric or not, but record fields themselves! We can have symmetric and asymmetric fields coexisting peacefully.

```
#{!a = 1; b = true};;
it:{b:abs; a:χ; π ⇒ a:pre (num); b:pre (bool); π}
```

Primitives to modify these properties of fields can easily be provided

$$\text{symmetric}^a : \{a:\theta; \chi \Rightarrow a:\text{pre}(\alpha); \chi\} \rightarrow \{a:\text{abs}; \chi \Rightarrow a:\text{pre}(\alpha); \chi\}$$

$$\text{asymmetric}^a : \{a:\theta; \chi \Rightarrow a:\text{pre}(\alpha); \chi\} \rightarrow \{a:\varepsilon; \chi \Rightarrow a:\text{pre}(\alpha); \chi\}$$

But it is not possible to make all fields of a record symmetric, or asymmetric; this has to be done field by field.

We can now better understand why symmetric concatenation is not so symmetric. Both `left` and `right` functions accept any argument, and one should not expect them to behave the same on a record of which some of the fields are asymmetric.

With asymmetric fields, the following examples reach the limit of ML polymorphism. For instance, the function

```
#fun r s → s.b, r ‖ s;;
it:{χ ⇒ b:abs; π} → {b:abs; π ⇒ b:pre (α); ξ} → α * {χ ⇒ b:pre (α); ξ}
```

does not accept a record r which has a b field, though the program would still run correctly if the b field of s is asymmetric. This is due to ML polymorphism weakness: the second argument is λ-bound and thus it is not polymorphic. The field b of s is observed by setting its input to abs, which has to be the output field b of r in r ‖ s.

Since s has definitely a b field, the concatenation r ‖ s is equal to the concatenation r\b ‖ s. We can rewrite the previous program as

```
#fun r s → s.b., (r\b ‖ s);;
it:{b:χ; π ⇒ b:ξ; φ} → {b:abs; φ ⇒ b:pre (α); ψ} →
    α * {b:abs; π ⇒ b:pre (α); ψ}
```

which can now be applied to any record r.

The restriction _\b of field b only changes the type of its arguments but does not modify it; it is called a *retyping function*. Many weaknesses of $\Pi^{\|}$ originating in the restricted polymorphism provided by the ML type system can be solved by adding retyping functions. They insert type information in the program helping the type inference engine. We will describe other ways of solving these examples by strengthening the type inference engine in section 2.3.

2.3 Strength and Weakness of $\Pi^{\|}$

We compare our language with Wand's proposal [Wan89], and Harper and Pierce's system and mention possible extensions.

Comparison with Other Systems There are only a few other systems that implement concatenation. Wand's proposal [Wan89] is still more powerful than our system $\Pi^{\|}$. For instance

$$\lambda r \,.\, r \,.\, a + (\{a = 1\} \| r) \,.\, a$$

is typable in Wand's system but not in ours. Wand's system polymorphism is carried by the concatenation operator, at the cost of bringing in the type system a restricted form of conjunctive types and having disjunction of principal types instead of unique principal types. In contrast, in our system, polymorphism is carried by records themselves. As mentioned above, we can regenerate polymorphism of records by inserting retyping functions. If the same restricted form of conjunctive types was brought in our system, then retyping functions would be powerful enough to regenerate all fields of a record without having to mention them explicitly. This would give back all the power of Wand's system.

This shows that the additional power of Wand's system comes from conjunctive types. Conversely, our system succeeds with only generic polymorphism on examples that needed conjunctive types in Wand's system. We are going to explain how this happens.

Wand's system can be reformulated in system Π. A simple idea is to type the concatenation operator by introducing an infix type operator $\|$ of arity two. Then concatenation has type:

$$\| : \Pi(\chi) \to \Pi(\pi) \to \Pi(\chi \| \pi)$$

But we have to eliminate $\|$ operators that might hide type collisions. In the system Π, we entice distributing concatenation on fields with the equations:

$$(a : \theta ; \chi) \| (a : \varepsilon ; \pi) = (a : \theta \| \varepsilon ; \chi \| \pi)$$

The operator $\|$ on fields can be defined by enumerating the triples $(\theta, \varepsilon, \theta \| \varepsilon)$. They are all triples of the form

$$(\theta, \mathrm{abs}, \theta) \quad \text{or} \quad (\theta, \mathrm{pre}(\beta), \mathrm{pre}(\beta)).$$

This disjunction in the relation $\|$ breaks the principal type property of type inference. Worse, disjunctions on different fields combine and make the resulting type (conjunction of types) explode in size.

Our system emphasizes that $\theta \| \varepsilon$ is uniform on θ: once we know ε, we can eliminate the conjunction in $\theta \| \varepsilon$. A field a, instead of carrying its type ε, carries the function $\theta \Rightarrow \theta \| \varepsilon$. For instance, if M has type τ, the record $\{a = M\}$ would have type $\Pi(a : \mathrm{pre}(\tau); \mathrm{abs})$ in Π. On field a, since ε is now $\mathrm{pre}(\tau)$, the merging $\theta \| \varepsilon$ is equal to $\mathrm{pre}(\tau)$. In the template, π is abs, and thus $\chi \| \pi$ is χ. We deduce the type of $\{a = M\}$ in $\Pi^{\|}$:

$$\{a : (\theta \Rightarrow \mathrm{pre}(\tau)); (\chi \Rightarrow \chi)\} \quad \text{i.e.} \quad \{(a : \theta; \chi) \Rightarrow (a : \mathrm{pre}(\tau); \chi)\}.$$

Another system with type inference was proposed by Ohori and Buneman in [OB88]. Their concatenation on records is recursive concatenation, which we do not provide. Note that they have a very restricted form of recursive concatenation since types in record fields must not contain any function type.

In explicitly typed languages, the only system with concatenation is the one of Harper and Pierce [HP90b]; it implements symmetric concatenation. Since their system is explicitly (higher order) typed, we say that typing a $\Pi^{\|}$ program M succeeds in HP90 if we can find a HP90 program whose erasure (the program obtained by erasing all type information) is M. Their system has not free restriction of fields, but we shall ignore this difference.

The following $\Pi^{\|}$ program cannot be typed in HP90:

```
#let either r s = (r ‖ s).a in
# if true then either {a = 1} {b = 2} else either {b = 2}
 {a = 1};;
it:num
```

In the expression $(r \| s).a$, one has to choose whether r or s is defining field a, and thus the function either cannot be used with the two alternatives. This breaks the symmetry of concatenation.

Conversely, there are programs that can be typed in HP90 but not in $\Pi^{\|}$ as a result of ML polymorphism restrictions. For instance the function

```
#let reverse r s = if true then r ‖ s else s ‖ r;;
reverse: {χ ⇒ χ} → {χ ⇒ χ} → {χ ⇒ χ}
```

cannot be applied to $\{a = 1\}$ and $\{b = 2\}$ in $\Pi^{\|}$. In HP90 it would have type

$$\forall \chi \cdot \forall \pi \# \chi \cdot \chi \to \pi \to (\chi \| \pi)$$

and could be applied to any two compatible records. It is difficult, though, to tell whether the failure comes from a limitation of polymorphism in general, or the inability to quantify with constraints, since the two are strongly related. The typability of the previous example in $\Pi^{\|}$ is somehow equivalent to the typability, in core ML, of the function:

```
#let reverse r s = if true then r ∘ s else s ∘ r;;
reverse:(α → α) → (α → α) → α → α
```

This is too weak a type! Whether a higher order language would give it a much better type is not so obvious. Next section provides a better basis for comparison between the two systems.

Limitations and Extensions   Since the type inference engine of $\Pi^{\|}$ is the same as the one of Π (only types of primitives have changed), both systems enjoy the same properties. Record polymorphism is provided by ML genericity introduced in let bindings. If this is too restrictive, then one should introduce type inclusion. One could also have a restricted conjunctive engine as in [Wan89]; however this would decrease considerably the efficiency of type inference, and the readability of types. Allowing recursion on types would also require an extension of the results (though in practice the mechanism is already present). In $\Pi^{\|}$, as in Π, present fields cannot be implicitly forgotten, but have to be explicitly removed, unless the structure of fields is enriched with flags. All these improvements are discussed in detail in [Rém92c].

3   Other Applications

The transformation can also be applied to other languages, which we illustrate in this section.

3.1   Application to Harper and Pierce's Calculus

The higher order typed language of Harper and Pierce [HP90a] already possesses concatenation, but records are not abstractions. It can still benefit from the encoding. Instead of presenting special constructs for operations on records, we could assume given the following primitives in their language:

Primitives for HP90

$\{\ \}:\Pi(\ )$

$\_.a:\forall\alpha\cdot\forall\chi\#a\cdot(\Pi(a:\alpha)\|\chi)\to\alpha$

$\{a=\_\}:\forall\alpha\cdot\alpha\to\Pi(a:\alpha)$

$\backslash a : \forall \alpha \cdot \forall \chi \# a \cdot (\Pi(a:\alpha) \| \chi) \to \chi$

$\| : \forall \chi \cdot \forall \pi \# \chi \cdot \chi \to \pi \to (\chi \| \pi)$

But the type system is not enough sophisticated to be able to type the primitive $\{\_ \text{ but } a \text{ from}\_\}$. Thus we apply the translation dropping the removal of fields. Using the encoding, the primitive operations on records in the language HP90$^\|$ have the following types:

Primitives for HP90$^\|$

$\{\ \} : \forall \chi \cdot (\chi \Rightarrow \chi)$

$\_ . a : \forall \alpha \cdot \forall \chi \# a \cdot \forall \pi \# a \cdot (\chi \Rightarrow \Pi(a:\alpha) \| \pi) \to \alpha$

$\{a = \_\} : \forall \alpha \cdot \alpha \to \forall \chi \# a \cdot (\chi \Rightarrow \Pi(a:\alpha) \| \chi)$

$\| : \forall \chi \cdot \forall \pi \cdot \forall \xi \cdot (\chi \Rightarrow \pi) \to (\pi \Rightarrow \xi) \to (\chi \Rightarrow \xi)$

We can define a function either:

$\Lambda \alpha . \Lambda \chi . \Lambda \pi \# a . \lambda r : (\Pi(\ ) \Rightarrow \chi) . \lambda s : (\chi \Rightarrow \Pi(a:\alpha) \| \pi).$
$\quad (\_. a[\alpha][\Pi(\ )][\pi](\| [\Pi(\ )][\chi][\Pi(a:\alpha) \| \pi] r s))$

and apply it to records $\{a = 1\}$ and $\{b = 2\}$ in any order. For instance,

either $[\text{num}][\Pi(a:\text{num})][\Pi(b:\text{num})](\{a = 1\}[\Pi(\ )])(\{b = 2\}[\Pi(a:\text{num})])$

This example is not typable in HP90.

Conversely, the program:

```
let reverse r s = if true then r ‖ s else s ‖ r in reverse
  {} {a = 1}, reverse {} {a = 1};;
```

can be typed in HP90, but we conjecture that it cannot be typed in HP90$^\|$. In fact its typability in HP90$^\|$ is equivalent to the following term being the erasure of a term of F:

```
(fun r → K (r I K) (r K I))
       (fun f g → (fun x → f (g x)) or
       (fun x → g (f x)))
```

where I is fun x → x and K is fun x y → x, and or is a constant assumed of type $\Lambda \alpha . \alpha \to \alpha \to \alpha$ in F.

To summarize, none of the language HP90 or HP90$^\parallel$ would be more powerful than the other. Remark that type applications and type abstractions are located at completely different places, thus a partial translation of explicitly typed terms from HP90$^\parallel$ to HP90 can only be global.

A previous language proposed by Harper and Pierce in [HP90a] had no concatenation, but shared the same spirit as HP90. The transformation applies to it as well, and results in a language with concatenation very closed to HP90$^\parallel$.

3.2 Application to Cardelli and Mitchell's Calculus

Unlike HP90, the language of Cardelli and Mitchell [CM89] does not already provide concatenation of records, but only strict extension. The application of our encoding to CM89 is not harder than to HP90. The language cannot be easily extended with the combining construct, therefore we skip the removal of fields. Using CM89 types, primitives for record operations in CM89$^\parallel$ have the following types:

Primitives for CM89$^\parallel$

$\{\ \}: \forall \chi \cdot (\chi \Rightarrow \chi)$

$\_.a: \forall \alpha \cdot \forall \chi < \langle\!\langle\ \rangle\!\rangle \backslash a \cdot \forall \pi < \langle\!\langle\ \rangle\!\rangle \backslash a \cdot (\chi \Rightarrow \langle\!\langle \pi \| a : \alpha \rangle\!\rangle) \to \alpha$

$\{a = \_\}: \forall \alpha \cdot \alpha \to \forall \chi < \langle\!\langle\ \rangle\!\rangle \backslash a \cdot (\chi \Rightarrow \langle\!\langle \chi \| a : \alpha \rangle\!\rangle)$
$\qquad \| : \forall \chi \cdot \forall \pi \cdot \forall \xi \cdot (\chi \Rightarrow \pi) \to (\pi \Rightarrow \xi) \to (\chi \Rightarrow \xi)$

We can again define the function either:

$\Lambda \alpha . \Lambda \chi . \Lambda \pi < \langle\!\langle\ \rangle\!\rangle \backslash a . \lambda r : (\langle\!\langle\ \rangle\!\rangle \Rightarrow \chi) . \lambda s : (\chi \Rightarrow \langle\!\langle \pi \| a : \alpha \rangle\!\rangle).$

$(\_.a[\alpha][\langle\!\langle\ \rangle\!\rangle][\pi](\| [\langle\!\langle\ \rangle\!\rangle][\chi][\langle\!\langle \pi \| a : \alpha \rangle\!\rangle] r s))$

and apply it to the records $\{a = 1\}$ and $\{b = 2\}$:

either $[num][\langle\!\langle a : num \rangle\!\rangle][\langle\!\langle b : num \rangle\!\rangle] (\{a = 1\}[\langle\!\langle\ \rangle\!\rangle]) (\{b = 2\}[\langle\!\langle a : num \rangle\!\rangle])$

3.3 Multiple Inheritance without Record Concatenation

Multiple inheritance has been encoded with record concatenation [Wan89]. We have encoded record concatenation with record extension. By composition, multiple inheritance can be encoded with record extension.

Given the strengthening of the type inference engine to recursive types, the system $\Pi^\parallel$ would support multiple inheritance as presented in [Wan89]. But multiple inheritance makes very little use of concatenation. It is only necessary for building new methods, but objects do not need it. Thus it may be worth revisiting the type-checking of multiple inheritance of [Wan89] and eliminating the need for concatenation by abstracting methods as we abstracted records.

The following encoding of multiple inheritance was used by Wand in [Wan89]. The definition of a class

$$\text{class } (\vec{x}) \text{ inherits } \overrightarrow{P(\vec{Q})} \text{ methods } \overrightarrow{a = M} \text{ end}$$

was encoded as

$$\lambda \vec{x} . \lambda \, self . \overrightarrow{P(\vec{Q})} \| \overrightarrow{\{a = M\}}$$

The creation of objects of that class

$$\text{instance } C(\vec{N})$$

was the recursive expression

$$Y(C(\vec{N}))$$

Sending a method a to an object x was the same as reading the field x of a. The problem with this encoding is that it requires record concatenation. We can easily get read of it, using our trick. We encode a class definition as

$$\lambda \vec{x} . \lambda u . \lambda \, self . u \| \overrightarrow{P(\vec{Q})} \| \overrightarrow{\{a = M\}}$$

i.e.

$$\lambda \vec{x} . \lambda u . \lambda \, self . \{ \overrightarrow{P(\vec{Q})} \circ u \text{ with } \overrightarrow{a = M} \}$$

which only requires record extension. Then creating an object of that class becomes

$$Y(C(\vec{N})\{ \ \})$$

and sending a method is unchanged.

Remarks Since removing of fields is not needed here, this section applies to all typed calculi with record extension.

This section uses Wand's conception of inheritance. Objects are carrying their dictionaries. Other views of objects do not encode with record operations. This section does not apply to them.

Conclusion

We have described how a functional language with records and record extension automatically provides record concatenation. Though records are data, they should be typed as if there were abstractions over an input row of fields that they modify. Their behavior can be observed at any time by giving them the empty row as input. Concatenation is then composition.

We have applied the method to a record extension of ML. We have obtained a language implementing all operations on records except the recursive merge, allowing type inference in a very efficient way in practice.

The kind of type system that we have obtained seems complementary to Harper and Pierce's one. Taking the best of the two systems would be interesting investigation.

The encoding also helps understanding concatenation. However, the relationship between the semantics of a program in the language with concatenation and the semantics of its translation need to be investigated closely before claiming that concatenation itself comes for free.

Acknowledgments

I am grateful for interesting discussions with Luca Cardelli, Georges Gonthier, Jean-Jacques Lévy, Benjamin Pierce and Mitchell Wand, and particularly thankful to Xavier Leroy whose comments on the presentation of this article were very helpful.

Notes

1. This is similar to the correspondence between *append* and *cons* on A-lists, in this particular case, the equality is $[M]$ *append* $r = M$ *cons* r.

2. For simplicity of examples we assume the existence a polymorphic equality `equal`.

References

[Car86]   Luca Cardelli. Amber. In *Combinators and Functional Programming Languages*, volume 242 of *Lecture Notes in Computer Science*, pages 21–47. Spinger Verlag, 1986. Proceedings of the 13th Summer School of the LITP.

[CH89]   Guy Cousineau and Gérard Huet. *The CAML Primer*. BP 105, F-78 153 Le Chesnay Cedex, France, 1989.

[CM89]   L. Cardelli and J. C. Mitchell. Operations on records. *Math. Structures in Computer Science*, 1(1):3–48, 1991. Summary in *Math. Foundations of Prog. Lang. Semantics*, Springer LNCS 442, 1990, pp 22–52.

[HMT91]   Robert Harper, Robin Milner, and Mads Tofte. *The definition of Standard ML*. The MIT Press, 1991.

[HP90a]   Robert W. Harper and Benjamin C. Pierce. Extensible records without subsumption. Technical Report CMU-C5-90-102, Carnegie Mellon University, Pittsburg, Pensylvania, February 1990.

[HP90b]   Robert W. Harper and Benjamin C. Pierce. A record calculus based on symmetric concatenation. Technical Report CMU-C5-90-157, Carnegie Mellon University, Pittsburg, Pensylvania, February 1990.

[JM88]   Lalita A. Jategaonkar and John C. Mitchell. ML with extended pattern matching and subtypes. In *Proceedings of the 1988 Conference on LISP and Functional Programming*, 1988.

[OB88]   Atsushi Ohori and Peter Buneman. Type inference in a database langage. In *ACM Conference on LISP and Functional Programming*, pages 174–183, 1988.

[Oho90]   Atsushi Ohori. Extending ML polymorphism to record structure. Technical report, University of Glasgow, 1990.

[Rém90]   Didier Rémy. *Algèbres Touffues. Application au Typage Polymorphe des Objects Enregistrements dans les Langages Fonctionnels*. Thèse de doctorat, Université de Paris 7, 1990.

[Rém91]   Didier Rémy. Type inference for records in a natural extension of ML. Technical Report 1431, Inria-Rocquencourt, May 1991.

[Rém92a]   Didier Rémy. Extending ML type system with a sorted equational theory. Technical report 1766, INRIA-Rocquencourt, BP 105, F-78 153 Le Chesnay Cedex, 1992. To appear. Also in [Rém90], chapter 3.

[Rém92b]   Didier Rémy. Syntactic theories and the algebra of record terms. Technical report 1869, BP 105, INRIA-Rocquencourt, BP 105, F-78 153 Le Chesnay Cedex, 1992.

[Rém92c]   Didier Rémy. Type inference for records in a natural extension of ML. This volume. Also in [Rém91].

[Wan87]   Mitchell Wand. Complete type inference for simple objects. In *Second Symposium on Logic In Computer Science*, 1987.

[Wan88]   Mitchell Wand. Corrigendum: Complete type inference for simple objects. In *Third Symposium on Logic In Computer Science*, 1988.

[Wan89]   Mitchen Wand. Type inference for record concatenation and multiple inheritance. In *Fourth Annual Symposium on Logic In Computer Science*, pages 92–97, 1989.

[Wei89]   Pierre Weis. *The CAML Reference Manual*. BP 105, F-78 153 Le Chesnay Cedex, France, 1989.

11 Extensible Records in a Pure Calculus of Subtyping

Luca Cardelli

Abstract

Extensible records were introduced by Mitchell Wand while studying type inference in a polymorphic λ-calculus with record types. This paper describes a calculus with extensible records, $F_{<:}\rho$, that can be translated into a simpler calculus, $F_{<:}$, lacking any record primitives. Given independent axiomatizations of $F_{<:}\rho$ and $F_{<:}$ (the former being an extension of the latter) we show that the translation preserves typing, subtyping, and equality.

$F_{<:}\rho$ can then be used as an expressive calculus of extensible records, either directly or to give meaning to yet other languages. We show that $F_{<:}\rho$ can express many of the standard benchmark examples that appear in the literature.

Like other record calculi that have been proposed, $F_{<:}\rho$ has a rather complex set of rules but, unlike those other calculi, its rules are justified by a translation to a very simple calculus. We argue that thinking in terms of translations may help in simplifying and organizing the various record calculi that have been proposed, as well as in generating new ones.

1 Introduction

Extensible records, and the associated notion of *row variables*, were introduced by Mitchell Wand while he was studying the problem of type inference in a polymorphic λ-calculus with record types [Wand 87]; a row variable is a type variable ranging over the possible field-extensions of a record type. Many calculi of row variables have been produced since then [Jategaonkar Mitchell 88] [Rémy 89] [Wand 89] [Harper Pierce 90] [Cardelli Mitchell 91], and many more can be imagined. As we try to increase the expressiveness of these calculi, the axiomatization techniques become more and more divergent and complex. To be able to compare and discuss these different calculi, we feel the need of some more fundamental framework. This paper suggests that a very simple calculus of subtyping can be used as a basis for studying much more complex calculi of extensible records.

In the search for a unifying framework, we can adopt the following working hypothesis: every reasonable calculus of row variables should be reducible to a calculus without row variables, via a well-behaved translation. The purpose of this hypothesis is not to eliminate row variables completely, since the translated programs would become too verbose to be be useful; the purpose is to gain insights in the study of

First appeared in Digital Equipment Corporation, Systems Research, Technical Report Number 81, 1992.

calculi with row variables. Even if our working hypothesis turns out to be false, which it may well be, we will have distinguished the easier features that can be translated from the more complex ones that cannot.

To carry out this plan, we need to fix a suitable target calculus for the translation. Since we are studying type variables, a likely choice would seem to be the second-order λ-calculus (*system F* [Girard 71] [Reynolds 74]). To express the idea that the translation is *well-behaved*, we require some basic soundness properties such as the preservation of typing, subtyping, and equality relations. But, in order to preserve subtyping relations, we need to translate to a target calculus that still has a notion of subtyping; otherwise we would gain little insight about the complex subtyping relations induced by extensible records. For a similar reason, we are not interested in untyped target calculi, for which translations are easily obtainable.

As target calculus we use therefore an extension of F with subtyping, called $F_{<:}$ (*F-sub*), which has been studied recently [Curien 90] [Curien Ghelli 91] [Cardelli Martini Mitchell Scedrov 91]. The fact that a translation of extensible records into $F_{<:}$ is at all possible also gives us new evidence about the expressiveness of $F_{<:}$, and reinforces our feeling that $F_{<:}$ can be regarded as a canonical calculus of subtyping.

Before the main discussion, we briefly review the motivations that led to the notions of row variables and extensible records.

In a calculus with records, a program may contain expressions like $r.l$ where r denotes a record value and the label l denotes a field of that record; then the *record selection* $r.l$ denotes the value of the field labeled l in record r.

Given the expression $r.l$ we can infer that r has a type of the form $Rcd(l:A)$, that is, a record type having a field labeled l of type A; the type A is to be determined later. Given another expression $r.l'$ in the same program, we can then infer that r has a type of the form $Rcd(l:A, l':A')$, and so on.

This form of typing, though, becomes insufficient when considering *record updates*. The expression $r.l \leftarrow a$ denotes a record similar to r, except that the value of its l component is updated to a. Consider now the program:

$$p \triangleq \lambda(r)r.l \leftarrow a$$

Assuming $a:A$, and for any type B, we can infer the typing:

$$p : Rcd(l:B) \rightarrow Rcd(l:A)$$

Given a record value $rcd(l = b, l' = b')$ having two fields labeled l and l' with respective values b and b', we consider legal the expression $p(rcd(l = b, l' = b'))$ because the argument has all the fields required by the type of p. This expression then receives the type $Rcd(l:A)$, because of the typing of p above. Unfortunately, by this typing we have forgotten that the argument of p, and hence its result, has another component labeled l'. This is unsatisfactory.

To capture the kind of polymorphism required by the record update operation, we introduce row variables. Record types are extended to the more general form $Rcd(l_1 : A_1, \ldots, l_n : A_n, X)$, where X is a *row variable* intended to represent "all the other fields" of a given record type; in this case all the fields except the ones labeled $l_1 \ldots l_n$. We can then assign to the program p the more informative type:

$$p : Rcd(l : B, X) \to Rcd(l : A, X)$$

Now, in $p(rcd(l = b, l' = b', l'' = b''))$, where $b' : B'$ and $b'' : B''$, the row variable X is bound to $l' : B'$, $l'' : B''$ (a *row type*), producing the expected result type $Rcd(l : A, l' : B', l'' : B'')$ by substitution of $l' : B', l'' : B''$ for X.

In this form of type inference we must keep track of constraints on the row variables, such as the fact that X in the example above must not come to contain l components (otherwise we would have a duplicate label). These constraints can be made manifest by adopting a type system featuring explicit polymorphism; then program p receives the typing:

$$p : \forall(Y)\forall(X \uparrow l)\, Rcd(l : Y, X) \to Rcd(l : A, X)$$

Here $X \uparrow l$ means that X is undefined at label l (that is, X can be bound only to row types that have no l components). Appropriate types and rows must then be explicitly supplied as arguments to p, as in:

$$p(B)(l' : B', l'' : B'')(rcd(l = b, l' = b', l'' = b''))$$

This is finally a satisfactory typing of p, although for practical reasons we may require some type inference to avoid writing down the type arguments (B) and $(l' : B', l'' : B'')$. We do not discuss type inference here, which we consider as a pragmatic variation on the basic calculus.

In Wand's original view, and in further developments [Rémy 89] [Harper Pierce 90], row variables are type variables of a different *kind*. In contrast, in [Cardelli Mitchell 91] we studied an explicitly polymorphic type system where both row variables and type variables are instances of second-order type variables, therefore unifying the two concepts. In this paper we go back to the original view that row variables are separate, but we show that they can ultimately be expressed as ordinary type variables.

In outline, this paper shows how a calculus with row variables, $F_{<:}\rho$, can be represented in a simpler calculus without row variables, $F_{<:}$, via a translation. Given independent axiomatizations of $F_{<:}\rho$ and $F_{<:}$ (the former being an extension of the latter) we prove that the translation is well-behaved, in that it preserves typing, subtyping, and equality.

The paper is organized as follows. Sections 2 and 3 recall the definition of $F_{<:}$ and its expressive power (borrowing from [Cardelli Martini Mitchell Scedrov 91]). Section 4 gives the main intuitions of the encoding of extensible records in $F_{<:}$. Section 5 describes $F_{<:}\rho$. Section 6 gives the translation of $F_{<:}\rho$ into $F_{<:}$, and finally section 7 shows that the translation is sound.

Examples of the expressive power of $F_{<:}\rho$ and comparisons with other calculi are delayed until section 5.5. We show there that $F_{<:}\rho$ can express many of the standard benchmark examples that appear in the literature. We encourage readers to examine these examples whenever convenient.

Readers who wish to learn about $F_{<:}\rho$ as a language of records but who are not interested in the translation into $F_{<:}$, may confine themselves to sections 1, 2.0, 2.1, 2.2, 5.0, 5.1, 5.2, 5.4, 5.5, and 8.

2   System $F_{<:}$

In this section we describe the target calculus, $F_{<:}$, for the translation that will follow. $F_{<:}$ can be translated in turn into a trivial extension of F called F_1 [Breazu-Tannen Coquand Gunter Scedrov 89]. However, the known translations from $F_{<:}$ to F_1 do not preserve subtyping in $F_{<:}$ [Martini 90]; this reinforces the point that translating to $F_{<:}$ is more informative than translating directly to F.

$F_{<:}$ is obtained by extending F with a notion of subtyping ($<:$). This extension allows us to remain within a pure calculus. That is, we introduce neither the basic types nor the structured types normally associated with subtyping in programming languages. Instead, we show that these programming types can be obtained via encodings within the pure calculus. In particular, we can encode record types with their subtyping relations [Cardelli 88].

2.1   Syntax

The snytax of $F_{<:}$ extends the syntax of F as follows. A new type constant *Top* denotes the supertype of all types. Second-order quantifiers acquire a subtype bound: $\forall(X <: A)A'$ (*bounded quantifiers* [Cardelli Wegner 85]). Ordinary second-order quantifiers are recovered by setting the quantifier bound to *Top*; we use $\forall(X)A$ for $\forall(X <: Top)A$. The syntax of values is extended by a constant *top* of type *Top*, and by a subtype bound on polymorphic functions, $\lambda(X <: A)a$. We use $\lambda(X)a$ for $\lambda(X <: Top)a$.

Syntax

$A, B ::=$	Types
X	type variable
Top	the supertype of all types
$A \rightarrow B$	function space
$\forall (X <: A)B$	bounded quantification

$a, b ::=$	Values
x	value variable
top	canonical value of type Top
$\lambda(x:A)b$	function
$b(a)$	application
$\lambda(X <: A)b$	bounded type function
$b(A)$	type application

A subtyping judgment is added to F's judgments. Moreover, the equality judgment on values is made relative to a type; this is important since values in $F_{<:}$ can have many types, and two values may or may not be equivalent depending on the type those values are considered as possessing.

Judgments

$\vdash E\ env$	E is a well-formed environment
$E \vdash A\ type$	A is a type
$E \vdash A <: B$	A is a subtype of B
$E \vdash a:A$	a has type A
$E \vdash a \leftrightarrow b:A$	a and b are equal members of type A

We use $dom(E)$ for the set of variables *defined* by an environment E.

As usual, we identify terms up to renaming of bound variables; that is, using $C\{X \leftarrow D\}$ for the substitution of D for X in C:

$$\forall (X <: A)B \equiv \forall (Y <: A)B\{X \leftarrow Y\}$$

$$\lambda(x:A)b \equiv \lambda(y:A)(b\{x \leftarrow y\})$$

$$\lambda(X <: A)b \equiv \lambda(Y <: A)(b\{X \leftarrow Y\})$$

These identifications can be made directly on the syntax, that is, without knowing whether the terms involved are the product of formal derivations in the system. By adopting these identifications, we avoid the need for a type equality judgment.

Environments, however, are not identified up to renaming of variables in their domains; environment variables are kept distinct by construction. A more formal approach would use de Bruijn indices for free and bound variables [deB 72].

2.2 Rules

The inference rules of $F_{<:}$ are listed below; we now comment on their most interesting aspects.

The subtyping judgment, $E \vdash A <: B$, defines, for any E, a reflexive and transitive relation on types with a *subsumption* property: a member of a type is also a member of any supertype of that type. Every type is a subtype of *Top*. The function space operator $\rightarrow$ is antimonotonic in its first argument and monotonic in its second. A bounded quantifier is antimonotonic in its bound and monotonic in its body.

The rules for the typing judgment, $E \vdash a : A$, are the same as the corresponding rules in F, except for the extension to bounded quantifiers. However, additional typing power is hidden in the subsumption rule, which for example allows a function to take an argument having a subtype of the function's input type.

Most of the equivalence rules, $E \vdash a \leftrightarrow b : A$, are unremarkable. They provide congruence over the syntax, and β and η equivalences. Two rules, however, stand out. The first, (Top collapse), states that any two terms are equivalent when "seen" at type *Top*. Since no operations are available on members of *Top*, all values are indistinguishable at that type; this fact will have many interesting consequences in the sequel. The second, (Eq appl2), is the congruence rule for polymorphic type application, giving general conditions under which two expressions $b'(A')$ and $b''(A'')$ are equivalent at a type C. This rule also has many intriguing consequences, but these will not be explored here. They are described in [Cardelli Martini Mitchell Scedrov 91].

Environments

$$\frac{}{\vdash \phi \; env} \tag{Env ϕ}$$

$$\frac{E \vdash A \; type \qquad x \notin dom(E)}{\vdash E, x : A \; env} \tag{Env x}$$

$$\frac{E \vdash A \; type \qquad X \notin dom(E)}{\vdash E, X <: A \; env} \tag{Env X}$$

Types

$$\frac{\vdash E, X <: A, E' \ env}{E, X <: A, E' \vdash X \ type} \qquad (Type \ X)$$

$$\frac{\vdash E \ env}{E \vdash Top \ type} \qquad (Type \ Top)$$

$$\frac{E \vdash A \ type \quad E \vdash B \ type}{E \vdash A \rightarrow B \ type} \qquad (Type \rightarrow)$$

$$\frac{E, X <: A \vdash B \ type}{E \vdash \forall(X <: A)B \ type} \qquad (Type \ \forall)$$

Subtypes

$$\frac{E \vdash A \ type}{E \vdash A <: A} \qquad (Sub \ refl)$$

$$\frac{E \vdash A <: B \quad E \vdash B <: C}{E \vdash A <: C} \qquad (Sub \ trans)$$

$$\frac{\vdash E, X <: A, E' \ env}{E, X <: A, E' \vdash X <: A} \qquad (Sub \ X)$$

$$\frac{E \vdash A \ type}{E \vdash A <: Top} \qquad (Sub \ Top)$$

$$\frac{E \vdash A' <: A \quad E \vdash B <: B'}{E \vdash A \rightarrow B <: A' \rightarrow B'} \qquad (Sub \rightarrow)$$

$$\frac{E \vdash A' <: A \quad E, X <: A' \vdash B <: B'}{E \vdash \forall(X <: A)B <: \forall(X <: A')B'} \qquad (Sub \ \forall)$$

Values

$$\frac{E \vdash a:A \quad E \vdash A <: B}{E \vdash a:B} \qquad (Subsumption)$$

$$\frac{\vdash E, x:A, E' \ env}{E, x:A, E' \vdash x:A} \qquad (Val \ x)$$

$$\frac{\vdash E \ env}{E \vdash top:Top} \qquad (Val \ top)$$

$$\frac{E, x : A \vdash b : B}{E \vdash \lambda(x : A)b : A \to B} \qquad\qquad (Val\ fun)$$

$$\frac{E \vdash b : A \to B \quad E \vdash a : A}{E \vdash b(a) : B} \qquad\qquad (Val\ appl)$$

$$\frac{E, X <: A \vdash b : B}{E \vdash \lambda(X <: A)b : \forall(X <: A)B} \qquad\qquad (Val\ fun2)$$

$$\frac{E \vdash b : \forall(X <: A)B \quad E \vdash A' <: A}{E \vdash b(A') : B\{X \leftarrow A'\}} \qquad\qquad (Val\ appl2)$$

Equivalence

$$\frac{E \vdash a \leftrightarrow b : A}{E \vdash b \leftrightarrow a : A} \qquad\qquad (Eq\ symm)$$

$$\frac{E \vdash a \leftrightarrow b : A \quad E \vdash b \leftrightarrow c : A}{E \vdash a \leftrightarrow c : A} \qquad\qquad (Eq\ trans)$$

$$\frac{E \vdash x : A}{E \vdash x \leftrightarrow x : A} \qquad\qquad (Eq\ x)$$

$$\frac{E \vdash a : Top \quad E \vdash b : Top}{E \vdash a \leftrightarrow b : Top} \qquad\qquad (Eq\ collapse)$$

$$\frac{E, x : A \vdash b \leftrightarrow b' : B}{E \vdash \lambda(x : A)b \leftrightarrow \lambda(x : A)b' : A \to B} \qquad\qquad (Eq\ fun)$$

$$\frac{E \vdash b \leftrightarrow b' : A \to B \quad E \vdash a \leftrightarrow a' : A}{E \vdash b(a) \leftrightarrow b'(a') : B} \qquad\qquad (Eq\ appl)$$

$$\frac{E, X <: A \vdash b \leftrightarrow b' : B}{E \vdash \lambda(X <: A)b \leftrightarrow \lambda(X <: A)b' : \forall(X <: A)B} \qquad\qquad (Eq\ fun2)$$

$$\frac{E \vdash b' \leftrightarrow b'' : \forall(X <: A)B \quad E \vdash A', A'' <: A \quad E \vdash B\{X \leftarrow A'\}, B\{X \leftarrow A''\} <: C}{E \vdash b'(A') \leftrightarrow b''(A'') : C} \qquad\qquad (Eq\ appl2)$$

$$\frac{E \vdash b \leftrightarrow b' : A \to B \quad y \notin dom(E)}{E \vdash \lambda(y : A)b(y) \leftrightarrow b' : A \to B} \qquad\qquad (Eq\ Eta)$$

$$\frac{E \vdash b \leftrightarrow b' : \forall(X <: A)B \quad Y \notin dom(E)}{E \vdash \lambda(Y <: A)b(Y) \leftrightarrow b' : \forall(X <: A)B} \qquad\qquad (Eq\ Eta2)$$

$$\frac{E, x:A \vdash b \leftrightarrow b':B \quad E \vdash a \leftrightarrow a':A}{E \vdash (\lambda(x:A)b)(a) \leftrightarrow b'\{x \leftarrow a'\}:B} \qquad (Eq\ Beta)$$

$$\frac{E, X <: A \vdash b \leftrightarrow b':B \quad E \vdash A' <: A}{E \vdash (\lambda(X <: A)b)(A') \leftrightarrow b'\{X \leftarrow A'\}:B\{X \leftarrow A'\}} \qquad (Eq\ Beta2)$$

This calculus was first extracted by Pierre-Louis Curien from the one in [Cardelli Wegner 85] and studied by him and Giorgio Ghelli [Curien Ghelli 91] under the name $F_\leq$. The present $F_{<:}$ is a refinement of $F_\leq$, achieved mostly by extending the (*Eq appl2*) rule. It is studied in [Cardelli Martini Mitchell Scedrov 91].

The following derived rules will be needed later. Their proofs follow from the lemmas listed in section 5.3 for $F_{<:}\rho$. (Those lemmas hold for $F_{<:}$ as well, when restricted to the syntax of $F_{<:}$.)

LEMMA (subsumption equivalence)   The subsumption rule extends to the equality judgment:

$$\frac{E \vdash a \leftrightarrow a':A \quad E \vdash A <: B}{E \vdash a \leftrightarrow a':B} \qquad (Eq\ subsumption)$$

LEMMA (domain restriction)   If $f:A \to B$, then f is equivalent to its restriction $f|_{A'}$ to a smaller domain $A' <: A$, when they are both seen at type $A' \to B$. That is:

$$\frac{E \vdash A' <: A \quad E \vdash B <: B' \quad E, x:A \vdash b \leftrightarrow b':B}{E \vdash \lambda(x:A)b \leftrightarrow \lambda(x:A')b':A' \to B'} \qquad (Eq\ fun')$$

LEMMA (bound restriction)   If $f:\forall(X <: A)B$, then f is equivalent to its restriction $f|_{A'}$ to a smaller bound $A' <: A$, when they are both seen at type $\forall(X <: A')B$. That is:

$$\frac{E \vdash A' <: A \quad E, X <: A' \vdash B <: B' \quad E, X <: A \vdash b \leftrightarrow b':B}{E \vdash \lambda(X <: A)b \leftrightarrow \lambda(X <: A')b':\forall(X <: A')B'} \qquad (Eq\ fun2')$$

3   Basic Encodings

Since $F_{<:}$ is an extension of F, it can express all the standard encodings of algebraic data types that are possible in F [Böhm Berarducci 85]. However, it is not clear that anything of further interest can be obtained from the subtyping rules of $F_{<:}$, which involve only an apparently useless type *Top* and the simple rules for $\to$ and $\forall$.

In this section we begin to show that we can in fact encode rich subtyping relations on familiar data structures. In section 4 the encodings become more involved; this increase in complexity then motivates the switch to an independently axiomatized system $(F_{<:}\rho)$ in section 5.

3.1 Booleans

In the sequel of section 3 we concentrate on inclusion of structured types, but for this to make sense we need to show that there are some non-trivial inclusions already at the level of basic types. We investigate here the type of booleans, and in the process we illustrate some interesting consequences of the $F_{<:}$ rules.

Starting from the encoding of Church's booleans in F, we can define three subtypes of *Bool* as follows (cf. [Fairbairn 89]):

$Bool \triangleq \forall(A)A \to A \to A$

$True \triangleq \forall(A)A \to Top \to A$

$False \triangleq \forall(A)Top \to A \to A$

$None \triangleq \forall(A)Top \to Top \to A$

where:

None <: True, None <: False, True <: Bool, False <: Bool

Looking at all the closed normal forms (that is, the *elements*) of these types, we have:

$true_{Bool} : Bool \triangleq \lambda(A)\lambda(x:A)\lambda(y:A)x$

$false_{Bool} : Bool \triangleq \lambda(A)\lambda(x:A)\lambda(y:A)y$

$true_{True} : True \triangleq \lambda(A)\lambda(x:A)\lambda(y:Top)x$

$false_{False} : False \triangleq \lambda(A)\lambda(x:Top)\lambda(y:A)y$

We obtain four elements of type *Bool*; in addition to the usual two, $true_{Bool}$ and $false_{Bool}$, the extra $true_{True}$ and $false_{False}$ have type Bool by subsumption. However, we can show that $true_{Bool}$ and $true_{True}$ are provably equivalent at type *Bool*, by using the domain restriction lemma ((*Eq fun'*), section 2.2).

$$\frac{E, A <: Top, x:A, y:Top \vdash x \leftrightarrow x:A \quad E \vdash A <: Top}{\begin{array}{c} E, A <: Top, x:A \vdash \lambda(y:Top)x \leftrightarrow \lambda(y:A)x:A \to A \\ \hline E, A <: Top \vdash \lambda(x:A)\lambda(y:Top)x \leftrightarrow \lambda(x:A)\lambda(y:A)x:A \to A \to A \\ \hline E \vdash \lambda(A)\lambda(x:A)\lambda(y:Top)x \leftrightarrow \lambda(A)\lambda(x:A)\lambda(y:A)x:\forall(A)A \to A \to A \\ \hline E \vdash true_{True} \leftrightarrow true_{Bool}:Bool \end{array}} \qquad (Eq\ fun')$$

Similarly, we can show that $E \vdash false_{False} \leftrightarrow false_{Bool} : Bool$. Hence, there really are only two different values in *Bool*.

3.2 Products

The standard encoding for pairs in F already exhibits useful subtyping properties:

$A \times B \triangleq \forall(C)(A \to B \to C) \to C$

Since both A and B occur in monotonic positions in $A \times B$ (being twice on the left of an arrow), we obtain the expected monotonic inclusion of products as a derived rule:

$$\frac{E \vdash A <: A' \qquad E \vdash B <: B'}{E \vdash A \times B <: A' \times B'}$$

The operations on pairs are defined, as usual, as:

$pair : \forall(A)\forall(B)A \to B \to A \times B \triangleq \lambda(A)\lambda(B)\lambda(a:A)\lambda(b:B)\lambda(C)\lambda(f:A \to B \to C)f(a)(b)$

$fst : \forall(A)\forall(B)A \times B \to A \triangleq \lambda(A)\lambda(B)\lambda(c:A \times B)c(A)(\lambda(x:A)\lambda(y:B)x)$

$snd : \forall(A)\forall(B)A \times B \to B \triangleq \lambda(A)\lambda(B)\lambda(c:A \times B)c(B)(\lambda(x:A)\lambda(y:B)y)$

We often use the following abbreviations, disambiguated by context:

$a, b \equiv a,_{A \times B}b \equiv pair(A)(B)(a)(b)$

$fst(c) \equiv fst_{A \times B}(c) \equiv fst(A)(B)(C)$

$snd(c) \equiv snd_{A \times B}(c) \equiv snd(A)(B)(c)$

3.3 Enumerations

Enumeration types (that is, finite sets) form another collection of base types with interesting inclusion relations. We describe them here because they show an interesting use of the *Top* type, and hint at the encoding of tuples in the next section.

The enumeration of *zero* elements can be defined as

$N_0 \triangleq \forall(A)Top \to A$

This type has no closed normal forms, hence no "elements".

The enumeration of *one* element is defined as:

$N_1 \triangleq \forall(A)A \times Top \to A$

This type has just one closed normal form:

$one_1 : N_1 \triangleq \lambda(A)\lambda(x : A \times Top)fst(x)$

Moreover, $N_0 <: N_1$ because $A \times Top <: Top$.

The enumeration of *two* elements is defined as:

$N_2 \triangleq \forall(A)A \times A \times Top \to A$

This type has the two closed normal forms:

$one_2 : N_2 \triangleq \lambda(A)\lambda(x : A \times A \times Top)fst(x)$

$two_2 : N_2 \triangleq \lambda(A)\lambda(x : A \times A \times Top)fst(snd(x))$

Moreover, $N_1 <: N_2$, and by subsumption:

$one_1 : N_2$

We find that N_2 has three elements. As for booleans, we can prove that two of these are equal in N_2:

$\vdash one_1 \leftrightarrow one_2 : N_2$

At this point the pattern of enumeration types should be clear:

$$N_n \triangleq \forall(A)A \times \underbrace{\cdots}_{n \text{ times}} \times A \times Top \to A$$

with $N_n <: N_{n+1}$, where N_n has n distinct elements.

3.4 Tuples

A *tuple type* $Tuple(A_1, \ldots, A_n, C)$ denotes an iterated product type. Its last slot, C, can be filled with any type. When C is a type variable, we have an *extensible tuple type*. When it is Top, we have a *simple tuple type*.

$Tuple(C) \triangleq C$

$Tuple(A_1, \ldots, A_n, C) \triangleq A_1 \times (\ldots \times (A_n \times C)\ldots) \qquad n \geq 1$

Hence we have:

$Tuple(A_1, \ldots, A_n, Tuple(B_1, \ldots, B_m, C)) \equiv Tuple(A_1, \ldots, A_n, B_1, \ldots, B_m, C)$

with derived rule:

$$\frac{E \vdash A_1 <: B_1 \ldots E \vdash A_n <: B_n \quad E \vdash C <: D}{E \vdash Tuple(A_1, \ldots, A_n, C) <: Tuple(B_1, \ldots, B_n, D)}$$

As a special case we obtain the rule for simple tuples:

$$\frac{E \vdash A_1 <: B_1 \ldots E \vdash A_n <: B_n \quad E \vdash A_{n+1} \, type \ldots E \vdash A_m \, type}{E \vdash Tuple(A_1, \ldots, A_n, \ldots, A_m, Top) <: Tuple(B_1, \ldots, B_n, Top)}$$

For example:

$Tuple(A, B, Top) <: Tuple(A, Top)$

    since $A <: A$, $B \times Top <: Top$, and $\times$ is monotonic.

We note here that the type *Top* assumes a very useful role, in allowing a longer tuple type to be a subtype of a shorter tuple type. The intuition is that a longer tuple value can always be regarded as a shorter tuple value, by "forgetting" the additional components, and this is possible since everything is forgotten in *Top*.

    For tuple values we have:

$tuple(c) \triangleq c$

$tuple(a_1, \ldots, a_n, c) \triangleq a_1, (\ldots, (a_n, c) \ldots) \qquad n \geq 1$

$tuple(a_1, \ldots, a_n, tuple(b_1, \ldots, b_m, c)) \equiv tuple(a_1, \ldots, a_n, b_1, \ldots, b_m, c)$

with derived rules:

$$\frac{E \vdash a_1 : A_1 \ldots E \vdash a_n : A_n \quad E \vdash a : A}{E \vdash tuple(a_1, \ldots, a_n, a) : Tuple(A_1, \ldots, A_n, A)}$$

$$\frac{E \vdash a_1 \leftrightarrow b_1 : A_1 \ldots E \vdash a_n \leftrightarrow b_n : A_n \quad E \vdash a \leftrightarrow b : A}{E \vdash tuple(a_1, \ldots, a_n, a) \leftrightarrow tuple(b_1, \ldots, b_n, b) : Tuple(A_1, \ldots, A_n, A)}$$

The basic tuple operations are: $a \perp i$, dropping the first i components of tuple a; and $a.i$, selecting the i-th component of a. These are defined by iterating product operations; we use the abbreviations:

$a \perp i \equiv a \perp_{A_i} i \equiv drop_i(A_i)(a) \equiv snd_i(a)$

$a.i \equiv a._{A_i} i \equiv sel_i(A_i)(a) \equiv fst(a \perp i)$

    More precisely:

$drop_0 : \forall(A_0) A_0 \to A_0 \triangleq \lambda(A_0)\lambda(t : A_0)t$

$sel_0 : \forall(A_0) A_0 \times Top \to A_0 \triangleq \lambda(A_0)\lambda(t : A_0 \times Top) fst_{A_0 \times Top}(drop_0(A_0 \times Top)(t))$

$drop_1 : \forall(A_1) Top \times A_1 \to A_1 \triangleq \lambda(A_1)\lambda(t : Top \times A_1) snd_{Top \times A_0}(drop_0(Top \times A_1)(t))$

$sel_1 : \forall(A_1) Top \times A_1 \times Top \to A_1$

$\quad \triangleq \lambda(A_1)\lambda(t : Top \times A_1 \times Top) fst_{A_1 \times Top}(drop_1(A_1 \times Top)(t))$

etc...

We obtain the derived rules:

$$\frac{E \vdash a : Tuple(A_0, \ldots, A_{i-1}, A)}{E \vdash a \angle i : A} \qquad \frac{E \vdash a : Tuple(A_0, \ldots, A_i, A)}{E \vdash a . i : A_i}$$

$$\frac{E \vdash a_0 : A_0 \ldots E \vdash a_{i-1} : A_{i-1} \quad E \vdash a : A}{E \vdash tuple(a_0, \ldots, a_{i-1}, a) \angle i \leftrightarrow a : A} \qquad \frac{E \vdash a_0 : A_0 \ldots E \vdash a_i : A_i \quad E \vdash a : A}{E \vdash tuple(a_0, \ldots, a_i, a) . i \leftrightarrow a_i : A_i}$$

Example:

$let \; f : \forall(X <: Tuple(B, Top)) \; Tuple(A, X) \to Tuple(A, A, X)$

$\quad = \lambda(X <: Tuple(B, Top))\lambda(t : Tuple(A, X)) \; tuple(t.0, t.0, t \angle 1)$

$f(Tuple(B, C, Top))(tuple(a, b, c, top)) \leftrightarrow tuple(a, a, b, c, top) : Tuple(A, A, B, C, Top)$

We have now developed the necessary techniques for encoding record types; this is the subject of the next section.

4   Records

The general plan, carried out in later sections, is to axiomatize the rules for records independently, and then provide a translation (encoding) into a calculus without records. In this section we are a bit more informal, and we discuss the encoding of record types without first discussing their derived type rules. Some pathologies caused by this approach will disappear later.

4.1   Simple Records

Let $\mathscr{L}$ be a countable set of *labels*, enumerated by a bijection $\iota \in \mathscr{L} \to Nat$. We indicate by l^i, with a superscript, the i-th label in this enumeration. Often we need to refer to a list of n distinct labels out of this enumeration; we then use subscripts, as in $l_1 \ldots l_n$. So we may have, for example, $l_1, l_2, l_3 = l^5, l^1, l^{17}$. More precisely, $l_1 \ldots l_n$ stands for $l^{\sigma(1)}, \ldots, l^{\sigma(n)}$ for some injective $\sigma \in 1 \ldots n \to Nat$.

A record type has the form $Rcd(l_1 : A_1, \ldots, l_n : A_n, C)$, where the final type C will normally be either Top or a type variable. Once the enumeration of the set of labels $\mathscr{L}$ is fixed, a record type is encoded as a tuple type where the record components are allocated to tuple slots as determined by the index of their labels. That is, the component of label l^i is allocated to the i-th tuple slot; the remaining slots are filled with *Top* "padding". For example:

$$Rcd(l^2:C, l^0:A, D) \triangleq Tuple(A, Top, C, D)$$

Since record type components are canonically sorted under the encoding, two record types that differ only in the order of their components will be equal under the encoding. Hence we can consider record components as unordered.

As an artifact of the encoding, a missing record field of label l^i is equivalent to a field $l^i: Top$. However, the type rules for these two situations will differ, and in the former case the extraction of the label l^i will not be allowed.

A record type whose final component is *Top* is called a *simple record*; one whose final component is a type variable, is called an *extensible record*, or simply a *record*. Only these two situations will be allowed by the type rules for records; for example, notice that $Rcd(l^0:A, Rcd(l^1:B, C))$ is not very meaningful under the translation.

From the encoding, we can derive the familiar rule for simple records [Cardelli 88]:

$$\frac{E \vdash A_1 <: B_1 \dots E \vdash A_n <: B_n \quad E \vdash A_{n+1} \; type \dots E \vdash A_m \; type}{E \vdash Rcd(l_1:A_1, \dots, l_n:A_n, \dots, l_m:A_m, Top) <: Rcd(l_1:B_1, \dots, l_n:B_n, Top)}$$

The conclusion holds because any additional field $l_k:A_k \; (n < k \leq m)$ on the left of $<:$ is absorbed either by the *Top* padding on the right, if $\iota(l_k) < max(\iota(l_1)\dots\iota(l_n))$, or by the final *Top*, otherwise. For example:

$$Rcd(l^0:A, l^1:B, l^2:C, Top) \equiv Tuple(A, B, C, Top)$$

$$<: Tuple(Top, B, Top) \equiv Rcd(l^1:B, Top)$$

Record values are similarly encoded, for example:

$$rcd(l^2 = c, l^0 = a, d) \triangleq tuple(a, top, c, d)$$

from which we obtain the rules for simple records:

$$\frac{E \vdash a_1:A_1 \dots E \vdash a_n:A_n}{E \vdash rcd(l_1 = a_1, \dots, l_n = a_n, top): Rcd(l_1:A_1, \dots, l_n:A_n, Top)}$$

$$\frac{E \vdash a_1 \leftrightarrow a_1':A_1 \dots E \vdash a_n \leftrightarrow a_n':A_n}{E \vdash rcd(l_1 = a_1, \dots, l_n = a_n, top) \leftrightarrow rcd(l_1 = a_1', \dots, l_n = a_n', top): Rcd(l_1:A_1, \dots, l_n:A_n, Top)}$$

Record selection is encoded as follows:

$$r.l_i \triangleq r.\iota(l_i)$$

with the rule:

$$\frac{E \vdash r : Rcd(l : A, Top)}{E \vdash r . l : A}$$

By subsumption, we have the following derived rules:

$$\frac{E \vdash a_1 : A_1 \ldots E \vdash a_n : A_n \ldots E \vdash a_m : A_m}{E \vdash rcd(l_1 = a_1, \ldots, l_n = a_n, \ldots, l_m = a_m, top) : Rcd(l_1 : A_1, \ldots, l_n : A_n, Top)}$$

$$\frac{\begin{array}{c} E \vdash a_1 \leftrightarrow b_1 : A_1 \ldots E \vdash a_n \leftrightarrow b_n : A_n \\ E \vdash a_{n+1} : B_{n+1} \ldots E \vdash a_p : B_p \quad E \vdash b_{n+1} : C_{n+1} \ldots E \vdash b_q : C_q \end{array}}{\begin{array}{c} E \vdash rcd(l_1 = a_1, \ldots, l_n = a_n, \ldots, l_p = a_p, top) \leftrightarrow rcd(l_1 = b_1, \ldots, l_n = b_n, \ldots, l_q = b_q, top) \\ : Rcd(l_1 : A_1, \ldots, l_n : A_n, Top) \end{array}}$$

$$\frac{E \vdash r : Rcd(l_1 : A_1, \ldots, l_n : A_n, Top)}{E \vdash r . l_i : A_i} \qquad i \in 1 \ldots n$$

The second rule above is particularly interesting. It expresses a form of observational equivalence: two records are equivalent at a given type if they coincide with the components that are observable at that type. Ultimately, this is because any two values are equivalent at type *Top*.

An interesting question about simple records remains: what is the equivalent of the $\angle$ operator on tuples? To answer this, we must turn to extensible records.

4.2   Extensible Records

In the next section we fully axiomatize a system with row variables, $F_{<:}\rho$. To understand that axiomatization better, it may be useful to have an idea of the translation into $F_{<:}$ that will follow. In this section we sketch the main ideas of that translation, but the reader can skip to section 5 at any point.

As we have done with tuples, we would like to place a type variable at the end of a record to capture all the "additional" components.

Tuple(A, B, C, X) X represents all the other tuple components

Rcd$(l^0 : A, l^2 : C, X)$ X represents all the other record components

When translating these records into tuples, we see that, to achieve the desired effect, the final type variable must split into a set of type variables. (We use the symbol $\approx$ to mean, informally, "translates to".)

Rcd$(l^0 : A, l^2 : C, X) \approx$ *Tuple*(A, X^1, C, X^3)

Here X cannot be bound to a single (record) type; it must be bound to a *labeled collection of types* that fills the slots X^1 and X^3 exactly. We call these collections *type rows*, and X a row *(type) variable*.

Consider, for example:

$Rcd(l^0:A, l^2:C, l^4:E, X)$

Here the row variable X can be instantiated only to a type row that does not contain components labeled l^0, l^2, or l^4, since these are already accounted for. For example, X can be instantiated to the type row $l^1:B$, $l^3:D$, *Top*.

We express this constraint on the instantiations of X by saying that X must have *kind* "$\uparrow l^0, l^2, l^4$", which reads "... is undefined (exactly) at l^0, l^2, l^4" or "... does not cover (exactly) l^0, l^2, l^4".

A constrained row variable $X \uparrow L$ is hence translated to a sequence of type variables with "gaps" at L; for example:

$X \uparrow (\ ) \approx X^0$

$X \uparrow l^0 \approx X^1 \qquad X \uparrow l^0, l^1 \approx X^2$

$X \uparrow l^1 \approx X^0, X^2 \qquad X \uparrow l^0, l^2 \approx X^1, X^3$

$X \uparrow l^2 \approx X^0, X^1, X^3 \qquad X \uparrow l^1, l^2 \approx X^0, X^3$

Therefore, the first step in extending $F_{<:}$ with row types is to allow constrained row variables in environments:

$E', X \uparrow L, E'' \vdash \ldots$

Then, if $X \uparrow L \approx X_1, \ldots, X_n$ we translate:

$E', X \uparrow L \vdash Rcd(l_1:A_1, \ldots, l_m:A_m, X)$ *type*

$\approx E', X_1, \ldots, X_n \vdash Tuple(B_1, \ldots, B_{n+m-1}, X_n)$ *type*

where the B_i are the $X_1 \ldots X_{n-1}$ and the $A_1 \ldots A_m$, in the proper order.

To manipulate type rows and row variables we introduce a new judgment form (described in detail in the next section):

$E \vdash R \uparrow L$

where R is a type row (including a row variable), and L is the set of labels that are not covered by the row R. In general we need to translate not just records, but rows, which may have missing components:

$(l^0:A, l^2:C, X) \uparrow l^1, l^4 \approx A, —, C, X^3, —, X^5$ (a row missing 1st and 4th).

Once row variables are allowed in environments, they give rise naturally to quanti-fiers $\forall(X \uparrow L)$, and binders $\lambda(X \uparrow L)$. These row quantifiers and row binders must decompose under translation into sequences of type quantifiers and type binders. For example, we have:

$$\forall(X \uparrow l^1) \, Rcd(l^1 : A \,; X) \to B$$

$$\approx \forall(X^0)\forall(X^2) \, Tuple(X^0, A, X^2) \to B$$

We now come to the most important issue of the translation: matching the number of arguments of a row type function $\lambda(X \uparrow L)a$ to the number of parameters in a row type application $(\lambda(X \uparrow L)a)(R \uparrow L)$. The application form for a function $b : \forall(X \uparrow L)B$ will have the shape:

$$b(R \uparrow L) : B\{X \leftarrow R\} \quad \text{for } R \uparrow L$$

where $B\{X \leftarrow R\}$ is a *row substitution* such that (for ξ a row variable or *Top*):

$$Rcd(l_1 : A_1, \ldots, l_n : A_n, X)\{X \leftarrow (l'_1 : B_1, \ldots, l'_m : B_m, \xi)\}$$

$$= Rcd(l_1 : A_1, \ldots, l_n : A_n, l'_1 : B_1, \ldots, l'_m : B_m, \xi)$$

We have seen that the translations of $\forall(X \uparrow L)B$ and $\lambda(X \uparrow L)b$ convert the single parameter $X \uparrow L$ into a sequence of parameters whose length can depend only on L. We call this length ∂L: the *dimension* of L. When translating an application $b(R \uparrow L)$ we must then produce a sequence of applications of size ∂L, irrespectively of the actual parameter R. This may require some regrouping of the components of an argument row R. For example:

$$b(l^2 : A^2, Y \uparrow l^1 l^3) \approx b(Y^0)(A^2)(Y^4)$$

(where $b : \forall(X \uparrow l^1 l^3)B$ and $Y \uparrow l^1 l^2 l^3 \approx Y^0, Y^4$ and $l^2 : A^2, Y \uparrow l^1 l^3 \approx Y^0, A^2, Y^4$)

$$b(l^3 : A^3, Y \uparrow l^1 l^2) \approx b(Y^0)(Tuple(A^3, Y^4))$$

(where $b : \forall(X \uparrow l^1 l^2)B$ and $Y \uparrow l^1 l^2 l^3 \approx Y^0, Y^4$ and $l^3 : A^3, Y \uparrow l^1 l^2 \approx Y^0, A^3, Y^4$)

In the second case, $b(Y^0)(A^3)(Y^4)$ would be wrong; we must group A^3 and Y^4 into $Tuple(A^3, Y^4)$, to match the two parameters (X^0 and X^3) expected by b. For uniform-ity in the translation, we always take the last parameter to be a tuple (since $Tuple(A) \equiv A$), so the first case above becomes:

$$b(l^2 : A^2, Y \uparrow l^1 l^3) \approx b(Y^0)(A^2)(Tuple(Y^4))$$

In conclusion, we can say informally that row variables translate to rows of variables, row types to rows of types, row quantifiers to rows of quantifiers, row applications to rows of applications, etc. The main difficulty in the translation is to ensure that all these rows match properly. For this, the precise relation between a row $R \uparrow L$ and its dimension ∂L, will be discussed in section 6.

We now turn to a formal system based on the intuitions about the translation of records into tuples developed in this section.

5   System $F_{<:}\rho$

We now extend $F_{<:}$ with records and row variables, as discussed in section 4; the resulting system is called $F_{<:}\rho$.

5.1   Syntax

Types in $F_{<:}$ are augmented by the following: record types $Rcd(R)$, where R is a *row type* that must be defined at all labels; row function types $R \uparrow L \to B$ from an input of row type $R \uparrow L$ to an output of type B; and row variable quantifications $\forall(X \uparrow L)B$, where L is a set of labels at which X is undefined.

A row type is either the constant *Etc*, standing for an "empty row" (more precisely, an unnamed extension of the current row type); a type variable X, standing for an extension of the current row type; or $l : A, R$, extending the row type R by a field of type A and label l.

Values are augmented by the following: records $rcd(r)$, where r is a *row value* defined at all labels; row functions $\lambda(x \therefore R \uparrow L)b$ accepting a row value for x of row type $R \uparrow L$; and row type functions $\lambda(X \uparrow L)b$ accepting a row type for X that is undefined at L. Record selection $a . l$ can be used on a record a that is defined at l. A row function b can be applied via $b(r \uparrow L)$ to a row value r undefined at L. A row type function b can be instantiated via $b(R \uparrow L)$ to a row type R undefined at L.

Finally, a row value is either the constant *etc*, standing for an "empty row" (or, an unnamed extension of the current row value); a row variable x; an extension $l = a, r$, extending row value r by a field of value a and label l; or a restriction $a\backslash L$, producing a row value undefined at L from a record a.

Syntax

$L ::= l_1, \ldots, l_n$	Label set
$A, B ::= \ldots$	Types as in $F_{<:}$, plus:
$\quad Rcd(R)$	record type
$\quad R \uparrow L \to B$	row function space
$\quad \forall(X \uparrow L)B$	row quantification

$R, S ::=$	Row types
X	row type variable
Etc	empty row type
$l:A, R$	row type R plus field A labeled l

$a, b ::= \ldots$	Values as in $F_{<:}$, plus:
$rcd(r)$	record value
$a.l$	record selection
$\lambda(x \therefore R \uparrow L)b$	row value function
$b(r \uparrow L)$	row value application
$\lambda(X \uparrow L)b$	row type function
$b(R \uparrow L)$	row type application

$r, s ::=$	Row values
x	row value variable
etc	empty row value
$l = a, r$	row value r plus field a labeled l
$a \backslash L$	row value of record a without fields in L

As discussed in section 2, we identify terms up to renaming of bound variables:

$$\forall(X \uparrow L)B \equiv \forall(Y \uparrow L)B\{X \leftarrow Y\}$$

$$\lambda(X \uparrow L)b \equiv \lambda(X \uparrow L)b\{X \leftarrow Y\}$$

$$\lambda(x \therefore R \uparrow L)b \equiv \lambda(y \therefore R \uparrow L)b\{x \leftarrow y\}$$

Moreover, we identify rows up to reordering of labeled components:

$$l:A, l':A', R \equiv l':A', l:A, R$$

$$l = a, l' = a', r \equiv l' = a', l = a, r$$

and we identify terms up to any permutation L' of a label set L:

$$\forall(X \uparrow L)B \equiv \forall(X \uparrow L')B \qquad R \uparrow L \rightarrow B \equiv R \uparrow L' \rightarrow B$$

$$\lambda(X \uparrow L)b \equiv \lambda(X \uparrow L')b \qquad b(R \uparrow L) \equiv b(R \uparrow L')$$

$$\lambda(x \therefore R \uparrow L)b \equiv \lambda(x \therefore R \uparrow L')b \qquad b(r \uparrow L) \equiv b(r \uparrow L')$$

$$a \backslash L \equiv a \backslash L'$$

Again, these identifications are legitimate because they depend only on the syntax of terms, and not on their derivations.

Given the identification of label sets above, we adopt the following notational convention used in the inference rules:

$l . L \triangleq \{l\} \cup L$ where $l \notin L$

We now add to $F_{<:}$ four judgments about rows, which all involve a set L at which the rows are undefined.

Judgments

. . .	Judgments as in $F_{<:}$, plus:
$E \vdash_\rho R \uparrow L$	R is a row type not covering L
$E \vdash_\rho r \therefore R \uparrow L$	r has row type $R \uparrow L$
$E \vdash_\rho R <\therefore S \uparrow L$	R is a subrow of S, both not covering L
$E \vdash_\rho r \leftrightarrow r' \therefore R \uparrow L$	r is equal to r' at row type $R \uparrow L$

It is important to notice that the L information is preserved exactly in $F_{<:}\rho$ derivations, in the sense that $E \vdash_\rho \vartheta \uparrow L \Rightarrow E \vdash_\rho \vartheta \uparrow L'$ is never derivable for $L \neq L'$ for any of the four judgments. Hence, when we say that a row is undefined at L, we always mean undefined *exactly* at L.

5.2 Rules

We indicate by $\vdash_\rho$ the judgments in $F_{<:}\rho$, to distinguish them from the judgments $\vdash$ in $F_{<:}$. The rules of $F_{<:}\rho$ consist of a copy of the rules of $F_{<:}$ (with $\vdash$ replaced by $\vdash_\rho$) plus the ones listed below. We now briefly comment on the $F_{<:}\rho$ rules.

A row type is formed by starting with a row variable $X \uparrow L$, or with a row $Etc \uparrow L$, and then prefixing fields $l : A$ with $l \in L$, at each step discarding l from L. Note that Etc can be assumed to lack any set of labels to start with. Informally, we can imagine either that an element of $Etc \uparrow L$ is a collection of $n = \#L$ empty slots that are later "filled in", or that an element of $Etc \uparrow L$ is an infinite row with "gaps" corresponding to L, and with all the other components filled with an error value.

A record type can be formed only from a *complete* row $R \uparrow (\ )$, one lacking no labels. (We call $R \uparrow (\ )$ complete even though we have only finite information about the labels of R; for example, $Etc \uparrow (\ )$ is complete but entirely unknown.) This completeness requirement is probably not essential, but gives us a simpler calculus where record types carry only positive information, while row variables carry only negative information [Harper Pierce 90].

The subrow judgment, $E \vdash_\rho R <\therefore S \uparrow L$, is mainly an auxiliary one used to define subtyping on records. According to this judgment, every row is a subrow of Etc; then we have componentwise subtyping on fields having the same label. Hence, a longer row ending in *Etc* is a subrow of a shorter row ending in *Etc* if their corresponding components are in subtype relation. Rows ending with the same type variables must have the same length (otherwise, assuming $X \uparrow l$, what could L be in $E \vdash_\rho l : A$, $X <\!:. X \uparrow L$?). Rows ending in distinct type variables are unrelated, since we have no information about the labeled types that may be substituted for the variables.

Record values can be created only from complete rows, as discussed above. Given a record $a : Rcd(l : A, R)$ we can select its l component by $a.l : A$. Moreover, given a record $a : Rcd(l_1 : A_1 .. l_n : A_n, R)$ we can extract a row $a \backslash L .\!:. R \uparrow L$ from it by removing all the components with labels in L.

In $F_{<:}$ any two values are equivalent in *Top*. Similarly, in $F_{<:}\rho$ any two row values are equivalent in *Etc*.

Environments

$$\frac{E \vdash_\rho R \uparrow L \quad x \notin dom(E)}{\vdash_\rho E, x .\!:. R \uparrow L \; env} \qquad\qquad (Env \; x \uparrow L)$$

$$\frac{\vdash_\rho E \; env \quad X \notin dom(E)}{\vdash_\rho E, X \uparrow L \; env} \qquad\qquad (Env \; X \uparrow L)$$

Types

$$\frac{E \vdash_\rho R \uparrow (\;)}{E \vdash_\rho Rcd(R) type} \qquad\qquad (Type \; Rcd)$$

$$\frac{E \vdash_\rho R \uparrow L \quad E \vdash_\rho B \; type}{E \vdash_\rho R \uparrow L \to B \; type} \qquad\qquad (Type \to \uparrow L)$$

$$\frac{E, X \uparrow L \vdash_\rho B \; type}{E \vdash_\rho \forall(X \uparrow L)B \; type} \qquad\qquad (Type \; \forall \uparrow L)$$

Row Types

$$\frac{\vdash_\rho E', X \uparrow L, E'' \; env}{E', X \uparrow L, E'' \vdash_\rho X \uparrow L} \qquad\qquad (Type \; X)$$

$$\frac{\vdash_\rho E \; env}{E \vdash_\rho Etc \uparrow L} \qquad\qquad (Type \; Etc)$$

$$\frac{E \vdash_\rho R \uparrow l.L \quad E \vdash_\rho A \; type}{E \vdash_\rho l : A, R \uparrow L} \qquad\qquad (Type \; cons)$$

Subtypes

$$\frac{E \vdash_\rho R <\therefore R' \uparrow (\ )}{E \vdash_\rho Rcd(R) <: Rcd(R')} \qquad (Sub\ Rcd)$$

$$\frac{E \vdash_\rho R' <\therefore R \uparrow L \quad E \vdash_\rho B <: B'}{E \vdash_\rho R \uparrow L \to B <: R' \uparrow L \to B'} \qquad (Sub \to \uparrow L)$$

$$\frac{E, X \uparrow L \vdash_\rho B <: B'\ type}{E \vdash_\rho \forall(X \uparrow L)B <: \forall(X \uparrow L)B'\ type} \qquad (Sub\ \forall \uparrow L)$$

Subrows

$$\frac{E \vdash_\rho R \uparrow L}{E \vdash_\rho R <\therefore R \uparrow L} \qquad (Sub\ Row\ refl)$$

$$\frac{E \vdash_\rho R <\therefore S \uparrow L \quad E \vdash_\rho S <\therefore T \uparrow L}{E \vdash_\rho R <\therefore T \uparrow L} \qquad (Sub\ Row\ trans)$$

$$\frac{E \vdash_\rho R \uparrow L}{E \vdash_\rho R <\therefore Etc \uparrow L} \qquad (Sub\ Etc)$$

$$\frac{E \vdash_\rho A <: B \quad E \vdash_\rho R <\therefore S \uparrow l.L}{E \vdash_\rho l : A, R <\therefore l : B, S \uparrow L} \qquad (Sub\ cons)$$

Values

$$\frac{E \vdash_\rho r \therefore R \uparrow (\ )}{E \vdash_\rho rcd(r) : Rcd(R)} \qquad (Val\ rcd)$$

$$\frac{E \vdash_\rho a : Rcd(l : A, R)}{E \vdash_\rho a.l : A} \qquad (Val\ sel)$$

$$\frac{E, x \therefore R \uparrow L \vdash_\rho b : B}{E \vdash_\rho \lambda(x \therefore R \uparrow L)b : R \uparrow L \to B} \qquad (Val\ fun\ \uparrow L)$$

$$\frac{E \vdash_\rho b : R \uparrow L \to B \quad E \vdash_\rho r \therefore R \uparrow L}{E \vdash_\rho b(r \uparrow L) : B} \qquad (Val\ appl\ \uparrow L)$$

$$\frac{E, X \uparrow L \vdash_\rho b : B}{E \vdash_\rho \lambda(X \uparrow L)b : \forall(X \uparrow L)B} \qquad (Val\ fun2\ \uparrow L)$$

$$\frac{E \vdash_\rho b : \forall(X \uparrow L)B \quad E \vdash_\rho R \uparrow L}{E \vdash_\rho b(R \uparrow L) : B\{X \leftarrow R\}} \qquad (Val\ appl2\ \uparrow L)$$

Row Values

$$\frac{E \vdash_\rho r \therefore R \uparrow L \quad E \vdash_\rho R <\therefore S \uparrow L}{E \vdash_\rho r \therefore S \uparrow L} \qquad (Row\ Subsumption)$$

$$\frac{\vdash_\rho E', x \therefore R \uparrow L, E'' \ env}{E', x \therefore R \uparrow L, E'' \vdash_\rho x \therefore R \uparrow L} \qquad (Val\ x \uparrow L)$$

$$\frac{\vdash_\rho E \ env}{E \vdash_\rho etc \therefore Etc \uparrow L} \qquad (Val\ etc)$$

$$\frac{E \vdash_\rho r \therefore R \uparrow l.L \quad E \vdash_\rho a : A}{E \vdash_\rho l = a, r \therefore l : A, R \uparrow L} \qquad (Val\ cons)$$

$$\frac{E \vdash_\rho a : Rcd(l_1 : A_1 .. l_n : A_n, R)}{E \vdash_\rho a \backslash l_1 .. l_n \therefore R \uparrow l_1 .. l_n} \qquad (Val\ restr)$$

Value Equivalence

$$\frac{E \vdash_\rho r \leftrightarrow r' \therefore R \uparrow (\ )}{E \vdash_\rho rcd(r) \leftrightarrow rcd(r') : Rcd(R)} \qquad (Eq\ rcd)$$

$$\frac{E \vdash_\rho a \leftrightarrow a' : Rcd(l : A, R)}{E \vdash_\rho a.l \leftrightarrow a'.l : A} \qquad (Eq\ sel)$$

$$\frac{E \vdash_\rho r \therefore R \uparrow l \quad E \vdash_\rho a \leftrightarrow a' : A}{E \vdash_\rho rcd(l = a, r).l \leftrightarrow a' : A} \qquad (Eq\ Eval\ sel)$$

$$\frac{E, x \therefore R \uparrow L \vdash_\rho b \leftrightarrow b' : B}{E \vdash_\rho \lambda(x \therefore R \uparrow L)b \leftrightarrow \lambda(x \therefore R \uparrow L)b' : R \uparrow L \to B} \qquad (Eq\ fun \uparrow L)$$

$$\frac{E \vdash_\rho b \leftrightarrow b' : R \uparrow L \to B \quad E \vdash_\rho r \leftrightarrow r' \therefore R \uparrow L}{E \vdash_\rho b(r \uparrow L) \leftrightarrow b'(r' \uparrow L) : B} \qquad (Eq\ appl \uparrow L)$$

$$\frac{E, X \uparrow L \vdash_\rho b \leftrightarrow b' : B}{E \vdash_\rho \lambda(X \uparrow L)b \leftrightarrow \lambda(X \uparrow L)b' : \forall(X \uparrow L)B} \qquad (Eq\ fun2 \uparrow L)$$

$$\frac{E \vdash_\rho b \leftrightarrow b' : \forall(X \uparrow L)B \quad E \vdash_\rho R \uparrow L}{E \vdash_\rho b(R \uparrow L) \leftrightarrow b'(R \uparrow L) : B\{X \leftarrow R\}} \qquad (Eq\ appl2 \uparrow L)$$

$$\frac{E, x \therefore R \uparrow L \vdash_\rho b \leftrightarrow b' : B \quad E \vdash_\rho r \leftrightarrow r' \therefore R \uparrow L}{E \vdash_\rho (\lambda(x \therefore R \uparrow L)b)(r) \leftrightarrow b'\{x \leftarrow r'\} : B} \qquad (Eq\ Beta \uparrow L)$$

$$\frac{E \vdash_\rho b \leftrightarrow b' : R \uparrow L \to R \quad y \notin dom(E)}{E \vdash_\rho \lambda(y \therefore R \uparrow L)b(y \uparrow L) \leftrightarrow b' : R \uparrow L \to B} \qquad (Eq\ Eta \uparrow L)$$

$$\frac{E, X \uparrow L \vdash_\rho b \leftrightarrow b' : B \quad E \vdash_\rho R \uparrow L}{E \vdash_\rho (\lambda(X \uparrow L)b)(R \uparrow L) \leftrightarrow b'\{X \leftarrow R\} : B\{X \leftarrow R\}} \qquad (Eq\ Beta2 \uparrow L)$$

$$\frac{E \vdash_\rho b \leftrightarrow b' : \forall(X \uparrow L)B \quad Y \notin dom(E)}{E \vdash_\rho \lambda(Y \uparrow L)b(Y \uparrow L) \leftrightarrow b' : \forall(X \uparrow L)B} \qquad (Eq\ Eta2 \uparrow L)$$

Row Value Equivalence

$$\frac{E \vdash_\rho r \leftrightarrow s \therefore R \uparrow L}{E \vdash_\rho s \leftrightarrow r \therefore R \uparrow L} \qquad (Eq\ Row\ symm)$$

$$\frac{E \vdash_\rho r \leftrightarrow s \therefore R \uparrow L \quad E \vdash_\rho s \leftrightarrow t \therefore R \uparrow L}{E \vdash_\rho r \leftrightarrow t \therefore R \uparrow L} \qquad (Eq\ Row\ trans)$$

$$\frac{E \vdash_\rho r \leftrightarrow r' \therefore R \uparrow L \quad E \vdash_\rho R <\therefore S \uparrow L}{E \vdash_\rho r \leftrightarrow r' \therefore S \uparrow L} \qquad (Eq\ Row\ Subsumption)$$

$$\frac{E \vdash_\rho r \therefore Etc \uparrow L \quad E \vdash_\rho s \therefore Etc \uparrow L}{E \vdash_\rho r \leftrightarrow s \therefore Etc \uparrow L} \qquad (Eq\ Row\ collapse)$$

$$\frac{E \vdash_\rho x \therefore R \uparrow L}{E \vdash_\rho x \leftrightarrow x \therefore R \uparrow L} \qquad (Eq\ x \uparrow L)$$

$$\frac{\vdash_\rho E\ env}{E \vdash_\rho etc \leftrightarrow etc \therefore Etc \uparrow L} \qquad (Eq\ etc)$$

$$\frac{E \vdash_\rho r \leftrightarrow r' \therefore R \uparrow l.L \quad E \vdash_\rho a \leftrightarrow a' : A}{E \vdash_\rho l = a, r \leftrightarrow l = a', r' \therefore l : A, R \uparrow L} \qquad (Eq\ cons)$$

$$\frac{E \vdash_\rho a \leftrightarrow a' : Rcd(l_1 : A_1 \ldots l_n : A_n, R)}{E \vdash_\rho a \backslash l_1 \ldots l_n \leftrightarrow a' \backslash l_1 \ldots l_n \therefore R \uparrow l_1 \ldots l_n} \qquad (Eq\ restr)$$

$$\frac{E \vdash_\rho r \leftrightarrow r' \therefore R \uparrow l_1 \ldots l_n \quad E \vdash_\rho a_1 : A_1 \ldots E \vdash_\rho a_n : A_n}{E \vdash_\rho rcd(l_1 = a_1 \ldots l_n = a_n, r) \backslash l_1 \ldots l_n \leftrightarrow r' \therefore R \uparrow l_1 \ldots l_n} \qquad (Eq\ Eval\ restr)$$

Example Derivations

$$\vdash_\rho E \ env$$
$$\frac{E \vdash_\rho Etc \uparrow l^3, l^5 \qquad E \vdash_\rho A \ type}{E \vdash_\rho l^3 : A, Etc \uparrow l^5 \qquad E \vdash_\rho B \ type}$$
$$\frac{E \vdash_\rho l^5 : B, l^3 : A, Etc \uparrow (\ )}{E \vdash_\rho Rcd(l^5 : B, l^3 : A, Etc) \ type}$$

$$\vdash_\rho E, X \uparrow l^3, l^5 \ env$$
$$\frac{E, X \uparrow l^3, l^5 \vdash_\rho X \uparrow l^3, l^5 \qquad E \vdash_\rho A \ type}{E, X \uparrow l^3, l^5 \vdash_\rho l^3 : A, X \uparrow l^5 \qquad E \vdash_\rho B \ type}$$
$$\frac{E, X \uparrow l^3, l^5 \vdash_\rho l^5 : B, l^3 : A, X \uparrow (\ )}{E, X \uparrow l^3, l^5 \vdash_\rho Rcd(l^5 : B, l^3 : A, X) \ type}$$

5.3 Properties

We now state some basic lemmas about the properties of $F_{<:}\rho$ derivations (and, implicitly, of $F_{<:}$ derivations). Unless otherwise noted, these are all proven by induction on the derivations; the proofs are long, but straightforward if done in the order indicated.

NOTATION   Let ϑ be any of

$$C \ type, \ S \uparrow M, \ C <: C', \ S <: \ \therefore \ S' \uparrow M, \ c : C, \ s \ \therefore \ S \uparrow M, \ c \leftrightarrow c' : C, \ s \leftrightarrow s' \ \therefore \ S \uparrow M$$

LEMMA   (renaming)   Let $\langle \xi, \xi', \beta, \beta' \rangle$ stand for either $\langle X, Y, X <: D, Y <: D \rangle$, $\langle X, Y, X \uparrow M, Y \uparrow M \rangle$, $\langle x, y, x : D, y : D \rangle$, or $\langle x, y, x \ \therefore \ T \uparrow M, y \ \therefore \ T \uparrow M \rangle$. Assume $\xi' \notin dom(E, \beta, E')$.

$$\vdash_\rho E, \beta, E' \ env \Rightarrow \vdash_\rho E, \beta', E'\{\xi \leftarrow \xi'\} \ env$$

$$E, \beta, E' \vdash_\rho \vartheta \Rightarrow E, \beta', E'\{\xi \leftarrow \xi'\} \vdash_\rho \vartheta\{\xi \leftarrow \xi'\}$$

LEMMA   (implied judgments 1)

$$\vdash_\rho E, F \ env \Rightarrow \vdash_\rho E \ env \qquad\qquad\qquad\qquad\qquad\qquad (\vartheta/env)$$

$$E, F \vdash_\rho \vartheta \Rightarrow \vdash_\rho E \ env$$

$$\vdash_\rho E, X <: D, E'env \Rightarrow E \vdash_\rho D \ type \qquad\qquad\qquad\qquad (env/type)$$

$$\vdash_\rho E, x : D, E' \ env \Rightarrow E \vdash_\rho D \ type$$

$$\vdash_\rho E, x \ \therefore \ R \uparrow L, E' \ env \Rightarrow E \vdash_\rho R \uparrow L \qquad\qquad\qquad (env/rowtype)$$

LEMMA   (bound change)

$$\vdash_\rho E, X <: D', E' \ env, \quad E \vdash_\rho D \ type \Rightarrow \vdash_\rho E, X <: D, E' \ env$$

$$E, X <: D', E' \vdash_\rho C \ type, \quad E \vdash_\rho D \ type \Rightarrow E, X <: D, E' \vdash_\rho C \ type$$

$$E, X <: D', E' \vdash_\rho S \uparrow M, \quad E \vdash_\rho D \ type \Rightarrow E, X <: D, E' \vdash_\rho S \uparrow M$$

LEMMA (weakening)   Let β stand for either $X \uparrow L$, $X <: D$, $x : D$, or $x \therefore T \uparrow L$. Assume $\vdash_\rho E, \beta\ env$, and $X, x \notin dom(E')$; then

$\vdash_\rho E, E'\ env \Rightarrow \vdash_\rho E, \beta, E'\ env$

$E, E' \vdash_\rho \vartheta \Rightarrow E, \beta, E' \vdash_\rho \vartheta$

   Assume $\vdash_\rho E, F\ env$ and $dom(F) \cap dom(E') = \phi$; then

$\vdash_\rho E, E'\ env \Rightarrow \vdash_\rho E, F, E'\ env$

$E, E' \vdash_\rho \vartheta \Rightarrow E, F, E' \vdash_\rho \vartheta$

LEMMA (implied judgments 2)

$$E \vdash_\rho C <: C' \Rightarrow E \vdash_\rho C\ type, \quad E \vdash_\rho C'\ type \qquad\qquad (sub/type)$$

$$E \vdash_\rho S <\therefore S' \uparrow M \Rightarrow E \vdash_\rho S \uparrow M, \quad E \vdash_\rho S' \uparrow M \qquad (subrow/typerow)$$

LEMMA (bound weakening)   Let $\langle \beta, \beta' \rangle$ stand for either

$\langle X <: D, X <: D' \rangle$, $\langle x : D, x : D' \rangle$, or $\langle x \therefore R \uparrow L, x \therefore R' \uparrow L \rangle$.

   Assume $E \vdash_\rho D' <: D$ and $E \vdash_\rho R' <\therefore R \uparrow L$.

$\vdash_\rho E, \beta, E'\ env \Rightarrow \vdash_\rho E, \beta', E'\ env$

$E, \beta, E' \vdash_\rho \vartheta \Rightarrow E, \beta', E' \vdash_\rho \vartheta$

LEMMA (type substitution)   Assume $E \vdash_\rho D' <: D$; then

$\vdash_\rho E, X <: D, E'\ env \Rightarrow \vdash_\rho E, E'\{X \leftarrow D'\}\ env$

$E, X <: D, E' \vdash_\rho \vartheta \Rightarrow E, E'\{X \leftarrow D'\} \vdash_\rho \vartheta\{X \leftarrow D'\}$

   Assume $E \vdash_\rho S \uparrow M$; then

$\vdash_\rho E, X \uparrow M, E'\ env \Rightarrow \vdash_\rho E, E'\{X \leftarrow S\}\ env$

$E, X \uparrow M, E' \vdash_\rho \vartheta \Rightarrow E, E'\{X \leftarrow S\} \vdash_\rho \vartheta\{X \leftarrow S\}$

LEMMA (value substitution)   Assume $E \vdash_\rho d : D$; then

$\vdash_\rho E, x : D, E'\ env \Rightarrow \vdash_\rho E, E'\ env$

$E, x : D, E' \vdash_\rho \vartheta \Rightarrow E, E' \vdash_\rho \vartheta\{x \leftarrow d\}$

Assume $E \vdash_\rho t \therefore T \uparrow N$; then

$\vdash_\rho E, x \therefore T \uparrow N, E'\ env \Rightarrow \vdash_\rho E, E'\ env$

$E, x \therefore T \uparrow N, E' \vdash_\rho \vartheta \Rightarrow E, E' \vdash_\rho \vartheta\{x \leftarrow t\}$

LEMMA (value strengthening)   Assume $x \notin FV(\vartheta)$; then, for $\vartheta \neq c \leftrightarrow c' : C$

$\vdash_\rho E, x : D, E'\ env \Rightarrow \vdash_\rho E, E'\ env$

$E, x : D, E' \vdash_\rho \vartheta \Rightarrow E, E' \vdash_\rho \vartheta\{x \leftarrow d\}$

Assume $x \notin FV(\vartheta)$; then, for $\vartheta \neq r \leftrightarrow r' \therefore R \uparrow L$

$\vdash_\rho E, x \therefore T \uparrow N, E'\ env \Rightarrow \vdash_\rho E, E'\ env$

$E, x \therefore T \uparrow N, E' \vdash_\rho \vartheta \Rightarrow E, E' \vdash_\rho \vartheta$

LEMMA (implied judgments 3)

$E \vdash_\rho c : C \Rightarrow E \vdash_\rho C\ type,$ (val/type)

$E \vdash_\rho s \therefore S \uparrow M \Rightarrow E \vdash_\rho S \uparrow M,$ (rowval/rowtype)

$E \vdash_\rho c \leftrightarrow c' : C \Rightarrow E \vdash_\rho c : C, E \vdash_\rho c' : C,$ (eq/val)

$E \vdash_\rho s \leftrightarrow s' \therefore S \uparrow M \Rightarrow E \vdash_\rho s \therefore S \uparrow M, \quad E \vdash_\rho s' \therefore S \uparrow M,$ (roweq/rowval)

LEMMA (subsumption equivalence)

$E \vdash_\rho c \leftrightarrow c' : C, \quad E \vdash_\rho C <: D \Rightarrow E \vdash_\rho c \leftrightarrow c' : D$

Proof   By subsumption and beta; see [Cardelli Martini Mitchell Scedrov 91]   ∎

LEMMA (implied judgments 4)

$E \vdash_\rho c : C \Rightarrow E \vdash_\rho c \leftrightarrow c : C$ (val/eq)

$E \vdash_\rho s \therefore S \uparrow M \Rightarrow E \vdash_\rho s \leftrightarrow s \therefore S \uparrow M$ (rowval/roweq)

LEMMA (exchange)   Let β stand for either $X <: D$, $Y \uparrow M$, $x : D$, or $x \therefore T \uparrow M$. Let β' stand for either $X' <: D'$, $Y' \uparrow M'$, $x' : D'$, or $x' \therefore T' \uparrow M'$. Assume $\vdash_\rho E, \beta'$ env.

$\vdash_\rho E, \beta, \beta', E'\ env \Rightarrow \vdash_\rho E, \beta', \beta, E'\ env$

$E, \beta, \beta', E' \vdash_\rho \vartheta \Rightarrow E, \beta', \beta, E' \vdash_\rho \vartheta$

We can now show that an *observational equivalence* rule for records is derivable. This rule asserts that two record values are equal at a given type if all the equally-labeled fields that can be observed at that type are equal.

PROPOSITION (observational equivalence for records)

$$E \vdash_\rho a_1 \leftrightarrow b_1 : A_1 \wedge \cdots \wedge E \vdash_\rho a_n \leftrightarrow b_n : A_n \wedge E \vdash_\rho r \therefore R \uparrow l_1 .. l_n \wedge E \vdash_\rho s \therefore S \uparrow l_1 .. l_n$$

$$\Rightarrow E \vdash_\rho rcd(l_1 = a_1, \ldots, l_n = a_n, r) \leftrightarrow rcd(l_1 = b_1, \ldots, l_n = b_n, s) : Rcd(l_1 : A_1, \ldots, l_n : A_n, Etc)$$

Proof

Let $L \equiv l_1 \ldots l_n$.

$E \vdash_\rho r \therefore R \uparrow L \Rightarrow \vdash_\rho E\ env$	(implied judgment)
$E \vdash_\rho r \therefore R \uparrow L \Rightarrow E \vdash_\rho R \uparrow L$	(implied judgment)

$E \vdash_\rho R \uparrow L \Rightarrow E \vdash_\rho R <\therefore Etc \uparrow L$	(Sub Etc)
$E \vdash_\rho r \therefore R \uparrow L \wedge E \vdash_\rho R <\therefore Etc \uparrow L \Rightarrow E \vdash_\rho r \therefore Etc \uparrow L$	(subsumption equiv.)

$\vdash_\rho E\ env \Rightarrow E \vdash_\rho etc \leftrightarrow etc \therefore Etc \uparrow L$	(Eq etc)
$E \vdash_\rho r \therefore Etc \uparrow L \wedge E \vdash_\rho etc \therefore Etc \uparrow L \Rightarrow E \vdash_\rho r \leftrightarrow etc \therefore Etc \uparrow L$	(Eq Row collapse)
$E \vdash_\rho s \therefore S \uparrow L \Rightarrow E \vdash_\rho etc \leftrightarrow s \therefore Etc \uparrow L$	(similarly)
$E \vdash_\rho r \leftrightarrow etc \therefore Etc \uparrow L \wedge E \vdash_\rho etc \leftrightarrow s \therefore Etc \uparrow L \Rightarrow E \vdash_\rho r \leftrightarrow s \therefore Etc \uparrow L$	(Eq trans)

$E \vdash_\rho r \therefore R \uparrow l_1 \ldots l_n \wedge E \vdash_\rho s \therefore S \uparrow l_1 \ldots l_n \Rightarrow E \vdash_\rho r \leftrightarrow s \therefore Etc \uparrow l_1 \ldots l_n$	(above)

$$E \vdash_\rho a_1 \leftrightarrow b_1 : A_1 \wedge \cdots \wedge E \vdash_\rho a_n \leftrightarrow b_n : A_n \wedge E \vdash_\rho r \leftrightarrow s \therefore Etc \uparrow l_1 \ldots l_n$$

$$\Rightarrow E \vdash_\rho l_1 = a_1, \ldots, l_n = a_n, r \leftrightarrow l_1 = b_1, \ldots, l_n = b_n, s \therefore l_1 : A_1, \ldots, l_n : A_n, Etc \uparrow (\ )$$
(Eq Row cons)

$$\Rightarrow E \vdash_\rho rcd(l_1 = a_1, \ldots, l_n = a_n, r) \leftrightarrow rcd(l_1 = b_1, \ldots, l_n = b_n, s) :$$
$$Rcd(l_1 : A_1, \ldots, l_n : A_n, Etc)$$
(Eq rcd) ∎

5.4 Some Useful Extensions

In preparation for examples in the next section, we discuss some useful extensions of our system: recursive types, label-set variables, and definitions. These extensions are not treated in the formal part of the paper.

5.4.1   Recursive Types   In order to introduce recursive types, we need to add type equivalence judgements to the system along with rules (omitted here) for making type equivalence into a congruence over the syntax:

$E \vdash_\rho A \leftrightarrow B\ type$ A and B are equivalent types

$E \vdash_\rho R \leftrightarrow S \uparrow L$ R and S are equivalent row types

A recursive type is, syntactically, a term $\mu(X)A$ where A is *contractive* in X (written $A \succ X$). This means that $A \neq X$, and if $A = \mu(Y)B$ then $B \succ X$. We immediately identify recursive types up to renaming of bound variables:

$$\mu(X)A \equiv \mu(Y)A\{X \leftarrow Y\}$$

Then, the rules for recursive types [Amadio Cardelli 91] are:

$$\frac{E, X <: Top \vdash_\rho A\ type \qquad A \succ X}{E \vdash_\rho \mu(X)A\ type}$$

$$\frac{E \vdash_\rho \mu(X)A\ type}{E \vdash_\rho \mu(X)A \leftrightarrow A\{X \leftarrow \mu(X)A\}\ type} \qquad (unfold)$$

$$\frac{E, X <: Top \vdash_\rho A \leftrightarrow B\ type \qquad A \succ X \qquad B \succ X}{E \vdash_\rho \mu(X)A \leftrightarrow \mu(X)B\ type}$$

$$\frac{E \vdash_\rho A \leftrightarrow C\{X \leftarrow A\}\ type \qquad E \vdash_\rho B \leftrightarrow C\{X \leftarrow B\}\ type \qquad C \succ X}{E \vdash_\rho A \leftrightarrow B\ type} \qquad (contract)$$

$$\frac{E \vdash_\rho \mu(X)A\ type \qquad E \vdash_\rho \mu(Y)B\ type \qquad E, Y <: Top, X <: Y \vdash_\rho A <: B}{E \vdash_\rho \mu(X)A <: \mu(Y)B}$$

A recursive value is, syntactically, a term $\mu(x:A)a$, with the identification:

$$\mu(x:A)a \equiv \mu(y:A)a\{x \leftarrow y\}$$

The standard rules for recursive values are:

$$\frac{E, x:A \vdash_\rho a:A}{E \vdash_\rho \mu(x:A)a:A} \qquad \frac{E, x:A \vdash_\rho a:A}{E \vdash_\rho \mu(x:A)a \leftrightarrow a\{x \leftarrow \mu(x:A)a\}:A}$$

$$\frac{E, x:A \vdash_\rho a \leftrightarrow b:A}{E \vdash_\rho \mu(x:A)a \leftrightarrow \mu(x:A)b:A}$$

5.4.2   Label Sets   The next extension involves variables W ranging over sets of labels. We allow these in environments, under an assumption $W \| L$ that W does not contain any of the labels in L.

$$\frac{E \vdash_\rho L \parallel M}{E \vdash_\rho M \parallel L} \quad \frac{E \vdash_\rho L \parallel M}{E \vdash_\rho L \parallel \phi} \quad \frac{E \vdash_\rho L \parallel l . M}{E \vdash_\rho L \parallel M}$$

$$\frac{\vdash_\rho E \; env}{E \vdash_\rho \phi \parallel l_1 \ldots l_n . \phi} \quad \frac{E \vdash_\rho L \parallel l . M}{E \vdash_\rho l . L \parallel M}$$

$$\frac{E \vdash_\rho L \parallel \phi \quad W \notin dom(E)}{\vdash_\rho E, W \parallel L \; env} \quad \frac{\vdash_\rho E, W \parallel L \; env}{E, W \parallel L, E' \vdash_\rho W \parallel L}$$

The rules of $F_{<:}\rho$ that involve label sets L, are extended to require $L \parallel \phi$, to make sure that L is well-formed. We do not define quantifiers or functions over label-set variables because we do not know how to translate them into $F_{<:}$; label-set variables will be used only in definitions.

5.4.3 Definitions   We now extend the system with various flavors of definitions. The simplest definitions are value and row value definitions (*let*'s):

$$\frac{E \vdash_\rho a : A \quad E, x : A \vdash_\rho b : B}{E \vdash_\rho let \; x : A = a \; in \; b : B} \quad \frac{E \vdash_\rho a : A \quad E, x : A \vdash_\rho b : B}{E \vdash_\rho let \; x : A = a \; in \; b \leftrightarrow b\{x \leftarrow a\} : B}$$

$$\frac{E \vdash_\rho r \therefore R \uparrow L \quad E, x \therefore R \uparrow L \vdash_\rho b : B}{E \vdash_\rho let \; x \therefore R \uparrow L = r \; in \; b : B} \quad \frac{E \vdash_\rho r \therefore R \uparrow L \quad E, x \therefore R \uparrow L \vdash_\rho b : B}{E \vdash_\rho let \; x \therefore R \uparrow L = r \; in \; b \leftrightarrow b\{x \leftarrow r\} : B}$$

There are several kinds of type-level definitions (*Let*'s); we may give a definition of either a type variable, a row type variable, or a label-set variable, in the scope of either a type, a row type, a value, a row value, or a label-set.

To compress several cases into one, we use the abbreviations:

$\mathcal{X}, \mathcal{Y}$ are either type, row type, or label-set variables;

$\mathcal{A}, \mathcal{B}, \mathcal{C}$ are either types, row type, or label sets;

$\mathcal{A}a, \mathcal{B}b, \mathcal{C}c$ are either values, row values, types, row types, or label-sets;

pred is either $: A$, $\therefore R \uparrow L$, *type*, $\uparrow L$, or $\parallel L$.

$\in \mathcal{K}$ is either $<: A$, $\uparrow L$, or $\parallel L$ (we often omit $<: Top$);

$\mathcal{A}a\{\mathcal{X}\}$ means $\mathcal{X}$ may occur in $\mathcal{A}a$, then $\mathcal{A}a\{\mathcal{B}\}$ stands for $\mathcal{A}a\{\mathcal{X} \leftarrow \mathcal{B}\}$

For type, row type, and label-set definitions, in various scopes, we have the rules:

$$Let \; \mathcal{X} = \mathcal{A} \; in \; \mathcal{B}b\{\mathcal{X}\} \equiv Let \; \mathcal{X}'' = \mathcal{A} \; in \; \mathcal{B}b\{\mathcal{X}'\}$$

$$\frac{E \vdash_\rho \mathcal{A} \in \mathcal{K} \quad E \vdash_\rho \mathcal{B}b\{\mathcal{A}\} \; pred}{E \vdash_\rho Let \; \mathcal{X} \in \mathcal{K} = \mathcal{A} \; in \; \mathcal{B}b\{\mathcal{X}\} \; pred}$$

$$\frac{E \vdash_\rho \mathcal{A} \in \mathcal{K} \quad E \vdash_\rho \mathcal{Bb}\{\mathcal{A}\} \; pred}{E \vdash_\rho Let \; \mathcal{X} \in \mathcal{K} = \mathcal{A} \; in \; \mathcal{Bb}\{\mathcal{X}\} \leftrightarrow \mathcal{Bb}\{\mathcal{A}\} \; pred}$$

Note that, unlike value definitions, we do not require $E, \mathcal{X} \in \mathcal{K} \vdash_\rho \mathcal{Bb}\{\mathcal{X}\} \; pred$; this might not be typeable on its own.

We also introduce *parametric* type-level definitions, for example:

$$Let \; \mathcal{X}[\mathcal{Y}, \mathcal{Z}] = \mathcal{A}\{\mathcal{Y}, \mathcal{Z}\} \; in \dots \mathcal{X}[\mathcal{B}_1, \mathcal{C}_1] \dots \mathcal{X}[\mathcal{B}_2, \mathcal{C}_2] \dots$$

$$\leftrightarrow \dots \mathcal{A}\{\mathcal{B}_1, \mathcal{C}_1\} \dots \mathcal{A}\{\mathcal{B}_2, \mathcal{C}_2\} \dots$$

for which we omit the obvious but technically complicated definitions.

Finally, we use *top level* declarations, in the following way:

$let \; x : A = a$
$let \; y : B = b$ stands for $let \; x : A = a \; in \; let \; y : B = b \; in \; c$
c

and similarly for *Let*.

We now have enough useful features, and we can turn to examples.

5.5 Examples

Many examples in this section are adapted from [Canning Cook Hill Olthoff Mitchell 89] [Harper Pierce 90] and [Cardelli Mitchell 91].

We start with a list of standard test cases and compare them with other calculi.

- *Extracting a field from a record that is known to possess it.*

$let \; select_x : Rcd(x : Nat, Etc) \to Nat =$
     $\lambda(a : Rcd(x : Nat, Etc))a . x$

$select_x(rcd(x = 3, y = true, etc)) \leftrightarrow 3 : Nat$

- *Extracting a field from a record that is not known to possess it.* This is a typing error in all the calculi that have been proposed.

- *Removing a field from a record that is known to possess it.*

$let \; restrict_x : \forall(X \uparrow x) \; Rcd(x : Nat, X) \to \dots X \dots =$
     $\lambda(X \uparrow x) \; \lambda(a : Rcd(x : Nat, X)) \dots a \backslash x \dots$ (in a row context)

$restrict_x(y : Nat, Etc \uparrow x)(rcd(x = 3, y = true, etc))$

• *Removing a field from a record that is not known to possess it.* This is the crucial feature in [Cardelli Mitchell 91]. It is not possible here because the translation (section 6) requires exact knowledge of the missing fields.

• *Adding a field to a record that is known not to possess it.* Not applicable; all records are already "complete". However, we can add a field to a row that is known not to possess it:

$$\lambda(r \therefore R \uparrow x . L) \ldots x = b, r \ldots \quad \text{(in a row context)}$$

• *Adding a field to a record that is not known to possess it.* Not applicable; all records are already "complete". Moreover, even for rows, "not knowing" is not a sufficient conditions for adding a field. This operation is possible in [Wand 87], [Rémy 89], and [Cardelli Mitchell 91].

• *Updating a field of a record that is known to possess it.* Although adding a field under these conditions is not possible because all records are "complete", there is no problem with updating. Note that type information about additional input fields is preserved. This example motivated the work [Cardelli Mitchell 91].

let replace$_x$: $\forall (X \uparrow x) \ \forall (A) \ Rcd(x : Top, X) \to A \to Rcd(x : A, X) =$
$\quad \lambda(X \uparrow x) \ \lambda(A) \ \lambda(r : Rcd(x : Top, X)) \ \lambda(a : A) \ rcd(x = a, r \backslash x)$

replace$_x$ $(y : Bool, Etc \uparrow x)(String)(rcd(x = 3, y = true, etc))("str")$
$\quad \leftrightarrow rcd(x = \text{"str"}, y = true, etc) : Rcd(x : String, y : Bool, Etc)$

A restricted version, called *consistent updating*, preserves the type of the field being updated.

let update$_x$: $\forall (X \uparrow x) \ \forall (A) \ Rcd(x : A, X) \to A \to Rcd(x : A, X) =$
$\quad \lambda(X \uparrow x) \ \lambda(A) \ \lambda(b : Rcd(x : A, X)) \ \lambda(a : A) \ rcd(x = a, b \backslash x)$

An interesting example of update occurs when "moving" the x field of a point. In this case we want to preserve the type of the y field (whatever subtype of *Int* that may be) and all the additional fields. If the input type of the x field is $0 \ldots 9$ (a proper subtype of *Int*), the corresponding output type must be *Int*, otherwise we could exceed the range $0 \ldots 9$ for x.

let move$_x$: $\forall (Y <: Int) \ \forall (Z \uparrow x, y) \ Rcd(x : Int, y : Y, Z) \to Rcd(x : Int, y : Y, Z) =$
$\quad \lambda(Y <: Int) \ \lambda(Z \uparrow x, y) \ \lambda(p : Rcd(x : Int, y : Y, Z)) \ rcd(p . x + 1, p \backslash x)$

$p : Rcd(x : 0 \ldots 9, y : 0 \ldots 9, c : Color, Etc)$

move$_x$ $(0 \ldots 9)(c : Color, Etc)(p) : Rcd(x : Int, y : 0 \ldots 9, c : Color, Etc)$

A more challenging task is to update "deep" in a structure, while preserving all the type information of the input. Here it can be achieved as follows, for a second-level boolean update.

let deep-update$_{xy}$:
$$\forall(X \uparrow x)\,\forall(Y \uparrow y)\,Rcd(x:Rcd(y:Bool, Y), X) \rightarrow Rcd(x:Rcd(y:Bool, Y), X) =$$
$$\lambda(X \uparrow x)\,\lambda(Y \uparrow y)\,\lambda(a:Rcd(x:Rcd(y:Bool, Y), X))$$
$$rcd(x = rcd(y = not(a.x.y), a.x\backslash y), a\backslash x)$$

$deepUpdate_{xy}(z:Nat, Etc \uparrow x)(w:Nat, Etc \uparrow y)(rcd(x = rcd(y = true, w = 3, etc), z = 4, etc))$
$\quad \leftrightarrow rcd(x = rcd(y = false, w = 3, etc), z = 4, etc)$
$\qquad : Rcd(x:Rcd(y:Bool, w:Nat, Etc), z:Nat, Etc)$

• *Updating a field of a record that is not known to possess it.* Again, "not knowing" is not a sufficient condition here.

• *Renaming.* Renaming is not possible in general. Consider, for example, $Rcd(x:A, X) \rightarrow Rcd(y:A, X)$; what would be the constraint on X?

We now pass to standard examples of "class hierarchies" and "methods". We use parametric type definitions, explained in section 5.4, to model record type extension, as in [Harper Pierce 90]. This technique compensates, up to a point, for the lack of the type operations of [Cardelli Mitchell 91].

• *Points and color points.* A point has components $x:Int$, $y:Int$, while a color point also has a component $c:Color$. The challenge is to define the *ColorPoint* type and values by reusing the *Point* type and values. Here we can reuse types in two steps by defining a parametric version of each type. (Similarly for values.) This is an instance of a powerful *generator* technique, widely employed in [Cook 89].

Let PointPlus$[Z \uparrow x, y] =$
$\quad Rcd(x:Int, y:Int, Z)$

Let Point $=$
$\quad PointPlus[Etc]$ $\qquad\qquad$ $(\equiv Rcd(x, y:Int, Etc))$

Let ColorPointPlus$[Z \uparrow x, y, c] =$
$\quad PointPlus[c:Color, Z]$ $\qquad$ $(\equiv Rcd(x, y:Int, c:Color, Z))$

Let ColorPoint $=$
$\quad ColorPointPlus[Etc]$ $\qquad$ $(\equiv Rcd(x, y:Int, c:Color, Etc))$

let originPlus$: \forall(Z \uparrow x, y)\,Z \uparrow x, y \rightarrow PointPlus[Z] =$
$\quad \lambda(Z \uparrow x, y)\,\lambda(z \therefore Z \uparrow x, y)\,rcd(x = 0, y = 0, z)$

let origin : *Point* =
    originPlus(*Etc* ↑ *x*, *y*)(*etc* ↑ *x*, *y*)
let whiteOriginPlus : ∀(*Z* ↑ *x*, *y*, *c*) *Z* ↑ *x*, *y*, *c* → *ColorPointPlus*[*Z*] =
    λ(*Z* ↑ *x*, *y*, *c*) λ(*z* ∴ *Z* ↑ *x*, *y*, *c*) *originPlus*(*c* : *Color*, *Z* ↑ *x*, *y*)(*c* = *white*, *z* ↑ *x*, *y*)
let whiteOrigin : *ColorPoint* =
    whiteOriginPlus(*Etc* ↑ *x*, *y*, *c*)(*etc* ↑ *x*, *y*, *c*)

• *Total orders.* Here we have a record type *TO* of total orders. The ordering is represented as a method *leq* : *TO* → *Bool*, that compares another element of *TO* to the *self* value. The type *TO* is then recursive in the input type of its only method.

The definition of *TO* is done in three steps; first we introduce a generator with open recursion (the *Self* type parameter), then a generator derived from it where the recursion is closed, and finally the actual type *TO*. In general, the last two steps are obtained uniformly from the first. This techique is a bit complex, but it should be seen as a standard way of translating a "class" written in some more amenable language.

Let TOGenPlus[*Self*, *X* ↑ *leq*] =
    Rcd(*leq* : *Self* → *Bool*, *X*)
Let TOPlus[*X* ↑ *leq*] =
    μ(*Self*) *TOGenPlus*[*Self*, *X*]   (≡ μ(*Self*) *Rcd*(*leq* : *Self* → *Bool*, *X*))
Let TO =
    TOPlus[*Etc*]   (≡ μ(*Self*) *Rcd*(*leq* : *Self* → *Bool*, *Etc*))

Next we define the total order to Naturals (by reusing *TOGenPlus*), as:

Let NatTOGenPlus[*Self*, *X* ↑ *leq*, *val*, *add*] =
    TOGenPlus[*Self*, (*val* : *Nat*, *add* : *Self* → *Self*, *X*)]
      (≡ *Rcd*(*leq* : *Self* → *Bool*, *val* : *Nat*, *add* : *Self* → *Self*, *X*))
Let NaTOPlus[*X* ↑ *leq*, *val*, *add*] =
    μ(*Self*) *NatTOGenPlus*[*Self*, *X*]
      (≡ μ(*Self*) *Rcd*(*leq* : *Self* → *Bool*, *val* : *Nat*, *add* : *Self* → *Self*, *X*))
Let NatTO =
    NatTOPlus[*Etc*]
      (≡ μ(*Self*) *Rcd*(*leq* : *Self* → *Bool*, *val* : *Nat*, *add* : *Self* → *Self*, *Etc*))
let zero : *NatTO* =
    rcd(*val* = 0, *add* = λ(*other* : *NatTO*) *other*,
      leq = λ(*other* : *NatTO*) 0 ≤ *other* . *val*, *etc*)

(The methods of *zero* are too specialized to be inherited; this problem can be amended by defining a value generator with open recursion and, for example, *leq* = $\lambda\,(other:NatTO)\;self.val \leq other.val$.)

We now discover that, although *NatTO* was obtained by adding components to *TO*, it is not a subtype of *TO* by the rules for recursive types. Here we have the unpleasant situation that operations defined on *TO* may not apply to particular total orders.

The solution is to define those operations on *TOPlus* instead of *TO*. (As pointed out in [Harper Pierce 90] this can be done even without *F-bounded quantification* [Canning Cook Hill Olthoff Mitchell 89] in a calculus of "negative information", such as $F_{<:}\rho$.) We can say that *NatTOPlus* is a *subclass* of *TOPlus* [Cook 89].

let $min : \forall (X \uparrow leq)\; TOPlus[X] \to TOPlus[X] \to TOPlus[X] =$
$\quad \lambda(X \uparrow leq)\; \lambda(a:TOPlus[x])\; \lambda(b:TOPlus[X])$
$\qquad if\; a.leq(b)\; then\; a\; else\; b$

We can then specialize *min* to *NatTO*:

let $minNat : NatTO \to NatTO \to NatTO =$
$\quad min(val:Nat, add:NatTO \to NatTO, Etc \uparrow leq)$

to see that this typechecks, compute:

$TOPlus[val:Nat, add:NatTO \to NatTO, Etc]$
$\equiv \mu(Self)\; TOGenPlus[Self,(val:Nat, add:NatTO \to NatTO, Etc)]$
$\equiv \mu(Self)\; Rcd(leq:Self \to Bool, val:Nat, add:NatTO \to NatTO, Etc)$ $(\mathscr{A})$
$\leftrightarrow NatTO$ $(\mathscr{B})$

The step from formula $\mathscr{A}$ to formula $\mathscr{B}$ proceeds as follows, using the rules for recursive types given in section 5.4. By unfolding, we have:

$\mathscr{A} \leftrightarrow Rcd(leq:\mathscr{A} \to Bool, val:Nat, add:\mathscr{B} \to \mathscr{B}, Etc)$

$\mathscr{B} \leftrightarrow Rcd(leq:\mathscr{B} \to Bool, val:Nat, add:\mathscr{B} \to \mathscr{B}, Etc)$

Consider the contractive context $\mathscr{C}[\mathscr{X}]$:

$\mathscr{C}[\mathscr{X}] \equiv Rcd(leq:\mathscr{X} \to Bool, val:Nat, add:\mathscr{B} \to \mathscr{B}, Etc)$

Then $\mathscr{A} \leftrightarrow \mathscr{C}[\mathscr{A}]$ and $\mathscr{B} \leftrightarrow \mathscr{C}[\mathscr{B}]$; hence $\mathscr{A} \leftrightarrow \mathscr{B}$ by the contract rule.

• *Movables.* Following the three-step schema, we now give type definitions for "things that can be moved". For added flexibility, the first step defines a row type instead of a record type, using a label-set parameter (explained in section 5.4).

Let $MovableGenPlus[Self, L \# move, X \uparrow move . L] \uparrow L =$
   $move : Int \rightarrow Int \rightarrow Self, X$

Let $MovablePlus[X \uparrow move] =$
   $\mu(Self) \, Rcd(MovableGenPlus[Self, \phi, X])$

$\qquad\qquad\qquad\qquad (\equiv \mu(Self) \, Rcd(move : Int \rightarrow Int \rightarrow Self, X))$

Let $Movable =$
   $MovablePlus[Etc] \qquad (\equiv \mu(Self) \, Rcd(move : Int \rightarrow Int \rightarrow Self, Etc))$

let $translate : \forall(X \uparrow move) \, MovablePlus[X] \rightarrow Int \rightarrow Int \rightarrow MovablePlus[X] =$
   $\lambda(X \uparrow move) \, \lambda(m : MovablePlus[X]) \, \lambda(dx : Int) \, \lambda(dy : Int) \, m . move(dx)(dy)$

We can see that in this case $Movable$ is a rather useless type. The interesting definition is $MovablePlus$, which however must be instantiated before it can be used. Hence, we combine movables with points:

Let $PointPlus[Z \uparrow x, y] =$
   $Rcd(x : Int, y : Int, Z)$

Let $Point =$
   $PointPlus[Etc] \qquad (\equiv Rcd(x : Int, y : Int, Etc))$

Let $MPointGenPlus[Self, X \uparrow x, y, move] =$
   $PointPlus[MovableGenPlus[Self, (x, y), X]]$

$\qquad\qquad\qquad (\equiv Rcd(x : Int, y : Int, move : Int \rightarrow Int \rightarrow Self, X))$

Let $MPointPlus[X \uparrow x, y, move] =$
   $\mu(Self) \, MPointGenPlus[Self, X]$

$\qquad\qquad\qquad (\equiv \mu(Self) \, Rcd(x : Int, y : Int, move : Int \rightarrow Int \rightarrow Self, X))$

Let $MPoint =$
   $MPointPlus[Etc] \quad (\equiv \mu(Self) \, Rcd(x : Int, y : Int, move : Int \rightarrow Int \rightarrow Self, Etc))$

let $move : \forall(X \uparrow x, y, move) \, MPointPlus[X] \rightarrow Int \rightarrow Int \rightarrow MPointPlus[X] =$
   $\lambda(Z \uparrow x, y, move) \, \lambda(self : MPointPlus[X]) \, \lambda(dx : Int) \, \lambda(dy : Int)$
      $rcd(x = self . x + dx, y = self . y + dy, self \backslash x, y)$

let $mOrigin : MPoint =$
   $\mu(self : MPoint) \, rcd(x = 0, y = 0, move = move(Etc \uparrow x, y, move)(self), etc)$

$translate(x : Int, y : Int, Etc \uparrow move)(mOrigin)(1)(1) : MPoint$

Note that in $MPointGenPlus$ we have successfully reused the definitions for both points and movables. Moreover, $move$ can be inherited by subclasses (as opposed to subtypes) of $MPointPlus$, by defining appropriate generators.

• *Concatenation.* Record concatenation can be handled by adapting a technique of Rémy [Rémy 91]. With an extra level of encoding, record concatenation can be modeled by function composition; in our system, this idea can be realized as follows.

We first define *segments*, as extensible records parameterized by their potential extensions:

$$Seg(l_1 : A_1, \ldots, l_n : A_n) \triangleq \forall(Z \uparrow l_1 \ldots l_n) \, Z \uparrow l_1 \ldots l_n \to Rcd(l_1 : A_1, \ldots, l_n, Z)$$
$$seg(l_1 = a_1, \ldots, l_n = a_n) \triangleq \lambda(Z \uparrow l_1 \ldots l_n) \, \lambda(z \therefore Z \uparrow l_1 \ldots l_n) \, rcd(l_1 = a_1, \ldots, l_n = a_n, z)$$

A field of a segment can be extracted by *precipitating* the segment to a record:

$$s . l_i \triangleq s(Etc \uparrow l_1 \ldots l_n)(etc \uparrow l_1 \ldots l_n) . l_i \quad \text{where } s : Seg(l_1 : A_1, \ldots, l_n : A_n), i \in 1 \ldots n$$

Then, given two segments with distinct sets of labels:

$$s : Seg(l_1 : A_1, \ldots, l_n : A_n) \equiv \forall(Z \uparrow l_1 \ldots l_n) \, Z \uparrow l_1 \ldots l_n \to Rcd(l_1 : A_1, \ldots, l_n : A_n, Z)$$
$$t : Seg(k_1 : B_1, \ldots, k_m : B_m) \equiv \forall(Z \uparrow k_1 \ldots k_m) \, Z \uparrow k_1 \ldots k_m \to Rcd(k_1 : B_1, \ldots, k_m : B_m, Z)$$

we can define their concatenation ($\|$) as follows:

$$s \| t \triangleq$$
$$\lambda(Z \uparrow l_1 \ldots l_n k_1 \ldots k_m) \, \lambda(z \therefore Z \uparrow l_1 \ldots l_n k_1 \ldots k_m)$$
$$s(k_1 : B_1, \ldots, k_m : B_m, Z \uparrow l_1 \ldots l_n)$$
$$(t(l_1 : Top, \ldots, l_n : Top, Z \uparrow k_1 \ldots k_m)(l_1 = top, \ldots, l_n = top, z \uparrow k_1 \ldots k_m) \backslash l_1 \ldots l_n)$$

so that we have:

$$s \| t : Seg(l_1 : A_1, \ldots, l_n : A_n, k_1 : B_1, \ldots, k_m : B_m)$$

It would now be possible to axiomatize an extension of $F_{<:}\rho$ with segments and concatenation, and define a translation of this extended calculus into $F_{<:}\rho$.

6 Translation of $F_{<:}\rho$ into $F_{<:}$

In this section we define the promised translation from a calculus with rows to one without rows. The basic idea is that row variables, row types, row values, and row judgments become rows or sequences of, respectively, variables, types, values, and judgments.

We start with some familiar notation from previous sections:

Notation

$\mathscr{L}$	the set of labels
$\iota: \mathscr{L} \to Nat$	(a bijection) a fixed enumeration of labels
$l^i \triangleq \iota^{-1}(i)$	the label whose index is i in the fixed enumeration
$L, M \dots$	finite sets of labels
$\# S$	size of a finite set

Next we define the set of indices of a set of labels, and its maximum index:

DEFINITION (indices and maximum index of a set of labels)

$$\iota L \triangleq \{\iota(l) | l \in L\} = \{i | l_i \in L\}$$

$$\Uparrow L \triangleq max(\iota L), \text{ where } \Uparrow \{ \ \} \triangleq -1$$

Finite sets of labels L are used mostly in contexts like $\uparrow L$, describing the labels a row *lacks*. If we need to talk about the labels a row *has*, we can consider the complement $\mathscr{L} - L$. This, though, is an infinite set, and the part beyond $\Uparrow L$ is uninteresting. Hence, it is natural to take its most interesting finite prefix, κL:

DEFINITION (finite complement prefix of a finite set of labels)

$$\kappa L \triangleq \{i | i < \Uparrow L \land l_i \notin L\}$$

A central concept in the sequel is that of the dimension of (the tuple translation of) a row. Take any row that is undefined at L; that is, any row whose tuple translation sketched in section 4.2 has gaps at L. Then the labeled components to the right of the last gap ($\Uparrow L$) are contiguous, and they can be collected into a single tuple; we call the result a *normal* row. The dimension ∂L of any row that has gaps at L is then defined as the number of components of the corresponding normal row. We emphasize that for any row $r \therefore R \uparrow L$ or $R \uparrow L$, its dimension depends only on L, and not on the structure of r or R. Hence ∂L can be defined very simply as:

DEFINITION (dimension of a row undefined at L)

$$\partial L \triangleq \#(\kappa L) + 1$$

When adding a new item to a row, the row dimension changes depending on whether the new item fills the last gap of the row or not. In the former case, a whole set of components may be compacted in the final tuple and the dimension decreases; in the latter case, the dimension increases by one. The following lemma is formulated in terms of adding or removing a gap.

LEMMA (row dimension)

For $l_i \notin L$,
  if $i < \Uparrow L$ then $\partial(l_i . L) = \partial L - 1$;
  if $i > \Uparrow L$ then $\partial(l_i . L) = \partial L + (i - (\Uparrow L + 1))$.

We now need some notation for describing complex sequences and rows, and for this purpose we use a notation similar to set comprehension. For example, we use $^i\langle i | 2 \leq i \leq 4\rangle$ to denote the sequence 2, 3, 4 in this order; the idea is that the superscript index i is increased monotonically to generate the elements of the sequence.

Notation (Sequences)

$\#(S)$	length of a sequence
S, S'	sequence concatenation
$^i\langle \varphi(i) | \Phi(i)\rangle$	sequence comprehension; the sequence, generated by increasing i, whose elements are $\varphi(i)$ for $i \in Nat \wedge \Phi(i)$.

A row is a sequence of labeled elements, sorted by label index, of length greater than zero. The last element of a row is special; as discussed in section 4.2 this is the *rest* of the row. For bookkeeping purposes, we use the special label $\angle^q$ for this last element, where q is intuitively the index of the beginning of the uninteresting part of the row (as we can see from the row structure lemma below).

Notation (Rows)

A type row R is a sequence of the form:

$l_1 : A_1 \ldots l_n : A_n$ where $n \geq 1$ and $l_n \equiv \angle^q$ for some q.

A value row r is a sequence of the form:

$l_1 = a_1 \ldots l_n = a_n$ where $n \geq 1$ and $l_n \equiv \angle^q$ for some q.

$\#(l_1 : A_1 \ldots l_n : A_n) \triangleq n;$ $\#(l_1 = a_1 \ldots l_n = a_n) \triangleq n$ size

$l_i : A_i \in l_1 : A_1 \ldots l_n : A_n;$ $l_i = a_i \in l_1 = a_1 \ldots l_n = a_n$ membership ($i \in 1 \ldots n$)

$l : A \rightsquigarrow R \triangleq {}^i\langle (l^i : A^i) | (l^i : A^i) \equiv (l : A) \wedge (l^i : A^i) \in R\rangle$ sorting (if $l : B \notin R$ for any B)

$l = a \rightsquigarrow r \triangleq {}^i\langle (l^i = a^i) | (l^i = a^i) \equiv (l = a) \wedge (l^i = a^i) \in r\rangle$ sorting (if $l = b \notin r$ for any b)

We can now define some basic sequences and rows that will be used in the translation. All these have dimension ∂L.

DEFINITION (basic sequences and rows)

$$VarSeq(X, \uparrow L) \triangleq {}^i\langle X^i | i \in \kappa L \rangle, X^{\Uparrow L+1}$$

$$VarRow(X, \uparrow L) \triangleq {}^i\langle (l^i : X^i) | i \in \kappa L \rangle, (\angle^{\Uparrow L+1} : X^{\Uparrow L+1})$$

$$TopRow(\uparrow L) \triangleq {}^i\langle (l^i : Top) | i \in \kappa L \rangle, (\angle^{\Uparrow L+1} : Top)$$

$$varSeq(x, \uparrow L) \triangleq {}^i\langle x^i | i \in \kappa L \rangle, x^{\Uparrow L+1}$$

$$varRow(x, \uparrow L) \triangleq {}^i\langle (l^i = x^i) | i \in \kappa L \rangle, (\angle^{\Uparrow L+1} = x^{\Uparrow L+1})$$

$$topRow(\uparrow L) \triangleq {}^i\langle (l^i = top) | i \in \kappa L \rangle, (\angle^{\Uparrow L+1} = top)$$

$$selRow(a, \uparrow L) \triangleq {}^i\langle (l^i = a . i) | i \in \kappa L \rangle, (\angle^{\Uparrow L+1} = a \angle \Uparrow L + 1)$$

EXAMPLES

$$VarRow(X, \uparrow (\ )) = \angle^0 : X^0 \qquad\qquad TopRow(\uparrow (\ )) = \angle^0 : Top$$

$$VarRow(X, \uparrow l^0) = \angle^1 : X^1 \qquad\qquad TopRow(\uparrow l^0) = \angle^1 : Top$$

$$VarRow(X, \uparrow l^1) = l^0 : X^0, \angle^2 : X^2 \qquad TopRow(\uparrow l^1) = l^0 : Top, \angle^2 : Top$$

$$VarRow(X, \uparrow l^0, l^2) = l^1 : X^1, \angle^3 : X^3 \quad TopRow(\uparrow l^0, l^2) = l^1 : Top, \angle^3 : Top$$

In defining the full translation, $[\![-]\!]$, we need an auxiliary translation, $\langle\!\!\triangleleft - \uparrow L \triangleright$, for converting row types $R \uparrow L$, and row values $r \uparrow L$, into rows of types and values, respectively. The results of $\langle\!\!\triangleleft - \uparrow L \triangleright$ are unnormalized, in the sense that they may have a dimension greater than ∂L; that is, the final tupleable components of the results need not be grouped together into a tuple. This auxiliary translation refers back to the proper translation, $[\![-]\!]$, but for exposition purposes we present it first.

DEFINITION (translation, part 1; auxiliary row translation)

$$\langle\!\!\triangleleft X \uparrow L \triangleright \triangleq VarRow(X, \uparrow L)$$

$$\langle\!\!\triangleleft Etc \uparrow L \triangleright \triangleq TopRow(\uparrow L)$$

$$\langle\!\!\triangleleft l : A, R \uparrow L \triangleright \triangleq l : [\![A]\!] \rightsquigarrow \langle\!\!\triangleleft R \uparrow l . L \triangleright$$

$$\langle\!\!\triangleleft x \uparrow L \triangleright \triangleq varRow(x, \uparrow L)$$

$$\langle\!\!\triangleleft etc \uparrow L \triangleright \triangleq topRow(\uparrow L)$$

$$\langle\!\!\triangleleft l = a, r \uparrow L \triangleright \triangleq l = [\![a]\!] \rightsquigarrow \langle\!\!\triangleleft r \uparrow l . L \triangleright$$

$$\langle\!\!\triangleleft a \backslash l_1 . . l_n \uparrow L \triangleright \triangleq selRow([\![a]\!], \uparrow L)$$

Hence, for the base cases $\langle\!\langle X \uparrow L \rangle\!\rangle$ and $\langle\!\langle Etc \uparrow L \rangle\!\rangle$ of the row type translation, we produce rows of X's or Top's of size ∂L. For $\langle\!\langle l : A, R \uparrow L \rangle\!\rangle$ we first compute $\langle\!\langle R \uparrow l . L \rangle\!\rangle$, which has an additional gap for l, and we sort $l : [\![A]\!]$ into the result.

Similarly for the row value translation. In addition, $\langle\!\langle a \backslash l_1 \ldots l_n \uparrow L \rangle\!\rangle$ produces a row of record selections; the idea here is that eliminating $l_1 \ldots l_n$ from a is the same as selecting and reassembling all the other components of a. (The type rules will ensure $(l_1 \ldots l_n) \equiv L$, if $a \backslash l_1 \ldots l_n \uparrow L$ is well-typed.)

Here is an example of the translation:

$$\langle\!\langle X \uparrow l^0, l^1, l^3, l^6 \rangle\!\rangle \equiv l^2 : X^2, l^4 : X^4, l^5 : X^5, \angle^7 : X^7 \quad (\text{of size } \partial(l^0, l^1, l^3, l^6))$$

$$\langle\!\langle (l^1 : A^1, l^6 : A^6, X) \uparrow l^0, l^3 \rangle\!\rangle \equiv l^1 : A^1, l^2 : X^2, l^4 : X^4, l^5 : X^5, l^6 : A^6, \angle^7 : X^7$$
$$(\text{of size greater than } \partial(l^0, l^3))$$

Next, we provide a kind of normal form for row types $l_1 : A_1 \ldots l_n : A_n, \xi$, based on the translations $\langle\!\langle R \uparrow L \rangle\!\rangle$ (under typing assumptions). As we have seen, the translation returns rows whose length (which depends both on L and $l_1 \ldots l_n$) may exceed ∂L. The normal form reveals that the portion beyond $\partial L - 1$ has in fact no gaps and therefore can be collected into a tuple to form a single ∂L^{th} element. Similarly for value rows.

LEMMA (row structure)

(1) Let $R \equiv l_1 : A_1 \ldots l_n : A_n, \xi$ where $\xi = X$ or $\xi = Etc$. Assume $E \vdash_\rho R \uparrow L$. Then $\langle\!\langle R \uparrow L \rangle\!\rangle$ has the following shape, for some B's:

$$^i\langle (l^i : B^i) | i \in \kappa L \rangle, \, ^j\langle (l^j : B^j) | \Uparrow L < j < q \rangle, (\angle^q : B^q)$$

$$\text{with } q = (\Uparrow L + 1) + (\partial(l_1 \ldots l_n . L) + n - \partial L) \quad (q > \Uparrow L)$$

(2) Let $r \equiv l_1 = a_1 \ldots l_n = a_n, \xi$ where $\xi = x$, $\xi = etc$, or $\xi = a \backslash M$. Assume $E \vdash_\rho r \therefore R \uparrow L$. Then $\langle\!\langle r \uparrow L \rangle\!\rangle$ has the following shape, for some b's:

$$^i\langle (l^i = b^i) | i \in \kappa L \rangle, \, ^j\langle (l^j = b^j) | \Uparrow L < j < q \rangle, (\angle^q = b^q)$$

$$\text{with } q = (\Uparrow L + 1) + (\partial(l_1 \ldots l_n . L) + n - \partial L) \quad (q > \Uparrow L)$$

Considering the previous example:

$$\langle\!\langle (l^1 : A^1, l^6 : A^6, X) \uparrow l^0, l^3 \rangle\!\rangle \equiv$$

$$(l^1 : A^1, l^2 : X^2), (l^4 : X^4, l^5 : X^5, l^6 : A^6), \angle^7 : X^7$$

of size $\partial(l^0, l^3) - 1$

tupleable, $\partial(l^0, l^3)^{th}$ item

Now we are ready for the full translation. The translation of the $F_{<:}$ fragment of $F_{<:}\rho$ is uninteresting, but we list it for completeness.

DEFINITION (translation, part 2; $F_{<:}$ fragment)

Environments

$$[\![\vdash_\rho E\ env]\!] \triangleq\ \vdash [\![E]\!]\ env$$

$$[\![\phi]\!] \triangleq \phi$$

$$[\![E, x : A]\!] \triangleq [\![E]\!], x : [\![A]\!]$$

$$[\![E, X <: A]\!] \triangleq [\![E]\!], X <: [\![A]\!]$$

Types

$$[\![E \vdash_\rho A\ type]\!] \triangleq [\![E]\!] \vdash [\![A]\!]\ type$$

$$[\![X]\!] \triangleq X$$

$$[\![Top]\!] \triangleq Top$$

$$[\![A \rightarrow B]\!] \triangleq [\![A]\!] \rightarrow [\![B]\!]$$

$$[\![\forall (X <: A)B]\!] \triangleq \forall (X <: [\![A]\!])[\![B]\!]$$

Subtypes

$$[\![E \vdash_\rho A <: B]\!] \triangleq [\![E]\!] \vdash [\![A]\!] <: [\![B]\!]$$

Values

$$[\![E \vdash_\rho a : A]\!] \triangleq [\![E]\!] \vdash [\![a]\!] : [\![A]\!]$$

$$[\![x]\!] \triangleq x$$

$$[\![top]\!] \triangleq top$$

$$[\![\lambda(x : A)b]\!] \triangleq \lambda(x : [\![A]\!])[\![b]\!]$$

$$[\![b(a)]\!] \triangleq [\![b]\!]([\![a]\!])$$

$$[\![\lambda(X <: A)b]\!] \triangleq \lambda(X <: [\![A]\!])[\![b]\!]$$

$$[\![b(A)]\!] \triangleq [\![b]\!]([\![A]\!])$$

Value Equivalence

$$\llbracket E \vdash_\rho a \leftrightarrow a' : A \rrbracket \triangleq \llbracket E \rrbracket \vdash \llbracket a \rrbracket \leftrightarrow \llbracket a' \rrbracket : \llbracket A \rrbracket$$

Finally, we can give the translation of the proper $F_{<:}\rho$ judgments and terms. An $F_{<:}\rho$ judgment $E \vdash_\rho \vartheta \uparrow L$ becomes a sequence of size ∂L of $F_{<:}$ judgments. A row variable $X \uparrow L$ in an environment becomes a sequence of ∂L type variables. The domain of row function space $R \uparrow L \to B$ becomes a sequence of ∂L domains; similarly for $\lambda(x \therefore R \uparrow L)$, with $b(r \uparrow L)$ becoming a sequence of ∂L applications. A row quantifier $\forall (X \uparrow L)$ becomes a nesting of ∂L type quantifiers; similarly for an abstraction $\lambda(X \uparrow L)$, with $b(R \uparrow L)$ becoming a nesting of ∂L type applications. Record types and values are translated by applying $\triangleleft - \uparrow L \triangleright$ to the respective rows, and then normalizing the results to size ∂L.

DEFINITION (translation, part 3; $F_{<:}\rho$ proper)

Environments (Continued)

$$\llbracket E, X \uparrow L \rrbracket \triangleq let\ X_1 \dots X_{\partial L} = VarSeq(X, \uparrow L)\ in\ \llbracket E \rrbracket, X_1, \dots, X_{\partial L}$$

$$\llbracket E, x \therefore R \uparrow L \rrbracket$$

$$\triangleq let\ x_1 \dots x_{\partial L} = varSeq(x, \uparrow L)\ and\ A_1 \dots A_{\partial L} = \llbracket R \uparrow L \rrbracket$$

$$in\ \llbracket E \rrbracket, x_1 : A_1 \dots x_{\partial L} : A_{\partial L}$$

Types (Continued)

$$\llbracket Rcd(R) \rrbracket \triangleq \llbracket R \uparrow (\ ) \rrbracket$$

$$\llbracket R \uparrow L \to B \rrbracket \triangleq let\ A_1 \dots A_{\partial L} = \llbracket R \uparrow L \rrbracket\ in\ A_1 \to \cdots \to A_{\partial L} \to \llbracket B \rrbracket$$

$$\llbracket \forall (X \uparrow L)B \rrbracket \triangleq let\ X_1 \dots X_{\partial L} = VarSeq(X, \uparrow L)\ in\ \forall (X_1) \dots \forall (X_{\partial L}) \llbracket B \rrbracket$$

Type Rows

$$\llbracket E \vdash_\rho R \uparrow L \rrbracket \triangleq let\ A_1 \dots A_{\partial L} = \llbracket R \uparrow L \rrbracket\ in\ \llbracket E \rrbracket \vdash A_1\ type \dots \llbracket E \rrbracket \vdash A_{\partial L}\ type$$

$$\llbracket R \uparrow L \rrbracket \triangleq let(l_1 : A_1 \dots l_{\partial L} : A_{\partial L} \dots l_n : A_n) = \triangleleft R \uparrow L \triangleright\ in\ A_1 \dots A_{\partial L - 1}, Tuple(A_{\partial L} \dots A_n)$$

Subrows

$$\llbracket E \vdash_\rho R <\therefore S \uparrow L \rrbracket$$

$$\triangleq let\ A_1 \dots A_{\partial L} = \llbracket R \uparrow L \rrbracket\ and\ B_1 \dots B_{\partial L} = \llbracket S \uparrow L \rrbracket$$

$$in\ \llbracket E \rrbracket \vdash A_1 <: B_1 \dots \llbracket E \rrbracket \vdash A_{\partial L} <: B_{\partial L}$$

Values (Continued)

$$\llbracket rcd(r) \rrbracket \triangleq \llbracket r \uparrow (\ ) \rrbracket$$

$$\llbracket a.l \rrbracket \triangleq \llbracket a \rrbracket . \imath(l)$$

$$\llbracket \lambda(x \therefore R \uparrow L)b \rrbracket$$

$$\triangleq \text{let } x_1 \ldots x_{\partial L} = varSeq(x, \uparrow L) \text{ and } A_1 \ldots A_{\partial L} = \llbracket R \uparrow L \rrbracket$$

$$\text{in } \lambda(x_1 : A_1) \ldots \lambda(x_{\partial L} : A_{\partial L}) \llbracket b \rrbracket$$

$$\llbracket b(r \uparrow L) \rrbracket \triangleq \text{let } a_1 \ldots a_{\partial L} = \llbracket r \uparrow L \rrbracket \text{ in } \llbracket b \rrbracket (a_1) \ldots (a_{\partial L})$$

$$\llbracket \lambda(X \uparrow L)b \rrbracket \triangleq \text{let } X_1 \ldots X_{\partial L} = VarSeq(X, \uparrow L) \text{ in } \lambda(X_1) \ldots \lambda(X_{\partial L}) \llbracket b \rrbracket$$

$$\llbracket b(R \uparrow L) \rrbracket \triangleq \text{let } A_1 \ldots A_{\partial L} = \llbracket R \uparrow L \rrbracket \text{ in } \llbracket b \rrbracket (A_1) \ldots (A_{\partial L})$$

Value Rows

$$\llbracket E \vdash_\rho r \therefore R \uparrow L \rrbracket$$

$$\triangleq \text{let } a_1 \ldots a_{\partial L} = \llbracket r \uparrow L \rrbracket \text{ and } A_1 \ldots A_{\partial L} = \llbracket R \uparrow L \rrbracket \text{ in } \llbracket E \rrbracket \vdash a_1 : A_1 \ldots \llbracket E \rrbracket \vdash a_{\partial L} : A_{\partial L}$$

$$\llbracket r \uparrow L \rrbracket \triangleq \text{let } (l_1 = a_1 \ldots l_{\partial L} = a_{\partial L} \ldots l_n = a_n) = \langle\!\langle r \uparrow L \rangle\!\rangle \text{ in } a_1 \ldots a_{\partial L - 1}, tuple(a_{\partial L} \ldots a_n)$$

Value Row Equivalence

$$\llbracket E \vdash_\rho r \leftrightarrow r' \therefore R \uparrow L \rrbracket$$

$$\triangleq \text{let } a_1 \ldots a_{\partial L} = \llbracket r \uparrow L \rrbracket \text{ and } a'_1 \ldots a'_{\partial L} = \llbracket r' \uparrow L \rrbracket \text{ and } A_1 \ldots A_{\partial L} = \llbracket R \uparrow L \rrbracket$$

$$\text{in } \llbracket E \rrbracket \vdash a_1 \leftrightarrow a'_1 : A_1 \ldots \llbracket E \rrbracket \vdash a_{\partial L} \leftrightarrow a'_{\partial L} : A_{\partial L}$$

EXAMPLES

$$\llbracket \lambda(x \therefore (l^0 : A, Etc) \uparrow l^1) \, rcd(l^1 = b, x) \rrbracket = \lambda(x^0 : \llbracket A \rrbracket) \, \lambda(x^2 : Top) \, tuple(x^0, \llbracket b \rrbracket, x^2)$$

$$\llbracket \lambda(x \therefore (l^2 : A, Etc) \uparrow l^1) \, rcd(l^1 = b, x) \rrbracket$$

$$= \lambda(x^0 : Top) \, \lambda(x^2 : Tuple(\llbracket A \rrbracket, Top)) \, tuple(x^0, \llbracket b \rrbracket, x^2)$$

$$\llbracket \lambda(X \uparrow l^0, l^1) \, \lambda(x \therefore (l^0 : A, X) \uparrow l^1) \, rcd(l^1 = b, x) \rrbracket$$

$$= \lambda(X^2) \, \lambda(x^0 : \llbracket A \rrbracket) \, \lambda(x^2 : X^2) \, tuple(x^0, \llbracket b \rrbracket, x^2)$$

$$\llbracket \lambda(X \uparrow l^1, l^2) \, \lambda(x \therefore (l^2 : A, X) \uparrow l^1) \, rcd(l^1 = b, x) \rrbracket$$

$$= \lambda(X^0) \, \lambda(X^3) \, \lambda(x^0 : X^0) \, \lambda(x^2 : Tuple(\llbracket A \rrbracket, X^3)) \, tuple(x^0, \llbracket b \rrbracket, x^2)$$

Using the row structure lemma, we can now show that the translation is well-defined, provided that the translated terms are well-typed.

LEMMA (translation dimensions)

$$\#(VarSeq(X, \uparrow L)) = \#(VarRow(X, \uparrow L)) = \#(TopRow(\uparrow L))$$

$$= \#(varSeq(x, \uparrow L)) = \#(topRow(\uparrow L)) = \#(varRow(x, \uparrow L)) = \#(selRow(a, \uparrow L))$$

$$= \partial L.$$

If $E \vdash_\rho R \uparrow L$ then $\#(\langle R \uparrow L \rangle) \geq \partial L$.

If $E \vdash_\rho R \uparrow L$ then $\#([\![R \uparrow L]\!]) = \partial L$.

If $E \vdash_\rho r \therefore R \uparrow L$ then $\#(\langle r \uparrow L \rangle) \geq \partial L$.

If $E \vdash_\rho r \therefore R \uparrow L$ then $\#([\![r \uparrow L]\!]) = \partial L$.

LEMMA (good translation)   If a judgment J is derivable, then the translation $[\![J]\!]$ is well-defined. That is, all the assumptions made in the translation about sizes of rows, are justified.

The row structure lemma is also the key to the following row analysis lemma, which is then used in the proof of all the technical lemmas in the next section. The row analysis lemma describes in detail what happens when a single element is added to a row, or removed from it.

LEMMA (row analysis)

(1) Assume $E \vdash_\rho l: A, R \uparrow L$. Let $B_1 \ldots B_{\partial l.L} = [\![R \uparrow l.L]\!]$ and $C_1 \ldots C_{\partial L} = [\![l: A, R \uparrow L]\!]$. If $\iota(l) < \Uparrow L$ then $\partial(l.L) = \partial L - 1$, and:

$$C_1 \ldots C_{\partial L} = B_1 \ldots B_{k-1}, [\![A]\!], B_k \ldots B_{\partial L - 1} \quad \text{where } k = \#\{i | i \in \kappa L \wedge i < \iota(l)\} \leq \partial L - 1.$$

If $\iota(l) > \Uparrow L$ then $\partial(l.L) = \partial L + (\iota(l) - (\Uparrow L + 1))$, and:

$$C_1 \ldots C_{\partial L - 1} = B_1 \ldots B_{\partial L - 1} \qquad C_{\partial L} = Tuple(B_{\partial L} \ldots B_{\partial l.L - 1}, [\![A]\!], B_{\partial l.L})$$

where $\partial(l.L) \geq \partial L$.

(2) Assume $E \vdash_\rho l = a, r \therefore R \uparrow L$. Let $b_1 \ldots b_{\partial l.L} = [\![r \uparrow l.L]\!]$ and $c_1 \ldots c_{\partial L} = [\![l = a, r \uparrow L]\!]$. If $\iota(l) < \Uparrow L$ then $\partial(l.L) = \partial L - 1$, and:

$$c_1 \ldots c_{\partial L} = b_1 \ldots b_{k-1}, [\![a]\!], b_k \ldots b_{\partial L - 1} \quad \text{where } k = \#\{i | i \in \kappa L \wedge i < \iota(l)\} \leq \partial L - 1.$$

If $\iota(l) > \Uparrow L$ then $\partial(l.L) = \partial L + (\iota(l) - (\Uparrow L + 1))$, and:

$$c_1 \ldots c_{\partial L-1} = b_1 \ldots b_{\partial L-1} \qquad c_{\partial L} = tuple(b_{\partial L} \ldots b_{\partial l.L-1}, [\![a]\!], b_{\partial l.L}) \quad \text{where } \partial(l.L) \geq \partial L.$$

(3) Assume $E \vdash_\rho a \backslash L \therefore R \uparrow L$. Let $b_1 \ldots b_{\partial l.L} = [\![a \backslash l.L \uparrow l.L]\!]$ and $c_1 \ldots c_{\partial L} = [\![a \backslash L \uparrow L]\!]$. If $\iota(l) < \Uparrow L$ then $\partial(l.L) = \partial L - 1$, and:

$$c_1 \ldots c_{\partial L} = b_1 \ldots b_{k-1}, [\![a.l]\!], b_k \ldots b_{\partial L-1} \quad \text{where } k = \#\{i | i \in \kappa L \wedge i < \iota(l)\} \leq \partial L - 1.$$

If $\iota(l) > \Uparrow L$ then $\partial(l.L) = \partial L + (\iota(l) - (\Uparrow L + 1))$, and:

$$c_1 \ldots c_{\partial L-1} = b_1 \ldots b_{\partial L-1} \qquad c_{\partial L} = tuple(b_{\partial L} \ldots b_{\partial l.L-1}, [\![a.l]\!], b_{\partial l.L})$$

where $\partial(l.L) \geq \partial L$.

7   The Translation Preserves Derivations

In this section we show that the translation from $\vdash_\rho$ to $\vdash$ is sound. That is, if a judgment J is derivable in $\vdash_\rho$, then all the judgments in the sequence $[\![J]\!]$ are derivable in $\vdash$.

The following group of lemmas is used in the hardest cases of the soundness proof. These lemmas are complicated by the fact that the translations are well-defined only under typing assumptions. First we have lemmas regarding rows; they have the structure of some of the inference rules, but concern the translation of those rules.

LEMMA (soundness of row inference rules)

(type row cons)

Assume $E \vdash_\rho R' \uparrow l.L$ and $E \vdash_\rho A$ type.

If $[\![E \vdash_\rho R' \uparrow l.L]\!]$ and $[\![E \vdash_\rho A$ type$]\!]$ then $[\![E \vdash_\rho l:A, R' \uparrow L]\!]$.

(sub row cons)

Assume $E \vdash_\rho A <: B$ and $E \vdash_\rho R' <\therefore S' \uparrow l.L$.

If $[\![E \vdash_\rho A <: B]\!]$ and $[\![E \vdash_\rho R' <\therefore S' \uparrow l.L]\!]$ then $[\![E \vdash_\rho l:A, R' <\therefore l:B, S' \uparrow L]\!]$.

(row cons)

Assume $E \vdash_\rho a:A$ and $E \vdash_\rho r \therefore R \uparrow l.L$.

If $[\![E \vdash_\rho a:A]\!]$ and $[\![E \vdash_\rho r \therefore R \uparrow l.L]\!]$ then $[\![E \vdash_\rho l = a, r \therefore l:A, R \uparrow L]\!]$.

(selection)

Assume $E \vdash_\rho a : Rcd(l : A, S)$.

If $[\![E \vdash_\rho a : Rcd(l : A, S)]\!]$ then $[\![E \vdash_\rho a . l : A]\!]$.

(restriction)

Assume $E \vdash_\rho a \backslash L \therefore l : A, S \uparrow L$.

If $[\![E \vdash_\rho a \backslash L \therefore l : A, S \uparrow L]\!]$ then $[\![E \vdash_\rho a \backslash l . L \therefore S \uparrow l . L]\!]$.

(eq-cons)

Assume $E \vdash_\rho r \leftrightarrow r' \therefore R \uparrow l . L$, and $E \vdash_\rho a \leftrightarrow a' : A$.

If $[\![E \vdash_\rho r \leftrightarrow r' \therefore R \uparrow l . L]\!]$ and $[\![E \vdash_\rho a \leftrightarrow a' : A]\!]$

  then $[\![E \vdash_\rho l = a, r \leftrightarrow l = a', r' \therefore l : A, R \uparrow L]\!]$

(eq-selection)

Assume $E \vdash_\rho a \leftrightarrow a' : Rcd(l : A, S)$.

If $[\![E \vdash_\rho a \leftrightarrow a' : Rcd(l : A, S)]\!]$ then $[\![E \vdash_\rho a . l \leftrightarrow a' . l : A]\!]$.

(eval-selection)

Assume $E \vdash_\rho r \therefore R \uparrow l$ and $E \vdash_\rho a \leftrightarrow a' : A$.

If $[\![E \vdash_\rho r \therefore R \uparrow l]\!]$ and $[\![E \vdash_\rho a \leftrightarrow a' : A]\!]$ then $[\![E \vdash_\rho rcd(l = a, r) . l \leftrightarrow a' : A]\!]$.

(eq-restriction)

Assume $E \vdash_\rho a \backslash L \leftrightarrow a' \backslash L \therefore l : A, S \uparrow L$.

If $[\![E \vdash_\rho a \backslash L \leftrightarrow a' \backslash L \therefore l : A, S \uparrow L]\!]$ then $[\![E \vdash_\rho a \backslash l . L \leftrightarrow a' \backslash l . L \therefore S \uparrow l . L]\!]$.

(eval-restriction)

(1) Assume $E \vdash_\rho r \leftrightarrow r' \therefore R \uparrow (\ )$. If $[\![E \vdash_\rho r \leftrightarrow r' \therefore R \uparrow (\ )]\!]$ then $[\![E \vdash_\rho rcd(r) \backslash \leftrightarrow r' \therefore R \uparrow (\ )]\!]$.

(2) Assume $E \vdash_\rho rcd(l = a, r) \backslash L \leftrightarrow l = a, r' \therefore l : A, R \uparrow L$. If $[\![E \vdash_\rho rcd(l = a, r) \backslash L \leftrightarrow l = a, r' \therefore l : A, R \uparrow L]\!]$ then $[\![E \vdash_\rho rcd(l = a, r) \backslash l . L \leftrightarrow r' \therefore R \uparrow l . L]\!]$.

Next we have substitution lemmas for all possible combinations of variables and terms.

LEMMA (soundness of substitution)

(type in type)

Assume $E \vdash_\rho A' <: A$ and $E, X <: A, E' \vdash_\rho B \, type$.

Then $[\![B\{X \leftarrow A'\}]\!]$ is well-defined.

Then $[\![B]\!]\{X \leftarrow [\![A']\!]\} \equiv [\![B\{X \leftarrow A'\}]\!]$.

(type in row-type)

Assume $E \vdash_\rho A' <: A$ and $E, X <: A, E' \vdash_\rho S \uparrow M$.

Then $[\![S\{X \leftarrow A'\} \uparrow M]\!]$ is well-defined.

Let $B_1 \ldots B_{\partial M} = [\![S \uparrow M]\!]$ and $C_1 \ldots C_{\partial M} = [\![S\{X \leftarrow A'\} \uparrow M]\!]$.

Then $B_1\{X \leftarrow [\![A']\!]\} \equiv C_1 \ldots B_{\partial M}\{X \leftarrow [\![A']\!]\} \equiv C_{\partial M}$.

(row-type in type)

Assume $E \vdash_\rho R \uparrow L$ and $E, X \uparrow L, E' \vdash_\rho B \, type$.

Then $[\![B\{X \leftarrow R\}]\!]$ is well-defined.

Let $X_1 \ldots X_{\partial L} = VarSeq(X, \uparrow L)$ and $A_1 \ldots A_{\partial L} = [\![R \uparrow L]\!]$

Then $[\![B]\!]\{X_1 \leftarrow A_1\} \ldots \{X_{\partial L} \leftarrow A_{\partial L}\} \equiv [\![B\{X \leftarrow R\}]\!]$.

(row-type in row-type)

Assume $E \vdash_\rho R \uparrow L$ and $E, X \uparrow L, E' \vdash_\rho S \uparrow M$.

Then $[\![S\{X \leftarrow R\} \uparrow M]\!]$ is well-defined.

Let $X_1 \ldots X_{\partial L} = VarSeq(X, \uparrow L)$ and $A_1 \ldots A_{\partial L} = [\![R \uparrow L]\!]$

Let $B_1 \ldots B_{\partial M} = [\![S \uparrow M]\!]$ and $C_1 \ldots C_{\partial M} = [\![S\{X \leftarrow R\} \uparrow M]\!]$

Then $B_i\{X_1 \leftarrow A_1\} \ldots \{X_{\partial L} \leftarrow A_{\partial L}\} \equiv C_i$ for i in $1 \ldots \partial M$.

(type in value)

Assume $E \vdash_\rho A' <: A$ and $E, X <: A, E' \vdash_\rho b : B$

Then $[\![b\{X \leftarrow A'\}]\!]$ is well-defined.

Then $[\![b]\!]\{X \leftarrow [\![A']\!]\} \equiv [\![b\{X \leftarrow A'\}]\!]$.

(type in row-value)

Assume $E \vdash_\rho A' <: A$ and $E, X <: A, E' \vdash_\rho s \therefore S \uparrow M$

Then $[\![s\{X \leftarrow A'\} \uparrow M]\!]$ is well-defined.

Let $b_1 \ldots b_{\partial M} = [\![s \uparrow M]\!]$ and $c_1 \ldots c_{\partial M} = [\![s\{X \leftarrow A'\} \uparrow M]\!]$.

Then $b_1\{X \leftarrow [\![A']\!]\} \equiv c_1 \ldots b_{\partial M}\{X \leftarrow [\![A']\!]\} \equiv c_{\partial M}$

(row-type in value)

Assume $E \vdash_\rho R \uparrow L$ and $E, X \uparrow L, E' \vdash_\rho c : C$.

Then $[\![c\{X \leftarrow R\}]\!]$ is well-defined.

Let $X_1 \ldots X_{\partial L} = VarSeq(X, \uparrow L)$ and $A_1 \ldots A_{\partial L} = [\![R \uparrow L]\!]$

Then $[\![c]\!]\{X_1 \leftarrow A_1\} \ldots \{X_{\partial L} \leftarrow A_{\partial L}\} \equiv [\![c\{X \leftarrow R\}]\!]$.

(row-type in row-value)

Assume $E \vdash_\rho R \uparrow L$ and $E, X \uparrow L, E' \vdash_\rho s \therefore S \uparrow M$.

Then $[\![s\{X \leftarrow R\} \uparrow M]\!]$ is well-defined.

Let $X_1 \ldots X_{\partial L} = VarSeq(X, \uparrow L)$ and $A_1 \ldots A_{\partial L} = [\![R \uparrow L]\!]$

Let $b_1 \ldots b_{\partial M} = [\![s \uparrow M]\!]$ and $c_1 \ldots c_{\partial M} = [\![s\{X \leftarrow R\} \uparrow M]\!]$

Then $b_i\{X_1 \leftarrow A_1\} \ldots \{X_{\partial L} \leftarrow A_{\partial L}\} \equiv c_i$ for i in $1 \ldots \partial M$.

(value in value)

Assume $E \vdash_\rho a : A$ and $E, x : A, E' \vdash_\rho b : B$

Then $[\![b\{x \leftarrow a\}]\!]$ is well-defined.

Then $[\![b]\!]\{x \leftarrow [\![a]\!]\} \equiv [\![b\{x \leftarrow a\}]\!]$.

(value in row-value)

Assume $E \vdash_\rho a : A$ and $E, x : A, E' \vdash_\rho s \therefore S \uparrow M$

Then $[\![s\{x \leftarrow a\} \uparrow M]\!]$ is well-defined.

Let $b_1 \ldots b_{\partial M} = [\![s \uparrow M]\!]$ and $c_1 \ldots c_{\partial M} = [\![s\{x \leftarrow a\} \uparrow M]\!]$

Then $b_1\{x \leftarrow [\![a]\!]\} \equiv c_1 \ldots b_{\partial M}\{x \leftarrow [\![a]\!]\} \equiv c_{\partial M}$.

(row-value in value)

Assume $E \vdash_\rho r \therefore R \uparrow L$ and $E, x \therefore R \uparrow L, E' \vdash_\rho c : C$.

Then $[\![c\{x \leftarrow r\}]\!]$ is well-defined.

Let $x_1 \ldots x_{\partial L} = varSeq(x, \uparrow L)$ and $a_1 \ldots a_{\partial L} = [\![r \uparrow L]\!]$

Then $[\![c]\!]\{x_1 \leftarrow a_1\} \ldots \{x_{\partial L} \leftarrow a_{\partial L}\} \equiv [\![c\{x \leftarrow r\}]\!]$.

(row-value in row-value)

Assume $E \vdash_\rho r \therefore R \uparrow L$ and $E, x \therefore R \uparrow L, E' \vdash_\rho s \therefore S \uparrow M$.

Then $[\![s\{x \leftarrow r\} \uparrow M]\!]$ is well-defined.

Let $x_1 \ldots x_{\partial L} = varSeq(x, \uparrow L)$ and $a_1 \ldots a_{\partial L} = [\![r \uparrow L]\!]$

Let $b_1 \ldots b_{\partial M} = [\![s \uparrow M]\!]$ and $c_1 \ldots c_{\partial M} = [\![s\{x \leftarrow r\} \uparrow M]\!]$

Then $b_i\{x_1 \leftarrow a_1\} \ldots \{x_{\partial L} \leftarrow a_{\partial L}\} \equiv c_i$ for i in $1 \ldots \partial M$.

Finally we have the soundness theorem, divided into mutual induction groups.

THEOREM (soundness)

(1) $\vdash_\rho E$ *env* $\Rightarrow [\![\vdash_\rho E$ *env*$]\!]$

$\quad E \vdash_\rho A$ *type* $\Rightarrow [\![E \vdash_\rho A$ *type*$]\!]$

$\quad E \vdash_\rho R \uparrow L \Rightarrow [\![E \vdash_\rho R \uparrow L]\!]$

(2) $E \vdash_\rho A <: B \Rightarrow [\![E \vdash_\rho A <: B]\!]$

$\quad E \vdash_\rho R <\therefore S \uparrow L \Rightarrow [\![E \vdash_\rho R <\therefore S \uparrow L]\!]$

(3) $E \vdash_\rho a : A \Rightarrow [\![E \vdash_\rho a : A]\!]$

$\quad E \vdash_\rho r \therefore R \uparrow L \Rightarrow [\![E \vdash_\rho r \therefore R \uparrow L]\!]$

(4) $E \vdash_\rho a \leftrightarrow a' : A \Rightarrow [\![E \vdash_\rho a \leftrightarrow a' : A]\!]$

$\quad E \vdash_\rho r \leftrightarrow r' \therefore R \uparrow L \Rightarrow [\![E \vdash_\rho r \leftrightarrow r' \therefore R \uparrow L]\!]$

Proof The proof is by simultaneous induction on the derivations, using the lemmas above in the hard cases. ∎

8 Conclusions

We have defined a calculus of row variables, $F_{<:}\rho$, and translated it into a simpler calculus with subtyping, $F_{<:}$. The constraints imposed by the translation have forced us into a restricted subset of the features that have been proposed for calculi of extensible records, but we can still express many benchmark examples.

The particular mixture of features chosen for $F_{<:}\rho$ is not uniquely determined. For example we might have attempted to incorporate bounds on row quantifiers $(\forall(X <: R \uparrow L)B)$, row-valued functions $(A \rightarrow_{\uparrow L} R)$, or record concatenation (sketched in section 5.5). The point is that many possible variations can be described and evaluated within a single basic framework. Underlying all these variations and bridging between them there is $F_{<:}$, often extended with recursion. This approach could provide us with a fundamental and unified framework in which to study complex features of object-oriented languages.

Acknowledgements

I would like to thank Martín Abadi for his careful reading of the draft.

References

[Amadio Cardelli 91] R. M. Amadio, L. Cardelli: *Subtyping recursive types*, Proceedings of the ACM Conference on Principles of Programming Languages, ACM Press, 1991.

[Böhm Berarducci 85] C. Böhm, A. Berarducci: *Automatic synthesis of typed λ-programs on term algebras*, Theoretical Computer Science, 39, pp. 135–154, 1985.

[Breazu-Tannen Coquand Gunter Scedrov 89] V. Breazu-Tannen, T. Coquand, C. Gunter, A. Scedrov: *Inheritance and explicit coercion*, Proc. of the Fourth IEEE Symposium on Logic in Computer Science, pp 112–129, 1989.

[Canning Cook Hill Olthoff Mitchell 89] P. Canning, W. Cook, W. Hill, W. Olthoff, J. C. Mitchell: *F-bounded polymorphism for object-oriented programming*, Proc. ACM Conference on Functional Programming and Computer Architecture, ACM Press, 1989.

[Cardelli Martini Mitchell Scedrov 91] L. Cardelli, J. C. Mitchell, S. Martini, A. Scedrov: *An extension of system F with subtyping*, to appear.

[Cardelli Mitchell 91] L. Cardelli, J. C. Mitchell: *Operations on records*, Proc. of the Fifth Conference on Mathematical Foundations of Programming Language Semantics, New Orleans, 1989. To appear in Mathematical Structures in Computer Science, 1991.

[Cardelli Wegner 85] L. Cardelli, P. Wegner: *On understanding types, data abstraction and polymorphism*, Computing Surveys, Vol 17 n. 4, pp 471–522, December 1985.

[Cardelli 88] L. Cardelli: *A semantics of multiple inheritance*, in Information and Computation 76. pp 138–164, 1988. (First appeared in Semantics of Data Types, G. Kahn. D. B. MacQueen and G. Plotkin Ed. Lecture Notes in Computer Science n. 173, Springer-Verlag 1984.)

[Cook 89]   W. Cook: *A denotational semantics of inheritance*, Ph.D. thesis, Technical Report CS-89-33. Brown University, 1989.

[Curien Ghelli 91]   P.-L. Curien, G. Ghelli: *Coherence of subsumption*, Mathematical Structures in Computer Science, to appear.

[de Bruijn 72]   N. G. de Bruijn: *Lambda-calculus notation with nameless dummies*, in Indag. Math. 34(5), pp. 381–392, 1972.

[Fairbairn 89]   J. Fairbairn: *Some types with inclusion properties in* $\forall$, $\rightarrow$, μ, Technical report No 171, University of Cambridge, Computer Laboratory.

[Girard 71]   J-Y. Girard: *Une extension de l'interprétation de Gödel à l'analyse, et son application à l'élimination des coupures dans l'analyse et la théorie des types*, Proceedings of the second Scandinavian logic symposium, J. E. Fenstad Ed. pp. 63–92, North-Holland, 1971.

[Harper Pierce 90]   R. Harper, B. Pierce: *A record calculus with symmetric concatenation*, Technical Report CMU-CS-90-157, CMU, 1990.

[Jategaonkar Mitchell 88]   L. A. Jategaonkar, J. C. Mitchell: *ML with extended pattern matching and subtypes*, Proc. of the ACM Conference on Lisp and Functional Programming, pp. 198–211, 1988.

[Martini 90]   S. Martini: personal communication.

[Rémy 89]   D. Rémy: *Typechecking records and variants in a natural extension of ML*, Proc. of the 16th ACM Symposium on Principles of Programming Languages, pp. 77–88, 1989.

[Rémy 91]   D. Rémy: *Record concatenation for free*, to appear.

[Reynolds 74]   J. C. Reynolds: *Towards a theory of type structure*, in Colloquium sur la programmation pp. 408–423, Springer-Verlag Lecture Notes in Computer Science, n. l9, 1974.

[Wand 87]   M. Wand: *Complete Type Inference for Simple Objects*, Proc. of the Second IEEE Symposium on Logic in Computer Science, pp 37–44, 1987.

[Wand 89]   M. Wand: *Type inference for record concatenation and multiple inheritance*, Proc. of the Fourth IEEE Symposium on Logic in Computer Science, pp. 92–97, 1989.

12 Bounded Quantification Is Undecidable

Benjamin C. Pierce

Abstract

$F_\le$ is a typed λ-calculus with subtyping and bounded second-order polymorphism. First introduced by Cardelli and Wegner, it has been widely studied as a core calculus for type systems with subtyping.

Curien and Ghelli proved the partial correctness of a recursive procedure for computing minimal types of $F_\le$ terms and showed that the termination of this procedure is equivalent to the termination of its major component, a procedure for checking the subtype relation between $F_\le$ types. This procedure was thought to terminate on all inputs, but the discovery of a subtle bug in a purported proof of this claim reopened the question of the decidability of subtyping, and hence of typechecking.

This question is settled here in the negative, using a reduction from the halting problem for two-counter Turing machines to show that the subtype relation of $F_\le$ is undecidable.

1 Introduction

The notion of *bounded quantification* was introduced by Cardelli and Wegner [15] in the language Fun. Based on informal ideas by Cardelli and formalized using techniques developed by Mitchell [29], Fun combined Girard-Reynolds polymorphism [24, 34] and Cardelli's first-order calculus of subtyping [6].

Fun and its relatives have been studied extensively by programming language theorists and designers. Cardelli and Wegner's survey paper [15] gives the first programming examples using bounded quantification; more are developed in Cardelli's study of power kinds [7] and in the documentation for his typechecker implementation [10]. Curien and Ghelli [20] and Ghelli [22, 23] address a number of syntactic properties of $F_\le$. Semantic aspects of closely related systems have been studied by Bruce and Longo [3], Martini [28], Breazu-Tannen, Coquand, Gunter, and Scedrov [1], Cardone [16], Cardelli and Longo [12], Cardelli, Martini, Mitchell, and Scedrov [13], Curien and Ghelli [20, 19], and Bruce and Mitchell [4]. $F_\le$ has been extended to include record types and richer notions of inheritance by Cardelli and Mitchell [14], Bruce [2], Cardelli [9, 11], Canning, Cook, Hill, Olthoff, and Mitchell [5], Mitchell [30], Pierce and Turner [33], and Hofmann and Pierce [25]. An extension with intersection types [18, 35] is the subject of the author's Ph. D. thesis [32]. The proof theory of a version of $F_\le$ with a rule of extensionality has been studied by Curien and Ghelli [19]. Bounded quantification also plays a key role in Cardelli's programing language Quest [8, 12] and in the Abel language developed at HP Labs [5, 17].

To appear in *Information and Computation* 113, Number 1 (August 1994). © 1994 Academic Press, Inc.

The original Fun was simplified by Bruce and Longo [3] for their investigation of its semantics, and again by Curien and Ghelli [20], who gave a proof of the coherence of typechecking. Curien and Ghelli's formulation, called *minimal Bounded Fun* or $F_{\leq}$ ("*F* sub"), is the one considered here.

As in other second-order λ-calculi, the terms of $F_{\leq}$ include variables, abstractions, applications, type abstractions, and type applications, with the refinement that each type abstraction gives a *bound* for the type variable it introduces and each type application must satisfy the constraint that the argument type is a *subtype* of the bound of the polymorphic function being applied. The well-typed terms of $F_{\leq}$ are defined by means of a collection of rules for inferring statements of the form $\Gamma \vdash e \in \tau$ ("*e* has type τ under assumptions Γ").

Variables, abstractions, and applications have the usual typing rules. (Here every free variable x is assumed to have some typing assumption $\Gamma(x)$.)

$$\Gamma \vdash x \in \Gamma(x)$$

$$\frac{\Gamma, x : \sigma \vdash e \in \tau}{\Gamma \vdash \lambda x : \sigma . e \in \sigma \to \tau}$$

$$\frac{\Gamma \vdash e_1 \in \sigma \to \tau \qquad \Gamma \vdash e_2 \in \sigma}{\Gamma \vdash e_1 e_2 \in \tau}$$

Type abstractions are treated as in other second-order λ-calculi, except that they also give a bound, with respect to the subtype relation, for the variable they introduce; they are checked by moving this assumption into the context and checking the body of the abstraction under the enriched set of assumptions:

$$\frac{\Gamma, \alpha \leq \theta \vdash e \in \tau}{\Gamma \vdash \Lambda \alpha \leq \theta . e \in \forall \alpha \leq \theta . \tau}$$

Type applications check that the type being passed as a parameter is indeed a subtype of the bound of the corresponding quantifier:

$$\frac{\Gamma \vdash e \in \forall \alpha \leq \theta . \tau \qquad \Gamma \vdash \sigma \leq \theta}{\Gamma \vdash e[\sigma] \in \{\sigma/\alpha\}\tau}$$

Finally, like other λ-calculi with subtyping, $F_{\leq}$ includes a rule of *subsumption* allowing the type of a term to be promoted to any supertype:

$$\frac{\Gamma \vdash e \in \sigma \qquad \Gamma \vdash \sigma \leq \tau}{\Gamma \vdash e \in \tau}$$

The rules for type application and subsumption rely on a separately axiomatized subtype relation $\Gamma \vdash \sigma \leq \tau$ ("σ is a subtype of τ under assumptions Γ"). This relation, which forms the main object of study in the present paper, is presented as follows.

Subtyping is both reflexive and transitive:

$$\Gamma \vdash \tau \leq \tau$$

$$\frac{\Gamma \vdash \tau_1 \leq \tau_2 \qquad \Gamma \vdash \tau_2 \leq \tau_3}{\Gamma \vdash \tau_1 \leq \tau_3}$$

Every type is a subtype of a maximal type called *Top*:

$$\Gamma \vdash \sigma \leq Top$$

One of the main uses of *Top* (and the one for which it was introduced by Cardelli and Wegner) is to recover ordinary unbounded quantification as a special case of bounded quantification: $\forall \alpha . \tau$ becomes $\forall \alpha \leq Top . \tau$.

Type variables are subtypes of their bounds:

$$\Gamma \vdash \alpha \leq \Gamma(\alpha)$$

The subtype relation between arrow types is contravariant in their left-hand sides and covariant in their right-hand sides:

$$\frac{\Gamma \vdash \tau_1 \leq \sigma_1 \qquad \Gamma \vdash \sigma_2 \leq \tau_2}{\Gamma \vdash \sigma_1 \to \sigma_2 \leq \tau_1 \to \tau_2}$$

Similarly, subtyping of quantified types is covariant in their bounds and contravariant in their bodies:

$$\frac{\Gamma \vdash \tau_1 \leq \sigma_1 \qquad \Gamma, \alpha \leq \tau_1 \vdash \sigma_2 \leq \tau_2}{\Gamma \vdash \forall \alpha \leq \sigma_1 . \sigma_2 \leq \forall \alpha \leq \tau_1 . \tau_2}$$

The last rule deserves a closer look, since it is the primary source of the difficulties we will be discussing for the rest of the paper. Intuitively, it reads as follows:

A type $\tau \equiv \forall \alpha \leq \tau_1 . \tau_2$ describes a collection of polymorphic values (functions from types to values) each mapping subtypes of τ_1 to instances of τ_2. If τ_1 is a subtype of σ_1, then the domain of τ is smaller than that of $\sigma \equiv \forall \alpha \leq \sigma_1 . \sigma_2$, so τ is a weaker constraint and describes a larger collection of polymorphic values. Moreover, if, for each type θ that is an acceptable argument to the functions in both collections (i.e., one that satisfies the more stringent requirement $\theta \leq \tau_1$), the θ instance of σ_2 is a subtype of the θ instance of τ_2, then τ is a "pointwise weaker" constraint and again describes a larger collection of polymorphic values.

Though semantically appealing, this rule creates serious problems for reasoning about the subtype relation. In a quantified type $\forall \alpha \leq \sigma_1 . \sigma_2$, free occurrences of α in σ_2 are naturally thought of as being bounded by their lexically declared bound σ_1. But this connection is destroyed by the second premise of the quantifier subtyping rule: when $\forall \alpha \leq \sigma_1 . \sigma_2$ is compared to $\forall \alpha \leq \tau_1 . \tau_2$, instances of α in *both* σ_2 and τ_2 are bounded by τ_1 in the premise $\Gamma, \alpha \leq \tau_1 \vdash \sigma_2 \leq \tau_2$. As we shall see, this "re-bounding" behavior makes it impossible to give a decision procedure for the subtype relation.

Cardelli and Wegner's original definition of Fun [15] used a weaker quantifier subtyping rule in which $\forall \alpha \leq \sigma_1 . \sigma_2$ is a subtype of $\forall \alpha \leq \tau_1 . \tau_2$ only if σ_1 and τ_1 are identical. (This variant of the system can easily be shown to be decidable.) Later authors, including Cardelli, have chosen to work with the more powerful formulation given here.

Curien and Ghelli used a proof-normalization argument to show that $F_\leq$ typechecking is *coherent*—that is, that all derivations of a statement $\Gamma \vdash e \in \tau$ have the same meaning. One corollary of their proof is the soundness and completeness of a natural syntax-directed procedure for computing minimal typings of $F_\leq$ terms with a subroutine for checking the subtype relation; the same procedure had been developed by the group at Penn and by Cardelli for use in his Quest typechecker [Gunter, personal communication, 1990]. The termination of Curien and Ghelli's typechecking procedure is equivalent to the termination of the subtyping algorithm. Ghelli, in his Ph.D. thesis [22], gave a proof of termination; unfortunately, this proof was later discovered—by Curien and Reynolds, independently—to contain a subtle mistake [23, 32]. In fact, Ghelli soon realized that there are inputs for which the subtyping algorithm does *not* terminate [personal communication, 1991]. Worse yet, these cases did not seem amenable to any simple form of cycle detection: when presented with one of them, the algorithm would generate an infinite sequence of different recursive calls with larger and larger contexts. This discovery reopened the question of the decidability of $F_\leq$.

The undecidability result presented here began as an attempt to formulate a more refined algorithm capable of detecting the kinds of divergence that could be induced in the simpler one. A series of partial results about decidable subsystems eventually led to the discovery of a class of input problems in which increasing the size the input by a constant factor would increase the search depth of a *succeeding* execution of the algorithm by an exponential factor. In addition to dispelling earlier intuitions about why the problem ought to be decidable, the technique used to construct this example suggested a trick for encoding natural numbers, from which it was a short step to an encoding of two-counter Turing machines.

After formally defining the $F_\leq$ subtype relation (Section 2), reviewing Curien and Ghelli's subtyping algorithm (Section 3), and presenting an example where the algorithm fails to terminate (Section 4), we identify a fragment of $F_\le$ that forms a convenient target for the reductions to follow (Sections 5 and 6). The main result is then presented in two steps:

1. We first define an intermediate abstraction, called *rowing machines* (Section 7). These machines bridge the gap between $F_\le$ subtyping problems and two-counter machines by retaining the notions of bound variables and substitution from $F_\le$ while introducing a computatonal abstraction with a finite collection of registers and an evaluation regime based on state transformation.

An encoding of rowing machines as $F_\le$ subtyping statements is given and proven correct in the sense that a rowing machine R halts iff its translation $\mathscr{F}(R)$ is a derivable statement in $F_\le$ (Section 8).

2. We then review the definition of *two-counter machines* (Section 9) and show how a two-counter machine T may be encoded as a rowing machine $\mathscr{R}(T)$ such that T halts iff $\mathscr{R}(T)$ does (Section 10).

Section 11 shows that the undecidability of subtyping implies the undecidability of typechecking. Section 12 briefly discusses the pragmatic import of our results.

2   The Subtype Relation

We begin the detailed development of the undecidability of $F_\le$ by establishing some notational conventions and defining the subtype relation formally.

2.1   NOTATION   We write $X \equiv Y$, where X and Y are types, contexts, statements, etc., to indicate that "X has the form Y." If Y contains free metavariables, then $X \equiv Y$ denotes pattern matching; for example

"If $\tau \equiv \forall \alpha \le \tau_1 . \tau_2$, then ..."

means

"If τ has the form $\forall \alpha \le \tau_1 . \tau_2$ for some α, τ_1, and τ_2, then ..."

2.2   DEFINITION   The *types* of $F_\le$ are defined by the following abstract grammar:

$$\tau ::= \quad \alpha \qquad\qquad\qquad \text{type variables}$$
$$| \tau_1 \to \tau_2 \qquad\quad \text{function types}$$
$$| \forall \alpha \le \tau_1 . \tau_2 \quad \text{bounded quantifiers}$$
$$| \mathit{Top} \qquad\qquad\quad \text{top type.}$$

2.3 DEFINITION *Typing contexts* in $F_\le$ are finite sequences of type variables and associated bounds,

$$\Gamma ::= \{\ \} \mid \Gamma, \alpha \le \tau$$

with all variables distinct. (If we were dealing formally with the $F_\le$ typing relation, we would also need bindings of the form $x : \tau$.)

The comma operator is used to denote both extension ($\Gamma, \alpha \le \tau$) and concatenation (Γ_1, Γ_2) of contexts. The set of variables bound by a context Γ is written $dom(\Gamma)$. When $\Gamma \equiv \Gamma_1, \alpha \le \tau, \Gamma_2$, we call τ the *bound* of α in Γ and write $\tau = \Gamma(\alpha)$.

2.4 DEFINITION A *subtyping statement* is a phrase of the form

$$\Gamma \vdash \sigma \le \tau.$$

The portion of a statement to the right of the turnstile is called the *body*.

2.5 DEFINITION The set of free type variables in a type τ is written $FTV(\tau)$.

2.6 DEFINITION A type τ is *closed* with respect to a context Γ if $FTV(\tau) \subseteq dom(\Gamma)$. A context Γ is closed if

1. $\Gamma \equiv \{\ \}$, or
2. $\Gamma \equiv \Gamma_1, \alpha \le \tau$, with Γ_1 closed and τ closed with respect to Γ_1.

A statement $\Gamma \vdash \sigma \le \tau$ is closed if Γ is closed and σ and τ are closed with respect to Γ.

2.7 CONVENTION In the following, we assume that all statements under discussion are closed. In particular, we allow only closed statements in instances of inference rules.

2.8 CONVENTION The metavariables σ, τ, θ, and ϕ range over types; α, β, and γ range over type variables; Γ ranges over contexts; J ranges over (closed) statements.

2.9 DEFINITION $F_\le$ is the least three-place relation closed under the following rules:

$$\Gamma \vdash \tau \le \tau \qquad\qquad\qquad\qquad\qquad\qquad\qquad\qquad (\text{REFL})$$

$$\frac{\Gamma \vdash \tau_1 \le \tau_2 \qquad \Gamma \vdash \tau_2 \le \tau_3}{\Gamma \vdash \tau_1 \le \tau_3} \qquad\qquad\qquad\qquad (\text{TRANS})$$

$$\Gamma \vdash \sigma \le Top \qquad\qquad\qquad\qquad\qquad\qquad\qquad (\text{TOP})$$

$$\Gamma \vdash \alpha \le \Gamma(\alpha) \qquad\qquad\qquad\qquad\qquad\qquad\qquad (\text{VAR})$$

$$\frac{\Gamma \vdash \tau_1 \leq \sigma_1 \qquad \Gamma \vdash \sigma_2 \leq \tau_2}{\Gamma \vdash \sigma_1 \to \sigma_2 \leq \tau_1 \to \tau_2} \qquad \text{(ARROW)}$$

$$\frac{\Gamma \vdash \tau_1 \leq \sigma_1 \qquad \Gamma, \alpha \leq \tau_1 \vdash \sigma_2 \leq \tau_2}{\Gamma \vdash \forall \alpha \leq \sigma_1.\sigma_2 \leq \forall \alpha \leq \tau_1.\tau_2} \qquad \text{(ALL)}$$

2.10   CONVENTION   Types, contexts, and statements that differ only in the names of bound variables are considered to be identical. (In a statement $\Gamma_1, \alpha \leq \theta, \Gamma_2 \vdash \sigma \leq \tau$, the variable α is bound in Γ_2, σ, and τ.)

It is formally clearer to think of variables not as names but, as suggested by deBruijn [21], as pointers into the surrounding context. This point of view is notationally too inconvenient to adopt explicitly in what follows, but can be a significant aid in understanding the behavior of the rules here (VAR and ALL) that manipulate variables.

2.11   DEFINITION   The capture-avoiding substitution of σ for α in τ is written $\{\sigma/\alpha\}\tau$. Substitution is extended pointwise to contexts: $\{\sigma/\alpha\}\Gamma$.

2.12   DEFINITION   In the examples below, it will be convenient to rely on a few abbreviations:

$$\forall \alpha.\tau \overset{\text{def}}{=} \forall \alpha \leq Top.\tau$$

$$\forall \alpha_1 \leq \phi_1 .. \alpha_n \leq \phi_n.\tau \overset{\text{def}}{=} \forall \alpha_1 \leq \phi_1 \ldots \forall \alpha_n \leq \phi_n.\tau$$

$$\neg\tau \overset{\text{def}}{=} \forall \alpha \leq \tau.\alpha$$

The salient property of the last of these is that it allows the right- and left-hand sides of subtyping statements to be swapped:

2.13   FACT $\Gamma \vdash \neg\sigma \leq \neg\tau$ is derivable iff $\Gamma \vdash \tau \leq \sigma$ is.

3   A Subtyping Algorithm

The rules defining $F_\leq$ do not constitute an algorithm for checking the subtype relation, since they are not syntax-directed. In particular, the TRANS rule cannot effectively be applied backwards, since this would involve "guessing" an appropriate intermediate type τ_2. Curien and Ghelli (as well as Cardelli and others) use the following reformulation:

3.1   DEFINITION $F_\leq^N$ (N for normal form) is the least relation closed under the following rules:

$$\Gamma \vdash \sigma \leq Top \tag{NTop}$$

$$\Gamma \vdash \alpha \leq \alpha \tag{NRefl}$$

$$\frac{\Gamma \vdash \Gamma(\alpha) \leq \tau}{\Gamma \vdash \alpha \leq \tau} \tag{NVar}$$

$$\frac{\Gamma \vdash \tau_1 \leq \sigma_1 \qquad \Gamma \vdash \sigma_2 \leq \tau_2}{\Gamma \vdash \sigma_1 \to \sigma_2 \leq \tau_1 \to \tau_2} \tag{NArrow}$$

$$\frac{\Gamma \vdash \tau_1 \leq \sigma_1 \qquad \Gamma, \alpha \leq \tau_1 \vdash \sigma_2 \leq \tau_2}{\Gamma \vdash \forall \alpha \leq \sigma_1 . \sigma_2 \leq \forall \alpha \leq \tau_1 . \tau_2} \tag{NAll}$$

The reflexivity rule here is restricted to type variables. Transitivity is eliminated, except for instances of the form

$$\frac{\Gamma \vdash \alpha \leq \Gamma(\alpha) \qquad \Gamma \vdash \Gamma(\alpha) \leq \tau}{\Gamma \vdash \alpha \leq \tau,}$$

which are packaged together as instances of the new rule NVar.

3.2 LEMMA [Curien and Ghelli] The relations $F_\leq$ and $F_\leq^N$ coincide: $\Gamma \vdash \sigma \leq \tau$ is derivable in $F_\leq$ iff it is derivable in $F_\leq^N$.

3.3 DEFINITION The rules defining $F_\leq^N$ may be read as an algorithm (i.e., a recursively defined procedure, not necessarily always terminating) for checking the subtype relation:

$check(\Gamma \vdash \sigma \leq \tau) =$
    $if \ \tau \equiv Top$
        $then \ true$
    $else \ if \ \sigma \equiv \sigma_1 \to \sigma_2 \ and \ \tau \equiv \tau_1 \to \tau_2$
        $then \quad check(\Gamma \vdash \tau_1 \leq \sigma_1)$
            $and \ check(\Gamma \vdash \sigma_2 \leq \tau_2)$
    $else \ if \ \sigma \equiv \forall \alpha \leq \sigma_1 . \sigma_2 \ and \ \tau \equiv \forall \alpha \leq \tau_1 . \tau_2$
        $then \quad check(\Gamma \vdash \tau_1 \leq \sigma_1)$
            $and \ check(\Gamma, \alpha \leq \tau_1 \vdash \sigma_2 \leq \tau_2)$
    $else \ if \ \sigma \equiv \alpha \ and \ \tau \equiv \alpha$
        $then \ true$
    $else \ if \ \sigma \equiv \alpha$
        $then \ check(\Gamma \vdash \Gamma(\alpha) \leq \tau)$
    $else$
        $false.$

We write $F_\leq^N$ to refer either to the algorithm or to the inference system.

The algorithm may be thought of as incrementally building a normal form derivation of a statement J, starting from the root and recursively building subderivations for the premises. By Lemma 3.2, if there is any derivation whatsoever of a statement J, there is one in normal form; the algorithm is guaranteed to recapitulate this derivation and halt in finite time.

3.4   FACT   [Curien and Ghelli] If $\Gamma \vdash \sigma \leq \tau$ is derivable in $F_\leq$, then the algorithm $F_\leq^N$ halts and returns *true* when give this statement as input.

4 Nontermination of the Algorithm

Ghelli dispelled the widely held belief that $F_\leq^N$ terminates on all inputs by discovering the following example.

4.1   EXAMPLE   Let

$$\theta \equiv \forall \alpha . \, \neg (\forall \beta \leq \alpha . \, \neg \alpha_2).$$

Then executing $F_\leq^N$ on the input problem

$$\alpha_0 \leq \theta \vdash \alpha_0 \leq (\forall \alpha_1 \leq \alpha_0 . \, \neg \alpha_1)$$

leads to the following infinite sequence of recursive calls:

$$\alpha_0 \leq \theta \vdash \alpha_0 \leq \forall \alpha_1 \leq \alpha_0 . \, \neg \alpha_1$$

$$\alpha_0 \leq \theta \vdash \forall \alpha_1 . \, \neg (\forall \alpha_2 \leq \alpha_1 . \, \neg \alpha_2) \leq \forall \alpha_1 \leq \alpha_0 . \, \neg \alpha_1$$

$$\alpha_0 \leq \theta, \alpha_1 \leq \alpha_0 \vdash \neg (\forall \alpha_2 \leq \alpha_1 . \, \neg \alpha_2) \leq \neg \alpha_1$$

$$\alpha_0 \leq \theta, \alpha_1 \leq \alpha_0 \vdash \alpha_1 \leq \forall \alpha_2 \leq \alpha_1 . \, \neg \alpha_2$$

$$\alpha_0 \leq \theta, \alpha_1 \leq \alpha_0 \vdash \alpha_0 \leq \forall \alpha_2 \leq \alpha_1 . \, \neg \alpha_2$$

$$\alpha_0 \leq \theta, \alpha_1 \leq \alpha_0 \vdash \forall \alpha_2 . \, \neg (\forall \alpha_3 \leq \alpha_2 . \, \neg \alpha_3) \leq \forall \alpha_2 \leq \alpha_1 . \, \neg \alpha_2$$

$$\alpha_0 \leq \theta, \alpha_1 \leq \alpha_0, \alpha_2 \leq \alpha_1 \vdash \neg (\forall \alpha_3 \leq \alpha_2 . \, \neg \alpha_3) \leq \neg \alpha_2$$

$$\alpha_0 \leq \theta, \alpha_1 \leq \alpha_0, \alpha_2 \leq \alpha_1 \vdash \alpha_2 \leq \forall \alpha_3 \leq \alpha_2 . \, \neg \alpha_3$$

$$\alpha_0 \leq \theta, \alpha_1 \leq \alpha_0, \alpha_2 \leq \alpha_1 \vdash \alpha_1 \leq \forall \alpha_3 \leq \alpha_2 . \, \neg \alpha_3$$

$$\alpha_0 \leq \theta, \alpha_1 \leq \alpha_0, \alpha_2 \leq \alpha_1 \vdash \alpha_0 \leq \forall \alpha_3 \leq \alpha_2 . \, \neg \alpha_3$$

etc.

(The α-conversion steps necessary to maintain the well-formedness of the context when new variables are added are performed tacitly here, choosing new names so as to clarify the pattern of regress.)

5   A Deterministic Fragment of $F_{\leq}$

The pattern of recursion in Ghelli's example is an instance of a more general scheme—one so general, in fact, that it can be used to encode termination problems for two-counter Turing machines. We now turn to demonstrating this fact.

5.1   DEFINITION   The *positive* and *negative occurrences* in a statement $\Gamma \vdash \sigma \leq \tau$ are defined as follows:

- The type σ and the bounds in Γ are negative occurrences; τ is a positive occurrence.
- If $\tau_1 \rightarrow \tau_2$ is a positive (respectively, negative) occurrence, then τ_1 is a negative (positive) occurrence and τ_2 is a positive (negative) occurrence.
- If $\forall \alpha \leq \tau_1 . \tau_2$ is a positive (negative) occurrence, then τ_1 is a negative (positive) occurrence and τ_2 is a positive (negative) occurrence.

5.2   FACT   The rules defining $F_{\leq}^N$ preserve the signs of occurrences: wherever a metavariable τ appears in a premise of one of the rules, it has the same sign as the corresponding occurrence of τ in the conclusion.

In what follows, it will be convenient to work in a fragment of $F_{\leq}^N$ with somewhat simpler behavior:

- we drop the $\rightarrow$ type constructor and its subtyping rule;
- we introduce the negation operator explicitly into the syntax and include a rule for comparing negated expressions;
- we drop the left-hand premise from the rule for comparing quantifiers, requiring instead that when two quantified typed are compared, the bound of the one on the left must be *Top*;
- we consider only statements where no variable occurs positively, allowing us to drop the NREFL rule; and
- we disallow *Top* in negative positions.

Since the $F_{\leq}^N$ rules preserve positive and negative occurrences, we may redefine the set of types so that positive and negative types are separate syntactic categories. At the same time, we simplify each category appropriately.

5.3 DEFINITION The sets of *positive types* τ^+ and *negative types* τ^- are defined by the following abstract grammar:

$$\tau^+ ::= Top \mid \neg\tau^- \mid \forall\alpha \le \tau^- . \tau^+$$

$$\tau^- ::= \alpha \mid \neg\tau^+ \mid \forall\alpha . \tau$$

A *negative context* Γ^- is one whose bounds are all negative types.

5.4 DEFINITION $F_\le^P$ (P for polarized) is the least relation closed under the following rules:

$$\Gamma^- \vdash \tau^- \le Top \tag{PTop}$$

$$\frac{\Gamma^- \vdash \Gamma^-(\alpha) \le \tau^+}{\Gamma^- \vdash \alpha \le \tau^+} \tag{PVar}$$

$$\frac{\Gamma^-, \alpha \le \phi^- \vdash \sigma^- \le \tau^+}{\Gamma^- \vdash \forall\alpha . \sigma^- \le \forall\alpha \le \phi^- . \tau^+} \tag{PAll}$$

$$\frac{\Gamma^- \vdash \tau^- \le \sigma^+}{\Gamma^- \vdash \neg\sigma^+ \le \neg\tau^-} \tag{PNeg}$$

$F_\le^P$ is almost the system we need, but it still lacks one important property: $F_\le$ is not a conservative extension of $F_\le^P$. For example, the non-derivable $F_\le^P$ statement

$$\vdash \neg Top \le \forall\alpha . \alpha$$

corresponds, under the abbreviations for $\neg$ and $\forall\alpha . \alpha$, to the derivable $F_\le$ statement

$$\vdash \forall\alpha \le Top . \alpha \le \forall\alpha \le Top . \alpha.$$

To achieve conservativity, we restrict the form of $F_\le^P$ statements even further so that negated types can never be compared with quantified types.

5.5 DEFINITION Let n be a fixed nonnegative number. The sets of *n-positive* and *n-negative types* are defined by the following abstract grammar:

$$\tau^+ ::= Top \mid \forall\alpha_0 \le \tau_0^- . . \alpha_n \le \tau_n^- . \neg\tau^-$$

$$\tau^- ::= \alpha \mid \forall\alpha_0 . . \alpha_n . \neg\tau^+$$

We stipulate, moreover, that an *n*-positive type $\forall\alpha_0 \le \tau_0^- . . \alpha_n \le \tau_n^- . \neg\tau^-$ is closed only if no α_i appears free in any τ_i.

An *n-negative context* Γ_n^- is one whose bounds are all *n*-negative types.

5.6 DEFINITION   An $F_\leq^D$ statement (D for deterministic) has the form $\Gamma_n^- \vdash \sigma_n^- \leq \tau_n^+$, where Γ_n^- is an n-negative context, σ_n^- is an n-negative type, and τ_n^+ is an n-positive type.

5.7 CONVENTION   To reduce notational clutter, we drop the superscripts $+$ and $-$ and usually leave n implicit.

5.8 DEFINITION $F_\leq^D$ is the least relation closed under the following rules:

$$\Gamma \vdash \tau \leq Top \qquad\qquad\qquad\qquad\qquad\qquad\qquad\qquad\qquad \text{(DTop)}$$

$$\frac{\Gamma \vdash \Gamma(\alpha) \leq \forall \alpha_0 \leq \phi_0 .. \alpha_n \leq \phi_n . \,\neg \tau}{\Gamma \vdash \alpha \leq \forall \alpha_0 \leq \phi_0 .. \alpha_n \leq \phi_n . \,\neg \tau} \qquad\qquad\qquad \text{(DVar)}$$

$$\frac{\Gamma, \alpha_0 \leq \phi_0 .. \alpha_n \leq \phi_n \vdash \tau \leq \sigma}{\Gamma \vdash \forall \alpha_0 .. \alpha_n . \,\neg \sigma \leq \forall \alpha_0 \leq \phi_0 .. \alpha_n \leq \phi_n . \,\neg \tau} \qquad \text{(DAllNeg)}$$

Using the earlier abbreviations for negation, multiple quantification, and unbounded quantification, we may read every $F_\leq^D$ statement as an $F_\leq^N$ statement. Under this interpretation, the two subtype relations coincide for statements in their common domain:

5.9 LEMMA $F_\leq^N$ is a conservative extension of $F_\leq^D$: if J is an $F_\leq^D$ statement, then J is derivable in $F_\leq^D$ iff it is derivable in $F_\leq^N$.

Proof   The implication $F_\leq^D \Rightarrow F_\leq^N$ is straightforward. The other direction, $F_\leq^N \Rightarrow F_\leq^D$, proceeds by induction on $F_\leq^N$ derivations, using the form of $F_\leq^D$ statements to constrain the possible forms of $F_\leq^N$ derivations whose conclusions are de-abbreviated $F_\leq^D$ statements.   ∎

These simplifications justify a useful change of perspective. Since the only rule in $F_\leq^N$ with two premises has been replaced by a rule with one premise, derivations in this fragment are linear: each node has at most one subderivation. Moreover, every metavariable in the premise of a rule also appears in the conclusion, which makes the step from conclusion to premise deterministic. The syntax-directed construction of such a derivation may be thus be viewed as a deterministic state transformation process, where the subtyping statement being verified is the current state and the single premise that must be recursively verified, if any, is the next state. In other words, a subtyping statement is thought of as an instantaneous description of a kind of automaton.

From now on, we use terminology that makes the intuition of "subtyping as state transformation" more explicit. Analogous terminology and notation will be used to describe the other calculi introduced below.

5.10   DEFINITION   The *one-step elaboration* function $\mathscr{E}$ for $F^D_\leq$-statements is the partial mapping defined by:

$$\mathscr{E}(J) = \begin{cases} J' & \text{if } J \text{ is the conclusion of an instance of DVAR or DALLNEG and } J' \text{ is the} \\ & \text{corresponding premise} \\ \text{undefined} & \text{if } J \text{ is an instance of DTOP.} \end{cases}$$

5.11   DEFINITION J' is an *immediate subproblem* of J in $F^D_\leq$, written $J \to_D J'$, if $J' = \mathscr{E}(J)$.

5.12   DEFINITION J' is a *subproblem* of J in $F^D_\leq$, written $J \xrightarrow{*}_D J'$, if either $J \equiv J'$ or $J \to_D J_1$ and $J_1 \xrightarrow{*}_D J'$.

5.13   DEFINITION   The *elaboration* of a statement J is the sequence of subproblems encountered by a subtyping algorithm given J as input.

6   Eager Substitution

To make a smooth transition between the subtyping statements of $F_\leq$ and the rowing machine abstraction to be introduced in Section 7, we need one more variation in the definition of subtyping, where, instead of maintaining a context with the bounds of free variables, the quantifier rule immediately substitutes the bounds into the body of the statement.

6.1   DEFINITION   The simultaneous, capture-avoiding substitution of ϕ_0 through ϕ_n, respectively, for α_0 through α_n in τ is written $\{\phi_0/\alpha_0 .. \phi_n/\alpha_n\}\tau$.

6.2   DEFINITION   An $F^F_\leq$ statement (F for flattened) is an $F^D_\leq$ statement with empty context.

6.3   DEFINITION $F^F_\leq$ is the least relation closed under the following rules:

$$\vdash \tau \leq Top \tag{FTOP}$$

$$\frac{\vdash \{\phi_0/\alpha_0 .. \phi_n/\alpha_n\}\tau \leq \{\phi_0/\alpha_0 .. \phi_n/\alpha_n\}\sigma}{\vdash \forall\alpha_0 .. \alpha_n . \neg\sigma \leq \forall\alpha_0 \leq \phi_0 .. \alpha_n \leq \phi_n . \neg\tau} \tag{FALLNEG}$$

6.4   REMARK   Of course, the analogous reformulation of full $F_\leq$ would not be correct. For example, in the non-derivable statement

$$\vdash (\forall\alpha \leq Top . Top) \leq (\forall\alpha \leq Top . \alpha)$$

substituting *Top* for α in the bodies of the quantifiers yields the derivable statement

$\vdash Top \leq Top.$

But having restricted our attention to statements where variables appear only negatively, we are guaranteed that the only position where the elaboration of a statement can cause a variable to appear by itself in a subproblem is on the left-hand side, where it will immediately be replaced by its bound. We are therefore safe in making the substitution eagerly.

In the remainder of this section, we verify that $F^D_\leq$ is a conservative extension of $F^F_\leq$.

6.5 LEMMA   Let $\phi_0 .. \phi_n$ be n-negative types and assume that the $F^D_\leq$ statement $\alpha_0 \leq \phi_0 .. \alpha_n \leq \phi_n, \; \Gamma \vdash \tau \leq \sigma$ is closed. Then if $\{\phi_0/\alpha_0 .. \phi_n/\alpha_n\}\Gamma \vdash \{\phi_0/\alpha_0 .. \phi_n/\alpha_n\}\tau \leq \{\phi_0/\alpha_0 .. \phi_n/\alpha_n\}\sigma$ is derivable in $F^D_\leq$, so is $\alpha_0 \leq \phi_0 .. \alpha_n \leq \phi_n, \; \Gamma \vdash \tau \leq \sigma$.

Proof   By induction on the size of the derivation. Note that by the stipulation in 5.5 that no α_i appears in any ϕ_i, the ϕ_i must all be closed.

Case DTop $\{\phi_0/\alpha_0 .. \phi_n/\alpha_n\}\sigma = Top$

Since variables can only occur negatively, σ cannot be a variable, so $\sigma \equiv Top$ and the result is immediate.

Case DVar $\{\phi_0/\alpha_0 .. \phi_n/\alpha_n\}\tau \equiv \beta$

We may assume that $\tau \not\equiv \alpha_i$ for any of the distinguished α_i's, since otherwise we would have $\phi_i \equiv \beta$ and the statement $\alpha_0 \leq \phi_0 .. \alpha_n \leq \phi_n, \; \Gamma \vdash \tau \leq \sigma$ would not be closed. So τ must itself be β. By assumption, we have a subderivation

$\{\phi_0/\alpha_0 .. \phi_n/\alpha_n\}\Gamma \vdash (\{\phi_0/\alpha_0 .. \phi_n/\alpha_n\}\Gamma)(\beta) \leq \{\phi_0/\alpha_0 .. \phi_n/\alpha_n\}\sigma,$

that is,

$\{\phi_0/\alpha_0 .. \phi_n/\alpha_n\}\Gamma \vdash \{\phi_0/\alpha_0 .. \phi_n/\alpha_n\}(\Gamma(\beta)) \leq \{\phi_0/\alpha_0 .. \phi_n/\alpha_n\}\sigma.$

By the induction hypothesis,

$\alpha_0 \leq \phi_0 .. \alpha_n \leq \phi_n, \; \Gamma \vdash \Gamma(\beta) \leq \sigma.$

By DVAR,

$\alpha_0 \leq \phi_0 .. \alpha_n \leq \phi_n, \; \Gamma \vdash \beta \leq \sigma.$

Case DAllNeg $\{\phi_0/\alpha_0 .. \phi_n/\alpha_n\}\tau \equiv \forall \beta_0 .. \beta_n. \; \neg\tau'_2$

$\qquad\qquad\qquad\quad \{\phi_0/\alpha_0 .. \phi_n/\alpha_n\}\sigma \equiv \forall \beta_0 \leq \psi'_0 .. \beta_n \leq \psi'_n. \; \neg\sigma'_2$

Since σ cannot be a variable (else $\alpha_0 \leq \phi_0 .. \alpha_n \leq \phi_n$, $\Gamma \vdash \tau \leq \sigma$ would not be an $F_{\leq}^D$ statement), we have

$$\sigma \equiv \forall \beta_0 \leq \psi_0 .. \beta_n \leq \psi_n . \, \neg \sigma_2$$

$$\psi_i' \equiv \{\phi_0/\alpha_0 .. \phi_n/\alpha_n\} \psi_i$$

$$\sigma_2' \equiv \{\phi_0/\alpha_0 .. \phi_n/\alpha_n\} \sigma_2.$$

For τ, there are two cases to consider:

Subcase $\tau \equiv \alpha_i$

Then

$$\phi_i \equiv \forall \beta_0 .. \beta_n . \, \neg \tau_2'.$$

By assumption, there is a subderivaton

$$\{\phi_0/\alpha_0 .. \phi_n/\alpha_n\} \Gamma, \beta_0 \leq \{\phi_0/\alpha_0 .. \phi_n/\alpha_n\} \psi_0 .. \beta_n \leq \{\phi_0/\alpha_0 .. \phi_n/\alpha_n\} \psi_n \vdash \sigma_2' \leq \tau_2',$$

i.e. (since we stipulated $\alpha_j \notin FTV(\phi_i)$, so $\alpha_j \notin FTV(\tau_i')$ for any j),

$$\{\phi_0/\alpha_0 .. \phi_n/\alpha_n\} \Gamma, \beta_0 \leq \{\phi_0/\alpha_0 .. \phi_n/\alpha_n\} \psi_0 .. \beta_n \leq \{\phi_0/\alpha_0 .. \phi_n/\alpha_n\} \psi_n$$

$$\vdash \{\phi_0/\alpha_0 .. \phi_n/\alpha_n\} \sigma_2 \leq \{\phi_0/\alpha_0 .. \phi_n/\alpha_n\} \tau_2,$$

By the induction hypothesis,

$$\alpha_0 \leq \phi_0 .. \alpha_n \leq \phi_n, \Gamma, \beta_0 \leq \psi_0 .. \beta_n \leq \psi_n \vdash \sigma_2 \leq \tau_2'.$$

By DALLNEG,

$$\alpha_0 \leq \phi_0 .. \alpha_n \leq \phi_n, \Gamma \vdash \forall \beta_0 .. \beta_n . \, \neg \tau_2' \leq \forall \beta_0 \leq \psi_0 .. \beta_n \leq \psi_n . \, \neg \sigma_2.$$

By DVAR,

$$\alpha_0 \leq \phi_0 .. \alpha_n \leq \phi_n, \Gamma \vdash \alpha_i \leq \forall \beta_0 \leq \psi_0 .. \beta_n \leq \psi_n . \, \neg \sigma_2.$$

Subcase $\tau \not\equiv \alpha_i$

Then

$$\tau \equiv \forall \beta_0 .. \beta_n . \, \neg \tau_2$$

$$\tau_2' \equiv \{\phi_0/\alpha_0 .. \phi_n/\alpha_n\} \tau_2.$$

By assumption, we again have a subderivation

$$\{\phi_0/\alpha_0 \mathinner{.\,.} \phi_n/\alpha_n\}\Gamma, \beta_0 \leq \{\phi_0/\alpha_0 \mathinner{.\,.} \phi_n/\alpha_n\}\psi_0 \mathinner{.\,.} \beta_n \leq \{\phi_0/\alpha_0 \mathinner{.\,.} \phi_n/\alpha_n\}\psi_n \vdash \sigma_2' \leq \tau_2',$$

that is,

$$\{\phi_0/\alpha_0 \mathinner{.\,.} \phi_n/\alpha_n\}\Gamma, \beta_0 \leq \{\phi_0/\alpha_0 \mathinner{.\,.} \phi_n/\alpha_n\}\psi_0 \mathinner{.\,.} \beta_n \leq \{\phi_0/\alpha_0 \mathinner{.\,.} \phi_n/\alpha_n\}\psi_n$$

$$\vdash \{\phi_0/\alpha_0 \mathinner{.\,.} \phi_n/\alpha_n\}\sigma_2 \leq \{\phi_0/\alpha_0 \mathinner{.\,.} \phi_n/\alpha_n\}\tau_2.$$

By the induction hypothesis,

$$\alpha_0 \leq \phi_0 \mathinner{.\,.} \alpha_n \leq \phi_n, \Gamma, \beta_0 \leq \psi_0 \mathinner{.\,.} \beta_n \leq \psi_n \vdash \sigma_2 \leq \tau_2.$$

By DALLNEG,

$$\alpha_0 \leq \phi_0 \mathinner{.\,.} \alpha_n \leq \phi_n, \Gamma \vdash \forall\beta_0 \mathinner{.\,.} \beta_n. \neg\tau_2 \leq \forall\beta_0 \mathinner{.\,.} \beta_n. \neg\sigma_2. \quad \blacksquare$$

6.6   LEMMA   If $\vdash \sigma \leq \tau$ is derivable in $F_{\leq}^F$, then it is derivable in $F_{\leq}^D$.

Proof   By induction on the original derivation, using Lemma 6.5 for the FALLNEG case.   ∎

6.7   LEMMA   If $\alpha \leq \phi, \Gamma \vdash \sigma \leq \tau$ is derivable in $F_{\leq}^D$, then $\{\phi/\alpha\}\Gamma \vdash \{\phi/\alpha\}\sigma \leq \{\phi/\alpha\}\tau$ has an $F_{\leq}^D$-derivation of equal or lesser size.

Proof   By induction on the given derivation.   ∎

6.8   LEMMA   If $\vdash \sigma \leq \tau$ is an $F_{\leq}^F$-statement and is derivable in $F_{\leq}^D$, then it is derivable in $F_{\leq}^F$.

Proof   By induction on the size of the original derivation, using Lemma 6.7 for the DALLNEG case.   ∎

6.9   LEMMA $F_{\leq}^D$ is a conservative extension of $F_{\leq}^F$.

Proof   By Lemmas 6.6 and 6.8.   ∎

7   Rowing Machines

The reduction from two-counter Turing machines to $F_{\leq}$ subtyping statements is easiest to understand in terms of an intermediate abstraction called a *rowing machine*, which makes more stylized use of bound variables.

A rowing machine is a tuple of *registers*

$$\langle \rho_1 \mathinner{.\,.} \rho_n \rangle,$$

where the contents of each register is a *row*. By convention, the first register is the machine's *program counter* (*PC*). To move to the next state, the *PC* is used as a template to construct the new contents of each of the registers from the current contents of all of the registers (including the *PC*).

7.1 DEFINITION The set of *rows* (of width *n*) is defined by the following abstract grammar:

$$\rho ::= \alpha_m \qquad\qquad 1 \leq m \leq n$$

$$| \quad [\alpha_1 .. \alpha_n] \langle \rho_1 .. \rho_n \rangle$$

$$| \quad \text{HALT}$$

The variables $\alpha_1 .. \alpha_n$ on the left of $[\alpha_1 .. \alpha_n] \langle \rho_1 .. \rho_n \rangle$ are binding occurrences whose scope is the rows ρ_1 through ρ_n. We regard rows that differ only in the names of bound variables as identical.

7.2 DEFINITION A *rowing machine* (of width *n*) is a tuple $\langle \rho_1 .. \rho_n \rangle$, where each ρ_i is a row of width *n* with no free variables.

7.3 DEFINITION The *one-step elaboration* function $\mathscr{E}$ for rowing machines of width *n* is the partial mapping

$$\mathscr{E}(\langle \rho_1 .. \rho_n \rangle)$$

$$= \begin{cases} \langle \{\rho_1/\alpha_1 .. \rho_n/\alpha_n\} \rho_{11} .. \{\rho_1/\alpha_1 .. \rho_n/\alpha_n\} \rho_{1n} \rangle & \text{if } \rho_1 = [\alpha_1 .. \alpha_n] \langle \rho_{11} .. \rho_{1n} \rangle \\ \text{undefined} & \text{if } \rho_1 = \text{HALT}. \end{cases}$$

(Since rowing machines consist only of closed rows, we need not define the evaluation function for the case where the *PC* is a variable. Also, since all the ρ_n are closed, the substitution is trivially capture-avoiding.)

7.4 NOTATIONAL CONVENTIONS

1. When the symbol "—" appears as the *i*th component of a compound row $[\alpha_1 .. \alpha_n] \langle \rho_1 .. \rho_n \rangle$, it stands for the variable α_i.

2. To avoid a proliferation of variable names in the examples and definitions below, we sometimes use numerical indices (like deBruijn indices [21]) rather than names for variables: the "variable" $\#n$ refers to the nth bound variable of the row in which it appears; $\#\#n$ *refers to the* n^{th} bound variable of the row enclosing the one in which it appears; and so on.

3. When these abbreviations are used, the bindings $[\alpha_1 .. \alpha_n]$ are omitted.

For example, the nested row

$$[\alpha_1 .. \alpha_3]\langle \alpha_1, [\beta_1 .. \beta_3]\langle \alpha_1, \beta_1, \beta_3 \rangle, \alpha_1 \rangle$$

would be abbreviated as

$$\langle -, \langle \# \# 1, \# 1, - \rangle, \# 1 \rangle.$$

4. It is convenient to introduce names for closed rows and use these to build up descriptions of other rows. For example, the compound now

$$\langle \langle \langle \# 1, \# 1, \# 1 \rangle, \# 3, \# 2 \rangle, \langle -, -, - \rangle, \langle \# 1, \# 1, \# 1 \rangle \rangle$$

might be written as

$$\langle Z, Y, X \rangle,$$

where

$$X \equiv \langle \# 1, \# 1, \# 1 \rangle$$

$$Y \equiv \langle -, -, - \rangle$$

$$Z \equiv \langle X, \# 3, \# 2 \rangle.$$

7.5 DEFINITION A rowing machine R *halts* if there is a machine R' such that $R \xrightarrow{*}_R R'$ and the PC of R' is the instruction HALT.

7.6 EXAMPLE The simplest rowing machine, $\langle \text{HALT} \rangle$, halts immediately. The next simplest, $\langle \langle \text{HALT} \rangle \rangle$, takes one step and then halts. Another simple one, $\langle \langle - \rangle \rangle$, leads to an infinite elaboration with every state identical to the first.

7.7 EXAMPLE The machine

$$\langle \text{LOOP}, \text{A}, \text{B} \rangle,$$

where

$$\text{LOOP} \equiv \langle -, \# 3, \# 2 \rangle$$

$$\text{A} \equiv \text{an arbitrary row}$$

$$\text{B} \equiv \text{an arbitrary row}$$

executes an infinite loop where the contents of the second and third register are exchanged at successive steps:

$\langle \text{LOOP}, \text{A}, \text{B} \rangle$

$\rightarrow_R \langle \text{LOOP}, \text{B}, \text{A} \rangle$

$\rightarrow_R \langle \text{LOOP}, \text{A}, \text{B} \rangle$

$\rightarrow_R \cdots$

7.8 EXAMPLE The row

$\text{BRI} \equiv \langle \#2, - \rangle$

encodes an *indirect branch* to the contents of register 2 at the moment when BRI is executed. The machine

$\langle \text{BRI}, \langle \text{BRI}, \langle \text{BRI}, \text{HALT} \rangle \rangle \rangle$

elaborates as follows:

$\langle \text{BRI}, \langle \text{BRI}, \langle \text{BRI}, \text{HALT} \rangle \rangle \rangle$

$\rightarrow_R \langle \langle \text{BRI}, \langle \text{BRI}, \text{HALT} \rangle \rangle, \langle \text{BRI}, \langle \text{BRI}, \text{HALT} \rangle \rangle \rangle$

$\rightarrow_R \langle \text{BRI}, \langle \text{BRI}, \text{HALT} \rangle \rangle$

$\rightarrow_R \langle \langle \text{BRI}, \text{HALT} \rangle, \langle \text{BRI}, \text{HALT} \rangle \rangle$

$\rightarrow_R \langle \text{BRI}, \text{HALT} \rangle$

$\rightarrow_R \langle \text{HALT}, \text{HALT} \rangle.$

8   Encoding Rowing Machines as Subtyping Problems

We now show how a rowing machine R can be encoded as a subtyping problem $\mathscr{F}(R)$ such that R halts iff $\mathscr{F}(R)$ is derivable in $F^F_{\leq}$. The idea of the translation is that a rowing machine $R = \langle \rho_1 .. \rho_n \rangle$ becomes a subtyping statement $\mathscr{F}(\rho)$ of the form

$$\vdash \ldots \leq (\ldots \mathscr{F}(\rho_1) \ldots),$$

(we use $\mathscr{F}$ to denote the translation of both rowing machines and rows), constructed so that

• if $\rho_1 = \text{HALT}$, then the elaboration of $\mathscr{F}(R)$ halts (by reaching a subproblem where *Top* appears on the right-hand side);

• if $\rho_1 = [\alpha_1 .. \alpha_n]\langle\rho_{11} .. \rho_{1n}\rangle$, then the elaboration of $\mathcal{F}(R)$ reaches a sub-problem that encodes the rowing machine $\mathcal{E}(\langle\rho_1 .. \rho_n\rangle) = \langle\{\rho_1/\alpha_1 .. \rho_n/\alpha_n\}\rho_{11} .. \{\rho_1/\alpha_1 .. \rho_n/\alpha_n\}\rho_{1n}\rangle$.

In more detail, if $R = \langle[\alpha_1 .. \alpha_n]\langle\rho_{11} .. \rho_{1n}\rangle .. \rho_n\rangle$, then $\mathcal{F}(R)$ is essentially the following:

$$\vdash \forall\gamma_1 .. \gamma_n. \qquad\qquad \neg(\forall\gamma'_1 \le \gamma_1 .. \gamma'_n \le \gamma_n. \neg \cdots)$$

$$\le \forall\gamma_1 \le \mathcal{F}(\rho_1) .. \gamma_n \le \mathcal{F}(\rho_n). \neg(\forall\alpha_1 .. \alpha_n. \qquad\qquad \neg(\forall\alpha'_1 \le \mathcal{F}(\rho_{11}) .. \alpha'_n \le \mathcal{F}(\rho_{1n}). \neg\mathcal{F}(\rho_{11}))).$$

The elaboration of this statement proceeds as follows:

1. The current contents of the registers $\rho_1 .. \rho_n$ are temporarily saved by matching the quantifiers on the right with the ones on the left; this has the effect of substituting the bounds $\mathcal{F}(\rho_1) .. \mathcal{F}(\rho_n)$ for free occurrences of the variables $\gamma_1 .. \gamma_n$ on the left-hand side. The right- and left-hand sides are also swapped (by the $\neg$ constructor on both sides), so that what now appears on the left is a sequence of quantifiers binding the free variables $\alpha_1 .. \alpha_n$ of ρ_1:

$$\vdash \forall\alpha_1 .. \alpha_n. \neg(\forall\alpha'_1 \le \mathcal{F}(\rho_{11}) .. \alpha'_n \le \mathcal{F}(\rho_{1n}). \neg\mathcal{F}(\rho_{11}))$$

$$\le \forall\gamma'_1 \le \mathcal{F}(\rho_1) .. \gamma'_n \le \mathcal{F}(\rho_n). \neg \cdots$$

2. The saved contents of the original registers now appear on the right-hand side. When these are matched with the quantifiers on the left, the result is that the old values of the registers are substituted for the variables $\alpha_1 .. \alpha_n$ in the body

$$\neg(\forall\alpha'_1 \le \mathcal{F}(\rho_{11}) .. \alpha'_n \le \mathcal{F}(\rho_{1n}). \neg\mathcal{F}(\rho_{11}))$$

of the left-hand side.

Swapping right- and left-hand sides again yields a statement of the same form as the original, where the appropriate instances of $\mathcal{F}(\rho_{11}) .. \mathcal{F}(\rho_{1n})$ appear as the bounds of the outer quantifiers on the right:

$$\vdash \cdots \le (\forall\alpha'_1 \le \{\mathcal{F}(\rho_1)/\alpha_1 .. \mathcal{F}(\rho_n)/\alpha_n\}\mathcal{F}(\rho_{11}) .. $$
$$\alpha'_n \le \{\mathcal{F}(\rho_1)/\alpha_1 .. \mathcal{F}(\rho_n)/\alpha_n\}\mathcal{F}(\rho_{1n}). $$
$$\neg\{\mathcal{F}(\rho_1)/\alpha_1 .. \mathcal{F}(\rho_n)/\alpha_n\}\mathcal{F}(\rho_{11}),$$

i.e.,

$$\vdash \cdots \le (\forall\gamma_1 \le \{\mathcal{F}(\rho_1)/\alpha_1 .. \mathcal{F}(\rho_n)/\alpha_n\}\mathcal{F}(\rho_{11}) .. $$
$$\gamma_n \le \{\mathcal{F}(\rho_1)/\alpha_1 .. \mathcal{F}(\rho_n)/\alpha_n\}\mathcal{F}(\rho_{1n}). $$
$$\neg\{\mathcal{F}(\rho_1)/\alpha_1 .. \mathcal{F}(\rho_n)/\alpha_n\}\mathcal{F}(\rho_{11}).$$

To get back to a statement of exactly the same form as the original, one further piece of mechanism is required: besides the n variables used to store the old state of the registers, a variable γ_0 holds the original value of the entire left-hand side of $\mathscr{F}(R)$. This variable is used at the end of a cycle to set up the left hand side of the statement encoding the next state of the rowing machine.

8.1 DEFINITION   Let ρ be a row of width n. The $F^F_{\le}$-translation of ρ, written $\mathscr{F}(\rho)$, is the n-negative type

$$\mathscr{F}(\rho) = \begin{cases} \alpha_i & \text{if } \rho = \alpha_i \\[2mm] \forall\gamma_0, \alpha_1 .. \alpha_n . \ \neg(\forall\gamma'_0 \le \gamma_0, \alpha'_1 \le \mathscr{F}(\rho_1)) .. \alpha'_n \le \mathscr{F}(\rho_n). \ \neg\mathscr{F}(\rho_1) & \text{if } \rho = [\alpha_1 .. \alpha_n]\langle\rho_1 .. \rho_n\rangle \\[2mm] \forall\gamma_0, \alpha_1 .. \alpha_n . \ \neg \ Top & \text{if } \rho = \text{HALT}, \end{cases}$$

where γ_0, γ'_0, and $\alpha'_1 .. \alpha'_n$ are fresh variables.

8.2 FACT

1. The free variables of ρ coincide with the free type variables of $\mathscr{F}(\rho)$.

2. $\mathscr{F}(\{\rho_1/\alpha_1 .. \rho_n/\alpha_n\}\rho) = \{\mathscr{F}(\rho_1)/\alpha_1 .. \mathscr{F}(\rho_n)/\alpha_n\}\mathscr{F}(\rho)$.

8.3 DEFINITION   Let $R = \langle\rho_1 .. \rho_n\rangle$ be a rowing machine. The $F^F_{\le}$-translation of R, written $\mathscr{F}(R)$, is the $F^F_{\le}$ statement

$$\vdash \sigma \le \forall\gamma_0 \le \sigma, \gamma_1 \le \mathscr{F}(\rho_1) .. \gamma_n \le \mathscr{F}(\rho_n). \ \neg\mathscr{F}(\rho_1),$$

where

$$\sigma \equiv \forall\gamma_0, \gamma_1 .. \gamma_n . \ \neg(\forall\gamma'_0 \le \gamma_0, \gamma'_1 \le \gamma_1 .. \gamma'_n \le \gamma_n. \ \neg\gamma_0)$$

and $\gamma_0, \gamma_1, \ldots, \gamma_n$ are fresh type variables. (Note that σ occurs on both sides of $\mathscr{F}(R)$.)

8.4 FACT   This definition is proper—i.e., $\mathscr{F}(R)$ is a well-formed $F^F_{\le}$-statement for every rowing machine R.

8.5 LEMMA   If $R \to_R R'$, then $\mathscr{F}(R) \overset{*}{\to}_F \mathscr{F}(R')$.

Proof   By the definition of the elaboration function for rowing machines,

$$R \equiv \langle\rho_1 .. \rho_n\rangle,$$

where

$$\rho_1 \equiv [\alpha_1 .. \alpha_n]\langle\rho_{11} .. \rho_{1n}\rangle,$$

and

$$R' \equiv \langle \{\rho_1/\alpha_1 .. \rho_n/\alpha_n\}\rho_{11} .. \{\rho_1/\alpha_1 .. \rho_n/\alpha_n\}\rho_{1n} \rangle.$$

Let

$$\sigma \equiv \forall \gamma_0, \gamma_1 .. \gamma_n . \neg(\forall \gamma_0' \le \gamma_0, \gamma_1' \le \gamma_1 .. \gamma_n' \le \gamma_n . \neg\gamma_0).$$

Now calculate as follows:

$$
\begin{aligned}
&\mathscr{F}(R) \\
&\equiv \vdash \sigma \\
&\qquad \le \forall \gamma_0 \le \sigma, \gamma_1 \le \mathscr{F}(\rho_1) .. \gamma_n \le \mathscr{F}(\rho_n) . \neg\mathscr{F}(\rho_1) \\
&\equiv \vdash \forall \gamma_0, \gamma_1 .. \gamma_n . \neg(\forall \gamma_0' \le \gamma_0, \gamma_1' \le \gamma_1 .. \gamma_n' \le \gamma_n . \neg\gamma_0) \\
&\qquad \le \forall \gamma_0 \le \sigma, \gamma_1 \le \mathscr{F}(\rho_1) .. \gamma_n \le \mathscr{F}(\rho_n) . \neg\mathscr{F}(\rho_1) \\
&\rightarrow_F \vdash \{\sigma/\gamma_0, \mathscr{F}(\rho_1)/\gamma_1 .. \mathscr{F}(\rho_n)/\gamma_n\}\mathscr{F}(\rho_1) \\
&\qquad \le \{\sigma/\gamma_0, \mathscr{F}(\rho_1)/\gamma_1 .. \mathscr{F}(\rho_n)/\gamma_n\}(\forall \gamma_0' \le \gamma_0, \gamma_1' \le \gamma_1 .. \gamma_n' \le \gamma_n . \neg\gamma_0) \\
&\equiv \vdash \mathscr{F}(\rho_1) \\
&\qquad \le \forall \gamma_0' \le \sigma, \gamma_1' \le \mathscr{F}(\rho_1) .. \gamma_n' \le \mathscr{F}(\rho_n) . \neg\sigma \\
&\equiv \vdash \forall \gamma_0, \alpha_1 .. \alpha_n . \neg(\forall \gamma_0' \le \gamma_0, \alpha_1' \le \mathscr{F}(\rho_{11}) .. \alpha_n' \le \mathscr{F}(\rho_{1n}) . \neg\mathscr{F}(\rho_{11})) \\
&\qquad \le \forall \gamma_0' \le \sigma, \gamma_1' \le \mathscr{F}(\rho_1) .. \gamma_n' \le \mathscr{F}(\rho_n) . \neg\sigma \\
&\equiv \vdash \forall \gamma_0, \alpha_1 .. \alpha_n . \neg(\forall \gamma_0' \le \gamma_0, \alpha_1' \le \mathscr{F}(\rho_{11}) .. \alpha_n' \le \mathscr{F}(\rho_{1n}) . \neg\mathscr{F}(\rho_{11})) \\
&\qquad \le \forall \gamma_0 \le \sigma, \alpha_1 \le \mathscr{F}(\rho_1) .. \alpha_n \le \mathscr{F}(\rho_n) . \neg\sigma \\
&\rightarrow_F \vdash \{\sigma/\gamma_0, \mathscr{F}(\rho_1)/\alpha_1 .. \mathscr{F}(\rho_n)/\alpha_n\}\sigma \\
&\qquad \le \{\sigma/\gamma_0, \mathscr{F}(\rho_1)/\alpha_1 .. \mathscr{F}(\rho_n)/\alpha_n\}(\forall \gamma_0' \le \gamma_0, \alpha_1' \le \mathscr{F}(\rho_{11}) .. \alpha_n' \le \mathscr{F}(\rho_{1n}) . \neg\mathscr{F}(\rho_{11})) \\
&\equiv \vdash \sigma \\
&\qquad \le \forall \gamma_0' \le \sigma, \\
&\qquad\qquad \alpha_1' \le (\{\mathscr{F}(\rho_1)/\alpha_1 .. \mathscr{F}(\rho_n)/\alpha_n\}\mathscr{F}(\rho_{11})) .. \\
&\qquad\qquad \alpha_n' \le (\{\mathscr{F}(\rho_1)/\alpha_1 .. \mathscr{F}(\rho_n)/\alpha_n\}\mathscr{F}(\rho_{1n})) . \neg(\{\mathscr{F}(\rho_1)/\alpha_1 .. \mathscr{F}(\rho_n)/\alpha_n\}\mathscr{F}(\rho_{11})) \\
&\equiv \vdash \sigma \\
&\qquad \le \forall \gamma_0 \le \sigma, \\
&\qquad\qquad \gamma_1 \le (\{\mathscr{F}(\rho_1)/\alpha_1 .. \mathscr{F}(\rho_n)/\alpha_n\}\mathscr{F}(\rho_{11})) .. \\
&\qquad\qquad \gamma_n \le (\{\mathscr{F}(\rho_1)/\alpha_1 .. \mathscr{F}(\rho_n)/\alpha_n\}\mathscr{F}(\rho_{1n})) . \neg(\{\mathscr{F}(\rho_1)/\alpha_1 .. \mathscr{F}(\rho_n)/\alpha_n\}\mathscr{F}(\rho_{11})) \\
&\equiv \mathscr{F}(R'). \quad \blacksquare
\end{aligned}
$$

8.6   LEMMA   If $R \equiv \langle \text{HALT}, \rho_2 .. \rho_n \rangle$, then $\mathscr{F}(R)$ is derivable in $F_{\le}^F$.

Proof   Let

$$\sigma \equiv \forall \gamma_0, \gamma_1 .. \gamma_n . \neg(\forall \gamma_0' \le \gamma_0, \gamma_1' \le \gamma_1 .. \gamma_n' \le \gamma_n . \neg\gamma_0).$$

Then

$$\mathscr{F}(R)$$
$$\equiv \vdash \sigma$$
$$\le \forall \gamma_0 \le \sigma, \gamma_1 \le \mathscr{F}(\text{HALT})..\gamma_n \le \mathscr{F}(\rho_n). \neg \mathscr{F}(\text{HALT})$$
$$\equiv \vdash \forall \gamma_0, \gamma_1..\gamma_n. \neg (\forall \gamma_0' \le \gamma_0, \gamma_1' \le \gamma_1..\gamma_n' \le \gamma_n. \neg \gamma_0)$$
$$\le \forall \gamma_0 \le \sigma, \gamma_1 \le \mathscr{F}(\text{HALT})..\gamma_n \le \mathscr{F}(\rho_n). \neg \mathscr{F}(\text{HALT})$$
$$\rightarrow_F \vdash \{\sigma/\gamma_0, \mathscr{F}(\text{HALT})/\gamma_1..\mathscr{F}(\rho_n)/\gamma_n\} \mathscr{F}(\text{HALT})$$
$$\le \{\sigma/\gamma_0, \mathscr{F}(\text{HALT})/\gamma_1..\mathscr{F}(\rho_n)/\gamma_n\} (\forall \gamma_0' \le \gamma_0, \gamma_1' \le \gamma_1..\gamma_n' \le \gamma_n. \neg \gamma_0)$$
$$\equiv \vdash \mathscr{F}(\text{HALT})$$
$$\le \forall \gamma_0' \le \sigma, \gamma_1' \le \mathscr{F}(\text{HALT})..\gamma_n' \le \mathscr{F}(\rho_n). \neg \sigma$$
$$\equiv \vdash \forall \gamma_0, \alpha_1..\alpha_n. \neg Top$$
$$\le \forall \gamma_0' \le \sigma, \gamma_1' \le \mathscr{F}(\text{HALT})..\gamma_n' \le \mathscr{F}(\rho_n). \neg \sigma$$
$$\rightarrow_F \vdash \sigma$$
$$\le Top,$$

which is an instance of FTOP. ∎

8.7   COROLLARY   The rowing machine R halts iff $\mathscr{F}(R)$ is derivable in $F_{\le}^F$.

8.8   REMARK   It is natural to ask whether Ghelli's nonterminating example (4.1) is the image of some rowing machine under this translation. The answer is "almost." Although the style of divergence in Ghelli's example is suggestive of the stepping behavior of translated rowing machines, every rowing machine translation involves a type σ of appropriate width, which is not present in Ghelli's example.

9   Two-Counter Machines

This section reviews the definition of two-counter Turing machines; see, e.g., Hopcroft and Ullman [26] for more details.

9.1   DEFINITION   A *two-counter machine* is a tuple

$$\langle PC, A, B, I_1..I_w \rangle,$$

where A and B are nonnegative numbers and PC and I_1 through I_w are instructions of the following forms:

INCA $\Rightarrow m$

INCB $\Rightarrow m$

TSTA $\Rightarrow m/n$

TSTB $\Rightarrow m/n$

HALT

with m and n in the range 1 to w.

9.2   DEFINITION   The *elaboration function* $\mathscr{E}$ for two-counter machines is the partial function mapping $T = \langle PC, A, B, I_1 .. I_w \rangle$ to

$$\mathscr{E}(T) = \begin{cases} \langle I_m, A + 1, B, I_1 .. I_w \rangle & \text{if } PC \equiv \text{INCA} \Rightarrow m \\ \langle I_m, A, B + 1, I_1 .. I_w \rangle & \text{if } PC \equiv \text{INCB} \Rightarrow m \\ \langle I_m, A, B, I_1 .. I_w \rangle & \text{if } PC \equiv \text{TSTA} \Rightarrow m/n \text{ and } A = 0 \\ \langle I_n, A - 1, B, I_1 .. I_w \rangle & \text{if } PC \equiv \text{TSTA} \Rightarrow m/n \text{ and } A > 0 \\ \langle I_m, A, B, I_1 .. I_w \rangle & \text{if } PC \equiv \text{TSTB} \Rightarrow m/n \text{ and } B = 0 \\ \langle I_n, A, B - 1, I_1 .. I_w \rangle & \text{if } PC \equiv \text{TSTB} \Rightarrow m/n \text{ and } B > 0 \\ \text{undefined} & \text{if } PC \equiv \text{HALT.} \end{cases}$$

9.3   CONVENTION   For the following examples, it is convenient to assign alphabetic labels to the instructions of a program. By convention, the instruction with label START is used as the initial PC, and the initial value in both registers is 0.

9.4   EXAMPLE   This program loads register A with the value 5 and then tests the parity of register A, halting if it is even and looping forever if it is odd:

START INCA $\Rightarrow$ I1

I1   INCA $\Rightarrow$ I2
I2   INCA $\Rightarrow$ I3
I3   INCA $\Rightarrow$ I4
I4   INCA $\Rightarrow$ E
E   TSTA $\Rightarrow$ OK/O
O   TSTA $\Rightarrow$ LOOP/E
LOOP INCA $\Rightarrow$ LOOP
OK   HALT.

9.5   EXAMPLE   This program loads 5 into register A and 3 into register B, then compares A and B for equality by repeatedly decrementing them until one or both become zero; if both do so on the same iteration, the program halts; otherwise it goes into an infinite loop.

START INCA ⇒ I1

I1   INCA ⇒ I2

I2   INCA ⇒ I3

I3   INCA ⇒ I4

I4   INCA ⇒ J0

J0   INCB ⇒ J1

J1   INCB ⇒ J2

J2   INCB ⇒ LL

LL   TSTA ⇒ AZ/AS

AZ   TSTB ⇒ AZBZ/AZBS

AS   TSTB ⇒ ASBZ/LL

AZBZ   HALT

AZBS   INCA ⇒ AZBS

ASBZ   INCA ⇒ ASBZ.

9.6   DEFINITION   A two-counter machine T *halts* if $T \xrightarrow{*}_T T'$ for some machine $T' \equiv \langle \text{HALT}, A', B', I_1 .. I_w \rangle$.

9.7   FACT   The halting problem for two-counter machines is undecidable.

Proof sketch   Hopcroft and Ullman [26, pp. 171–173] show that a similar formulation of two-counter machines is Turing-equivalent. (Their two-counter machines have test instructions that do not change the contents of the register being tested, and separate decrement instructions. It is easy to check that this formulation and the one used here are inter-encodable.)   ■

10   Encoding Two-counter Machines as Rowing Machines

We can now finish the proof of the undecidability of $F_\le$ subtyping by showing that any two-counter machine T can be encoded as a rowing machine $\mathcal{R}(T)$ such that T halts iff $\mathcal{R}(T)$ does.

The main trick of the encoding lies in the representation of natural numbers as rows. Each number n is encoded as a *program* (i.e., a row) that, when executed, branches indirectly through one of two registers whose contents have been set beforehand to appropriate destinations for the zero and nonzero cases of a test; in other words, n itself encapsulates the behavior of the test instruction on a register containing n. The increment operation simply builds a new program of this sort from an existing one. The new program saves a pointer to the present contents of the register in a local variable so that it can restore the old value (i.e., one less than its own value) before executing the branch.

The encoding $\mathscr{R}(T)$ of a two-counter machine $T \equiv \langle PC, A, B, I_1 .. I_w \rangle$ comprises the following registers:

$\#1$	$\mathscr{R}^w(PC)$
$\#2$	$\mathscr{R}_A^w(A)$
$\#3$	$\mathscr{R}_B^w(B)$
$\#4$	address register for zero branches
$\#5$	address register for nonzero branches
$\#6$	$\mathscr{R}^w(I_1)$

$\ldots$

$\#6 + w - 1 \quad \mathscr{R}^w(I_w)$.

We use four translation functions for the various components:

1. $\mathscr{R}(T)$ is the encoding of a the two-counter machine T as a rowing machine of width $w + 5$;

2. $\mathscr{R}^w(I)$ is the encoding of a two-counter instruction I as a row of width $w + 5$;

3. $\mathscr{R}_A^w(n)$ is the encoding of the natural number n, when it appears as the contents of register A, as a row of width $w + 5$;

4. $\mathscr{R}_B^w(n)$ is the encoding of the natural number n, when it appears as the contents of register B, as a row of width $w + 5$.

10.1 DEFINITION   The *row-encoding* (for w instructions) of a natural number n in register A, written $\mathscr{R}_A^w(n)$, is defined as follows:

$$\mathscr{R}_A^w(0) = \langle \#4, -, -, \text{HALT}, \text{HALT}, \underbrace{- .. -}_{w \ times} \rangle$$

$$\mathscr{R}_A^w(n + 1) = \langle \#5, \mathscr{R}_A^w(n), -, \text{HALT}, \text{HALT}, \underbrace{- .. -}_{w \ times} \rangle.$$

The row-encoding (for w instructions) of a natural number n in register B, written $\mathscr{R}_B^w(n)$, is defined as follows:

$$\mathscr{R}_B^w(0) = \langle\, \#4, -, -, \text{HALT}, \text{HALT}, \underbrace{-..-}_{w\ times}\,\rangle$$

$$\mathscr{R}_B^w(n+1) = \langle\, \#5, -, \mathscr{R}_B^w(n), \text{HALT}, \text{HALT}, \underbrace{-..-}_{w\ times}\,\rangle.$$

10.2 DEFINITION The *row-encoding* (for w instructions) of an instruction I, written $\mathscr{R}^w(I)$, is defined as follows:

$\mathscr{R}^w(\text{INCA} \Rightarrow m)$

$\quad = \langle\, \#m+5, \langle\, \#5, \#\#2, -, \text{HALT}, \text{HALT}, -..-\,\rangle, -, \text{HALT}, \text{HALT}, -..-\,\rangle$

$\mathscr{R}^w(\text{INCB} \Rightarrow m)$

$\quad = \langle\, \#m+5, -, \langle\, \#5, -, \#\#3, \text{HALT}, \text{HALT}, -..-\,\rangle, \text{HALT}, \text{HALT}, -..-\,\rangle$

$\mathscr{R}^w(\text{TSTA} \Rightarrow m/n) = \langle\, \#2, -, -, \#m+5, \#n+5, -..-\,\rangle$

$\mathscr{R}^w(\text{TSTB} \Rightarrow m/n) = \langle\, \#3, -, -, \#m+5, \#n+5, -..-\,\rangle$

$\mathscr{R}^w(\text{HALT}) = \langle\, \text{HALT}, -, -, \text{HALT}, \text{HALT}, -..-\,\rangle.$

10.3 DEFINITION Let $T \equiv \langle PC, A, B, I_1 .. I_w \rangle$ be a two-counter machine. The *row-encoding* of T, written $\mathscr{R}(T)$, is the rowing machine of width $w+5$ defined as follows:

$$\mathscr{R}(T) = \langle\, \mathscr{R}^w(PC), \mathscr{R}_A^w(A), \mathscr{R}_B^w(B), \text{HALT}, \text{HALT}, \mathscr{R}^w(I_1) .. \mathscr{R}^w(I_w)\,\rangle.$$

10.4 LEMMA If $T \to_T T'$, then $\mathscr{R}(T) \overset{*}{\to}_R \mathscr{R}(T')$.

Proof Let $T = \langle PC, A, B, I_1 .. I_w \rangle$. Proceed by cases on the form of PC.

Case $PC = \text{INCA} \Rightarrow m$

Then $T' = \langle I_m, A+1, B, I_1 .. I_w \rangle$. Calculate as follows:

$\quad \mathscr{R}(T)$

$\equiv \quad \langle\langle\, \#m+5, \langle\, \#5, \#\#2, -, \text{HALT}, \text{HALT}, -..-\,\rangle, -, \text{HALT}, \text{HALT}, -..-\,\rangle,$
$\qquad \mathscr{R}_A^w(A), \mathscr{R}_B^w(B),$
$\qquad \text{HALT}, \text{HALT},$
$\qquad \mathscr{R}^w(I_1) .. \mathscr{R}^w(I_w)\rangle$

$\rightarrow_R \quad \langle \mathscr{R}^w(I_m),$
$\qquad \langle \#5, \mathscr{R}_A^w(A), -, \text{HALT}, \text{HALT}, - .. - \rangle, \mathscr{R}_B^w(B),$
$\qquad \text{HALT}, \text{HALT},$
$\qquad \mathscr{R}^w(I_1) .. \mathscr{R}^w(I_w) \rangle$

$\equiv \quad \mathscr{R}(T').$

Case $\quad PC = \text{INCB} \Rightarrow m$
   Similar.

Case $\quad PC = \text{TSTA} \Rightarrow m/n$
   Calculate as follows:

$\qquad \mathscr{R}(T)$

$\equiv \quad \langle\langle \#2, -, -, \#m + 5, \#n + 5, - .. - \rangle,$
$\qquad \mathscr{R}_A^w(A), \mathscr{R}_B^w(B),$
$\qquad \text{HALT}, \text{HALT},$
$\qquad \mathscr{R}^w(I_1) .. \mathscr{R}^w(I_w) \rangle$

$\rightarrow_R \quad \langle \mathscr{R}_A^w(A),$
$\qquad \mathscr{R}_A^w(A), \mathscr{R}_B^w(B),$
$\qquad \mathscr{R}^w(I_m), \mathscr{R}^w(I_n),$
$\qquad \mathscr{R}^w(I_1) .. \mathscr{R}^w(I_w) \rangle$

There are two subcases to consider:

Subcase $\quad A = 0$
   Then

$\mathscr{R}^w(A) = \langle \#4, -, -, \text{HALT}, \text{HALT}, - .. - \rangle$

$T' = \langle I_m, A, B, I_1 .. I_w \rangle.$

Continue calculating as follows:

$\qquad \langle\langle \#4, -, -, \text{HALT}, \text{HALT}, - .. - \rangle,$
$\qquad \mathscr{R}_A^w(A), \mathscr{R}_B^w(B),$
$\qquad \mathscr{R}^w(I_m), \mathscr{R}^w(I_n),$
$\qquad \mathscr{R}^w(I_1) .. \mathscr{R}^w(I_w) \rangle$

$\rightarrow_R \quad \langle \mathscr{R}^w(I_m),$
$\qquad \mathscr{R}_A^w(A), \mathscr{R}_B^w(B),$
$\qquad \text{HALT}, \text{HALT},$
$\qquad \mathscr{R}^w(I_1) .. \mathscr{R}^w(I_w) \rangle$

$\equiv \quad \mathscr{R}(T').$

Subcase $A > 0$

Then

$$\mathscr{R}_A^w(A) = \langle \#5, \mathscr{R}_A^w(A-1), -, \mathrm{HALT}, \mathrm{HALT}, -..-\rangle$$

$$T' = \langle I_n, A-1, B, I_1 .. I_w \rangle.$$

Continue calculating as follows:

$$\langle\langle \#5, \mathscr{R}_A^w(A-1), -, \mathrm{HALT}, \mathrm{HALT}, -..-\rangle,$$
$$\mathscr{R}_A^w(A), \mathscr{R}_B^w(B),$$
$$\mathscr{R}^w(I_m), \mathscr{R}^w(I_n),$$
$$\mathscr{R}^w(I_1) .. \mathscr{R}^w(I_w)\rangle$$

$\rightarrow_R \quad \langle \mathscr{R}^w(I_n),$
$$\mathscr{R}_A^w(A-1), \mathscr{R}_B^w(B),$$
$$\mathrm{HALT}, \mathrm{HALT},$$
$$\mathscr{R}^w(I_1) .. \mathscr{R}^w(I_w)\rangle$$

$\equiv \quad \mathscr{R}(T').$

Case $PC = \mathrm{TSTB} \Rightarrow m/n$

Similar.

Case $PC = \mathrm{HALT}$

Can't happen. ∎

10.5 LEMMA   If $T = \langle \mathrm{HALT}, A, B, I_1 .. I_w \rangle$, then $\mathscr{R}(T)$ halts.

Proof Immediate. ∎

10.6 COROLLARY T halts iff $\mathscr{R}(T)$ does.

10.7 THEOREM   The $F_\leq$ subtyping relation is undecidable.

Proof Assume, for a contradiction, that we had a total-recursive procedure for testing the derivability of subtyping statements in $F_\leq$. Then to decide whether a two-counter machine T halts, we could use this procedure to test whether $\mathscr{F}(\mathscr{R}(T))$ is derivable, since

T halts

iff $\mathscr{R}(T)$ halts   by Corollary 10.6

iff $\mathscr{F}(\mathscr{R}(T))$ is derivable in $F_\le^F$ by Corollary 8.7

iff $\mathscr{F}(\mathscr{R}(T))$ is derivable in $F_\le^D$ by Lemma 6.9

iff $\mathscr{F}(\mathscr{R}(T))$ is derivable in $F_\le^N$ by Lemma 5.9

iff $\mathscr{F}(\mathscr{R}(T))$ is derivable in $F_\le$ by Lemma 3.2. ∎

11   Undecidability of $F_\le$ Typechecking

From the undecidability of $F_\le$ subtyping, the undecidability of typechecking follows immediately: we need only show how to write down a term that is well typed iff a given subtyping statement

$$\vdash \sigma \le \tau$$

is derivable. One such term is:

$$\lambda f : \tau \to Top \,.\, \lambda a : \sigma \,.\, fa.$$

12   Discussion

The undecidability of $F_\le$ came as a surprise to many who have studied, extended, and applied it since its introduction in 1985. But it seems probable that language designs and implementations based on $F_\le$ will not be greatly affected by this discovery. Here are some reasons for optimism:

1. The algorithm has been used for several years now without any sign of misbehavior in any situation arising in practice. Indeed, constructing even the simplest nonterminating example requires a contortion that is difficult to imagine anyone performing by accident.

2. A number of useful fragments of $F_\le$ are easily shown to be decidable. For example:

• The prenex fragment, where all quantifers appear at the outside and quantifiers are instantiated only at monotypes (types containing no quantifiers).

• A predicative fragment where types are stratified into universes and the bound of a quantified type lives in a lower universe than the quantified type itself.

• Cardelli and Wegner's original formulation where the bounds of two quantified types must be identical in order for one to be a subtype of the other. Though semantically unappealing, this formulation of $F_\leq$ appears strong enough to include essentially all useful programming examples. The only known examples that require the more general quantifier subtyping rule are those involving bounded existential types, which correspond to "partially abstract types" (c.f. [15]) under Mitchell and Plotkin's correspondence between abstract types and existential types [31]. Partially abstract types are a generalization of abstract types where some of the structure of the representation type is known but its exact identity remains hidden. Interesting subtype relations between partially abstract types can only arise from the full $F_\leq$ quantifier subtyping rule.

3. The best known subtyping algorithms for these fragments are essentially identical to the algorithm $F_\leq^N$.

4. On well-typed expressions, a type synthesis algorithm based on $F_\leq^N$ is guaranteed to terminate, since it will only ask questions to which the answer is "yes."

Acknowledgements

I am grateful for productive discussions with John Reynolds, Robert Harper, Luca Cardelli, Giorgio Ghelli, Daniel Sleator, and Tim Freeman.

This research was sponsored in part by the Avionics Laboratory, Wright Research ad Development Center, Aeronautical Systems Division (AFSC), U.S. Air Force, Wright-Patterson AFB, OH 45433-6543 under Contract F33615-90-C-1465, Arpa Order No. 7597; in part by the Office of Naval Research under Contract N00013-84-K-0415; in part by the National Science Foundation under Contract CCR-8922109; and in part by Siemens. The views and conclusions contained in this document are those of the author and should not be interpreted as representing the official policies, either expressed or implied, of the U.S. Government.

References

[1] Val Breazu-Tannen, Thierry Coquand, Carl Gunter, and Andre Scedrov. Inheritance as implicit coercion. *Information and Computation*, 93:172–221, 1991.

[2] Kim B. Bruce. The equivalence of two semantic definitions for inheritance in object-oriented languages. In *Proceedings of Mathematical Foundations of Programming Semantics*, Pittsburgh, PA, March 1991.

[3] Kim B. Bruce and Giuseppe Longo. A modest model of records, inheritance, and bounded quantification. *Information and Computation*, 87:196–240, 1990. An earlier version appeared in the proceedings of the IEEE Symposium on Logic in Computer Science, 1988.

[4] Kim Bruce and John Mitchell. PER models of subtyping, recursive types and higher-order polymorphism. In *Proceedings of the Nineteenth ACM Symposium on Principles of Programming Languages*, Albequerque, NM, January 1992.

[5] Peter Canning, William Cook, Walter Hill, Walter Olthoff, and John Mitchell. *F*-bounded quantification for object-oriented programming. In *Fourth International Conference on Functional Programming Languages and Computer Architecture*, pages 273–280, September 1989.

[6] Luca Cardelli. A semantics of multiple inheritance. *Information and Computation*, 76:138–164, 1988. An earlier version appears in Semantics of Data Types, Kahn, Mac-Quenn, and Plotkin, eds., Springer-Verlag LNCS 173, 1984.

[7] Luca Cardelli. Structural subtyping and the notion of power type. In *Proceedings of the 15th ACM Symposium on Principles of Programming Languages*, pages 70–79, San Diego, CA, January 1988.

[8] Luca Cardelli. Typeful programming. Research Report 45, Digital Equipment Corporation, Systems Research Center, Palo Alto, California, February 1989.

[9] Luca Cardelli. Notes about $F^{\omega}_{<:}$. Unpublished notes, October 1990.

[10] Luca Cardelli. An Implementation of $F_{<:}$. Research Report 97, DEC Systems Research Center. Feb. 1993.

[11] Luca Cardelli. Extensible records in a pure calculus of subtyping. Research report 81, DEC Systems Research Center, January 1992.

[12] Luca Cardelli and Giuseppe Longo. A semantic basis for Quest: (Extended abstract). In *ACM Conference on Lisp and Functional Programming*, pages 30–43, Nice, France, June 1990. Extended version available as DEC SRC Research Report 55, Feb. 1990.

[13] Luca Cardelli, Simone Martini, John C. Mitchell, and Andre Scedrov. An extension of system *F* with subtyping. In Ito and Meyer [27], pages 750–770.

[14] Luca Cardelli and John Mitchell. Operations on records (summary). In M. Main, A. Melton, M. Mislove, and D. Schmidt, editors, *Proceedings of Fifth International Conference on Mathematical Foundations of Programming Language Semantics*, volume 442 of *Lecture Notes in Computer Science*, pages 22–52, Tulane University, New Orleans, March 1989. Springer Verlag. To appear in Mathematical Structures in Computer Science; also available as DEC Systems Research Center Research Report #48, August, 1989.

[15] Luca Cardelli and Peter Wegner. On understanding types, data abstraction, and polymorphism. *Computing Surveys*, 17(4), December 1985.

[16] Felice Cardone. Relational semantics for recursive types and bounded quantification. In *Proceedings of the Sixteenth International Colloquium on Automata, Languages, and Programming*, volume 372 of *Lecture Notes in Computer Science*, pages 164–178, Stresa, Italy, July 1989. Springer-Verlag.

[17] William R. Cook, Walter L. Hill, and Peter S. Canning. Inheritance is not subtyping. In *Seventeenth Annual ACM Symposium on Principles of Programming Languages*, pages 125–135, San Francisco, CA, January 1990.

[18] M. Coppo, M. Dezani-Ciancaglini, and B. Venneri. Principal type schemes and lambda calculus semantics. In *To H. B. Curry: Essays on Combinatory Logic, Lambda Calculus, and Formalism*, pages 535–560, New York, 1980. Academic Press.

[19] Pierre-Louis Curien and Giorgio Ghelli. Subtyping + extensionality: Confluence of $\beta\eta$-reductions in $F_{\leq}$. In Ito and Meyer [27], pages 731–749.

[20] Pierre-Louis Curien and Giorgio Ghelli. Coherence of subsumption. *Mathematical Structures in Computer Science*, 2:55–91, 1992.

[21] Nicolas G. de Bruijn. Lambda-calculus notation with nameless dummies: a tool for automatic formula manipulation with application to the Church-Rosser theorem. *Indag. Math.*, 34(5):381–392, 1972.

[22] Giorgio Ghelli. *Proof Theoretic Studies about a Minimal Type System Integrating Inclusion and Parametric Polymorphism*. PhD thesis, Università di Pisa, March 1990. Technical report TD-6/90, Dipartimento di Informatica, Università di Pisa.

[23] Giorgio Ghelli. Divergence of $F_\leq$ type checking. Technical Report 5/93. Dipartimento di Informatica, Università di Pisa, 1993.

[24] Jean-Yves Girard. *Interprétation fonctionelle et élimination des coupures de l'arithmétique d'ordre supérieur*. PhD thesis, Université Paris VII, 1972.

[25] Martin Hoffman and Benjamin Pierce. An abstract view of objects and subtyping. Technical Report ECS-LFCS-92-225, University of Edinburgh, LFCS, 1992.

[26] John E. Hopcroft and Jeffrey D. Ullman. *Introduction to Automata Theory, Languages, and Computation*. Addison-Wesley, 1979.

[27] T. Ito and A. R. Meyer, editors. *Theoretical Aspects of Computer Software (Sendai, Japan)*, number 526 in Lecture Notes in Computer Science. Springer-Verlag, September 1991.

[28] Simone Martini. Bounded quantifiers have interval models. In *Proceedings of the ACM Conference on Lisp and Functional Programming*, pages 174–183, Snowbird, Utah, July 1988. ACM.

[29] John C. Mitchell. Polymorphic type inference and containment. *Information and Computation*, 76:211–249, 1988.

[30] John C. Mitchell. Toward a typed foundation for method specialization and inheritance. In *Proceedings of the 17th ACM Symposium on Principles of Programming Languages*, pages 109–124, January 1990.

[31] John Mitchell and Gordon Plotkin. Abstract types have existential type. *ACM Transactions on Programming Languages and Systems*, 10(3), July 1988.

[32] Benjamin C. Pierce. *Programming with Intersection Types and Bounded Polymorphism*. PhD thesis, Carnegie Mellon University, December 1991. Available as School of Computer Science technical report CMU-CS-91-205.

[33] Benjamin C. Pierce and David N. Turner. Object-oriented programming without recursive types. Technical Report ECS-LFCS-92-226, University of Edinburgh, LFCS, 1992.

[34] John Reynolds. Towards a theory of type structure. In *Proc. Colloque sur la Programmation*, pages 408–425, New York, 1974. Springer-Verlag LNCS 19.

[35] John C. Reynolds. Preliminary design of the programming languages Forsythe. Technical Report CMU-CS-88-159, Carnegie Mellon University, June 1988.

V INHERITANCE

13 Two Semantic Models of Object-Oriented Languages

Samuel N. Kamin and Uday S. Reddy

Abstract

We present and compare two models of object-oriented languages. The first we call the *closure model* because it uses closures to encapsulate side effects on objects, and accordingly makes the operations on an object a part of that object. It is shown that this denotational framework is adequate to explain classes, instantiation, and inheritance in the style of Simula as well as SMALLTALK-80. The second we call the *data structure model* because it mimics the implementations of data structure languages like CLU in representing objects by records of instance variables, while keeping the operations on objects separate from the objects themselves. This yields a model which is very simple, at least superficially. Both the models are presented by way of a sequence of languages, culminating in a language with SMALLTALK-80-style inheritance. The mathematical relationship between them is then discussed and it is shown that the models give equivalent results. It will emerge from this discussion that more appropriate names for the two models might be the *fixed-point model* and the *self-applicaton model*.

1 Introduction

Object-oriented languages, such as SMALLTALK-80[1] [GR83], have recently received a lot of attention. However, the term "object-oriented" does not seem to have a commonly accepted meaning. It is sometimes used to refer to the presence of *data objects with local state*, sometimes to the *coupling* of data with operations, sometimes to record *subtyping*, sometimes to the notion of *class inheritance*, and sometimes to the specific notion of inheritance in Smalltalk which involves a kind of "dynamic binding". The first of the these notions, viz., objects with local state, has long been used in the functional programming community to encapsulate "side effects" whenever they were necessary [ASS85, KL85]. These are sometimes loosely referred to as *closures*. A closure is essentially a function (or a data structure containing functions) with some local bindings to values or storage locations. In describing the semantics of object oriented languages, it seems natural that such a notion of closure should play a role. The second notion, that of coupling data with structures of operations, is used in data abstraction languages like CLU [LAB+81]. A distinguishing feature of these languages is that the structure of operations is shared by many data objects.

SMALLTALK and other object oriented languages, of course, go much beyond data objects with local states or coupling of data with operations. They allow classes to be defined, objects to be created as instances of classes, class descriptions to refer to the receiving object in terms of *self*, and subclasses to be derived from superclasses.

Whether all these concepts can be explained in terms of closures or data structures is an interesting quesiton. If so, the denotational semantics of object oriented languages can be defined in terms of such concepts.

In this chapter, we present two semantic models of object-oriented languages. The closure-based model has been presented previously in [Car84, Coo89, Red88]. The data structure model appeared in [Kam88]. Reddy [Red88] also gave an abstracted version of the model in [Kam88] and commented on their relationship. The present chapter is an expansion of [Red88], in which the data structure model is presented more fully and the relationship between the models is formalized. In particular, the models are shown to give equivalent results. The assertion in [Red88] that the closure model is more abstract than the data structure model is discussed, though we have not succeeded in proving it.

To present the semantics, we discuss a series of small abstract languages. Firstly, *ObjectTalk* is a language in which objects can be defined, but no classes. In the second language, *ClassTalk*, classes can be defined and objects can be created as instances of classes. The third language, *InheritTalk*, provides subclasses to be defined by inheriting from other classes. The bindings of messages used by superclasses are not affected by inheritance. The inheritance of Simula [DN66] and C++ [Str86] work in this fashion (when virtual functions are excluded). Finally, we define a language called *SmallTalk*, which implements inheritance in the style of SMALLTALK-80, by rebinding messages in subclasses.[2]

The four languages are defined in each of the two models in sections 3 and 4, respectively. Section 2 establishes our notations and gives the semantics of simple imperative language constructs. Section 5 comments on the relationship between the two models and, in Section 6, we formalize the relationship and prove the computational equivalence of the two models.

2 Denotational Framework

Our style of presentation will be to consider a series of small abstract languages with increasingly more expressive power. For obvious reasons, we will not treat a full language, but only those portions which are of interest to object-oriented programming. To set the context, let us first give some examples of syntactic constructs:

$x, y \in variable$

$\quad e \in expression$

$\quad e ::= x \,|\, \texttt{valof}\ e \,|\, x := e \,|\, \texttt{let}\ x = e_1\ \texttt{in}\ e_2$

Here, we have only two kinds of syntactic objects *variable* and *expression*, and three kinds of expression constructs. For pedagogical reasons, we use the dereferencing operator `valof` to access the contents of a location. (It allows us to use a single semantic function, rather than two separate ones for the *l-* and *r-values* of expressions).

Conventionally, the meaning of an expression [Sto77] is of the type

env → *state* → *val* × *state*.

So, an expression valuation $[\![e]\!]\eta\sigma$ is some $\langle v, \sigma' \rangle$. The bindings of free variables in e, which may be values or locations, are obtained from η, and the contents of locations are obtained from the state σ. Our semantic domains and a sampler of semantic definitions are given below:

$$\alpha \in loc$$
$$v, w \in val \ = basicval + loc + \cdots$$
$$\eta \in env \ = variable \rightharpoonup val$$
$$\sigma \in state = loc \rightharpoonup val$$

$$[\![-]\!] : env \rightarrow state \rightarrow (val \times state)$$
$$[\![x]\!]\eta\sigma = \langle \eta x, \sigma \rangle$$
$$[\![\texttt{valof } e]\!]\eta\sigma = \textbf{let } \langle \alpha, \sigma' \rangle = [\![e]\!]\eta\sigma$$
$$\textbf{in } \alpha \in loc \rightarrow \langle \sigma'\alpha, \sigma' \rangle; ?$$
$$[\![x := e]\!]\eta\sigma = \textbf{let } \alpha = \eta x$$
$$\langle v, \sigma_1 \rangle = [\![e]\!]\eta\sigma$$
$$\textbf{in } \alpha \in loc \rightarrow \langle v, \sigma_1[\alpha \rightarrow v] \rangle; ?$$
$$[\![\texttt{let } x = e_1 \texttt{ in } e_2]\!]\eta\sigma = \textbf{let } \langle v_1, \sigma_1 \rangle = [\![e_1]\!]\eta\sigma$$
$$\textbf{in } [\![e_2]\!](\eta[x \rightarrow v_1])\sigma$$

Let us make a few comments about our notation. The symbol ? denotes an error value. We do not elaborate its meaning any further. (See [Sto77] for a detailed discussion.) Environments and states are finite *partial* functions, and we often need to update them (like in the semantics of assignment above). The notation $f[x \rightarrow v]$ means a copy of the function f that maps x to v leaving everything else unchanged. Similarly, $f[x_1 \rightarrow v_1, \ldots, x_k \rightarrow v_k]$ or $f[\bar{x} \rightarrow \bar{v}]$ denotes simultaneous multiple updates. A second notational device is $f; f'$ which means the update of f with all the bindings in f' (note: f' should be a finite mapping). The symbol $\eta_\perp$ denotes the empty environment and $\sigma_\perp$ denotes the empty state.

Closures   The notion of *closure* arises from the fact that expressions may have free (nonlocal) variables. The type *env* → *state* → (*val* × *state*) shows that an expression valuation depends on an environment and a state. Given both, the value of the expression is fixed. Now, consider a procedure-valued expression with free variables, *e.g.*,

$$\text{let } f(\ ) = (x := \text{valof } y) \text{ in } f$$

The "value" (i.e. the *val* part in the above type) of such an expression is, in turn, of the type

$$procedure = val^* \rightarrow state \rightarrow (val \times state)$$

It can be applied to a tuple of value arguments $\bar{v}$ and then executed in a state σ, producing a result value and a new state. The environment at the point of its application does not affect its meaning. Thus, if the definition of f is evaluated (not applied) in an environment η with $\eta x = \alpha_1$ and $\eta y = \alpha_2$, then the value of f is

$$c \equiv \lambda\langle\ \rangle.\lambda\sigma.\langle(\sigma\alpha_2), \sigma[\alpha_1 \rightarrow (\sigma\alpha_2)]\rangle$$

The variables x and y have been replaced by their bindings α_1 and α_2, and this procedure will forever transfer the contents of the location α_2 to the location α_1. A procedure value, such as c, is called a *closure*[3]. The expression of which it is a value may have had free variables. But, they have all been eliminated before we obtain the value. The closure itself now does not "depend" on any variables.

Another programming language feature concerned with closures is the declaration of mutable variables in local contexts. To make this precise, let us add another construct to our example language:

$$e ::= \text{local } x; e \text{ end}$$

Its semantics is given by

$$[\![\text{local } x; e \text{ end}]\!]\eta\sigma = \tag{1}$$
$$\quad \textbf{let } \alpha = newloc\ \sigma \qquad \text{—new location for } x$$
$$\qquad \sigma_1 = extend\ \sigma\ \alpha \quad \text{—allocation of the location}$$
$$\qquad \eta_1 = \eta[x \rightarrow \alpha] \quad \text{—local environment for } e$$
$$\quad \textbf{in } [\![e]\!]\eta_1\sigma_1$$

newloc is the operation on states that delivers a new location; it returns that location, and *extend* returns a state in which the location has been allocated (i.e. is no longer available to *newloc*); see [Sto77, p. 287–288] for further discussion of these functions.

This sequence of definitions arises so often in this paper that we introduce a new function *alloc* for it:

$$alloc\ \sigma\langle x_1, \ldots, x_n \rangle = \textbf{let}\ \alpha_1 = newloc\ \sigma \tag{2}$$
$$\sigma_1 = extend\ \sigma\ \alpha_1$$
$$\ldots$$
$$\alpha_n = newloc\ \sigma_{n-1}$$
$$\sigma_n = extend\ \sigma_{n-1}\ \alpha_n$$
$$\eta_0 = \eta_\perp[x_1 \to \alpha_1, \ldots, x_n \to \alpha_n]$$
$$\textbf{in}\ \langle \eta_0, \sigma_1 \rangle$$

Now, (1) can be simply rewritten as

$$[\![\texttt{local}\ x; e\ \texttt{end}]\!] \eta\sigma = \textbf{let}\ \langle \eta_0, \sigma_1 \rangle = alloc\ \sigma\langle x \rangle \tag{3}$$
$$\textbf{in}\ [\![e]\!](\eta; \eta_0)\sigma_1$$

Returning to our discussion of closures, suppose the expression e in such a context defines and returns a procedure, as in

$$\texttt{local}\ x; \textbf{let}\ f(\ ) = (x := \texttt{valof}\ y)\ \textbf{in}\ f\ \texttt{end} \tag{4}$$

then the location assigned to x is built into f. Moreover, only f can access this location. The rest of the program can affect the value of the location only by calling f. It is often said that, in such a situation, the location of x makes up the *local state* of f. More accurately, f has an exclusive "local window" on the *global* state (since it can access or modify the rest of the state as well). The rest of the program has neither access to, nor interest in, the structure of this local window or the variables used for accessing it.

We will show that objects in object oriented languages can be modeled by such closures with local windows to the state. Further, the model can be extended to cover the notion of classes and inheritance as well.

Data structures   The second semantic concept we use in this paper is that of a *data structure*. A data structure is a compound object whose components include data values as well as operations on those values. (Thus our use of the term "structure" draws from the mathematical notion of structure.) This is in contrast to closures which only contain operations as components. Data structures are familiar from languages supporting abstract data types such as CLU [LAB⁺81] and Ada [DoD82], except that the operations in such languages are often associated with static types rather than with data values. The treatment of CLU in [Kam90] is closer to our notion of data structure.

The closure defined in (4) can be expressed as a data structure by making the local variable a part of the result:

$$\texttt{local}\ x; \textbf{let}\ f(x) = (x := \texttt{valof}\ y)\ \textbf{in}\ (x, f)\ \texttt{end} \tag{5}$$

Note that both the location x as well as the operation on x are available to users. It may appear that data structures violate the principle of data encapsulation by offering the users direct access to representations. However, they provide flexibility in defining "privileged" users who require access to representations. We will see that inheritance as in SMALLTALK-80 involves such privileged users.

3 Closure Semantics

In this section, we develop semantics for a series of small abstract languages based on the closure model. For quick reference, we define below the various semantic domains involved in this development:

$v \in val = basicval + loc + objectval + classval + superclassval$

$o \in objectval = menv$

$\rho \in menv = message \rightarrow method$

$\mu \in method = val^* \rightarrow state \rightarrow (val \times state)$

$\xi \in classval = state \rightarrow (menv \times state)$

$\psi \in superclassval = state \rightarrow (env \times (menv \rightarrow menv) \times state)$

3.1 ObjectTalk

The simplest of our abstract languages is *ObjectTalk*. In this language, an object can be defined using the syntax

$e ::= \mathtt{obj}(x_1, \ldots, x_n)\{m_1(\bar{y}_1) = e_1, \ldots, m_k(\bar{y}_k) = e_k\}$

Here $x_1, \ldots, x_n$ are the local variables of the object (also called *instance variables*), and $m_1, \ldots, m_k$ are the "messages" (or operations) that the object responds to. The definition of a message is called its "method". There is no notion of a class. However, methods can create objects each time they are called, so the effect of classes can still be achieved by objects. The syntax for sending messages to objects is

$e ::= e_o . m(\bar{e}_a)$

where e_o is the *receiver object*, m is the message and $\bar{e}_a$ are the argument expressions. The following definition of a point object illustrates these constructs:

$$p = \mathtt{obj}(x, y)\{put(a, b) = \mathtt{begin}\ x := a;\ y := b\ \mathtt{end}, \qquad\qquad (6)$$
$$dist(\ ) \quad = sqrt(sqr(\mathtt{valof}\ x) + sqr(\mathtt{valof}\ y)),$$
$$closer(q) = \mathtt{self}.dist(\ ) < q.dist(\ )\}$$

This declares two local variables x and y for the coordinates of the point, and three messages. The *put* message sets the coordinates of the points; the *dist* message gives the distance of the point from the origin; and *closer* takes another "point-like" object q as a parameter, and checks if the current point is closer to the origin than q. The special variable `self` denotes the very object being defined (p, in this case). We could have used p in place of `self`. But, note that p is an external name being given to the `obj` expression. We would want to define objects without giving them names. The variable `self` is useful to refer to the object, in such contexts.

What should objects denote? From the point of view of a user, an object simply responds to a set of messages. So, the meaning of an object can simply be an environment binding messages to their methods (message environments). The summand *objectval* of *val* can thus be defined by

$$\rho \in objectval = menv = message \to method$$

$$\mu \in method = val^* \to state \to (val \times state)$$

The domain *method* is similar to the type of procedure values discussed in the last section. Here is a first attempt at the semantics for `obj`-expressions:

$$\begin{aligned}
&\llbracket \text{obj}(\bar{x})\{m_i(\bar{y}_i) = e_i\} \rrbracket \eta \sigma = \\
&\quad \textbf{let } \langle \eta_o, \sigma_1 \rangle = alloc\ \sigma\ \bar{x} \qquad\qquad \text{—value environment of the object} \\
&\qquad \rho = \rho_\perp[m_i \to \lambda\bar{w} . \llbracket e_i \rrbracket(\eta; \eta_o[\bar{y}_i \to \bar{w}])] \quad \text{—message environment} \\
&\quad \textbf{in } \langle \rho, \sigma_1 \rangle
\end{aligned}$$

Note that the message environment ρ produced as the value of the object expression is a closure, since the loal environment η_o is absorbed in it. Thus the object has an exclusive window to the locations allocated in η_o.

This semantics is not yet complete because we would like to have recursive references to an object's messages in the methods defining those messages. This recursion is achieved indirectly by sending a message to the special variable `self`. The use of `self` is accommodated in our semantics as follows:

$$\begin{aligned}
&\llbracket \text{obj}(\bar{x})\{m_i(\bar{y}_i) = e_i\} \rrbracket \eta \sigma = \qquad\qquad\qquad\qquad\qquad\qquad (7) \\
&\quad \textbf{let } \langle \eta_o, \sigma_1 \rangle = alloc\ \sigma\ \bar{x} \\
&\qquad \rho = fix\ (\lambda\rho . \rho_\perp[m_i \to \lambda\bar{w} . \llbracket e_i \rrbracket(\eta; \eta_o[\bar{y}_i \to \bar{w}, \text{self} \to \rho])]) \\
&\quad \textbf{in } \langle \rho, \sigma_1 \rangle
\end{aligned}$$

The only change is in the environment in which the method-expressions are interpreted. We bind the variable `self` to the message environment ρ that is being constructed for the object. But this makes the definition of ρ recursive, and we resolve it by introducing the fixed point operator *fix*. The use of fixed points to model references to `self` first appeared in [Car84].

The meaning of a message send is defined as follows:

$$[\![e_o.m(\bar{e})]\!]\eta\sigma = \textbf{let } \langle \rho, \sigma_1 \rangle = [\![e_o]\!]\eta\sigma \quad \text{—message environment of } e_o \qquad (8)$$
$$\langle \bar{v}, \sigma_2 \rangle = [\![\bar{e}]\!]\eta\sigma_1 \quad \text{—values of arguments}$$
$$\textbf{in } \rho m\bar{v}\sigma_2$$

Using the semantic definitions (7) and (8), the meaning of the point object p defined in (6) can be expressed as follows: (where α_x and α_y are the locations allocated for x and y)

$$\rho_p = fix\,(\lambda\rho.[put \quad \rightarrow \lambda\langle w_a, w_b \rangle . \langle w_b, \lambda\sigma.\sigma[\alpha_x \rightarrow w_a, \alpha_y \rightarrow w_b]\rangle,$$
$$dist \quad \rightarrow \lambda\langle\,\rangle.\lambda\sigma.\langle\sqrt{(\sigma\alpha_x)^2 + (\sigma\alpha_y)^2}, \sigma\rangle,$$
$$closer \rightarrow \lambda\langle\rho_q\rangle.\lambda\sigma.\textbf{let } \langle v_1, \sigma_1 \rangle = \rho\,dist\,\langle\,\rangle\sigma$$
$$\langle v_2, \sigma_2 \rangle = \rho_q\,dist\,\langle\,\rangle\sigma_1$$
$$\textbf{in } \langle v_1 < v_2, \sigma_2 \rangle])$$

Since this recursion converges finitely, it simplifies to:

$$\rho_p = [put \quad \rightarrow \lambda\langle w_a, w_b \rangle.\lambda\sigma.\langle w_b, \sigma[\alpha_x \rightarrow w_a, \alpha_y \rightarrow w_b]\rangle, \qquad (9)$$
$$dist \quad \rightarrow \lambda\langle\,\rangle.\lambda\sigma.\langle\sqrt{(\sigma\alpha_x)^2 + (\sigma\alpha_y)^2}, \sigma\rangle,$$
$$closer \rightarrow \lambda\langle\rho_q\rangle.\lambda\sigma.\textbf{let } v_1 = \sqrt{(\sigma\alpha_x)^2 + (\sigma\alpha_y)^2}$$
$$\langle v_2, \sigma_2 \rangle = \rho_q\,dist\,\langle\,\rangle\sigma$$
$$\textbf{in } \langle v_1 < v_2, \sigma_2 \rangle]$$

3.2   ClassTalk

In this language, we introduce classes without inheritance. The syntax is similar to that of objects:

$$e ::= \texttt{class}\,(x_1, \dots, x_n)\{m_1(\bar{y}_1) = e_1, \dots, m_k(\bar{y}_k) = e_k\}$$

Instance objects of classes are created by the expression

$$e ::= \texttt{new } e_c$$

Now, we can define a generic point class instead of a specific point as in (6):

$$point = \texttt{class}\,(x, y)\{put(a, b) = \texttt{begin } x := a;\, y := b \texttt{ end}, \qquad (10)$$
$$dist(\,) = sqrt(sqr(\texttt{valof } x) + sqr(\texttt{valof } y)),$$
$$closer(q) = \texttt{self}.dist(\,) < q.dist(\,)\}$$

Every evaluation of `new` *point* yields a new instance of *point*.

The semantics of classes should naturally satisfy the property

$$[\![\text{new } \text{class}(x_1,\ldots,x_n)\{m_1(\bar{y}_1) = e_1,\ldots,m_k(\bar{y}_k) = e_k\}]\!]$$

$$= [\![\text{obj}(x_1,\ldots,x_n)\{m_1(\bar{y}_1) = e_1,\ldots,m_k(\bar{y}_k) = e_k\}]\!] \qquad (11)$$

since instantiating a class expression to get an object is the same as directly using an obj-expression. So, the class construct provides a *generator* which can be invoked to obtain an *objectval*. The simplest such generators are given by the domain

$$\xi \in classval = state \rightarrow (menv \times state)$$

and we add it as a new summand to the *val* domain. The semantics of the constructs is given by:

$$[\![\text{class}(\bar{x})\{m_i(\bar{y}_i) = e_i\}]\!]\eta\sigma = \qquad (12)$$
$$\langle \lambda\sigma'. \textbf{let } \langle \eta_o, \sigma_1' \rangle = alloc \, \sigma' \, \bar{x}$$
$$\rho = fix(\lambda\rho.\rho_\perp[m_i \rightarrow (\lambda\bar{w}.\lambda\sigma.[\![e_i]\!](\eta;\eta_o[\bar{y}_i \rightarrow \bar{w}, \text{self} \rightarrow \rho])\sigma)])$$
$$\textbf{in } \langle \rho, \sigma_1' \rangle,$$
$$\sigma \rangle$$
$$[\![\text{new } e_c]\!]\eta\sigma = \textbf{let } \langle \xi, \sigma_1 \rangle = [\![e_c]\!]\eta\sigma \textbf{ in } \xi\sigma_1$$

Classes do not add any expressive power to ObjectTalk owing to the equivalence (11). In fact, the effect of classes can be achieved in ObjectTalk by the following translation

$$\text{class}(\bar{x})\{\overline{M}\} \equiv \text{obj}(\ )\{new(\ ) = \text{obj}(\bar{x})\{\overline{M}\}\}$$

$$\text{new } c \equiv c.new(\ )$$

However, ClassTalk has an advantage from a software engineering perspective. There are good reasons to disallow free variables denoting objects in obj or class expressions. That way, we can treat every object as a self contained unit. In fact, in SMALLTALK-80 no object references are allowed in class descriptions. But, we do want class descriptions to refer to other classes. This is like importation of modules. The above simulation of classes in terms of objects does not allow such preferential treatment to free class references. So, even without inheritance, classes are useful.

3.3 InheritTalk

In this language, we introduce a simple form of class inheritance. A subclass of another class can be expressed by the construct:

$$e ::= \text{subclass } e_c(x_1,\ldots,x_n)\{m_1(\bar{y}_1) = e_1,\ldots,m_k(\bar{y}_k) = e_k\}$$

An instance of such a subclass would have all the variables $x_1, \ldots, x_n$ as well as the instance variables of the superclass e_c even though none of them would be visible to the users. Similarly, it would accept all the messages $m_1, \ldots, m_k$ as well as the messages specified in e_c. There is also a notion of overriding. That is, if a message is specified in both the superclass and the subclass, then the subclass method overrides that of the superclass. However, the behavior of the superclass instances are (reasonably) not modified by the subclass specification; only the instances of the subclass use the overriding methods. This is similar to the overriding caused by statically nested scopes. In fact, our semantics of inheritance in InheritTalk closely follows that of nested scopes:

$$
\begin{aligned}
&[\![\texttt{subclass}\ e_c(\bar{x})\{m_i(\bar{y}_i) = e_i\}]\!]\eta\sigma = \\
&\quad \textbf{let}\ \langle \xi_c, \sigma_1 \rangle = [\![e_c]\!]\eta\sigma \\
&\quad \textbf{in}\ \langle \lambda\sigma'.\ \textbf{let}\ \langle \rho_c, \sigma_1' \rangle = \xi_c\sigma' \\
&\qquad\qquad\quad \langle \eta_o, \sigma_2' \rangle = alloc\ \sigma_1'\bar{x} \\
&\qquad\qquad\quad \rho = fix(\lambda\rho.\ \rho_c[m_i \to \lambda\bar{w}.\ [\![e_i]\!](\eta; \eta_o[\bar{y}_i \to \bar{w}, \texttt{self} \to \rho])]) \\
&\qquad\quad\ \textbf{in}\ \langle \rho, \sigma_2' \rangle, \\
&\qquad \sigma_1 \rangle
\end{aligned}
$$

When instantiated in a state σ', the *classval* of the subclass first instantiates the *classval*, ξ, of the superclass. This yields a message environment ρ_c. The subclass then allocates storage for the additional instance variables $\bar{x}$, and constructs the message environment ρ by updating ρ_c. The essential difference between this and the semantics of the `class` construct (12) is in the use of ρ_c instead of $\rho_\perp$ in constructing ρ. The default inheritance of Simula [DN66] and C++ [Str86] work in this fashion (when virtual functions are not used).

3.4 SmallTalk

Note that, in InheritTalk, the variable `self` means different message environments in a superclass and its subclass. It can be justifiably argued that `self` should denote the message environment of the receiver object, and therefore should have the same meaning in both classes. Consider, for example, the following subclass *manpoint* (for Manhattan point) of the *point* class:

manpoint $=$ `subclass` point ( ) $\{dist(\ ) = (\texttt{valof}\ x) + (\texttt{valof}\ y)\}$

The class *manpoint* inherits *put* and *closer* messages from the *point* class, but uses a different notion of "distance from origin" (the sum of the x and y coordinates). We want to be able to compare *manpoints* using the *closer* operation inherited from the *point* class. But, such a use of the *closer* operation should use the *dist* method defined in *manpoint* rather than that defined in *point*. Note that InheritTalk does not achieve this kind of inheritance. What is inherited by *manpoint* in InheritTalk is a fixed behavior of an object as a *point*, as in (9). The recursion over `self` is already resolved in such behavior, and *closer* can only compare the Euclidean distance. Inheritance in SMALLTALK-80 does not make such early commitment to the meaning of `self`. Any instance of *manpoint* consistently uses the new method for *dist* defined in the subclass definition. Similar inheritance can be achieved in C++ using "virtual" functions. We call this form of inheritance *dynamic inheritance* (and, by contrast, the inheritance of InheritTalk *static inheritance*) since the meaning of `self` is not determined statically by the `class` expression in which at appears, but dynamically when the class is instantiated.

This form of inheritance poses an interesting semantic issue. If *manpoint* inherits the "behavior" of *closer* from the *point* class, then *closer* cannot behave differently in the instances of *point* and the instances of *manpoint*. So, what is inherited from *point* is the "behavior of *closer* parameterized by the behavior of `self`". This means that the semantic description of a `class`-expression cannot directly bind `self`. Its binding would be known only when the class is instantiated by `new`. So, the meanings of `class`-expressions would now involve transformation *functionals* of the kind

$$\tau \in menv \to menv$$

We can think of τ as accepting the *menv* of `self` as a parameter, and producing a new *menv* for `self`. Such functionals were also involved in the semantics of ClassTalk and InheritTalk; but they were immediately eliminated in favor of their fixed points.

Another semantic issue of SMALLTALK-80 that we would like to model is that the instance variables specified in a class c are visible to its subclasses. For instance, *manpoint* references the instance variables x and y specified in *point*. This means that it is not possible to hide the local environment in a class definition. These two issues motivate us to replace the subdomain *classval* of *val* by

$$\psi \in superclassval = state \to (env \times (menv \to menv) \times state)$$

The *superclassval* of a class is its meaning as seen by a subclass of it. But, to instantiate a class using `new`, we need its *classval*. The following functon *close* coerces *superclassvals* to *classvals*:

$$close \; : \; superclassval \to classval$$
$$close \; \psi = \lambda\sigma \, . \, \textbf{let} \; \langle \eta, \tau, \sigma_1 \rangle = \psi\sigma$$
$$\textbf{in} \; \langle \, fix \; \tau, \sigma_1 \rangle$$

When instantiated in a state σ, a *superclassval* produces a triple $\langle \eta, \tau, \sigma_1 \rangle$. If the instantiation is done using *new* then the environment η is ignored and the fixed point of τ is produced as the object (using the above coercion *close*). But, if the instantiation is from a subclass, then the subclass can extend η with additional variables and τ with additional messages, to produce another such triple. The following definitions state this:

$$[\![\text{class}(\bar{x})\{m_i(\bar{y}_i) = e_i\}]\!]\eta\sigma =$$
$$\langle \lambda\sigma' . \text{let } \langle \eta_o, \sigma_1' \rangle = alloc \; \sigma' \; \bar{x}$$
$$\tau = \lambda\rho . \rho_{\perp}[m_i \to \lambda\bar{w} . [\![e_i]\!](\eta; \eta_o[\bar{y}_i \to \bar{w}, \text{self} \to \rho])]$$
$$\text{in } \langle \eta_o, \tau, \sigma_1' \rangle,$$
$$\sigma \rangle$$
$$[\![\text{subclass } e_c(\bar{x})\{m_i(\bar{y}_i) = e_i\}]\!]\eta\sigma =$$
$$\text{let } \langle \psi, \sigma_1 \rangle = [\![e_c]\!]\eta\sigma$$
$$\text{in } \langle \lambda\sigma' . \text{let } \langle \eta_c, \tau_c, \sigma_1' \rangle = \psi\sigma'$$
$$\langle \eta_o, \sigma_2' \rangle = alloc \; \sigma_1' \; \bar{x}$$
$$\tau = \lambda\rho . \tau_c\rho[m_i \to \lambda\bar{w} . [\![e_i]\!](\eta; \eta_c; \eta_o[\bar{y}_i \to \bar{w}, \text{self} \to \rho])]$$
$$\text{in } \langle \eta', \tau, \sigma_2' \rangle,$$
$$\sigma_1 \rangle$$

The significant part of this semantics is the definition of τ. Given a binding ρ of self, $\tau\rho$ first finds $\tau_c\rho$ (the *menv* determined by the superclass e_c) and then extends it with new message bindings. This technical meaning of SMALLTALK-80 style inheritance was independently discovered by Cook [Coo89].

SMALLTALK-80 also has a special variable super which, appearing inside a method expression, denotes the receiver object viewed as an instance of the superclass. This can be modeled by modifying the environment used for method expressions e_i to be

$$\eta'[\bar{y}_i \to \bar{w}, \text{self} \to \rho, \text{super} \to \tau_c\rho]$$

The semantics of new is to close the *superclassval* to a *classval* and instantiate it in the current state:

$$[\![\text{new } e_c]\!]\eta\sigma = \text{let } \langle \psi, \sigma_1 \rangle = [\![e_c]\!]\eta\sigma$$
$$\text{in } close \; \psi \; \sigma_1$$

Let us use the *point* and *manpoint* classes to illustrate these semantic definitions. To make the meanings intuitive, we use an informal description. The *menv* transformation functionals (for an object with local environment η_o) are

$$\tau_{point}[\eta_o] = \lambda\rho.\,[put \to \text{set } \eta_o x \text{ and } \eta_o y, \qquad\qquad\qquad (13)$$
$$dist \to \text{Euclidean distance,}$$
$$closer \to \text{compare } \rho\ dist \text{ and argument's } dist\,]$$
$$\tau_{manpoint}[\eta_o] = \lambda\rho.\,[put \to \text{set } \eta_o x \text{ and } \eta_o y,$$
$$dist \to \text{Manhattan distance,}$$
$$closer \to \text{compare } \rho\ dist \text{ and argument's } dist\,]$$

Notice that only the binding of *dist* is changed. When we *close* the *superclassvals* for instantiation, we get the respective *menvs* as fixed points.

$$\rho_{point}[\eta_o] = [put \to \text{set } \eta_o x \text{ and } \eta_o y, \qquad\qquad\qquad (14)$$
$$dist \to \text{Euclidean distance,}$$
$$closer \to \text{compare Euclidean distance and argument's } dist\,]$$
$$\rho_{manpoint}[\eta_o] = [put \to \text{set } \eta_o x \text{ and } \eta_o y,$$
$$dist \to \text{Manhattan distance,}$$
$$closer \to \text{compare Manhattan distance and argument's } dist\,]$$

This illustrates that SMALLTALK-80 style inheritance occurs at the *superclassval* level rather than at the *classval* level. This fact can be used for reasoning about object oriented programs as follows. When a class (or a subclass) is defined, we cannot make any assumptions about the behavior of `self` except that it looks something like the *menv* being defined. When a class is instantiated, the instance object fixes the meaning of `self` and its behavior becomes determined. Another way to think about programs is by giving two meanings to each class, in terms of *superclassvals* and *classvals*. The *superclassval* meaning is as just mentioned. The *classval* meaning assumes that `self` has the same behavior as the *menv* being defined. In this view, we have to remember that what is inherited is the *superclassval* and what is instantiated is the *classval*.

The fixed point involved in the above semantic definition merely models the recursion involved in references to `self`. There may be other kinds of recursion involved in a program, *e.g.*, recursive references to classes in creating instance variables.

4 Data Structure Semantics

As discussed in the introduction, Kamin [Kam88] gave a different framework for describing the denotational semantics of SMALLTALK-80. The essential difference is that, in that framework, each object contains an explicit value environment. This corresponds to the notion of *data structure* mentioned in Section 2. Accordingly, rather than methods seeing `self` as a variable bound at object-creation time, they receive it as an argument each time they are applied. In this section, we develop the semantics of our four languages using the data structure model. Again, for quick reference, we list the semantic domains involved in this development.

$v \in val = basicval + loc + objectval + classval$

$o \in objectval = env \times menv$

$\rho \in menv = message \to method$

$\mu \in method = objectval \to val^* \to state \to (val \times state)$

$\langle \phi, \rho \rangle \in classval = (state \to env \times state) \times menv$

4.1   ObjectTalk

Again, objects are no longer simply message environments, but also include a value environment for the bindings of instance variables.

$$\llbracket \text{obj}(\bar{x})\{m_i(\bar{y}_i) = e_i\} \rrbracket \eta \sigma = \textbf{let } \langle \eta_o, \sigma_1 \rangle = alloc\ \sigma\ \bar{x}$$
$$\rho_o = \llbracket \{m_i(\bar{y}_i) = e_i\} \rrbracket \eta$$
$$\textbf{in } \langle \langle \eta_o, \rho_o \rangle, \sigma_1 \rangle$$
$$\llbracket \{m_i(\bar{y}_i) = e_i\} \rrbracket \eta = [m_i \to \lambda \langle \eta_o, \rho_o \rangle. \lambda \bar{v}. \llbracket e_i \rrbracket (\eta; \eta_o[\text{self} \to \langle \eta_o, \rho_o \rangle, \bar{y}_i \to \bar{v}])]$$

Each method takes an additional implicit argument, $\langle \eta_o, \rho_o \rangle$, representing `self`. Whenever a message is sent, its receiver is passed as an additional argument:

$$\llbracket e_0.m(\bar{e}) \rrbracket \eta \sigma = \textbf{let } \langle \langle \eta_o, \rho_o \rangle, \sigma_1 \rangle = \llbracket e_0 \rrbracket \eta \sigma$$
$$\langle \bar{v}, \sigma_2 \rangle = \llbracket \bar{e} \rrbracket \eta \sigma_1$$
$$\textbf{in } \rho_o(m)\langle \eta_o, \rho_o \rangle \bar{v} \sigma_2$$

As an example, consider again the definition of a point object:

$$p = \text{obj}\ (x, y)\{put(a, b) = \textbf{begin } x := a; y := b \textbf{ end},$$
$$dist(\ ) = sqrt(sqr(\text{valof } x) + sqr(\text{valof } y)),$$
$$closer(q) = \text{self}.dist(\ ) < q.dist(\ )\}$$

Suppose α_x and α_y are the two locations that are allocated in the current state for the variables x and y when this expression is evaluated. It will produce the following object:

$$\langle [x \to \alpha_x, y \to \alpha_y], \tag{15}$$
$$[put \to \lambda \langle \eta_r, \rho_r \rangle . \lambda \langle v_a, v_b \rangle . \lambda \sigma . \langle v_b, \sigma[\eta_r(x) \to v_a, \eta_r(y) \to v_b] \rangle,$$
$$dist \to \lambda \langle \eta_r, \rho_r \rangle . \lambda \langle \rangle . \lambda \sigma . \langle \sqrt{\sigma(\eta_r(x))^2 + \sigma(\eta_r(y))^2}, \sigma \rangle,$$
$$closer \to \lambda \langle \eta_r, \rho_r \rangle . \lambda \langle \langle \eta_a, \rho_a \rangle \rangle . \lambda \sigma.$$
$$\textbf{let } \langle v_1, \sigma_1 \rangle = \rho_r \ dist \ \langle \eta_r, \rho_r \rangle \langle \rangle \sigma$$
$$\langle v_2, \sigma_2 \rangle = \rho_a \ dist \ \langle \eta_a, \rho_a \rangle \langle \rangle \sigma_1$$
$$\textbf{in } \langle v_1 < v_2, \sigma_2 \rangle]$$

What most clearly distinguishes this object from the one in section 3.1 is that the locations α_x and α_y do not appear in any of the methods, and the definition of *dist* is not used in the semantics of *closer*. The meanings of the methods in an object are independent of that object. In this sense, these methods are far more general than necessary, since they are equipped with the ability to be applied to any object, when in reality they will always be applied to the object in which they are contained (as can be seen in the semantics of message sends). On the other hand, this flexibility turns out to be useful for the semantics of inheritance.

4.2 ClassTalk

As in the closure model, ClassTalk does not require major changes in the semantics. As in Objecttalk, but in contrast to [Kam88], we keep the method environment defined by the class in each object. Note that the meanings of methods are not dependent on the state:

$$(\phi, \rho) \in classval = (state \to env \times state) \times menv$$

$$[\![class(\bar{x})\{m_i(\bar{y}_i) = e_i\}]\!]\eta\sigma = \langle \langle \lambda\sigma . alloc \ \sigma \ \bar{x}, [\![\{m_i(\bar{y}_i) = e_i\}]\!]\eta \rangle, \sigma \rangle$$

$$[\![new \ e]\!]\eta\sigma = \textbf{let } \langle \langle \phi, \rho \rangle, \sigma_1 \rangle = [\![e]\!]\eta\sigma$$
$$\langle \eta_1, \sigma_2 \rangle = \phi(\sigma_1)$$
$$\textbf{in } \langle \langle \eta_1, \rho \rangle, \sigma_2 \rangle$$

A *classval* has two components: an allocator for instance variables and a message environment. The former is used for each creation of an instance and the latter is directly shared by all instances.

In [Kam88], objects contained class *names*, which indirectly referred to message environments (via a separate global environment). In this reformulation, we eliminate the indirect reference and directly model *classvals* to contain the message environments.

4.3 SmallTalk

The straightforward form of inheritance in the data structure model immediately gives SMALLTALK-80 style inheritance. So, we present the semantics of SmallTalk first and postpone its adaptation to InheritTalk to the following section.

Unlike the closure semantics, the data structure model does not use a fixed point to bind self. Hence, there is no need to define a separate *superclassval* which contains functionals. To put this differently, any method is perfectly able to be sent to any object—it does not "assume" it will be sent only to an object of its own class (recall the flexibility mentioned in Section 4.1). Thus, a class inherits a method simply by copying it:

$$
\begin{aligned}
[\![\text{subclass } e_c(\bar{x})\{m_i(\bar{y}_i) = e_i\}]\!]\eta\sigma = {}& \textbf{let } \langle\langle\phi_c, \rho_c\rangle, \sigma'\rangle = [\![e_c]\!]\eta\sigma \\
& \phi_o = \lambda\sigma.\, \textbf{let } \langle\eta_1, \sigma_1\rangle = \phi_c\sigma \\
& \qquad\qquad\quad \langle\eta_2, \sigma_2\rangle = alloc\; \sigma_1\bar{x} \\
& \qquad\quad \textbf{in } \langle\eta_1; \eta_2, \sigma_2\rangle \\
& \rho_o = \rho_c;\, [\![\{m_i(\bar{y}_i) = e_i\}]\!]\eta \\
& \textbf{in } \langle\langle\phi_o, \rho_o\rangle, \sigma'\rangle
\end{aligned}
\tag{16}
$$

The allocator of the subclass extends the allocator of the superclass to account for the extra variables and the message environment of the subclass is a mere extension of that of the superclass.

It hardly seems worth repeating the *point/manpoint* example here. The only difference between *point* objects, as in (15), and *manpoint* objects is that, in the message environment of the latter, *dist* is bound to the Manhattan distance. The functions bound to *closer* are identical in both the classes. This contrasts with the closure semantics (14), where the different bindings of *dist* entail different bindings for *closer*. However, whenever a *closer* message is sent to an instance of *manpoint*, the desired behavior is still obtained because the method uses the binding of *dist* contained in the instance. Thus, *classvals* in the data structure semantics resemble the *superclassvals* of the closure semantics.

Finally, let us consider how to define "super" in this model. Even though the syntax of message send treats super as if it were an object, it is not really an object in the usual sense. For, suppose it denoted an object $o = \langle\eta_s, \rho_s\rangle$. Then, the semantics of the message send super.$m(\bar{e})$ would be to invoke $\rho_s(m)$, passing o as the self argument. But here's the dilemma: the message m should be "sent" to self, i.e., self should be passed as the implicit self argument to $\rho_s(m)$. Giving the name super as the receiver really only indicates where to start the method search, not who the receiver is. So, super really denotes a message environment—a particular view of self—rather than a real object. We need to define a special kind of message send to such views of self (note that super is being overloaded as both a "reserved word" and as a variable):

$$[\![\texttt{super}.m(\bar{e})]\!]\eta\sigma = \textbf{let } \rho_s = \eta(\texttt{super})$$
$$o = \eta(\texttt{self})$$
$$\langle \bar{v}, \sigma_1 \rangle = [\![\bar{e}]\!]\eta\sigma$$
$$\textbf{in } \rho_s(m)o\bar{v}\sigma_1$$

The variable super needs to be bound in the environment at the point of m's definition. To do this, modify the semantics of subclass expressions (16) so that methods have the variable super bound in their static environments, by letting the *menv* of the class value be:

$$\rho_c; [\![\{m_i(\bar{y}_i) = e_i\}]\!]\eta[\texttt{super} \to \rho_c]$$

Interestingly, this special treatment of super is not involved in the closure semantics because objects in that semantics are precisely message environments.

4.4 Inherittalk

The crucial property of Inherittalk is that when a method m defined in a class C is applied to an object o, m effectively *assumes* that o is an instance of class C and not of a subclass. Indeed, if o is an object of a subclass, as soon as it becomes the receiver of m it loses all ability to receive messages of its own class. This is because all message sends in C's methods are statically bound; it follows that they can only send messages defined either in C or in a superclass of C. Similarly, any instance variables of o that were declared in o's class cannot be accessed by m or by any method called by m with o as receiver.

Thus, inheritance can be treated by a very simple mechanism: whenever an inherited method is invoked, the receiver object is coerced up to the class in which the method is defined.

$$[\![\texttt{subclass } e_c(\bar{x})\{m_i(\bar{y}_i) = e_i\}]\!]\eta\sigma =$$
$$\textbf{let } \langle \langle \phi_c, \rho_c \rangle, \sigma' \rangle = [\![e]\!]\eta\sigma$$
$$\phi_o = \lambda\sigma . \textbf{let } \langle \eta_1, \sigma_1 \rangle = \phi_c\sigma$$
$$\langle \eta_2, \sigma_2 \rangle = alloc\ \sigma_1\bar{x}$$
$$\textbf{in } \langle \eta_1; \eta_2, \sigma_2 \rangle$$
$$\rho_o = (\lambda m . \lambda o . \rho(m)(coerce\ \bar{x}\rho_c o)); [\![\{m_i(\bar{y}_i) = e_i\}]\!]\eta$$
$$\textbf{in } \langle \langle \phi_o, \rho_o \rangle, \sigma' \rangle$$

where (*coerce* $\bar{x}\rho$) modifies an *objectval* up to its superclass:

$$coerce\ \bar{x}\rho_c : objectval \to objectval$$
$$: \langle \eta, \rho \rangle \mapsto \langle \eta - \bar{x}, \rho_c \rangle$$

5 Relationship between the Semantic Models

The most obvious relationship between these two models is that they give the same results (if one were an operational semantics and the other denotational, this would be called *adequacy* [Gun92]). This is proven in section 6.

A deeper relationship is that, as observed in [Red88] and [CP93], the closure model is more abstract than the data structure model. Unfortunately, we do not yet have a formal proof of this, but we have good reasons to believe it is so, and in the rest of this section we present those reasons.

There are two ways in which the closure model (which we refer to as the $\mathscr{C}$-model in this section) is more abstract than the data structure model (the $\mathscr{D}$-model). The more obvious one is that, by including an explicit value environment in each object, the $\mathscr{D}$-model fails to abstract away from instance variable names. The less obvious is that the two models rely on different models of recursion: an explicit fixed point in the $\mathscr{C}$-model vs. self-application in the $\mathscr{D}$-model. The use of self-applicaton essentially entails that $\mathscr{D}$-objects contain functionals, while the $\mathscr{C}$-objects contain their fixed points. Since there are "more" functionals than fixed points, there are more $\mathscr{D}$-objects than $\mathscr{C}$-objects. In this section, we explain how these two models of recursion are employed.

First, let us briefly examine the first source of non-abstractness in $\mathscr{D}$, the presence of value environments in objects. It is easy to see that a kind of α-equivalence applies to object definitions in $\mathscr{C}$:

$$\mathscr{C}[\![\texttt{obj}(\bar{x})\{m_i(\bar{y}_i) = e_i\}]\!] \equiv \mathscr{C}[\![\texttt{obj}(\bar{z})\{m_i(\bar{y}_i) = e_i[\bar{z}/\bar{x}]\}]\!]$$

as long as the usual name conflicts are avoided. This equivalence fails to hold in $\mathscr{D}$. The semantics of obj-expressions exports the value environment to the outside and then receives it back as part of the receiver arguments of methods. Thus, even though renaming is not observationally distinguishable, the equivalence is not present in the semantic values themselves.

On the other hand, this rule does not extend to class or subclass expressions in SmallTalk. Since a subclass sees the instance variables of its superclass, those variables are part of the superclass's meaning.

We can now focus on the other source of non-abstractness in the $\mathscr{D}$-model: it and the $\mathscr{C}$-model are based on distinct models of recursion. The former uses self-application familiar from (untyped) lambda calculus while the latter uses explicit fixed points.

To get to the heart of the matter, we use a functional version of ObjectTalk (i.e., without states or locations). We also assume that objects have no instance variables and that all messages take a single argument. Further, we represent message environments as tuples of methods rather than as maps from message names to methods. All these simplifications, except for the one regarding states, are essentially benign. Since the functional ObjectTalk has all the expressive power of untyped lambda calculus, the other features can be defined within the simplfied language. The semantic domains for the language are

$$val_C = basicval + objectval_C \tag{17}$$

$$objectval_C = [val_C \rightarrow val_C]^*$$

$$val_D = basicval + objectval_D$$

$$objectval_D = [objectval_D \rightarrow val_D \rightarrow val_D]^*$$

The semantic functions for object definitions and message sends are as follows

$$\mathscr{C}[\![\text{obj}(\ )\{m_i(x) = e_i\}_{i=1,n}]\!]\eta = fix\,(\lambda\rho\,.\,\langle\lambda v\,.\,\mathscr{C}[\![e_i]\!]\eta[\text{self} \rightarrow \rho, x \rightarrow v]\rangle_{i=1,n})$$

$$\mathscr{C}[\![e_0\,.\,m_i(e_1)]\!]\eta = (\mathscr{C}[\![e_0]\!]\eta)_i(\mathscr{C}[\![e_1]\!]\eta)$$

$$\mathscr{D}[\![\text{obj}(\ )\{m_i(x) = e_i\}_{i=1,n}]\!]\eta = \langle\lambda\rho\,.\,\lambda v\,.\,\mathscr{D}[\![e_i]\!]\eta[\text{self} \rightarrow \rho, x \rightarrow v]\rangle_{i=1,n}$$

$$\mathscr{D}[\![e_0\,.\,m_i(e_1)]\!]\eta = (\mathscr{D}[\![e_0]\!]\eta)_i(\mathscr{D}[\![e_0]\!]\eta)(\mathscr{D}[\![e_1]\!]\eta)$$

Now, consider an object with a single message m:

$$E \equiv \text{obj}(\ )\{m(x) = e\}$$

Assume that all the uses of self in e are message sends of the form self.$m(e')$. The $\mathscr{C}$-semantics of such an object is of the form $fix\ t_c$ where t_c is a functional of type $[val_C \rightarrow val_C] \rightarrow [val_C \rightarrow val_C]$. The $\mathscr{D}$-semantics of the object is a function t_d of type $[objectval_D \rightarrow val_D \rightarrow val_D] \rightarrow [val_D \rightarrow val_D]$. The meaning of each message send to self is of the form $\rho\rho v$ where ρ is the argument of t_d. So, there is a function t_d': $[val_D \rightarrow val_D] \rightarrow [val_D \rightarrow val_D]$ such that

$$t_d'(\rho\rho) = t_d(\rho)$$

The meaning of the object in the two semantics is

$$o_c = fix\ t_c$$

$$o_d = \lambda\rho . t'_d(\rho\rho)$$

Modulo the fact that the two semantics work in different domains, t_c and t'_d are essentially equivalent. They both express the meaning of e as a function of what can be written as `self.m` and the formal parameter x. ("`self.m`" is the $[val \rightarrow val]$ function obtained by invoking the message. It is simply ρ in the $\mathscr{C}$-semantics, and $\rho\rho$ in the $\mathscr{D}$-semantics). Finally, consider a use of the object, such as

$$E.m(e')$$

The function denoted by $E.m$ in the $\mathscr{C}$-semantics is $o_c = fix\ t_c$, and the function denoted in the $\mathscr{D}$-semantics is

$$o_d o_d = (\lambda\rho . t'_d(\rho\rho))(\lambda\rho . t'_d(\rho\rho))$$

The latter is $\mathbf{Y}t'_d$ for the familiar $\mathbf{Y}$ combinator of lambda calculus which is equivalent to the fixed point operator [Par70, Wad76]. Thus, both the closure semantics and the data structure semantics express the same meaning by different means.

In Fig. 1 these ideas are illustrated for three examples: the simple case just described of an object with one message; an object with two messages; and an object that inherits a method.[4] In each case, it may be verified that the functions denoting the messages have the same infinite expansions.

Closure semantics	Data abstraction semantics
An object with a single message:	
let $m = fix\ t$ **in**...m...	**let** $m' = \lambda s . t'(ss)$ **in**...$(m'm')$...
An object with two messages:	
let $\langle m_1, m_2 \rangle = fix\ (t_1 \times t_2)$ **in**...m_1...	**let** $\langle m'_1, m'_2 \rangle = \langle \lambda\langle x_1, x_2\rangle . t'_1([x_1, x_2]\langle x_1, x_2\rangle),$ $\lambda\langle x_1, x_2\rangle . t'_2([x_1, x_2]\langle x_1, x_2\rangle)$ **in**...$(m'_1\langle m'_1, m'_2\rangle)$...
An object inheriting a method from another:	
let $\langle m_{11}, m_{12} \rangle = fix\ (t_1 \times t_{12})$ $\langle m_{21}, m_{22} \rangle = fix\ (t_1 \times t_{22})$ **in**...m_{21}...	**let** $\langle m'_{11}, m'_{12} \rangle = \langle \lambda\langle x_1, x_2\rangle . t'_1([x_1, x_2]\langle x_1, x_2\rangle),$ $\lambda\langle x_1, x_2\rangle . t'_{12}([x_1, x_2]\langle x_1, x_2\rangle)\rangle,$ $\langle m'_{21}, m'_{22} \rangle = \langle m'_{11},$ $\lambda\langle x_1, x_2\rangle . t'_{22}([x_1, x_2]\langle x_1, x_2\rangle)\rangle$ **in**...$(m'_{21}\langle m'_{21}, m'_{22}\rangle)$...

Figure 1
Interpretations of simple example objects

Having seen how the two models of recursion are employed, it is clear how the $\mathscr{C}$-model is the more abstract: there is, roughly speaking, a function from $\mathscr{D}$-meanings of objects to their $\mathscr{C}$-meanings, namely $(\mathscr{D} \to \mathscr{C})(o_d) = o_d o_d$. The discussion above also is a preview of the proof of equivalence of the two semantics. As mentioned before, the simplifications made to the syntax are benign and they can be easily removed while retaining the spirit of the proof. However, the assumption about the restricted use of self (all the uses of self in a method are message sends) is a serious restriction. In the next section, we formally prove that the two semantics give the same computed results for all expressions.

6 Equivalence

In this section, we formally prove that the data structure semantics and the closure semantics are equivalent for functional ObjectTalk. For this theoretical study, we use a simplified version of ObjectTalk where objects have no instance variables and support a single message. This language is defined by the abstract syntax:

$$e ::= x \mid k \mid \text{obj}\{\lambda x . e'\} \mid e_0(e_1)$$

where x ranges over variables, k over constants, obj-expressions define objects with a single message $\lambda x . e'$, and $e_0(e_1)$ denotes the invocation of the unique message of e_0 with the argument e_1.

The domain of the closure semantics is[5]

$$C = B + [C \to C]$$

An object here is denoted by a function for its unique message. For simplicity, we assume that all constants denote atomic values and there is a function *Const* mapping constant symbols to their denotations in B. The semantics of the constructs is specified by:

$$\mathscr{C}[\![x]\!]\eta = \eta x$$

$$\mathscr{C}[\![k]\!]\eta = Const(k)$$

$$\mathscr{C}[\![\text{obj}\{\lambda x . e'\}]\!]\eta = fix\,(\lambda o . \lambda v . \mathscr{C}[\![e']\!]\eta[\text{self} \to o, x \to v])$$

$$\mathscr{C}[\![e_0(e_1)]\!]\eta = \begin{cases} \bot, & \text{if } \mathscr{C}[\![e_0]\!]\eta \text{ is } \bot \text{ or is in } B \\ \mathscr{C}[\![e_0]\!]\eta\,\mathscr{C}[\![e_1]\!]\eta, & \text{otherwise} \end{cases}$$

Note that the meaning of obj-expressions involves the fixed point operator and message send is simply function application.

The domain of the data structure semantics is simply

$$D = B + [D \to D \to D]$$

Objects here represent functions of two arguments, one for `self` and the second for the explicit argument. (The domain is slightly larger than in (17) in that the first argument is not restricted to $objectval_D$). The semantics of the language is then specified as

$$\mathscr{D}[\![x]\!]\eta = \eta x$$

$$\mathscr{D}[\![k]\!]\eta = Const(k)$$

$$\mathscr{D}[\![\mathtt{obj}\{\lambda x. e'\}]\!]\eta = \lambda o. \lambda v. \mathscr{D}[\![e']\!]\eta[\mathtt{self} \to o, x \to v]$$

$$\mathscr{D}[\![e_0(e_1)]\!]\eta = \begin{cases} \bot, & \text{if } \mathscr{D}[\![e_0]\!]\eta \text{ is } \bot \text{ or is in } B \\ \mathscr{D}[\![e_0]\!]\eta \bullet \mathscr{D}[\![e_1]\!]\eta, & \text{otherwise} \end{cases}$$

The binary operator $\bullet$ corresponding to message send is defined by $f \bullet x = ffx$. Note that it involves a self-application of the object.

The most direct way to establish a relationship between the two semantics would be to exhibit a relation θ between D and C which is respected by the two semantics. The relation should be the identity on B and two objects must be related if, given θ-related arguments, they return θ-related results, i.e., $\theta(o_d, o_c)$ iff, for all v_d and v_c, $\theta(v_d, v_c) \Rightarrow \theta(o_d o_d v_d, o_c v_c)$. Unfortunately, such a relation does not seem to exist because of the self-application o_d. The standard techniques for establishing such relations [Mil74, MS76, Rey74] fail. Therefore, we follow a circuitous approach and show that each semantics approximates the other. The next two subsections are devote to this problem.

6.1   Data Structure Semantics Approximates Closure Semantics

Since the data structure semantics models message send by self-application, the equivalence proof mirrors the inverse limit construction for the domain D. Specifically, the domain is the inverse limit D_∞ of the sequence $D_0 \leftrightarrows D_1 \leftrightarrows D_2 \leftrightarrows \cdots$ where $D_0 = \{\bot\}$ and each D_i is a retraction of D_{i+1} as determined by the functor

$$T(D) = B + [D \to D \to D]$$

The details of the construction may be found in the Appendix. For the present purpose, it is adequate to note that each D_i has an isomorphic image in D_∞ and there is a retraction P_i from D_∞ to this image. The objects in D_i (and, hence, those in the isomorphic image of D_i in D_∞) are able to perform message sends at most $i - 1$ levels deep, either to themselves or to other objects.

To model this state of affairs, we extend the language as follows:

$$e ::= x \mid k \mid \mathtt{obj}\{\lambda x . e'\} \mid e_0(e_1) \mid \mathtt{obj}^i\{\lambda x . e'\}$$

The interpretation of the new expressions is

$$\mathscr{D}[\![\mathtt{obj}^i\{\lambda x . e'\}]\!]\eta = P_i(\mathscr{D}[\![\mathtt{obj}\{\lambda x . e'\}]\!]\eta)$$

$$\mathscr{C}[\![\mathtt{obj}^i\{\lambda x . e'\}]\!]\eta = \mathscr{C}[\![\mathtt{obj}\{\lambda x . e'\}]\!]\eta$$

That is, in the data structure semantics, the labeled expressions denote approximate objects but, in the closure semantics, the labels have no effect. An expression in which all $\mathtt{obj}$-expressions have labels is called an *approximate expression*.

LEMMA 1 $\mathscr{D}[\![\mathtt{obj}\{\lambda x . e'\}]\!] = \bigsqcup_i \mathscr{D}[\![\mathtt{obj}^i\{\lambda x . e'\}]\!]$

That is, every expression in the original language is expressible as the lub of approximate expressions in the extended language. The proof uses the fact that $\bigsqcup_i P_i = id$.

We would like to prove that the meanings assigned by the data structure semantics are "smaller" than those assigned by the closure semantics. However, this cannot be simply stated as $\mathscr{D}[\![e]\!]\eta \sqsubseteq \mathscr{C}[\![e]\!]\eta$ because, for higher-order values, the two meanings do not even have the same type. So, we should be satisfied if all the observable atomic values obtained in the data structure semantics are smaller than the corresponding atomic values obtained in the closure semantics. The following is the most natural requirement:

THEOREM 2   For every $c \in C$, there exists a relation over D denoted by $d \lesssim c$ such that $d \lesssim c$ if and only if

1. $d = \bot$,
2. $d \in B$, $c \in B$, and $d \sqsubseteq c$, or
3. $d \in [D \to D \to D]$, $c \in [C \to C]$, and, for all d' and c', $d' \lesssim c' \Rightarrow d \bullet d' \lesssim cc'$.

The existence of such a relation is established using the standard techniques [Mil74, MS76, MP87, Rey74]. See Appendix for the technical details. It may also be verified by induction on n that:

LEMMA 3   For $d \in D$ and $c \in C$, $d \lesssim c$ if and only if, whenever $d_1 \lesssim c_1, \ldots d_n \lesssim c_n$ (for $n \geq 0$), $d \bullet d_1 \bullet \cdots \bullet d_n \in B \Rightarrow d \bullet d_1 \bullet \cdots \bullet d_n \sqsubseteq cc_1 \ldots c_n$.

The advantage of this restatement of $\lesssim$ is that it does not have recursive references to $\lesssim$ in the consequent. Now, we are able to present the main result of this section:

THEOREM 4   If η_d and η_c are environments such that $\eta_d x \lesssim \eta_c x$ for all x, then $\mathscr{D}[\![e]\!]\eta_d \lesssim \mathscr{C}[\![e]\!]\eta_c$ for all expressions e.

Proof   We first prove the statement for *approximate* expressions in the extended language (i.e., all obj-expressions have integer labels). The proof is by structural induction on expressions and the integer labels on the obj-expressions.

- $e = x_i$. The result follows from the assumption on η_d and η_c.

- $e = k$. The result is trivial because both the semantics assign the meaning $Const(k)$.

- $e = e_0(e_1)$. By inductive hypothesis, $\mathscr{D}[\![e_0]\!]\eta_d \lesssim \mathscr{C}[\![e_0]\!]\eta_c$. If the former is $\bot$ or is in B, $\mathscr{D}[\![e_0(e_1)]\!]\eta_d = \bot$ and the result is trivial. Assume it is in $[D \to D \to D]$. Then, by definition of $\lesssim$, $\mathscr{C}[\![e_0]\!]\eta_c$ is also in $[C \to C]$ and, whenever $d' \lesssim c'$, $\mathscr{D}[\![e_0]\!]\eta_d \bullet d' \lesssim \mathscr{C}[\![e_0]\!]\eta_c c'$. So, using the inductive hypothesis for e_1,

$$\mathscr{D}[\![e_0]\!]\eta_d \bullet \mathscr{D}[\![e_1]\!]\eta_d \lesssim \mathscr{C}[\![e_0]\!]\eta_c \mathscr{C}[\![e_1]\!]\eta_c$$

- $e = \mathtt{obj}^0\{\lambda x.e'\}$. $\mathscr{D}[\![e]\!]\eta_d = P_0(\mathscr{D}[\![\mathtt{obj}\{\lambda x.e'\}]\!]) = \bot \lesssim \mathscr{C}[\![e]\!]\eta_c$.

- $e = \mathtt{obj}^i\{\lambda x.e'\}$ and $i > 0$. To show that $\mathscr{D}[\![e]\!]\eta_d \lesssim \mathscr{C}[\![e]\!]\eta_c$ we use Lemma 3. Assume that $d_1 \lesssim c_1, \ldots, d_n \lesssim c_n$ and $\mathscr{D}[\![e]\!]\eta_d \bullet d_1 \bullet \cdots \bullet d_n \in B$. The objective is to show that $\mathscr{D}[\![e]\!]\eta_d \bullet d_1 \bullet \cdots \bullet d_n \sqsubseteq \mathscr{C}[\![e]\!]\eta_c c_1 \ldots c_n$. If $n = 0$, $\mathscr{D}[\![e]\!]\eta_d \notin B$, contradicting the assumption. Assume that $n > 0$. First, calculate

$$\mathscr{D}[\![e]\!]\eta_d = P_i(\mathscr{D}[\![\mathtt{obj}\{\lambda x.e'\}]\!]\eta_d)$$

$$= P_i(\lambda o.\lambda v.\mathscr{D}[\![e']\!]\eta_d[\mathtt{self} \to o, x \to v])$$

$$= \lambda o.\lambda v.P_{i-1}(\mathscr{D}[\![e']\!]\eta_d[\mathtt{self} \to P_{i-1}(o), x \to P_{i-1}(v)])$$

Next, notice that

$$P_{i-1}(\mathscr{D}[\![e]\!]\eta_d) = P_{i-1}(P_i(\mathscr{D}[\![\mathtt{obj}\{\lambda x.e'\}]\!]\eta_d)) = P_{i-1}(\mathscr{D}[\![\mathtt{obj}\{\lambda x.e'\}]\!]\eta_d)$$

$$= \mathscr{D}[\![\mathtt{obj}^{i-1}\{\lambda x.e'\}]\!]\eta_d$$

So,

$$\mathscr{D}[\![e]\!]\eta_d \bullet d_1 \bullet \cdots \bullet d_n$$

$$= (\lambda o.\lambda v.P_{i-1}(\mathscr{D}[\![e']\!]\eta_d[\mathtt{self} \to P_{i-1}(o), x \to P_{i-1}(v)])) \bullet d_1 \bullet \cdots \bullet d_n$$

$$= P_{i-1}(\mathscr{D}[\![e']\!]\eta_d[\mathtt{self} \to P_{i-1}(\mathscr{D}[\![e]\!]\eta_d), x \to P_{i-1}(d_1)] \bullet d_2 \bullet \cdots \bullet d_n$$

$$\sqsubseteq \mathscr{D}[\![e']\!]\eta_d[\mathtt{self} \to \mathscr{D}[\![\mathtt{obj}^{i-1}\{\lambda x.e'\}]\!]\eta_d, x \to d_1] \bullet d_2 \bullet \cdots \bullet d_n$$

Similarly,

$$\mathscr{C}[\![e]\!]\eta_c c_1 \ldots c_n = \mathit{fix}\,(\lambda o.\,\lambda v.\,\mathscr{C}[\![e']\!]\eta_c[\texttt{self} \rightarrow o, x \rightarrow v])c_1 \ldots c_n$$

$$= \lambda v.\,\mathscr{C}[\![e']\!]\eta_c[\texttt{self} \rightarrow \mathscr{C}[\![e]\!]\eta_c, x \rightarrow v]c_1 \ldots c_n$$

$$= \mathscr{C}[\![e']\!]\eta_c[\texttt{self} \rightarrow \mathscr{C}[\![e]\!]\eta_c, x \rightarrow c_1]c_2 \ldots c_n$$

Now, by inductive hypothesis (for the smaller label $i - 1$),

$$\mathscr{D}[\![\texttt{obj}^{i-1}\{\lambda x.\,e'\}]\!]\eta_d \precsim \mathscr{C}[\![\texttt{obj}^{i-1}\{\lambda x.\,e'\}]\!]\eta_c = \mathscr{C}[\![e]\!]\eta_c$$

Since $d_1 \precsim c_1$ by assumption, the inductive hypothesis applied to e' gives

$$\mathscr{D}[\![e']\!]\eta_d[\texttt{self} \rightarrow \mathscr{D}[\![\texttt{obj}^{i-1}\{\lambda x.\,e'\}]\!]\eta_d, x \rightarrow d_1] \precsim \mathscr{C}[\![e']\!]\eta_c[\texttt{self} \rightarrow \mathscr{C}[\![e]\!]\eta_c, x \rightarrow c_1]$$

Hence, by Lemma 3,

$$\mathscr{D}[\![e']\!]\eta_d[\texttt{self} \rightarrow \mathscr{D}[\![\texttt{obj}^{i-1}\{\lambda x.\,e'\}]\!]\eta_d, x \rightarrow d_1] \bullet d_2 \bullet \cdots \bullet d_n$$

$$\sqsubseteq \mathscr{C}[\![e']\!]\eta_c[\texttt{self} \rightarrow \mathscr{C}[\![e]\!]\eta_c, x \rightarrow c_1]c_2 \ldots c_n$$

Thus,

$$\mathscr{D}[\![e]\!]\eta_d \bullet d_1 \bullet \cdots d_n \sqsubseteq \mathscr{C}[\![e]\!]\eta_c c_1 \ldots c_n$$

This shows the result for all the approximate expressions.

Next, consider the full extended language. The only interesting case is $e = \texttt{obj}\{\lambda x.\,e'\}$. (The other cases are similar to the above treatment). We again use Lemma 3 and assume that $d_i \precsim c_i$ for $i = 1,\ldots,n$, and $\mathscr{D}[\![e]\!]\eta_d \bullet d_1 \bullet \cdots \bullet d_n \in B$. By Lemma 1, $\mathscr{D}[\![e]\!]\eta_d$ is equal to $\bigsqcup_i \mathscr{D}[\![\texttt{obj}^i\{\lambda x.\,e'\}]\!]\eta_d$, and, since $\bullet$ is continuous,

$$\mathscr{D}[\![e]\!]\eta_d \bullet d_1 \bullet \cdots \bullet d_n = \bigsqcup_i (\mathscr{D}[\![\texttt{obj}^i\{\lambda x.\,e'\}]\!]\eta_d \bullet d_1 \bullet \cdots \bullet d_n)$$

Use the same reasoning as above to conclude that

$$\mathscr{D}[\![\texttt{obj}^i\{\lambda x.\,e'\}]\!]\eta_d \bullet d_1 \bullet \cdots \bullet d_n \sqsubseteq \mathscr{C}[\![\texttt{obj}\{\lambda x.\,e'\}]\!]\eta_c c_1 \ldots c_n$$

and the lub of the LHS's is smaller than the right hand side.

Since the result holds for the extended language, it must hold for the subset representing the original language as well. ∎

6.2 Closure Semantics Approximates Data Structure Semantics

This proof follows the same line of argument as the previous one. It is slightly simpler because there is no self-application involved in message send.

THEOREM 5 For every $d \in D$, there exists an inclusive relation over C denoted by $c \lesssim d$ such that $c \lesssim d$ if and only if

1. $c = \bot$,

2. $c \in B$, $d \in B$ and $c \sqsubseteq d$,

3. $c \in [C \rightarrow C]$, $d \in [D \rightarrow D \rightarrow D]$ and, for all c' and d', $c' \lesssim d' \Rightarrow cc' \lesssim d \bullet d'$.

This relation is constructed by induction on C_∞ construction. We also have:

LEMMA 6 For $c \in C$ and $d \in D$, $c \lesssim d$ if and only if, whenever $c_1 \lesssim d_1, \ldots, c_n \lesssim d_n$ (for $n \geq 0$), $cc_1 \ldots c_n \in B \Rightarrow cc_1 \ldots c_n \sqsubseteq d \bullet d_1 \bullet \cdots \bullet d_n$.

THEOREM 7 If η_c, η_d are environments such that $\eta_c x \lesssim \eta_d x$ for all x, then $\mathscr{C}[\![e]\!]\eta_c \lesssim \mathscr{D}[\![e]\!]\eta_d$ for all expressions e.

Proof The proof is by structural induction on expressions.

- $e = x$. Follows by assumption on η_c and η_d.

- $e = k$. Both the semantics assign $Const(k)$.

- $e = e_0(e_1)$. By inductive hypothesis, $\mathscr{C}[\![e_0]\!]\eta_c \lesssim \mathscr{D}[\![e_0]\!]\eta_d$. If $\mathscr{C}[\![e_0]\!]\eta_c$ is $\bot$ or is in B, $\mathscr{C}[\![e]\!]\eta_c = \bot$ and the result is trivial. If $\mathscr{C}[\![e_0]\!]\eta_c$ is in $[C \rightarrow C]$ then, by definition, $\mathscr{D}[\![e_0]\!]\eta_d$ is in $[D \rightarrow D \rightarrow D]$ and, whenever $c' \lesssim d'$, $\mathscr{C}[\![e_0]\!]\eta_c c \lesssim \mathscr{D}[\![e_0]\!]\eta_d \bullet d'$. Since $\mathscr{C}[\![e_1]\!]\eta_c \lesssim \mathscr{D}[\![e_1]\!]\eta_d$ by inductive hypothesis, the result follows.

- $e = \mathtt{obj}\{\lambda x . e'\}$. First, calculate

$\mathscr{C}[\![\mathtt{obj}\{\lambda x . e'\}]\!]\eta_c$
$\quad = fix(\lambda o . \lambda v . \mathscr{C}[\![e']\!]\eta_c[\mathtt{self} \rightarrow o, x \rightarrow v])$
$\quad = \bigsqcup_i (\lambda o . \lambda v . \mathscr{C}[\![e']\!]\eta_c[\mathtt{self} \rightarrow o, x \rightarrow v])^i(\bot)$

Call the functional involved here F, so that the semantics is $\bigsqcup_i F^i(\bot)$. Since $\lesssim$ is inclusive in its C argument, this holds if $F^i(\bot) \lesssim \mathscr{D}[\![e]\!]\eta_d$. We show the latter by induction on i. For $i = 0$, $F^0(\bot) = \bot \lesssim \mathscr{D}[\![e]\!]\eta_d$. Next, consider $i > 0$. To use Lemma 6, assume that $c_1, \ldots, c_n \in C$ and $d_1, \ldots, d_n \in D$ are such that $c_i \lesssim d_i$ and $cc_1 \ldots c_n \in B$. (So, $n > 0$). Note that $F^i(\bot) = F(F^{i-1}(\bot)) = \lambda v . \mathscr{C}[\![e']\!]\eta_c[\mathtt{self} \rightarrow F^{i-1}(\bot), x \rightarrow v]$. Hence,

$$F^i(\bot)c_1 \ldots c_n = \mathscr{C}[\![e']\!]\eta_c[\mathtt{self} \rightarrow F^{i-1}(\bot), x \rightarrow c_1]c_2 \ldots c_n$$

Similarly,

$$\mathscr{D}[\![e]\!]\eta_d \bullet d_1 \bullet \cdots \bullet d_n = \mathscr{D}[\![e']\!]\eta_d[\mathtt{self} \rightarrow \mathscr{D}[\![e]\!]\eta_d, x \rightarrow d_1] \bullet d_2 \cdots \bullet d_n$$

Since

$$\mathscr{C}\llbracket e' \rrbracket \eta_c[\mathtt{self} \to F^{i-1}(\bot), x \to c_1] \lesssim \mathscr{D}\llbracket e' \rrbracket \eta_d[\mathtt{self} \to \mathscr{D}\llbracket e \rrbracket \eta_d, x \to d_1]$$

(by inductive hypothesis applied to e', the inductive hypothesis $F^{i-1}(\bot) \lesssim \mathscr{D}\llbracket e \rrbracket \eta_d$, and the assumption $c_1 \lesssim d_1$), we obtain, by Lemma 6,

$$\mathscr{C}\llbracket e' \rrbracket \eta_c[\mathtt{self} \to F^{i-1}(\bot), x \to c_1]c_2 \ldots c_n$$

$$\sqsubseteq \mathscr{D}\llbracket e' \rrbracket \eta_d[\mathtt{self} \to \mathscr{D}\llbracket e \rrbracket \eta_d, x \to d_1] \bullet d_2 \bullet \cdots \bullet d_n$$

Thus,

$$F^i(\bot)c_1 \ldots c_n \sqsubseteq \mathscr{D}\llbracket e \rrbracket \eta_d \bullet d_1 \bullet \cdots \bullet d_n$$

and, by Lemma 6, $F^i(\bot) \lesssim \mathscr{D}\llbracket e \rrbracket \eta_d$. ∎

6.3 Discussion

From the two theorems, it follows that, for all closed basic-valued expressions e, $\mathscr{C}\llbracket e \rrbracket \eta_\bot = \mathscr{D}\llbracket e \rrbracket \eta_\bot$. While this result guarantees that the two semantics give the same computed results for all programs, it falls short of what is ideally desired: a direct correspondence between the higher-type abstractions (for objects) constructed by the two semantics.

Intuitively, it seems that the correspondence should be precisely what is stated in Theorem 2, condition 3. A $\mathscr{D}$-object d and a $\mathscr{C}$-object c are equivalent if dd and c are equivalent as functions. However, strengthening conditions 1 and 2 to represent equivalence poses harder theoretical problems. The "downward closed" property used in establishing the existence of the relation becomes unavailable and it seems that the approximations of dd in the iterative construction of D_∞ do not grow as fast as the corresponding approximations of c in the constructions of C_∞. Some other technique must be found for establishing the existence of the equivalence relation. Secondly, the proof of Theorem 4 also uses the fact that the relation is an approximation rather than an equivalence. To strengthen it, one would have to find approximate forms of objects which grow in parallel in the two semantics. (Our $\mathtt{obj}^i$ expressions denote approximate objects only in the $\mathscr{D}$-semantics, not in the $\mathscr{C}$-semantics). We leave these tantalizing problems open.

7 Conclusion

We presented two semantic models of object-oriented languages focusing on the inheritance aspects. The closure model completely hides instance variables and gives an abstract semantic framework. The data structure model treats objects as structures containing both data and operations, and provides a somewhat lower level semantic framework.

At a deeper level, the closure model treats `self` via explicit fixed point operators while the data structure models uses self-application familiar from the untyped lambda calculus. Thus, the two models may also be appropriately called the fixed point and self-application models. The relationship between these two approaches brings to surface the sophisticated semantic structure inherent in object-oriented programming languages. Because self-application uses universal reflexive domains, the fixed point approach is better suited for typed languages.

Inheritance in the sense of SMALLTALK-80 has a somewhat awkward presentation in the fixed point approach. A class has two levels of meaning: as seen by its subclasses and as seen by the instances. On the other hand, the self-application model treats inheritance in a more straightforward fashion, but its apparant simplicity may be deceptive.

Our study leads to important theoretical questions regarding the relationship between self-application and fixed point methods of semantic analysis, some of which are still unanswered. Further work is needed to clarify this relationship.

Appendix

We discuss the technical details of the construction of the reflexive domains involved in Section 6 and the existence proof of the relations involved in Theorems 2 and 5. The essential technique of constructing reflexive domains using embedding-projection pairs is due to Scott [Sco72] and a more expository treatment is found in [MP87, Rey72, SP82, Wad76]. In the following, we use the notation of [MP87] uniformly.

Construction of D   We would like to define a domain satisfying the isomorphism

$$D \cong B + [D \to D \to D]$$

where B is some arbitrary domain and $+$ is the separated sum construction. For this purpose, we first define an ω-chain of domains $D_0, D_1, \ldots$ and a pair of maps between consecutive domains of the form $f_n : D_n \leftrightarrows D_{n+1} : f_n^R$. ($f_n$ is an *embedding* and f_n^R is a *projection* satisfying $f_n^R \circ f_n = \mathrm{id}$ and $f_n \circ f_n^R \sqsubseteq \mathrm{id}$). The definitions are as follows:

$$D_0 = \{\bot\}$$

$$D_{n+1} = B + [D_n \to D_n \to D_n]$$

$$f_0 = \lambda d . \perp$$

$$f_{n+1} = \mathrm{id}_B + (\lambda d . \lambda a . f_n \circ d(f_n^R a) \circ f_n^R)$$

$$f_0^R = \lambda d . \perp$$

$$f_{n+1}^R = \mathrm{id}_B + (\lambda d . \lambda a . f_n^R \circ d(f_n a) \circ f_n^R)$$

where $f + g$ is the notation for the function that maps $\perp$ to $\perp$ and the two summands of the domain to the respective summands of the codomain by f and g respectively. We can define embedding-projection pairs between arbitrary domains in the chain by $f_{nm} = f_{m-1} \circ \cdots \circ f_n$ and $f_{nm}^R = f_n^R \circ \cdots \circ f_{m-1}^R$.

The domain D is the colimit of the chain D_i. An element of D is an infinite sequence $d_0 d_1 d_2 \ldots$ of values drawn from the domains D_i such that, for every n, $d_n = f_n^R(d_{n+1})$. There is a cone of embedding-projection pairs from the chain to D defined by:

$$\mu_n : D_n \leftrightarrows D : \mu_n^R$$

$$(\mu_n(d_n))_m = \begin{cases} f_{nm}(d_n) & (m \geq n), \\ f_{mn}^R(d_n) & (m < n) \end{cases}$$

$$\mu_n^R(d) = d_n$$

Note that μ_n is the inclusion of D_n in D. Further, we can define a projection $P_n : D \to D$ which projects D to the image of D_n in D. This is defined by $P_i = \mu_n \circ \mu_n^R$.

By applying the functor $T(D) = B + [D \to D \to D]$ to the above cone, we obtain another cone from the subchain $D_1, D_2, \ldots$ to $B + [D \to D \to D]$. The embedding-projection pairs of the latter cone are defined by:

$$v_n : D_{n+1} \leftrightarrows B + [D \to D \to D] : v_n^R$$

$$v_n = \mathrm{id}_B + (\lambda d . \lambda a . \mu_n \circ d(\mu_n^R a) \circ \mu_n^R)$$

$$v_n^R = \mathrm{id}_B + (\lambda d . \lambda a . \mu_n^R \circ d(\mu_n a) \circ \mu_n^R)$$

Then the isomorphism pair $\Phi : D \leftrightarrows B + [D \to D \to D] : \Psi$ is given by the formulae:

$$\Phi = \bigsqcup_{n \geq 0} v_n \circ \mu_{n+1}^R$$

$$\Psi = \bigsqcup_{n \geq 0} \mu_{n+1} \circ v_n^R$$

It is easy to calculate that

$$(d \bullet (\mu_n d'))_n = (\Phi(d) d d')_n = d_{n+1} d_n d'$$

We often write $\Phi(d)$ simply as d.

Construction of C   The construction of the domain C satisfying

$$C \cong B + [C \to C]$$

is similar to that of D. The essential difference is in the embedding-projection pairs:

$$f_n : C_n \leftrightarrows C_{n+1} : f_n^R$$

$$f_0 = \lambda d . \perp$$

$$f_{n+1} = \mathrm{id}_B + (\lambda d . f_n \circ d \circ f_n^R)$$

$$f_0^R = \lambda d . \perp$$

$$f_{n+1}^R = \mathrm{id}_B + (\lambda d . f_n^R \circ d \circ f_n^R)$$

Construction of the logical relations   The technique used here is that of [MP87; Appendix II]. First, define relations $\lesssim^n \subseteq D_n \times C$ as follows: $d \lesssim^n c$ if and only if one of the following holds:

1. $d = \perp$,
2. $d \in B$, $c \in B$ and $d \sqsubseteq c$, or
3. $n > 0$, $d \in [D_{n-1} \to D_{n-1} \to D_{n-1}]$, $c \in [C \to C]$ and $\forall d' \in D_{n-1}$, $c' \in C . d' \lesssim^{n-1} c' \Rightarrow d \bullet_n d' \lesssim^{n-1} cc'$ where $d \bullet_n d' = d(f_{n-1}^R d)d'$.

Some elementary properties of the $\lesssim^n$ relations follow:

LEMMA 8   Each $\lesssim^n$ is downward closed in the first argument, i.e., $d \lesssim^n c$ and $d' \sqsubseteq d$ implies $d' \lesssim^n c$.

Proof   Easy induction on n.   ■

LEMMA 9   Each $\lesssim^n$ is inclusive in the first argument, i.e., if d_i is an increasing sequence in D_n and $d_i \lesssim^n c$ then $(\bigsqcup_i d_i) \lesssim^n c$.

Proof   By induction on n.   ■

LEMMA 10   The relations $\lesssim^n$ respect the embedding-projection pairs between D_n's. That is,

1. $d \lesssim^n c \Rightarrow f_n(d) \lesssim^{n+1} c$.
2. $d \lesssim^{n+1} c \Rightarrow f_n^R(d) \lesssim^n c$.

Proof   By simultaneous induction on n. For (1), $d \lesssim^n c$ gives three cases: If $d = \perp$ then $f_n(d) = \perp \lesssim^{n+1} c$. If $d \in B$ then $f_n(d) = d$ and, since $d \sqsubseteq c$, $d \lesssim^{n+1} c$. The final case is that of $d \in [D_{n-1} \to D_{n-1} \to D_{n-1}]$, $c \in [C \to C]$ and $\forall d'' \in D_{n-1}$, $c'' \in C . d'' \lesssim^{n-1} c'' \Rightarrow d \bullet_n d'' \lesssim^{n-1} cc''$. To show the result, assume $d' \in D_n$ and $c' \in C$ such that $d' \lesssim^n c'$. First, calculate

$$(f_n d) \bullet_{n+1} d' = (f_n d)(f_n^R(f_n d))d'$$

$$= (f_n d)dd'$$

$$= (f_{n-1} \circ d(f_{n-1}^R d) \circ f_{n-1}^R)d'$$

$$= f_{n-1}(d \bullet_n (f_{n-1}^R d'))$$

By inductive hypothesis (2), $f_{n-1}^R d' \lesssim^{n-1} c'$. So, by assumption, $(d \bullet_n (f_{n-1}^R d')) \lesssim^{n-1} cc'$. By using the inductive hypothesis (1), we obtain $f_{n-1}(d \bullet_n (f_{n-1}^R d')) \lesssim^n cc'$. Thus, for all $d' \in D_n$, $c' \in C$, $d' \lesssim^n c' \Rightarrow (f_n d) \bullet_{n+1} d' \lesssim^n cc'$.

For (2), $d \lesssim^{n+1} c$ gives three cases: If $d = \perp$ or $d \in B$, the result is obvious. For the case where $d \in [D_n \to D_n \to D_n]$, $c \in [C \to C]$ and $\forall d'' \in D_n$, $c'' \in C . d'' \lesssim^n c'' \Rightarrow d \bullet_{n+1} d'' \lesssim^n cc''$, as usual, assume $d' \in D_{n-1}$, $c' \in C$ such that $d' \lesssim^{n-1} c'$. Calculate

$$(f_n^R d) \bullet_n d' = (f_n^R d)(f_{n-1}^R(f_n^R d))d'$$

$$= (f_{n-1}^R \circ (d(f_{n-1}(f_{n-1}^R(f_n^R d)))) \circ f_{n-1})d'$$

$$\sqsubseteq (f_{n-1}^R \circ (d(f_n^R d)) \circ f_{n-1})d'$$

$$= f_{n-1}^R(d \bullet_n (f_{n-1} d'))$$

By inductive hypothesis (1), $f_{n-1} d' \lesssim^n c'$. So, by assumption, $d \bullet_n (f_{n-1} d') \lesssim^n cc'$. By inductive hypothesis (2), $f_{n-1}^R(d \bullet_n (f_{n-1} d')) \lesssim^{n-1} cc'$. Since $\lesssim^{n-1}$ is downward closed, we obtain the result $(f_n^R d) \bullet_{n-1} d' \lesssim^{n-1} cc'$. ∎

Proof of Theorem 2 We define the relation $\lesssim \subseteq D \times C$ by

$$d \lesssim c \quad \text{iff} \quad \forall n . d_n \lesssim^n c$$

This is clearly inclusive using Lemma 9. Next, we show that it satisfies the recursive specification given in Theorem 2, *i.e.*, $d \lesssim c$ iff

1. $d = \perp$,

2. $d \in B$, $c \in B$, and $d \sqsubseteq c$, or

3. $d \in [D \to D \to D]$, $c \in [C \to C]$, and, for all d' and c', $d' \lesssim c' \Rightarrow d \bullet d' \lesssim cc'$.

(d in the above conditions is really Φd, but we ignore to write this coercion).

$\Rightarrow$ Suppose $d \lesssim c$. There are three possibilities for d. If $d = \perp$, there is nothing to be proved. If $d \in B$, $\mu_n^R(d) = d$ for all $n > 0$. By assumption, $d \lesssim^n c$ and this shows that

$c \in B$ and $d \sqsubseteq c$. If $d \in [D \to D \to D]$, $d_{n+1} \in [D_n \to D_n \to D_n]$ for all n. Since $d_{n+1} \lesssim^{n+1} c$, we have that $c \in [C \to C]$. Assume $d' \in D$, $c' \in C$ such that $d' \lesssim c'$. By definition, $d'_n \lesssim^n c'$ and, so, $d_{n+1} \bullet_n d'_n \lesssim cc'$. Since $(d \bullet d')_n = d_{n+1} \bullet_n d'_n$, by definition, $d \bullet d' \lesssim cc'$.

$\Leftarrow$ If $d = \bot$ then $\mu_n^R(d) = \bot$. Since $\bot \lesssim^n c$, we have $d \lesssim c$. If $d \in B$, $c \in B$ and $d \sqsubseteq c$ then $\mu_0^R(d) = \bot$ and $\mu_{n+1}^R(d) = d$. So, we have $\mu_n^R(d) \lesssim^n c$ for all n. Finally, suppose $d \in [D \to D \to D]$, $c \in [C \to C]$ and $\forall d'' \in D$, $c'' \in C$. $d'' \lesssim c'' \Rightarrow d \bullet d'' \lesssim cc'$. We need to show that $d_n \lesssim^n c$ for all n. For $n = 0$, the result is trivial. For $n > 0$, Consider $d' \in D_{n-1}$ and $c' \in C$ such that $d' \lesssim^{n-1} c'$. We have $\mu_{n-1}(d') \lesssim c'$ and, by assumption, $d \bullet \mu_{n-1}(d') \lesssim cc'$. The definition of $\lesssim$ gives $(d \bullet \mu_{n-1}(d'))_{n-1} \lesssim^{n-1} cc'$, but, the LHS is the same as $d_n \bullet_n d'$. Thus, for all $d' \in D_{n-1}$, $c' \in C$, $d' \lesssim^{n-1} c' \Rightarrow d_n \bullet_n d' \lesssim cc'$. This shows $d_n \lesssim^n c$ for all n. $\blacksquare$

The construction of the logical relation mentioned in Theorem 5 proceeds similarly.

Notes

1. "SMALLTALK-80" is a trademark of ParcPlace Systems. We use here a language called "SmallTalk" (with different capitalization) as an abstraction of SMALLTALK-80.

2. In the terminology of P. Wegner [Weg87], ObjectTalk is a prototypical "object-based" language, ClassTalk is a "class-based" language while InheritTalk and SmallTalk are "object-oriented" languages.

3. We are using the term here to denote the general notion of an abstraction with no free variables, rather than the particular representation of such abstractions as pairs of expressions and environments [Sto77, p. 44].

4. If $f: X \to A$ and $g: Y \to B$, we use the notation $f \times g$ for the function $\lambda \langle x, y \rangle . \langle fx, gy \rangle$ of type $X \times Y \to A \times B$. If $f: X \to A$ and $g: X \to B$, we use the notation $[f, g]$ for the function $\lambda x . \langle fx, gx \rangle$ of type $X \to A \times B$.

5. In this section, we abbreviate *basicval* to B, val_C to C and val_D to D.

References

[ASS85]   H. Abelson, G. J. Sussman, and J. Sussman. *Structure and Interpretation of Computer Programs.* MIT Press, Cambridge, Mass., 1985.

[Car84]   L. Cardelli. A semantics of multiple inheritance. In *Semantics of Data Types*, pages 51–67. Springer-Verlag LNCS Vol. 173, 1984.

[Coo89]   W. R. Cook. *A Denotational Semantics of Inheritance.* PhD thesis, Dep. of Computer Science, Brown Univ., May 1989. (Tech. Report CS-89-33).

[CP93]   W. Cook and J. Palsberg. A denotational semantics of inheritance and its correctness. *Information and Computation*, 1993. (to appear).

[DN66]   O.-J. Dahl and K. Nygaard. An Algol-based simulation language. *Communications of the ACM*, 9(9):671–678, Sep 1966.

[DoD82]   DoD. *Reference Manual for the ADA Programming Language.* United States Department of Defense, 1982.

[GR83]   A. Goldberg and D. Robson. SMALLTALK-80: *The Language and its Implementation.* Addison-Wesley, Reading, MA, 1983.

[Gun92]   C. A. Gunter. *Semantics of Programming Languages: Structures and Techniques.* MIT Press, 1992.

[Kam88]   S. Kamin. Inheritance in SMALLTALK-80: A denotational definition. In *ACM Symp. on Princ. of Program. Lang.,* January 1988.

[Kam90]   S. N. Kamin. *Programming Languages: An Interpreter-Based Approach.* Addison-Wesley, Reading, MA, 1990.

[KL85]   R. M. Keller and G. Lindstrom. Approaching distributed database implementations through functional programming concepts. In *Intl. Conf. on Distributed Computing Systems.* IEEE, May 1985.

[LAB+81]   B. Liskov, R. Atkinson, T. Bloom, E. Moss, J. C. Schaffert, R. Scheiffler, and A. Snyder. *CLU Reference Manual,* volume 114 of *Lect. Notes in Comp. Science.* Springer-Verlag, 1981.

[Mil74]   R. E. Milne. *The Formal Semantics of Computer Languages and their Implementation.* PhD thesis, Univ. of Cambridge, 1974.

[MP87]   P. D. Mosses and G. D. Plotkin. On proving limiting completeness. *SIAM J. Computing,* 16(1):179–194, Feb 1987.

[MS76]   R. E. Milne and C. Strachey. *A Theory of Programming Language Semantics.* Chapman and Hall, London, 1976.

[Par70]   D. M. R. Park. The *Y*-combinator in Scott's lambda-calculus models. In *Symposium on Theory of Programming,* Warwick, 1970. University of Warwick.

[Red88]   U. S. Reddy. Objects as closures: Abstract semantics of object oriented languages. In *ACM Symp. on LISP and Functional Programming,* pages 289–297. ACM, July 1988.

[Rey72]   J. C. Reynolds. Notes on a lattice-theoretic approach to the theory of computation. Lecture notes, Systems and Information Science, Syracuse University, Oct 1972.

[Rey74]   J. C. Reynolds. On the relation between direct and continuation semantics. In *Intern. Colloq. Automata, Languages. and Programming,* pages 141–156. Springer-Verlag, Berlin, 1974.

[Sco72]   D. S. Scott. Continuous lattices. In F. W. Lawvere, editor, *Toposes, Algebraic Geometry and Logic,* pages 97–136. Springer-Verlag, 1972. (Lecture Notes in Mathematics, Vol. 274).

[SP82]   M. B. Smyth and G. D. Plotkin. The category-theoretic solution of recursive domain equations. *SIAM J. Computing,* 11:761–783, 1982.

[Sto77]   J. E. Stoy. *Denotational Semantics: The Scott-Strachey Approach to Programming Language Theory.* MIT Press, 1977.

[Str86]   B. Stroustrup. *The C++ Programming Language.* Addison-Wesley, Reading, MA, 1986.

[Wad76]   C. P. Wadsworth. The relation between computational and denotational properties for Scott's D_∞-models of the lambda calculus. *SIAM J. Computing,* 5:488–521, 1976.

[Weg87]   P. Wegner. Dimensions of object-based language design. In *Object Oriented Prog. Systems, Lang. and Applications.* ACM SIGPLAN, 1987.

14 Inheritance Is Not Subtyping

William R. Cook, Walter L. Hill, and Peter S. Canning

Abstract

In typed object-oriented languages the subtype relation is typically based on the inheritance hierarchy. This approach, however, leads either to insecure type-systems or to restrictions on inheritance that make it less flexible than untyped Smalltalk inheritance. We present a new typed model of inheritance that allows more of the flexibility of Smalltalk inheritance within a statically-typed system. Significant features of our analysis are the introduction of polymorphism into the typing of inheritance and the uniform application of inheritance to objects, classes and types. The resulting notion of *type inheritance* allows us to show that the type of an inherited object is an inherited type but not always a subtype.

1 Introduction

In strongly-typed object-oriented languages like Simula [1], C++ [28], Trellis [25], Eiffel [19], and Modula-3 [9], the inheritance hierarchy determines the conformance (subtype) relation. In most such languages, inheritance is restricted to satisfy the requirements of subtyping. Eiffel, on the other hand, has a more expressive type system that allows more of the flexibility of Smalltalk inheritance [14], but suffers from type insecurities because its inheritance construct is not a sound basis for a subtype relation [12].

In this paper we present a new typed model of inheritance that supports more of the flexibility of Smalltalk inheritance while allowing static type-checking. The typing is based on an extended polymorphic lambda-calculus and a denotational model of inheritance. The model contradicts the conventional wisdom that inheritance must always make subtypes. In other words, we show that incremental change, by implementation inheritance, can produce objects that are not subtype compatible with the original objects. We introduce the notion of *type inheritance* and show that an inherited object has an inherited type. Type inheritance is the basis for a new form of polymorphism for object-oriented programming.

Much of the work presented here is connected with the use of self-reference, or recursion, in object-oriented languages [3, 4, 5]. Our model of inheritance is intimately tied to recursion in that it is a mechanism for incremental extension of recursive structures [11, 13, 22]. In object-oriented languages, recursion is used at

First appeared in P. Hudak, editor, *Principles of Programming Languages*, 1990, pages 125–135. © The Association for Computing Machinery, Inc., 11 West 42nd Street, New York, NY 10036.

three levels: objects, classes, and types. We apply inheritance uniformly to each of these forms of recursion while ensuring that each form interacts properly with the others. Since our terminology is based on this uniform development, it is sometimes at odds with the numerous technical terms used in the object-oriented paradigm. Our notion of object inheritance subsumes both delegation and the traditional notion of class inheritance, while our notion of class inheritance is related to Smalltalk metaclasses.

Object inheritance is used to construct objects incrementally. We show that when a recursive object definition is inherited to define a new object, a corresponding change is often required in the type of the object. To achieve this effect, polymorphism is introduced into recursive object definitions by abstracting the type of *self*. Inheritance is defined to specialize the inherited definition to match the type of the new object being defined. A form of polymorphism developed for this purpose, called F-bounded polymorphism [3], is used to characterize the extended types that may be created by inheritors.

Class inheritance supports the incremental definition of classes, which are parameterized object definitions. A class is recursive if its instances use the class to create new instances. When a class is inherited to define a new class, the inherited creation operations are updated to create instances of the new class. Since class recursion is also related to recursion in the object types, the polymorphic typing of inheritance is extended to cover class recursion. We also introduce a generalization of class inheritance that allows modification of instantiation parameters.

A final application of inheritance is to the definition of recursive types. Type inheritance extends a recursive record type to make a new type with similar recursive structure but more fields. Because of an interaction between function subtyping and recursion, an inherited type is not necessarily a subtype of the type from which it was derived. This is a second sense in which inheritance is not subtyping. Type inheritance is useful for constructing the types of objects produced by object inheritance. In addition, F-bounded polymorphic functions can be applied to the types of objects that inherit from a given object definition and then to objects of that type; objects with different inherited types are prevented from being mixed together.

The typed model of inheritance is directly relevant to the analysis and design of programming languages. It indicates how object-oriented languages could be extended to support more flexible forms of inheritance while retaining static typing. Several other theories of typed inheritance have also been proposed [15, 20, 30]. A preliminary comparison reveals a similarity of approach. However, the models are based on a wide range of theoretical foundations, and more research is required to resolve the differences.

The next section surveys terminology and background on objects, types, and inheritance for our model of object-oriented programming. The following three sections are organized to address the use of inheritance for the three kinds of recursion found in object-oriented programs. Section 3 examines the relationship between object recursion and type recursion, and introduces a polymorphic typing of inheritance to allow more flexibility in the presence of recursive types. Section 4 introduces recursive classes with instantiation parameters and extends inheritance to allow modification of parameters by subclasses. Section 5 defines a notion of inheritance for types and demonstrates its connection to object inheritance. Section 6 illustrates these features with a practical programming example. Section 7 applies the model to the analysis of object-oriented languages and compares it to other models of typed inheritance.

2 Background

2.1 A Typed Record Calculus

A typed polymorphic lambda-calculus with records is used to describe the typing of inheritance. The language is functional and explicitly typed; no provision is made for imperative constructs or type inference. Imperative constructs, which support mutable object state, are not included because they do not affect the analysis of inheritance. An untyped version of the calculus is used to introduce new constructs before giving a typed presentation.

2.2 Records

A record is a finite mapping of labels to values. A record with fields $x_1,\ldots,x_n$ and associated values $v_1,\ldots,v_n$ is written $\{x_1 = v_1,\ldots,x_n = v_n\}$. If the values have type $\sigma_1,\ldots,\sigma_n$ then the record has type $\{x_1:\sigma_1,\ldots,x_n:\sigma_n\}$. Selecting the a component of a record r is given by $r.a$.

Cardelli [6, 8] identified record subtyping as an important form of polymorphism in object-oriented programming. The main idea is that if a record r has fields $x_1:\sigma_1,\ldots,x_k:\sigma_k$ and also $x_{k+1}:\sigma_{k+1},\ldots,x_l:\sigma_l$, then a record r' with fields $x_1:\sigma_1,\ldots,$ $x_k:\sigma_k$ can be constructed from r by omitting fields. Therefore, any record with type $\{x_1:\sigma_1,\ldots,x_k:\sigma_k,\ldots,x_l:\sigma_l\}$ can be coerced into a record of type $\{x_1:\sigma_1,\ldots,x_k:\sigma_k\}$. The general form of this coercion allows the field values to be coerced as well:

$$\frac{\sigma_1 \leq \rho_1,\ldots,\sigma_k \leq \rho_k,}{\{x_1:\sigma_1,\ldots,x_k:\sigma_k,\ldots,x_l:\sigma_l\} \leq \{x_1:\rho_1,\ldots,x_k:\rho_k\}}$$

In our model, record types indicate exactly what fields a record contains. This differs from Cardelli, who uses a *subsumption* model in which a record type represents all records that have at least the specified fields. We do not use subsumption because it complicates the problem of record combination.

2.3 Record Combination

The language supports a simple record combination operator, **with**, that joins two records. The typing of **with** is defined by a typed introduction rule.

$$\frac{e_1 : \{x_1 : \sigma_1, \ldots, x_j : \sigma_j, x_{j+1} : \tau_{j+1}, \ldots, x_k : \tau_{k-j}\} \qquad e_2 : \{x_{j+1} : \sigma_{j+1}, \ldots, x_n : \sigma_n\} \quad (k \le n)}{e_1 \text{ with } e_2 : \{x_1 : \sigma_1, \ldots, x_n : \sigma_n\}}$$

If there are common fields, $x_{j+1}, \ldots, x_k$, they may have different types in the two records. The conflict is resolved by taking the value from e_2. An analogous operator, $+$, is defined on record types. The evaluation rule performs the corresponding operation on record values. The operator **with** is well-behaved because our types are exact specifications of the fields in a record. If subsumption were allowed, the actual value of e_2 could have more fields than mentioned in its type. According to the evaluation rule, these fields would take precedence over the fields in e_1 resulting in a unsound typing.

Our record combination operator is simpler than the ones proposed by Rémy [23] and Wand [29, 30]. The simply typed version of **with** is sufficient for the analysis in this paper.

2.4 Recursive Types

The notation for a recursive type defined by $T = F[T]$ is $\mu t . F[t]$. A recursive type is equal to its infinite expansion. One step in this expansion is given by the *unrolling* rule:

$$\mu t . F[t] = F[\mu t . F[t]]$$

One recursive type is a subtype of another if their infinite expansions are in a subtype relation. An induction rule is used to specify the subtype relation [7].

$$\frac{\Gamma, s \le t \vdash \sigma[s] \le \tau[t]}{\Gamma \vdash \mu s . \sigma[s] \le \mu t . \tau[t]}$$

To illustrate, the types T_1 and T_2 below are subtypes of T. These subtypes do not have the same pattern of recursion as T. T_3 is not a subtype of T, even though it has the same recursive structure, because of the contravariance [6] of the function type in the b field.

$$T = \mu t.\{a:int, c:t, b:t \to t\}$$

$$T_1 = \{a:int, c:T, b:T \to T, d:bool\}$$

$$T_2 = \mu t.\{a:int, c:t, b:T \to t, d:bool\}$$

$$T_3 = \mu t.\{a:int, c:t, b:t \to t, d:bool\}$$

2.5 Polymorphism

Subtype-bounded polymorphism [10] allows functions to be written that operate uniformly over all subtypes of a given type. A bounded polymorphic function is defined by the expression $\Lambda t \le \sigma.e$. If assuming $t \le \sigma$ gives e type τ, then the polymorphic function has type $\forall t \le \sigma.\tau$. For recursive types, however, there are forms of structural similarity not captured by subtyping, as illustrated above. The types that have the *recursive structure* of $T = \mu t.F[t]$ are those that satisfy the constraint $t \le F[t]$. In the example above, $F[t] = \{a:int, c:t, b:t \to t\}$. Of types T_1, T_2 and T_3, only T_3 satisfies the constraint $T_3 \le F[T_3]$. *F-bounded polymorphism* [3], written $\forall t \le F[t].\sigma$, supports parametric quantification over the recursive types that share the recursive structure specified by F. Examples demonstrating the use of F-bounded polymorphism in typing functions involving recursive types are given in [3].

2.6 Objects

As in [5, 11, 22, 31], we represent objects as records whose fields contain methods. The methods of an object may refer to each other, so objects are naturally viewed as mutually recursive definitions. The traditional interpretation of mutual recursion from denotational semantics is as a fixed point of a function on environments of identifiers. For example, an object handling messages $m_1, \ldots, m_j$ by methods $e_1, \ldots, e_j$ is a fixed point of the function P.

$$P = \lambda(self).\{m_1 = e_1, \ldots, m_j = e_j\}. \tag{1}$$

The expressions $e_1, \ldots, e_j$ may contain references to *self*; for example, to call the m method with argument 3 one would write $self.m(3)$. The function P is a definition of the object $Y(P)$. The type of an object is a record type, and is often a recursive record type [2, 3, 4, 5, 24]. Recursion in object types is associated, for example, with a method that simply returns the pseudovariable *self*.

While our language does not support mutable object state, lexically bound variables can be used to parameterize objects (see Section 4.1). If mutable variables were supported, any pattern of shared state among different objects could be defined, including those characteristic of delegation systems [18]. To simplify the presentation, some methods are simple values instead of functions; if state were introduced then lambda-abstractions would be required on all methods to delay evaluation.

2.7 Inheritance

An untyped, compositional model of inheritance based on the fixed-point function, $\mathbf{Y}$, was developed independently by Cook [11, 13] and Reddy [22]. Given a definition, P, of a *parent* recursive value $\mathbf{Y}(P)$ and a self-referential modifier M, one may construct a *child* value $\mathbf{Y}(\lambda(s).M(s)(P(s)))$. This example illustrates inheritance as an operation on recursive definitions.

Inheritance allows a new object definition to be derived from an existing one where self-reference in the inherited object definition is unified with self-reference in new methods.

$$C = \lambda(self).P(self) \text{ with } \{m'_1 = e'_1, \ldots, m'_k = e'_k\} \tag{2}$$

The use of the pseudovariable *super* to refer directly to parent methods is also supported in the model. This generalization is illustrated in Section 6.

A simple typing of inheritance is easily derived by adding type-constraints to the basic inheritance model [11]. If P has type $\sigma \to \sigma$ for some σ, then the object $\mathbf{Y}(P)$ has type σ. If the modifier has type $\tau \to \sigma \to \tau$ to produce an object of type τ from one of type σ, then $\lambda(s).M(s)(P(s))$ has type $\tau \to \tau$ and its fixed point is an object of type τ. The significant constraint introduced by inheritance is that τ must be a subtype of σ for the application $P(s)$ to be type-correct.

3 Object Inheritance

3.1 Problems in the Simple Typing of Inheritance

In this section we illustrate some problems in using the simple typing of inheritance to define objects with recursive types. One problem arises because the simple typing of inheritance does not always provide the most precise type possible. Consider a simple object definition with a method i returning the value 5 and a method *id* that returns the object itself.

$$P = \lambda(self).\{i = 5, id = self\}$$

The object $\mathbf{Y}(P)$ has type $\sigma = \mu t.\{i : int, id : t\}$, thus the simple typing of inheritance gives P the type $\sigma \to \sigma$. A child C is defined by inheriting P and adding a single boolean field b.

$C = \lambda(self) . P(self)$ **with** $\{b = true\}$

In the simple typing of inheritance, $\mathbf{Y}(C)$ has type $\sigma + \{b:bool\}$, or $\tau_1 = \{i:int, id:\sigma, b:bool\}$. Note that τ_1 is not directly recursive in the type of the *id* method.

Expanding C to eliminate $P(self)$ and combine records gives an equivalent expression.

$C_1 = \lambda(self) . \{i = 5, id = self, b = true\}$

$\mathbf{Y}(C_1)$ has type $\tau_2 = \mu t . \{i:int, id:t, b:bool\}$. Since $\tau_2 < \tau_1$ the simple typing has resulted in less precise type for the inherited object than is possible.

A more serious problem occurs when attempting to use contravariant [6] recursive types. Consider a new object definition with an equality method instead of an identity method.

$P' = \lambda(self) . \{i = 5, eq = \lambda(o) . (o.i = self.i)\}$

Although several typings for $\mathbf{Y}(P')$ are possible, the one that expresses *eq* as a binary method is recursive in the type of the *eq* method.

$\sigma' = \mu t . \{i:int, eq:t \to bool\}$

Now C' can be defined by inheriting P' while adding a b field and redefining *eq*.

$C' = \lambda(self) . P'(self)$ **with**
$\qquad \{b = true,$
$\qquad eq = \lambda(o) . (o.i = self.i$ and
$\qquad\qquad\qquad o.b = self.b)$
$\qquad \}$

Before examining possible typings for C, consider the object it defines. The object $\mathbf{Y}(C')$ has a recursive type, τ'_2.

$\tau'_2 = \mu t . \{i:int, b:bool, eq:t \to bool\}$

The simple typing of C' fails because $\tau'_2 \not\leq \sigma'$. Simple types cannot be assigned to the definition of C' because P' of type $\sigma' \to \sigma'$ cannot be applied to *self* which has type τ'_2 as required by the inheritance. It is important to note that in an untyped framework this use of inheritance is meaningful, but the type system is simply not expressive enough to describe the relevant constraints. The simple typing of inheritance, with its subtype assumption, cannot give a typing for this example.

3.2 Polymorphism and Inheritance

To overcome these problems we introduce polymorphism directly into the mechanism of inheritance. This is motivated by observing the type-dependency within a recursive definition: the type of object created depends on the type of *self*. We provide a more flexible typing by abstracting the type of *self* and replacing type recursion by type-dependency. The type recursion is reintroduced when the object is constructed. Let $F[t] = \{m_1 : \sigma_1, \ldots, m_j : \sigma_j\}$ be a type function defining a recursive type $\sigma = \mu t . F[t]$. An object with methods e_i of type σ_i is defined by an expression in which the type of *self* is polymorphic.

$$P : \forall t \leq F[t] . t \to F[t] \tag{3}$$
$$P = \Lambda t \leq F[t] . \lambda(self:t) . \{m_1 = e_1, \ldots, m_j = e_j\}$$

The F-bounded constraint $t \leq F[t]$ is central to the model. It provides information about the methods defined by the object denoted by *self*. For example, if $F[t] = \{m : t \to t, n : t\}$, the n method could return $self . m(self)$. Of course, the exact type t is unknown—it is supplied by inheritors to indicate the type of the complete object into which the methods in P are being incorporated.

Object instantiation must now include the type of the object being created, as in $\mathbf{Y}(P[\sigma])$. The simple typing is recovered by forming $P[\sigma] : \sigma \to F[\sigma]$, which, by unrolling, is equal to $\sigma \to \sigma$.

For inheritance, it is necessary to define a type $\tau = \mu s . G[s]$ such that $G[t] \leq F[t]$. Any type satisfying $t \leq G[t]$ also satisfies $t \leq F[t]$.

The typing of inheritance involves defining a new polymorphic function that specializes its parent to the appropriate type before modifying its methods.

$$C : \forall t \leq G[t] . t \to G[t] \tag{4}$$
$$C = \Lambda t \leq G[t] . \lambda(self:t) . P[t](self) \textbf{ with } \{m'_1 = e'_1, \ldots, m'_k = e'_k\}$$

The fields m'_1 must be assigned values as specified in $G[t]$. The use of $P[t]$ is type-correct because $G[t] \leq F[t]$. The simple record combination operator, **with**, is sufficient because it is applied to values whose types are constant. Although it might seem reasonable to abstract over P to produce an *abstract subclass*, or *wrapper* [21], the resulting function cannot be assigned a useful type without a more expressive record combination operator.

To illustrate the polymorphic typing of inheritance, the examples from Section 3.1 are combined into a single construct.

$$P = \Lambda t \leq F[t].\lambda(self:t).$$
$$\{i = 5,$$
$$id = self,$$
$$eq = \lambda(o:t).(o.i = self.i)\}$$

The type function $F[t] = \{i:int, id:t, eq:t \to bool\}$ specifies the recursive type of the objects, and P has type $\forall t \leq F[t].t \to F[t]$.

The inheriting definition adds a method b and redefines the equality method.

$$C = \Lambda t \leq G[t].\lambda(self:t).$$
$$P[t](self) \text{ with}$$
$$\{b = true,$$
$$eq = \lambda(o:t).(o.i = self.i \text{ and}$$
$$o.b = self.b)$$
$$\}$$

The new object has type $\tau = \mu t.G[t]$.

$$G[t] = \{i:int, id:t, b:bool, eq:t \to bool\}$$

The polymorphic application $P[t]$ is valid because $t \leq G[t]$ and $G[t] \leq F[t]$ imply $t \leq F[t]$. Despite this relationship between G and F, their fixed points are not in a subtype relation.

4 Class Inheritance

4.1 Classes

A class is a parameterized object definition. In the previous section we used simple classes that were just descriptions of a single object. A more sophisticated notion of class includes instantiation parameters so that multiple objects, called the *instances* of the class, may be created. In this interpretation classes are functions that create object specifications. Classes may be inherited to define other classes.

A class is recursive if its instances use the class to make new instances. When a method using class recursion is inherited, the recursive use of the class is modified so that the method constructs subclass instances instead. Smalltalk is a good illustration of class recursion and inheritance: an object can determine the class that created it with the expression *self class*. To create a new instance like itself an object sends its class a *new* message: *self class new*. In Smalltalk, *new* messages are handled by metaclasses, which support specialization of object creation by inheritance.

A recursive class is defined using fixed points, just as objects are fixed points of mutually recursive method specifications. For objects, the functional argument represented *self*, to which recursive messages are sent. For classes, the argument represents the class to use in constructing new instances. This argument is called *myclass*. The general untyped form of a recursive class definition has two levels of recursion, *myclass* and *self*.

$$\mathscr{P} = \lambda(myclass).\,\lambda(x).\,\lambda(self).\,\{m_1 = e_1, \ldots, m_j = e_j\}$$

The argument x represents the instantiation parameter. The class recursion variable, *myclass*, is used in the expressions e_i to construct new instances of the class. Let $P = \mathbf{Y}(\mathscr{P})$ be the class associated with the class definition $\mathscr{P}$. An object is instantiated with parameter a by applying the class to a and then taking the fixed point: $\mathbf{Y}(P(a))$. The complete equation for making an instance from a recursive class definition involves a double fixed point: $\mathbf{Y}(\mathbf{Y}(\mathscr{P})(a))$. Two applications of the fixed-point function are used because class recursion and object recursion are independent.

In the child class definition, $\mathscr{P}$ is passed a new value for *myclass* so that the inherited methods m_i create instances of $\mathscr{C}$, not instances of $\mathscr{P}$.

$$\mathscr{C} = \lambda(myclass).\,\lambda(x).\,\lambda(self)$$
$$\mathscr{P}(myclass)(x)(self) \text{ with } \{m'_1 = e'_1, \ldots, m'_k = e'_k\}$$

4.2 Typed Class Inheritance

The typing of class recursion uses the same technique of polymorphism introduced in Section 3.2. Although the scope of class-level recursion contains the scope of object recursion, the polymorphism associated with the type of *self* must be moved outside of the class recursion variable.

$$\mathscr{P} : \forall t \le G[t].\,(\alpha \to (t \to t)) \to (\alpha \to (t \to F[t])) \tag{5}$$
$$\mathscr{P} = \Lambda t \le F(t).\,\lambda(myclass : \alpha \to (t \to t)).$$
$$\lambda(y : \alpha).\,\lambda(self : t).$$
$$\{m_1 = e_1, \ldots, m_k = e_k\}$$

Note that *myclass* produces values of type $t \to t$ rather than $t \to F[t]$ as in the final result-type of $\mathscr{P}$. This allows the fixed point of *myclass* to be used without complete knowledge of the final binding of t. The objects created by this class definition have type $\sigma = \mu t.\,F[t]$. Instantiation of a class definition with polymorphic typing, $P = \mathbf{Y}(\mathscr{P}[\sigma])$, involves binding the type argument the instance type and then taking the fixed point. The class P has type $\alpha \to (\sigma \to \sigma)$.

The typing of an inheriting class definition is straightforward.

$$\mathscr{C} : \forall t \le G[t] . (\alpha \to (t \to t)) \to (\alpha \to (t \to G[t])) \tag{6}$$

$$\mathscr{C} = \Lambda t \le G(t) . \lambda(myclass : \alpha \to (t \to t)).$$
$$\lambda(x : \alpha) . \lambda(self : t).$$
$$\mathscr{P}[t](myclass)(x)(self)$$
$$\textbf{with } \{m'_1 = e'_1, \ldots, m_k = e'_k\}$$

4.3 Changing Instantiation Parameters

Class inheritance is complicated by the common need to change the form of the instantiation parameters of the subclass to be of some type β. The problem is that the inherited definition expects a value of *myclass* with type $\alpha \to (t \to t)$, but the subclass definition of *myclass* has type $\beta \to (t \to t)$. Unless $\alpha \le \beta$, the types will not match. This condition is too restrictive: it is common for the subclass to require more information, not less.

The difference between the initialization parameters is bridged by two translation functions. The first translation, $Q : \beta \to \alpha$, converts child parameters to the form required by the parent class. The second translation, $T : \alpha \to \beta$, converts parent parameters to the form required by the child so that uses of *myclass* in parent methods will construct child instances. With these translation functions, the inheritance construct supports modification of instantiation parameters.

$$C : \forall t \le G[t] . (\beta \to (t \to t)) \to (\beta \to (t \to G[t])) \tag{7}$$

$$\mathscr{C} = \Lambda t \le F(t) . \lambda(myclass : \beta \to (t \to t)).$$
$$\lambda(y : \beta) . \lambda(self : t).$$
$$\mathscr{P}[t](myclass \circ T)(Q(y))(self) \textbf{ with } \{m'_1 = e'_1, \ldots, m'_k = e'_k\}$$

T and Q are defined in a context in which y and *self* are bound. The context is particularly relevant in the case of T, since the additional information required for subclass instantiation is often computed from *self*.

5 Type Inheritance

As an operation on recursive definitions, inheritance can also be applied to recursively defined record types. Let $F[t] = \{x_1 : \sigma_1, \ldots, x_n : \sigma_n\}$ be a type function defining a recursive record type $\sigma = F[\sigma]$. Type inheritance allows the definition F to be modified to define a new type. A definition that inherits F has the form

$$G[t] = F[t] + \{x'_1 : \sigma'_1, \ldots, x'_n : \sigma'_n\}$$

G defines the type $\tau = G[\tau]$, a child of σ. Note that $G[t]$ need not be a subtype of $F[t]$ because the field types may be changed. The replacement of field types during type inheritance is analogous to the replacement of field values (methods) during object inheritance.

There is a close connection between type inheritance and class/object inheritance. In the polymorphic typing defined in Section 3.2, the type function G which specifies the type of the inheriting object may be expressed by inheriting F. The types of methods $m'_1, \ldots, m'_k$ that are changed can be identified in a type-function R for which $G[t] = F[t] + R[t]$ Thus the type of an inherited object is an inherited type.

The properties of types of inherited objects are analogous to those of subtypes. The constraint imposed by object inheritance, $G[t] \leq F[t]$, ensures that inherited objects can be used as arguments to F-bounded polymorphic functions just as values of subtypes can be used as arguments to subtype-bounded polymorphic functions. Thus F-bounded polymorphism is useful in object-oriented programming for writing functions that work uniformly over the subclasses of a class.

6   Example

The following example illustrates the recursive structure of objects, classes and types, and the typing of inheritance given in Sections 3 and 4. The class definition exhibits both object and class recursion, and gives an example of typed class inheritance. The type of the objects created from the inherited class is defined using the type inheritance operation described in Section 5. For a more complete discussion of a version of this example and the informal object-oriented notation used below, see [4].

A type *Point* specifies the interface of movable planar points. When a point is moved it returns a new point at the new location.

interface *Point*
    x : *Real*
    y : *Real*
    move(*Real*, *Real*) : *Point*
    equal(*Point*) : *Boolean*

More formally, *Point* is the fixed point of a type function derived from the interface definition.

$$F[t] = \{x : Real, y : Real, move : Real \times Real \to t, equal : t \to Boolean\}$$

Type inheritance can be used to extend the recursive *type Point*.

interface *ColorPoint* **inherits** *Point*
    color : *Color*

Type inheritance is explained as extension of type functions in Section 5. *ColorPoint* is the fixed point of *G*.

$$G[t] = F[t] + \{color : Color\}$$

ColorPoint $\not\leq$ *Point* because the equality method is contravariant. Intuitively, a *ColorPoint* can't be used where a *Point* is expected because it does not make sense to compare *Points* and *ColorPoints* for equality. The problem is that *Points* do not have color. The system could also have been designed to allow the comparison, but then the *ColorPoint* equality method could not determine the color of its argument.

On the other hand, *ColorPoint* does have the same recursive structure as *Point*: *ColorPoint* $\leq F[ColorPoint]$ and for all t, $G[t] \leq F[t]$. These are exactly the constraints required by inheritance.

The class *cart_point* implements objects of type *Point*. It has two initialization parameters, x and y, that specify the location of the point in cartesian coordinates.

class *cart_point* $(x : Real, y : Real)$
    implements *Point*
    method $x : Real$
        return x
    method $y : Real$
        return y
    method $move(dx : Real, dy : Real) : Point$
        return new $myclass(self.x + dx, self.y + dy)$
    method $equal(p : Point) : Boolean$
        return $(self.x = p.x)$ and $(self.y = p.y)$

Instances of *cart_point* are recursive because they send messages to *self*. The class *cart_point* is also recursive because the *move* method uses *myclass* to create a new point at a given distance from itself. Both the *equal* method and the *move* method involve the type *Point* in association with object recursion, so there is an opportunity to encode these types so that they may be specialized. The definition above is easily translated into the format of Equation 5.

$\mathscr{P} = \Lambda t \leq F[t] . \lambda(myclass : (Real \times Real) \to (t \to t)).$

$\quad \lambda(x : Real, x : Real) . \lambda(self : t).$

$\quad \{x = x,$

$\quad\quad y = y,$

$\quad\quad move = \lambda(dx : Real, dy : Real).$

$\quad\quad\quad \mathbf{Y}(myclass(self.x + dx, self.y + dy)),$

$\quad\quad equal = \lambda(o : t).$

$\quad\quad\quad (self.x = o.x) \text{ and } (self.y = o.y)$

$\quad\quad \}$

Instances of *cart_point* have type *Point*. The class associated with this definition is

$cart\_point = \mathbf{Y}(\mathscr{P}[Point])$

To illustrate, consider the point at location $(2, 5)$. Of course, the object has an infinite expansion, so it can only be written using fixed points.

$p = \mathbf{Y}(cart\_point(2, 5))$

$\quad = \mathbf{Y}(\mathbf{Y}(\mathscr{P}[Point])(2, 5))$

$\quad = \{x = 2, y = 5,$

$\quad\quad move = \lambda(dx : Real, dy : Real) . \mathbf{Y}(cart\_point(2 + dx, 5 + dy)),$

$\quad\quad equal = \lambda(o : t) . (2 = o.x) \text{ and } (5 = o.y)\}$

Using inheritance, a new class *color_point* is defined. Instances of *color_point* have an additional method *color* that is defined using an additional instantiation parameter for the class. The equality method is redefined so that two points are equal only if their colors match.

class *color_point* $(x : Real, y : Real, c : Color)$

$\quad$ **implements** *ColorPoint*

$\quad$ **inherit** *cart_point*(x, y)

$\quad\quad$ **translating new** *myclass*(x', y')

$\quad\quad\quad$ **to new** *myclass*$(x', y', self.color)$

$\quad$ **method** *color* : *Color*

$\quad\quad$ **return** c

$\quad$ **method** *equal*$(p : ColorPoint) : Boolean$

$\quad\quad$ **return** *super.equal*(p) and

$\quad\quad\quad (self.color = p.color)$

The class *color_point* inherits *cart_point* and indicates the two translations. The first translation is given by *cart_point*(*x*, *y*); it indicates how to instantiate the inherited point class. The second translation is more explicit; it indicates how recursive calls within *cart_point* are to be translated to construct *color_point* objects. In this example the moved point simply retains its color. It is also possible to define an arbitrary computation of the new color from the point's position and previous color. The modified *equal* method uses *super* to invoke the original notion of equality and add a new constraint. The treatment of *super* simply involves an additional let variable.

$$\mathscr{C} = \Lambda t \le G[t]$$
$$\lambda(myclass : (Real \times Real \times Color) \to (t \to t)).$$
$$\lambda(x : Real, y : Real, c : Color).$$
$$\lambda(self : t).$$
$$\textbf{let } super = \mathscr{P}[t](\lambda(x', y') . myclass(x', y', c))(x, y)(self)$$
$$\textbf{in } super \textbf{ with } \{color = c$$
$$equal = \lambda(o : t).$$
$$super.equal(o) \text{ and}$$
$$(self.color = o.color)$$
$$\}$$

Most of the work occurs in the value bound to *super*. First, the parent class definition is applied to *t*, a polymorphic type variable constrained by $t \le G[t]$. This polymorphic application is legal because $\mathscr{P}$ accepts any type $t \le F[t]$ and we know that $G[t] \le F[t]$. The result is applied to a translated form of the class recursion variable *myclass*. Recursive class instantiation in *cart_point* are translated to construct colored points. Finally, the parent component is initialized by *x* and *y*, and *self* is bound to interpret method recursion properly.

Instances of *color_point* and *cart_point* cannot be intermixed in a program because their types are not subtype compatible (they cannot be compared for equality). However, it is possible to write F-bounded polymorphic functions that operate uniformly over either *Points* or *ColorPoints*.

7   Related Type Systems for Inheritance

7.1   Eiffel

Eiffel is based on an identification of classes with types and of inheritance with subtyping. Within this context, however, Eiffel is able to express many of the constructs described in this paper. The correspondence is not complete, because the identification of inheritance and subtyping makes Eiffel's type system insecure [12].

In Eiffel, the pseudovariable *Current* is used instead of *self* to indicate object recursion. Class recursion and a form of type inheritance are expressed by the type expression *Like Current*, which refers to the current class. That is, it denotes the class in which it appears or into which it is inherited. *Like Current* acts somewhat like the type variable *t* in the polymorphic typing of inheritance. The following code illustrates its use to implement the example from Section 3.2.

```
class P feature
    i : Integer is 5;
    id : Like Current is Current
    eq(other : Like Current) : Boolean is
        begin
            Result := (other.i = Current.i)
        end
end P
```

```
class C inherit P redefine eq feature
    b : Integer is 5;
    eq(other : Like Current) : Boolean is
        begin
            Result := (other.i = Current.i) and (other.b = Current.b)
        end
end P
```

This code illustrates the problem of assuming that subclasses are subtypes. With this assumption, one can assign an instance *c* of class *C* to a variable *v* : *P* *v* := *c*. It is then legal to send the *eq* message to *v* with parameter *p* of class *P*. However, *v.eq(p)* cannot execute properly because *p* does not have a *b* attribute. A modified conformance rule that eliminates this problem was proposed in [12].

Like Current also allows Eiffel to express class recursion. For example, the following *clone* method always creates an instance of the same class as the receiver of the message because it uses *Like Current* for the class. Unfortunately, Eiffel has no way to translate instantiation parameters uniformly.

```
class Copier feature
    clone: Like Current is
        local
            temp: Like Current;
        begin
            temp.Create;
            Result := temp;
        end
end
```

The typed model of inheritance presented in this paper provides a formal model in which Eiffel may be explained. It also indicates why Eiffel's type-system is insecure and how the language may be corrected and extended.

7.2   Other Languages

Like Eiffel, most other strongly-typed object-oriented languages, including Modula-3, C++, Trellis and Simula, are based on the identification of classes and types. Their subtype relations are based on their inheritance hierarchies. Unlike Eiffel, these languages are type-safe because they restrict inheritance to satisfy subtyping. In Modula-3, C++ and Simula, the types of methods may not be changed. Trellis allows the types to be changed according to the rules for function subtypes.

None of the languages provide support for class inheritance, as we define it. It can be simulated manually by defining a method in a root class P called *mynew* which simply executes **new** P. If *mynew* is redefined manually in each subclass C to return **new** C, then class inheritance can be achieved by always using *mynew* instead of **new**. Except in Trellis, the typing does not work correctly because *mynew* must have result-type P in all classes.

Simula and C++ are interesting because they provide mechanisms for translating the subclass instantiation parameters into a form appropriate for instantiation of the parent. This mechanism is explained by the Q translation introduced in Section 4.3.

7.3   Mitchell

Mitchell [20] has developed a typed object model based on extensible records and self-application. Object types are defined by a special **class** notation.

$$T = \mathbf{class}\ t\ \{m_1:\sigma_1,\ldots,m_k:\sigma_k\}$$

Objects of type T are similar to records of functions representing methods, except that record component selection is replaced by a *message send* operation. The methods are polymorphic functions with an additional hidden argument. The polymorphism, over a domain of type functions, is used to specialize method types, while the extra argument represents *self*. They are both bound by the message sending operator, $\Leftarrow$, which binds the polymorphic argument to an empty type function, and binds the argument *self* to the object itself. Thus recursion in objects is implemented by self-application.

$$o \Leftarrow m = o \, . \, m[\lambda(t :: TYPE). \{ \ \}](o)$$

A new object may be created by replacing methods or adding new methods in an existing object. Recursion in the types of existing methods are adjusted during extension.

There is a close relationship between Mitchell's work and the model presented in this paper. Although expressed in a different framework, the polymorphic typing of methods achieves the same effect. One advantage of Mitchell's framework is that the type of the *self* argument of each method can be different, giving a more precise typing of methods. Our system has the advantage of simplicity: it does not require special **class** types, extensible records, quantification of type functions, etc.

The systems also differ in their basic object models. Mitchell uses extensible objects, self-application, and a form of delegation [18, 27], while we use records, fixed points, inheritance, and recursive classes. In the models this difference manifests itself in the relative order of record construction and *self* abstraction. In our system, polymorphism (F-bounded) and *self* occur outside the record of methods, requiring type application and a fixed-point function to create an object, which is a simple record. Mitchell places the polymorphism (over type functions) and *self* within each method of an object and binds them during message passing.

Since record formation and *self* abstraction are independent, it appears that the two systems are isomorphic at the value level. Even so, there are tradeoffs. One advantage of the delegation system is that classes and objects are unified. However, class recursion does not seem to be supported, since all object creation is done by extending existing objects. This makes it difficult to construct objects with hidden state, as is possible with recursive classes. Our system has the advantage of a uniform treatment of inheritance on objects, classes and types. A formal investigation of relationship between the models may provide useful insights into implementation techniques and possible extensions.

7.4 Wand

Wand [29, 31] and Remy [23] have developed a type-inference scheme for dealing with records and record extension. Wand's system also allows recursive types. Record types are total functions from labels to a union of *present* and *absent* fields. The system uses ML-style parametric polymorphism instead of record subtype polymorphism: a record type has the form $\Pi[l_i : f_i]\rho$, where l_i are the explicitly defined fields and f_i is either *present*(τ) or *absent*. The *record extension variable* ρ represents any additional fields the record may have. In these systems there is no notion of subtyping; there is only parametric polymorphism. In a recent manuscript, Wand [30] proposes a type-inference rule in the style of ML for object inheritance with recursive types. With first-order extension variables and recursive types, his system can express F-bounded polymorphism. Thus his system can type the examples given in this paper.

A practical drawback to using first-order polymorphism to implement record subtype polymorphism is that records and record functions cannot be passed as arguments and then used with subtype polymorphism; the first-order constraint requires that the types be bound when the record is passed. A more serious problem arises in the presence of recursive types. In a traditional type-system with record subtypes, a subtype of a recursive type may have different fields at each level of unrolling in its infinite expansion. If restricted to first-order quantification, the extension variables in a recursive type cannot be instantiated at each level of unrolling. To achieve the effect of record subtyping, quantifiers would have to be included in the scope of recursion.

These problems could be solved by introducing explicit quantification, at the cost of making type-inference much more complex. A detailed comparison of Wand's type-inference approach based on record extension and our explicitly-typed approach with F-bounded polymorphism is an important topic for future research.

7.5 TS

The TS project [15, 16, 17] has recognized that inheritance does not necessarily produce subtypes. To type-check existing Smalltalk programs, which may contain ad-hoc combinations of code, their system copies the text of methods from parent to child before type-checking. These inherited method expressions are type-checked in their new context and may have very different types than they did in the parent class. As a result, a particular expression may be type-checked many times depending on the depth of the inheritance hierarchy. They also perform type inference, using ML-style unification and first-order polymorphism.

The polymorphic typing of inheritance presented here supports a somewhat more abstract notion of typed inheritance, since a single (polymorphic) type must be assigned to a class. Our polymorphic typing of inheritance uses only the type of the parent, not its method expressions; the type of an inherited method may change but only according to its polymorphic typing. The polymorphic typing provides a degree of encapsulation not found in TS, but TS can type-check some programs that do not have polymorphic typings.

8 Conclusion

We present a typed model of inheritance that preserves more of the flexibility of inheritance in untyped object-oriented languages. Our typing applies to both object and class inheritance. In addition, a notion of inheritance for types is introduced. Type inheritance is analogous to subtyping, but is useful for object-oriented programming because inherited objects have inherited types, not subtypes.

Previously, typed languages allow either modification of instantiation parameters (Simula and C++) or provide class inheritance (Eiffel), but not both. Smalltalk provides both but is untyped. Our model provides a explicit higher-order formalism in which class inheritance, inheritance over recursive types, and modification of instantiation parameters are all supported.

Acknowledgment

We would like to thank Luca Cardelli, David Chase, Jim Donahue, John Mitchell and Benjamin Pierce for the discussions on this work. We would also like to thank Alan Snyder for his support and inspiration [26].

References

[1] G. M. Birtwistle, O.-J. Dahl, B. Myhrhaug, and K. Nygaard. *SIMULA Begin*. Auerbach, 1973.

[2] A. H. Borning and D. H. Ingalls. A type declaration and inference system for Smalltalk. In *Proc. of Conf. on Principles of Programming Languages*, pages 133–141, 1982.

[3] P. Canning, W. Cook, W. Bill, J. Mitchell, and W. Olthoff. F-bounded polymorphism for object-oriented programming. In *Proc. of Conf. on Functional Programming Languages and Computer Architecture*, pages 273–280, 1989.

[4] P. Canning, W. Cook, W. Hill, and W. Olthoff. Interfaces for strongly-typed object-oriented programming. In *Proc. ACM Conf. on Object-Oriented Programming: Systems, Languages and Applications*, pages 457–467, 1989.

[5] P. Canning, W. Hill, and W. Olthoff. A kernel language for object-oriented programming. Technical Report STL-88-21, Hewlett-Packard Labs, 1988.

[6] L. Cardelli. A semantics of multiple inheritance. In *Semantics of Data Types, LNCS 173*, pages 51–68.. Springer-Verlag, 1984.

[7] L. Cardelli. Amber. In *Combinators and Functional Programming Languages, LNCS 242*, pages 21–47, 1986.

[8] L. Cardelli. Structural subtyping and the notion of power type. In *Conf. Rec. ACM Symp. on Principles of Programming Languages*, pages 70–79, 1988.

[9] L. Cardelli, J. Donahue, M. Jordan, B. Kaslow, and G. Nelson. The Modula-3 type system. In *Conf. Rec. ACM Symp. on Principles of Programming Languages*, pages 202–212, 1989.

[10] L. Cardelli and P. Wegner. On understanding types, data abstraction, and polymorphism. *Computing Surveys*, 17(4):471–522, 1985.

[11] W. Cook. *A Denotational Semantics of Inheritance*. PhD thesis, Brown University, 1989.

[12] W. Cook. A proposal for making Eiffel type-safe. In *Proc. European Conf. on Object-Oriented Programming*, pages 57–70. BCS Workshop Series, 1989. Also in *The Computer Journal*, 32(4):305–311, 1989.

[13] W. Cook and J. Palsberg. A denotational semantics of inheritance and its correctness. In *Proc. ACM Conf. on Object-Oriented Programming: Systems, Languages and Applications*, pages 433–444, 1989.

[14] A. Goldberg and D. Robson. *Smalltalk-80: the Language and Its Implementation*. Addison-Wesley, 1983.

[15] J. Graver. *Type-Checking and Type-Inference for Object-Oriented Programming Languages*. PhD thesis, University of Illinois, 1989.

[16] R. Johnson and J. Graver. A user's guide to Typed Smalltalk. Technical Report UIUCDCS-R-88-1457, University of Illinois, 1988.

[17] R. Johnson, J. Graver, and L. Zurawski. TS: An optimizing compiler for Smalltalk. In *Proc. ACM Conf. on Object-Oriented Programming: Systems, Languages and Applications*, 1988.

[18] H. Lieberman. Using prototypical objects to implement shared behavior in object-oriented systems. In *Proc. ACM Conf. on Object-Oriented Programming: Systems, Languages and Applications*, pages 214–223, 1986.

[19] B. Meyer. *Object-Oriented Software Construction*. Prentice-Hall, 1988.

[20] J. C. Mitchell. Towards a typed foundation for method specialization and inheritance. In *Proc. of Conf. on Principles of Programming Languages*, 1989.

[21] D. Moon. Object-oriented programming with Flavors. In *Proc. ACM Conf. on Object-Oriented Programming: Systems, Languages and Applications*, pages 1–9, 1986.

[22] U. S. Reddy. Objects as closures: Abstract semantics of object-oriented languages. In *Proc. ACM Conf. on Lisp and Functional Programming*, pages 289–297, 1988.

[23] D. Rémy. Typechecking records and variants in a natural extension of ML. In *Conf. Rec. ACM Symp. on Principles of Programming Languages*, pages 77–88, 1989.

[24] J. Reynolds. User-defined data types and procedural data structures as complimentary approaches to data abstraction. In *New Advances in Algorithmic Languages*. INRIA, 1975.

[25] C. Schaffert, T. Cooper, B. Bullis, M. Kilian, and C. Wilpolt. An introduction to Trellis/Owl. In *Proc. ACM Conf. on Object-Oriented Programming: Systems, Languages and Applications*, pages 9–16, 1986.

[26] A. Snyder. Inheritance and the development of encapsulated software components. In B. Shriver and P. Wegner, editors, *Research Directions in Object-Oriented Programming*, pages 165–188. MIT Press, 1987.

[27] L. A. Stein. Delegation is inheritance. In *Proc. ACM Conf. on Object-Oriented Programming: System, Languages and Applications*, pages 138–146, 1987.

[28] B. Stroustrup. C++. Addison-Wesley, 1987.

[29] M. Wand. Complete type inference for simple objects. In *Proc. IEEE Symposium on Logic in Computer Science*, pages 37–44, 1987.

[30] M. Wand. Type inference for objects with instance variables and inheritance, 1989. manuscript.

[31] M. Wand. Type inference for record concatenation and multiple inheritance. In *Proc. IEEE Symposium on Logic in Computer Science*, pages 92–97, 1989.

15 Toward a Typed Foundation for Method Specialization and Inheritance

John C. Mitchell

Abstract

This paper discuss the phenomenon of *method specialization* in object-oriented programming languages. A typed function calculus of objects and classes is presented, featuring method specialization when methods are added or redefined. The soundness of the typing rules (without subtyping) is suggested by a translation into a more traditional calculus with recursively-defined record types. However, semantic questions regarding the subtype relation on classes remain open.

Introduction

In spite of the increasing popularity of object-oriented programming, several issues do not seem to be well understood. In particular, although preliminary formal semantics have been proposed [Kam88, Red88, Yel89], there is neither an accepted basis for reasoning about basic issues such as program transformation or optimization, nor a sound basis for flexible typing disciplines. This paper presents a typed function calculus with simple forms of "objects" and "classes" which illustrate an essential feature of inheritance we call method specialization. To give some insight into the connection between this calculus and previous formal analysis, we also give a translation of objects and classes into records and recursively-defined record types. This clarifies some of the challenges involved in giving compositional, typed semantics to realistic object-oriented languages.

Apart from typing and mathematical semantics, the basic calculus used in this paper is relatively straightforward. The main idea is to provide a functional (*i.e.,* side-effect free) form of "prototyping," or "delegation" [Bor86, Lie86, LTP86, US87] so that one object may be created by inheriting methods from another. For simplicity, we treat methods and instance variables uniformly; methods may be replaced, and therefore instance variables may be regarded as methods that return a constant value. The set of messages an object will answer, and the types of their results, are specified by a form of type we call a class. One class will be considered a subclass (or subtype) of another if every object of the first is guaranteed to behave properly when considered as an element of the second. Thus, in our view, classes are types whose

First appeared in P. Hudak, editor, *Principles of Programming Languages*, 1990, pages 109–124. © The Association for Computing Machinery, Inc., 11 West 42nd Street, New York, NY 10036.

elements are objects, and inheritance is a mechanism for constructing one object from another. The subclass relation is determined by behavioral characteristics of objects rather than program declarations. While this may not be the predominant view of object-oriented programming, it is consistent with at least one important practical view and it is a convenient model for our purposes.

Method specialization, which is described in some detail in Section 2, is achieved by treating objects as collections of functions, each representing a method of the object. When a method is invoked, the appropriate function is applied to the object itself. In other words, instead of using a special symbol *self* to allow a method to refer to the object to which it belongs, we use the first argument of the method. This approach is also used directly in *T* [RA82, AR88], which we were not aware of when we first began experimenting with this idea, and in the implementation of Modula 3 [CDG+88, CDJ+89]. The main point of the paper is not to promote this view of objects, but to develop typing rules for methods which usefully reflect the way they are inherited.

One long-term goal is to develop a flexible, polymorphic typing discipline which could prevent such common run-time errors as *message not understood*. This is not an easy task, as illustrated by the vagaries of the early proposals for typing in Smalltalk [BI82, Suz81] and the subtle bugs surrounding *like self* [Coo89b] in the more recent language Eiffel [Mey88]. Another reason to develop typing rules is that in giving types, we are forced to specify exactly what kind of value is defined by each kind of expression in the language. This seems quite valuable when we consider substitution equivalence, which is critical to understanding or reasoning about transformation and optimization.

The calculus presented in this paper owes much to the recent line of work on record calculi with subtyping, beginning with Cardelli's 1984 paper [Car88]. A number of influential typing ideas, including bounded quantification, were sketched out in [CW85], and summarized in [DT88]. More recently, type inference techniques been presented in [Wan87], followed up by [Sta88, JM88, Rém89, Wan89]. From an untyped, denotational point of view, the primary studies seem to be Cook's thesis [Coo89a], which highlights method specialization, and the denotational semantics presented in [Kam88, Red88, Yel89]. The general perspective of this paper has developed from a tutorial presentation at the 1988 OOPSLA conference with Luca Cardelli [CM88], a subsequent joint paper [CM89], and numerous conversations with members of the ABEL group at HP Labs (Peter Canning, William Cook, Walt Hill and Walter Olthoff).

2   Method Specialization

An important phenomenon that seems essential to object-oriented programming will be referred to as *method specialization*. Although there is really only one basic idea, it will be helpful to separate method specialization into two forms, one involving the addition of methods, and the other involving method replacement, or "overriding." Both forms may be illustrated using example classes of points (*c.f.* [CW85, JM88]). The class *point* contains objects that have *x*, *y* and *move* methods. If points have integer coordinates, then the functionality of point objects may be summarized by the signature,

class *point* **methods**
> $x : int, y : int,$
> $move : int \times int \rightarrow point$

which we will regard as the type of all objects having *x*, *y*, and *move* methods of the indicated functionality. Note that we allow methods to return functions, which reduces method parameterization to ordinary function application. A more specialized class of points are the colored points, which have an additional method returning their color

class *colord_point* **methods**
> $x : int, y : int, c : color,$
> $move : int \times int \rightarrow colored\_point$

and an appropriately revised type of *move* method. In a language such as Smalltalk [GR83], we might first define a *point* class and use *point* objects in writing a graphics package. Later, after upgrading to a color display, we might define the subclass of *colored_point*'s and use these instead. In a delegation or prototype-based language such as Self, we might use a similar programming technique, although we would define the basic point methods in a prototype point, instead of a class declaration. An important aspect of object-oriented languages in general is that much of the code we write for *point*'s may be used directly on *colored_point*'s, eliminating what could otherwise be a significant amount of reprogramming.

   When we define *colored_point*'s, either as a subclass (as in Smalltalk) or by prototyping (as in Self), the *move* method is *specialized* as it is inherited. In particular, the type of *move* changes when it is inherited. If we send the *move* message to a point, along with integer "displacements" δ_x and δ_y, we obtain a point with modified *x* and *y* coordinates. However, when we send the *move* message to a colored point, we obtain a colored point instead of an uncolored point. While this will be completely familiar to anyone who has written a program in an object-oriented language, it is worth noting that it is difficult to simulate this behavior within traditional typed languages such as Pascal and Ada; the typing constraints interfere (see [DCBA89], for example). In particular, the correct behavior of *move* on colored points cannot be simulated using only a "conversion" function mapping *colored_point* to *point* (c.f. [BL88, BTCGS89]). If we convert a *colored_point p* to a *point p'* and then send the *move* message to *p'*, we obtain a *point* instead of a *colored_point*.

A more complex form of method specialization occurs when a method is overridden. To give an example, we need one method which depends on another. Let us assume we have another class of points, each having a method *slide* which moves the point one unit up and to the right.

class *sl_point* **methods**
$$x : int, \ y : int,$$
$$move : int \ \times \ int \to sl\_point,$$
$$slide : sl\_point$$

Since we have a *move* method, the natural implementation of *slide* is to send *move* with argument $\langle 1, 1 \rangle$. We now get an interesting form of method specialization if we replace *move* in some object (or subclass) which inherits *slide*. One subclass of *sl_point* might be the class *dir_point* of directed points which have *x*, *y* coordinates and a direction, say an angle *theta*.

class *dir_point* **methods**
$$x : int, \ y : int, \ theta : real,$$
$$move : int \ \times \ int \to dir\_point,$$
$$slide : dir\_point$$

Let us assume that when we move a directed point, we wish to maintain its orientation toward some position on the perimeter of some bounding box, such as the boundary of the window or screen on which it is displayed. To achieve this behavior, we would redefine the *move* method to calculate a new direction whenever the *x* and *y* coordinates are altered. However, *slide* may be inherited directly from sliding points, because of the following phenomenon. With *slide* implemented by invoking *move*, the inherite *slide* method will invoke the more specialized *move* method associated with directed points. In other words, when *slide* is inherited by *dir_point*, this method is specialized in accordance with the *move* method on directed points, even though *slide* was declared as part of *sl_point*. This kind of behavior is relatively easy to implement.

However, from a mathematical point of view, this form of specialization seems to be a fairly complex operation on functions.

While method specialization is very useful in a variety of programming situations, method specialization seems to complicate static analysis. In particular, let us say two expressions are *substitution equivalent* (or observationally congruent) if we may substitute one for the other any place inside any program, without changing the overall program behavior. This is an important relation in any language, since it characterizes the local program transformations or optimizations that may be applied safely in any context. In a Pascal-like language, it is relatively easy to state a simple condition guaranteeing substitution equivalence of two procedures: if both return the same results and have the same side-effects, for all possible values of the input parameters, then either may be substituted for the other in any program. However, looking only at a single method body in an object-oriented language, it is difficult to se whether a simple local transformation could change the behavior of the entire program. The novice might suspect, for example, that in-line substitution of a method body might preserve program meaning. However, if we replace the reference to *move* in the method body of *slide* by in-line code, this would change the way that *slide* works when inherited by directed points. Specifically, if *slide* does not refer to *move*, then overriding *move* has no effect on the behavior of *slide*.

3   Method Specialization and Natural Transformation

There is a simple and intuitive connection between method specialization and natural transformation. We will illustrate the main idea using an elementary view of objects resembling [Car88]. Although the formal development of the paper does not depend on this section, the correspondence will hopefully gives some insight into the typing rules of the calculus presented in Section 4. For the remainder of this section, we will use *simple object* to mean a record of some type, and *simple method* to mean a certain kind of function on simple objects. A *simple class* is therefore a record type.

At the risk of overdoing a single example, let us consider simple classes of cartesian points. The most basic is the class *simple_point* whose elements are simple objects (records) with integer x and y components. Using the notation of [CM89], we may write this record tyype as follows[1].

$simple\_point ::= \langle\!\langle x : int, y : int \rangle\!\rangle$

It is also useful to consider a simple class of colored points

$simple\_col\_point ::= \langle\!\langle x : int, y : int, c : color \rangle\!\rangle$

Writing $<:$ for the subtype relation, we have *simple_col_point* $<:$ *simple_point* by accepted subtyping rules explained in [Car88, CM89] and summarized in Appendices A and B.

A function which moves points as in Section 2 should change the x and y coordinates of any record with integer x and y fields, and preserve any additional components, such as $c:color$. If we define *simple_move* as a function from *simple_point* to *simple_point*, then we may apply *simple_move* to any simple object of any subtype of *simple_point* (see rule (subsum) in Appendix B). However, this always gives us a *simple_point*, rather than an element of a subtype such as *simple_col_point*. In order to get a map from *simple_col_point* to *simple_col_point*, and similarly for any other type of records with $x:int$, $y:int$ and additional components, *simple_move* must be a function of a more complicated type. The correct functionality in this case corresponds to a natural transformation.

Since natural transformations are maps between functors over categories, it might seem that we should now introduce a lot of categorical machinery. However, by working within a calculus that has the appropriate form of polymorphic functions, we may define functors and natural transformations using syntactic expressions of the calculus. In doing so, we consider the types of the calculus as objects (in the categorical sense of the word) of a category. There are two choices of morphisms. One might be the class of morphisms given by closed function expressions (or, equivalently, open expressions with exactly one free variable; see [MS89]). However, the more appropriate category seems to be the preorder given by the provable subtyping assertions of our calculus. We will be primarily concerned with subcategories of this category which consist of all subtypes of a given type. Since these categories are preorders, a functor is determined by a function F from subtypes of some A to types such that whenever $s <: t <: A$, we have $Fs <: Ft$. In type systems based on [CW85], the "kind" $\forall s <: A \,.\, T$ is the collection of all functions which map every subtype s of A to a type (element of the kind T of all types). It is a helpful notational convention to use a double colon "$::$" for kind membership and reserve the single colon for types. Using this notation, the functors we consider are given by type functions $F :: \forall s <: A \,.\, T$. Rather than explain the general idea in any more detail (*c.f.* [Rey84, RP89]), we will illustrate the approach by the example at hand. It is hoped that the main ideas will be immediately clear to those familiar with category theory, and still reasonably accessibe to those without.

To consider *simple_move* as a natural transformation, we must generalize *simple_point* from a type to a functor. The codomain of the functor we want should be the collection of subtypes of *simple_point*, since *simple_move* acts as a function on each subtype of *simple_point*. Using record type expressions of [CM89], we may define the map

$$F ::= \lambda R <: \langle\!\langle\,\rangle\!\rangle \backslash xy . \langle\!\langle R | x : int, y : int \rangle\!\rangle$$

from subtypes of $\langle\!\langle\,\rangle\!\rangle \backslash xy$ to record types, which is explained below. It is easy to verify that F is a functor. In words, this type function maps any type R of records without x and y fields to the type $\langle\!\langle R | x : int, y : int \rangle\!\rangle$ of all records obtained by adding integer x and y fields to some record from R. In more detail, $\langle\,\rangle$ is the type of all records, and (consequently) $\langle\,\rangle \backslash xy$ is the type of all records without x or y fields. The constraint that formal parameter R of F must be a subtype of $\langle\,\rangle \backslash xy$ first implies that the domain of F is the collection of all subtypes of $\langle\,\rangle \backslash xy$, and second guarantees that the type expression $\langle\!\langle R | x : int, y : int \rangle\!\rangle$ is well-formed, since in the [CM89] calculus we may only add fields to records which are known not to already have these fields. The range of the functor F is the collection of all subtypes of *simple_point* which are obtained by adding new fields[2]. Thus F is a functor on the subcategory of our language whose objects are record types without x and y fields and whose morphisms are given by the subtyping preorder on these types.

The natural extension of *simple_move* to a map on arbitrary types of the form $\langle\!\langle R | x : int, y : int \rangle\!\rangle$ is the polymorphic function

$$
\begin{aligned}
simple\_move ::= \\
&\lambda R <: \langle\!\langle\,\rangle\!\rangle \backslash xy . \\
&\quad \lambda a : \langle\!\langle R | x : int, y : int \rangle\!\rangle . \\
&\quad\quad \langle a \backslash xy | x = a . x + 1, y = a . y + 1 \rangle .
\end{aligned}
$$

In words, the first parameter of this function may be any type R which is a subtype of $\langle\,\rangle \backslash xy$, which means that R may be any type of records without x and y fields. The second parameter is a record a of type $\langle\!\langle R | x : int, y : int \rangle\!\rangle$. Since R may be arbitrary, we know that a has integer x and y fields, but do not know what other fields this record might have. The record expression $a \backslash xy$ denotes the result of removing x and y fields from a, and the form $\langle r | x = M, y = N \rangle$ is used to extend a record r by adding x and y fields with values M and N, respectively. Thus the function body $\langle a \backslash xy | x = a . x + 1, y = a . y + 1 \rangle$ defines a record a' which is identical to a, but with x and y fields each incremented by 1. An elementary calculation within the record calculus shows that *simple_move* defines a natural transformation. This means that if $R <: S$, and consequently

$$\langle\!\langle R | x : int, y : int \rangle\!\rangle <: \langle\!\langle S | x : int, y : int \rangle\!\rangle$$

are two subtypes of *simple_point*, and if we begin with any element r if the smaller subclass $\langle\!\langle R | x : int, y : int \rangle\!\rangle$, the following two computations yield the same result. The first applies move to r, and then "converts" r to the larger subclass $\langle\!\langle S|x:int, y:int\rangle\!\rangle$ according to the subtyping assertion $R <: S$. The second computation converts r to the larger subclass before applying *move*. The fact that these two give the same result seems to capture the intuitive property that however we specialize *simple_move* on subclasses, it should respect the behavior of *simple_move* on *simple_point*'s.

It is worth mentioning that the view of methods as natural transformations not only gives us a reasonable "default" for specializing a method to subclasses with additional properties, but allows for the possibility of "redefining" methods in any way that is consistent with our interpretation of subtyping. However, within the framework of "simple objects," we have no linguistic or semantic mechanism for redefining methods. This leads us to include methods as components of objects, as we do in the next section.

4   Classes and Objects

4.1   Class Types

In the record calculus of [CM89], a record type determines a finite map from field names to types. Since the type of an object would naturally be a list of method names and their types, it is expedient to use record field names as method names, and define class types using record types. As a consequence of using the type expressions of [CM89], we get variables ranging over finite maps with certain method names guaranteed *not* to be in their domain. This is exactly what we need in order to type methods on objects (*c.f.* [JM88]). While it is certainly possible to define class types without mentioning records, it is convenient to use the following formaton rule.

$$\frac{\Gamma, t :: T \rhd R <: \langle\,\rangle}{\Gamma \rhd \mathbf{class}\, t.\{R\} :: T}$$

In words, if R is any record type expression, possible containing a free type variable t, then **class**.$\{R\}$ is a type. The type variable t is bound in **class** $t.\{R\}$ If R is an explicit record type of the form $\langle\ldots\rangle$, then it is convenient to omit the angle brackets from the corresponding **class** type expression. For example, the class of points may be written

$$point ::= \mathbf{class}\, t.\{x:int, y:int, move:int \times int \to t\}$$

In words, the type expression for *point* defines the class t with methods $x:int$, $y:int$ and $move:int \times int \to t$.

4.2 Operations on Objects

An object is a value which accepts messages. The simplest object is the "empty" object, which accepts no messages at all. We will write { } for the empty object, and $o \Leftarrow m$ for the result of sending message m to object o. Since the result of sending a message may be a function (from objects to objects, for example), there is no special syntax for message parameters.

In addition to sending a message, there are two basic operations on objects, adding a method and replacing a method. Suppose o is an object accepting messages $m_1, \ldots, m_k$ and that we want to extend o to an object o' accepting an additional message n. We begin by choosing a "method body" e, which must be a function; the result of sending message n to the new object o' will be the result of the application eo' of method body e to object o'. A reasonable syntax for the object obtained by extending o with method body e for n might be

extend o **with** $n = e$

Using the syntax $o \Leftarrow n$ for sending message n to o, we could then evaluate message send by a rule such as

(**extend** o **with** $n = e$) $\Leftarrow n = e$(**extend** o **with** $n = e$)

Since e is passed the entire object as a parameter, the method body may send any other message $m_1, \ldots, m_k$ to the object, or send the message n if desired. In this way, recursion and "self-reference" become inherent parts of our object model.

There is a minor technical difficulty with the simple syntax presented above. Suppose we send a message m_i to the object o' above. This is not the "most recently added" method, but a method implemented in the "old" object o. The method body for m_i is therefore designed to be applied to some object that does not have an n method, but only methods among $m_1, \ldots, m_k$. Therefore, before we apply the appropriate method body to o', we must somehow alter the method body to accept an argument with additional methods. As a "bookkeeping" mechanism for keeping the types of methods straight, we will use a syntax for objects that indicates, for each method, the list of methods that were known at the time this method was added. Specifically, if o is an object accepting messages $m_1, \ldots, m_k$, we will write $\{o \mid n(m_1, \ldots, m_k, n) = e\}$ for the result of extending o with method body e for n. The equational rules for manipulating object expressions will allow us to "update" the types of method bodies to account for methods added later (see Table 2 and related discussion).

If we replace a method, then we write $\{o \leftarrow m_i(m_1, \ldots, m_k) = e\}$ for the object obtained from o by redefining m_i to be e. Since an object containing a method e may later be altered by adding or replacing methods, our typing rules must guarantee that e makes sense for any object obtained in this way.

4.3 Typing Rules for Objects

The first typing rule specifies that the empty object belongs to the class which does not promise any methods.

$$\frac{\Gamma \text{ context}}{\Gamma \rhd \{\ \} : \textbf{class } t.\{\ \}}$$

In words, if Γ is a well-formed context (designating types for variables; see Appendix B), then we have the *judgement* $\Gamma \rhd \{\ \} : \textbf{class } t.\{\ \}$ asserting that in context Γ, the expression $\{\ \}$ has type $\textbf{class } t.\{\ \}$.

The next rule describes method addition, which is relatively complicated. There are two main features of this rule. The first is that a method must be a function applicable to the object obtained by adding this method, and that the type of the result of sending a message is the type of this function application. The second overall objective is to guarantee that the method will make sense for all "future" objects constructed from this one. In intuitive terms, we require that a method have the polymorphic type of a "natural transformation" on the "functor" which produces extensions of the present class. (Technically, it is worth noting that the "functor" is actually a map from types to types which does not always seem to respect the subtyping preorder.) If we begin with an object o of type $\textbf{class } t.\{m_1 : \sigma_1, \ldots, m_k : \sigma_k\}$; then every object obtained by adding or redefining methods will have a type of the form $\textbf{class } t.\{Ft | m_1 : \sigma_1, \ldots, m_k : \sigma_k\}$, where F is a function from types to record types such that Ft never involves the names $m_1, \ldots, m_k$ of methods of o. Since the types of "future" objects are characterized by type functions, we want any method we add to o to define a natural transformation on a functor whose domain is a category of maps from types to types. (The morphisms of this category correspond to the point-wise subtyping preorder on $T \Rightarrow T$ described in Appendix B). In a notation following [CM89], we require that the new method body have a type of the form

$$\forall F <: (\lambda t :: T. \langle\!\langle\ \rangle\!\rangle \backslash m_1 \ldots m_k n).$$
$$[\textbf{class } t.\{Ft | m_1 : \sigma_1, \ldots, m_k : \sigma_k, n : \tau\}/t](t \rightarrow \tau)$$

where the constraint $F <: (\lambda t :: T. \langle\!\langle\ \rangle\!\rangle \backslash m_1 \ldots m_k n)$ guarantees that the function F from types to types always produces a record type without $m_1 \ldots m_k n$, and the square brackets in the subexpression $[\dots/t](t \to \tau)$ indicate substitution. In words, the new method body must be a polymorphic function which, for any "possible future" type **class** $t . \{Ft | m_1 : \sigma_1, \dots, m_k : \sigma_k, n : \tau\}$, maps objects of this type to some result type possibly depending on the type of objects involved. The formal rule, which is illustrated by example in Section 4.4, appears at the top of Table 1. Reading the rule in words, we begin with an object e_1 which has methods $m_1, \dots, m_k$ and wish to add another method n implemented using method body e_2. For this to make good sense, e_2 must be a function which, for any addition methods Ft, makes sense on an object of type **class** $t . \{Ft | m_1 : \sigma_1, \dots, m_k : \sigma_k, n : \tau\}$, where τ is the type of result of sending message n to the new object. The constraint at the binding occurrence of F is that for any argument t, the type Ft must be a subtype of $\langle\!\langle\ \rangle\!\rangle \backslash m_1 \dots m_k$. This is a formal way of saying that Ft may be any finite function from field names to types "containing" t which does not associate a type to any $m_1, \dots, m_k, n$.

The rule for replacing one method by another is similar, but somewhat less complicated. If we begin with an object $e_1 : $ **class** $t . \{m_1 : \sigma_1, \dots, m_k : \sigma_k\}$ and wish to replace m_i, then we need an alternate method body with the type required to produce a result of type σ_i. While it seems reasonable to allow the new method body to have a type corresponding to some subtype of σ_i, we will make the simplifying assumption that the new method returns the same type of result as the old. The formal rule which accomplishes this appears in Table 1.

Since we may only add methods one-at-a-time, the reader may wonder whether it is possible to define an object with two mutually recursive methods, m and n, for example. It is generally possible to do this, but in a fuller development of the calculus it would probably be worthwhile to use more general rules allowing simultaneous addition of several methods. There is no technical problem in doing this, but the typing rules become more difficult to read.

The typing rule for message send specifies that the result of sending the message has whatever type is specified. The formal rule (**class** E) appears in Table 1. To illustrate (**class** E) by example, a object representing a number, with its own addition method (as described in [GR83], for example) might be defined by an expression with type $e : $ **class** $t . \{val : num, plus : t \to t\}$. Sending the addition message to this object produces a function from this class to itself

$$e \Leftarrow plus : \textbf{class } t . \{val : num, plus : t \to t\} \to \textbf{class } t . \{val : num, plus : t \to t\}$$

Therefore, $e \Leftarrow plus\ e$ produces another object of the same class.

The evaluation rules for objects compute the result of message send by applying the appropriate method to the object itself. The equational axiom at the bottom of

Table 1
Typing and evaluation rules for objects

$$\frac{\Gamma \rhd e_1 : \mathbf{class}\, t.\{m_1 : \sigma_1, \ldots, m_k : \sigma_k\}}{\Gamma \rhd e_2 : \forall F <: (\lambda t :: T. \langle\!\langle\,\rangle\!\rangle \backslash m_1 \ldots m_k n).\, [\mathbf{class}\, t.\{Ft|m_1 : \sigma_1, \ldots, m_k : \sigma_k, n : \tau\}/t]\,(t \to \tau)}{\Gamma \rhd \{e_1|n(m_1, \ldots m_k, n) = e_2\} : \mathbf{class}\, t.\{m_1 : \sigma_1, \ldots, m_k : \sigma_k, n : \tau\}} \qquad (add\ meth)$$

$$\frac{\Gamma \rhd e_1 : \mathbf{class}\, t.\{m_1 : \sigma_1, \ldots, m_k : \sigma_k\}}{\Gamma \rhd e_2 : \forall F <: (\lambda t :: T. \langle\!\langle\,\rangle\!\rangle \backslash m_1 \ldots m_k).\, [\mathbf{class}\, t.\{Ft|m_1 : \sigma_1, \ldots, m_k : \sigma_k\}/t]\,(t \to \sigma_i)}{\Gamma \rhd \{e_1 \leftarrow m_i(m_1, \ldots, m_k) = e_2\} : \mathbf{class}\, t.\{m_1 : \sigma_1, \ldots, m_k : \sigma_k\}} \qquad (ovw\ meth)$$

$$\frac{\Gamma \rhd e : \mathbf{class}\, t.\{m_1 : \sigma_1, \ldots, m_k : \sigma_k\}}{\Gamma \rhd e \Leftarrow m_i : [\mathbf{class}\, t.\{m_1 : \sigma_1, \ldots, m_k : \sigma_k\}/t]\,\sigma_i} \qquad (class\ E)$$

$$\{o|m(m_1, \ldots, m_k) = e\} \Leftarrow m = e(\lambda t :: T. \langle\!\langle\,\rangle\!\rangle)\{o|m(m_1, \ldots, m_k) = e\}\,XS$$

Table 1 is based on this idea, with type application to the constant "empty record type" function used to make the application type correct. The corresponding axiom for a redefined method is similar.

There are several equational axioms for manipulating object expressions, most of them following the pattern of record axioms explained in [CM89]. One nontrivial axiom allows us to permute the order of methods. In general, an object which has been extended twice will have the form

$$\{\{o|n(m_1, \ldots, m_k, n) = e\}|n'(m_1, \ldots, m_k, n, n') = e'\}$$

Note that the method body e does not assume the object has a method named n', since the second method was added later. However, e' assumes a method named n. The equational axiom for exchanging the order of methods is given in Table 2, where the change in method body accounts for the presence of n'. Intuitively, this type manipulation is related to the fact that a natural transformation must be applied to the type of an argument before it is applied to the argument itself. However, in our calculus, we do not have a basic operation that returns the type of an expression. Therefore, we must "precompute" the type of a method argument incrementally as we build the object itself.

4.4 An Example

As an example, we will show how to define an object of class *point*. Recall that a point has x, y and *move* methods. We will define a point whose x and y methods are constant functions, returning integer coordinates x_0 and y_0. The *move* method will return a function which, given a pair of integers, returns a point with x and y coordinates altered accordingly. We begin by adding polymorphic constant functions (as methods) to the empty object $\{\ \}:$**class** $t.\{\ \}$. Since we will also use constant functions in the definition of *move*, it is helpful to introduce the following general form for methods returning constant methods,

$$c\_meth_{\bar{m},\bar{\sigma}}[e] ::= \lambda F <: (\lambda t :: T. \langle\!\langle \ \rangle\!\rangle \backslash \bar{m}).$$
$$\lambda x : (\textbf{class}\ t.\{Ft|\bar{m}:\bar{\sigma}\}).e$$

for any sequence $\bar{m}$ of method names, sequence $\bar{\sigma}$ of corresponding types, and expression e not containing F of x free. (If $\bar{m} = m_1 \ldots m_k$ and $\bar{\sigma} = \sigma_1 \ldots \sigma_k$, we write $\bar{m}:\bar{\sigma}$ for $m_1:\sigma_1 \ldots, m_k:\sigma_k$.) For any integer expression e without F or x free, the constant function $c\_meth_{\bar{m},\bar{\sigma}}[e]$ has the following "bounded polymorphic type."

$$\forall F <: (\lambda t :: T. \langle\!\langle \ \rangle\!\rangle \backslash \bar{m}).$$
$$(\textbf{class}\ t.\{Ft|\bar{m}:\bar{\sigma}\}) \to int$$

Therefore, by the object extension rule, the object

$$\{\{\ \}|x(x) = c\_meth_{x,int}[x_0]\}$$

with method x returning the integer coordinate x_0 has type **class** $t.\{x:int\}$. This object may be extended with a constant y method returning integer coordinate y_0.

$$p_{xy} ::= \{\{\{\ \}|x(x) = c\_meth_{x,int}[x_0]$$
$$\}|y(x,y) = c\_meth_{(xy),(int\ int)}[y_0]$$
$$\}$$

This gives us an object with two integer methods.

It useful to make several observations about the object $p_{x,y}$. First, note that the first method added, x, "expects" to be passed an object with only one method, while the second method expects both x and y. This is indicated by the lists of method names in the object expression. If we send the message y to $p_{x,y}$, the result may be computed directly using the equational rule at the bottom of Table 1. However, if we send the x message, then we must first permute the order of methods using the equational rule on Table 2. This rule changes the type of the method body for x so that the function may be applied to any object with at least the two methods x and y. We now continue the example by adding a *move* method to $p_{x,y}$.

The move method for $p_{x,y}$ will be a polymorphic function of type

$$\forall F <: (\lambda t :: T. \langle\!\langle \ \rangle\!\rangle \backslash xy\ move).$$
$$\textbf{class}\ t.\{Ft|x:int, y:int, move:int \times int \to t\}$$
$$\to int \times int \to$$
$$\textbf{class}\ t.\{Ft|x:int, y:int, move:int \times int \to t\}$$

Table 2
Equational rule for permuting methods

$$\frac{\Gamma \rhd \{\{o|n(\overline{m}, n) = e\}|n'(\overline{m}, n, n') = e'\} : \textbf{class } t \, . \, \{Ft|n : \tau, n' : \tau'\}}{\Gamma \rhd \{\{o|n(\overline{m}, n) = e\}|n'(\overline{m}, n, n') = e'\}} \quad n' \text{ not among } \overline{m}, n$$

$$= \{\{o|n'(\overline{m}, n, n') = e'\}|n(\overline{m}, n, n') = \lambda G <: (\lambda t :: T. \langle\!\langle \, \rangle\!\rangle \backslash \overline{m}nn') \, . \, e(\lambda t :: T. \langle\!\langle Gt|n' : \tau' \rangle\!\rangle)\}$$

Table 3
Move method body and example calculation

$$move\_meth ::= \lambda F <: (\lambda t :: T. \langle\!\langle \, \rangle\!\rangle \backslash x \, y \, move).$$
$$\lambda o : \textbf{class } t \, . \, \{Ft|x : int, y : int, move : int \times int \to t\}.$$
$$\lambda d : int \times int.$$
$$\{\{o \leftarrow x(x, y, move) = c\_meth[(o \Leftarrow x) + fst \, d]\}$$
$$\leftarrow y(x, y, move) = c\_meth[(o \Leftarrow y) + snd \, d]\}$$
$$pt \Leftarrow move = \{p_{xy}|move(x, y, move) = move\_meth\} \Leftarrow move$$
$$= (move\_meth)(\lambda t :: T. \langle\!\langle \, \rangle\!\rangle)pt$$
$$= \lambda d : int \times int.$$
$$\{\{pt \leftarrow x(x, y, move) = c\_meth[(pt \Leftarrow x) + fst \, d]\}$$
$$\leftarrow y(x, y, move) = c\_meth[(pt \Leftarrow y) + snd \, d]\}$$

since *move* must map any object with x, y, *move* and additional methods to another object of the same type. An appropriate method body for *move* is given at the top of Table 3. This function takes any object with x, y and *move* methods and replaces the x and y methods by constant functions returning new coordinates. Note that the new coordinates are calculated by sending x and y messages to the object and incrementing the results. We obtain a point object by adding this method to the object p_{xy}

$$pt ::= \{p_{xy}|move(x, y, move) = move\_meth\}$$

To complete the example, we will compute the value of $pt \Leftarrow move$ in Table 3. Thus $pt \Leftarrow move$ is a function which, given a displacement $d : int \times int$, returns an object which is identical to pt, but with x and y coordinates incremented by the first and second components of d.

One very important fact about this calculation is that if we had a more "specialized" kind of point pt', with any number of additional methods, the same calculation would give us a new point identical to pt', but with x and y methods replaced by constant functions returning new coordinates. It is exactly this uniform behavior of methods, guaranteed by the typing rules, that allows us to inherit *move* from pt and use it on extensions of pt.

5 A Translation of Objects into Records

The object and class expressions introduced in the previous section may be interpreted in the calculus with records and recursive type definitions summarized in Appendix B, in the sense that under an appropriate syntactic translation, all of the typing and equational rules for objects are derived rules of the record calculus. Although we have not studied the semantics of the target record calculus when recursive type declarations are allowed [CM89], the calculus is close enough to other systems so that semantic soundness seems very likely (see [BTCGS89]). However, as outlined in Section 6, this translation does not respect the natural subtyping relation on classes. Thus a semantic account of class subtyping remains an open problem.

The translation into records is syntax-directed, proceeding by induction on the formation of an expression. The translation of an object is essentially a record containing the methods of the object. More precisely, we translate the empty object to the empty record, and $\{e_1|m(m_1,\ldots,m_k,m) = e_2 : F\}$ to the record expression $\langle Trans_{m:F}(e_1)|m = e_2\rangle$, where $Trans_{m:F}$ is a translation which makes sure that the type of each method in e is "adjusted" to take the presence of the additional method into account. A class type expression **class** $t \,.\, \{m_1 : \sigma_1,\ldots,m_k : \sigma_k\}$ may be interpreted as the recursive type expression

$$\mu t \,.\, \langle\!\langle m_1 : t \to \sigma_1,\ldots,m_k : t \to \sigma_k \rangle\!\rangle$$

Note however that we may select components directly from a record of this type, whereas message send only gives us "indirect" access to the methods of an object. This is the main reason why the translation of objects into records does not respect the natural subtype ordering on class types. The translation becomes slightly more complicated in the presence of record type variables (which must also be translated), but is essentially routine given the development of [CM89]. Details are omitted from this conference paper.

6 Subtyping

The subtype relation on classes is relatively subtle. However, since ordinary bounded quantification is not the only way to define polymorphic functions over all classes of a certain from [CCH+89], our ability to write useful programs is not as dependent on the subtyping relation as might at first appear. By analogy with record types, one might think that if one class type is obtained from another by adding methods, this should be a subclass. However, consider the classes

$A ::= \textbf{class } t \, . \, \{ x : int, y : int, plus : t \to t \}$

$B ::= \textbf{class } t \, . \, \{ x : int, plus : t \to t \}$

Should we consider $A <: B$? The bottom line is that we may only adopt $A <: B$ if, in any context, any expression of type B could safely be replaced by an expression of type A. But consider the expression $o \Leftarrow plus\ o$, where $o : B$. If the *plus* method for some $o' : A$ is implemented by using both x and y methods, then it certainly does not make sense to replace the first occurrence of o by $o' : A$. Thus $A <: B$ is unsound. On the other hand, it certainly seems reasonable that any class of the form

class $t \, . \, \{ \ldots , print : string, \ldots \}$

should be a subtype of *printable* $::= \textbf{class } t \, . \, \{ print : string \}$. This would be useful, for example, in writing a print queue which collects *printable* objects and prints each one in turn (each using its own *print* method).

This example raises an important issue regarding the difference between the natural subtyping relation on classes and subtyping on recursive record types. For example, a class with print method might be interpreted, under the translation mentioned above, as the recursive record type

$R ::= \mu t \, . \, \langle\!\langle x : t \to \sigma, print : t \to string \rangle\!\rangle$

while the class *printable* would be interpreted as

$printable\_rcd ::= \mu t \, . \, \langle\!\langle print : t \to string \rangle\!\rangle$

Under the accepted notion of subtyping for recursive record types (see Appendix B), we do *not* have $R <: printable\_rcd$. (This is similar to the $A <: B$ example above.) This illustrates that in semantic models of the calculus of objects and classes, it is important to take seriously the fact that methods may not be selected from objects, only applied to the object itself. For without this consideration, the expected subtyping relation on classes cannot be semantically justified.

7 Conclusion

We have developed a preliminary function calculus with objects and classes, and justified the typing rules by translation into a more commonly studied calculus which is believed sound. Although we may explain method specialization using the more familiar framework of recursively-defined record types, semantic justification of reasonable subtyping rules seems a difficult open problem.

The calculus of objects and classes is presented using record type expressions from the record calculus of [CM89]. This is convenient when it comes to translating objects into records, but from a programming point of view it seems unnecessarily complex. In future work, it might be useful to simplify the language to those type expressions that are absolutely necessary to program realistic object-oriented examples, and eliminate records in favor of objects.

The main long-term objectives of this work are to provide a basis for reasoning about object-oriented programming languages, and to design flexible polymorphic type systems. In future work, it seems worthwhile to consider languages with different sets of basic operations, in hopes that we could more easily guarantee that the meanings of expressions have the types outline here, without requiring as much type information in the syntax itself. Although type inference algorithms might help, it seems more useful to take up the connection with natural transformations in earnest and define a language in which application of natural transformation is a basic operation. Or, since many of the type functions do not induce functors (*i.e.*, do not respect subtyping), a treatment based on presheaf categories seems more promising. This might alleviate much of the complication and could lead to a more elegant language. Another research direction is to try to adapt the typing concepts presented here to a prototyping-based language such as Self. It is hoped that some of the optimizations achieved through dynamic typig [CU89], for example, could be guaranteed by a static typing discipline along the lines suggested here.

Acknowledgments

I am grateful to Luca Cardelli of DEC Systems Research Center and the members of the ABEL group at HP Laboratories (Peter Canning, William Cook, Walt Hill and Walter Olthoff) for many discussions. Thanks also to Eugenio Moggi, Gordon Plotkin and Andre Scedrov for their comments and insight.

Notes

First appeared in P. Hudak, editor, *Principles of Programming Languages*, 1990, pages 109–124. © The Association for Computing Machinery, Inc., 11 West 42nd Street, New York, NY 10036.

Supported in part by an NSF PYI Award, matching funds from Digital Equipment Corporation, the Powell Foundation, and Xerox Corporation, and NSF grant CCR-8814921.

1. In [CM89], a record type may be written by enclosing a list of labels (or field names) and types within double angle brackets $\langle\!\langle$, $\rangle\!\rangle$, as described in Appendix A.

2. In general, a subtype of *simple_point* may have the form $\langle R | x : \sigma, y : \tau \rangle$ where $R <: \langle \; \rangle \backslash xy$ and both σ and τ are subtypes of *int*. However, since arbitrary subtypes of *int* may not be closed under addition, the appropriate types to use in discussing the functionality of *simple_move* have the form $\langle R | x : int, y : int \rangle$. Put another way, we wish to describe the functionality of *simple_move* using a functor whose range is the collection of all types which are closed under *simple_move*. When we apply *simple_move* to a simple object of some arbitrary subtype $\langle R | x : \sigma, y : \tau \rangle$, the best our type system can do is guarantee that the result has "more generous" type $\langle R | x : int, y : int \rangle$.

References

[AR88]   N. Adams and J. Rees. Object-oriented programming in Scheme. In *Proc. ACM Symp. Lisp and Functional Programming Languages*, pages 277–288, July 1988.

[BI82]   A. H. Borning and D. H. Ingalls. A type declaration and inference system for Smalltalk. In *ACM Symp. Principles of Programing Languages*, pages 133–141, 1982.

[BL88]   K. Bruce and G. Longo. A modest model of records, inheritance and bounded quantification. In *Third IEEE Symp. Logic in Computer Science*, pages 38–51, 1988.

[BMM89]   K. B. Bruce, A. R. Meyer, and J. C. Mitchell. The semantics of second-order lambda calculus. *Information and Computation*, 1989. (to appear).

[Bor86]   A. H. Borning. Classes versus prototypes in object-oriented languages. In *ACM/IEE Fall Joint Computer Conf.*, pages 36–40, 1986.

[BTCGS89]   V. Breazu-Tannen, T. Coquand, C. A. Gunter, and A. Scedrov. Inheritance and explicit coercion. In *Fourth IEEE Symp. Logic in Computer Science*, page (to appear), 1989.

[Car86]   L. Cardelli. Amber. In *Combinators and Func. Programming*, pages 21–47. Springer-Verlag LNCS 242, 1986.

[Car88]   L. Cardelli. A semantics of multiple inheritance. *Information and Computation*, 76:138–164, 1988. Special issue devoted to *Symp. on Semantics of Data Types*, Sophia-Antipolis (France), 1984.

[CCH⁺89]   P. Canning, W. Cook, W. Hill, J. Mitchell, and W. Olthoff. F-bounded quantification for object-oriented programming. In *Functional Prog. and Computer Architecture*, 1989. To appear.

[CDG⁺88]   L. Cardelli, J. Donahue, L. Galssman, M. Jordan, B. Kalsow, and G. Nelson. Modula-3 report. Technical Report SRC-31, DEC systems Research Center, 1988.

[CDJ⁺89]   L. Cardelli, J. Donahue, M. Jordan, B. Kalsow, and G. Nelson. The Modula-3 type system. In *Sixteenth ACM Symp. Principles of Programming Languages*, pages 202–212, 1989.

[CM88]   L. Cardelli and J. C. Mitchell. Semantic methods for object-oriented languages. Unpublished OOPSLA tutorial, 1988.

[CM89]   L. Cardelli and J. C. Mitchell. Operations on records. In *Math. Foundations of Prog. Lang. Semantics*, 1989. To appear.

[Coo89a]   W. R. Cook. *A Denotational Semantics of Inheritance*. PhD thesis, Brown University, 1989.

[Coo89b]   W. R. Cook. A proposal for making Eiffel type-safe. In *European Conf. on Object-Oriented Programming*, pages 57–72, 1989.

[CU89]   C. Chambers and D. Ungar. Customization: Optimizing compiler technology for Self, a dynamically-typed object-oriented programming language. In *SIGPLAN '89 Conf. on Programming Language Design and Implementaton*, pages 146–160, 1989.

[CW85]   L. Cardelli and P. Wegner. On understanding types, data abstraction, and polymorphism. *Computing Surveys*, 17(4):471–522, 1985.

[DCBA89]   A. DiMaio, C. Cardingno, R. Bayan, and C. Atkinson. Dragoon: an Ada-based object-oriented language. In *Proc. Ada-Europe Conference*, 1989. To appear.

[DT88]   S. Danforth and C. Tomlinson. Type theories and object-oriented programming. *ACM Computing Surveys*, 20(1):29–72, 1988.

[Gir71]   J.-Y. Girard. Une extension de l'interpretation de Gödel à l'analyse, et son application à l'élimination des coupures dans l'analyse et la théorie des types. In J. E. Fenstad, editor, *2nd Scandinavian Logic Symposium*, pages 63–92. North-Holland, 1971.

[Gir72]   J.-Y. Girard. Interpretation fonctionelle et elimination des coupures de l'arithmetique d'ordre superieur. These D'Etat, Universite Paris VII, 1972.

[GR83]   A. Goldberg and D. Robson. *Smalltalk-80: The language and its implementation*. Addison Wesley, 1983.

[JM88]   L. Jategaonkar and J. C. Mitchell. ML with extended pattern matching and subtypes. In *Proc. ACM Symp. Lisp and Functional Programming Languages*, pages 198–212, July 1988.

[Kam88]   S. Kamin. Inheritance in smalltalk-80: a denotational definition. In *ACM Symp. Principles of Programming Languages*, pages 80–87, 1988.

[Lie86]   H. Lieberman. Using prototypical objects to implement shared behavior in object-oriented systems. In *Proc. ACM Symp. on Object-Oriented Programming: Systems, Languages, and Applications*, pages 214–223, October 1986.

[LTP86]   W. R. LaLonde, D. A. Thomas, and J. R. Pugh. An exemplar based Smalltalk. In *Proc. ACM Symp. on Object-Oriented Programming: Systems, Languages, and Applications*, pages 322–330, October 1986.

[Mey88]   B. Meyer. *Object-Oriented Software Construction*. Prentice-Hall, 1988.

[Mit84]   J. C. Mitchell. Coercion and type inference (summary). In *Proc. 11-th ACM Symp. on Principles of Programming Languages*, pages 175–185, January 1984.

[MPS86]   D. MacQueen, G. Plotkin, and R. Sethi. An ideal model for recursive polymorphic types. *Information and Control*, 71(1/2):95–130, 1986.

[MS89]   J. C. Mitchell and P. J. Scott. Typed lambda calculus and cartesian closed categories. In *Proc. Conf. Computer Science and Logic June 14–20, 1987, Univ. Colorado Boulder*, volume 92 of *Contemporary Mathematics*, pages 301–316. Amer. Math. Society, 1989.

[RA82]   J. Rees and N. Adams. T, a dialect of Lisp, or lambda: the ultimate software tool. In *Proc. ACM Symp. Lisp and Functional Programming Languages*, pages 114–122, August 1982.

[Red88]   U. S. Reddy. Objects as closures: Abstract semantics of object-oriented languages. In *Proc. ACM Symp. Lisp and Functional Programming Languages*, pages 289–297, July 1988.

[Rém89]   D. Rémy. Typechecking records and variants in a natural extension of ML. In *16-th ACM Symposium on Principles of Programming Languages*, pages 60–76, 1989.

[Rey84]   J. C. Reynolds. Polymorphism is not set-theoretic. In *Proc. Int. Symp. on Semantics of Data Types, Sophia-Antipolis (France), Springer LNCS 173*, pages 145–156. Springer-Verlag, 1984.

[RP89]   J. C. Reynolds and G. D. Plotkin. On functors expressible in the polymorphic lambda calculus. *Information and Computation*, page to appear, 1989.

[Sta88]   R. Stansifer. Type inference with subtypes. In *Proc. 15-th ACM Symp. on Principles of Programming Languages*, pages 88–97, January 1988.

[Suz81]   N. Suzuki. Inferring types in Smalltalk. In *ACM Symp. Principles of Programming Languages*, pages 187–199, 1981.

[US87]   D. Ungar and R. B. Smith. Self: The power of simplicity. In *Proc. ACM Symp. on Object-Oriented Programming: Systems, Languages, and Applications*, pages 227–241, 1987.

[Wan87]   M. Wand. Complete type inference for simple objects. In *Proc. 2-nd IEEE Symp. on Logic in Computer Science*, pages 37–44, 1987. Corrigendum in *Proc. 3-rd IEEE Symp. on Logic in Computer Science*, page 132, 1988.

[Wan89]   M. Wand. Type inference for record concatenation and simple objects. In *Proc. 4-nd IEEE Symp. on Logic in Computer Science*, pages 92–97, 1989.

[Yel89]   P. M. Yelland. First steps towards fully-abstract semantics for object-oriented languages. In *European Conf. on Object-Oriented Programming*, pages 347–367, 1989.

A   Summary of Cardelli-Mitchell Record Operations

A.1   Introduction

This appendix contains an intuitive summary of the record operations presented in [CM89]. The general idea of [CM89] is to extend a polymorphic type system with a notion of subtyping at all types. Record types are then introduced as specialized type constructures with some specialized subtyping rules.

A.2   Record Values

A record value is essentially a finite map from labels to values, where the values may belong to different types. Syntactically, a record value is a collection of fields, where each field is a labeled value. To capture the notion of a map, the labels in a given record must be distinct. Hence the labels can be used to identify the fields, and the fields should be regarded as unordered. This is the notation we use:

$\langle \rangle$ the empty record.

$\langle x = 3, y = true \rangle$ a record with two fields, labeled x and y, and equivalent to
$\qquad\qquad\qquad\qquad \langle y = true, x = 3 \rangle$.

There are three basic operations on record values, *extension*, *restriction*, and *extraction*. These have the following basic properties.

Extension $\langle r | x = a \rangle$ adds a field of label x and value a to a record r, provided a field of label x is not already present. This restriction will be enforced statically by the type system. The additional brackets placed around the operator help to make the examples more readable; we also write $\langle r | x = a | y = b \rangle$ for $\langle \langle r | x = a \rangle | y = b \rangle$.

Restriction $r \backslash x$ removes the field of label x, if any, from the record r. We write $r \backslash xy$ for $(r \backslash x) \backslash y$.

Extraction $r.x$ extracts the value corresponding to the label x from the record r, provided a field having that label is present. This restriction will be enforced statically by the type system.

We have chosen these three operations because they seem to be fundamental constituents of more complex operations. Some examples ae given in Table 4.

Some additional operators may be defined in terms of the ones above.

Table 4
Example record expressions

$\langle\langle x = 3\rangle | y = true\rangle = \langle x = 3, y = true\rangle$	extension
$\langle x = 3, y = true\rangle \backslash y = \langle x = 3\rangle$	restriction (canceling y)
$\langle x = 3, y = true\rangle \backslash z = (x = 3, y = true\rangle$	restriction (no effect)
$\langle x = 3, y = true\rangle . x = 3$	extraction
$\langle\langle x = 3\rangle | x = 4\rangle$	invalid extension
$\langle x = 3\rangle . y$	invalid extraction

Renaming $r[x \leftarrow y] \stackrel{\text{def}}{=} \langle r\backslash x | y = r.x\rangle$ changes the name of a record field.

Overriding $\langle r \leftarrow x = a\rangle \stackrel{\text{def}}{=} \langle r\backslash x | x = a\rangle$. If x is present in r, replace its value with one of a possibly unrelated type, otherwise extend r with $x = a$ (compare with [Wan89]). Given adequate type restrictions, this can be seen as an updating operator, or a method overriding operator. We write $\langle r \leftarrow x = a, y = b\rangle$ for $\langle\langle r \leftarrow x = a\rangle \leftarrow y = b\rangle$.

It is clear that any record may be constructed from the empty record using extension operations. In fact, it is convenient to regard the syntax for a record of many fields as an abbreviation for iterated extensions of the empty record, *e.g.*,

$$\langle x = 3, y = true\rangle \stackrel{\text{def}}{=} \langle\langle\langle \rangle | x = 3\rangle | y = true\rangle.$$

This approach to record values allows us to express the fundamental properties of records using combinations of simple operators of fixed arity, as opposed to n-ary operators. Hence we never have to use schemas with ellipses, such as $\langle x_1 = a_1, \ldots, x_n = a_n\rangle$, in our formal treatment.

Since $r\backslash x = r$ whenever r lacks a field of label x, we may write $\langle x = 3, y = true\rangle$ using any of the following expressions:

$$\langle\langle \rangle | x = 3 | y = true\rangle = \langle\langle\langle \rangle \backslash x | x = 3\rangle \backslash y | y = true\rangle$$

$$= \langle\langle \rangle, x = 3, y = true\rangle$$

The latter forms match a similar definition for record types, given in the next section.

A.3 Record Types

In describing operations on record values, we made positive assumptions of the form "a field of label x must occur in record r" and negative assumptions of the form "a field of label x must not occur in record r". These constraints will be verified statically by the type system. To accomplish this, record types must convey both positive and negative information. Positive information describes the fields that members of a record type must have, while negative information describes the fields the members of that type must not have. Within these constraints, the members of a record type may or may not have additional fields or lack additional fields. It is worth emphasizing that both positive and negative constraints restrict the elements of a type, hence increasing either kind of constraint will lead to smaller sets of values. The smallest amount of information is expressed by the "empty" record type $\langle\!\langle\,\rangle\!\rangle$. The "empty" record type is empty only in that it places no constraints on its members—every record has type $\langle\!\langle\,\rangle\!\rangle$, since all records have at least no fields and lack at least no fields. Some examples are given in Table 5.

As with record values, we have three basic operations on record types.

Extension $\langle\!\langle R|x:A\rangle\!\rangle$ This type denotes the collection obtained from R by adding x fields with values in A in all possible ways (provided that none of the elements of R have x fields). More precisely, this is the collection of those records $\langle r|x=a\rangle$ such that r is in R and a is in A, provided that a positive type field x is not already present in R (this will be enforced statically). We sometime write $\langle\!\langle R|x:A|y:B\rangle\!\rangle$ for $\langle\!\langle\langle\!\langle R|x:A\rangle\!\rangle|y:B\rangle\!\rangle$.

Restriction $R\backslash x$ This type denotes the collection obtained from R by removing the field x (if any) from all its elements. More precisely, this is the collection of those records $r\backslash x$ such that r is in R. We write $R\backslash xy$ for $(R\backslash x)\backslash y$.

Extraction $R.x$ This is the type associated to label x in R, provided R has such a positive field. This provision will be enforced statically. Again, several derived operators can be defined from these.

Renaming $R[x,y] \stackrel{\text{def}}{=} \langle\!\langle R\backslash x|y = R.x\rangle\!\rangle$ changes the name of a record type field.

Table 5
Example record type expressions

$\langle\!\langle\,\rangle\!\rangle$	the type of all records. Contains, *e.g.*, $\langle\,\rangle$ and $\langle x=3\rangle$.
$\langle\!\langle\,\rangle\!\rangle\backslash x$	the type of all records which lack a field labeled x. E.g., $\langle\,\rangle$, $\langle y = true\rangle$, *but not* $\langle x=3\rangle$.
$\langle\!\langle x:Int, y:Bool\rangle\!\rangle$	the type of all records which have at least fields labeled x and y, with values of types *Int* and *Bool*. E.g., $\langle x=3, y=true\rangle$, $\langle x=3, y=true, z=str\rangle$ but not $\langle x=3, y=4\rangle$, $\langle x=3\rangle$.
$\langle\!\langle x:Int\rangle\!\rangle\backslash y$	the type of all records which have at least a field labeled x of type *Int*, and no field with label y. E.g., $\langle x=3, z=str\rangle$, but not $\langle x=3, y=true\rangle$.

Overriding $\langle\!\langle R \leftarrow x:A\rangle\!\rangle \overset{\text{def}}{=} \langle\!\langle R\backslash x | x:A\rangle\!\rangle$ if a type field x is present in R, replaces it with a field x of type A, otherwise extends R. Given adequate type restrictions, this can be used to override a method type in a class signature (i.e. record type) with a more specialized one, to produce a subclass signature.

One crucial formal difference between these operators on types and the similar ones on values is that $\langle\!\langle\rangle\!\rangle\backslash y \neq \langle\!\langle\rangle\!\rangle$, since records belonging to the "empty" type may have y fields, whereas $\langle\rangle\backslash y = \langle\rangle$. In forming record types, one must always make a field restriction before a type extension, as illustrated by example in Table 6.

It helps to read the examples in terms of the collections they represent. For example, the first example for restriction says that if we take the collection of records that have x and y (and possibly more) fields, and remove the y field from all the elements in the collection, then we obtain the collection of records that have x (and possibly more) but no y. In particular, we do not obtain the collection of records that have x and possibly more fields, because those would include y.

The way positive and negative information is formally manipulated is actually easier to understand if we regard record types as abbreviations, as we did for record values:

$$\langle\!\langle x:Int, y:Bool\rangle\!\rangle \overset{\text{def}}{=} \langle\!\langle\langle\!\langle\rangle\!\rangle\backslash x | x:Int\rangle\!\rangle\backslash y | y:Bool\rangle\!\rangle$$

Then, when considering $\langle\!\langle y:Bool\rangle\!\rangle\backslash y$, we actually have $\langle\!\langle\langle\!\langle\rangle\!\rangle\backslash y | y:Bool\rangle\!\rangle\backslash y$. If we allow the outside positive and negative y labels to cancel, we are still left with $\langle\!\langle\rangle\!\rangle\backslash y$. The inner y restriction reminds us that y fields have been eliminated from records of this type.

A.4 Subtyping

The subtyping rules for record types are essentially that every record type is a subtype of $\langle\!\langle\rangle\!\rangle$, and the subtyping relation respects the type operations of extension,

Table 6
Record type extension examples

$\langle\!\langle\langle\!\langle x:Int\rangle\!\rangle\backslash y | y:Bool\rangle\!\rangle = \langle\!\langle x:Int, y:Bool\rangle\!\rangle$ extension

$\langle\!\langle x:Int, y:Bool\rangle\!\rangle\backslash y = \rangle\!\rangle x:Int\rangle\!\rangle\backslash y$ restriction (canceling y)

$\rangle\!\rangle x:Int, y:Bool\rangle\!\rangle\backslash z = \langle\!\langle x:Int, y:Bool\rangle\!\rangle\backslash z$ restriction (no effect)

$\langle\!\langle x:Int, y:Bool\rangle\!\rangle . x = Int$ extraction

$\langle\!\langle\langle\!\langle\rangle\!\rangle | x:Bool\rangle\!\rangle$ invalid extension

$\langle\!\langle x:Int\rangle\!\rangle . y$ invalid extraction

---

restriction and extraction. Writing $A <: B$ for A *is a subtype of* B, we have the following examples.

$$\langle x:Int, y:Bool \rangle <: \langle \rangle$$

$$\langle R|x:A \rangle <: \langle S|x:A \rangle \quad \text{if } R <: S <: \langle \rangle \backslash x$$

$$R \backslash x <: S \backslash x \quad \text{if } R <: S <: \langle \rangle$$

$$R.x <: S.x \quad \text{if } R <: S <: \langle x:A \rangle$$

In general, a record type R will be a subtype of another record type S if every positive constraint (labeled field) associated with R is also a positive constraint imposed by S, and similarly for negative constraints (fields required to be absent). There are some subtleties. For example, $\langle R \backslash x | x : Int \rangle$ is not necessarily a subtype of R, and *never* a subtype of $R \backslash x$, even though this might seem consistent with the point of view expressed in [Car88], for example.

B Summary of Full Typed Calculus

B.1 Overview

The basic calculus we use is a higher-order typed lambda calculus, in the general style of Girard's F_ω [Gir71, Gir72] and many subsequent systems. In addition to function types and polymorphism, we will use recursive type definitions, subtyping and a relatively elaborate form of record types and operations. All of this is quite "standard," in the sense of being syntactically familiar to type theorists, with the exception of the record calculus and subtyping. The main subtyping notions are primarily due to Cardelli [Car88, CW85], with some remnants of [Mit84]. The record calculus with subtyping is explored in some depth in [CM89], although certain semantic and pragmatic questions remain. While many of the syntactic aspects of this calculus will be familiar, the reader should not take this as an indication that the semantics are well-understood. In particular, the combination of record operations, subtyping and recursive types poses a number of mathematical challenges. However, it seems that the bulk of the problems here have been identified and discussed in the literature (see, for example, [BTCGS89, BL88, CM89]). Due to space limitations, we will only summarize the basic parts of the calculus.

B.2 Kinds

The types and type-producing functions of the calculus are characterized by *kinds*, following [Gir72, MPS86, BMM89]; kinds are called *orders* in [Gir72] and some subsequent work. The kinds consist of the base kind T, the kind of all types, and kinds of functions over T. Since we wish to consider type constructors defined only on subtypes of some type A, for example, we will allow "dependent" kinds of the form $\forall s <: A \,.\, \kappa_1$, where $A :: \kappa_2$. While we could also introduce product kinds $\kappa_1 \times \kappa_2$, we have no immediate need for them in this paper. We write "κ kind" if κ is a well-formed kind expression.

B.3 Contexts

Free variables are given types or kinds using *contexts*, which are ordered lists of assumptions about variables. We write "Γ context" if Γ is a well formed context. The basic rules for context are standard, with $\emptyset$ context. We write $v :: \kappa$ to indicate that v has kind κ, and $x : \tau$ to indicate that x has type τ. Kinded variables are added to contexts using the rule

$$\frac{\Gamma \text{ context}, \quad \kappa \text{ kind}}{\Gamma, v :: \kappa \text{ context}} \qquad v \notin Dom(\Gamma).$$

We omit the analogous rule for typed variables.

Since subtyping is a basic notion of the calculus, we may assert in a context that a fresh type variable denotes a subtype of a given type. It is also useful to have "subtyping" at higher kinds, with the intuitive meaning that $<:$ on kind $\kappa_1 \Rightarrow \kappa_2$ is the pointwise ordering

$$F <:_{\kappa_1 \Rightarrow \kappa_2} G \quad \text{iff} \quad \forall v : \kappa_1 \,.\, fv <:_{\kappa_2} gv.$$

We generally omit subscripts from the subtype relation.

Subtyping assumptions are added to contexts according to the rule

$$\frac{\Gamma \rhd A :: \kappa}{\Gamma, U <: A \text{ context}}.$$

B.4 Subtyping

The main typing rule associated with subtyping is called *subsumptions*.

$$\frac{\Gamma \rhd e : \sigma, \quad \Gamma \rhd \sigma <: \tau}{\Gamma \rhd e : \tau} \qquad\qquad \textit{(subsum)}$$

This rule lets us apply a function $f : \sigma \to \tau$ to an argument $x : \sigma'$, whenever $\sigma' <: \sigma$, for example.

B.5 Function Types

We have ordinary function types, formed according to the typing rule

$$\frac{\Gamma \rhd A :: T, \quad \Gamma \rhd B :: T}{\Gamma \rhd A \to B :: T} \tag{$\to$}$$

and polymorphism over all kinds, as in F_ω.

$$\frac{\Gamma, v :: \kappa \rhd A :: T}{\Gamma \rhd \forall v :: \kappa . B :: T} \tag{$\forall$}$$

In addition, as in [CW85], we have bounded polymorphism.

$$\frac{\Gamma, u <: A \rhd B :: T}{\Gamma \rhd \forall u <: A . B :: T} \tag{$\forall \, bdd$}$$

Introduction and elimination rules defining terms of these types are standard and omitted.

We do not seem to need the so-called F-bound polymorphism of [CCH$^+$89], since most useful cases seem to be handled by ordinary bounded quantification over kind $T \Rightarrow T$. (We have not done a thorough study of this point, and it may eventually be necessary to introduce F-bounded polymorphism.)

B.6 Record Types

The "empty" or "universal" record type is written $\langle\!\langle \; \rangle\!\rangle$, following [CM89].

$$\frac{\Gamma \text{ context}}{\Gamma \rhd \langle\!\langle \; \rangle\!\rangle :: T}$$

This type contains all records.

Additional types of records are formed by adding constraints of the form $x : \tau$, which assert that all elements of this type must have an x component of type τ, and constraints of the form $\backslash x$, which assert that no elements of this type may have an x component.

$$\frac{\Gamma \rhd R <: \langle\!\langle \; \rangle\!\rangle \backslash x, \quad \Gamma \rhd A :: T}{\Gamma \rhd \langle\!\langle R | x : A \rangle\!\rangle :: T}$$

$$\frac{\Gamma \rhd R <: \langle\!\langle \; \rangle\!\rangle}{\Gamma \rhd R \backslash x : T}$$

In [CM89], if R is a type of records, with every record guaranteed to have an x component, then $R.x$ is the type of all x components of records from R. However, we do not seem to need type expressions of the form $R.x$ in this paper.

Using equational rules, which we omit, every record type of the pure calculus may be simplified to the form

$$\langle\!\langle R\backslash x_1 \backslash x_2 \ldots | y_1 : A_1 | \ldots \rangle\!\rangle$$

where R is either the empty record type $\langle\!\langle\,\rangle\!\rangle$, a record type variable, or an application begining with a variable of some functional kind. It is convenient to write $\langle\!\langle x_1 : A_1, \ldots, x_k : A_k \rangle\!\rangle$ for $\langle\!\langle\,\langle\!\langle\,\rangle\!\rangle\backslash x_1 \backslash x_2 \ldots | x_1 : A_1 | \ldots | x_k : A_k \rangle\!\rangle$.

B.7   Record Subtyping

Every record type is a subtype of the type $\langle\!\langle\,\rangle\!\rangle$ containing all records. Moreover, subtyping respects record type extension and restriction.

$$\frac{\Gamma \rhd R <: S <: \langle\!\langle\,\rangle\!\rangle\backslash x, \quad \Gamma \rhd A <: B}{\Gamma \rhd \langle\!\langle R | x : A \rangle\!\rangle <: \langle\!\langle S | x : B \rangle\!\rangle}$$

$$\frac{\Gamma \rhd R <: S <: \langle\!\langle\,\rangle\!\rangle}{\Gamma \rhd R\backslash x <: S\backslash x}$$

A derived rule is that from $\Gamma \rhd \sigma_1 <: \tau_1, \ldots, \Gamma \rhd \sigma_k <: \tau_k$ we may drive that $\langle\!\langle m_1 : \sigma_1, \ldots, m_k : \sigma_k, n_1 : \rho_1, \ldots, n_l : \rho_l \rangle\!\rangle$ is a subtype of $\langle\!\langle m_1 : \tau_1, \ldots, m_k : \tau_k \rangle\!\rangle$, which may be familiar from [Car88].

B.8   Recursive Types

Recursive types will be used to describe records which contain methods applicable to the records themselves. Rather than write recursive types in the common programming language form

$$tree = leaf + \langle\!\langle l : tree, r : tree \rangle\!\rangle$$

we will use the more concise syntax

$$\mu t . leaf + \langle\!\langle l : t, r : t \rangle\!\rangle.$$

The formation rule for record types is

$$\frac{\Gamma, v :: T \rhd \sigma :: T}{\Gamma \rhd \mu v :: T . \sigma :: T}$$

and the natural subtyping rule for record types [Car86, BTCGS89] is

$$\frac{\Gamma, (s <: t) \rhd \sigma <: \tau, \quad \Gamma \rhd t :: T}{\Gamma \rhd (\mu v :: T . \sigma) <: (\mu v :: T . \tau)}$$

The usual term formation rules associated with recursive types are

$$\frac{\Gamma \rhd e : [\mu v :: T . \sigma / t] \sigma}{\Gamma \rhd abs\, e : \mu v :: T . \sigma} \qquad (\mu\ I)$$

$$\frac{\Gamma \rhd e : \mu v :: T . \sigma}{\Gamma \rhd rep\, e : [\mu v :: T . \sigma / t] \sigma} \qquad (\mu\ E)$$

where *abs* and *rep* are names for the isomorphism between $\mu v :: T . \sigma$ and $[\mu v :: T . \sigma / t] \sigma$. For simplicity of notation, we will omit *abs* and *rep* from expressions.

Contributors

Val Breazu-Tannen
Department of Computer and
Information Science
University of Pennsylvania
200 South 33rd Street
Philadelphia, PA 19104
val@cis.upenn.edu

Kim B. Bruce
Department of Computer Science
Williams College
Williamstown, MA 01267
kim@cs.williams.edu

Peter Buneman
Department of Computer and
Information Science
200 South 33rd Street
University of Pennsylvania
Philadelphia, PA 19104
peter@cis.upenn.edu

Peter S. Canning
Apple Computer, Inc.
20525 Mariani Avenue
Cupertino, CA 95014
canning@apple.com

Luca Cardelli
DEC Systems Research Center
130 Lytton Avenue
Palo Alto, CA 94301
luca@src.dec.com

William R. Cook
Apple Computer, Inc.
20525 Mariani Avenue
Cupertino, CA 95014
cook@apple.com

Thierry Coquand
Department of Computer Science
Chalmers University
Chalmers, Sweden
coquand@cs.chalmers.se

Pierre-Louis Curien
Laboratoire d'Informatique
Ecole Normale Superieure
45 rue d'Ulm
75230 Paris Cedex 05, France
curien@dmi.ens.fr

Giorgio Ghelli
Dipartimento di Informatica
Università di Pisa
Corso Italia 40
56125 Pisa, Italy
ghelli@di.unipi.it

Carl Gunter
Department of Computer and
Information Science
200 South 33rd Street
University of Pennsylvania
Philadelphia, PA 19104-6389
gunter@cis.upenn.edu

Walter L. Hill
777 Bay Street
San Francisco, CA 94109
whill@netcom.com

Samuel N. Kamin
Computer Science Department
University of Illinois
1304 W Springfield Avenue
Urbana, IL 61801
kamin@cs.uiuc.edu

Giuseppe Longo
Laboratoire d'Informatique
Ecole Normale Superieure
45 rue d'Ulm
75005 Paris, France
longo@dmi.ens.fr

John C. Mitchell
Stanford University
Department of Computer Science
Stanford, CA 94305
mitchell@cs.stanford.edu

Atsushi Ohori
Research Inst. for Math. Sciences
Kyoto University
Sakyo-ku, Kyoto 606-01
Japan

Benjamin C. Pierce
Lab for Foundations of
Computer Science
University of Edinburgh
King's Buildings
Edinburgh, EH9 3ZJ, United Kingdom
benjamin.pierce@dcs.ed.ac.uk

Uday S. Reddy
Computer Science Department
University of Illinois
1304 W Springfield Avenue
Urbana, IL 61801
reddy@cs.uiuc.edu

Didier Rémy
INRIA
P.O. Box 105
Domain de Voluceau
Rocquencourt
78150 Le Chesnay, France
remy@margaux. inria.fr

John C. Reynolds
School of Computer Science
Carnegie Mellon University
5000 Forbes Ave
Pittsburgh, PA 15213
John.Reynolds@cs.cmu.edu

Andre Scedrov
Department of Mathematics
University of Pennsylvania
209 South 33rd Street
Philadelphia, PA 19104-6395
andre@saul.cis.upenn.edu

Mitchell Wand
College of Computer Science
Northeastern University
360 Huntington Avenue
Boston, MA 02115
wand@ccs.neu.edu